W9-BCE-099

Gregory of Tatev
Homilies

This publication was made possible
by a generous grant from
The Dolores Zohrab Liebmann Fund

Gregory of Tatev
(Grigor Tat'ewac'i)

Homilies

Seventy homilies from the "Book of Homilies which Is Called Summer Volume"

Translation by
Vatche Ghazarian
Introduction by
Sergio La Porta

Mayreni Publishing
Monterey - California

Library of Congress Control Number: 2018953119

Gregory of Tatev
Homilies

ISBN: 978-1-931834-13-1

Mayreni Publishing, Inc.
P.O. Box 5881
Monterey, California 93944

Printed and bound in the United States of America

Contents

Illustrations from the 1741 print of *Amaran*

Hübschmann-Meillet Transliteration System for Armenian Characters

Ա	ա	A	a	Յ	յ	Y	y
Բ	բ	B	b	Ն	ն	N	n
Գ	գ	G	g	Շ	շ	Š	š
Դ	դ	D	d	Ո	ո	O	o
Ե	ե	E	e	Չ	չ	Č‘	č‘
Զ	զ	Z	z	Պ	պ	P	p
Է	է	Ē	ē	Ջ	ջ	J̌	ǰ
Ը	ը	Ə	ə	Ռ	ռ	Ṙ	ṙ
Թ	թ	T‘	t‘	Ս	ս	S	s
Ժ	ժ	Ž	ž	Վ	վ	V	v
Ի	ի	I	i	Տ	տ	T	t
Լ	լ	L	l	Ր	ր	R	r
Խ	խ	X	x	Ց	ց	C‘	c‘
Ծ	ծ	C	c	Ւ	ւ	W	w
Կ	կ	K	k	Փ	փ	P‘	p‘
Հ	հ	H	h	Ք	ք	K‘	k‘
Ձ	ձ	J	j	Օ	օ	Ō	ō
Ղ	ղ	Ł	ł	Ֆ	ֆ	F	f
Ճ	ճ	Č	č	Ու	ու	Ow	ow
Մ	մ	M	m		և		ew

ԳԻՐՔ ՔՐ. ՐՈ ՁՈՒ ԹԷ
Որ կոչի Մաւսան Հատոր
Ըլարեալ նա Հօրն մերոյ Գրիգո
րէ Տաթեավղոյն եօԹնելոյս վար
դապետէ։ Տպագրեցեալ օրնակա
նուԹ̅ե̅ նբ առապքլոյն [Ժտագեոսէ
էԲարեՓուղղեբէնոսի. ենրէն Գրիգո
րէ մերոյ լուսաեօրզին։ էէ արտագա
Հսա մլբայէն նբյն Մէնասայ։
Ի Հայրապետութե նա էՔմեածնէ
լուսնկաւցյ՝ տերանիկար եանղյողեէ
 էէ աճեողն, ՏՆ ՂՐ.ՁՐՈՒ
այս Հայոց երիցս երանել գեբբրնեեր
երշանիկ եաճաբան ԿաԹ̅ո̅ կոսէ
էէ ՚ֆպատբարգոււ նբյ եէմ̅ ջս
ակին տեղեածն ՏՆ Գրեգերէ աճ
աբան Վարդապետէ:
է Հ՚իկոստանծնուպոշսյ ջաՆ.ջես
պատբբարուե՛ ՏՆ Ցակոբա աճ
 աբան Վարդապետէ
Հրամանաւ մերոյգրեցեալ սրբա
ջան մէւ̅ջին մերոյ։
Ujle Հրամանաւ երիւցս սրբաջա
նեց մեբոյգբեբելցղ պատբբարգւ։
Ընդ Հոյանեաւ նբ Մ̅ ՚Գածնէն բաց
մ̅ ՀՀաջ եկեղեցայն ՚իկոստանճնու
պոլսս՝ Ul արեամբ եՃախիւ.ք Դ
փանցի Մատւեոս Շ̅նՀագարին
Թուին. աՃԲ ։ Փետրվար. Բ̅Ե:

Preface

The challenging venture to translate homilies or sermons from *Amaran*,[1] the second volume of Grigor Tat'ewac'i's collection of homilies, is the product of a discussion with a friend which occurred in 1999, shortly after translating a portion of Tat'ewac'i's *Girk' Harc'manc'* (Book of Questions) in partnership with the late Fr. Dajad Davidian, the former Pastor of St. James Armenian Church in Watertown, MA.

Grigor Tat'ewac'i—a reformist theologian canonized into sainthood by the Armenian Apostolic Church and honored as *Eramec* (Trismegistus) in Armenian sources—was the Armenian Apostolic Church's most celebrated and prolific theologian of the late fourteenth-early fifteenth century. At a time when the Armenian nation was no longer independent and the very foundation of the Armenian Apostolic Church was under threat, Tat'ewac'i's work fortified it against adverse forces and influences.

Today, he remains widely considered an Illuminator of the Armenian Nation[2] and is, to Apostolic Armenians, the counterpart of Saint Thomas

---

[1] The title of this book of sermons appears in two different spellings in Armenian sources: one as *Amaran*, the other as *Amaran*. The latter appears on both the title page of the collection originally published in Constantinople in 1741 and its reproduction in Jerusalem in 1998. The word is derived from *amarn* (summer). Linguistically, *Amaran* is the accurate form, as the consonant *r* turns into *r* when it is separated from a following *n*. Besides, *Amaran* is the form Tat'ewac'i himself used in naming his volume.

[2] Armenian chronicler T'ovma Mecop'ec'i (1378–1446), who was an apprentice of Tat'ewac'i, declared his teacher the Second Illuminator of the Armenian Nation and "a sun that does not set" in his *Patmut'iwn Lank-T'amowray ew yajordac' iwroc'* [History of Tamerlane and His Successors] (Paris, 1860), p. 17. However, Łazar I Jahkec'i, Catholicos of All Armenians (1737–1751), who wrote the preface for *Amaran*'s first print, designated Tat'ewac'i as the Forth Illuminator of the Armenian nation, referring to St. Gregory the Illuminator or Grigor Lusaworič' (c. 257 – c. 331) as the First Illuminator, and naming St. Mesrop Maštoc' (361/2–440) and St. Yovhannēs Ōjnec'i (688–728) Second and Third Illuminators, respectively (*Girk' K'arozut'ean Or Koč'i Amaran Hator: Arareal s[r]b[o]y hōrn meroy Grigori Tat'ewac'woyn eōt'naloys vardapeti* [Book of Homilies which Is Called Summer Volume, created by our Holy Father Grigor Tat'ewac'i, the Seven-lighted Doctor] (Constantinople, 1741), p. 6).

xiii

Aquinas[3] and other great Western theologians of the Middle Ages.[4]

* * *

Excluding incidental writings incorporated in Tatʿewacʿi's *Amaran,* the sermonary contains 184 homilies,[5] of which twenty-two are explicitly mentioned as written by authors other than Tatʿewacʿi, all of whom are unnamed. Of the 184, the first seventy homilies are included in this translation. The translated sermons are based on the facsimile reprint of *Amaran* published in 1998 through a generous grant from the Dolores Zohrab Liebmann Fund.[6]

The 1741 original print of *Amaran* was accomplished in Constantinople by orders of Archbishop Yakob Nalean Zmmaracʿi, Patriarch of Armenians in Constantinople (1741–1749). Mahtesi Šahnazar of Łapʿan, a devout Armenian of means, funded the project and Łazar I Ĵahkecʿi, Catholicos of All Armenians (1737–1751), wrote the preface. Therein, Ĵahkecʿi praises Tatʿewacʿi as the "blessed sun of the church," who, being well versed in the Old and New testaments and in philosophical works, "quenched the fire of sins" and

---

[3] Saint Thomas Aquinas (1225–1274), a Doctor of the Catholic Church, is most notably known for his profound influence upon Western theological thought. Tatʿewacʿi's voluminous *Girkʿ Harcʿmancʿ* [Book of Questions] is to the Armenian Apostolic Church what Aquinas's *Summa Theologiae* is to the Catholic Church.

[4] Małakʿia Ōrmanean, *Azgapatum: Hay Ułłapʿaṙ Ekełecʿwoy ancʿkʿerə skizbēn minčʿew mer ōrerə yarakicʿ azgayin paraganerov patmuac* [National History: The Events of the Armenian Orthodox Church from Beginning to Our Days, Told in Conjunction with National Events] (Constantinople, 1914), vol. 2, p. 2029.

[5] In an encyclopedia dedicated to the 1700th Anniversary of Armenia's conversion to Christianity, the authors attribute 160 sermons to *Amaran* and 184 to *Jmeran,* the first volume of the book of sermons (*Kʿristonya Hayastan Hanragitaran* [Encyclopedia Christian Armenia], Editor-in-Chief Hovhannes Ayvazyan (Erevan, 2002), p. 249). It is *Jmeran* that contains 160 sermons (*Girkʿ Karozutʿean Or Kocʿi Jmeṙan Hator* [Book of Homilies which Is Called Winter Volume], repr. Jerusalem, 1998 (original edition printed in Constantinople, 1740)). The authors were misled most likely by a segment of Fr. Gēorg Karpisean's thesis on Tatʿewacʿi and the role of the School of Tatʿew in the history of Armenian culture published in the official monthly of the Catholicosate of All Armenians in Etchmiadzin, Armenia. There, Fr. Karpisean says: "Tatʿewacʿi's other important work is 'Profession of Faith, Sermonary,' completed in 1407. The book consists of two volumes: *Jmeran* and *Amaran*. The first volume includes ... 184 sermons, while the second ... includes 160 sermons" (Gevorg Vardapet Karpisyan, *Grigor Tatʿewacʿi: Erkerə* [Grigor Tatʿewacʿi: The Works], Ēĵmiacin paštōnakan amsagir Hayrapetakan Atʿoṙoy S. Ēĵmiacni, 1959/4, p. 21).

[6] Grigor Tatʿewacʿi, *Girkʿ Karozutʿean Or Kocʿi Amaṙan Hator* [Book of Homilies which Is Called Summer Volume], repr. Jerusalem, 1998 (original edition printed in Constantinople, 1741).

"enlightened the souls with vivifying teaching."[7] To emphasize Tatʿewacʿi's holiness, Ĵahkecʿi likened him to the class of angels referred to as Thrones that receive wisdom directly from the Holy Spirit and pass it on to disciples.[8]

Given the peculiar structure of these homilies, along with the frequent references used by Tatʿewacʿi to ancient and medieval philosophers and theologians, it is assumed that these homilies were not composed for delivery at church services attended by lay people. As Małakʿia Ōrmanean, a theologian, church historian, and the Patriarch of Armenians in Constantinople at the turn of twentieth century (1896–1908), indicates in his writings, Tatʿewacʿi's intent was to train his apprentices in preaching and rhetorical art.[9] In other words, the sermonaries were composed in order to play the role of textbooks and serve as practical, instructional, and educational tools.[10]

It is to be noted, also, that Tatʿewacʿi wrote the homilies to reach audiences beyond the walls of his monastery, and to prepare apprentices, both near and far, to ready themselves asexemplary clergy for spiritual battle in defense of the orthodox doctrine of the Armenian Apostolic Church.

After all, penning his two volumes of homilies in 1407 was a means for an aging and ailing Tatʿewacʿi to achieve his ambition of reaching out to a broad audience and ease the work of others as they engage in sermon writing by distancing themselves from temptations to plagiarize or "sermonize dishonestly by taking [sermons] belonging to others."[11]

In addition to facilitating the study of Tatʿewacʿi's religio-philosophical thoughts and positions, his homilies shed light on the way of life of Armenians during mediaeval times and their popular traditions and beliefs, as noted by various Armenologists.[12]

* * *

Identifying the Biblical verses referenced in the original text was challenging in great part because they are denoted without corresponding

---

[7] *Ibid.,* p. 5.

[8] *Ibid.*

[9] Ōrmanean, *op. cit.,* p. 1998.

[10] Karpisyan, *op. cit.,* p. 22.

[11] *Amaran,* p. 720. In Tatʿewacʿi's words: "zaylocʿn ařeal anparkešt kʿarozel."

[12] Abr[aham] Zamin[ean], *Hay Grakanutʿean Patmutʿiwn* [History of Armenian Literature] (Nor Naxiĵewan, 1914), p. 212; Manuk Abełyan, *Hayocʿ Hin Grakanutʿyan Patmutʿyun,* [History of Ancient Armenian Literature], vol. 2 (Erevan, 1941), p. 364.

numbers, except in chapter titles. The verse numbers presented within square brackets in this translation indicate that the verses are not denoted explicitly in the original text.

Rendition of verses of the Old Testament are based primarily on *The Septuagint*,[13] while *The New Oxford Annotated Bible* is used as the primary reference for verses of the New Testament,[14] with some reliance on other translations included in *The Word*.[15]

This translation contains ten sermons written by other Church Fathers or ecclesiastics. To distinguish such sermons, Tatʿewacʿi clearly states that they are *by another*. I chose not to exclude them, since they reflect beliefs which Tatʿewacʿi more than likely felt were in accord with his teachings or in harmony with positions he conceived to be of the orthodox approach.

In order to deliver the translated sermons to readers without further delay, minimal time was dedicated to identifying the *others* and the philosophical and theological sources referenced in the original work.

Where needed, the Hübschmann-Meillet transliteration system is applied throughout (see table on page ix).

* * *

I would like to express my gratitude to the Dolores Zohrab Liebmann Fund for funding this project and to Dr. Sergio La Porta for writing the introductory biography of Tatʿewacʿi.

I would also like to acknowledge Father Dr. Krikor Maksoudian's help in clarifying some sentences that seemed ambiguous to me.

Words of profound thankfulness are also due to my wife, Barbara, who patiently helped bring my translation to its publishable stage.

Vatche Ghazarian, Ph.D.

---

[13] *The Septuagint with Apocrypha: Greek and English*, [Translated by] Sir Lancelot C[harles] L[ee] Brenton, 6th Printing, Hendrickson Publishers, [Peabody], 1997.

[14] *The New Oxford Annotated Bible with the Apocryphal/Deuterocanonical Books*, edited by Bruce M. Metzger and Roland E. Murphy, New revised standard edition, Oxford University Press (New York, 1994).

[15] *The Word – The Bible from 26 Translations*, Ed. Curtis Vaughan, Mathis Publishers, Inc. (Moss Point, 1993).

ԳՐԻԳՈՐ   ԼՈՒՍ-ՈՉ   ԱՍՐ ԳՐԻԳՈՐՈՒՁՍ ԼԻԿ ԱՑՈՅ

ՍԲԵՅՈՀԱՆՆՕՐՈՆՅՆՒ   ԳՐԳՐՏՍԱԹԵԱՅԻ

Grigor Tatʻewacʻi (1344–1409)

Grigor Tatʻewacʻi was born in 1344 in Vayocʻ Jor and raised by his brother in the fortress of Tmokʻ in Javaxeti, then part of the Kingdom of Georgia.[1] His given name was Xutʻlušah, derived from Tatar *qutlu*, "blessed," and Persian *šāh*, "king." This was a popular name among Armenians in the thirteenth and fourteenth centuries and attests to the diverse and multi-lingual environment in which young Xutʻlušah grew up. His father, Amir Sargis, was from Arčēš, and his mother was a lady from Pʻarp, whose name is unfortunately unknown. Grigor's birth coincided with the unraveling of the Il-Khān empire—that is, the Mongol empire in Iran—which took place in the 1330s due to civil strife. The collapse of centralized power resulted in an increase in raiding activities particularly by Türkmen tribes. According to the *Yaysmawurkʻ*, the Armenian collection of saints' lives arranged calendrically, Tatʻewacʻi's family fled from the Kajberunikʻ region around Lake Van to Siwnikʻ on account of the destabilization of the area.[2]

At the age of fourteen, Xutʻlušah met and was taken under the wing of the famous teacher, Yovhannēs Orotnecʻi. Orotnecʻi was the last disciple of the great master of the renowned monastic school at Glajor, Esayi Nčʻecʻi; he seems to have been a member of the princely house of Siwnikʻ. Orotnecʻi brought his student to Tiflis where King David VIII Bagrationi of Georgia had once again set the court of the Georgian monarchy in 1358. Orotnecʻi was certainly in Tiflis by 1363 when a colophon notes that he requested a copy of the complete works of John of Damascus in that year.[3] Tiflis had a large Armenian community as is witnessed by the *Yaysmawurkʻ*'s reference to it as "an Armenian city," and there were at least two Armenian monasteries in the environs of the city in the fourteenth century.

Sometime in or shortly prior to 1371, Yovhannēs took his young disciple

---

[1] For a detailed examination of Tatʻewacʻi's life, see Sergio La Porta, "'The Theology of the Holy Dionysius,' Volume III of Grigor Tatʻewacʻi's *Book of Questions*: Introduction, Translation, and Commentary," Ph.D. diss. (Harvard University, 2001), ch. 1.

[2] *Yaysmawurkʻ* (Constantinople, 1706), pp. 698–704.

[3] The colophon is to codex 297 of the Armenian Patriarchate of Jerusalem.

west and ordained him at the monastery of St. Grigor Lusaworič' (the Illuminator) on Mt. Sepuh in the environs of Erznka (Erzinjan), giving him the appropriate name of Grigor. Orotnec'i's association with the mountain was so close, that the church of St. Karapet there was more commonly known as the church of Yovhannēs Orotnec'i. The monastic complexes on Mt. Sepuh were home to a thriving intellectual community.[4] The city of Erznka rested on the trade route that crossed Anatolia, linking Iran with the Mediterranean. Mt. Sepuh, as the traditional burial site of St. Grigor, constituted an important locus of pilgrimage that was a popular spot for Armenian pilgrims on their way to and from the Holy Land. The monasteries that established themselves on the mountain benefited from their location near a significant urban center and from the passage of scholars, pilgrims, and merchants along the route. Texts and traditions from Greater Armenia, Cilicia, and Jerusalem crossed paths and mixed together in their scriptoria. While for most of the thirteenth century, such traffic was primarily from west to east, the flow of intellectual transfer reversed course in the latter part of the century. This shift in direction resulted partially from the new economic prosperity in the east that coincided with the *pax Mongolica* and the rise of the monastic schools of Siwnik'.

From Erznka, Orotnec'i took his young student Grigor to Jerusalem, where he was ordained a priest in 1373.[5] Jerusalem had been a site of pilgrimage for Armenians since at least the fourth century. The archbishop Macarius (sed. 314–335/6) communicated with a delegation of Armenian priests who were visiting the Holy City concerning questions about the administration of the rites of baptism and the eucharist.[6] Armenian pilgrims continued to flock to the city in subsequent centuries, as epigraphical evidence attests.[7] It is also apparent that a community of Armenians, possibly monastic scholars, settled in Jerusalem and formed the core of an Armenian community there during the

---

[4] On the monasteries on Mt. Sepuh, see Jean-Michel Thierry "Le Mont Sepuh: Étude Archéologique," *Revue des études arméniennes* 21 (1988-89), pp. 385–449.

[5] Sergio La Porta, "Grigor Tat'ewac'i's Pilgrimage to Jerusalem," in *The Armenians in Jerusalem and the Holy Land*, ed. R. Ervine, M. Stone, and N. Stone (Leuven, 2002), pp. 97–110.

[6] Abraham Terian, *Macarius of Jerusalem: Letter to the Armenians, Ad 335* (St. Vladimir's Seminary Press, 2008).

[7] See, e.g., Michael E. Stone, "Holy Land Pilgrimage of Armenians before the Arab Conquest," *Revue Biblique* 93 (1986), pp. 93–110; Abraham Terian, "Armenian Writers in Medieval Jerusalem," in *Patterns of the Past Prospects for the Future: The Christian Heritage in the Holy Land*, ed. T. Hummel, K. Hintlian, and U. Carmesund (London, 1999), pp. 139–156.

fifth century. This attraction, both physical and spiritual, to Jerusalem persisted through the middle ages and inspired the greatest of the Armenian poets, including Grigor Narekac'i (d.1003), Nersēs Šnorhali (1102–1173), and Grigor Pahlawuni (1093–1166). The city left its mark on Tat'ewac'i as well. He penned a homily for the feast of the Entry of Christ into Jerusalem included in his *Winter Sermonary* which can be described as an exhortation to pilgrimage.[8] In it, he proceeds through ten praises that guide the reader or auditor through the holy places. The praises commence with Adam and Eve and progress chronologically and geographically through the patriarchs and the Exodus, to the city of Jerusalem as the center of the world, to the economic activity of the Lord within the city, to the final judgment which will take place there. A scriptural verse or passage, whose full meaning is elicited by its inclusion within this pilgrimage, provides the touchstone for each "praise." Grigor concludes with an exclamation of a vision of Christ: "Now if the place is worthy of being where God descends in just examination and all the angels and saints with Him, then it is worthy for everyone to run there, as if [running] before Christ, and to be physically face to face and to see Christ and the place of His Incarnation."[9]

Following his ordination in Jerusalem he returned to Erznka with Orotnec'i where he received the lower degree of *vardapet* (monastic teacher)[10] between 1374 and 1376. This rank permitted him to preach and teach lower classes but not yet compose works of his own. In order to receive that rank, he had to pass an exam based upon his knowledge of the Old and New Testament, of the confession of faith, as well as of selections from the Church Fathers and previous *vardapet*-s. It is likely that he also had to deliver a graduation oration before the title of *vardapet* was officially conferred upon him. Yovhannēs and Grigor returned to Siwnik' by 1376 when a student of Orotnec'i mentions his teacher's presence in the canton of Orotn. In the meantime, they may have been informed of the fall of the city of Sis in 1375 to Mamluk forces and of the capture of the last king of Cilicia, Levon V.

Upon returning to Siwnik' Grigor continued his studies in order to advance

---

[8] *Girk' K'arozut'ean Or Koč'i Jmeṙan Hator* (Jerusalem, 1998), pp. 610–613.

[9] *ard et'ē aržani ē tełin ur astuac iǰanē i datastan k'nnut'ean ew amenayn hreštakk' ew amenayn surbk' ǝnd nma, apa aržani ē amenayn umek' ǝnt'anal and. ibr t'ē dēm ǝnd aṙaǰ k'ristosi. ew marmnov dēm yandiman linil ew tesanel zk'ristos ew ztełi mardełut'ean nora*, p. 613.

[10] On the title of *vardapet*, see Robert Thomson, "*Vardapet* in the Early Armenian Church," *Le Muséon* 102 (1989), pp. 131–145.

to the rank of higher or eminent *cayragoyn vardapet*, which he achieved by 1385. While his lower degree authorized preaching and some introductory teaching, this higher degree was required to compose and publish works of his own and lead instruction at a school. In 1386 he finished his first work of biblical exegesis, a commentary on the book of Isaiah. Unfortunately, Yovhannēs Orotnecʻi died just before its completion. Upon his teacher's death, Grigor assumed his position as the head of the school of the monastery at Vałand. He was not, however, able to stay there long.

In 1387 the invasions of Tīmūr forced Grigor to flee to the fortress of Šahapōnkʻ in Naxičewan, where he remained for three months. While besieged in the fortress, he completed his *Questions of the Vardapet Gēorg* [Erznkacʻi] *and Grigorʻs Explanations*. In the colophon to that work, he describes in detail the horror of the Tīmūrid invasions.[11]

Grigor survived the devastation and by 1391 he assumed directorship of the school at the monastery of Tatʻew, at which point he was recognized as the chief *vardapet* of Armenia. Under his leadership, the school at Tatʻew became the most famous throughout Armenian lands, and students flocked there from not only Siwnikʻ and Arcʻax, but also Tabriz, Tiflis, Crimea, Kʻajberunikʻ, Tarōn, and Cilicia.

The popularity and renown of the school appears to have rested largely on Tatʻewacʻiʻs personality and guidance. One of his last students, Tʻovma Mecopʻecʻi, expounds upon the effect Grigor exerted on those who studied with him:

> He was generous and rich in speech, there not being [anyone] like him among all peoples, neither in the past nor present, a second Theologian [i.e., Gregory Nazianzenus] and John Chrysostom. In such a manner that when he taught and we closed our eyes, we saw an old man seated by him. And again, sometimes he distributed bread, and sometimes apples. And blessed of the spectators and auditors were those who saw him, for he had an awe-inspiring appearance, and many times we heard from men that Christ had come into this world in such a form.[12]

Although the exact number of students that were trained at Tatʻew is unknown, Tʻovma Mecopʻecʻi is able to provide some idea of the size of the

---

[11] Levon Xačʻikyan, *ŽD dari jeṙagreri hišatakaranner* (Erevan, 1950), pp. 567–569.

[12] Tʻovma Mecopʻecʻi, *Patmagrutʻiwn*, ed. Levon Xačʻikyan (Erevan, 1999), p. 47.

monastic community. According to Mecop'ec'i, when he arrived at Tat'ew in 1406 Tat'ewac'i had many students—he names sixteen—and more than sixty priests. T'ovma brought an additional eleven students to Tat'ew, bringing the student population to at least twenty-five in 1406. Mecop'ec'i also informs us that the normal number of monks residing at a monastery in the region at this time was anywhere between sixty and one hundred and sixty monks. Among that group, approximately eight to maybe twenty-five were engaged in higher studies.

A manuscript preserved in the Matenadaran in Erevan provides a description of the curriculum at Tat'ew according to which Grigor Tat'ewac'i maintained three 'classrooms' (*usumnarank'*):

> In the monastery of Tat'ew he [i.e., Grigor] had three classrooms. In one he taught the music with sweet-sounding chants of the former singer-*vardapet*-s, so that at once they came from the entire land and from the cities and studied at his feet. And in the other, [he taught] the art of portrait painting[13] and various [types of] painting. And in the third, [he taught] the 'internal' and 'external' writings in particular the Old and New Testaments, with 'internal' and 'external'[14] commentary and translation.[15]

Students thus received some instruction in music, the scribal arts, illumination, grammar, and biblical exegesis.[16] After a preliminary introduction to these fields, students focused upon one of the fields that best suited their abilities. A good example of someone who was instructed in all these areas is Grigor Tat'ewac'i himself who was a skilled painter,[17] an exegete, and knowledgeable about hymnography. Although his handwriting leaves something to be desired—to judge from the autograph of his *Book of*

---

[13] 'Portrait painting' (*patkerahanut'iwn*) refers to the depiction of the Evangelists, Mary, other biblical figures, and saints of the Church.

[14] 'Internal' (*nerk'in*) signifies religious literature while 'external' (*artak'in*) denotes profane literature, in this case likely works of philosophy, Mane Širinyan, "'*Artak'in' ew 'Nurb' greank'*," *Aštanak* 2 (1998), pp. 15–45.

[15] Thomas Mathews and Avedis Sanjian, *Armenian Gospel Iconography: The Tradition of the Glajor Gospel*, (Washington, DC 1991), pp. 23–24.

[16] For a discussion of the composition of the Glajor-Tat'ew school curriculum, see Sergio La Porta, "Les sept arts libéraux et l'école de Glajor-Tat'ew," in *Les arts libéraux et les sciences dans l'Arménie ancienne et médiévale*, ed. V. Calzolari (Paris, forthcoming).

[17] La Porta, "'Theology of the Holy Dionysius'," pp. 61–62.

Questions[18]—he was a trained scribe who commented upon the theological meaning of the scribal art.[19]

Tat'ewac'i was able to remain at Tat'ew for seventeen years; however, at the end of his life, Grigor was once again forced into flight. In 1408 he and his students were harassed by marauders who emerged in the several years of chaos following Tīmūr's death in 1405. Grigor fled with his students to his father's home of Arčēš and established himself at the monastery of Mecop'. T'ovma Mecop'ec'i gives details of Tat'ewac'i's death in his *History* and in a colophon that he composed in 1410 shortly after his teacher's death. While in his history he notes that in 1409 Grigor died on the road back to Tat'ew, in his colophon he relates an enigmatic story in which a group of Grigor's "beloved students," otherwise unidentified, stole Grigor from Mecop'. T'ovma and his band of students caught up with them in Ayrarat but could not convince Grigor to return to Mecop'; he, unfortunately, died soon thereafter.[20]

From this brief overview, we can observe that Grigor's life was very uprooted. By the end of his twenties, he had spent time in Georgia, Siwnik', Erznka, and Jerusalem, and at the end of his life he was forced to move to K'ajberunik' on the shores of Lake Van whence his family had fled. He was thus familiar with a wide variety of Armenian experiences, and this background may have been one of the reasons for his popularity among students who hailed from different locales. Furthermore, during his travels, Grigor was exposed to a number of non-Armenian communities, particularly in the urban centers of Tiflis, Erznka, and Jerusalem, diverse cities, inhabited by varied Muslim, Jewish, and Christian populations.

Much of Tat'ewac'i's mobility was the result of political upheaval, but he was not merely a passive actor fleeing changes in his socio-political environment. Contrary to our often idealized picture of the monastic vocation as a cloistered life, Grigor was very much involved in the world and its conflicts. At least twice he acted as a political intermediary. During the later Tīmūrid invasions, he mediated on behalf of the Christian population of

---

[18] The manuscript is cod. 3616 of the Mesrop Maštoc' Institute of Armenian Manuscripts (Matenadaran) in Erevan, Armenia.

[19] Sergio La Porta, "Translation and Transformation: Armenian Meditations on the Metamorphic Power of Language," in *The Poetics of Grammar and the Metaphysics of Sound and Sign*, ed. S. La Porta and D. Shulman (Leiden-Boston, 2007), pp. 342–367.

[20] T'ovma Mecop'ec'i, *Patmagrut'iwn*, pp. 94-95; Levon Xač'ikyan, *ŽE dari jeṙagreri Hišatakaranner* (Erevan, 1955), vol. 1, p. 101.

Siwnik', securing a promise for their safety from Tīmūr's son, Mīrān-Shāh.[21] And when Qara-Yūsuf, leader of the Türkmen Qara-Qoyunlu tribe, seized the province of Orotn from Smbat Ōrbēlean in late 1407, Tat'ewac'i went to him as an intercessor.[22] Although he was unsuccessful in his embassy, Grigor's undertaking of this mission is indicative of the wider role he played beyond the walls of a monastery.

Two interconnected religious conflicts in particular occupied Tat'ewac'i during his life. The first concerned the schism within the Armenian Church between the Cahtolicosates of Sis in Cilicia and Ałt'amar.[23] The disagreement between the two Sees arose in the early twelfth century when the Archbishop of Ałt'amar, Dawit', refused to acknowledge the election of Grigor III Pahlawuni due to his youth and declared himself Catholicos. The matter was of significance to Tat'ewac'i because his father and grandfather had been born under the excommunication of the Catholicosate in Sis as the region of K'ajberunik' fell under Ałt'amar's jurisdiction. Motivated partially by this family history, Tat'ewac'i took a personal interest in trying to resolve the dispute between the two hierarchies. Although he did not manage to secure a lasting harmonization, he did succeed in having the bonds of excommunication lifted from those who lived under the jurisdiction of Ałt'amar.

The split within the Armenian Church was further exacerbated by the other, perhaps even greater, fissure between those ecclesiastics who favored a closer relationship with the Latins, some to the point of union, and others who wanted to maintain a greater distance from both Latin practices and the Papacy.[24] As the ecclesiastical hierarchy in Sis generally moved in a latinophile direction, the Catholicos of Ałt'amar was able to position himself as the bulwark of an independent Armenian Apostolic Church and attracted support from beyond the borders of his jurisdiction. Relations between the Armenian and Latin hierarchies had been ongoing since the late eleventh century and deepened with the establishment of Armenian and Crusader states in the Levant. The Papacy attempted to effect a union between the two Churches beginning with the coronation of King Lewon I in 1198, and successive councils reiterated how

---

[21] T'ovma Mecop'ec'i, *Patmagrut'iwn*, p. 110.

[22] T'ovma Mecop'ec'i, *Patmagrut'iwn*, p. 46.

[23] La Porta, "'Theology of the Holy Dionysius'," pp. 77–86.

[24] Sergio La Porta, "Armeno-Latin intellectual exchange in the fourteenth century: Scholarly traditions in conversation and competition," *Medieval Encounters* 21 (2015), pp. 269–294.

Armenian ecclesiastical belief and praxis should be brought into conformity with Latin ones. In the late thirteenth century, Franciscan and Dominican missionaries began to penetrate Anatolia and Iran, shifting the lines of encounter between the two Christian communities eastwards away from the Mediterranean coast.

The missionaries attracted both followers and opponents rather quickly. With the accession of Pope John XXII in 1316, who disliked the Franciscans, the Dominicans became the dominant missionary force in eastern Anatolia and Iran. In 1330, the Armenian brotherhood at the monastery of K'ṙna voted to unite with Rome; in 1356 they were recognized by Pope Innocent VI as the Unitor brotherhood.[25] At this time, they numbered about fifty houses with some 700 monks. Early responses to the missionaries by the Armenian hierarchy in Siwnik' largely consisted of literary polemics, but in the second half of the thirteenth century they became much more aggressive. Yovhannēs Orotnec'i and his students, including Grigor Tat'ewac'i, were at the forefront of this movement. They not only disseminated literary refutations of Latin beliefs and practices, they also took physical action against Armenian converts, conducting a *de facto* inquisition against them. For example, a colophon reports that Orotnec'i and Tat'ewac'i attempted to convince some converts to change their minds, but were unsuccessful. Local princes were summoned, the transgressors were arrested and then they were boiled to death in a bronze cauldron.[26] Our sources do not indicate that European missionaries were ever attacked or harmed; this treatment seems to have been reserved for Armenian converts alone.

Another way Orotnec'i and Grigor contested Latin influence was through education. Above I mentioned that Tat'ewac'i received the rank of lower *vardapet* in 1374 and that of higher or eminent *vardapet* in 1385. Orotnec'i seems to have introduced the distinction between *vardapet*-al degrees to enhance the prestige and requirements of the rank. The course of instruction for eminent *vardapet* focused on the exegesis of primarily Aristotelian texts, which Orotnec'i adapted from the Dominican *logica vetus* used by the Unitor

---

[25] On the Unitors, see Marcus van den Oudenrijn "Uniteurs et Dominicains d'Arménie," *Oriens Christianus* 40 (1956), pp. 94–112; 42 (1958), pp. 110–33; 43 (1959), pp. 110–119.

[26] The colophon is to MS 138 (=Or. 6798) of the British Museum, Frederick Conybeare, *A Catalogue of the Armenian Manuscripts in the British Museum* (London, 1913), pp. 339–340.

Order.[27] In 1383 Grigor completed compilations of his master's teachings on Arisotle's *Categories* and *de Interpretatione*, as well as possibly his own remarks on Ps.-Aristotle's *de Virtutibus*, and the writings of Porphyry.

The changes inaugurated by Yovhannēs Orotnecʻi concerning the levels of *vardapet*-al authority were formalized by Grigor Tatʻewacʻi in a long rite that proceeds through fourteen degrees. His ceremony for the bestowal of the *vardapet*-al degree remains the basis of the rite to the present and is incorporated within the Armenian Ritual Book, the *Maštocʻ*.[28] The rite is replete with biblical readings and hymns recalling the responsibilities of the preacher and the teacher.[29] Many of the selections from the hymnal are taken from the hymns sung during Pentecost.[30] The biblical readings likewise evoke the activity of the Holy Spirit in the Old and New Testaments. Most of the degrees include a reading from the Pentateuch (Exodus or Numbers) or the historical books (I Kings or III Kings); at least one prophetic book, usually Isaiah; a reading from Acts of the Apostles; at least one Epistle, usually Pauline; and a reading from one of the Gospels.

Tatʻewacʻi divided the series of fourteen degrees into two major categories. The first consists of four degrees called the lesser (*pʻokʻr*) or particular (*masnawor*) degrees. The second category consists of ten degrees that are called the greater (*mec*) or eminent (*cayragoyn*) degrees. The four particular degrees are granted by a bishop to the candidate. The bishop questions the candidate whether he knows the Old and New Testaments, the profession of the Orthodox faith, and has rejected every heretical sect. At the conclusion of the fourth category the bishop bestows a staff to the candidate and delivers a pronouncement that emphasizes the candidate's position and duties as a preacher. A chief *vardapet*, rather than a bishop,[31] administers the ten degrees

---

[27] Yovhannēs appears to be the most probable force behind the innovations to monastic education. First, as the Unitors only adopted the Dominican model in 1344, the Armenian Orthodox reform must post date that time as it occurred in reaction to it. Second, the anthology of Matenadaran MS 3902 demonstrates Orotnecʻi's interest in those texts which formed part of the new curriculum.

[28] La Porta, "'Theology of the Holy Dionysius'," pp. 58–61.

[29] *Girkʻ Mec Maštocʻ Kočʻeal* (Ejmiacin,1807), pp. 281–334. I have followed the *Mayr Maštocʻ* (*Mother Maštocʻ*); there are slight differences between the *Mayr Maštocʻ* and *Jeṙnadrutʻean Maštocʻ* (*Maštocʻ of Ordination*).

[30] On these hymns, see Abraham Terian, "The Holy Spirit in the Liturgy of the Armenian Church: The Significance of the Hymns of Pentecost," *St. Nersess Theological Reivew* 4/1-2 (1999), pp. 33–49.

[31] This is according to *Mayr Maštocʻ*; the *Jeṙnadrutʻean Maštocʻ* retains a bishop as the

of eminent *vardapet*. Some of the degrees resemble those of the first four and the rite encourages the candidate to live in accordance with his preaching. It concludes with the officiant's proclamation that the candidate may now perform all the tasks required by his rank, including biblical interpretation.

In addition to his political and pedagogic activity, Tat'ewac'i was incredibly prolific. During his lifetime, Grigor composed or compiled over twenty works including philosophical and biblical commentaries,[32] two theological compilations, a two-volume sermonary, a number of liturgical tractates, and several epistles. A commentary on Grigor Narekac'i's *Book of Lamentation* has also been attributed to him.[33] Of his many works, his *Sermonary* (*K'arozgirk'*) was the most popular to judge from the extremely large number of surviving manuscript copies, both whole and partial, of this two-volume work. The homilies were compiled in 1407 into a *Winter* and *Summer* volume. These were published in Constantinople in 1740 and 1741 respectively and reprinted in Jerusalem in 1998. Between the two volumes, Grigor collected 344 sermons; 160 in the *Winter Sermonary* and 184 in the *Summer*. While he apparently composed most of the sermons, he also selected fifty-four sermons by other people for inclusion. Although these authors are not explicitly named, the sermons are designated as "by another" (*yaylmē*). He explains his reason for this in the colophon to the *Winter* volume: "Whereas those that have been subtitled 'of the same' and 'by another' [is] so that they may be distinguished from each other, and lest they be deemed stolen to foolish minds. Moreover the useful and good ones 'by another' were selected, while the superfluous ones were discarded."[34]

Despite the vigorous measures taken against Armenian converts to the Latin Church, Tat'ewac'i remained more receptive towards Latin texts.[35] Beginning in 1331, the Unitor Yakob K'ṙnec'i *T'argmann* (the Translator) had

---

officiant.

[32] His early philosophical works were compilations of his teacher's remarks on various subjects gathered from class notes and possibly should be included among Orotnec'i's works. Grigor explicitly notes that the explanation of Aristotle's *Categories* and *de Interpretatione*, his *Commentary on Isaiah*, and his *Commentary on the Scholia of Cyril of Alexandria* are based on Orotnec'i's teachings. It is also possible that his early works on Aristotle's *de Virtutibus* and his *Explanations on the Exposition of David's Analysis of Porphyry's Isagogē* likewise derive from his teacher's comments.

[33] This is according to codices 437 and 2091 of the Matendaran.

[34] Xač'ikyan, *ŽE dari jeṙagreri Hišatakaranner*, p. 72.

[35] Even the scribe of the colophon in which Armenian converts are approvingly boiled alive admits that the translated homilies of Augustine were full of useful and wise sayings.

translated many Latin works into Armenian with the assistance of Bartholomew of Poggio. At first, they communicated through Persian as Yakob did not know Latin and Bartholomew did not know Armenian. Over time, they succeeded in doing away with Persian as each learned the language of the other. The translators began with Bartholomew's own *Sermonary* (*K'arozgirk'*), and also translated Aristotelian works with commentaries, liturgical texts, and theological works. Many of these works were to be found in the library collection at the monastery of Glajor, where Orotnec'i studied, and even more in that at Tat'ew. Grigor incorporated passages from many Latin texts within his own work, although he often did not cite their origin.[36] We may also attribute his use of tables of contents, the arrangement of his sermonary into summer and winter volumes, and even his adoption of the question and answer format to his familiarity with Latin modes of textual construction. Grigor's juxtaposition of Armenian and Latin texts and employment of Latin forms of composition reflected his desire to negotiate between the two traditions. While Armenian converts needed to be combatted, physically if necessary, Latin ideas and texts required careful reading and re-contextualization to be converted into acceptable Armenian doctrine. In his response to and engagement with Latin texts, Tat'ewac'i contributed to the consolidation and codification of Armenian theological and exegetical positions.

Grigor composed all of his works, including his sermons, in the form of questions and answers. Question and answer texts are attested in Armenian from the fifth century, but no previous author writing in Armenian employed the format so widely.[37] The numerous copies of his works produced in his lifetime and afterwards attest to its appreciation by Grigor's contemporaries and intellectual descendants. Tat'ewac'i was conscious of making his writings accessible to his students through choosing to write in what he described as a medium register and by providing an organized layout. Undoubtedly one of the reasons for the popularity of his works is their clear systematization.

---

[36] Several examples are provided in La Porta, "'Theology of the Holy Dionysius',"; idem, "A fourteenth-century Armenian polemic against Judaism and its Latin source," *Le Muséon* 122 (2009), pp. 93-129"; Nona Manukyan, "Interrelations Between Scholarship and Folklore in Medieval Armenian Culture." *Le Muséon*, 110 (1997), pp. 81-89; see also Diana Tsaghikyan, "Grigor Tatevatsi and the Sacraments of Initiation," Pd.D. diss. (Univ. of Edinburgh, 2014).

[37] Grigor's use of this mode of composition has led to frequent comparisons between him and Latin scholastic theologians. Nonetheless, there are formal differences between the compositions of the thirteenth-century scholastics and Tat'ewac'i's method which more closely resembles that of twelfth-century monastic masters.

Although Tat'ewac'i's programmatic use, regardless of genre, of neatly enumerated series of questions and answers leaves a modern reader somewhat cold, it must have provided much comfort to a monk living in the chaotic socio-political environment of the late fourteenth and fifteenth centuries and served as a reminder that a divine order did permeate the cosmos. Tat'ewac'i may be most remembered today as an encyclopedic compiler of Armenian tradition, but his students and colleagues saw him differently. For them, he was someone who not only shared their troubles, but also worked to alleviate them. He did not just gather a great amount of information, but provided a spiritual vision of an ordered and harmonious universe. In recognition of his literary and ecclesiastical efforts, the Armenian Apostolic Church recognizes Tat'ewac'i as a saint and commemorates his life and achievements with those of his teacher on the third Saturday of Great Lent.

Dr. Vatche Ghazarian's translation of seventy of Grigor Tat'ewac'i's sermons from his *Summer Sermonary* makes available for the first time to an English-reading audience a significant amount of this work. These sermons address issues concerning personal conduct, the meaning of faith, and the sacraments of the Church. They therefore provide insight into contemporary social ideals and ecclesiology. As the reader will notice, each sermon is replete with allusions to biblical verses as well as to patristic and philosophical texts, and so they also invite us to explore Grigor's exegetical methodology. It is hoped that this English translation will encourage readers to delve further into the literary legacy of one of the most consequential thinkers and reformers of the Armenian Church.

Sergio La Porta
Haig and Isabel Berberian Professor of Armenian Studies
California State University, Fresno

Օգնեա՛ Հո
գիդ սուրբ աստ
ծմարխս։

Գրիգորի կատեճէլ թէ
զքրիստ կրքթոռակէ է, էջ
Հակտորդէ խաշնարուէ է
նոստուծրէ ձգհայգէոց մԶ

Ահ խոսյողը էէլխսոով. Աշէերը Յշճննաս որգմ եղյսայ Հործէս է՛էխոռսկը զոսգ խ՛էՊ
գսայս շսորգո. յսսէր էՀգրէյոսէ բոսխգ օէրմէն Հոսմ և՛խ ոս ս շչձ է՛էէ է խէրսո
զսյս Ադ էդ ոռձմոա գորէ խոս բոսխը ոս գմրե խ տորոռս. Յո սգ սա ՛Ե Լ Ս Տ սսո բոսխս
ош ой. ховлотой 'оилер соройшоо щащои оойшшх в'х 'зоилы х э ыл щшоо 'х
Ստէրս. Պ ս ս ս շ ս   Տ   ս ս հ ս Հ ս ս   է ս ս ս ս սա շ ս ս ս ս ս ս ս ս ս ս ս շ ս ս ս շ ս ս ս ս
ш ј шь ј. Јшй   ишј шшшоой шиши ишо шы 'щй ыыойй шо шоиый шыо.
Եմ ս ս շ ս Հ ս ս Ք ս ս Գ ս ս. 'ս ս ս ս ս ս ս ս ս ս Պ ս ս ս ս ս (Ս ս ս ս ս ս ս ի ս ճ
' ш ишй щшишхбшой щшу из'шй ишй 'й Հш'шзшз.) Սши. 118.35.   (Գ', ш. Բ')

ՆԱՊԱՐՀԻՔ ԿԵՆՑԱՂՈՅՍ ՄԱՐԴ
ԿԱՆ ԲԱՐԻ ԵՒ ՀԱԿ ԲԱՐԻ ՃԱՆԱՊԱՐՀՆ ԵՒՓՈԾ

ըն՛ բնական է մարդյս. զի անդստին'խստեղծմանէ եդ աստ զբարբն՛բքնուխս մէր.
Զէ Հոգէ Մարմեն ևմաք մարդյս բաթէ են. Ե՛է բարւոյն ած լստեղծեաս. Իսկ
չարն՛ եկամուտ է. որ յետոյ մուծաձ 'քէնութիս մէր 'է լչերկես պատճառ է.
'կահ՛ 'խստանայե. որ սերմանեաց բզգասն 'էՀոգէ ե՛էմասրէն ե՛է խորՀարդս
մարդկան: էջ երկրորդ'յանձնէխեան համաց մերոց. որ մէր կամ՞ես Հաէ անեսմք ստ
տանայե սերմանէն. խաունևմը գզար: Ապ՛ օբեէն այ' դարձուցանեն զմեզ 'է
չար ճանապարՀէն ստանանայե. եկեբքն յուղեղ ճանտապարՀն ե՛է գորձս բարիս.
ած ասէ մարզարէն:

(Օրեէք

The Second Volume of My
Book of Homilies

CHAPTER I

On the statement of David the Prophet who says: "Lead me in the path of your commandments, O Lord, for I delight in it" (Ps 119:35).

There are two ways of life for humankind—good and evil. The good way and [good] deed is intrinsic to man, for God placed the good within our nature at creation. The soul, the body, and the mind of man are good and created by good God; whereas evil is extrinsic, it entered our nature because of two causes: First, because of Satan, who sowed evil in man's soul, body, and thoughts; second, because of our free will, since we willfully consent to what Satan sowed, and commit evil [acts].

Now, God's ordinances turn us from Satan's evil path and bring us to the straight path and to good deeds. As the Prophet says: "The ordinances of the Lord are right, rejoicing the heart" (Ps 19:8). Concerning law, it is to be known that God's ordinances and commandments are fulfilled in three ways.

First, by listening to the ordinances and accepting their instruction; second, by fearing God and keeping [the ordinances] in mind; third, by complying with God's commandments and implementing them, as Solomon the Wise says: "My child, hear everything, and fear God, and keep his commandments" (cf. Eccl 12:13). As my obedient child and a follower of my doctrine, listen and pay attention to all that God's ordinances say to you, so you may not be ignorant and perish with sacrilegious people because of ignorance, by saying "I don't know God's law." Moreover, do not question the ordinances, asking why should I keep them, or how do I benefit by doing so?

It is said, do not question and listen to all [commandments] without objection.

Second, the statement exhorts and says: "Fear God"; that is, whenever you hear the ordinances of God, fill yourself with fear and awe, that God is judge

1

and revengeful toward sinners, and He punishes those who do not keep [the law]. Keep a fear of this nature always in your mind, as the Prophet David begged God, saying: "Penetrate my flesh with your fear, for I am extremely afraid of your judgments" (Ps 118:120).

Third, it says "Keep His commandments," because when man fears God, he can keep the commandments, as David says: "Blessed is he who fears the Lord; he will delight greatly in his commandments" (Ps 112:1). Thus, by keeping the commandments, man does not commit sins. Moreover, if he had committed them, he would repent and be justified, because man has been created absolutely for this [purpose]; that is, man was created by God for this, and to this he has been designated. He was placed in Paradise to listen to God's commands, to fear Him, and to fulfill His commandments. This is evident from what was said to man: "Of the tree of the knowledge [of good and evil] you shall not eat, for if you eat thereof you shall surely die" (Gen 2:17).

Behold God's command, and behold the fear of death that follows the command. Had he [man] kept the commandment, he would have been transferred to life eternal. Likewise, the whole of God's creation was called and brought to the world for this [purpose]. As Moses said: "Hear, O Israel, and fear from God, and observe his commandments" (cf. Deut 4:1, 6:2). Thus, every person should first listen to the law, then fear God, and, finally, keep what the ordinances dictate.

Fear and adherence to the ordinances of God enlighten the mind of man, and with the light of the commandments, he attains divine love and perfection. As the Prophet says: "Guide me in the path of your commandment, for I have delighted in it" (Ps 118:35).

Fulfillment of the law generally has three benefits: First, he [man] fulfills the canons and the obligations of law; second, he frees himself of embarrassment before God the lawmaker; third, he stores goodness in his person. These benefits are important, for they are the three countenances of God; that is, the lawmaker, the law, and the executor [of law].

The righteous man is happy to fulfill the laws. First, because physical delights, such as pleasures, glory, and wealth are perishable. Second, because these [physical delights] are reckoned as transgression and sin to the righteous, wherefore the righteous do not rejoice by these; rather, they rejoice by the fulfillment of the law. For the law is joy and life to those who fulfill it, while it is grief and death to those who do not fulfill it, as the Apostle says: "The very commandment that promised life proved to be death to me" (Rom 7:10).

Understand [this] in three ways: First, God's commandment is life for those who keep it, and is death to those who are guilty. Second, they [the ordinances] are death for the body and life for the soul. Third, transgressors are killed in accordance with the law, as has been said: "You shall not commit adultery, you shall not steal" (Deut 4:18–19). When we commit adultery or theft, the same law punishes us, as the Apostle says elsewhere: "If it had not been said in the law, I would not have known sin" (Rom 7:7). Thus, God's law and commandments are life for those who keep them and death to those who do not. Wherefore, the Prophet prayed to God: "Guide me in the path of the commandment; for I have delighted in it" (Ps 118:35). It should be known also that God's law is a barrier and a fence for man; wherefore, Isaiah says: "I made a hedge round it" (Isa 5:2). And there are three [kinds of] fortifications and barriers for man; a city, for example, is fortified twice or thrice.

Prudence is the first inner barrier. Anything man does wisely and prudently will surely be successful. Virtuous acts, such as fasting, prayer, and alms, that protect man from evil are the second barrier. Abstinence cements this barrier, strengthening the fortification, for everything is accomplished by abstinence and patience. The third fortification is God's law, which protects us from the tricks of the adversary, Satan. Of these, prudence is the first fortification, [virtuous] acts are the middle, and law is the last. Further, wisdom functions at the beginning, abstinence during action, and law at the end. Moreover, with wisdom we fortify the mind, with action the soul, and with law all the senses of the body, as well as the soul and the mind.

Should someone question: "How can the ordinances protect us? Behold! Although we keep the ordinances, all kinds of calamities surround us; that is, diseases, pains, plagues, hail, storms, winter, and all the seasons and elements are changed into disorder upon us." The doctors say to the confused that God honored man and put in him three orders—personal, natural, and required. The personal order in essence is the mastery of soul upon the body, which should be obedient [to the soul]. The natural order is the inferiority of desire to passion, which in turn is [inferior] to reason, for reason is always sovereign, and desire is always subject. Passion is both sovereign and subject—it is the master of desire and the slave of reason. In required order man should obey God's ordinances.

Man possessed these three orders before he passed from Paradise. When he voluntarily changed these three orders, the body ruled the soul, reason became the slave of passion and desire, and he himself forsook the commandments of God. Then, indeed, all of the elements transformed into disorder; beasts and animals disobeyed man and became his foes. This [happened] because of God's allowance. In exchange for his forsaking the commandment of God, man was excluded from God's providence, and because of the natural disorder, the elements changed their order. Because of the rebellion of the internal beasts—passion and desire—the external beasts and animals rebelled against man. Because of the tyranny of the body, pain and disease dominated the body. And it has always worked in the same fashion: whenever we forsake the commandment of God, God lets temptations and troubles dominate us—insubordination of elements, hail, drought, pains, plagues. Particularly famine, [death by] sword, and all kinds of punishments and catastrophes take hold of us. And this is good, too, for these troubles become exhortation, fear, and training for us; that is, at the time of such calamities, distant people are advised, and close people are frightened, while the punished are trained and educated. Again, it is exhortation and punishment for sins that have already been committed, awe and fear for the future, and training and education for the present, so we may stay away from sins.

Thus, the forsaking of God's commandments excludes us from God's providence. First, for God's commandments are a visible light descended upon us; hence: "The commandments of the Lord are light, enlightening the eyes" (Ps 19:8). When we forsake them, we are lost in darkness. Moreover, God's ordinances are direction for us in our life's path; when we forsake them, we err and stray. The law is also a support for us, like a pillar for a house; when we forsake the law, our spiritual structure crumbles. The ordinances are also a strong rod; when we throw them away, we easily stumble and fall. Again, they are a path leading us to God in heaven; hence: "Go by the King's Highway; do not turn aside to the right hand or to the left" (Num 20:17).

When we forsake [the ordinances], we stray in this world. It is also a spiritual life; hence: "That commandment is an eternal life" (Jn 12:50); when we distance ourselves from it, we die by death. Again, God knows us through the commandments; when we forget them, God forgets us. And behold! For so long as Adam kept the commandments, he saw God, but when he forsook them, he was excluded from God's sight, as we are. The law shows us the sins, and the law cleanses us from sins.

Like water that cleanses the filth of the body, God's commandments cleanse the filth and sins of the spirit. The law keeps us in the service of God; when we forsake it, we distance ourselves from God, like Adam who so long as he kept the established laws, saw God in Eden, but when he forgot the law, he distanced himself from God and exited Eden. The ordinances are the tree of the knowledge of good and evil, which God commanded, "Eat not that fruit"

(Gen 3:3). When they [Adam and Eve] ate, they broke God's commandment, and were therefore condemned to death. For example, when a man tears apart the decree of the king, he is not fined for the paper; rather, he is sentenced to death for having torn apart the name and the word of the king. A king's decrees are all equal in importance, because all are his words. Likewise, the ordinances are equally important, for they all are God's even commands and we ought to keep them, so we may communicate with God's entire goodness. For God grants us all the goodness of the soul and the body through the ordinances. When we forsake them, we will be deprived of all good things.

And how do we forsake the law? When each person goes according to his own will, he forsakes the will of God. The will of God is referenced in His commandments, and we ought to follow them; that is why we are referred to as law-abiding and Christian people. Christians are like an ox with a yoke on its shoulder that cannot turn aside to the right hand or the left, nor can it become slothful; and if it swerves, the whip straightens it. And pagans and unlawful people are like a wild goat in a herd of black cattle that sits, eats, and moves in whichever direction it chooses, according to its will. The ordinances speak to, govern, and instruct the lawful, not those who are unlawful.

Do not be like the unlawful, for those who have not accepted the law and those who either do not know or do not implement [the law] are perceived to be unlawful indiscriminately. Likewise, those who have accepted the ordinances but have forgotten them, forsaken them, or do not implement them are unlawful. God has excluded such people from His providence and has forgotten them; hence: "I let them go after the ways of their own hearts" (Ps 81:12). And when God lets man go, all kinds of accidents and temptations overtake him, from heaven and earth, from devils and men, pain in the soul, bitterness in the mind, disease in the body, plague, and various accidents.

It is to be known that God's ordinances contain two kinds of recompense: reward for those who work [the law], and punishment for those who sin. There are two kinds of rewards: bodily here [in this life], and spiritual in the life to come. Punishment also is of two kinds: temporal here, and eternal there [in the life to come]. And this is so, for there are two kinds of violators of the law: some violate intentionally, and some unintentionally.

In the same fashion, the punishment of those who violate intentionally is everlasting and eternal, whereas those who sin against the law unintentionally are punished bodily here. In the same fashion, the reward of those who willingly keep the law is eternal, whereas the reward of those who keep it unwillingly or obligatorily is material here [on earth]. It is to be known also

5

that God's promises and their results also are rewards. The promise antecedes here, whereas the result follows in the life to come. Similarly, threats and sentences make up God's punishments. The threat antecedes here, whereas the sentence follows in the life to come. It is to be known also that a pure man is distinguished from an impure [man] through two things, just like clean and unclean animals.

They [animals] are first distinguished by law, and then by the sign they carry. So is man. Whoever has received the law is pure, whereas whoever lacks it is impure, because the ordinances were given to man as guidance and holiness. Second, whoever has the sign and acts as dictated by the law is pure, and whoever lacks the sign and violates the law is impure and is also referred to as unlawful. For unlawful are those who have not accepted the law, as are those who have accepted the law but do not act accordingly. Again, as the clean and unclean animals are distinguished from each other by their location, food, and other elements, such as a kite and dove, wolf and lamb, believers are distinguished from unbelievers by their actions, food, and speech. A person consumes contention and fight, and so on, whereas another is gentle, peaceful, conciliatory, and so on. Thus they were distinguished from one another, "for a believer has no part with an infidel" (2 Cor 6:15).

Again, there are four kinds of recompense: good for good, evil for evil, good for evil, and evil for good. Good for good is moderately good, and evil for evil is moderately evil; whereas good for evil is absolutely good, and evil for good is absolutely evil. The first, good for good, relates to civil law. The second, evil for evil, is of the ordinances of Moses. The third, good for evil, relates to the new law of Christ. Hence, the fourth, evil for good, relates to the unlawful who possess none of the three laws, as Agidopel [did] to David and the betrayer [did] to Christ by exchanging good with evil. Wherefore, their conscience choked them, and they physically drowned and sank into the torments prepared [for them]. Christ our God will save us from these and all the accidents of the evil devil for the glory of God, who is blessed forever and ever. Amen.

CHAPTER II

[Homily] of the same [Tat'ewac'i] on the beginning of the Ten Commandments, according to the verse: "I am the Lord your God, you shall not make to yourself an idol, and you shall have no other God beside me" (Ex 2[0]:2[–3]).

Man is created with an intelligible soul and a perceptible body. The perceptible body has so overpowered the intelligible soul and augmented it that many think we are [made of] body alone. The Scripture testifies to God's saying: "My Spirit shall not remain among these men forever, because they are flesh" (Gen 6:4). Wherefore, [people] considered the function of the senses alone to be true in perceptible creatures, and attempted to create things that please the senses— beautiful appearances for the eyes, pleasant sounds for the ears, loquacity for the tongue, fattening of the abdomen, and softness for the hands. The mind [has become] mingled in these and adapted to be pleased with them. It delights when it sees through the eyes many things serving [human beings], and when it hears through the ears obedience and praise, and finds reverence and prostration.

But human beings did not know that there was an intelligible God, or an intelligible life, and that it would be natural for intelligence to think of Him and to delight mentally. Wherefore, God gave the law, and lifted human minds to His intelligible knowledge, so they might abandon the perceptible ill delights through the law and touch God through intelligent reason. And since people were dull and imprudent, He condescended to their level, and appeared perceptibly with trumpets and thunders, with fire and cloud, with an awesome appearance from which they took fright. And He gave bounties as quail and manna, and material promises—a perceptible altar, and sacrifices and gifts made of irrational [creatures], so they might establish familiarity with the intelligible and God might free Himself from such needs [for perceptible presence]. But when did He give these ordinances?

The all-merciful God wrote the law by the hand of Moses the Great, and gave it to the people [persecuted under the pharaoh] after He sympathized with them; saved them from slavery; struck Egypt with ten strikes; cut the sea and submerged the pharaoh in exchange for their suffering; and led them to the

7

desert. [He did this] first, to be a path for direction and salvation, so they would not return to Egypt to perish. Second, so they would live not by the body alone, but also by the soul with the law of God, and consequently emerge to the land of bounties. With divine fingers, He wrote the Ten Commandments on two tablets: five imperative [in nature] to keep the command, and five prohibitive [in nature] to prevent evil. And [He gave] two tablets, so that we keep God's ordinances in our soul and body, and write them in our hearts. Five relate to God, so we may love Him and come close to Him, and five relate to men, so we may love our neighbors and distance ourselves from evil. For virtue is twofold, like the person who stands on two feet; as the Prophet teaches: "Cease to do evil and learn to do good" (Isa 1:16–17).

Wherefore, He wrote the laws on two tablets—one to avoid evil and one to do good. Again, He wrote the Ten Commandments on two tablets, because originally He had created ten senses for us—five for the spirit and five for the body—and He gave Ten Commandments so we may adorn them [the senses]. Moreover, the sages say that there are two kinds of piety—theoretical and practical—and that each is divided into five: wisdom, sight, hearing, unforgetfulness, and truth as their completion. For a wise soul can see, and can always see that which is straight. And those who have seen, hear from others and learn, and those who have learned keep remembering and truly become the true image of true God, thus knowing the Creator and the creatures, for He [the Creator] is the cause and origin of all, whereas we are caused and made by Him. This is what we learn from the first five [commandments] written on the tablet.

[The sages] also say that reason is divided into five components: thought, action, virtue, faith, and goodness as their completion. For the thoughtful always thinks that which is appropriate, and works that which has been thought, and virtue becomes accomplished through his actions, and faith is established afterward. When we perform a virtue, faith appears in us, and our audience becomes strengthened in faith, be it through seeing or hearing. Then goodness is accomplished, for faith is established through works and goodness is completed through them. Thus, man becomes perfect in faith and works. God, therefore, wrote the Ten Commandments to adorn in us all parts of the soul and the body.

The first commandment says: "I am the Lord your God, . . . you shall have no other God beside me" (cf. Ex 20:2–3). The first goodness of man is to know God, as Paul says: "One must believe that God exists" (cf. Heb 11:6), then to approach God through good works and implement His will. Now, God is one, and He is the Lord and Creator of all; however, the Trinity is worshipped and prostrated before, as Deuteronomy says: "Hear, O Israel, the Lord our God is one Lord" (Deut 6:4), while here [in the Decalogue] He says: "I am the Lord your God" (Ex 20:2–3), who has three countenances—Father, Son, and Spirit. The Son and the Spirit are from God the Father, but they are not alien to Him, as our Lord says: "I came from the Father and have come into the world" (Jn 16:28), and "The Spirit comes from the Father" (cf. Jn 15:26). If you seek an example, the sun is one, but it has three properties: the ring [of fire], light, and heat, and these three properties have one nature. Likewise, the Trinity is one nature, one Godhead, one glory, and one kingdom.

The second commandment says: "You shall not make for yourself an idol, whether in the form of anything that is in heaven, or that is on the earth" (Ex 20:4). This obviously means: Unlike the Egyptians who worshipped reptiles and animals, or the Babylonians who worshipped the image of man, while others [worshipped] the sun and the moon, and yet others [worshipped] fire and water, and other things, we should not worship idols of silver and gold or anything else, and should not erect images of man, or birds, or beasts, or reptiles. Therefore, it [the commandment] says: "In the form of anything that is in heaven, or that is on the earth, or that is in the water" (Ex 20:4).

It is to be known that there are three kinds of idolatry from which we are instructed to stay away [in this commandment]. First, avoid worshipping as God immaterial objects, such as angels. Wherefore He says: "You shall have no other God beside me." Silver and golden casts comprise the second type of idols. He says: "You shall not make yourself an idol," for "The idols of the heathen are devils" (Ps 96:5), the Prophet says. The third [type of idol] is the icon—the replica of living or lifeless things, as is said: "You shall not make for yourself an idol, whether in the form of anything that is in heaven, or that is on the earth" (Ex 20:4). Should someone question: Why do we worship the icon? We briefly say that it is apparent that the icons before which we prostrate are not of demons and idols, but of Christ, the Mother of God, angels, or other holy beings. We do not worship these icons as God; rather, we prostrate before and revere Him whom the icon resembles. It is to be known that we prostrate before blessed images, but we worship the cross, for Christ is united with it and is nailed to it inseparably.

Prostration is bodily obedience, whereas worship is [accomplished] within the spirit and with passion, as is written: "Worship the Lord your God, and serve only Him" (Mt 4:10). We worship the cross alone with faith and spirit, and we are designated as worshippers of the cross. Concerning prostration, our prostration before God is different from our bowing before the angels, man, or saints. For example, we bow before the king and those who are prominent; however, we obey them differently. Likewise, bowing before God is different from bowing before man. But who are those who bow before unfamiliar gods and icons? With regard to the first commandment—"You shall not bow to other gods" (Ex 20:3)—[note that] the Hebrews and Saracens worship satanic figures. The Hebrews [worship] the Anti-Christ, whereas the Saracens [worship] the forerunner of the Anti-Christ—their erroneous leader.

With regard to the second [commandment], [note that] the heretics make prints and casts, because a heretic accepts only whatever his mind can cast and figure; he neither knows nor accepts what is pertinent to the canons of faith. Those who cast figures are sinful Christians who submit to sins and serve them. The Lord says: "He who commits sin is the servant of sin" (Jn 8:34). The proud man worships the figures of those who are in the heavens above, for he always likes to be higher than his peer is. The avaricious worships the figures that are on earth, indulging excessively and drinking excessively, just like animals. The voluptuous worships those that are in the waters with lascivious desire. And he whose mind always wanders on the earth worships the reptiles.

Likewise, the beastly man worships the beasts, the glutton worships the belly, the womanizer worships women, and so on, as the Apostle says: "Whose God is their belly, and whose glory is their shame" (Phil 3:19).

Elsewhere, [God] divides the worship of idols into four [categories], when He says: "You shall make for yourselves no handmade idols and no images, and no statues, and no figured stones" (cf. Lev 26:1). The handmade [refers to] those who abandon the worship of God and preoccupy themselves with bodily works and avarice. They sin twofold: first, because "Greed is idolatry by itself" (Col 3:5), as the Apostle says; second, [because] they detach themselves from the worship of God and time [reserved] for prayers, and give themselves to bodily works, [engaging] in husbandry, labor, trade, and [breeding] animals. God tolerates them that they may not reduce their prayers to nothing; otherwise, the state of poverty would distance them more [from God]. And it is a work befitting to the adversary when man sometimes gets intrigued by wealth, and sometimes through poverty wonders if God has caused wealth and poverty for a good reason, so people might inherit the kingdom through them [wealth and poverty]. Satan turned this around and brought the inheritance of hell [to human beings] by causing wealth and poverty. For this reason, He says: "You shall make for yourselves no handmade idols, and no images" (Lev 26:1).

Factually, man gives himself up to lechery by always looking at faces or reproducing faces in his mind; the Lord designated that looking with such desire equates to committing adultery in the heart; and evil thoughts in the heart are seeds, which then grow in the body as sinful actions. Therefore, we ought to stay away from such evil looks, for the blindness of the eyes is virginity to man, as Job says: "I made a covenant with my eyes, and I will not think upon a virgin" (Job 31:1). For this reason He says: "You shall make no images."

He also says: "No statues." Statues are [perceived in] two [ways]: first, when man remains in the sin without repentance and strengthens the sins within himself and fortifies them; second, when man leaves an evil memory after his death—people brand him as evil and curse him so long as they remember him, while others learn his wickedness and practice it [themselves], increasing [by doing so] his punishment, as the Apostle says: "There are sins that precede man, and there are those that follow man to the grave" (cf. 1 Tim 5:24); that is, the statue of sins. The figured stone indicates those who constantly pile sins upon their sins either by committing various sins or by finding pleasure in one sin and repeating it many times addictively; [thus] they create in their soul a heap of stones by which the soul gets stoned and loaded in hell. With this interpretation, some have developed the habit of building heaps of stones for evil men, as an indication to the wicked, whose soul will likewise be stoned and descend into hell with a heavy burden.

As commanded in the law, a notorious adulterer should be taken out of the camp, and those who have witnessed him should lay their hands on his head, and the whole congregation should stone him. Laying the hands on the head seems to mean: "You deserve death according to our testimony, and let your blood be on your own head." In the new law, we take [the sinner] out of the church, separate him, and stone his soul with excommunication, and the entire congregation ceases greeting him and interacting with him. This comprises a monumental sin [in the form of figurative stone]. May the Savior of all, Christ the God, save us from all evil sins, and make us worthy of His mercy. Amen.

This [the above] was [about] the second commandment.

The third [commandment] says: "You shall not take the name of God in vain" (Ex 20:7); meaning, you shall not swear falsely. Pagans falsely take the name of God upon images that are not God. Likewise, people who swear falsely take the name of God upon falsehood. This [swearing] is of two kinds: without reason and with reason. Nobody requires [swearing] without reason; nevertheless, [a swearer] habitually always takes the name of God in every false thing when receiving, giving, trading, measuring, weighing, and so on.

11

[Swearing] with reason is of two kinds. The first kind is a person who has not seen, has not caught, and does not know [a sinner], and yet bears false witness for the wrongdoings of others. The other [kind] is a person who covers his sins by [using] God's name, thinks that the never-sleeping eye, the One that is next to everybody is blind, and deceives men. Concerning those, the law says: "God will not acquit him who takes his name in vain" (Deut 5:11); that is, He will not expiate the sin through minor penance, for although presently He does not torment [the sinner], He lends [the sinner's life] by mercy so that he may pay for it through severe penance.

And it is to be known here that man commits three kinds of sins through the misuse of God's name: First, by taking God's name in vain—despite knowing his wrongness—and swearing on expense of despising God. Second, by breaking his word and lying after [swearing]. Third, by inappropriate swearing—such as swearing by the white hair and the beard of God, and so on—which is a major sin. Likewise, it is inappropriate when someone swears negatively or affirmatively by mentioning God's awesome name as testimonial, or in writing, as some men are used to, for they write their soul to Satan. These are extremely great sins. Christians should not swear, because Christ commanded: "Let your 'yes' be yes, and 'no' no" (Mt 5:37).

Christians should demonstrate faith and manners that eliminate the need to swear to one another, except when people demonstrate lack of belief, and when the work is of great significance to [matters of] faith or salvation of the kin. In such a case, they can swear within the following limits: [I swear that] this is so by the Glory of this cross or this Gospel; or the Lord, the cross, and the church know [that I speak the truth]. And this [is allowed only] when necessary, [provided] he [who swears] would still seek expiation through penance.

It is to be known that God's name is taken in three kinds of falsehood: by heart, by mouth, and by action. [God's name is taken] by heart by the wicked faithful—false Christians—who have received baptism but lack the grace of baptism, for they do not love God by heart, but only by their false name and lying tongue. Those who swear falsely, make a vow but do not fulfill it, pray in false words and not by warm heart, or preach [driven] by greed, glory, or heresy lie by the mouth. It is those who call God's name with a deceitful mouth; hence: "This people honors me with their lips, but with heart they are far separated from me" (Mt 15:8). Elsewhere it is said: "You are near in their mouths, yet far from their kidneys [hearts]" (Jer 12:2). Those who call God's name upon superficial external works, and not by a pure heart, lie through their works, like the hypocrites, because they give God's name in vain upon these [external works], for they receive the reward from human beings but not God. Moreover, [the Gospel] says: "He will cut the sinners in pieces, and put their pieces with the hypocrites in the eternal fire" (cf. Mt 24:51). This [explanation was about] the third commandment.

The fourth [commandment] says: "Remember the Sabbath day" (Ex 20:8). Sabbath is perceived as rest, or devotion, when we rest from physical work and devote ourselves to God's spiritual works, such as praying, worshipping, meditating upon God, and so on. Also, by resting we cease from evil works and engage in good works. This is the first [kind] of cessation from work. The second [kind of] Sabbath is the rest of God, who created the world in six days and rested on the seventh, and [therefore] we ought to cease and rest from physical works. The third [kind of] Sabbath is the Great Sabbath, when Christ entered the grave, and rested from the agony of the cross, and descended into hell, and rested by delivering the souls from torments. The fourth [kind of Sabbath occurs] when we die in the body, are placed in the grave, and rest from life's suffering, for "Death is rest to a man" (Job 3:23); because if he was sinful, [by dying] he escaped the multitude of sins, and if he was righteous, he escaped the traps of the hunters and physical pains. This is what is meant by "Remember the Sabbath day." The fifth [kind of] Sabbath is the rest of the eternal life which is prepared for the saints and for those who love Him after their transition from this life. This is the Sabbath, which He commanded: "Remember the Sabbath day."

"You shall work six days, but you shall rest on the seventh day" (Ex 34:21). First, because God created the world in six days and rested on the seventh, we ought to follow suit—work six days, and rest on the seventh, because the God of eternities does not labor and rests.[1] And as He said: "I repent that I have made the man" (cf. Gen 6:6), so that we may repent our sins. It [the Scripture] also said: "God rested," so we may work six days and rest on the seventh; [and] we were taught to observe the Sunday [in the new law] as the Sabbath was observed in the old [law].

Second, since [God] worked material works during six ages, and rest followed during the seventh, we ought to work six days and rest on the seventh.

Third, since there are six things in man that motivate him to sin, and [only] one thing moves us toward holiness by which we are justified, we ought to work six days and rest on the seventh.

---

[1] The original text mistakenly says, "does not rest."

13

Fourth, since number seven is sacred and is God's gift, we perform physical works six days, and sanctify the seventh and give God His share.

Fifth, because the people of Israel were hard-hearted and merciless, He commanded them to rest, so their servants, whether male or female, their hirelings, their oxen, their donkeys, and every other laboring creature could rest.

Sixth, so that men might dedicate at least one day to see the creatures for the glory of God, and understand the Creator, and thankfully praise the Creator of all.

Seventh, because the seventh day is the day of confession and expiation of sins, so that those who have committed sins throughout the week might repent on Sunday.

Eighth, so that on Sunday [men] may learn to do good and keep it in their mind in order to observe throughout the next week [what they have learned], because man is very forgetful. For this reason man ought to continuously learn, so he may not forget that which is good. For this reason [God] commanded in the old [law] the observance of Sabbath, and in the new [law] the Apostles instructed us to change [the day] and observe the Sunday.

Ninth, we ought to observe the Sunday because it is the first day of the creation of the world, and many wonders occurred on Sunday in the old times. It was Sunday when the sea was divided and the people passed through; and it was Sunday when God appeared in Sinai and gave the law. In the new [times] also some say that it was on Sunday that Christ was born, although others say the birth occurred on Saturday and the tidings on Wednesday. Moreover, the resurrection of Christ happened on Sunday, when He rose from the grave and delivered us from our servitude to death and corruption. Likewise, the descent of the Holy Spirit [upon the Apostles] occurred on Sunday, wherefore we ought to observe it, so that we may deserve the grace.

Tenth, because the last ever luminous day, when the [general] resurrection, the judgment, and the compensation for the works of all men will take place, will coincide with Sunday.

Wherefore, we ought to cease from sins today [this Sunday] and hope for the coming of Christ and the sound of trumpets on that [last] day. We ought to rest from physical works and sins on Sunday, because it is the prototype of the last Sunday, which is the ever luminous and immutable day of the end [of the world], the end of this age, and the beginning of eternity. For this reason, [God] commanded us to observe the Sabbath in the old and Sunday in the new [law].

Moreover, God commanded us to keep one of each seven Sabbaths and one of each seven months, and repose. And [commanded us] to cease from working the earth every other seven years: not seeding, harvesting, [planting] trees, or collecting the fruits of the fields. First, so that beasts and wild animals may eat them, for they, too, are the creation of God, and the earth, where we took abode, was their place, and the earthly things that we ravished belonged to them; [so] we ought to give them what belongs to them every other seventh year. Second, so that the earth and the elements might rest from those who labor, because the elements of the earth labor and suffer with us through our evil works. When we roam the world with evil [intentions and deeds], and turn the air into substance for evil things, and carry the water in our desires for sins, and [also use] the heat of fire for the love and inflammation of evil things, the elements of the earth suffer with us; but when we work good deeds, they rest and share our joy.

And should someone say, how can the breathless and lifeless elements suffer or repose? We say that each element has guardian and protector angels; they suffer with our wickedness, and rest with our good works. Because good works can be worked always and continually, as the Lord said: "My Father is still working, and I also am working" (Jn 5:17); that is, the work of providence that makes the animals and the plants give birth, changes kings and rulers, puts the heavens and the luminous bodies into motion, and sustains the earth. It is evident, then, that when [the Scripture] says: "God rested from all his works" (Gen 2:3), it meant [God ceased] to create new species, but He always works through providence. Thus, we ought to refrain from physical and evil works, and increase spiritual and good works.

Just as the priests circumcised the children on their eighth day in the temple and it was not [considered] sin, and [just as] they served the sacred bread with the baked lamb morning and evening on the Sabbath, and [just as] they gave water to the ox and the ass, and brought the fallen animal out of the well, so should we bring our souls, which are submerged in deep sins, out on Sunday, and give water to all ill-mannered people. And on any given day when human beings do good, God considers it Sabbath and rest. And on Sunday we should refrain from sinning, trading, [visiting] theaters, [watching] plays, intriguing, drunkenness, and the pleasures of bed. And if it has been canonized not to genuflect on Sunday, [it was done so] because [on Sunday] Christ rose from the dead and made us stand; [therefore] we should not prostrate ourselves, and more so, we should stay steady and avoid falling in the pleasures of the body. Now, to refrain from physical work is everybody's obligation; to refrain from sins is [an obligation] particular to Christians and saints; and to preoccupy oneself with good works is more pertinent to perfect and God-pleasing men for the glory of Christ our God who is blessed forever, amen.

The fifth commandment, "Honor your father and your mother" (Ex 20:12), seals the first five commandments, beginning with God and ending with the parents, because the parents are reckoned to be "second gods" to their descendants, for the true God is [parent] to all, whereas the parents are [parent] to individual descendants. And just as God creates the invisible soul, the parents [create] the visible body, wherefore it is impossible [for the descendants] to remunerate their parents for their suffering day and night, for the food and clothing [they provide], and for their compassion and protection. Even if the descendants compensate for all of these, they will stop short of one thing—giving birth to their parents.

Parents are to be honored for many reasons. First, parents are the images of God, as has been demonstrated; therefore, they should be honored second to God. Second, they are the instruments of the image of the great God in us, for God neither would create the soul, nor would He compose the body in the womb without parents. Third, we learn to love God and man from our parents: whoever loves his parents loves God and men, and whoever does not love his parents is ungrateful toward God and hateful toward men.

Fourth, parents are to be honored so that they may be compensated somewhat for their many favors. Fifth, parents are to be honored so that [the descendants of] their descendants may honor them, because whatever you do to your parents, your descendant does to you, be it evil or good. Sixth, parents are to be honored to fulfill God's [fifth] commandment: "Honor your father and your mother."

Seventh, [parents are to be honored] because of the promise of the tidings: "It may be well with you, and you may be long-lived" (cf. Deut 4:40); for, indeed, whoever sustains the lives of others deserves his life to be sustained.

Eighth, parents need to be obeyed because of the [threat of] the punishment stated in the law: "Anyone who dishonors his father or his mother will die the death" (Lev 20:9), for the parents are the second cause [of human existence], and speaking evil of them relates to God—the first cause. Hence: "Whoever dishonors you dishonors me, and whoever receives you receives me" (cf. Lk 10:16).

Ninth, parents are to be honored so that [the descendants] may deserve the last blessing of the parents, just as Isaac was blessed by Abraham, and Jacob by Isaac; and through such blessing their descendants grew and multiplied on earth like the multitude of stars in heaven. However, whoever does not deserve his parents' blessing will inherit curse, like Reuben [inherited] from Jacob, and Canaan from Noah, who said: "Cursed be young Canaan, a slave shall he be to his brethren" (Gen 9:25). It was because of this curse that the Canaanites underwent famine and death by the sword by Israel. "And the earth opened her mouth and swallowed Korah and Dathan" (cf. Num 26:10) because of Reuben's curse. Thus is the curse of the parents, and thus is their blessing.

Tenth, honoring the parents can be learned from irrational animals, such as a righteous stork that feeds its old-aged parents, or young pewits that do not mate unless they pay their debt to their parents and mate [only] upon their consent. If men are not able to learn from the Scripture, they ought to learn to obey their parents from the irrational beings.

A parent owes four things to the descendants. First, attendance to their bodily needs: food, clothing, and other nourishment. Second, teaching them professions and useful instruction. Third, giving them to marriage. Fourth, training them in faith and good works. The first [obligation] relates to the protection of the individual and his body. The second is the well-being of the same and his mental education. The third is the multiplication of the [human] kind and blessed births. The fourth is for the goodness of the soul and the memory, for he [the descendant] becomes known to God by his faith and work, which weigh more than the perishable treasures of gold and silver. A pious person will lack nothing in the world; hence: "For a believer the whole world is full of possessions; but for the unbeliever it holds not even a gerah" (Prov 17:4).[2] It is evident, then, that the fourth [obligation] is more necessary for the parents than the previously mentioned three [obligations].

Likewise, the descendants owe their parents four things. First, obeying the commands of their parents and not deviating from their commands, for Solomon says: "A disobedient son will be destroyed, but an obedient son is exempt from destruction" (cf. Prov 13:1). Second, honoring their parents in their needs for physical food and drink, and clothing and other things unto the day of their death. Third, keeping the will of the parents in effect and unaltered, whatever their will may be, "For a will takes effect only at death" (Heb 9:17). Fourth, making the day of [the parents'] death glorious, and being a good reminder of their parents' souls so long as they live. By doing so, they may pay, somewhat, what they owe to his parents.

It needs to be taken into consideration that the designation "father" is given

---

[2] In the Armenian Bible this sentence follows the text found in English translations of the Bible; that is: "An evildoer gives heed to false lips; [and] a liar gives ear to a naughty tongue."

to many people. First, the corporeal parents are the corporeal creator of the body, as we have mentioned. Second, [there is] the spiritual father of the second birth, such as the primate or the priest—the creators of grace. Third, [there is] the rational father—the creator of minds, such as the instructors of apprentices, "For in Christ Jesus I became your father through the Gospel" (1 Cor 4:15). Fourth, the leaders of a covenant and old-aged people also are referred to as fathers, for they are fathers of exhortation and fear, because Amon says: "Anyone who is not at the feet of the elderly is an easy prey to Satan." Fifth, kings and rulers are referred to as fathers; they protect and care for the population and provinces.

The obligation to obey these [fathers] differs from one father to another. We ought to obey a corporeal father in corporeal matters as we have said, and [we have to show] spiritual obedience to the spiritual father. Apprentices [should obey] by listening to the instructors, for [the Apostle] says: "Obey your leaders and submit to them, for they are keeping watch over your souls" (Heb 13:17). Members of a brotherhood should obey the primate in fear and awe of him, so that they may overcome their own wills and fulfill his will, thus meeting the pleasure of God's will. And we ought to obey the king or the ruler in temporal and common matters, "For there is no authority except from God, and those authorities that exist have been instituted by God. Therefore, whoever resists authority, opposes God's command" (Rom 13:1–2).

Should someone say: Do we have to accept everything a ruler might say? We say that we ought to fulfill the nonspiritual tasks he puts forth, so long as it does not lack faith and soul. As I have previously mentioned, they ought to be obeyed in temporal and common matters, for they have authority over the body and temporal things. But the ruler and judge of your faith and soul is God; [therefore] matters related to faith and good works should be offered to Him. And if a ruler turns into a tyrant, it is better for him to die physically with sword, rather than fall spiritually with the sword of God, as Christ said: "Do not fear those who kill the body but cannot kill the soul; rather fear him who can destroy both soul and body in hell" (Mt 10:28). Just as the ranks of the martyrs who died for Christ and came back to life with Him were saved from the fire of hell and admitted to the kingdom of heaven, may Christ, through their intercession and the intercession of all saints, save all those who believe in His name from the fire of hell and the never-ending torments, ranking them with the saints and the loved ones in the kingdom of heaven; and glory to Him forever. Amen.

This [was] about the imperative [commandments].

CHAPTER III

Homily of the same according to the verse: "You shall not murder. You shall not commit adultery. You shall not steal. You shall not bear false witness against your neighbor. You shall not covet your neighbor's wife; you shall not covet your neighbor's house; [etc.]" (Ex 20:13–17).

The Decalogue divided the law into two groups of five [commandments] because man possesses ten senses: five related to the soul, for which [God] commanded five clauses of law, and five related to the body, for which [the other] five clauses are placed—"You shall not murder. You shall not commit adultery"—and so on. Again, the five clauses, already discussed, are positive by nature, and the five [clauses], which are to be discussed, are prohibitive by nature. Again, the five [already discussed clauses] are imperative commandments, and the five [to be discussed] are prohibition and instruction. Again, the [first] five ordinances pertain to God, and the [last] five to man and to [his] neighbors.

For this reason, those pertinent to God were prior to those concerning human beings, which state: "You shall not murder. You shall not commit adultery," and so on. It is to be known that this commandment and instruction are from the natural law that was planted in our natures from the beginning. The first patriarchs, such as Enos, Enoch, Noah, [and] Abraham, were justified by this [natural law]. Instructed by nature, they installed judges and inquisitors over the sinners. They decreed death and prison and torture, as Paul says: "Those who practice such things deserve to die" (Rom 1:32). In this way they [the patriarchs] met the law of God, in accordance with the prohibitive divine commandment—"You shall not murder." But why does the law address the public as one person and not many? This is so to have all relate the precepts to themselves, take ownership of the instruction, and avoid inactiveness through their negligence [as unrelated to individuals, since they are] addressed to many. Besides, an individual keeping God's ordinances is as precious to God as all of humankind.

Therefore, He [God] said: "You shall not murder." [To kill] is a great and absolute iniquity, which He placed before [the other four commandments pertinent to humankind]. He commanded to Noah: "He who sheds man's blood, instead of that blood shall his own be shed, for in the image of God I made man" (Gen 9:6). God created humankind in His image, and [therefore] a murderer goes against God in two ways. First, for he has ravished God's work; because the action befits Him who binds, sets loose, and binds insolubly—Him who said: "I kill and I will make to live" (Deut 32:39). Whosoever cannot give life does not have the right to kill. Second, since God brought [man] into life and being, he [the murderer] goes against God by turning [a man] into death and nonbeing. Independent philosophers prohibited murder for this reason. According to Plato, "we are reminiscent to a prisoner and no one has the right to bring himself or someone like him outside the body."[3]

Should someone question whether a person who commits suicide is a greater murderer than a manslayer, some answer: It seems that manslaughter as sin is greater than suicide, for he [the murderer] is responsible twice—first, for his own sins; second, for the sins of him who he murdered. But the doctors say: No, suicide is a greater sin than [manslaughter] for three reasons. First, because by being alive, [the manslayer] can later seek expiation through penance, as Lucianus and many Jews who crucified Christ were expiated through penance. Judas, however, was unable to repent, and he descended to hell with sins. Second, a manslayer is the adversary and enemy of him who he murdered; while anyone who commits suicide antagonizes God, for to bind and set loose of the body is God's prerogative, as Plato says, "we are reminiscent to a prisoner and no one has the right to take away his own life until he who bound it sets it loose again."[4]

Besides, the doctors say: "We [need to] wait for Him who binds and sets loose, and binds again insolubly." Third, a manslayer can pay for the blood [that he shed] with his own blood, as the law mandates. "He that sheds man's blood, instead of that blood shall his own be shed" (Gen 9:6) and it will be paid here [in this world or life]. But a suicide will be punished in the life to come perpetually; then, therefore, just as eternal torment is greater than [the torment] of the body, so also suicide is greater as sin and reason for unending torment than manslaughter for which the manslayer was punished in this life.

[Consider] also this when [God] says: "You shall not murder." He prohibits all kinds of unlawful murders. And the unlawful murder occurs in three ways. First, when a man is killed without offense and without being sentenced to death. Second, when someone kills a man without having authority, or without

---

[3] See Socrates' dialogue with Cebes in Plato's *Phaedo*.

[4] *Ibid.*

being a servant of the law. Third, when a man of authority kills because of an ill intention and not because he is driven by vengeance for God's law; this is unlawful killing; [the murderer] is liable for the blood [he shed].

But murder is not exhausted by these. Other acts also are considered murder. First, a man who finds someone in ultimate need and subject to great hardship, both spiritually and physically, yet neglects and helps not, is a murderer, because he did not do good to his neighbor. Second, he who works evil and hates his neighbor in his mind is a murderer, according to what has been said: "All who hate a brother are murderers" (1 Jn 3:15). Third, anyone who speaks slander or defamation or betrayal is a murderer. Since kings and princes order executioners verbally to stone or strangle [people], they are murderers. Likewise, explicitly murderers are the betrayers who by their words cause murder or seizure of possessions, for possessions are man's life—he has gathered them by sweat. It is said about [expropriated] possessions that when the blood was shed, or when the possessions are taken away, [men] die of famine. Fourth, murderers are reckoned to be those who, through their actions, are evil influence, causing others' destruction by making them sin, or by leading a voluptuous life, or by deceiving them. "Murderers do not have [eternal] life abiding in them" (1 Jn 3:15).

More on murder.

There are many kinds of murderers. There is murder that stems from hatred—Cain's case. And there is murder that stems from revenge—Absalom's case. There is murder [motivated by] envy—the case of Satan, the first manslayer. There is murder stemming from greed—the case of thieves and robbers. There is murder caused by calumny and treachery. And there is murder that is [committed] by expropriating the orphan and the widow. And this kind of murder is presented by the Prophet: "They have slain the widow and the stranger, and murdered the fatherless" (Ps 94:6). And there is murder stemming from neglecting the needs of the neighbor. Moreover, this is to be known that the ordinances of the Decalogue are fundamental. [Perceive them] as totality and a single class composed of parts and divisions that are delivered concisely.

"You shall not murder." [This commandment] prohibits all kinds of murders, whether by heart, mouth, or action. It commands refraining from anger, grudge, hatred, envy, knavery, and rancor, for these are murders by heart. Also, [it commands] refraining from treachery, blasphemy, envy, intrigue, curse, and insult, for these are murders by tongue. Also, [it commands] refraining from giving the deathblow to those who are not [sentenced] to death, beating, [or] tearing out the hair or the beard, for these constitute murder by action. The ordinances stipulate not to commit these [kinds of acts].

The seventh clause of the law says: "You shall not commit adultery." This is not a minor trespass but rather one of the capital mortal sins— lasciviousness—which is the lewd copulation of the body, instigated by impure desires, which [God] prohibits by saying: "You shall not commit adultery," because it causes many physical harms.

First, it weakens the steadiness of the soul and makes man sluggish and cowardly in everything. Second, it corrupts the body, according to the Apostle: "The fornicator sins against the body itself" (1 Cor 6:18). Third, it causes frenzy and makes man savage. Just as [these happen to] the drunkard, so also [they happen to] the fornicator; as Hosea says: "Wine and woman take away the understanding" (Hos 4:11);[5] they cause illusion and thereby the person is called frenetic, wandering around as if he is possessed. It [adultery] also makes man fornicate without shame; hence: "You have a whore's face; you did become shameless toward all" (Jer 3:3). Fourth, it leads to intemperance and impurity, for man cannot resist desires, and just as the candle is consumed by fire, so is man consumed by impure desires, whether he looks or thinks, because his desire is insatiable, like the flame that burns everything it touches and remains unquenchable. Fifth, it corrupts the heritage. A husband and a wife are lawful heirs to one another; when they go to a different bed, they corrupt the heritage of others, besides confusing and corrupting themselves.

Sixth, [adultery] causes animosity and commotion, for as the dogs fight over a bitch, so [do] fornicators over women. Seventh, it makes either the fornicator or the woman commit murders—Solomon says: "For the jealousy arouses a husband's fury, and will not spare in the Day of Judgment" (Prov 6:34)—either [people] will kill the fornicator in lieu of others, or others will kill for the fornicator. Or the guardians of the law will kill [the fornicator], as Phinehas slew Zimri and Cozbi, and then death for prostitution in the name of Baal-Peor [Num 25] ceased. And as the men of Shechem were killed by the sword because they had defiled Dinah daughter of Jacob; the men [who defiled] were first circumcised and then Simeon and Levi killed everybody with the sword [Gen 34].

Eighth, it [adultery] excites people to sedition, as is written in Judges about the woman who died because of rape, and all the tribes [of Israel] gathered together and killed twenty-six thousand armed men, and put the Benjamites to the sword. Only six hundred men survived and fled toward the mountains [Judg

---

[5] "Wine and new wine . . ." and not "wine and woman . . ."

20]. Ninth, it destroys houses, as is evident from the fornicators who lose all their possessions because of adultery, and their houses get destroyed. Otherwise, the law allows the fornicators to be stoned and their houses to be destroyed. Tenth, it curtails the hope of the legitimate sons [for fair inheritance], because they do not know who is born of whom, and often sons of fornication inherit the patrimony of the legitimate sons, who then are deprived of inheritance. It is with these and with their likes that adultery physically harms adulterers.

But it harms [adulterers] much more spiritually. First, because it [adultery] dishonors God by violating His temple. [The Apostle] says: "You are God's temple and God's Spirit dwells in you" (1 Cor 3:16). Second, for it becomes a rest and abode for demons, as Job says: "Behemoth lies in marshy places" (cf. Job 40:15–24), which are the souls of lustful people. And just as a possessed person is driven by Satan, so is the frenetic driven by passion. Third, the mind becomes blind at sight [of adultery], for reason becomes consumed and forgets the grievance of death and hell. Moreover, [man] becomes uncertain in his thoughts, sometimes thinking one thing and sometimes another.

Fourth, it [adultery] seduces the neighbor, enticing him to sin, as Hosea says: "You have been a snare at the watch-tower, and a net spread upon the mountain" (Hos 5:1),[6] for by adultery [men] entrap the flying soul. And "Woe to anyone who puts a stumbling block before one of these little ones," says the Lord (Mt 18:6), and woe to anyone who puts a trap for a blind man on the road. Fifth, it judges the mind with conscience, as was said to David: "The sword shall not depart from your house forever" (2 Kings 12:10). And this was said because he [David] had sinned with Bathsheba. The sword of conscience torments the souls of adulterers daily, for sin seems pleasant briefly, but upon occurrence it becomes more bitter than gall, as Solomon says: "Honey drops from the lips of a harlot; but in the end you will find her more bitter than gall" (cf. Prov 5:3). Sixth, it [the soul] is subdued by indignation; the spirit, which is master, serves the senses and the body. Moreover, man yields to the associate of passionate sin and obeys [the associate]; wherefore it was said: "Because you have listened to the voice of your wife and have eaten the fruit" (Gen 3:17).

Seventh, it makes man love himself and the worldly life, for he desires longevity in order to accomplish his lustful desires. He also desires health, strength, wealth, honor, and the likes through which adultery is accomplished. Eighth, man hates God who punishes those who follow the lustful desires of

---

[6] "You have been a snare at Mizpah, and a net spread upon Tabor."

the body, when He sends them sickness, poverty, and other kinds of instruction. Moreover, man hates the saints who reproach him for such [adulterous] deeds. Solomon says: "They hated those who reproved them in court" (cf. Prov 15:12). They do not open their ears to instruction, because "Like adder and aspic his ears are blocked" (Ps 58:4)[7] with the relaxation of adultery. Ninth, [man feels] desperation for the life and glory to come, and for the forgiveness of sins or repentance. He [the adulterer] also neglects physical punishments and the state of ignominy before judges and rulers, for he dissolutely proceeds in lustfulness. Tenth, the vain and the abrupt flare of pleasure is substance for ever-burning hell. As adding wood [to a fire] intensifies the fire, likewise the filth of voluptuous desire intensifies the eternal fire "which is prepared for the devil and his angels" (Mt 25:41). These are the losses of adulterers, wherefore the law prohibits it and commands: "You shall not commit adultery."

Adultery is divided into numerous kinds, for it is multifaceted and ought to be forbidden to adulterers. First, there is simple fornication, through which a free person commits adultery with a free person, be it man or woman.

Second, there is prostitution, which either is committed with many or is limited to sleeping with a notorious prostitute.

Third, there is an adultery which spoils the wedding bed and is committed with strangers, in the likeness of dogs, whether they are men or women.

Fourth, there is fornication [committed] either by having two wives [while the first is still] alive, or, after the death of the first, by having a third and even a fourth wife who [then] are called whores, because only the first wedding is lawful—one woman to one man as it is with priests. The second [wife] is forgiven and allowed to the laity because of [their] weakness. But [to have] a third, a fourth, and more [wives] is fornication and unlawful marriage, as the Lord commanded the Samaritan woman by saying: "You have had five husbands, and the one you have now is not your husband" (Jn 4:18); it is fornication.

Fifth, the defilement of virgins is adultery, for it corrupts virgins' integrity.

Sixth, the desecration [committed] by those who have dedicated themselves to God [is adultery]. Those who have vowed themselves to God, such as clergymen, penitents, and others, lose their temperance through desecration—the higher the rank, the heavier the sin.

Seventh, incest [is adultery]. Whether the [close] relationship is through blood or marriage, or is a spiritual relationship, [intercourse] spoils.

---

[7] In *The Septuagint:* "As that of a deaf asp, and that stops her ears."

Eighth, sinning through the eyes, and being execrable by the scurrility of hands, ears, or tongues, or through other filthy things, are adultery by heart. The Lord designates these as adultery: "Whoever looks [at a woman] with lust" (Mt 5:28), even when the time, the place, or the person hampers the completion of the act [of adultery], that person has already committed adultery in his heart. Moreover, adultery is what has been committed already through [other body] parts. Wherefore, looking with lust, speaking with lust, and so on is called adultery.

Ninth, the cursed unspeakable crimes of males and females and of those who copulate with animals and their likes are adultery. They sin against nature by practicing sodomy, for not only men, but also animals run away from such copulation. Those deserve a thousand deaths and punishments if they refuse to expiate their sins through bitter and severe penitence. The Holy Scripture did not want to stain itself and the listeners [by writing about them]; it simply said: "You shall not commit adultery."

Tenth, the lustful copulation of a man and a woman [is adultery]. For example, [the eating of] clean food, like lamb, during Lent, or in an inappropriate place, or in violation of restrictions is always as condemnable as eating unclean food. Otherwise, it [the clean food], too, will be unclean and filthy.

Likewise, if the lawful matrimony is not maintained by discretion, it will be adultery and fornication. For matrimony has two modes: proper and improper. The proper is exercised for reproducing children to serve God, to keep the husband away from fornication, or to fulfill a responsibility; and the responsibility is that just as the woman is indebted because she was made of man, so is the man indebted because he was born of a woman. For these reasons, marriage is noble and beds are sacred, [especially] when the place and time [of copulation] are chosen with decency because of the weakness of [human] nature. This [the aforementioned] is the proper and honest matrimony.

The improper occurs in five modes, whereby this noble thing [proper matrimony] turns to be considered adultery. First, when [copulation] is performed in honest matrimony impetuously and [to] always satisfy licentious lust with whorish adulation, it is considered similar to that [copulation] of whores and adulterers. Second, when it is against the regular habit, as was said in the law: "You shall not sow your field with two kinds [of seed]" (Lev 19:19). Third, when it occurs in inappropriate time—during feasts, Sundays, Lent, and so on. For when a wedding is not permitted during a [particular] day, then [men] are not allowed to intermingle in beds [on that particular day]. Fourth, when they are in a holy place, next to a church, to a cross, or to other forbidden places. Fifth, when a man makes love to a pregnant woman who is close to giving birth or is having the menses. With these five modes, lawful matrimony turns into adultery and fornication, wherefore it is commanded: "You shall not commit adultery."

Again, as Ecclesiastes says: "A woman is the prey and trap of man's heart and is bands on his hands" (Eccl 7:27). It means that the lust of women is like a snare that captures birds, like a trap that captures beasts, and like a handcuff during action.

Although women harm men in numerous ways, they in particular harm them in three ways. First, [man's] mind is like a bird; it becomes bewitched and caught in the lust of women. Second, the body, like a beast, becomes entrapped when it fulfills the desire. Third, in the end [the lust] becomes an impediment for virtue, which is destroyed. And this happens because of three reasons. First, the mind is bewitched and dazzled by the sight and the beauty of women; hence: "Souls entrapped in sins lose also their mind." Then, passionate pleasures catch the body and entrap it, and lust diverts the soul from virtuous acts. As stated elsewhere: "The lust of wicked women entraps men as a dog bound by rope, and as a stag struck, and as an ox driven to slaughter" (Prov 7:2–22). If you want to learn the strength of women, you can see it in relation with Solomon the Wise, as the Scripture relates. Solomon's heart was straight toward his God since childhood, but when he aged and fell after women, his heart was no longer straight toward his God, for wine and women distanced him from God.

You can also see it in relation with mighty Samson: a woman tied him and his eyes were gouged out, and he was delivered to the hands of the Philistines. But this does not [apply] to all women and men. For it is said: "Those [sinners] who are abandoned by God are taken by her, and those who are good [in the sight of God] escape her" (Eccl 7:21). Susanna the prudent escaped the lustful old men just as Joseph the prudent escaped the tipsy whore. Likewise, those who have the fear of God fastened in their heart avoid their [women's] traps. But those who are weak and lewd, who follow their desires, and who are abandoned by God, fall in their [women's] traps.

But how do we escape adultery? First, avoid looking at, sitting close to, or talking to [a woman], or [doing] any other [tempting act], as Job says: "I made a covenant with my eyes, and I will not look at a virgin" (Job 31:1). And the proverb says: "Whoever touches pitch gets dirty" (Sir 13:1). And Sirach says: "He who holds her is like him who grasps a scorpion, a serpent, and fire" (Sir

26:7). Besides, as a saint[8] said: "Flee Martianus; flee and do not linger." This is the first means to escape fornication.

Second, put pressure on the body through hunger, thirst, and labor, for when the substance is reduced, the fire would be extinguished, as the Lord says: "This kind of demon goes not out but by prayer and fasting" (Mt 17:21).

Third, do physical work and sweat, or read, [or get involved] in studies or any other good work, for the doctors say: "Always do something good so that Satan may find you busy," since "Idleness is mother of all that is evil."

Fourth, oppose temptation, evil counsel, or evil actions from the beginning. As once inside a hole, the head of the serpent pulls its whole body in, likewise [man] should exercise caution at the beginning of a sin, in order to prevent its full penetration in him. The beginning of sin and evil counsel is as weak as the head of a serpent and can be smashed easily, wherefore God said: "He will strike your head" (Gen 3:15).

Fifth, think about the day of death and the tortures of hell. As the doctors say: "Remember the end of your life and then you will never sin" [Sir 7:36].

Sixth, do not trust yourself and always live in suspicion and fear, for if you are fallen, you should fear torments, and if you are not fallen, you should fear that you might fall, as the Apostle [Paul] says (cf. 1 Cor 10:12). David, who was a holy man, fell, Solomon the Wise erred, and the mightiest Samson lost his strength; therefore, [man] ought to live always in suspicion and fear, to watch out through the six [aforementioned] means, and to request alertness and protection from God our Savior who is blessed forever, amen.

The eighth commandment of the law says: "You shall not steal." These instructions are useful and beneficial in our life. They need to be taught to children at an early age, and prevent them from stealing, so they may not find the greater [theft] agreeable after being allowed the smaller, because according to the philosopher [Aristotle], habit transcends nature.[9] Habit extended over a long period becomes adventitious nature, and theft becomes as natural as sleeping, hunger, and thirst. [Prohibit] also minor theft so that a person would not commit a major theft, as the Lord instructs: "Whoever is faithful in a very little is faithful also in much; and whoever is dishonest in a very little is dishonest also in much" (Lk 16:10). For this reason, people say: "He who steals an egg and he who steals a horse are equal," because both are equally referred

---

8   Reference befits St. Martianus, the monk revered by the Coptic and Ethiopian churches for his resistance to the temptation of a harlot.

9   Cf. Aristotle, *Metaphysics*.

to as thieves, as people who deprive others from their possessions, and as avaricious [individuals].

Now, we were commanded by God to eat [our] bread by the sweat of [our] brows and not [to eat] what others earn, let aside stealing [what belongs to others]. [God] wrote in the law and prohibited stealing other peoples' belongings. Now, these two commandments are of the natural law: to eat the fruit of our labor and to steal not what others earn. Our Lord Jesus Christ added a third component [to this commandment, saying] that we should economize and distribute to others our lawful earning, and then we shall be perfect.

First, because we absolutely distance ourselves from ravishing strangers, for since we are commanded to give ours away, then we should not steal what belongs to others. Second, love toward our neighbor is demonstrated through almsgiving, and God's commandment is fulfilled when [you] "love your neighbor as yourself" (Lev 19:18). Third, through almsgiving we pile our treasures in heaven; first, because the heavenly treasure remains protected against thieves and spoilers, and then: "where your treasure is, there your heart will be also" (Lk 12:33). For this reason, [the Lord] commands: "Sell your possessions and give alms. Make purses for yourselves that do not wear out in heaven" (Lk 12:33).

Fourth, through almsgiving an enemy reconciles, a tyrant becomes humble, and an angry person calms down. For this reason, it was commanded: "If the tyrant takes your coat away, give him the other too. Give to everyone who begs from you, and do not refuse anyone who wants to borrow from you" (cf. Mt 5:40–42). It is evident, then, that the law of Christians is perfect. For this reason, it is important to exercise caution against theft as the Lord commanded. "You shall not steal." Moreover, this commandment includes the following: you shall not expropriate, you shall not usurp, you shall not cut off a deposit, or a debt, or a wage, and so on. Because theft occurs in many ways. Whoever covertly takes away possessions from a house is a thief. Likewise, whoever trades with [stolen things] is a dispossessor, for whoever sells [something] for more than its worth, or buys it for less than its worth, is a thief and dispossessor. Likewise, whoever practices double measures—big and small—as well as [double] cubits and weights by taking with the greater and giving with the lesser, is a thief and dispossessor. For this reason, their [thieves' and dispossessors'] abode is called "stall,"[10] which indicates a thief's circuit.

---

[10] The Armenian word *kulpak* [կուլպակ] is misspelled in the manuscript as *kolpak* [կոլբակ]. A variation of the same appears later in Chapter IV.

28

And whoever is the head of a village but deprives the village, [practically] robs the whole village. And whoever causes damage to or adulterates in a [given] profession, or reduces the substance which he has received, is a thief and dispossessor. They and those resembling them who defraud covertly are referred to as thieves and dispossessors, whereas those who openly take away [possessions of travelers] on the roads are referred to as ravishers and robbers. The tyrants and princes who deprive the poor of their rights are ravishers, and the judges who twist sentences by bribes are ravishers. Whoever loans silver or receives food and interest is a ravisher. And all those others who explicitly deprive are ravishers, while [those who deprive] covertly are thieves. Likewise, to cut off a deposit and a trust is conceived to be theft. Failure to return debts and pay wages to laborers is also theft, dispossession, and ravishing. For those cry out to God and He listens to them; hence: "Whoever is deprived among you cries out, and the cries of the harvesters have reached the ears of the Lord of hosts" (Jas 5:4).

What is the punishment of a thief? That which the angel showed to the Prophet Zechariah coming out of the temple with a scroll in his hand of twenty cubits long and ten cubits wide. The angel said to him, I will go and take my scroll to the houses of the thieves and robbers (cf. Zech 5:1–4), so that the angel may cut [them] off with the fiery sword physically here [in this world] and both physically and spiritually during the eternal torment. Behold, brethren, this is the punishment of thieves according to the Prophet, as has been demonstrated. In civil law, it is known that those who are guilty in trading [are subject to] fines, blows, reproach, and spit. The burglar and the robber are put to death, and the left foot and the right hand of the thief are cut off so that he may no longer steal. If he appears [stealing] again, [authorities] hang him from the hook. Indeed, whoever has stolen covertly is hanged from a high place manifestly. The robber is put to death as a notorious thief, and [authorities] sever the [robber's] right hand so that he may no longer steal. [They] also sever the left foot so that he may walk on the right side of his colleague when the latter sets off [for robbery]. [Authorities] also [allocate] fines and ignominy to the booths of thieves. And those who deceive covertly are dishonored explicitly so you may know that their physical punishment resembles the punishment of their soul, as we have mentioned. For this reason, and in order to spare us, [God] warned: "You shall not steal."

How are thieves treated? Whatever God commands in the law: "If the theft be certainly found in the thief's hand, he shall restore double" (Ex 22:4); one to be given to the [rightful] owner, and the other to the ruler; thereafter, he is beaten to death. But if the stolen belongings are already consumed when the thief is caught, he shall restore four or five times as much [for what he has stolen] and give them to the owners and the ruler. If the stolen good is a sheep, [the thief] restores four sheep for a sheep, and if it is an ox, [he restores] five for one, because to steal something big is a greater impudence than stealing something small. It is for this reason that [thieves] restore four for one [if it is a sheep].

If someone borrows one, he shall compensate that one with one. If someone dispossesses [another] unintentionally, [he shall restore] double. Then, indeed, anyone who steals should pay four times as much—two for dispossessing, and two for stealing. Also, [since] properties are [composed] of the four elements, the thief restores four times as much, and since the five senses have cooperated [in the theft], the [thief's] fine is five times as much. Similarly, in the new [law], thieves receive similar punishment. As Zacchaeus said to the Lord: "I will give to the poor half of my possessions; and if I have dispossessed anyone, I will compensate four times as much" (Lk 19:8), wherefore [the Lord] said: "Today salvation has come to this house of dispossessors because he [Zacchaeus] has compensated four times as much" (Lk 19:9).

If a thief is not caught, but he himself repents and goes to confess to the priest, the law commands the following: First, the thief shall confess to the priest, then restore as much as he has stolen, adding to it one fifth of the theft's worth for God. Moreover, he shall restore one fifth of the stolen belongings— as a fine for the five senses—to the [rightful] owner, and if he [the owner] is dead, to his blood relative, and if there is none, he shall give [the one fifth] to the priest who is an intercessor between the dead and the living. Thereafter, they [the thief and the owners of the stolen possessions] reconcile with one another. Afterward, [the thief] shall take a ram worth fifty piasters and make [with it] an offering to God, whereupon he will be forgiven.

Thus was the [old] law, and justly so.

The thief is guilty before the law of God, who said: "You shall not steal." He is guilty before the canons of the church and the priests, and he is indebted to the [rightful] owner of the [stolen] possessions. It is for this reason that he shall offer a ram to God, confess according to the canons, and restore the possessions to the owner, in order to be justified. Pay attention to the repentance, for only he who repents is exempt [of the obligation] of compensating four or five times as much, such as a caught thief is obliged to do.

The new [law] also is similar. A thief cannot be justified by confessing alone; he has to return the stolen possessions to the [rightful] owner, or to the poor, or to the priests and the church, and [only] then will he be reckoned a person who has paid. Instead of the ram, he has to offer his body and his soul to God through fasting and prayers, and [only] then will the sin of theft be expiated. With this in mind, penance, almsgiving, or fasting and prayers are designated for all sins, and more so for a thief. It is to be known that theft is exempt of punishment in three cases: First, when a sword is stolen from an enraged man so he would not harm himself or others; this is precaution and not theft. Second, when a dying person is extremely hungry and takes bread to fill [his stomach]; this is a necessity and not theft. Third, when it [theft] is committed by a command, such as when the Israelites took away the vessels of the Egyptians and did not give them back, because they [the Egyptians] owed them [the Israelites] the wage of the bricks; God commanded them to betray [the Egyptians] so they would be compensated.

Should someone say: So-and-so person dispossessed me, would I be justified if I steal his possessions? We say that [theft] should not occur [in such instances] because he [who dispossessed] will be judged with dispossessors, while you [will be judged] with thieves [if you do so]. God commanded the people [of Israel] to steal not only for compensation, but also so that they [the Israelites] would not dare to return to Egypt, for they had stolen their [the Egyptians'] possessions. Therefore, under no circumstance should a person dispossess [another] and steal others' possessions, because by stealing from others he forfeits his good works to others during the righteous judgment of God, and if he is not credited with good works, he gives away his faith and baptism [during the judgment]. And if [these others whom he has stolen from] belong to a different religion, then he [who steals] takes [upon himself] the sins [of these] and will be tortured in the fire [of hell], while they will receive God's reward.

Thus, brethren, to dispossess and to steal, whether from the church, the priest, or the laity, are most heavy [sins] when Christians or the church are dispossessed; but if [Christians] dispossess people of different religions, they carry the sins [of others], whether wealthy or poor. For this reason [God] warns: "You shall not steal."

Do not lose your soul for perishable possessions, but love your neighbor and give alms to the needy, and be compassionate! Feed the poor, clothe the naked, open your house to the homeless, and provide shelter to strangers. Assist those who are sick, and comfort those who are grieved, and you shall deserve

31

an indescribable mercy and a delightful life in Jesus Christ our Lord, who is blessed forever, amen.

The ninth clause of God's commandments says: "You shall not bear false witness." A [person who bears] false witness is liable to numerous evil things, whether he stands unaware of the matter and deceived by a neighbor, or he knows the truth and yet bears false witness by partiality. First, this brings great harm, for it distorts the truth and contradicts it, just as darkness contradicts light, evil [contradicts] good, and nothingness [contradicts] being. In addition, falsehood is nothingness, evil, and darkness, and it comes forth from darkened minds and contradicts the truth.

But what is truth? First, it is praise to Him, because truth is the sun and light of all virtues, for truth illuminates all virtuous acts, just as the sun enlightens intellectual beings and their eyes. Second, truth is attributed to God in numerous instances, such as when Christ said: "I am the truth" (Jn 14:6) and: "God of the truth, and Father, and the Spirit of truth" (cf. Jn 15:26), because He hates and makes all that is false vanish, and nothing hides from the beautiful light of truth. Third, there are no presents and offerings more pleasing than truth to God. Because God is truth, He loves truth more [than other things] and wills it as something of His own kind. Fourth, truth has descended within us from God, just like goodness, light, and life, and since it is from God, it is valuable and praiseworthy. Falsehood is of Satan, just as evil and sin are; therefore, it is despicable.

Fifth, [truth] being delivered to us works the truth in us. As the fire provides warmth to those whom it approaches, and as the light enlightens, likewise truth works the truth in man and distances him from falsehood and darkness. Sixth, truth is everlasting and imperishable; it is eternal, whereby the old law and the offerings were demolished, because they were a ghost and an apparition, while the new [law], which is the truth, will last forever. Seventh, truth is both a reality and a substance, while falsehood is nothingness and intangible, as we have mentioned. Eighth, there is only one truth—nothing contradicts it; but there are numerous false things like evil, and they contradict each other. Ninth, truth is the fulfillment of the word, just as goodness is the completion of works. This is the theoretical wisdom and the practical virtue within us, proceeding from the soul and the body. The theoretical wisdom stems from the word and is accomplished in truth, while the practical virtue originates from the will and is accomplished in goodness. Thereafter, man is completed in soul and in body. Tenth, truth is strongest of all things, as Zerubbabel wrote before King Darius. [There, before the king] someone wrote that wine is the strongest, another [wrote] a woman is the strongest, and someone else [wrote] sleep [is the strongest]; but Zerubbabel [wrote] truth [is the strongest], and the king rose and honored him, and sent him to Jerusalem with great glory.

Now, this is the first harm of a [person who bears] false witness: he wants to corrupt the truth and destroy that which possesses all the blessings. A person might ask, how can truth be destroyed? We say that truth in itself is not destroyed; it is distanced from falsehood. This is what we can say about it [truth]: [It is] like the sun which is not lost at night, but has distanced its light, or [we can say] that those who close their eyes are deprived of light. The philosophers[11] formulate this in the following fashion: When an object corresponds to its name, the result is truth, for what we say conforms to the object, such as when we say for a man that he is man, and a being, and rational, and so on, that is true. But when we say that a man is stone, or wood, and the object does not conform to its designation, then this is falsehood. Others say that a being that exists is true, as is true a nonbeing that does not exist, such as when we say snow is white and not black, for we affirm [the property] that it possesses and negate [the property] that it does not possess. Falsehood relates to nonbeing, which [we claim] to exist, and to being, which [we claim] to be inexistent; [in this way] we affirm [the property] that it does not possess and negate [the property] that it possesses, such as when we say milk is black and not white. The true and the false are distinguished in these terms, according to the philosophers. Therefore, we should possess truth, which is praiseworthy before both God and man, and forsake falsehood, which is unworthy before God and man, as it is before the Holy Scripture and independent philosophers.

Furthermore, falsehood is in a way the source of every evil thing. First, all sins and evil things, such as adultery, fornication, and so on, are the products of falsehood. Second, everyone intends to lie before doing evil, so that when [people] interrogate them, they reply, I did not do that, such as a thief, a murderer, an adulterer, an avaricious person, and others. Thus, falsehood is the source and origin of all sins; and, therefore, truth is the source and origin of all goodness.

Again, falsehood is Satan, for he spoke the first lie to man about God, by saying: "Did God say 'You shall not eat from any tree in the garden'?" (Gen 3:2). And the woman [Eve] lied to him that it was not so, but that [God] commanded to eat from all, except one. Then, influenced by Satan, she

---

[11] To identify which philosophers Tat'ewac'i refers to collectively would be speculative, since the "correspondence theory of truth" is manifested in various works of various philosophers and theologians, to begin with Aristotle and Plato.

deceived the simple-minded [Adam] and caused him death. Likewise, whoever lies is the son of Satan from whom he has received the seed of lies. Hence: "Whoever lies, lies according to his own nature, for false is his father Satan" (cf. Jn 8:44) who himself is the eternal fire. Hence: "Depart from me into the eternal fire prepared for Satan" (Mt 25:41). For this reason, it is said: Fire is the share of a [person who bears] false witness. Then, therefore, since a liar is the son of Satan, he who speaks truth is the son of God and the co-inheritor of Christ who is the kingdom of heaven. Again, a liar can never justify himself, for God forgives all the sins we commit when we confess—confession is truthfulness before God and the priest [when we say] I did this and that, and I have sinned before God, and for this and that reason forgive me [Lord] my sins. Now, if we confess through true repentance, God forgives us all our sins; but if we lie and deceive the priest, God does not forgive us. When God asked Adam: "Where are you?" (Gen 3:9), He gave him an opportunity to speak. Adam said: "I was naked, and I hid myself" (Gen 3:10). Then God said: "Have you eaten from the tree of which I commanded you not to eat?" (Gen 3:11), so that [Adam] might confess and receive forgiveness. But [Adam] said: "My wife deceived me" (cf. Gen 3:12).

The woman [Eve], too, did not repent, and accused the serpent, wherefore they [Adam and Eve] were not justified, because to avoid sin is the first goodness, and to repent and find forgiveness after [committing] sin is the second [goodness]. When [a sinner] exercises penance for a long period, he becomes like a nonsinner. As one of the saints said: "If you have not been righteous in your actions, be righteous in your words." If someone practices the same [speaking righteously] for long, he becomes also righteous in his actions. Behold! A true word justifies man, while a lie condemns [him], as [happened with] Adam and Eve. Why did [God] not interrogate the serpent? Because the serpent was not given a tongue and [the ability to] speak; [therefore] why interrogate it? Also, since the serpent was a liar, [God] did not interrogate it. For this reason, a [person who bears] false witness is like the first cursed serpent and he should not be interrogated in a tribune.

Afterward, [God] condemned Adam: "Cursed is the ground because of what you did" (Gen 3:17), and He said to the woman: "In pain you shall bring forth children" (Gen 3:16). He also cursed the serpent, saying: "Cursed are you among all animals; upon your belly you shall go, and dust you shall eat all the days of your life" (Gen 3:14). A [person who bears] false witness is a partaker of these curses, for he is cursed among all men, and he creeps in his heart, and eats the food of the serpent—dust and sins. This is the share of a [person who bears] false witness, brethren! Again, a liar's sin is that which the Lord specified: "Whoever denies me before men, I also will deny him before my Father" (Mt 10:33). Because He [Christ] does not deny the wicked, the murderer, and the adulterer, but shows mercy and pity for them when they repent for their sins. However, He denies the denier, whose sin is his tongue's [sin]. Find this from the examples: He justified the tax collector, cleansed the fornicator, [and] mentioned the kingdom for the thief, but denied the denier.

Should someone say, Peter denied [Christ], yet he was forgiven; we say, yes, he was forgiven, but after much crying and bleeding with bitter tears, and [Peter did] this through repentance for the sake of hope. However, deniers who do not repent will not be forgiven; hence: "Whoever speaks a word against the Son of Man will be forgiven" (Mt 12:32); that is, a denier who repents and confesses will be forgiven. "But whoever speaks against the Holy Spirit will not be forgiven, either in this world or in the life to come" (Mt 12:32); that is, whoever denies and blasphemes the faith, the church, and things of the sort, and despairs and remains without repentance, shall not receive forgiveness for his sins here [in this age], nor will he be exempt from punishment in the life to come. Because sins that are not forgiven here by the priest will not be forgiven there by God.

Watch also the sins of the tongue. The denier is referred to as sacrilegious and ungodly, like idolaters, and whoever sins practically is guilty and sinful before God. Again, when we confess by tongue and profess God, we shall be justified from all sins, as [it happened when] we believed and were justified at baptism. Hence: "Abraham believed God and God reckoned it to him as righteousness" (Gen 15:6). Then, therefore, whoever denies God and his faith by his tongue will invite upon him all [kinds of] sins and punishments.

It is to be known that all lies are divided into three [kinds]. First, into the harmful [kind], which harms man, such as perjury and slandering. Second, into the funny [kind], which amuses and makes fun [of things]. Third, into the harmless [kind], which can be useful in certain instances, such as when an outraged person asks for a sword and we lie that we do not have one; or when [people] ask a dishonest question, and we say that we do not know [the answer]. Lies of this caliber are useful and good. But the first [harmful kind of] lie is a great mortal sin. And the second [funny kind] is a forgivable sin if it occurs infrequently or [if it is exercised] among the laity. Otherwise, if it occurs always and [is exercised] within churches, it is a mortal sin. For the Holy Father, Nilus suggests that a buffoon clergyman is like a demon from Gergesenes, while the Lord says: "Woe to you who are laughing now" (Lk 6:25). It is the jester who

35

causes [laughter], and that is a useless discourse, as the Lord says: "You will have to give account for every careless word you utter" (Mt 12:36). Wherefore, [man] should never lie, as God has commanded.

"You shall not bear false witness." Moreover, this commandment includes the prohibition of telling tales and talking nonsense, and although falsehood and vanity are of the same kind, a person can distinguish them. Falsehood is the negation of goodness—the property possessed by an object; whereas vanity is the attribution of properties to an object that is void of such properties; that is, evil. Vanity is the affirmation of evil, and falsehood is the negation of goodness. Therefore, [man] should neither lie nor speak in vain, speak heresy, betray, cry loudly, denounce, insult, cuss, curse, blaspheme, or do anything like these, because the mouth of those who blaspheme will be filled by worms and they will provoke God against people, for blaspheming invokes the memory of all sins before God.

God is provoked against people mostly through three things: the offerings of unworthy priests, false vows, and profane blasphemers, because not only the blasphemers but also the listeners bring condemnation upon themselves. It is because of the sins of such people that the heavens and the earth turn dry, trees become fruitless, seeds are destroyed, and births become corrupted; havoc, beasts, and plague move upon the face of the earth.

For this reason, such things should be prohibited for all Christians, offerings should be forbidden to unworthy priests, and those who make false vows and blasphemous offenses [should be banned]. The blasphemer is the wickedest of all, for he offends God in His presence. If he dishonors the faith, faith is God; or [if he dishonors] the cross, the church, or the priest, the cross is Christ, the church is the temple and the throne of God, and the priest is an earthly angel. Or if [the blasphemer dishonors] faces and the mouth, the face of a Christian is Christ, [as] the Prophet says: "The spirit of our faces is the Lord Christ" (cf. Lam 4:20), while our mouth is Christ's grave. Furthermore, the grave and the bones of a Christian are relics anointed and confirmed by holy chrism, while the grave also is sealed by the cross and the Gospel; [the blasphemer] dishonors these.

For this reason, [blaspheming] is the heaviest of all sins and is unforgivable. It is written in the canons of the fathers that if a blasphemer refused to repent and regret, he should not receive communion at his death, nor should he be buried in a Christian cemetery. Laypeople should drag him and bury him in the ground outside the cemetery, without cross and without priest, and [they will do so] justly. Since during his life he blasphemed all these [sacred things], he should be deprived of them and their grace at his death. May Christ save us from such wicked swearwords, and help us be worthy—through our true knowledge and true words, and true actions—to the true and real promise of Christ the God who is blessed forever, amen.

The tenth verse of the commandment says: "You shall not covet your neighbor's house; nor his wife; nor his servants, male or female; nor his ox, nor his donkey, nor anything that belongs to him" (Ex 20:17). At the end of the Decalogue, [God] prohibits desires, and extends this prohibition upon many [other] things, by saying: "You shall not covet your neighbor's wife, nor anything that belongs to him." First, because all desires fall under two major categories: the desire of the body and of the eyes. The desire of the body is that which we bring to our bodies from outside. The desire of the eyes is that which is related to other people's belongings and possessions. Through these two [kinds of desires], our corruptible nature becomes more attracted toward, first, physical pleasures through inner passion, and then visual pleasures through external [stimulants]. [God] prohibits both: "You shall not covet your neighbor's wife, nor anything that belongs to him."

Second, [God] extends [prohibition] upon many [things], because all sins come forth from desires, for [sinners] desire and then fornicate, desire and then steal, or kill, or get drunk, or are provoked, or blaspheme, and so on. Third, our wicked will and wicked intelligence attract us toward all [kinds of] sins, for the will is like a tyrant ruler, while the intelligence is like a judge who sees and examines. [God] says: Do not covet the wife [of your neighbor] through wicked will, and do not covet the possessions and belongings [of your neighbor] through wicked intelligence. Fourth, [God] extends [the commandment] upon many things because many men are destroyed through desire, while few are those who escape it. Some desire glory, others authority or possessions, others the wives of other men, and others desire what belongs to others, and a few among those many manage to avoid it [desire]. The vice of desire is like a multitude of traps for birds; if [a bird] escapes one, it will get caught in the other. For this reason, [God] strictly instructs: "You shall not covet your neighbor's wife, nor anything that belongs to him."

Fifth, desire is part of the irrational soul. Philosophers claim that the soul is composed of three parts—reason, wrath, and desire.[12] The reason within us is angelic, the wrath is bestial, and the desire is [pertinent to] irrational beings.

---

[12] The most significant claimer seems to be Plato, who in his *Republic* speaks of the "logical, spirited, and appetitive" parts of the soul.

The reason is initial, the passion is medial, and the desire is last. Similarly, in our body parts, reason and wisdom operate in the brain of the head; passion [functions] in the heart; and desire [works] in the kidneys. Thus, desire pulls down a soul that lacks fortitude and the fear of God, and disturbs the peace of soul, attracting it toward sin. For this reason, [God] prohibited desiring, by saying: "You shall not covet." Sixth, there are three kinds of souls: rational, sentient, and instinctive. We understand and speak through the rational [soul]. We see, hear, smell, taste, and touch through the sentient [soul]. And we receive nourishment, grow, and give birth to our kind through the instinct. The desires within us are innate; they always strive for nourishment, growth, and reproduction, just like a plant.

Sometimes the rational and the sentient [souls] take a break at night when we sleep. But the instinct—the desire within us—never ceases; it functions day and night without interruption, and always attracts us toward sins. It is for this reason that [God] prohibited this more.

Seventh, it is said that desires resemble the serpent. As the serpent easily creeps on its belly, likewise desire easily attracts man toward an action. Again, as the serpent makes five turns when it moves, likewise man is attracted to pleasure through the five senses. He finds pleasure in color through the eyes, and in sound through the ears. Likewise, man finds pleasure through smelling, tasting, and touching. Also, the serpent's head is [its] weak [part], but the body is firm; wherever it inserts its head, [it can] pull its body in and can hardly be pulled out. Similarly, the desire enters [in man] through [his] weakness and pulls in the [performance of a given] action. Man can hardly be distanced from that action. For this reason, the head of the serpent should be smashed, as God said: "He will strike your head" (Gen 3:15).

Desire—the source and the origin of sins—should be destroyed within us; otherwise, we will not be able to avoid its effect. Thus it is said that within us desire is the head of the serpent, passion is its tail, and sinful actions constitute the part in between, because we desire and consequently act and grieve, whether in adultery, fornication, theft, or murder. We grieve after all sinful actions. Therefore, the bitter venom of the deadly serpent affects us, as Moses wrote in Numbers: "Because the people in the wilderness desired and complained, God was provoked and sent poisonous deadly serpents among the people, and they bit the people and the people died" (cf. Num 21:5–6). Hence: "I will gather irremediable evils upon them, wild beasts, [etc.]" (cf. Deut 32:23–24).

God punished [the Israelites] through the serpent for two reasons: First, because God allocated dust to the serpent as food and it did not complain, while [the Israelites] complained against God, even though He had sent them manna from the heavens. Second, because they [the Israelites] desired a desire, God punished them with a similar vice; that is, by the serpent which symbolizes desire, as we have mentioned. Then God commanded [Moses] to make a brazen serpent and lift it up high, and everyone who was bitten looked at the serpent, and the serpent died while the [bitten] people survived; and those who were not bitten remained without fear. Our Lord Jesus Christ himself left the following advice: "Just as Moses lifted up the serpent in the wilderness, so must the Son of Man be lifted up" (Jn 3:14). This is evident from the cross. Just as those who looked at the brazen serpent were healed, so will those who lift their eyes to Christ in faith be healed from the deadly venom of the serpent—sin. Furthermore, there we see the opposite—the brazen serpent killed the [living] serpent of its [own] kind, and gave life to the adversary—man. And Christ gave life to people [who are] of His own kind, while he persecuted and destroyed the adversary—Satan. Again, just as the lifeless serpent killed the [living] serpent and gave life to those bitten, likewise Christ killed the sins through himself in his lifeless body, and gave life to people in His living divinity. Since the desire of sins is so evil, [God] therefore prohibited it, by saying: "You shall not covet the wife, [etc.]"

Eighth, desire is evil in the following fashion: All sins are committed toward those who are nigh and by taking control of them, but desire [makes us] commit sins toward those [who are] distant and without taking control of them. Hence: "They desired a desire in the wilderness" (Num 11:4). If a man has abundant treasures and wealth, he is not [necessarily] avaricious, as Abraham and David [were not]. However, whoever does not possess even a piaster, and yet covets properties, is avaricious and greedy. If a man is honestly married, he is not an adulterer; but if he has no wife, nor has he ever seen one, and yet covets [a woman] in his mind, he is an adulterer in his heart. Similarly, whoever is content with [only] necessary food and moderate drink and [only necessary] clothes is not voracious. However, he who has no belongings, does not drink and does not wear [what is only necessary], but always covets and complains and voices dissatisfaction, is voracious and flaunty and so on. [They are] like those who desired meat in the wilderness and complained, wherefore God sent them quails, which they ate until they were saturated. Moreover, they preserved some of the quails, whereby they provoked God and He killed many [Israelites], as David says: "When their food was yet in their mouth, then the indignation of God rose up against them, and overthrew the choice men of

39

Israel" (Ps 78:30–31). The place was called grave of desires; that is, the body of coveters, because he who covets through his eyes and ears and mind is a grave of desire; he is a grave of death and sins. Again, the grave of desire is hell, for all the desires of sins and all sinners are gathered there, and the body, which desires, is called hell and house of sins.

Although man desires through all [five] senses, the greater instrument of desire is the eyesight, which wounds [a man] like an arrow [released] from a distance. While other weapons kill that which is close, the arrow [kills] from a distance; likewise, the eyes see and desire that which is remote. It is said that the reason [for this] is the following: Most veins of desire covering the head are distributed in the eyes and the face, wherefore [man] desires by sight. It is also said that the four major colors—black, white, red, and yellow—of the four elements are gathered in the face; it is for this reason that [eyes] desire more [than other parts of the body]. Therefore, man should always and primarily avoid looking in order to prevent desire, as was mentioned earlier about adulterers.

Ninth, desire burns and is referred to as fire. If we do not obstruct the substance of fire, it will not cease. Since desire burns, whoever lustfully desires is always drained and consumed, because desire consumes fat and fatness, as James says: "You ask and receive not, because you ask wrongly, that you may consume it upon your lusts" (Jas 4:3). He [James] applies the same to the love of world: "Adulterers! Do you not know that friendship with the world is enmity with God?" (Jas 4:4). Thus, the desires of the body are enmity with God, and a coveter is called adulterer; he is drained and consumed bodily. For this reason [God] says: "You shall not covet the wife, [etc.]" Tenth, as fire is luminous in nature and moves upward, likewise when our desire is alive and luminous in nature, and burns with love for God, it moves upward toward God. This is called love, and love and desire are distinguished in the following fashion: a burning, luminous, and upward-moving love is referred to as love for God and the saints. Whereas desire is that which has no light but burns and moves downward; this is referred to as desire, which burns violently and is inclined toward the body. The fire which came down on Sodom and possessed only burning [characteristics], and which fell upon the earth against [the law of] nature because they [the inhabitants of Sodom] acted against nature outside [the limitations of] habits, burned them with the burning of an extraordinary fire. Likewise, all those who replace their love for God with desire—that is, [they replace] the spiritual with the physical, and the eternal with the temporal—will similarly burn with the eternal fire on the judgment [day];

wherefore [the Lord] said to the sinners: "You that are accursed, depart from me into the eternal fire" (Mt 25:41).

As we have separated the love for God from our desires, likewise the voice of God separates the flame from the fire; that is, the light from burning. He turns the light into a crown for the righteous, and gathers the fire in the bottom of the hell where He burns them [sinners], [and where] "The fire is never quenched, and the worm never dies" (Mk 9:47), [and] where "will be weeping of the eyes and gnashing of teeth" (Mt 8:12). [In hell] darkness cannot be penetrated, and torment is eternal, grievance is without joy, tears are from within, all evil [things] are abundant, goodness is absent, and in addition to all of these, there is a deprivation of God's vision and [there is] the vision of demons which is a greater evil than all torments. May Christ save all those who believe in His name and are born in His holy font from these [torments] and make them worthy of the portion of the heritage of the saints in light. Amen.

CHAPTER IV

[Homily] of the same, again, on the ordinances of the Decalogue, in general.

God creates through creation, and gratifies through attendance, and regulates through ordinances, because He creates from nothing, and attends to the creation by sustaining them, and regulates through His benevolence. Moreover, because man possesses nature, grace, and glory, He creates the nature, attends for the grace, and establishes ordinances for the glory. For the ordinances guide man, make him attain grace, and complete him for the glory.

For this reason, when [God] created Adam, He gave him the natural law, [commanding him] not to eat of the fruit of knowledge. And [God commanded] Seth's sons not to mix with Cain's generations. And [commanded] Noah not to eat any suffocated thing. And [made with] Abraham and other Patriarchs the covenant of circumcision. But He delivered the Decalogue and other particular precepts through Moses in writing, because, first, they were many and could have been forgotten, and then, because kings were used to communicating with distant people in writing and through intermediaries.

Likewise, when sins distanced us from God, He made the great Moses intercessor and gave the ordinances in writing. First, so that people may not be totally distanced and alienated from God. Second, so that people may not excuse themselves [by saying] that they were unaware of the ordinances. Third, so that people may hurry to follow the direction of the ordinances and the right path in accordance with God's will. Fourth, so He may show that people are the masters of their own decisions in both keeping or breaking [the law]. Fifth, so He may show that God, who established the commandments, is great. Sixth, so that people may learn obedience in keeping [the ordinances], otherwise [there will be] punishment from the Creator.

For these and many more reasons, He gave us the commandments as from Father to son. And [gave] the ordinances like a lord to his servants. And [gave] command as from the Creator to the creation, for He is our father, birth-giver, Creator, and Lord. Wherefore, He provides for us and establishes ordinances in order to regulate us and guide us to the path of benevolence. And the first commandment says: "I am the Lord your God" (Ex 20:2). This first [commandment] teaches us to believe in the Holy Trinity. "I" means the Father, and "Lord" and "God" indicate the Son and the Spirit. As He says elsewhere: "Hear, O Israel, the Lord is our God, the Lord alone" (Deut 6:4). That is, hear, O Christians who have seen God and who wish to see God through faith, believe in God as three countenances and one nature; they are the Father, the Son, and the Holy Spirit. "You shall have no other gods except me" (Ex 20:3).

The Son from the Father is not a different God [simply] because He [Christ] says: "I came from the Father and have come to the world" (Jn 16:28). The Holy Spirit also comes forth from the Father and fills the creation. Let no one dare to separate those who are alike, for they are three countenances but one nature, one Godhead, and one glory, and so on. And other gods are idols that only erroneously are named [God], and are not [God] by essence and nature, and are distant [from being God] functionally. Also, the false prophets who make themselves subject to worship and prostration as gods [are erroneously named God].

The second [commandment says]: "You shall not make for yourselves idols whether in the form of anything that is in heaven above, or that is on earth beneath" (Ex 20:4). First, it leads to the worship of God. Second, it distances [man] from idols. The human-made idol symbolizes abandoning the worship of God and serving objects, for if someone loves something more than God, that [item] is god to him, or if [he cherishes] himself, or his wife, or his body, and so on [more than God, they are his gods]. Hence: "I tell them in tears . . . their god is their bellies, and their glory is their shames" (Phil 3:19). They are enemies of Christ's cross, for they should have brought the cross and the agony upon themselves, but instead, and contrary to Christ, they embraced pleasure. And since Christ introduced God's worship through the cross, they abandon [the worship of God] and worship objects. It is required that [man] quit his job in the morning and the evening, and go to pray and worship God. They [idolaters] abandon prayers and go after physical works, pillaging, trading, laboring, and so on. God sends poverty to them so they may not preoccupy [themselves with idolatry]; but they use the increased poverty as an excuse and become lazy in worshipping.

The third commandment [says]: "You shall not use God's name in vain" (Ex 20:7). That is, do not commit perjury. Moreover, do not break an oath, and do not lie when you swear or make an oath, for perjury is heavy [sin]. Although at the time [of perjury God] does not punish man, and [even] forgives him mercifully when he repents; [later] however, God punishes him heavily, if he does not repent. For this reason, the Lord commands in the Gospel: "Do not swear at all" (Mt 5:34). If an opponent argues that swearing for the sake of truth is not harmful, such as saying: I swear that Christ is a true God; or: I swear that this bread is a bread; we say that although swearing that Christ is a true God is not harmful, truth does not require swearing. First, that which is true does not need to be declared true through swearing, for it is true and evident by itself.

Second, we are not sure if that which is definitely true is indubitable or dubitable; therefore we should not swear for that which is indubitably true, or for the dubitable. Besides, we should not swear in general, whether for the false, or for the true. First, because the Lord commands: "Do not swear at all." And this "at all" means not to swear for both that which is true and that which is false. Second, because perjury comes forth from the habit [of swearing]. Now, if [man] swears for that which is true, he breaks the oath, and if [he swears] for that which is false, he violates and [again] breaks the oath. Third, when [man] becomes accustomed [to swearing], he loses the ability to differentiate the false from the true; rather, he swears for all things indiscriminately, and [thus] the false becomes like the true. For this reason, the Lord made a distinction: "Let your 'yes' be yes and 'no' no" (Mt 5:37).

Fourth, there will also be another great harm: when [man swears] for only that which is false, he is condemned, for he has become the son of falsehood and Satan. [Imagine] how stronger and unforgivable swearing in the name of God would be! For this reason, the Lord commanded: "Do not swear at all." To call the name of God wrongly occurs also in the following way: when men trade, they are accustomed to always swearing and mentioning the mighty name of God over false objects [even at the expense of] provoking Him against them. Man knows that a specific object is not worth its price, [therefore] he puts God's name on the worthless as a confinement, and then deceives not his neighbor, but God, and deprives not him [the neighbor], but his soul. Since trading in our times cannot be accomplished without perjury, a pious man should distance himself from the profit of trading, because the honest bread becomes desecrated by extortion and perjury. Priests, in particular, should avoid and watch such things. For this reason, it is written in the canons that when a priest trades, [authorities] counsel, dismiss, and banish him. Again, the misuse of God's name occurs when [a man], driven by the hardness of his heart, curses and anathematizes a man, for to curse means to kill, and to anathematize [means] to excommunicate. And to do this by the name of God is a greater sin; as if [the curser] associates God with his wrath and also makes Him his servant and says [to Him]: Go and curse so-and-so person. God's forgiveness [in such a case] is amazing. And watch the heavy sins; [even] an enemy should not be cursed, but this [curser], contrary to [the teaching of] Christ, curses him who is to be loved. He [Christ] commanded to bless him who is to be cursed (cf. Lk 6:28), whereas this [curser] curses him who is to be loved. And [he does] this by the name of God, when God's name should never be used for cursing, but rather always for blessing, because God is the source of blessing and fills [the universe] with goodness. The Prophet says concerning this: "God is not before their eyes" (cf. Ps 10:4). Cursing should not be used except for two [kinds] of people. For either he who is a heretic, or he who is impenitent in evil. This kind is cursed after being counseled two or three times. Cursing should not be practiced because of [man's] avarice, glory, or sins. Solomon says: "As a fowl flies away from the nest and returns to settle in the nest, likewise curse settles in the fool" (Wis 5:11).

The fourth [commandment says]: "Remember the Sabbath day" (Ex 20:8), which is [our] Sunday. Work six days for your body, and [dedicate] Sunday to your soul. And [on Sunday] rest from your physical labor, and [give rest to] the livestock and servants, both male and female, for they, too, are created by God. Sunday is a day [for man] to confess his sins, which he committed during the week and which are not forgotten yet. Also, [Sunday is a day] to hear diverse instructions and sermons about the ordinances and live the following week in the fear of God, for man forgets and [therefore] always needs to learn that which is good. In addition, Christ's resurrection occurred on Sunday; [a faithful person] should follow suit of the myrrophores. Moreover, the general resurrection [will occur] on Sunday; [the faithful] should think about God the judge on that day, as well as [about] the compensation for evil and good works. Since [man] should not do physical work on Sunday, he can [thus] avoid many more sins [that he would have otherwise committed]. He should not go to the theater, to concerts, to wine drinking, to fornication, to distribute goods, to trade, to travel. He should only go to church and pray to God.

The fifth [commandment] says: "Honor your father and your mother" (Ex 20:12). [Thus God] seals the first five [commandments] that begin with God and end with parents. Parents also are referred to as gods, because [as] God is the Creator of all, parents are [the creators] of their children. God creates the soul, and parents [create] the body. [Parents] also provide for and suffer with their children night and day; [something] a son cannot compensate for. Even if he pays for everything else, he cannot give birth to his parents. For this reason, [God] promises eternal reward: "That it may be well with you and that you may live long" (Deut 5:16). Elsewhere [God] says: "Anyone who speaks evil of his father or of his mother, let him die the death" (Lev 20:9).

It is written that a prodigal son who is tipsy and disobedient to his parents will be taken to the elders; the hands of the son will be placed on his head, all the people will stone him, and [thus] evil will be lifted from within and others will take fright.

If [a son] strikes his parents and strangles them, [people] will lift him on the cursed wood—the cross—and will throw him in the grave that very day, as if the wood and the ground were cursed because of Adam, to whom [God] said: "Thorns and thistles the ground shall bring forth for you, and cursed is the ground because of you" (cf. Gen 3:17). For this reason, [people] curse a prodigal son and hang him from the cursed wood, they put him that very day in the ground, and [only] then the ground would be expiated. Burdensome is the honor of parents.

A prodigal son indicates the following: we deserved death, and in our stead "the elements groan[ed] and travail[ed]" (cf. Rom 8:22) for our sins, and we never accomplished God's will. But the all-merciful God sent the Only Begotten Son for our sake. "He was called sin and curse for our sake" [cf. Gal 3:13], He was lifted on the wooden cross, placed in the grave the same day, and resurrected three days later, thus turning the wooden cross and the grave into a source of blessing for us, as Paul says: "Christ redeemed us from the curse of the law," and so on (Gal 3:13), and blessed us all with spiritual blessing. Also, [note this], parents are mentors for their disciples, and leaders for their followers, and priests for the faithful, and rulers for a country; we ought to obey them as if they were the representatives of God, as well as to listen to and execute their commands. These are the five articles of the law. It should be known at this point that of the Ten Commandments, five are affirmative [ordinances] and five are prohibitive, because through [the first] five we do good, while through [the other] five we turn away from evil as [God] restricts us and dictates.

Sixth, "You shall not murder" (Ex 20:13). Murder is a great and heavy sin, and it is against God. For he who cannot create is not entitled to kill. Hence, He says: "I kill and I make alive" (Deut 32:39). For this reason, He commanded Noah: "Whoever sheds man's blood, [instead of that blood] his blood will be shed" (Gen 9:6), because the price of [human] blood is the blood of a man and nothing else, for all human beings equally are the image of God.

There are three types of manslaughter. First, when [a man] is guilty and is killed. Second, when [a man] is killed unknowingly and unintentionally, as well as suddenly and accidentally. Third, when [a man] is killed knowingly and intentionally, without [him having] any sin. The first [type of] killing is a right judgment because the guilty are killed by their guilt and not by us [other human beings]; [it is in this way that a guilty man] receives restitution for his sins. Kings and rulers are installed in order to interrogate the guilty and avenge the law of God. [Concerning] the second [type of killing], which is accidental and occurs unknowingly and unintentionally, the law commands to build refuges in forty-eight cities where those who have murdered unintentionally may be taken and set loose, until the judges examine [the case]. If he [the manslayer] has murdered intentionally, he will be handed to the avengers of the blood so they may kill him, and if [he has murdered] unintentionally, he will be returned to the city of refuge to stay there until the death of the high priest; thereafter, he is free to go home. Now, the unintentional murderer indicates the sinner who repents, and when he repents and confesses, the sin turns into an unintentionally [committed sin].

The forty-eight cities symbolize the penance of the forty days of Lent through which we are liberated. And the great high priest [symbolizes] Christ who died, and consequently we were liberated from our sins. This is [concerning] the blood [shed] unintentionally.

The third, intentionally [shed] blood, has no deliverance, nor is it possible to compensate for, to [pay] ransom for, or to escape [from]. Even when [the manslayers] have entered the temple [for refuge], they were taken away and put to death. Intentional bloodshed is so costly that there is no way of forgiveness until [the murderer] dies. And a father should not [be killed] instead of his son, nor a son instead of his father; but "The soul that sins, it shall die" (Ezek 18:4). For this reason, He says: "You shall not murder."

Murder is performed not only by sword, but also by tongue. When [people] slander, they murder, or when they ravish possessions, [the ravished person] dies. Kings and rulers kill a man when they order: take him and kill him. Behold, they are murderers. Likewise, if someone hates his friend in his heart, he is a murderer like Cain. Also, if [a man] defames his neighbor or makes him do evil things, he is a murderer, for he has killed his [neighbor's] soul.

The seventh commandment says: "You shall not commit adultery" (Ex 20:14). It is a great trespass to leave the lawful bed and to commit adultery or fornication, whether according to the law of nature [heterosexuality], or outside [the realm of] nature [homosexuality]. Because incest is adultery, similar to going to the wife of another man, or to notorious whores, or to a person dedicated to God. To violate virgins also [is adultery].

The law commanded as follows. If a man commits adultery with the wife of another man, they should be stoned together for they have desecrated a lawful bed (Deut 22:22). Likewise, if a man commits adultery with an engaged woman in the city, both should be stoned, for both wanted to commit adultery (Deut 22:23). But if a man violates a virgin in the open country, only the man should suffer death and not the virgin, for she was forced and there was no one to help her (Deut 22:25). When a man murders another violently [he] is [considered a] manslayer, whereas the murdered [man] is not [considered] guilty. Similarly, the [male] adulterer is guilty [in this case] and the virgin is guiltless.

Committing adultery with the wife of another man is greater evil than [exercising it] with whores in the city for four reasons. First, because there is only one punishment to the whore—the fire of hell; whereas these [adulterers with other men's wives] have three [punishments]: One is the [punishment of] man "whose jealousy is stronger than the wife and will not spare in the day of vengeance" (Prov 6:34). The second is the punishment of civil judges, and then [comes the punishment of] the fire of hell. Second, whoever goes to the wife of another man unbinds from the wife the bond of love and blessed matrimony, while the whores do not possess such things. Third, a whore causes loss to two souls—her own and that of her associate; while a wife of another man causes loss to three souls—her own, that of he who copulates with her, and her husband's; because the matrimony is unbound, it will be adultery also for him [the husband, to be with] that woman. Fourth, they [the married couple] do not know whose is the legitimate son; is he the whore's, or the lawful husband's? [Therefore,] the son will not have a proper inheritance, nor will he have sincere love and compassion; whereas a whore does not have a child.

Furthermore, adultery brings forth seven kinds of harm and defects. First, it violates the law of God, which dictates: "You shall not commit adultery." The Apostle says: "Abstain from fornication absolutely" (1 Thess 4:3). Second, it is a violation of the limit established by God—[the limit of] one husband in matrimony. Third, it constitutes ravishing and avarice, as Paul says: "Do not wrong or exploit a brother in this matter" (1 Thess 4:6). Fourth, because, [as Paul] says: "The Lord is avenger in all these things" (1 Thess 4:6). Fifth, because [as Paul] says: "No fornicator, no adulterer, [etc.], will inherit the kingdom of heaven" (1 Cor 6:9). Sixth, because [as Paul] says: "Therefore, whoever dishonors this dishonors no man, but God who also gave the Holy Spirit" (1 Thess 4:8). Seventh, because it is said: "My spirit shall not abide in them, for they are flesh" (Gen 6:3). In addition to these, there is the adultery through the eyes, the heart, and all the senses; [therefore, the Scripture] says: "You shall not commit adultery by your heart, and you shall not look with lustful eyes, nor shall you commit adultery by your hands or any other part of the body" (cf. Mt 5:27–30).

The eighth verse [of the ordinances] says: "You shall not steal" (Ex 20:15). And this is beneficial and instructional for life. Precaution should be made from childhood, so that they [children] may not be accustomed to theft, otherwise they will not be able to restrain [themselves]. A whore, a drunkard, and a murderer are capable of distancing themselves from sins, but a thief is not. And thieves are of many kinds. Whoever breaks into a house is a thief. Whoever robs on the road is a thief and robber. He who cheats a man during trading is a thief; whereby [his trading place] is called stall, which is the circuit of a thief situated in the street.[13] Besides, to measure and weigh with double [standards]; that is, to take with the greater [measure] and give with the lesser, is theft, and God detests it, as Solomon says. Ravishing and pillaging a village is also [considered] theft. It is theft to not return a deposit to its owner. It is theft to find [something] and to keep it, as well as to deprive and pillage. God commanded in the ordinances that a thief, when caught, should pay five times as much to the owners because of the five senses that [helped him] sin. If the thief repents and confesses, [the ordinances demand of him] to return the principal, and to additionally pay one-fifth [of the principal] as fine, and to offer a ram that is worth fifty piasters as sacrifice. Expiation is contingent on all these.

Similarly, we, in the new [covenant], ought to return the stolen belongings either to the owner or to his relatives, or, if there are none, to the priest, for he is the intercessor for reconciliation between the dead and the living. Or else, [the thief] has to give [the stolen belongings] to the poor in order to be freed from the stolen belongings. Otherwise, beware, the punishment is [reminiscent to] the Prophet Zechariah's vision. The angel of God came out of the temple with a scroll on his shoulder, its length twenty cubits and its width ten [cubits]. [The Prophet] asked: "Where do you go?" [The angel] replied: "I will go to the houses of the thieves and robbers in order to exterminate them" (cf. Zech 5:1–4). It is to be known that in civil law there are punishments established for all kinds of offenses for thieves, murderers, and others, in the following fashion: First, they [authorities] seize the properties of the thief, and then they either cast him into prison and impose fines upon him, or gouge out his eyes. If he commits [theft] for a second time, they sever his right hand and left foot. If he

---

[13] The text suggests an analogy between *stall* (*kułbak/kułpak* [կուլբակ/ կուլպակ]) and a thief's circuit (*gołi bak* [գողի բակ]).

does it again, they finally decapitate him or put him to death on a pole. Also, if a thief has stolen only properties, they take away the properties, or cut his hand and then execute him. The reason [for this is] the following. First, because the law forgave the first and second [thefts]; but when [thieves] became increasingly wicked, the punishments were increased, for the [popular] proverb says: "All things break when they become thinner, except for sins, which break when they become thicker." Second, [authorities] gouge out the eyes because a thief, first, sees through the eyes and then digs the hole; and they [sever] the left foot, for he has failed in his action, and [sever] the right hand by which he caught and stole, and [shed the thief's] blood for blood [shed by him], and [give him] blows for blows [he has given], and return the belongings [he has stolen to the owners]. Afterward, they [authorities] decapitate [the thieves], because thieves do not move by hands and feet only, they also see and steal by their mind, wherefore they are beheaded. And they [authorities] crucify [a thief] so that everybody may see and say: "He deserved it."

They also [lift the thief] on a high pole, first, because the ugliness of evil works becomes beautiful through severe punishments, and second, because punishment is [given] against evil [works]; since a thief covertly steals at night, the punishment against it is [given] on a high place and manifestly.

Third, so that they [thieves] might not die with common people on earth, but their death might occur with demons in the air, as happened to Judas who was hanged and suffocated, so that he might not live with the angels in heaven, nor with people on earth, but swing in the air where demons live. Besides, his [Judas's] brain dropped into his belly and stomach, for he had plotted against Christ; his mouth, however, remained incorrupt, because he had kissed Christ. His heart and stomach, however, fell out because he had thought and planned to betray Christ. The punishment of thieves is reminiscent of this. For this reason, they are hanged from a pole high in the air.

The ninth verse [of the ordinances] says: "You shall not bear false witness" (Ex 20:16). This imposes upon man the liability of great wickedness when he gives false testimony for things he has not seen or touched. The punishment [for perjury] is what the ordinances commanded—when caught, [authorities] should treat a [bearer of] false witness just as he had intended to treat another person: "Soul for soul, eye for eye, and tooth for tooth" (Deut 19:21).

Since the Jews testified wrongly against Jesus at his death, they carried the same punishment [in this world] through the swords of Titus and Vespasian, and there [in the afterlife] through the eternal fire.

Additionally, lying is the head of all sinful things, because people first plan to lie and then commit their sins. Falsehood is Satan, because he spoke the first lie against God. A liar is the son of Satan, wherefore the Prophet says: "You hate all them that work iniquity; you will destroy all that speak falsehood" (Ps 5:5–6). For this reason, the Lord restricted: "Let your 'yes' be yes, and 'no' no" (Mt 5:37). Likewise, all evil things that come forth from the tongue—cuss, blasphemy, defamation, heresy, and so on—are all falsehood.

[The] tenth [commandment] commands: "You shall not covet" (Ex 20:17) and extends [the prohibition] over many things: "You shall not covet your neighbor's wife, or anything that belongs to him," and so on, because all sins begin with desire. Man thinks in his mind and desires, and then acts physically, just as the seed makes roots in the ground and then grows. Few are those who can avoid it [coveting]—one desires wealth, another glory, and another authority. And [desire] comes in many kinds; it is invisible, no one can see it. For this reason, [God] substantiated in the last commandment of the ordinances: "You shall not covet."

It is to be known that [God] commanded [people] to write the Decalogue and keep it handy like a ring, and have it in sight, and always [follow it] when talking, sitting at home, traveling on the road, sleeping, and waking up. Also, [God commanded people] to write it on the thresholds of their houses, so that it may be read while traversing, and if not [the entire Decalogue], at least five [of the commandments], which are: "You shall not murder," "You shall not steal," and so on. Thus, it is our duty to write the ordinances of God—to write them more in our minds and senses than on the thresholds or the doors, and to recall each one of them. When desire moves us, we [should] say: "Do not covet." When theft [moves] us, we [should] say: "Do not steal, do not lie, do not get angry," and so on. Because by thinking about the ordinances we become fearless during the day, and keep ourselves away from adultery or theft at night. Bringing the ordinances to the mind and the mouth when we are awake [helps us] do the same at night when we dream. And [we should] thus instruct all the children. Fathers [should instruct] their sons, mothers their daughters, and lovers one another. Mentors [should instruct] their apprentices, and masters their servants: to think the same and to proceed [according] to God's ordinances, because "The ordinances of God are perfect, converting souls. The testimony of the Lord is faithful, instructing babes" (Ps 19:7).

Moreover, the ordinances [of God] are a road leading us to God. Also: "The ordinances are light and enlighten the eyes of our soul in the darkness of our life" (cf. Ps 19:8). Also, the ordinances are instruction and canon that direct us; the ordinances for the lawful [people] are like a string to someone who measures. They do not exceed their limits, nor do they fall short of them. Just as the yoked ox swerves neither right nor left, so the yoke of the ordinances works like an instructing whip upon us if we become slothful or pertinacious. Should someone ask: "How are they a whip?" They are [a whip in a sense] that ordinances are good bounties descended unto us from God; they also are witness to the good and wicked, and a cause for death and life. Because if we keep the ordinances, they bring us life, blessing, peace, and abundance of everything that is good; but if we violate the ordinances of God, they bring us death, like Adam, and dissension, and famine, and thirst, and captivity, and so on. Not only the ordinances of God [should be] listened to, but they should also be kept in mind and transpire through works. "It is not the hearers of the law who are righteous in God's sight, but the doers" (Rom 13:17). The Lord says: "If you know these things, you are blessed if you do them" (Jn 13:17).

All the ordinances of God should be implemented at all times. A person should not execute one and refrain from another, or keep one and neglect another, or implement today and abstain tomorrow. They should be implemented at all times, without boredom, as the Lord commanded: "Go and make disciples of all nations, teaching them to obey everything that I have commanded you" (cf. Mt 28:20). But for what? Because "I am with you always, to the end of the age" (Mt 28:20). That is, as long as we keep the law of God, He [Christ] will be with us and protect us; but when we go astray, He will depart us and no longer provide for us. We should keep two major things among the ordinances of God: first, fasten His love in our souls; second, fasten His fear in our bodies, because we are both soul and body. "To love God with all the heart" (Mk 12:33) spiritually, and to fasten His fear in our bodies physically.

For this reason, [God] established five commandments so that we may love Him, and [another] five so that we may fear Him and walk in the path of righteousness. Whoever chooses fine silver and gold appreciates jewels well and recognizes the nature of precious stones and pearls. The most precious gold is the soul of man; [the most precious] silver [is] the body [of man]. They are precious and should be kept pure. The precious stone is the law of God, and the pearl is the faith descended unto us. We ought to know the nature of the law and faith.

For this reason, I beg you with the love of Christ to befriend and know the laws of God, and to walk according to His exhortations in this short period of our relocation on this earth. Love God and fear Him, so that He may lead us on the path of life and bring us to the kingdom of heaven, to our Lord Jesus Christ who is blessed forever, amen.

CHAPTER V

Homily of the same on the ten strikes of Egypt, [according] to the verse:
"One is punished by the very things by which one sins" (Wis 11:16).

All Holy Scriptures and all of the orthodox doctors say that God the Creator is merciful, and preach that He is righteous. As the Prophet says: "The Lord is pitiful, merciful, and righteous" (Ps 112:4). Moreover: "I will bless you, O Lord, of mercy and judgment" (Ps 101:1). God's mercy is evident, first, through the act of creation. God established the world because of His benevolence and mercy, so that all creatures may enjoy His mercy; hence: "You have said that you will create the world by mercy" (Ps 88:3). Second, mercy is evident through the act of providence: God protects all creatures, so that each creature may maintain its nature, whether in heaven or on earth—each and every creature, human and irrational [being], living and lifeless, evil and good; hence: "He makes the sun rise on the evil and on the good, and sends rain on the righteous and on the unrighteous" (Mt 5:45).

These are regulated by God's mercy. And God's justice is evident, first, from life's lessons: He torments some, so that others may be instructed and fear [him], as He tormented [people] in Egypt with many strikes, so that the Canaanites and all other nations may fear God. He torments some through punishment, so that they may suffer in the body, and hardship may weigh less in their soul, such as through the flood and through the Sodomeans' [example], for they were physically tormented in this age with water and fire, so that they might suffer spiritually less in the life to come; hence: "It will be more tolerable for the land of Sodom and Gomorrah on the Day of Judgment than for this town" (Mt 10:15). This is God's first act of justice in this life. The second act of justice will occur on the Day of Judgment in the life to come, when He will restitute in righteousness according to each action taken by the good and the wicked: eternal torment to the wicked and never-ending life to the good. As the Apostle says: "All of us must appear before the judgment seat of Christ, so that each may receive recompense for what has been done in the body, whether good or evil" (2 Cor 5:10). These are God's two wills of merciful and righteous acts as we have mentioned. With the first will, God acts in mercy, for God's will is to create and maintain the creation. God exercises this act through His nature, disposition, and first will. [God] exercises in justice with the second will, for He does not want to subject people to calamities or punishments. It is the iniquitous works of people that bring God's calamities upon them, and He reluctantly and with His second will avenges and punishes those guilty for the sake of justice.

There was a time when sin and iniquity increased among the Egyptians, who tortured the Israelites during [their] bitter bondage. The Israelites cried out to God in the heavens, and God sent the Prophet Moses to save the people. Strengthened by the Spirit of God, he [Moses] made Egypt and the pharaoh suffer through ten strikes, and then liberated the people.

The ten strikes of Egypt

The first strike was turning the river into blood. The Egyptians could no longer drink, and both people and animals suffered from thirst. This meant that God did not forget the blood of the children drowned in the river; He made them [the Egyptians] drink it [the blood].

Moreover, [He did so] as a pattern for those who turn from purity to sin and become flesh and blood. "[Wrongdoers] will not inherit the kingdom of God" (1 Cor 6:9), unless they are cleansed through penance and tears; hence: "Though your sins are like scarlet, I will make them white like snow" (Isa 1:18). And it was a miracle, because the same river was clear water to the Israelites who drank it, whereas it was blood to the Egyptians.

This meant that our Lord Jesus Christ was God and simultaneously became man—rehabilitation and salvation for those who believe, and falling and stumbling for unbelievers. Also, [it meant] that the holy body and blood [of Christ] are life and holiness to the worthy, and death and corruption to the unworthy. This was the first sign and strike—the Prophet turning the river into blood.

The second strike was that of frogs coming out of the river, invading everywhere, inside and outside, houses and plains. The Prophet David says: "And he spoiled them with the frog" (Ps 78:45). This means, first, that their deeds had turned them into filthy people and their sins into lepers; for this reason, He spoiled them with abominable animals. It was as if the children, who had been drowned in the river, came to life to torture them.

The third strike was that of gnats—small flies or mosquitoes. He took the dust of the earth, spread it in the air, and [the dust] turned into gnats that caused them [the Egyptians] pain, an indication that they were harsh in their conduct, and that their words wounded and caused pain to the Israelites, wherefore He tortured them in this manner.

The fourth [strike was that of] the dog-fly, for they were demonstrating doglike manners by sleeping with the wives of others. It is the habit of dogs to copulate in a manner different from other animals, wherefore numerous poisonous flies came forth from dogs and bit them [the Egyptians].

The fifth punishment was the death of livestock, for they [the Egyptians] by their five senses had been like animals and had lost their reason and wisdom; that is, they [were] addicted to women like horses, stubborn like a donkey, cunning like a camel, and so on. For this reason, to instruct them, He wreaked havoc on their livestock, so that they might come to their senses and fear for their souls.

The sixth strike was that of the blain and the boil, for the blain galled the skin and the boil festered and caused pain to their bodies.

The seventh strike was that of hail mixed with fire, for the two opposites— fire and water—combined, without spoiling one another, penalized the sacrilegious [Egyptians]. The hail struck down everything, and the fire burned trees, plants, and shrubs. This meant that they [the Egyptians] harbored coldness toward God and warmth toward vanity.

The eighth [strike was that of a] dense swarm of locusts that ate all that the hail had left [untouched]. This signified their multiplied weaknesses, piled and intensified like locusts. It also [meant] that as locusts are insatiable and eat everything, likewise they [the Egyptians] torturously oppressed the Israelites and ate the fruits of their labor.

The ninth strike was darkness that could be felt. It was so dense that [people] touched it, or were able to move around only by feeling by the hands or [relying] on canes. It was so dense that a seated person was unable to stand up, and the fire or the light of a lamp could not penetrate it, whereas the Israelites enjoyed light and freedom [in their places]. [This] indicated the darkness of their [the Egyptians'] absurdity [by which] they were obscured, more than any other nation, for they came to worship all abominable animals. The Israelites had light that indicated that they worshipped God.

Pay attention to the severity of the torment. First, those far from Moses and those close to him suffered equally when he gave the strike. It was not similar to others [other strikes] when the close one suffers and the distant one remains unharmed. Second, it is evident that they experienced twofold suffering—they grieved from the memories of the dead, and feared future probable strikes, and thus they were tortured perpetually. But notice also the benevolent forgiveness of God in two matters. First, He offered intervals and periods [to the Egyptians] to breathe and repent, and did not deliver [the strikes] one after another uninterruptedly. While they admitted during the torments that it [the strike] was the work of God, once it [a torment] was over, they stopped believing in God. Second, the strikes gradually increased in severity; had they repented after the minor [strike], they would have been saved from the greater; they, however, did not repent, and [the Scripture] says: "The pharaoh hardened his heart more and would not let the people go" (Ex 8:32).

The tenth strike, the death of the firstborns, was the harshest, for all the firstborns [of the Egyptians] died, whether human or animal, and then [only] the Israelites were set free. They [the Egyptians] lost their firstborns, because they had tortured and killed God's first children. Also, because they had lost the prime mystery of the worship of God, so their firstborns were spoiled. It also meant that by Christ's coming, the firstborn of Satan would perish; that is, arrogance and idolatry, for Christ came in humility, invited humanity to worship one God, and destroyed the worship of demons.

Should someone ask, why did [God] strike Egypt with ten strikes? We say, because the Israelites were tormented by five kinds of tortures, they [the Egyptians] received double restitution for their evil [actions]. All sinners are charged double for their wickedness; that is, spiritually and physically, or here and in the hereafter, as Isaiah says: "She has received from the Lord's hand double for all her sins" (Isa 40:2).

The five torments exercised by Egypt are the following:

First, they [the Egyptians] kept the Israelites as servants and slaves. Second, they drowned the [Israelite] boys in the river. Third, [because of] the potter and the adobe, for they [the Egyptians] required an account for the bricks from each individual [Israelite]. Fourth, [the Israelites were forced to gather] stubbles instead of the straw. Fifth, because [the Egyptians] opposed the religion [of the Israelites]. For this reason, they suffered through ten strikes.

Again, it could be asked, why did [God] torture the Egyptians through abominable, weak animals, such as frogs, dog-flies, gnats, and locusts? He could have punished them by sending against them bears and lions, and beasts with fiery breath. Solomon the Wise answers in love [righteousness][14] and mentions four reasons: First, because they became more foolish than any other [nation] and worshipped flies, reptiles, rivers, and animals. For this reason, He tortured them by abominable, weak animals, so that they may learn that "One is punished by the very things by which one sins" (Wis 11:16).

---

[14] The first line of the *Book of Wisdom*.

Second, in order to demonstrate the weakness of the Egyptians who could not stand the weak hosts of God and who were defeated by the smallest insects and suffered in many ways from them. Third, [Solomon] says, because God arranges tortures for the sinners righteously, according to size, quantity, and weight: the size, whether large or small, indicates deficiency and fullness; the quantity indicates abundance and scarcity; and the weight [indicates] heaviness and lightness.

This shows that God remunerates punishments righteously, according to the dimension of sins, both here—physically—and in the hereafter—physically and spiritually—although we do not know the dimension of the punishment [in the hereafter]. Fourth, [Solomon] says that God spared them because they were people created by Him, for God is called benevolent. Although they were guilty, He instructed them by forgiving them, so that they might repent and be saved from greater [tortures] through lesser [tortures] and to teach us that a righteous [being] should increase its benevolence and judge by forgiveness, as God did with the Egyptians. But they [the Egyptians] were hardened and did not repent, until they suffered all the strikes and all of them—the pharaoh and all of his carts and armies—were drowned in the Red Sea. As [Solomon] the Wise says: "One is punished by the very things by which one sins" (Wis 11:6).

Although this verse is short and concise, it is widely observed through numerous aspects. First, it is seen through the flood: "They were eating and drinking, marrying and giving in marriage" (Mt 24:38), wherefore they were killed by the flood. Because they were caught by wet lustful vice and gave themselves to pleasures, they were tortured and spoiled with water. Noah, with his family, was the only one to survive. He remained virgin in his sacred body for five hundred years, and was a righteous man among those of his kind. Therefore, he remained [as] seed for humankind and [became] the second beginning of humanity.

Second, this [Solomon's] statement can be related to the Sodomeans who perished by fire that came down from the heavens. Their burning passion made them commit unrighteous acts; therefore, they were killed by the burning fire. This [happened] for three reasons: First, they acted in strange ways and against nature, wherefore they were burned by a strange fire that came down from the heavens. Second, because they committed new evil acts on earth, they were tormented by new and severe torments. Cain, who committed a new evil act by murdering his brother, was tortured by a new and bitter torment. The same will happen to us. Third, to be a reminder for all people that those who commit such acts shall encounter such torments at the end of the age; hence: "He shall rain upon sinners snares, fire, and brimstone, and a stormy blast shall be the portion of their cup" (Ps 11:6). Lot's wife turned into a pillar of salt, when she looked back [while fleeing Sodom], for two reasons. First, turning back was a sign of her disbelief; [therefore] she was petrified as a reminder to unbelievers that the hardness of disbelief petrifies humans, as she was [petrified] bodily, whereas others [shall be petrified] spiritually. Second, she turned into a pillar of salt so that she would wash away and nothing of her would remain; in this way, [people] would not be able to worship her. They suffered in this way due to the similarity of their sins: Lot's wife was petrified for her disbelief, and the land of Sodom was burned because of the evil works [of Sodomeans]; plants would not grow in the soil of that land; fire would not proceed from the stone that was burned; water would remain still, undisturbed by the waves; [the land] would not feed the animals; trees would not give fruits, for although the peel [of a fruit] would look like a fruit, the inside would be dust and soil. All of this was to remain as a source for fear and a reminder for all nations.

Third, it [Solomon's statement] is demonstrated through the Egyptians, as we have mentioned: "One is punished by the very things by which one sins" (Wis 11:16). Because they sinned and worshipped all kinds of abominable animals and the river as divinity, [God] tortured them through their deities: he changed the river into blood, and spoiled them with frogs, and [sent against them] dog-flies and other things that we mentioned earlier. [These took place] first, in order for everybody to know that only the true God loves man, and that He is benevolent to everybody, because He has created them. False and strange deities cannot be good to men, because they have not created men. Second, it shows that all those who befriend Satan and submit to his will shall be tortured by Him in the eternal fire in a similar fashion. For example, when man befriends the fire he gets burned as he goes near, or gets pricked when he [befriends and] goes near the thorn. Likewise, those who befriend Satan and follow his will participate in and share the eternal fire with him, suffering with him. As the Lord commands: "Depart from me into the eternal fire prepared for the devil and his angels" (Mt 25:41).

Fourth, the verse relates to the laws of Moses, because God delivered them [the Israelites] ordinances, [saying] that: "I am the Lord your God and there is no other God except me. And you shall not make wrongful use of the name of God, . . . And you shall not commit adultery, and you shall not murder, and you shall not covet" (cf. Ex 20:2–17). In the precepts, He promised rewards and punishments. Rewards—health, life, peace, descendants, wealth, and so on—to those who keep [the commandments], for they behaved like children and were simpleminded, and kept the precepts because of physical promises; whereas the guilty were punished by the laws, as was said: "Eye for eye, tooth for tooth, and blood for blood" (Ex 21:24). Similarly, the laws designated punishments to the thieves, the adulterers, and [those who bear] false witness, as the Apostle said: "The very commandment that promised life proved to be death to me" (Rom 7:10), because the law is life to those who keep it, and death to sinners. The law punished so mercilessly and harshly for two reasons: First, because pagans and idolaters did not fear their idols, for they [the idols] did not punish them; God established ordinances for them so that they would fear the laws and cease their evil deeds. Second, [God] spared their souls, because they were not graced to be forgiven through Christ. He punished their bodies, so that they would suffer less spiritually. Thus, God tormented and tortured them with the same laws against which they sinned.

Fifth, the verse relates to the Israelites whom [God] brought out of Egypt by means of miracles; He divided the sea and made them cross it; drowned their enemies; sustained them in the wilderness for forty years without shortage, for their clothes grew with them and their footwear did not wear out; made them drink water from the rock; brought quail for them out of the sea; and fed them by manna from the heavens. But when they complained and spoke against God, saying: What have you given us to eat? We would have preferred to die by the fleshpots of the pharaoh, eating the flesh of pigs with watermelons, God sent them the serpent that killed them because of their complaints. This was so, because God gave the serpent dust as food, and it did not complain, while they [the Israelites] complained despite being nourished by manna. Wherefore, He sent against them "a string of irremediable serpents; beasts of wilderness that will spoil them here and there together with the grounds" (Deut 32:24).

Then the Prophet Moses, upon God's command, made a brazen serpent and lifted it up on a rod; those who looked at it in faith lived, while the serpent died. Those who looked at it with lack [of faith] perished. This indicates the cross of Christ, for it gives life to the faithful; hence: "Whoever believes in Him shall not perish, but shall receive eternal life" (cf. Jn 3:18, 36). Whereas, whosoever does not believe in the cross and in Christ who was crucified "will not see life, but must endure God's wrath" (Jn 3:36).

Complaint causes great harm and kills the soul. Miriam and Aaron, too, complained against Moses, and Miriam became leprous and was shut out of the camp for seven days. This means that the souls of complainers become spoiled in similar fashion, and they are excluded from the camp of God—the kingdom of heaven.

As the Apostle says; "Revilers will not inherit the kingdom of God" (cf. 1 Cor 6:10). For this reason, the wise [Solomon] says: "One is punished by the very things by which one sins" (Wis 11:16).

Sixth, the verse relates also to the Prophet David. When he took a census of the people of Israel to find out whether presently they were more than at the time of Moses in the wilderness, and found their numbers doubled and even more, God was provoked, saying: I increased your population, and they are mine. Why do you pride yourself over them? And He sent a prophet to David, saying: Choose one of the punishments so I give it to your people: famine to last three years, a sword that will last three months, or three days of pestilence. He [David] chose the three-day pestilence for two reasons. The three-year famine and the three-month sword were harsher than the three-day pestilence. Second, famine and the sword punish the good and the wicked together, whereas the pestilence is through God's choice and falls upon those who have sinned. This shows that the Prophet David was not guilty; he was not punished with the people. He [David] saw how the angel struck down seventy thousand people from morning until three o'clock in the afternoon: all killed in accordance with the righteous punishment. Thereafter, God's mercy prevented [the execution for] the rest of the days; otherwise, the entire population would have died within one day, just as the angel of God had struck down one hundred eighty-five thousand in the camp of Rabshakeh in one night. And why is it that David alone saw the killer angel? So that he would mediate and ask for God's interference. For this reason, he tore his collar, fell on his face, and said to God: "Let your sword [fall] on me and on my father's house, why should innocent people be plagued?" (cf. 2 Kings 24:17). Then he went to Ornan's threshing floor, purchased the oxen, [and] presented them as burned offerings, and the sword [of the angel] was lifted from the people. It was there that God promised to judge all men. It was the same spot, also, where He [later] sent the Only Begotten Son who was sacrificed on the cross and lifted the sins of men. The conclusion of this is that the sword of anger is put back into its sheath through worship and offerings; [otherwise] God would send untimely death and other plagues unto the world.

Seventh, the verse relates [also] to King Hezekiah, whom God healed and for whom He turned the sun back ten intervals, which was ten hours; it [the sun] turned by ten hours back to the East, and reached the same [initial] point after ten hours, and the sun sat after an additional two hours, whereby that day was thirty-two hours. Envoys from all countries came to him [Hezekiah] with presents. But when the envoys of the king of Babylon came to him with presents, he boasted and showed them his entire treasure house. Then the Prophet Isaiah came to him and said: "Who are these and where from they came to you?" The king said: "They have come from a remote country." Then [the Prophet] asked: "What did they see in your house?" The king said: "They saw all that was in my house; there was nothing that they did not see." Then the Prophet turned to him and spoke to him by God's command: "All that they saw in your house shall be carried to Babylon as booty; and your own sons who were born to you shall be taken captive." This was realized later: Nebuchadnezzar came to Jerusalem, captured his son, Manasseh, took him to Babylon, and put him in prison. He [Manasseh] was freed and returned to Jerusalem through prayer. Then, Jerusalem and its entire wealth were captured thrice, the sacred objects of the temple were looted and taken away, and [the Israelites] remained in captivity seventy years. Thus, he was punished by that very sin and arrogance of his.

Eighth, this verse [also] relates to King Ahab and [Queen] Jezebel. He was a wicked king of Israel and went astray in idolatry, while Jezebel persecuted and killed God's prophets. Because of their sins, Elijah was enraged and bound the heavens. It did not rain for three years and six months. Men and animals died of famine. Drought prevailed over the land until Elijah came out and killed all the prophets of Baal, eight hundred fifty in number, and then it rained over the earth.

Afterward, [King Ahab] coveted Naboth's vineyard. Jezebel sent after him [Naboth], killed him, ravished the vineyard, and gave it to Ahab as his possession. Because of this, God sent Elijah to Ahab to say: "Since you have ravished Naboth's vineyard without right, instead of it I will take your kingdom away from you and give it to your servant. Just as you have shed an innocent blood, so, instead, I will kill your seventy sons with the sword, I will put you and your house through sword, and hogs will wash in your blood"; which happened. King Ahab died during that war. After him reigned his servant Jehoshaphat, who killed all his [Ahab's] sons and grandsons: [a total of] seventy males. Jezebel was trampled to death by running horses. Dogs ate her body and hogs washed in her blood, as was said by the Prophet. Thus he [Ahab] was punished by the very things by which he sinned.

[These occurred] as a paradigm for us, because ravishing is a heavy sin, and shedding innocent blood on earth is an absolute [sin].

Ninth, this verse shall be true in our times as well, so long as we live, because we shall be punished by the very things by which we sin. God's providence watches us: If authority makes [man] sin, He removes him [the man of authority], and if wealth [does so], He makes the same [wealthy person] poor. If health is the cause [of sinning], He sends sickness. If [the cause] is peace, He stirs trouble. If eating and drinking [are the cause], He gives famine and brevity; and thus He punishes us and makes us suffer. For example, when a skilled physician finds out whether a [sick] man's pain is caused by heat or cold, he heals him by the opposite medicine; likewise, God watches us and provides for us, so "we shall be punished by the very things by which we have sinned."

Similarly, if we sin by our thoughts, God finds out and sends pain and anxiety into our minds, thus torturing us. If [we sin] by the body, the eyes, the tongue, or the hands, He strikes in the very same parts of the body so that we would be straightened from strayings with that [strike]. For this reason, He always maintains physical exhortations upon humankind and spreads famine, or sword, or death, or illness, or anything else here and there, so that some would hear from a distance and be instructed, while others would suffer from the lesser, to be saved from the greater [punishment]; some others would see the same and repent for their evil actions, practice penance for their past sins, and refrain from committing others. For this reason, He says: "One is punished by the very things by which one sins" (Wis 11:16).

Tenth, this verse points at the Day of Judgment at the end of the age, when Christ will sit in the tribune and the entirety of creation will gather before Him. He will then put the righteous on His right-hand side as sheep and the sinful on His left-hand side as goats. Then they will be placed in the just balance and He will compensate through a just judgment each according to their actions, indiscriminately and impartially, before the terrible and dreadful tribune, for all eloquent tongues will be silenced, words will be consumed, and actions will reign.

With such a careful examination, God will review all the actions of man on the Day of Judgment and will judge the sins of thoughts, words, and actions. Concerning the thoughts, it is said: "Who examines the hearts and the reigns; God is righteous judge" (cf. Ps 7:9). Concerning the words, it is said: "On the Day of Judgment you will have to give an account for every careless word you utter" (Mt 12:36). Concerning the actions, the Apostle said: "All of us must appear before the judgment seat of Christ, so that each may receive recompense for what has been done in the body, whether good or evil" (2 Cor 5:10). He will condemn man with the same body part and send him to the torments of the eternal fire; if he [man] has committed sin by the eyes, the ears, or another part of the body, He will make him suffer by the same part.

If [sinners] have sinned by their whole body, He will torture the entirety of the sinners in soul, in body, and in mind. When He said to the king: "Depart from me into the eternal fire" (Mt 25:41), He also said to the righteous: "Come, you that are blessed by my Father, inherit the eternal life" (Mt 25:34). God, without exception, puts all those who believe in His name and who prostrate themselves before the life-giving cross in the class of the saints. He also pardons and forgives our numerous sins and mistakes through His holy cross, which is stained by His blood and suffering, and through the wishes and the intercession of all those in heaven and on earth, and all the saints and their beloved ones in Christ our God.

Glory to Him with His Father and the Holy Spirit, forever and ever. Amen.

CHAPTER VI

Homily of the same on vision and dreams, according to Hosea's verse: "I have multiplied visions, and have spoken to you through dreams"
(cf. Hos 12:10).

God is good in nature, and He provides for all beings through His benevolence: "Who desires everyone to be saved and to come to the knowledge of the truth" (1 Tim 2:4). Wherefore, He gave us the commandments as a lamp, so that we may come to the knowledge of the truth of God by its light. If someone ever errs in his journey of righteousness, He instructs [him] and turns him to the straight [path] through His benevolent will.

He provides for us through five means. First, He gave us a rational mind by which we may choose and distinguish the good from evil, avoid evil, and pursue the good, as the Prophet advised: "Turn away from evil, and do good; seek peace, and pursue it" (Ps 34:14). Many think in this way and by thinking [so], they recognize the consequences through experience, and [eventually] turn away from evil. If we swerve from this [path], He provides for us by the second [means], to turn us away from evil through visions and dreams. Third, by [means of] physical movements [He reveals] the real meaning of things, just as when a part of the body moves—the eye, the back, or anything else—people think about the consequences based on knowledge obtained through experience. Fourth, by means of the animals, such as ravens, magpies, or others that serve man, [He] warns us to watch for what is to come. Fifth, there occurs a sign in nature and in the luminous bodies of the sky, such as their eclipse, or a comet, a cloud, an earthquake, thunder, and so on, as the Scripture said: "[God] made them to be for signs and for seasons" (Gen 1:14), so that we may see them from everywhere and prepare ourselves for the life to come.

[God] makes people prepare themselves according to what they are accustomed to. For example, the Egyptians were oneiromancers and diviners; [therefore God] wanted to guide them through dreams.

As it is written, the pharaoh dreamed of seven fat and seven sleek cows coming up out of the river. [He saw] also seven plump ears of grain and seven blighted. The sleek cows were swallowing the fat cows, and the blighted grains the full. He called for all the sages of Egypt, but they could not explain the dream. However, when Joseph came, he explained the dream. He said that the seven fat cows and the seven plump ears of grain meant that there will come seven years of great plenty. Thereafter, there will be seven years of famine, which the seven sleek cows and the seven blighted ears of grain referred to.

Now, first, we must know how many kinds of dreams there are. The doctors say that there are four kinds of dreams: first, natural; second, inconstant; third, demonic; fourth, intellectual visions.

The natural [dream] consists of the disorderly prattling of that which is innate, for when man sleeps, sentience halts, intellect becomes idle and obscured, and, therefore, the innate wanders in the mind and the memory; it recalls either a past action, or that which is still in the thoughts [waiting] to be implemented, projecting these imaginatively. This is the natural [dream]. The inconstant [dream] is that which occurs from an excess of the elements, from external or internal nourishment, or from illness. If the fire is increased, [the dreamer] sees the same [fire], and if the water, the air, or the earth [is increased], the same [elements] are projected in the dreams. The demonic [dream] occurs when demons, through the sharpness of their mind, project to man that which will come, whether evil or good, and thus deceive man. Man sees the fourth—which is vision and divine revelation, and intends to prepare us to turn from evil to the good—as a vision, as it is said: "I have multiplied visions, and have spoken to you through dreams" (Hos 12:10).

Second, it needs to be queried why unworthy people, such as the pharaoh, Nebuchadnezzar, and others, see divine visions. We say that unworthy people saw the visions for the sake of worthy people, such as the pharaoh for the sake of Joseph the Worthy, so that he [Joseph] would be acknowledged and honored. Likewise, Nebuchadnezzar for the sake of Daniel, who by explaining the dream revealed "He has within him the Spirit of God" (Dan 4:5). Likewise, the diviner Balaam saw the angel, and the donkey spoke for the sake of Israel. He [Balaam] then blessed and did not dare to curse the people of God. Similarly, Caiaphas prophesied about Christ, the Savior of humanity, by saying: "It is better to have one person die for the people" (Jn 18:14).

Third, it needs to be queried what is the use of foreknowing and foretelling the future through dreams or prophecy. We say that there are three major benefits: First, when they [the dreams or the prophecies] foretell the good, we make ourselves worthy of the good to come, so that we might not be deprived of it. Second, when they foretell evil, we watch and avoid the evil to come. Third, so that we may turn and repent for our sins, if we are evildoers presently. It is for these reasons that the future is foreseen through prophecy and dreams.

Joseph explained the pharaoh's dream, saying that there will come seven years of great plenty and seven years of famine. God showed you [this] in your dream, so that you may store wheat during the plenty so your country will survive the famine. Consequently, the pharaoh appointed Joseph ruler of the whole country. He put his ring on the hand [of Joseph], [arrayed on him] a fine linen tunic, and [put] a gold chain around his neck; also, he had him ride in the chariot.

He [Joseph] gathered five times as much throughout the country and stored up the grain [in such abundance] that the stores were beyond measure. Now, the ring indicates the image of the Immortal King, which was pure within him. The silk [indicates] the tunic of the innocent soul. The gold necklace [shows] the integral and incorrupt faith. The chariot—in the likeness of Elijah with the fiery chariot—[symbolizes] his rising unto God in his mind. This means that those who are holy and unstained with sins, just like Joseph, will please the heavenly king, become rulers and commanders of the earth, escape God's punishment, and bring salvation to many.

Now, seven is a holy number and is the feast [day] of the true God, for "God sanctified the seventh day" (Gen 2:3). And the seventh day is the feast [day] of God, such as Sunday is within the week. Moreover, the Holy Spirit possesses seven powers, which provide for and do good to people. But if people prove themselves to be unworthy of God's benevolent acts, God punishes them with the sevenfold severity of the same number [seven].

It is for this reason that it was said: Seven years of great plenty and seven years of famine. It is God's custom to provide an extended period of peace before sending punishments for the sins, such as at Noah's time, [when God gave] one hundred years and then sent the flood. Such was in Egypt: seven years of plenty and then [only] famine. Or [God provides] an extended period [of ease], so that [people] might repent and turn from sins, so that they avoid perishing from the sudden punishment. Or, so that they know that peace will be followed by trouble. [God gave] famine after abundance, so that people prepare themselves and survive.

What is famine? There are many kinds. First, famine is the lack of food, when the heavens turn into copper and the earth into iron because of sins. As God said through the Prophet: "The sky shall withhold rain and the earth shall keep back her produce" (Hag 1:10). Likewise, plants will dry, so will dry all kinds of seeds and roots that replace the bread, and the fish will decrease and livestock perish, so that they may not be milked, as was said: "There came great suffering throughout Canaan" (cf. Acts 7:11). This occurs because the abundance of food and drink leads to sins. As it was said: "This was the guilt of your sister Sodom: fullness of food and abundance of wine" (cf. Ezek 16:49), by which people committed [unlawful] acts; for this reason, God terminates the cause of sins and sends famine.

There is also a famine of the mind, when God's wisdom decreases in man, as the Prophet said: "I will send not a famine of bread, or a thirst of water, but of hearing the Word of God" (cf. Am 8:11). Because as food is life for the body, so is the Word of God life for the soul. Hence: "One does not live by bread alone, but by every word of God" (cf. Mt 4:4). God sends this [kind of] famine when man is unworthy of hearing God's Word, as it was said: "I will command the clouds to rain no rain upon my vineyard" (cf. Isa 5:6). The cloud is [analogous to] the prophet, the doctor, the instructor: when men sin and deserve punishment, [God] prohibits the instructors, "So they may not listen with their ears, and comprehend with their hearts [minds], and turn and be healed" (cf. Isa 6:10 and Jn 12:40).

There is also a famine of [good] works. When [good] works and purity decline in man, sins and offenses surround us and we become hungry for and in need of good works. As the parable of the prodigal indicates: "A severe famine and a need for good works took place throughout that country. So he hired himself out to a man, and began to feed the pigs of the desires of sins, and did not get saturated from the pigs' nourishment" (cf. Lk 15:14). It was because of such a famine that the Prophet David prayed to God: "Save me! for godliness is diminished; truth is diminished from among the children of men" (Ps 12:1). Because when truth and the godliness of words and deeds are diminished, man is destroyed through falsehood and impure works, for a liar poses two dangers: first, he becomes the son of Satan through falsehood, because Satan is the liar; and second, no one believes in what he says. It is said in [folk] proverbs: "What is the liar's profit, if people would not believe in his true word, either?" On the contrary, he who speaks the truth is godly, first, because God is truth, and [therefore] the speaker of truth will resemble God. Second, when his audience confirms the truth of his words, they will accept all of his words and utterances. For this reason, the Lord commands: "Let your 'yes' be yes, and 'no,' no; anything more than this comes from the evil one" (Mt 5:37).

There is also the famine of faith. When true faith diminishes in people, they become deniers, heretics, or blasphemers. Each individual follows his own will, choice, and erroneous leader. They go after those who preach as they wish. The Apostle says: "They will accumulate for themselves teachers to suit their own desires; that is, conciliation, and will wander away to myths" (cf. 2 Tim 4:3). They turn away their faces from true doctors, for ungodly people despise and dishonor the instructions of wise men and are pleased with the myth of liars. "By smooth talk and flattery they deceive men," says the Apostle (Rom 16:18), and the Lord cautions: "[They] come to you in sheep's clothing" (Mt 7:15), because they have two covers—that of a sheep and that of a wolf; one worn atop the other.

A heretic, however, deceives man with three covers and tears him into pieces like an Arabian wolf: First, with the vestment of a priest, which he wears as a man of order. Second, with the words of his daily preaching and teaching. Third, by presenting superficial instruction in law and faith, while covertly mixing in unlawfulness and imperfection that simpleminded people cannot distinguish and [therefore they] err. What else? It is said: "You will know them by their fruits" (Mt 7:16); that is, recognize them by what they do and do not be deceived by their words, for the Lord refers to them, saying: "They bind heavy burdens on others, but they themselves do not lift a finger; and you are not to follow them, for they say but do not do" (cf. Mt 23:4).

Because when faith is diminished in people, it signals the end of the world, as the Lord says: "When the Son of Man comes, will he find faith on earth?" (Lk 18:8). Love, too, will be diminished, as the Lord says: "Because of the increase of lawlessness, the love of many will be drained" (Mt 24:12). As we nowadays witness, the hope in God is decreased and the love of God and their neighbor is drained among those whose faith has been diminished. These are referred to as a famine of faith, hope, and love.

Furthermore, there is an intelligible postmortem famine in the hereafter, because this life is fullness and is made up of many discoveries, whereas the other [life] is famine and idleness from all works, for [people] neither can sow, nor can they harvest or store, just as [happened] at the time of famine [in Egypt]. And as famine destroys the fullness and leaves nothing for the sight, so does the other life to this life, because nothing would be left for the sight after death—neither possessions, nor wealth, glory, beauty, or anything [else] that exists in this life—since all would be destroyed. In addition, [people] would not function with the senses—the eye would not see, the ear would not hear, the mouth would not speak, the hand would not operate, and the foot would not move, because the other life is like night, whereas this [life] is [like] day, [in which instance] people work until night and stop at night. This is what the Lord teaches: "Work while it's day; the night of death is coming when no one can work" (cf. Jn 9:4).

Analogous to the summer and winter, this life is summer—[time to] sow, harvest, and store; whereas the other [life] is winter and interruption of the works—[people] enjoy [only] that which they have earned, and those who have nothing will perish of famine. People harvest what they have sown, whether wheat, barley, or thorn. Whoever has sown wheat in his soul—God-pleasing good works—shall harvest the incorrupt life in his soul, for the soul is immortal and [therefore] its seeds are immortal. And whoever has sown barley, which is food for animals, in his body—sins that please the bestial body but wound the soul like thorns—shall harvest corruption and torments in his body, for the body is corruptible and its plants are [therefore] corruptible: "Wood, hay, straw, which are sources for the eternal fire" (cf. 1 Cor 3:12). The fullness of a saturated person lasts short after he has eaten, whereas hunger and want last longer, until he eats again. Similarly, our life of abundance is short and temporal, whereas the hereafter, which is famine, is prolonged and eternal, without limit and without end, as the Apostle says: "What can be seen is temporary, but what cannot be seen is eternal" (2 Cor 4:18).

What should we do, then? The following [is what we should do]. Just as Joseph the Wise took one fifth during the years of plenty and filled many granaries, and gathered the possessions and belongings of the Egyptians in the house of the pharaoh, so shall we wisely give our bodies their share from the four elements, and give the fifth portion, which is the spiritual, to our soul as its share, [thus] storing treasures in the house of the king of heavens, "where neither moth consumes it, nor thieves steal it" (cf. Mt 6:20).

What does this mean? If you have spiritual grace, such as wheat, and if you have material possessions such as gold and silver, and if [you have] irrational [faculties] such as your five irrational senses, or [if you have] a land and a house for your body, relinquish all of them, put your own soul in the service of God, and store all your goodness in the heavenly treasury of the king of heavens.

But what is heaven? Heaven is your soul; and that which is heavenly is above your material body; [therefore] store everything in your soul. Store also in the holy church, which is heaven on earth. Provide for the needs of the poor and the needy. If they need spiritual words and instruction, teach them; and if [they need] material clothes, food, or comfort, attend to their needs; they are members of Christ's [body]. Whatever you do to the members, you do to the head [Christ]. Your reward is not lost [even] when you give a glass of cold water; [imagine, then] how greater [a reward you will have] if you do greater works. Solomon said: "Send forth your bread upon the face of the water, for you shall find it after some time" (Eccl 11:1). The bread is not lost in the water, because the fish—God's creation—eat the bread and God rewards [the bread giver]. [Imagine] the extent [of your reward] when you give to a poor man, for the poor man is the image of Christ. Christ comes to your door through the poor, through the hand of the poor Christ himself receives the alms out of your hands, and compensates for it, for the Wise [Solomon] says: "He who has pity on the poor, lends to God" (cf. Prov 14:21). And the Lord himself says: "What you have done to one of these little ones, you have done it to me; come, you that are blessed by my Father, inherit the eternal life" (cf. Mt 18:6, 25:34). Christ, to his pleasure, will receive the alms and the presents of your souls through the prayers of all saints, and will reward hundreds for your one here [in this world], and will make you inherit the eternal life there [in the hereafter] for the glory of his Father and the Holy Spirit, forever and ever. Amen.

CHAPTER VII

Homily and instruction of the same to everybody according to the verse:
"Watch yourself that there be not a secret thing in your heart" (Deut 15:9).

The new lawmaker, our Lord Christ, commands us to put the lamp of law on a lamp stand so that it may illuminate everyone in the house—that is, in the holy church—and not to place it under the beds of pleasure or indifference. Because those who are reluctant to put the parables of the Scripture on the lamp stand of commentaries and work with them, [actually] put the lamp under the bed. Whoever [puts the lamp] under the bushel basket—which is a measurement— does not engage himself in this limited life of ours in interpreting the Word of God, but rather cares for his body [alone]. Whereas whoever wants to hear the Word of God has to have Martha's verse in mind, as the Lord criticized her: "You are distracted by many things; there is need of a few things here" (cf. Lk 10:41). Also, [have in mind the verse of] Mary, for she chose the better part: always sitting at the feet of the doctors and learning from them.

Now, encouraged by Him, we will lift up the lamp stand of our simple words. First, [we will lift up] the vessel containing the light, and then [we will show] the flame of the verse, saying: "Watch yourself that . . ." This expression belongs to great Moses, who wrote it in Deuteronomy among many and extended ordinances. Moses is the one who knew the Lord face-to-face through signs and miracles, and God spoke to him face-to-face, directly and not metaphorically. Moses is the first prophet and the one who spoke about God. He by his own mouth—which God moved and the Spirit came out of it— uttered these ordinances, which are very useful to everybody—clergy and laity, kings and subjects, wealthy and poor, healthy and sick, men of all ages, and the various craftsmen of the world. Because the Holy Spirit is the Creator of all and their provider, and [the Holy Spirit] instructs all those who have accepted the law, the prophets, and the Gospels, and who can think and see with their souls: "Watch yourself." Now, it should be known that man possesses two [kinds of] eyes: one is the sentient eye that sees the visible, and the other is the intelligible mind that sees the invisible. If we relate what was said ["Watch yourself"] to [only] the sentient eyes, we will fail to fully utilize the commandment, because the corporeal eye cannot see itself, the head, and the

71

back; and [it is known that] ordinances do not command things that are impossible. It is evident, then, that it ["Watch yourself"] was said for the mind that constitutes the eyes of the soul and is capable of visualizing the whole man. Hence: "No one knows man, except the soul that is within [the man]" (1 Cor 2:11).

We learn two things from irrational animals: First, those that choose digestible food and stay away from the harmful [food] know the healing medicine when they become sick. Likewise, the rational man, by watching himself, ought to make a choice and stay away from evil action and heretical words that bring death upon the soul, and ought to follow good actions and the orthodox teaching that are healthy nourishment for the soul. Second, we ought to learn from those irrational [beings] that manage to escape the traps of the hunters, such as the roe [that escapes] thanks to its sharp eyes and [fast running] feet, and the birds that fly with their wings. Likewise, we should clear the spring of our heart from envy, arrogance, filth, and other things that darken the mind. Then we can see by sharp eyes the traps that Satan digs everywhere. Hence: "They stretched out ropes for snares for my feet, and they set a stumbling-block for me near the path" (Ps 139:6). And [we should avoid the traps] by our two feet and two hands; that is, we should always remember the two testaments in our soul and body, and fly by them unto the heavens. For neither traps nor hunters can reach there. Hence: "Our souls have been delivered as sparrows from the snare of the fowlers" (Ps 123:7). Concerning this, it has been said: "Watch yourself."

The second message of this verse, "Watch yourself," is [the following]: As the philosopher says, we, what belongs to us, and what is around us are different things. We are souls and minds, because man is the image of God and is immortal. What belongs to us is our bodies and our five senses, by which we see, hear, smell, taste, and feel, and by which we find pleasure in this world. What is around us is our clothes, the food, the house, and all possessions. Now, when it is said: "Watch yourself," we ought to watch the soul and the mind, and keep them clean from various vices. We should not watch for bodily pleasures attainable through the senses. Whoever does such a thing is profane and abominable, and measures up to animals. We should not watch for the charm of a dress, or an abode, or the multitude of possessions, because these do not travel with us to the hereafter.

The Apostle Paul says that man has dual nature—internal and external, the soul and the body, each desiring opposite desires. One desires to rise sacredly toward God, while the other is pulled down toward the vices of sin and pleasures. Therefore, he [Paul] instructs: "Do not attend to the pleasures of the body, for the more our outward man suffers and is weakened, our inward man is renewed and strengthened" (cf. 2 Cor 4:16). Therefore, it has been said: Watch the soul and not the desires of the body.

The third meaning suggests that, if you are healthy and innocent in soul and in body, if you have the image of God intact [in you], if the angels favor you as much as they favored Daniel, and you are as beautiful in appearance as the head of Christ and the prototype of Christians, [then] watch yourself, and keep yourself pure from all evil [things], for if you sin, you will become ugly, abominable, and hated by angels and men. Again, if you sin or are sickened by sins, watch yourself and make use of the medicine of penance so that you may not die the eternal death. Behold! If the sin is heavy and great, heavy penance and bitter tears will be required, as happened to Peter after his denial; but if the sin is light and minor, it can easily be expiated through fasting and giving alms to the homeless.

The fourth meaning concerns the virtues. There are seven virtues—three divine and four human. Faith, hope, and love are [the three] divine and sublime virtues, while prudence, fortitude, temperance, and righteousness are human and perfect virtues.

Now, it ["Watch yourself"] says in reference to these: First, if you have faith in the Holy Trinity and the humanization of Christ, watch yourself; do not become distrustful or heretic. Again, do not be condescending like Eve, disbeliever, or as stubborn in believing as Zechariah, who was punished. If you possess hope, watch yourself and do not become frustrated from God, and do not place your hope upon the unworthy or the weak, for whoever sins with hope is destroyed hopelessly. Establish your hope in Christ, and He will strengthen you. If you possess love for God and for your neighbor, watch yourself; do not mix deceit [in your love], nor love God falsely by your tongue [alone] and not in your heart. Wherefore God says: "This people worships me in vain; they are close to me with their lips, but their heart is far from me" (Isa 29:13). Likewise, if you love your neighbor, watch yourself; do not love with raving desire, but by purity and spiritually; and not by word, but by deed and effectively. Divine virtues are accomplished in this way. Again, if you possess prudence and wisdom, watch yourself; you might become cunning and deceitful, and you might fall into disbelief by boasting with knowledge. Or [you might] think by roguery that you are a wise man. Instead, thinking wisely, keep yourself humble, worship God, and keep His commandments.

If you possess fortitude in any given task, avoid audacity and exaggerated boldness, for God detests an impudent person more than a sinner. Also, avoid sloth and timidity, for both of them are edged with evil, but stay in the middle of the path: "You shall not turn aside to the right hand or to the left" (Deut 5:32). If you are prudent and virgin, watch yourself so that you may not be virgin in your body alone, but rather in your soul, body, and mind, as well as by all of your senses. Bring the fear of God to yourself in order to avoid licentiousness. Likewise, if you are righteous, watch yourself so that you may not do injustice whether to man, to the ordinances, or to God. Moreover, respect your obligations, as the Apostle says: "[Respect] to whom respect [is due], honor to whom honor [is due], and owe no one anything" (cf. Rom 13:7–8). Watching yourself thus, you will regulate all the parts of your soul.

The fifth meaning refers to the seven deadly sins—pride, envy, anger, sloth, avarice, gluttony, and lust. St. Evagrius speaks of eight thoughts, because various kinds of demons covertly sow in [people's] thoughts the evil seeds of sins and then make them grow in the sensual faculties. Knowing this, fortitudinous and wise people oppose and defeat the sins and the demons, and receive the crown of triumph from Christ.

Pride is the first [sin] Satan plants and presents as virtue, knowledge, or other things. Therefore, [the Scripture] says: "Watch yourself," because you are dust and ashes, worm and corruptible, and boast not and perish not. Likewise, if the demon troubles you with envy in view of your neighbor's success and honor, envy not, because this is how envy is interpreted. First, [a man] commits evil to himself and then to his neighbor. Solomon says: "Through envy of the devil came death into the world" (Wis 2:24). Thus, if anger troubles you, the Prophet says: "Be you angry, and sin not" (Ps 4:4). A person whose anger is provoked cannot do justice. As God instructed the Prophet Elijah, the Lord is absent where earthquakes, fires, and storms exist, but when there is a quiet breeze, the Lord is there. These three evil thoughts [pride, envy, and anger] are mostly found in the fine people whom Satan turns rightward and makes them sin. And Satan brings sloth, boredom, and sadness upon the lascivious, and [thus] causes laziness and boredom toward good things, and sadness for the diminution of evil things, wherefore it has been said in reference to people who are mentally slow in learning and physically lazy in actions: the gate of God's chamber is closed before the slothful and lazy, as it was before the foolish virgins.

When he [Satan] places avarice in the mind, due to old age or sickness, or for any other reason, say: "Greed, which is idolatry" (Col 3:5). The Lord said: "You cannot serve God and wealth" (Mt 6:24). Theft, robbery, lies, murder, and many more evil things come forth from avarice. Wherefore the Apostle instructs: "Do not ask for more and be content with what is at hand, for we have clothing and food and we will be content with these" (cf. 1 Tim 6:8). This [was said] about the laity.

Concerning the clergy, the doctors say: "Should a monk possess a piaster, he would be worth not even a piaster." When Satan brings gluttony [to you], watch yourself and look into abstinence and modesty, and speak against it [gluttony] like the Lord: "One does not live by bread alone, but by every word that comes from the mouth of God" (Mt 4:4). When [Satan] opposes [God through you] by [instilling] lust, remember the agony of Christ—the thorn, the spit, the slapping, the cross, and the piercing of his side. Remember the day of death and the destruction of the soul. Remember also the impartial judgment of God and the fire of hell prepared for the sinners; or remember the punishment of the extremely lustful ancient men—the deluge, the fire in Sodom, and many other things. By watching yourself in this fashion, you shall be able to avoid all deadly sins.

The sixth meaning of the verse is understood in relation to the mysteries of the church. The seven mysteries of the church are: first, Baptism, [then] Confirmation, Anointment, Communion, Penance, Order of Priesthood [Ordination], and Matrimony. First, since you are enlightened through baptism and born as the child of God, and since the faith in Christ is placed [in you] as a foundation, watch yourself so that you may not lose the grace of God's adoption. The faith is placed as a foundation, so assemble not upon it wood, grass, and reed—the materials for hell—which are the wealth and riches in this world. But build gold, silver, and precious stones that are the fasting, prayers, alms, and so on. Likewise, if you have received confirmation and anointment, you are a soldier of God; watch yourself and be brave in the battle, put on the armor of justice and place hope as a helmet, take the Word of the Gospel as a sword and fill yourself with the strength of the entire Scripture. Above all, put up the shield of faith so that you may be able to quench the thunderbolt, the fume of evil.

Likewise, if you receive communion during Holy Liturgy, watch yourself and see if you are worthy, for one should be God-like in order to approach God. Watch the mystery if you are offering Christ or receiving communion, for the Apostle says: "Man will examine himself and then will eat of the bread, and he who eats and drinks unworthily, eats and drinks judgment against himself" (cf. 1 Cor 11:28–29). The Apostles tasted Christ in the Upper Room and were justified, while Judas tasted [him] and was punished. If you are distant [from

God], that is disbelief and desperation, yet you approach [Him] unworthily, that is audacity and boldness. David says: "Those who remove themselves from you shall perish" (Ps 73:27). And the Apostle says: "How much worse punishment will be deserved by those who have spurned the Son of God" (cf. Heb 10:29). Likewise, if you repent your sins, watch yourself and, first, repent by your heart and distance yourself from the root of sins, and then confess all of your sins, one by one, before the priest, hiding nothing. Because you will be put to shame before the last judgment of Christ, for whatever you hide here and whatever you confess here will be covered and lost there. After [doing] all of these, make the penance for [your] sins and compensate for them with fasting, prayers, and alms. And watch yourself, stop falling down, and do not despair.

[People] find themselves through two things: fear and hope. Fear is useful to those who are innocent, and hope to those who have sinned, because fear prevents [people] from falling into sins and hope restores [them] and does not let them [remain entrapped] in sins. Likewise, if you have taken the blessed matrimony and have become one body, watch yourself. See what the Apostle says: "This is a great mystery, and I am applying it to Christ and the church. For just as Christ is the head of the church, so the husband is the head of the wife. And just as the church is subject to Christ, so also wives ought to be subject to their husbands" (cf. Eph 5:22–24, 32). Whoever destroys the blessed matrimony by adultery or fornication will be deprived of the blessed matrimony and join the class of adulterers, "For marriage is honorable, and the bed undefiled; but God will judge fornicators and adulterers" (Heb 13:4).

The seventh meaning of the verse is extended over all the ranks and orders of priesthood. If you are a catholicos, watch yourself. The catholicos is referred to as universal [entity] and overseer of bishops. Attend to your holy jurisdiction with a clear and impartial view. Walk among them [the faithful of your jurisdiction] like an apostle, sell not the grace of the Spirit for silver to those who are ignorant and unworthy, and associate not yourself with the sins of others and with ignorant people who are responsible for bloodshed, by assigning them to high positions, wherefrom they soon fall and lose their sanity. If you are a priest, watch yourself, for you are called expiator and intercessor between God and man, and your sin is sacrilege before God. Because when someone sins against man, they [the priests] pray to God [as intercessors]. But if someone sins against God, whom will they pray to [for forgiveness]? If you as an expiator commit a sin that has no expiation, nothing can cover you, no matter how deep you hide. And if you stop short of expiating the flock, "God will require their blood at your hand" (Ezek 33:8). If you are a monk and you are about to become a clergyman [of rank], watch yourself; the monk is referred to as father, and [a ranking] clergyman is [perceived to be] one who carries the cross of Christ on his shoulder. The Prophet [Isaiah] regards Christ as "father of the world to come" (Isa 9:6).

The one who gave birth to all Christians through the font stood them before the Father by saying: "Here am I and the children" (Heb 2:13). A monk is like Christ who gives birth to himself and then becomes his own father, as Isaiah says: "We have conceived because of your fear, and have brought forth our souls" (cf. Isa 26:18), redeemed through fasting, prayers, and relentless penance; bearing the awe and fear of God, without food, without drink, honest, meek, and humble, with broken heart and consumed soul, crucified in the world and living only for God. If you are a deacon, an acolyte, or a seminarian of the holy church, watch yourself, for the deacon belongs to the order of the seventy disciples who walked before the Apostles in pairs. St. Stephen the Protomartyr was a deacon who served all the orphans and the poor.

Watch your task, O you who incenses with the censer! You now possess that which the ancient high priest possessed. Likewise, the acolyte—the flabellum that he carries is patterned after the six-winged seraphim that surround the throne of God. Thus, all nine ranks of the church [hierarchy] resemble the nine classes of the angels, [and therefore] they ought to be as holy as the heavenly hosts are and ought to attend to their ranks in a fashion that will be accountable to God. And if you were called a doctor or a teacher, watch yourself, for you carry the same name of Christ whom [people] called Rabboni. Through your work you ought to be like Christ "who worked and taught" (cf. Mk 9:31), because if you work and teach, you will be considered great in the kingdom of heaven. However, if you teach others but work not [what you teach], you will resemble a bell that sounds but is empty; it invites us to the church but itself remains outside. Watch your rank, as the Apostle says: "God has appointed in the church first apostles, second prophets, third doctors; then deeds of power and [gifts of] healing, and various ranks of the church" (cf. 1 Cor 12:28). The tasks are as great as the ranks: "From everyone to whom much has been given, much will be required" (Lk 12:48).

If you are a student and a servant of the Word, watch yourself. You are similar to Christ's disciples who served the Word of God. Are you a student of the Scripture? Serve [then] the Spirit and not the letter, "for the letter kills, but the Spirit gives life" (2 Cor 3:6). [If] you examine the words, [then] you are an image of the Spirit, "for the Spirit searches everything, even the depths of God"

(1 Cor 2:10). [If] you examine others, first examine yourself, for Solomon says: "They that are judges of themselves are wise" (Prov 13:10). Receive a bright mind, an orthodox faith, a firm hope, and pure love in your heart; [be] humble and obey your leaders; [be] alert in soul and in body, [and be] diligent and brave in all theoretical and practical teachings of virtues.

The eighth meaning of the verse relates to lay leaders. If you are a king, a prince, or a judge, watch yourself. Recognize, first, that you do not possess your kingdom and dominion by nature, "For God empowered you," as Solomon says (Wis 6:4). Second, you are not always a ruler; sometimes you give your power away. Third, because just as you hold others accountable, so will God hold you, as Solomon says: "An impartial judgment shall be to rulers, for the mightiest shall be asked of the mighty men" (cf. Wis 6:7). Likewise, you, O judge, who is seated on the seat of judgment, just like Christ "who is to judge the living and the dead" (2 Tim 4:1), watch yourself.

First, judge and straighten yourself and then others, and make an honest, impartial, fearless, and wise judgment. Just as you judge others, so will God judge you. Likewise, [the verse extends] over all lords and nobles who have subjects and servants under their authority [requiring them] to watch their natures, which are similarly perishable in all human beings. They can take with them [to the hereafter] neither their lands, nor their possessions, nor their power, but rather [only] their deeds—if evil, they will be tormented, and if good, they will find rest.

The ninth meaning of the verse relates to the six kinds of praises on earth. Because there are six things that bring praise to man—beauty, strength, possessions, wisdom, nobility, and skill. First, watch yourself. If you possess beauty, present it to God and deposit it where it cannot be stolen, and do not trade your beauty with the ever-burning hell. If you are physically strong and healthy, dedicate your strength to the vineyard and the plain of God's commandments, and provide for the sick and the poor with the goodness God granted you. If you own possessions, distribute them to the needy; give your material [belongings] to receive [instead] that which is spiritual. Hence: "Sell what you own, and give to the poor, and you will have treasure in heaven" (Mk 10:21). If you have the grace of wisdom, increase it spiritually, by distributing the spiritual nourishment abundantly to your associates in the church. If you possess physical skills, feed the poor with material nourishment; work without ravishing and stealing; earn what is lawful by your hands, and eat what is lawful by your mouth. Also, "Honor the Lord with your just labors," as Solomon says (Prov 3:9). If you are noble and pride yourself for that, watch yourself, for we all are from the same soil, children of one father, Adam, we all will be disintegrated into the same soil, and the size of the grave will be the same for all. Receive, if you wish, a great virtue and, through it, relate yourself to the angels. That is what constitutes the nobility and glory of man, and not the boasting with paternal and decayed ashes.

The tenth meaning of the verse covers all human beings in general, male and female, old and young, wealthy and poor, healthy and sick, lords and subjects, and so on. If you are male physically, watch yourself and do not be weak and fainthearted; rather, just as you are male physically, stay brave and active spiritually in all kinds of virtuous works. Masculinity is perceived to be an image; if you are the image of God, do not bring to yourself an alien form that does not exist in God. Watch yourself! If you are lustful and fond of women, you are [then] an image of a horse and an ass, but not of God. If you are arrogant, [you are an image] of a lion; if you are revengeful, of a camel; if voracious, of a pig; if deceitful and a cheater, of a serpent and a fox; if thief, of a mouse, and so on. If you are female, watch yourself, for you, too, are an image of God with your inner body. Adam named the woman life; if you are life, do not sin so that you may not die: "The person who sins shall die," says God through the Prophet (Ezek 18:4). If you make a man sin, then you are a mother of sins, just like Eve who caused Adam's exodus from the Garden of Eden. Stay innocent so that you may become a mother of life, just like Mary, the Holy Mother of God.

If you are an old person, watch yourself, for you have approached death and your heel is in the grave. Give your few remaining days to God and pray with tears, so that you may leave this irreparable life behind with provision. If you are a young man or a child, watch yourself; do not stain or corrupt yourself; keep the cleanliness of the font; stay in Christ's Paradise, which is the church and which is the brightest of all things you may find [in the material world]; fast and pray a lot; do good to the extent the energy of your age allows; serve God; and do not forget death, for death is for both the old and the young. If you are wealthy and rich, follow the instructions of the Lord: "Sell and give to the poor" (Mk 10:21). Remember the wealthy person who neglected the poor man; he was thirsty in the fire there [in hell], but did not deserve even a drop of water. It was Christ who told [us] this, and not a [common] person.

If you are a poor man, watch yourself and do not diminish virtues in you; fill your soul and body with the treasures of virtue; be thankful to God; bear your martyrdom patiently; remember the poor man, Lazarus, who was carried to be with Abraham—to the kingdom of heaven—to be a partaker of the delight, as the Lord said: "Blessed are the poor in spirit, for theirs is the kingdom of heaven" (Mt 5:3). Whether you are healthy or sick, watch yourself; dedicate your healthy life to God and do good; and when you are sick, be thankful to God who instructed you; remember sicknesses when you are healthy and fear God, and remember death when you are sick and confess your sins. If you are a lord, watch yourself and do not be disgusted by your servant, for he has the same nature you have and is a servant of God who created him; also, do not deprive him of the wage of his service, for the Apostle[15] says: "Whoever is deprived among you cries out, and the complaints of the harvesters have reached the ears of the Lord of hosts" (cf. Jas 5:4). If you are a servant, watch yourself; be obedient in your service and serve faithfully, not by partiality and deceit, because God has given him [your master] authority and has given you obedience; whoever obeys the command of his master, obeys God's command, and [whoever] opposes [his master], opposes God. Disobey a master [only] in two things: in matters of faith and evil actions. Because faith and good actions are God's share and not the share of the master, listen to him [your master] obediently except in these [two instances].

If you are a wise man, watch yourself; do not engage in wickedness and embrace goodness. Never acquaint yourself with evil, and share your goodness, skill, and intellect with everybody, according to God. If you have a foolish mind, watch yourself, for you need [the help of] the learned; do nothing on your own and learn obediently from those who are wise. And if you are a mindless person, benefit from the minds of others, for everybody's goodness and wisdom is from God.

Now let us briefly add the following. Christians are divided into two [categories]—the clergy and the laity. Each one of these [groups] is straightened by watching itself [each in its own way]. If you are a clergyman, watch yourself: "How you should behave in the household of God, which is the church of the living God, the pillar and bulwark of the world" (1 Tim 3:15).[16] The pure and sacred life and prayer of a clergyman are the pillar and bulwark of the world. When corruption and harm appear among clergymen, the world becomes dislodged and ruined, and we find ourselves responsible for much destruction and bloodshed. We should extremely fear and tremble for the sins clergymen commit. Because just as fornication in a church is greater and more terrible [a sin] than fornication outside the church, so is the sin of clergymen

---

[15] Prophet, in the original.

[16] "the pillar and bulwark of the truth" elsewhere.

greater and tremendous than the sin of laity, because the laity can pretend unawareness [of God's ordinances], while we [the clergy] cannot. We are designated to be salt and light; if we lose our taste, we shall be good for neither taste nor the earth: "If the light in you is darkness, how great is the darkness!" (Mt 6:23). This is the Word of God and not man. God said: "Heaven and earth will pass away, but my words will not pass away" (Mk 13:31). "It is a fearful thing to fall into the hands of the living God," says the Apostle (Heb 10:31), and to be subject to His righteous judgment.

Likewise, if you belong to the laity, you have to watch yourself, because you will be taken to a different life and a different world; one can in no way return to this life therefrom. Whoever labors here [in this world] will rest there [in the hereafter], and whoever rests here will suffer there. A layperson is called mourner,[17] indicating mourning and wailing, for a layperson is deplorable because of many ghosts and phantoms, women and children, elders and tyrants, demons and physical needs. Much strength, alertness, prayers to God, and intercessions by the saints is required of him so that he may not be drowned in the depths and the whirlpool of abysses. And a person should always keep in mind, first, his own death, which is God's inevitable punishment to all human beings. Second, the fear of God's judgment and the account he has to present before God's last tribune for his trespasses. Third, the eternal torments of the never-ending fire, the relentless worms, the weeping of eyes and gnashing of teeth, the refusal of God's sight, and the traceless loss. By having all of these in mind through God's grace, [a layman] keeps himself [away] from sins. But if he sins, he can be expiated by God's mercy through confession and penance, and [he can] always exercise caution in life to never again sin, as the Lord says: "Sin no more, that nothing worse befall you" (Jn 5:14). Otherwise, if you return like a dog to your vomit and roll like a pig in mud, God, the angels, and the saints will detest you. Wherefore the holy Prophet says: "Watch yourself that there be not a secret thing in your heart" (Deut 15:9). This commands us to not only hamper obvious actions but also cleanse the hidden thought of the heart from sins. This is how this statement was interpreted by our holy and orthodox doctors, as an exhortation and caution for people of all ages.

He, who is the provider for the entire world and the protector of Israel, may protect and provide for all of His common and specific creatures, whether intelligible or touchable, rational or irrational; may see through His never-

---

[17] This sentence is structured as a pun in the original Armenian text, where the words *ašxarhakan* [աշխարհական] and *ašxarakan* [աշխարական] are used to indicate a layman and a mourner, respectively.

sleeping and merciful eye the needs and deficiencies of the Christians gathered in the holy church; and may fill the deficiencies of all from the inconsumable sea of His benevolence. May He—who came for the sake of the lost sheep and the lost image, completed our salvation through the cross and His death, liberated the souls that followed Adam through the destruction of hell, was resurrected as God and ascended to the heavens in His body, and will come with the glory of the Father to judge the living and the dead—see to help our weakened nature, and may hurry to support the humankind that is fallen and destroyed in diverse abysses of sins, forgiving us our sins and harboring compassion for us through His benevolent will. Glory, might, and prostration to Him with His Father and the most Holy Spirit, now, always, and forever and ever. Amen.

CHAPTER VIII

Homily of the same on the Holy Trinity, according to the verse: "God is spirit, and those who worship Him must worship in spirit and truth" (Jn 4:24).

O You Sublime Trinity! O Absolute Godhead and absolute goodness, guardian of the Christians, Godhead of three lights! Light, and light, and light—unbegotten, begotten, and unspeakable procession. Father and Son and Holy Spirit. You shone light in the darkness at the beginning of our creation! Later, You revealed yourself to Moses on Mount Sinai in a cloud of light. You also descended on that day [of Pentecost] through fiery tongues among the ranks of the Apostles as a Holy Spirit. You, the Only Begotten Son! You will come on the same day with the glory of the Father and with Your Holy Spirit to renew the entire face of the earth. Shine the beams of Your grace in our dark souls and minds, and with the fiery tongues give us reason and wisdom. For because of You and by You we shall be able to speak and understand Your words about You, saying: "God is spirit, and those who worship Him must worship in spirit and truth" (Jn 4:24).

All of the Holy Scriptures inspired by God, and all of the doctors filled with the Spirit, taught and professed the uncreated divine essence as three countenances and one nature. Wherefore, we ought to worship [the three countenances] and kneel before them equally. The blind person should believe those who can see the diverse colors. And a deaf person should believe that there are pleasant tunes. This is so for two reasons: First, although the person lacks one sense, he still possesses four [other] senses that enable him to become well versed in sensible things. Second, because those who witness are numerous and their senses are intact. Then, therefore, those who lack sharp eyes should believe those who see. Likewise, we, blinded by sins, should believe the holy Apostles, the Prophets, and the theologian doctors, because they can see that which is spiritual. For example, when a child is born in darkness, although he has not seen the sun or the moon, he should believe that both the sun and the moon exist. Likewise, those who are born in the darkness of sins and ignorance should believe the saints and good men to whom God revealed Himself. As the Lord said to the Apostles: "I have made known to you everything that I have heard from my Father; and you are witnesses for me" (cf. Jn 15:15). Nicodemus came to Jesus and said: "We know that you are a teacher who has come from God; for no one can do these things that you do if God is not with him" (Jn 3:2). This verse is reminiscent of the Holy Trinity, because when it mentions God, it refers to God the Father, and He who came is the Son, while "God is with him" [indicates] the Holy Spirit as associate. And [the following verse] also refers to the Holy Trinity by saying: "No one can enter the kingdom of God without being born of water and Spirit" (Jn 3:5). Also, [by saying]: "What is born of the Spirit" (Jn 3:6). Elsewhere, He [Christ] says: "Baptize them in the name of the Father and of the Son and of the Holy Spirit" (Mt 28:19). And here [in this verse] He says: "God is Spirit"; that is, the Father, the Son, and the Holy Spirit constitute a divinity. Now, the truth of the Holy Trinity is confirmed through three testimonies. First, through the Scriptures that are inspired by God. Second, through independent philosophers. Third, through theologian doctors and paradigms.

Let us explore the first [group of evidence] from the Scriptures that are inspired by God. First, Moses says: "In the beginning God created" (Gen 1:1); that is, the Father [created]. God, that is, the Son, said: "And the Spirit of God moved over the waters" (Gen 1:2). [The Scripture] also says: "Hear, O Israel: The Lord your God is one Lord" (Deut 6:4). [The Scripture] mentions Lord and God thrice as one person, referring to them as one due to the oneness of [their] nature. Again, Noah says: "Blessed be the Lord God, God of Sem" (Gen 9:26). Also three persons appeared to Abraham in Mambre and [he] did obeisance to the ground as to one person. Also, Moses spoke of constructing four city refuges, each at equal distance from the other.

Second, David says in Psalms: "The Lord lives; and blessed be God; and let the God of my salvation be exalted" (Ps 17:46). Also: "The earth is full of the mercy of the Lord. By the Word of the Lord the heavens were established; and all their host by the breath of his mouth" (Ps 33:5–6). Also: "The voice of the Lord is upon the waters; the God of glory has thundered; and the Lord is upon many waters" (Ps 29:3). And he says: "The God of Gods the Lord has spoken, and called the earth" (Ps 50:1). He also says: "Let God our God bless us; let God bless us" (Ps 67:6). Elsewhere it has been said: "You are my Son; today I have begotten you" (Heb 1:5).

Elsewhere it has been said: "He shall cry unto me, You are my father" (Ps 88:27). Also, it has been said: "The Lord said to my Lord, 'Sit at my right hand'" (Mt 22:44). Also, it has been said: "I have begotten you from the womb before the morning star" (Ps 110:3). Also: "Where shall I go from your Spirit?

And where shall I flee from your presence?" (Ps 139:7).

Third, Solomon says in Proverbs: "I am the Son of my Father, only begotten from my mother; before all the mountains and the hills he begot me; and when he established all, I was present with him, suiting myself to him" (cf. Prov 8:22–30). [Solomon] also says: "God by wisdom founded the earth, and by his understanding broke up the depths" (cf. Prov 3:19–20). He also says: "In her is an understanding spirit, holy, only begotten" (Wis 7:22). [He] also says: "There are three things impossible for me to understand" (Prov 30:18).

Fourth, Isaiah says: "Holy, holy, holy Lord of hosts" (Isa 6:3). By saying "holy" thrice, Isaiah refers to the three persons of the Trinity and the one nature of the Lord. [Isaiah] also says: "He stretched the heavens like a tent, and hanged the earth by three fingers, and you the Lord our Father forever is your name" (cf. Isa 40:22). [He] also says: "I, who give bearing to all, how can I not give birth says the Lord Almighty?" (cf. Isa 66:8–9). [Isaiah] also says: "My Spirit shall go forth from me, and I have created all breath" (Isa 57:16). Of the twelve [minor] prophets, Haggai says: "I am, and my Word and my Spirit are in the midst of you, says the Lord Almighty" (cf. Hag 2:6). Zechariah says: "The Lord rebuke you" (Zech 3:2). Job says: "The divine Spirit is that which created all" (cf. Job 33:4). The king told Daniel: "The Spirit of God is in you" (Dan 4:15). Referring to the Son, he [Daniel] says: "Did I not cast three men into the furnace? . . . And the fourth is like the Son of God" (cf. Dan 3:24–25). He also says: "The Ancient of the days sat" (Dan 7:9); that is, the Father, and the Son of God came unto Him, and "His kingdom is an everlasting kingdom, which shall not pass away" (Dan 7:14).

These and many others are testimonies on the Holy Trinity in the Holy Scripture. We shall see the second [group of evidence] through independent philosophers, of whom the doctors[18] have taken [the arguments] and confirmed as follows: First, the good communicates itself to others by nature; and the better it is, the more it communicates itself; and since God is absolutely good, He communicates Himself entirely. Since nobody has been created as limitless as God, we need to say that God has a Son to whom He communicates Himself totally. Second, what is good and begets the good and produces the endless is nobler and better than that which is only good and endless; otherwise, the power would be more honorable than the activity. God is nobler and better than all beings; then, therefore, He produced from within the endless good, which

---

[18] Reference, most likely, to Pseudo-Dionysius and Thomas Aquinas. The idea of communicable goodness is present in their works; namely, *The Divine Names* (Chapter IV) and *Summa Theologica* (Article Four of "The Divine Government"), respectively.

is God. Third, all created things have limitations, and everything within them is limited; likewise, since God is unlimited, everything within Him is unlimited. God has intellect and will; God's intellect and will, alike, are unlimited, wherefore they constitute the countenance. Fourth, the eternal and unfathomable energy operates unfathomably and eternally; then, therefore, it acts the eternal and unfathomable good.

Fifth, it is evident that God has intellect and will, and as He begets the Word from within by [His] intellect, likewise He makes the Holy Spirit proceed by willing it.

Sixth, just as there is one prime being among all beings, so is there one prime action among all actions. Since birth is an action, thereby God, who is the absolute prime being, has two processions—one natural, which is His intellect, and one voluntary, which is His will. Thus, the Son is the wisdom of the Father, and the Holy Spirit is His will. And this is the same that was mentioned earlier.

Seventh, every orderly thing has to have first [order], middle [order], and last [order]. God has the order [in the persons of the Father, the Son, and the Holy Spirit]. [Therefore], as Aristotle says: "[since] God has all of the orders, He has to be worshipped with the number three";[19] [that is, as Trinity.] Eighth, each individual object, whether material or immaterial, has essence, power, and energy; and since it is confessed that God exists and is an essence, then the Son is His power and the Holy Spirit, His energy. Besides, each object has three dimensions—length, width, and depth. Take a house as an example. It is impossible to eliminate any one of these [dimensions] there, because the object will no longer exist. Ninth, an imperfect father can beget a perfect son, just like a blind father who begets a son with sight. Although [an imperfect] man does not become perfect by the birth of his [perfect] son, it is because of man's perfection that a man can beget persons like him. All kinds of perfections should be in God, wherefore Isaiah says: "I give bearing to all; how can I not give birth, says the Lord?" (cf. Isa 66:8–9).

Tenth, angels and men are honorable beings and they possess intelligence and animation. Whatever is deprived of these [two attributes] is irrational and lifeless, like a stone. The idols, which are referred to as deities, are irrational and lifeless, but God is an honorable being and has intelligence and animation—the Son and the Holy Spirit. Should the adversary say: "God has intelligence but it is a being and not begotten," concerning this we say: First,

---

[19] Aristotle, *On the Heavens*, Book I, Part 1.

our words are born of our minds and they are not created; likewise, [God's Word is born and not created]. Second, [the adversary says] He was irrational until He created the Word. The adversaries also say, If the Word of God and the Spirit are persons in God, then there are many persons in God and not three, because God has Word [intelligence], sight, hearing, power, energy, eternity, kindness, goodness, and so on. Concerning this we say: First, whatever has been mentioned—sight, hearing, power, and so on—is not directed inwardly, toward Him, but outwardly, toward creatures. Wherefore, these are not persons. But the Word and the Spirit are innate and exist within Him, wherefore these are personified. Again, all that has been mentioned—goodness, kindness, power, and so on—is related to the three persons, as was demonstrated earlier. This [much about] the second section.

Let us discuss the third [group of evidence] through the theologian doctors who establish the Holy Trinity in our minds by numerous examples. First, as the sun has its own circle, light, and heat, likewise the Father, the Son, and the Holy Spirit are equal to one another. Or, just as two lights—that is, the yellow and white lights—proceed from the sun, likewise the Son and the Holy Spirit [come forth] from the Father. Or, [Trinity is] just like a lamp where three lights are intermingled as one. Second example: The doctors refer to man as the image of God; he is one in soul, in body, and in mind. If he lacks soul, then he is dead; if he lacks speech, [then] he is mute. Third example: Like Adam, Eve, and Seth from her—one of them was born but the other not; [and yet] the three had one nature. Fourth, like the rational soul of man that has mind, will, and memory, which are three faculties but one substance. Likewise, the Holy Trinity is one divinity but three persons. Again, the mind, the intellect, and the will have one nature but three properties. Fifth example: Like an apple that has three properties—taste, scent, and color—recognized through the senses. Again, for example, like fire and its light and heat. Just as heat is somehow separated from fire—that is, when water gets warm—and yet remains inexhaustible in fire, likewise the scent of the apple can be separated from it. Thus, the Son of God alone was humanized and born of the Holy Mother of God, always remaining on the right hand of God the Father. Sixth example: The soul, the word [intelligence], and the breath are one and three—the word is born, while the breath proceeds from the soul. Seventh, [Trinity] is like the body, the hand, and the finger that are one; these three [parts] have one nature but three properties. Eighth, like the sea, the river, and the spring, all having the same nature of water. Ninth, like the root, the tree, and the fruit that are one. Also, [like] the flower, its color, and its scent that are one. Tenth example: Every substance, whether material or immaterial, has nature, power, and energy. It also has essence, beauty, and goodness. And the doctors present numerous other examples of the Holy Trinity as a support for the weak minds of men.

But He [God the Father] Himself is exceptional, unique, and above all created things. He resembles only Himself, as well as the Only Begotten Son and the Holy Spirit. Should someone argue that the Gospel says: "No one is good but God alone" (Lk 18:19), while the Apostle in 1 Corinthians says: "For us there is one God, the Father, from whom are all things" (1 Cor 8:6). Concerning this, we say: Saying "one God" does not separate the Son and the Holy Spirit. First, because the Son and the Holy Spirit are from the one God. Also, the Son and the Holy Spirit are God just as the Father is God.

Saying "one" is conceivable in four ways. First, God is referred to as one to negate the many idol-gods that are not divine by nature or by energy, whether in heaven or on earth. Second, God is one by nature, power, glory, and dominion, although there are three persons with specific countenances. Third, [God] is one numerically, like the sun that is one numerically, and not three numerically with regard to the three persons, while three people are three [separate] persons and three [beings] numerically. The Holy Trinity is three persons and one [entity] numerically—one God and one king. Fourth, [there are] one Father, one Son, and one Holy Spirit. Because God is one and He begets the Son and proceeds the Holy Spirit—the Son is one and not two, although both the Son and the Spirit are from the Father; and the immutable Spirit is one, for it does not change to the Father and the Son. Thus, the Holy Trinity is one and three, and three and one, beyond the intellect and reason of angels and men. It is understood only by itself. We can [only] believe in it through the Holy Scripture and paradigms, and cannot examine it, because to examine [the Holy Trinity] is audacity, and to believe is salvation, and to know is eternal life. Therefore, let us be worthy to prostrate ourselves before the Holy Trinity. And glory to it forever. Amen.

CHAPTER IX

Homily of the same on the Lord's word, saying: "When you pray, say: 'Our Father in heaven, hallowed be your name'" (Lk 11:2).

Prayers, all in all, are extremely venerable and praiseworthy, because they equal man to the angels and make him communicate with God. This [particular] prayer, however, is sublime and most venerable for four reasons. First, God taught it. Our Lord, not just an apostle or a prophet, taught it to us. Second, it is concise and everybody can say it. Third, everybody ought to learn it; this prayer is as necessary as the profession of faith. As in the old [covenant] everybody had to learn the Decalogue, likewise in the new [covenant] this [prayer ought to be learned by everybody]. Fourth, this is a fruitful prayer and contains a multitude of produce; that is, it contains all of the spiritual and material solutions, whether for this life or for the hereafter. Therefore, everybody should learn it and say: "Our Father." Concerning this, we need to discuss three things. First, why is He called *Father*? Second, [why should we] say *our*? Third, [why] does it say *in heaven*?

[Concerning] the first, it should be known that God is called "Father" in six ways. First, by nature, for He is the cause of the Son's birth and the Spirit's procession. Hence: "The Spirit who comes from the Father" (Jn 15:26), and "The Lord said to him, 'You are my Son'" (Heb 5:5). Second, He is called Father by creation, for He is the Creator of all beings. Hence: "Is not He your father, who created you, who made you . . . ?" (Deut 32:6). Third, He is called Father through restoration, for He who creates from nothing, restores from corruption. Hence: "They received power to become children of God" (Jn 1:12). Fourth, He is called Father because of His wisdom and teaching; He instructs and teaches. Hence: "O my God, you have taught me from my youth" (Ps 71:17). Fifth, He is called Father for His compassion and care. He feeds and provides nourishment. Hence: "Every act of giving is goodness from the Father of lights" (cf. Jas 1:17). Sixth, He is called Father because of the paternal heritage, which He distributes to His children, as the youngest son said: "Father, give me my share, so He divided the properties" (Lk 15:12).

He is called God the Father particularly by us [Christians] in the following six ways. First, He is the father of Christians by grace and designation, and not by nature, as He is the father and cause of the Son's birth and the Spirit's procession. We are called Christ's brothers and Christians, and we receive the Holy Spirit within us. [Then] it is evident that we become children of God the Father by designation, although not by nature, as [Christ] stated: "I am ascending to my Father by nature and your Father by designation, to my God by designation and your God by nature" (cf. Jn 20:17). Second, He is our Father by creation; and more so [He is Father] for us, Christians, because every child is the image and the likeness of his father. We were created in the image of God, conforming to His image. Hence: "We are conformed to the image of the Son of God" (cf. Rom 8:29). He is our Father through our birth from the font, because the image that has been corrupted by corporeal birth is restored in us through spiritual birth. Hence: "Who were born not of blood or the flesh, but of God" (cf. Jn 1:13). Fourth, He is called Father by wisdom and teaching, for He taught us the Gospel and the wisdom of the Holy Trinity. Hence: "O Father, you have hidden these things from the wise and the intelligent, and have revealed them to the infants" (Lk 10:21), and infants are innocent. Fifth, He is called our Father through His care; He gives us nourishment and feeds us not only materially, but also spiritually, which is the body and blood of the Son of God, and He thus unites us with the head, Christ. Sixth, He is called our Father through paternal heritage; He promised us the kingdom of heaven. Hence: "Just as my Father has conferred on me, so I confer on you a kingdom" (Lk 22:29).

There is also another notion about saying "Father." It indicates ten kinds of goodness to us. First, saying "Father" points at the compassion and love He has for us. Hence: "As a father pities his children" (Ps 103:13). Also: "The Father loves the Son" (Jn 3:35). Second, it reveals to us the hidden knowledge, for he [John] says: "Shows him [the Son] all" (Jn 5:20). Third, He forgives and does not torment us, and sometimes He instructs us with love like father to son. Fourth, He appropriately gives us what we have asked for. Hence: "The Father will give you whatever you ask Him" (Jn 15:16); also: "The heavenly Father knows how to give gifts to his children" (cf. Mt 7:11). Fifth, He cares for us and protects us like father to son. Hence: "The heavenly Father knows what you need" (Mt 6:32).

Sixth, because He is the Father, He makes man deserve the forgiveness of sins, and makes man partaker of justice and sanctity. Hence: "O God, give your judgment to the king, and your righteousness to the king's son" (Ps 72:1). Seventh, when He finds us subjected to evil and the grievance of temptation, He does not tolerate it and helps and gives [human beings] His hand like father to son. Hence: "My deliverer from angry enemies" (Ps 17:48); also: "By you

I shall be delivered from temptation" (Ps 17:30). Eight, He sends the true Spirit to comfort us. Hence: "I will pray the Father, and He will give you another comforter, the Spirit" (cf. Jn 14:16–17).

Ninth, when we refer to God as Father, He elevates us to the supreme honor of being Christ's brothers and not servants, according to the Apostle who says: "We cry 'Abba! Father!' We are no longer servants, but children; heirs and joint heirs with Christ" (cf. Rom 8:15–17). Tenth, when we say "Father," He not only allows us to nominally be called [His] children, but also demands of us works worthy of this name. Because the work confirms the designation, as He [Christ] said to the Hebrews: "If you were Abraham's children, you would be doing the works of Abraham" (Jn 8:39). Then He [Christ] said to the unbelievers: "If I am not doing the works of God, then do not believe me. But if I do them, even though you do not believe me, believe through the works that I am the Son of God" (cf. Jn 10:37–38).

Similarly, we refer to God as Father in many ways, such as by creation, by the font, and by other ways that we have mentioned and that are hidden.

Now, if we refer to God as Father through [our] works, all the ways of fatherhood should be evident and true in us. Should someone ask: What is the work of God, which we should make ours? We say that God's work is goodness, holiness, righteousness, mercy, humility, truth, and other similar things. Now, when we carry goodness in our minds, righteousness in our souls, holiness in our bodies, humility in our wills, [and] truth on our tongues, and bring other virtues into us, then we shall be called the worthy children of the heavenly Father, as the Lord said: "Be perfect, as your heavenly Father is perfect" (Mt 5:48). [Only] then we shall obtain the right to refer to God as "our father." But if we are unworthy in deeds, yet we refer to God as Father, we sin with six kinds of blasphemy. First, because we will be illegitimate and not legitimate children, for every legitimate son demonstrates in himself a likeness to his father, while the illegitimate son does not inherit the patrimony. Second, because if we are not doing [God-pleasing] works, we lie when we say: "You are our Father." And the liar is the son of Satan, as the Gospel says. Third, [it will appear that] Christ, who is truth, falsely taught us to refer [to God] as Father, and this is a greater blasphemy, and a great sin. Fourth, it is audacity and impudence to refer to God as Father through unworthy works. Fifth, because with our profane voice we stain the holy name of God, as the Prophet said: "Why do you recite my righteousness," and so on (cf. Ps 50:16). Sixth, we dishonor God's name and curse Him when we are wicked in our deeds, and yet we call Him Father.

We will [thus] discuss the statement ["Our Father"] further. When we call [God] "Father" by words, but we are evil in [our] actions, what would His answer be after He hears our prayers and sees our actions? [He would say] you lie in your words, and you are not my son by your actions. I am the Father of incorruption, while you are corrupt by your actions; you are not my son, because my image is absent in you; instead, you are the son of Satan and you carry his image in you; you are alien to me, because I am good, but you are evil; I am merciful, but you are merciless; I am righteous, but you are unrighteous; and I am light, but you are darkness by your mind and actions; light cannot unite with darkness, nor can evil unite with goodness, and so on. I will not listen to you and will not fulfill your prayers, for I do not recognize you; but your father is Satan and he will listen to you. The heavenly Father will give this kind of answer when our prayers are unworthy. Should someone wonder how can we be children of Satan, for he is not our creator, nor did he beget us, nor do we call him "Father," we say, although Satan did not give birth to us or create us, and we are never called his children, man becomes the son of Satan in four ways. First, by will; second, by action; third, by likeness; fourth, by image.

First, by will: since every son executes the will of his father, when we abandon God's will and execute the will of Satan, we are called his [Satan's] son. Second, by action: just as anyone who performs God's works is called the son of God, so is called the son of Satan whoever performs Satan's works. Third, by likeness: A person possessing luminous mind is called the son of light and day, while a strong person [is called] the son of strength; likewise, an angry person is called the son of anger, and a person who is dead through sins [is called] the son of peril, and a liar the son of falsehood, and so on. Fourth, by image: a person possessing a good image in Him is called the son of goodness; likewise, he who has the image of Satan [in him] is called the son of Satan.

Satan's distinguishing marks are envy, hatred, calumny, arrogance, avarice, lustful desires, and so on. Envy is of Satan who first envied the glory of the Creator, then envied the glory of man. Hatred [is of Satan], for he first hated God, then the angels and the saints. The slanderer is of Satan, first, because he sowed his word in the angels and troubled them; then [he did the same] in the first created beings, and now constantly sows his words in us and in our neighbors. Pride is from him [Satan], first, because he swelled with pride against the Creator, then against the angels. Avarice [is from Satan], because he coveted and ravished the glory of heavenly beings, then ruled the world avariciously. Lustful desires [are of Satan], because he changed the sacred love and developed sinful habits, and now continues to always be fond of fornication. All of these, and many more, are Satan's distinguishing marks, and whoever carries these in his person becomes the son of Satan. Then, therefore, so long as we dwell in sins, we should not say: "Our Father in heaven." Otherwise, if someone says [so], the heavenly Father will not listen, but the infernal one, who is Satan, [will listen], as has been shown.

The second question [relates to] saying "our" and not "my." It is to be known that Christ's statement, "Our Father," was discussed in ten paragraphs [demonstrating] the compassion and love [God] has for us. Also, [discussed were] in six paragraphs the ways of fatherhood by which we are called children of our Father. Now we shall briefly mention, in six ways, why we should not say "My Father." First, because to say "My Father" is appropriate only to the Son by nature who is our Lord Jesus Christ. But to say "Our Father" is appropriate to us who are called children of God by grace, as He [Christ] said: "I am ascending to my Father and your Father" (Jn 20:17). Second, it shows that the common is good everywhere and is more pleasing to God than the unique, because while He does not want us to pray solitarily, more so He does not want our individual possessions and belongings. For this reason, He [Christ] said: "Where two or three are gathered in my name, I am there among them" (Mt 18:20). Third, it eliminates avarice, because one should not pray for himself only, but also for the neighbor and the whole world. Fourth, it eliminates hatred and strengthens love, for to pray for all is an indication of love. Fifth, it eliminates arrogance and strengthens humility, for to say "My Father" indicates arrogance, as the Pharisee said: "I thank you my God" (Lk 18:11). Sixth, it shows that all of us, Christians, are equally children of God and He loves us equally and not [one] more and [the other] less: "For God shows no partiality" (Rom 2:11), and He equally grants us forgiveness of sins, kingdom, immortality, and all other bounties. This [much about] the second section on "Our Father."

The third question is: Why does it [the prayer] say "in heaven"? The Prophet said: "Our God is in the heavens and on earth" (cf. Ps 113:3). He also said: "His dominion is everywhere" (cf. Ps 103:22). It is to be known that "in heaven" is evidently said for ten reasons. Although God is everywhere by providence, essence, and power, He is exalted in heaven by substance. Primarily, He [Christ] praises us as the children of such heavenly Father, as elsewhere He says: "Call no one your father on earth, for you have one Father—the one in heaven" (Mt 23:9). Second, heaven is lofty, and by mentioning Him, He [Christ] implores in us the lofty and heavenly virtues, which are spiritual and angelic. Third, saying "in heaven" indicates our abode. Since we fell from heaven because of Adam, we will ascend again unto heaven through Christ's help. Fourth, saying "in heaven" indicates that we are related to the heavenly Father in whose image we were created, and that we are related to the angels who praise [God] in the heavens. Fifth, mentioning heaven revives in our minds the heavenly goodness that we lost, and when we recall our desire [to return to heaven], it incites us [to be in heaven]. Sixth, He [Christ] said "in heaven," because through the mind's thoughts we rise there and depart from that which is earthly, as the Apostle says: "Set your minds on things that are above, not on things that are on earth" (Col 3:2).

Seventh, He [Christ] said "in heaven" so that we establish the foundation of our habitation in heaven and build the "gold, silver, and precious stones" there (1 Cor 3:12), as the Apostle says. Eighth, when we build our house in heaven, we gather all our proceeds there, where they remain safe from violators. Hence: "Store up for yourselves treasures in heaven, where thieves do not break in" (Mt 6:20). Ninth, because we will be with the heavenly Father by our hearts and disposition, for "Where your treasure is, there your heart will be also" (Mt 6:21). Tenth, saying "in heaven" directs us to heaven, which we ought to seek and go toward. This path is not designed to travel to heaven; rather, to escape there. Because a path is something we travel on voluntarily and peacefully, while fleeing has three characteristics. First, we flee from evil. Second, we move fast. Third, we do not look back. That is how we must flee from evil on earth, as the Prophet said: "Go and hide for a little while" (cf. Isa 16:20), and hasten to travel to the good. We should not look at the world with desire at all, as the Apostle said: "I have forgotten what lies behind and am strained forward to what lies ahead; I pass on toward the good" (Phil 3:13–14). It is thus, then, that we can ascend unto heaven.

Should someone doubt, [saying]: "Our bodies are heavy and are made of earth, how can we ascend unto heaven?" The doctors say that we do not need material ladders, or ropes, or any other means to elevate us unto heaven, but we can easily ascend unto heaven through six means that we possess. The first is to turn from evil and stay with that which is good by the mind, soul, and body; and this goodness is implanted in us by God and lifts us unto God in heaven. Second, after we imprint the image of God by sanctity and righteousness within ourselves, we will be with God inseparably in heaven, where our archetype God is. Third, since all of our virtues are light and conceivable, when we carry them within ourselves, we fly by them and rise to the conceivable heaven, just as the bird flies by wings, or the weight of an arrow is lifted by its wings. Fourth, faith and hope have descended into us from God as a string of light; we rise unto heaven with it [this light of faith and hope]. Fifth, through love we unite with God, for love is an indivisible bond; therefore, necessarily, where God is, there we shall be with Him in heaven. Sixth, through prayers, for what we ask of Him now in prayers, we receive them from Him, as He [Christ] said: "Strive first for the kingdom of God and his righteousness, and all these things will be given to you as well" (Mt 6:33).

Thus, one can ascend unto heaven in six ways; therefore, He [Christ] said: "Our Father in heaven." So did the prodigal son who is mentioned in the Gospel. He [Jesus] refers to the angels as elder son, because they are elder when considering time, and they came to existence with the light. They are elder by glory, honor, and position; they are incorporeal and reside in heaven; and they praise God. Whereas man, Adam, is younger; he was created on Friday; he was placed in the dust-made earthly paradise; and he was less honorable than the angels, as David said: "You made him a little less than angels," and so on (Ps 8:5). "The younger said to his father, 'Give me my share,' so he divided his property" (Lk 15:11). He gave to the angels that which is heavenly and to man that which is earthly. And [man] traveled to a distant country and squandered his property in dissolute living, and he joined the demons, because sinners dwell with sinners and in hell.

And [the prodigal son's] feeding the pigs is a lustful desire. First, because pigs are fond of wetness and they return immediately into the mud after being washed. The desire of sins is insatiable. Therefore, He [Christ] said: "He wanted to fill his belly with the horn" (Lk 15:16). When he wanted to go to his father, he first came to himself and recognized himself by saying: "I am dying of hunger" (Lk 15:17), and then he composed a confession in his mind and said: "Father, I have sinned against heaven and before you" (Lk 15:18). [Christ] refers to the Garden of Eden as heaven, for [Adam] sinned there and fell down unto the earth. The prodigal son signifies the sinner who first ought to recognize himself as a sinner and return, then repent and think, and then confess to the priest. The heavenly Father went to him; that is, "ran to him, put his arms around him, and kissed him" (Lk 15:20).

What we have said has four meanings. First, as the prodigal [son] was returning, the father ran to him, kissed him because he had repented, and adorned him with cloths and other things because he had confessed. The merciful heavenly Father treats all sinners in a similar fashion. Second, there are three kinds of kisses: on the feet, on the hands, and on the face. That of the feet is for enemies. That of the hands is for strangers. But that of the face is for beloved ones. Thus, by love he [the father] received the prodigal [son]. Third, putting of the arms around him [the son] indicates the rational yoke of the Gospel, which He [Christ] placed upon him, who distanced from himself the first obligation of the commandment. Thus, when we confess, we ought to accept the yoke of penance. Fourth, since the hugging takes place in a crosslike fashion, this means that the prodigal son was accepted through the intercession of Christ's cross. Thus, a sinner finds forgiveness of sins through the cross.

The second adornment is that [the father] took away the filthy garb and put on him [the son] the original robe, which is the innocence and radiance that he possessed in the Garden of Eden. Because [the first man] became naked by his disobedience, and when he tasted the fruit, he saw his nakedness; similarly, the sinner first disobeys the ordinances and then, by committing the sins, becomes stripped of grace. But when he confesses, he puts innocence on again. Third, the ring on the finger of the hand. The hand is a symbol of labor and the ring of dominion. The finger is our rational mind. The circle [of the ring] indicates faith, while the substance [of the ring indicates] uncorrupted and pure hope. The shiny stone [on the ring means that] God's image is beautified within us. Fourth, the sandals on his [prodigal son's] feet are the durability of the soul and the body, so that the cursed serpent might not wound [him] again, but strengthened by the Gospel, [he might] crush its head. Hence: "I have given you authority to tread on snakes and scorpions; and nothing will harm you" (Lk 10:19). [Sacrificing] the fattened calf [symbolizes] sacrificing the Only Begotten who was offered for our sake, because one ought to receive communion after confession, and that should happen through the hands of other priests. Because He [the father] ordered others to bring the fattened calf. The expression [of the son] "Father, I have sinned against heaven and before you" is a confession, while the expression "Our Father in heaven" is a prayer. For if they [sinners] are not worthy of prayer, [at least] they can confess with the prodigal son, saying: "Father, I have sinned against heaven and before you."

And may He, the heavenly Father, with His benevolent compassion, make all sinners worthy of His loving kiss, and return us to heaven, to our patrimony, in our Lord Jesus Christ, glory and power [to Him] forever. Amen.

CHAPTER X

Homily of the same, again, on the same verse: "Our Father in heaven"
(Lk 11:21).

There are three modes of priesthood: established by the law, true, and sacramental. The established [mode] is the priesthood of the old [covenant] given through Moses. The true [mode] is the new grace consigned to us through Christ, whereby: "The law was given through Moses; grace and truth came through Jesus Christ" (Jn 1:17).

Now, our Lord transformed the shadow into light and the idea into truth in four ways. First, they [the Israelites of the old covenant] had one priest, in one place, who made an offering once a year, whereas our Lord commanded all men to offer prayers everywhere and at all times. Second, they cleansed themselves with incidental water, while we cleanse ourselves through repentance, confession, and the water of tears. Third, they wore robes made of four colors, while our dress is [made of] four virtues of the soul, beautified within us. Gold for us [signifies] incorrupt thought, silver [signifies] unconfused word; and it is the commandments of God that adorn us instead of various [precious] stones, and [it is through] the precious oil poured on our heads that we anoint our minds with wisdom, which is faith, hope, and love for God. Fourth, they offered the blood of animals, incense, and burned sacrifices, while we offer God the Eucharist, our sweet-scented prayers instead of incense, and our living works [instead of] blood, together with our bodies and souls as burned offering. Thus, we all become sacramental priests. For this reason, our Lord taught us to pray and say: "Our Father in heaven."

Now, saying "Father" has a double meaning. First, it indicates the Son of God by nature who is our Lord Jesus Christ. Second, [the word] indicates the children by grace—us—the faithful and the baptized by the font. But when we are referred to as Christ's brothers and children of the heavenly Father, we ought to demonstrate worthy works that are appropriate to this designation, so that we may resemble Christ. We will discuss this in ten paragraphs.

First, we ought to love our God the Father and keep His commandments, as the Son said: "I have kept my Father's commandments and abide in his love" (Jn 15:10).

97

Second, [we ought to] love our neighbors as ourselves, as He [Christ] said: "No one has greater love than this, to lay down one's being for his friends, as I did" (Jn 15:13).

Third, [we ought to] yield for the poor and the needy, just as the wealthy Son yielded to us, the humble ones, and alleviated our need.

Fourth, [we ought to] be gentle in heart, just as our archetype Christ Himself was meek and humble. Hence: "Learn from me, for I am gentle and lowly in heart" (Mt 11:29). David said: "The meek shall inherit the earth" (Ps 37:11).

Fifth, [we ought to] give up whatever is important for the body; that is, a father, a mother, a field, and their likes [for Christ's sake] in accordance with His [Christ's] commandment, and then we shall be worthy of becoming His [God's] children.

Sixth, [we ought to] deny ourselves, too, and take the cross and the suffering, and lose [ourselves] to become His [God's] children, so that we may find Him, as He [Christ] said.

Seventh, [we ought to] be peacemaker and reconciler between people, just as the Son became an intercessor between men and God and reconciled [God] with us. Indeed, then, such a person can be called a child of God. Hence: "Blessed are the peacemakers, for they shall be called children of God" (Mt 5:9).

Eighth, [we ought to] forgive one another's debts and trespasses, just as the Son of God granted us [forgiveness] for our many debts; then, indeed, He [Christ] promises the name of a child [of God, by saying]: "Your heavenly Father will forgive you your trespasses" (Mt 6:14).

Ninth, [we ought to] be able to endure with joy and patience for His [Christ's] sake, even if [others] trouble, insult, persecute, and slander us by all untrue words, just as the Son of God forgave the persecutions, the [attempt of] hurling [Him] off the cliff, the insults, and the slanders.

Tenth, in addition to all of the above, [we ought to] submit ourselves to death and crucifixion when the [moment for] bloodshed arrives, for the sake of His [Christ's] name, just as our first [brother] Christ did. Then, therefore, indeed, they will be called children of the heavenly Father, and they will deservedly dare to say: "Our Father in heaven." This is the first clause of the prayer.

The second clause [of the prayer] says: "Hallowed be your name" (Lk 11:12). That is, may your name be sacred and glorious. First, when we do good, God's name becomes glorified, because those who see our good work will glorify God. Hence: "They may see your good works [and give glory]," and so on (Mt 5:16). But if we do not do good, pagans will dishonor God's name. When they see us slothful in prayer, in fasting, and in almsgiving, [and also see us as] unjust, drunkards, adulterers, fornicators, disobedient, and blasphemers, then they will not say "That person is wicked"; instead, they will blaspheme our ordinances and faith. Wherefore [God] threatened through the Prophet: "Woe to you, for my name is blasphemed among the Gentiles on account of you" (Isa 52:5). Second, it is to be understood that since we have the faith of a Christian, we ought to do sacred works, so that the name of Christianity might be sacred and true; otherwise, we would be called false Christians. Since the works we do will be false, so will be our name and faith. Also, we first ask the following of God: Let our works be as sacred as the name and the faith of a Christian. Again, when we keep our mouths exempt from blasphemy, no one will have the right to mention and give God's awesome name with a filthy tongue. This [is] the second clause of the prayer.

The third clause says: "Your kingdom come" (Lk 11:2). That is, let your kingdom come upon us. But when and in which period is God not king? That is, although God is always the only Lord and King of all creatures, He is not a king by force or coercion, unlike the worldly kings who rule by force. Rather, He is king of those who want Him and love Him. And we say so for four reasons. First, Satan became king and ruler of people by force, wherefore he is referred to as the prince of the world, and he leads everybody toward destruction by his will. And when we beg God and He becomes our king, He saves us from Satan and leads us toward life. Hence: "He has rescued us from the power of darkness and transferred us into the kingdom of his beloved Son" (Col 1:13). Second, sins and evil works enslave us and rule us, and it is as if they tie us with a rope. Hence: "Everyone who commits sin is a slave to sin" (Jn 8:34). The Prophet says: "Transgressors shall be bound through their works" (Ps 9:16). But when God reigns over us, He saves us from all slavery to sins and liberates us from the chains and torments of sins. Third, when wicked tyrants rule and oppress us by all means, God allows this because of our sins, just as the pharaoh tortured the Israelites. [But] when they cried to God, He listened and sent Moses as their savior. Likewise, when we ask God for His protection, He saves us from wicked tyrants, or replaces them, or turns their hearts toward goodness. Fourth, we say this: During prayer hour, the hordes of demons gather together, surround us like a wall, and lead our minds astray by various vices, [such as] arrogance, anger, fornication, and so on, as David said: "O Lord, why are they that afflict me multiplied?" (Ps 3:2). And when God's kingdom arrives with chariots and a great number of angels, He will persecute the multitude of demons and vices. For Daniel says: "The chariots of God are ten thousand fold, and thousands of demons shall fall at your side, and ten thousand angels at your right hand" (91:7). Just as fire burns the candle and wind diminishes the smoke, so shall sins and demons be diminished and lost. Hence: "Let God arise and [His enemies] be scattered; let them vanish as smoke vanishes" (Ps 68:1). For these four reasons, we say: "Your kingdom come."

It is also written in other versions of the Gospel: "Let your Holy Spirit come and cleanse us." First, this shows that the Holy Spirit is King and Lord, and it is holy and cleanses us; then, therefore, the Holy Spirit also is God with the Father and the Son. Second, it indicates that our prayers are directed to the Holy Trinity. To the Father, since we say: "Our Father in heaven." To the Son: "Hallowed be your name." To the Holy Spirit: "Come to us and cleanse us of all the impurity of evil." Again, there is [yet] another hidden wisdom [in this prayer]. Saying "Our Father" indicates our glory, which will be [designated] to the saints at the resurrection to come, for they are called children of God and resurrection. Because we will truly become children of the heavenly Father only when He elevates us from the dust, lifts us up unto heaven, and makes us inherit the kingdom. And it is then, also, that the holy name of God will be called upon His saints. Hence: "God shall come in the saints" (cf. 2 Thess 1:10). And the Gospel says: "Then the righteous will shine like the sun" (Mt 13:43), and will share the kingdom with Christ, and will inherit the kingdom. Hence: "If we endure, we will also reign with him" (2 Tim 2:12) in our Lord Jesus Christ, glory and power [to Him] forever. Amen.

CHAPTER XI

Homily of the same on the same subject: "Your will be done on earth as it is in heaven" (Lk 11:2).

Doctors say there are five reasons for the sickness of the body and five for its health. First, if the elements are commingled in the body equally, the body is healthy—[equal] warmth and cold, dryness and wetness. But [if one element is] more and [the other is] less, sickness comes forth. Second, well-natured weather brings health, while the ill-natured [causes] sickness. Third, useful and moderate food is healthy, but excessive and harmful [food] is sickening. Fourth, when the vital strength of the soul becomes weak, that is sickness, and when it is drained, that is death. But the increase [of vital strength] is healthy for the body.

Fifth, people become sick or healthy because of God's providence for a variety of reasons. Now, the first three [kinds of sicknesses] can be cured with medical treatment, but the last two cannot. Likewise, these five reasons are found for the sickness and health of the soul. First, [if] the four virtues are equally [distributed] in the parts of the soul, that is health, but if [one is] more and [the other is] less, that is sickness to the soul. Second, the soul becomes sick from external sensations and evil spirits, and is recovered by the same sensations and good influences. Third, the same moderate food and fasting are healthy for the soul. Hence: "Whenever I am weak, then I am strong" (2 Cor 12:10). Debauchery, however, brings sickness [to the soul] just as to the body. Fourth, there are four kinds of formal strengths: knowledge, faith, hope, and love. Their weakness is sickness to the soul, and their diminution is death; whereas their abundance is health and life to the soul. Fifth, God's providence keeps some without stumbling and straightens those who have gone astray, such as those chosen from the beginning. And He lets others be destroyed, such as the scorned who knows the reason, but keeps it to himself.

Now, the first three sicknesses of the soul are treatable by us or by other physicians. The [cure of the] fourth is limited only to God who gives knowledge, faith, hope, and love. But the fifth [sickness] is incurable. The substances for healing medications, such as roots, leaves, and various flowers, are numerous. Equally numerous and various are the vices of the soul, and [consequently] there are various treatments for these gathered from the Holy Scripture. I mentioned this because God's will is the reason for our health and sickness, whether spiritually or physically. As it is evident from our nature, so long as the patriarch Adam obeyed God, he lived in the Garden of Eden and possessed immortal life. He was healthy in body and exempted from aging, sicknesses, and vices. He was also healthy in the soul; he spoke to God, the angels served him, and he always saw God and delighted. But when he disobeyed God's will and violated the command, he was overtaken by sickness and death of the soul and the body. Hence: "The day that you eat of it you shall die" (Gen 2:17).

Now, our Lord wanted to take us [back] to the prime health of the soul and the body; [therefore He wanted us] to put the will before us, pray, and say: "Your will be done." That is, we seek your consent and your providence, for the will of God indicates His providence and consent. And we say so for three reasons. First, we seek the prime life of the Garden of Eden; and just as Adam abandoned God's will and lost all good things, so do we seek God's will that He may give us back [the prime life of Paradise]. Second, just as the patient says to the physician: "Heal me as your will," similarly we—the sickened through various sins—beg the healer of the souls to recover us according to His will. And just as we tell the doctor about pain and its cause, so are we required to, first, confess our sins and point them out, and then He will heal us. Hence: "Confess your sins . . . that you may be healed" (Jas 5:16). Third, because we abandoned God's will and followed the will of the evil one and fulfilled the desires of our body—adultery, fornication, drinking, hatred, murder, and so on—we now say: "O God, your will be done and not Satan's; take us out of our wills and lead us toward you through your will." And should someone ask, "Where is God's will? Behold! We follow evil, because our will is evil." We say that God's will is incomprehensible to those who are foolish, for only the wise can perceive it. Besides, God's will is found primarily in the Holy Scripture of the Apostles, the Prophets, and the Gospel; God's will is that which they command. Second, God's will is in the leaders; whatever the leader or the supervisor says is good and is the will of God, and whoever listens to them fulfills the will of God. Third, we say that God's will assists in all good works—righteousness, fortitude, prudence, piety, and so on. Just as Satan's will leads man toward wickedness, so does God's will lead toward goodness.

Because man sins easily and performs good [works] with difficulty, evil works please him more than the good [works]. And this has two reasons. First, Satan has enervated goodness and strengthened evil in our nature. Second, our body is voluptuous by nature and prefers sins, because they are more convenient [to commit], like a rock that rolls down the slope easily but requires effort to be pushed up the slope. Likewise, sinners go to hell easily, but they need help [to ascend] to heaven. And just as the body is easily wounded and sickened, but its recovery is difficult, so are we readily wounded by sins, whether caused by Satan or men, but we recover spiritually with much effort.

Health requires three things. First, a skilled physician. Second, fasting from the first pain onward. Third, receiving a bitter medicine or [undergoing an] operation. Likewise, in the spiritual realm, Christ is the wise healer and the priest is His representative. We ought to repent and turn from the first sins, sever them by confession, and then heal spiritually through painful penance. Wherefore we ask for God's will—since all good works are through God's will—that He may lead us toward goodness. And just as light drives darkness away, health [drives] sickness [away], and life [drives] death [away], so does the good will of God drive Satan's evil wills and sins away from us, and they disappear.

Fourth, what does "in heaven and on earth" mean? It is to be known that rational beings have two natures: angelic and human. Angels are intelligible, whereas human beings are perceptible. Angels reside up in heaven. God allotted intelligible, luminous, and light places to the angels, because they are intelligible, light, and luminous. And because our body is earthen, heavy, and dense, and it pulls us down, it received the lower places and earthen territories as abode. Just as wine or oil clears after the residues have settled in the bottom [of a container], so did the angels remain innocent and pure in heaven through the will of God, while Satan the evil and his demons and evil works weigh more and descend upon earth. So did Adam fall from the Garden of Eden because of his sins.

The world is caught in dark sins and we cannot see the light of God, and all human beings walk toward various evil things according to their own choice. Now, we first ask [God], saying, since the angels remained in goodness in heaven by Your will, and [since] Your will is accomplished among them, maintain us in a similar fashion by Your will, lead us toward goodness, and let Your will be accomplished among us. Also, when all men are resurrected in the life to come, lift us unto heaven and place us with the angels according to Your true promise: "I go and prepare a place for you, I will come again and will take you to myself, so that where I am, there my servant may be also" (Jn 14:3), because we believe in You, are baptized in Your font, were saved by the blood of Your Only Begotten, and are named after You. Briefly, this is the meaning of "Your will be done on earth as it is in heaven." This is the fourth clause of the prayer in an orderly manner.

The fifth clause says: "Give us this day our daily bread" (Lk 11:3). All that has been said previously [relates to] spiritual matters, but this one [relates to] corporeal needs. "Our bread" indicates four things. First, prayers need to be made for all people in general, and not to be restricted to oneself, because that [the general] is loving the neighbor, while the second [the restricted] is selfishness. For this reason, [Christ] phrased all the clauses of the prayer in plural. Second, it indicates moderation—give us what is necessary to us, and not more than what we need. Third, it indicates our want for a lawful earning, and not something that belongs to others or is unlawful. Fourth, "our bread" means the body and the blood of Christ, which is bread to us, the believers, and the cause of our life. Hence: "The bread of God is that which comes down from heaven and gives life to the world" (Jn 6:33).

God gives us bread in two ways. First, He gives us bread from the elements, vegetation, and animals, as well as through the sun and rain from heaven, and fruits from the earth, and so on. Hence: "The eyes of all wait upon you; and you give them their food in due season" (Ps 145:15). Second, God gives bread through our lawful labor and work. Hence: "By the sweat of your face you shall eat bread" (Gen 3:19). We can give God a portion of that bread, which is the gift of God and the fruit of our lawful labor. Hence: "Honor the Lord with your just labor" (Prov 3:9). But the bread of others, and that [which is obtained] by ravishing and theft, is not bread from God; rather, it is from Satan, for he is the father of iniquity and ravishing. Satan is the one who accepts such offering, not God. Hence: "I will take no bullocks out of your house" (Ps 50:9). Or: "That ox to me is as he that slaughters a dog," and so on. (Isa 66:3). A sacrifice of this kind is received by Satan, not by God.

Behold! We ask for bread that is necessary and not more than that, and [we ask] not for gold, silver, land, or any other material comfort that heathens seek. [We ask for] bread, which is nourishment by which our bodies are kept alive. We ask it daily, which indicates moderation and not the greed for more. Saying "today" unfolds two meanings. First, it indicates our daily life, because this one is our day, for yesterday is past and lost, and it [this day] is not in the future. Our whole life is this one day for us. Past and future do not belong to us, for they are appropriate to God and things that are everlasting. Second, "This day" indicates that we need to care for today only, not for tomorrow, because tomorrow is unknown. We do not know what it will bring—evil or good, death or life? Wherefore the Lord said: "Do not worry about tomorrow, for it will bring worries of its own" (Mt 6:34); that is, today's troubles and worries are enough; do not trouble yourselves today by worrying about tomorrow, otherwise the troubles and worries of each day will be doubled.

And should someone say: "Since we are moderate, then we should not cultivate the garden, nor should we till this fall, because these [the fruits of these labors] are for next year. We say, that is not what constitutes a worry for tomorrow; because when we cultivate the vineyard or anything else this fall, we do today's work and [face] today's trouble. God does not prohibit this, for this is prosperity for the earth. However, He prohibits worrying more than necessary and troubling the body excessively, and [suggests] to worry moderately about the needs of the body and excessively for [the needs of] the soul.

Should someone argue: "The Lord says: 'Do not worry about tomorrow,' and elsewhere [God] says: 'By the sweat of your face you shall eat bread,' whereas Solomon says: 'Go to the ant and the bee, O sluggard, and emulate his ways'" (cf. Prov 6:6). We say that these do not contradict one another; they are in accord very much. Solomon exhorts the slothful—the sluggard and lazy in laboring for their needs—while the Lord dispels excessive possession and avarice. Saying "By the sweat of your . . ." also dispels theft and ravishing, and commands fair labor. Thus, when He [Christ] says: "Look at the birds of the air; they neither sow," and so on (Mt 6:26), He does not say, do not labor and do not work; rather, do not exert excessive efforts for your bodies; be content with moderate [effort and outcome], just like the birds that seek only their daily food. This is the meaning of "Give us this day our daily bread."

The sixth clause of the prayer says: "Forgive us our debts, as we forgive our debtors" (Lk 11:4). This clause refers to philanthropy, which is the foremost good work, for "Love is the fulfilling of the law" (Rom 13:10). This clause has six meanings. It indicates that man is God's associate, because it is God's prerogative to forgive sins, as the Gospel says: "Who can forgive sins but God alone?" (Mk 2:7). Here [we face] two questions. First, why is it that God alone can forgive sins? We say that through our sins we break God's commandments and become indebted to His commands; [then] indeed, God [alone] can forgive, for we have sinned against Him only. The second question is: Why do men forgive sins on earth? We say that man can forgive through his words what people owe him, and this is acknowledged; then, therefore, God's Word can forgive the debts men owe Him. Now, the priest [also] can forgive man's debts, not as a human being [though]; rather, because he is authorized to forgive the debts of man through the Word of God. This is the first notion of the clause that shows man as God's associate.

Second, it indicates [humans'] worthiness to the point where they are [deservedly] called children of the heavenly Father and, eventually, also other things, and therefore they are empowered to ask God's forgiveness and say: "Forgive us our debts"; otherwise, if they were unworthy, they would not have asked. Third, it indicates those who are entitled to find God's forgiveness, for those who wish forgiveness and ask for it by word [only] will not find it, but those who do it through work, and forgive others, will find God's forgiveness. Fourth, it indicates that man resembles God the good, merciful, forgiving, kind, and so on. He forgives everybody's debts and sins. Likewise, a man who is good, merciful, forgiving, and so on, and who forgives all the sins of those who are indebted to him, does, indeed, resemble God, and is benevolent. Fifth, [the clause] has another profound and sublime meaning: God is the archetype and paradigm of all good things, and just as we learn all good things from Him, as Paul says: "Be imitators of me, as I am of Christ" (1 Cor 11:1), likewise, by changing the order, we become models of love and God learns from us. This is exactly what [the clause] "as we also have forgiven our debtors" means. You, too, learn it, and forgive your debtor. Man speaks to God thus: "I have forgiven, so forgive also You; I have released, so release also You. Because You commanded: 'Forgive, and you will be forgiven; release, and you will be released; give, and it will be given to you' (cf. Lk 6:37–38). And if my sin against you is greater than that of my neighbor's against me, yes, I will say: 'O, greater are You than me. You are God, Almighty, and King, while I am human, weak, and poor; indeed, You do forgive according to Your greatness.'"

Sixth, saying "Forgive us our debts" indicates humility, for when we pray, we do not consider ourselves holy and sinless like the Pharisee who perished because of his arrogance. Although one can be stainless from corporeal sins, he is [still] sinful and indebted to God in his mind, as Solomon says: "Who will boast that he has a pure heart?" (Prov 20:9). And although he may be stainless from sin by his works, he is indebted by the original sin, as Job says: "Even if man's life should be but one day, it would be impossible to be pure of sins" (cf. Job 14:4–5). And even if he is clean from deadly sins, he is unclean in the venial [sin]. It is known, otherwise, that man's nature is sinful because of Adam's sin, and whoever possesses human nature, possesses [also] Adam's sin. This is how one should understand the clause "Forgive us our debts, as we forgive our debtors."

If we forgive not, the prayers [will cause] many harms. First, we will be damning ourselves by our own tongues: just as we have not forgiven others, forgive us not [O Lord]. Hence: "If you do not forgive others, neither will your Father forgive your trespasses" (Mt 6:15). Second, because rancor turns man into Satan, for a man filled with rancor is Satan who is full of rancor against God, angels, and man; and just as Satan is distant from God, so is a rancorous man. Third, because he will be frightened by human fear if he does not forgive the debts. Fourth, because his conscience will torture and trouble him. Fifth, because he [man] supplicates and deceives God [as if saying] "You forgive my debts, but I will not forgive my neighbor." Sixth, whoever asks forgiveness by [his] tongue, but forgives not in [his] heart, contradicts the knowledge of God who first reads the mind and then listens to the words and [examines] all other works. Since man is corporeal, he understands the mind [of man] through actions and words, but God is incorporeal, [therefore] He recognizes the abstract mind before the actions and words. Thus, [the prayer] is harmful to a rancorous man in six ways when he does not forgive his neighbor.

Let us see what you owe your Lord and what your neighbor owes you. Your neighbor owes you a few things either in words if he insulted, slandered, or calumniated you, and so on; or in possessions if he cannot pay [his debt], robbed or ravished [you], and so on. But you are indebted to God and have sinned against Him by many things: so long as you think evil in your mind, speak evil by your tongue, sin by the eyes and [other] senses, curse and become slothful in keeping His commandments, you are indebted by everything to your Lord who created you and gave you soul and body, and gave the creatures goodness and the promise of a life to come. Now, if you are not willing to forgive the few debts [of your neighbors], do not ask God's [forgiveness for] the many [sins you have committed]. As the parable of the Gospel says, one owed ten thousand talents [to his lord]; when he begged his lord, he [the lord] forgave him the debt, but as the servant went out, he saw another servant who owed him one hundred piasters, and seizing him by the throat, demanded: "Pay what you owe me." When the servants reported this to their lord, he [the lord] said to the servant: "You evil and wicked servant! You pleaded with me and I forgave you all your debt; since you did not forgive your debtor, pay all your debt by endless torture" (cf. Mt 18:32–34). See how easy it is to forgive the neighbor's debt, and how harsh [the consequence] is for those who do not forgive. Wherefore we say: "Forgive us our debts, as we forgive our debtors."

The seventh and eighth clauses [of the prayer] say: "Do not lead us into temptation, but save us from evil" (Lk 11:4). There are two questionable items here. First, how does God lead us into temptation? We say that God does not lead us into temptation and evil, but when we follow our sins by our own free will, He allows us [to do so] and does not prohibit by force. This is [how we should understand] His leading us into evil, as He said: "I will harden Pharaoh's heart" (Ex 7:3); that is, will allow him to be hardened in evil. The second questionable aspect of the expression "Do not lead us into temptation" arises from the Apostle's saying: "Blessed is anyone who endures temptation, for he will receive the crown of life" (Jas 1:12). We say that there are two kinds of temptation: one relates to sins, which we carry in our bodies and are caused by Satan; this is evil; we pray [to God] to not lead us into such temptation; and the other is the temptation we face from strangers who torment and torture us because of our faith; this is good [temptation]: "Whoever endures, will receive the crown of Christ" (cf. Jas 1:12).

Now we shall discuss the kind of evil and temptation we pray [to God] to save us from. Our enemy Satan is occasionally referred to in many names: Diabolus, Adversary, Beelzebub, Evil Spirit, and Tempter who tempts man and pulls him into evil traps. Tempting is interpreted elsewhere as examination and choice. Here, however, it [tempting] means Satan's deception and seduction. Like bait that covers the hook and the snare, and captures the fish and bird, Satan places pleasure as a bait for sins, and [thus] seduces the senses and catches us in the trap of sins. A sea wave is evil, because it drowns man; inflaming the fire is evil, because it burns and corrupts [man]; and war is evil, because it kills man. Whoever wants to avoid these must distance himself from them. Similarly, the tempest of desires, the fire of anger, and Satan's battle are evil in nature, wherefore we ask God to help us stay away from them. Also, sinning unintentionally and unknowingly is temptation, while sinning intentionally and knowingly is evil, [wherefore] we pray to God that He may save us from both. Again, sinning by the senses is temptation when someone unexpectedly sees, hears, and sins; but wicked is he who premeditates, consents to, and then commits [sins] intentionally. Again, Satan's deception is temptation and his violent power is evil, for its two arms—knavery and violence—are satanic. Again, the corporeal punishment we are subjected to in this world is temptation, while the eternal torment in the world to come is evil. We pray [to God] to save us from these.

Then, He [Christ] adds the ninth clause that says: "For yours is the kingdom and the power and the glory, forever," in a sense that You [Father] should save us, for You are our Lord and King, and You have the mighty power to save us, the weak ones, from the tyranny of evil, and our salvation is Your glory and name, O You who saves and liberates us from eternal torments through His mercy!

The tenth clause says: "Amen." That is, let what we asked of You be realized; let our various requests be accomplished. Also, indeed, You are the mighty King and Lord, and glory and praise to You in all eternities, in the past, in the present, and in the life to come. From all creatures, whether in heaven, on earth, or infernal, and from all tongues, mouths, and breaths, glory and prostration to the Father Almighty, and the Only Begotten Son our Savior, and the life-giving and liberating Holy Spirit; praise and benediction and glory forever, amen.

CHAPTER XII

The first homily of the same on faith, according to the verse of the Apostle in Hebrews: "Whoever would approach God, must believe that God exists, and that He rewards those who seek Him" (Heb 11:6).

Isaiah, the theologian Prophet, teaches that the pattern of God's worship is made of three elements: first, hearing by the ears; second, understanding by the mind; third, the sight of the eyes. Concerning the first, he says: "Have you not heard? Has it not been told you?" (Isa 40:21). Concerning the second [Isaiah says]: "Have you not understood? Have you not known?" (Isa 40:28). Concerning the third [Isaiah says]: "Lift up your eyes on high and see, who has established all these things?" (Isa 40:26). In this way, we come to know true God, as was said in the law, through the narrations of the ancient people: "I am the Lord God the first and the last, and besides me there is no God" (Isa 44:6). And we ought to believe that God exists. Second, we come to know God by the mind, through the order of things, for every being has to have a beginning and a cause, because something cannot be its own beginning and cause. Then, therefore, God is the beginning and cause of all things, just as number one is [the beginning] of the multitude of numbers. Third, by the sight of the eyes [we come to know God], for we see the firmament, the running waters, the wide arch of sky, and the movement of the stars and other things. And we learn through these that they have a creator. As the Apostle says in Romans: "God's invisible things are understood and seen through the visible creation" (cf. Rom 1:20). A philosopher[20] described the first origin by the following theory: "There is One who stirs the heavenly body, and He is one, and is incorporeal, and has infinite power, and is uncreated, and therefore has no end. And He is the creator of all beings, and He should be worshipped and believed in." The Apostle also teaches us the same: "Whoever would approach God, must believe that God exists, and that He rewards those who seek Him" (Heb 11:6). We will discuss six aspects of the present verse.

First, what is faith? Second, which of these perceives more: faith, the mind,

---

[20] Possibly Diogenes Laërtius, who in his *Lives and Opinions of Eminent Philosophers* refers to both Aristotle and Plato as saying that God in incorporeal and his providence extends over all heavenly bodies (Book 5, "The Peripatetics").

or the eyes? Third, where does faith come from? Fourth, which part of the soul does it [faith] comprise? Fifth, how many kinds of faith are there? Sixth, [what are] the stages and profession of faith?

Let us find out, first, what faith is. The Apostle defines it as follows: "Faith is the assurance of things hoped for and the manifestation of things not seen" (cf. Heb 11:1). That is, faith confirms in us the goodness of the life to come, which we hope for, and manifestly indicates God and confirms in our souls the giver of goodness, who cannot be seen through the eyes. St. Dionysius attests that faith is the solid foundation [of those who believe], establishing them in the truth and truth in them.[21] That is, since God and His goodness-to-come are truth, man adheres to true God and approaches Him through faith, and receives the promised goodness, as it is taught here: "Whoever would approach God, must believe that God exists, and that He rewards those who seek Him" (Heb 11:6). This [was] about the first matter.

The second matter [relates to examining] which of these perceives more: faith, the mind, or the eyes? It is to be known that all creatures are of two kinds: intelligible or incorporeal, such as angels and heavenly life, and perceivable or corporeal, such as visible things and the present life. Man's knowledge [also] is of two kinds: [knowledge gained] by the mind and by the sensate eyes, for by the mind [man] perceives the incorporeal essence of angels, and by the eyes [he perceives] perceivable bodies. Wherefore God gave us faith to perceive Him through faith, because perception by faith is greater than perception by the mind and the eyes, is not it?

This is evident from four things. First, an eye is able to see what lies before the eyes, such as a wall, a mountain, and the sky. It cannot pass beyond [the limit of vision]. The mind perceives these and adds [to what has been perceived by the eyes] what is beyond the wall and the mountain, and then perceives the classes of angels and incorporeal things that are above the world. But it [the mind] falls short of perceiving God for two reasons: First, the mind is created, while God is uncreated; a creation cannot perceive the uncreated. Second, the mind is limited, while God is unlimited; the limited cannot understand and perceive the unlimited. Faith, however, can perceive and understand God, because it has come unto us from God. This is evident, first, through numerous philosophers who, although possessing intellectual knowledge, could not understand God. Second, it is evident that intellectual knowledge adheres to the nature of things; it cannot perceive the supernatural, for the mind cannot

---

[21] Pseudo-Dionysius, *The Divine Names*, Chapter 7.

reach where nature cannot reach. Faith, however, perceives the supernatural, such as God, and believes in supernatural miracles. Third, it is evident that the philosophers who possessed intellectual knowledge spoke many true things, but many of their perceptions were false and wrong, such as those about the existence of heaven and earth, and the world's beginning and end. Everything the prophets and the apostles said, however, was unmistakably true, because they had received the knowledge of God through faith. Therefore, we ought to accept the true words of the philosophers, but refute their teachings that contradict the doctors of the church, considering them vain and false. Fourth, it is evident that those who possessed intellectual knowledge were not justified [simply] because of [possessing] the knowledge, nor did anyone die because of his knowledge. However, many possessors of faith died because of their faith, such as the scores of martyrs, and [many] were justified through their faith. As the Scripture says: "Abraham believed God, and it was counted to him for righteousness" (Gen 15:6). Then, therefore, it is evident from what we have said that perception by faith is greater than perception by the mind and eyes. This [concludes] the second matter.

The third question addresses the source of faith. The doctors say: The eye, for example, has intrinsic lighting, but it needs the external light of the sun or a lamp to unite with it in order to see. In a similar fashion, God placed an intrinsic lighting in the eye of our soul, which is the mind, but it needs to unite with the light pouring down from God so that it may perceive God, the goodness to come, and the eternal life through it. Wherefore doctors suggest the following definition: "Faith is the illumination of the mind poured in the rational person by the first light, that he may understand the spiritual goodness."[22] Also, for example, if one of the two lights is missing—whether the intrinsic [light] as in a blind person, or the extrinsic, as at night—we can see nothing. Likewise, if the inherent reason is missing, as in irrational animals, or the light pouring down from God is absent as among other faith-lacking nations, a person will not be able to perceive the life to come. A third example: A blind person is completely darkened and cannot see, whereas a watery eye has blurry sight and a clear eye's sight is bright. Similarly, those who do not believe and those who belong to other religions are completely blind, whereas a heretic has deficiency of faith and has confused sight. The orthodox [believer], however, possesses the true and perfect light of faith and [therefore] bright sight.

---

[22] Pseudo-Dionysius, *The Divine Names*, Chapter 7.

It is to be known that there are three kinds of intelligible lights: natural [inherent/ intrinsic] light, the light of grace, and the light of glory. Natural light is the inherent reason, such as in philosophers. The light of grace is reminiscent of the light of the faith of prophets and Christians. The light of glory is possessed by angels and the blessed saints in the upper domain. Now, natural light is like the light of the stars, which is lesser. The light of grace, which is that of faith, is like the [light of] the moon, which is greater [than the light of the stars]. The light of glory is like the [light of] the sun, which is the greatest and brightest. Independent philosophers possessed only the inherent light, but we, Christians, the apostles, and the prophets have received the light of grace beyond natural light—faith—and with this light we attain the light of glory, which the angels possess.

These three kinds of lights are differentiated in the following fashion. First, natural light is hypothetical knowledge, such as the knowledge of the philosophers, and [therefore] it is false. The light of grace is true knowledge, such as the knowledge of the faithful, but it is lesser. The light of glory is the most sublime and bright knowledge, such as the knowledge of the saints in heaven. For this reason, the knowledge of faith is in between the other two [kinds of] knowledge; it is greater than the hypothetical knowledge of man, but inferior to the knowledge of angels. The prophets and the faithful perceive by way of reflection, while the saints in heaven see face to face, as the Apostle says: "Now we see by the way of reflection, but then [we will see] face to face" (cf. 1 Cor 13:12). The three lights are differentiated [in that] natural light is first, [and] then there is the light of grace followed by the light of glory. Natural light transforms into the light of grace, and that of grace [transforms] into the light of glory, and where the light of faith is absent, there the light of glory is nonexistent. Then, therefore, it is evident that believers who now possess the light of grace can perceive the light of God's glory, whereas unbelievers who do not possess the light of grace can see the light of glory neither in this world nor in the one to come. This [much about] the third matter.

The fourth question is: Which part of the soul does faith comprise? The doctors say that the soul has three powers and parts—innate, sentient, and rational. The innate is completely beyond man's control, such as the power of disintegration and growth, and so on. We can never regulate these [powers] and they operate according to their nature. They function more when man is asleep, rather than when he is awake. The sentient parts [of the soul], such as wrath and desire, sometimes obey us and sometimes disobey, because these [parts] are sometimes subject to reason through fear or shame, and they cease stirring desire and anger. The rational parts [of the soul], such as intellect and will, are absolutely obedient to man. The intellect consists of intelligence and thought; by these we conceive the truth, and by the sovereign will we do good.

Now, faith is not included in the innate, disobedient part of the tripartite soul, because, like the plants and shrubs, the innate cannot be subject to virtue. Faith is not included in the part where the sentient power exists, either, for although there may be room for virtues there—there is honesty in desire and fortitude in wrath—they cannot be subject to the divine virtue, which faith is. This pattern is also found in irrational beings, which lack the sublime virtue— faith. Then, therefore, faith is in the third part of the soul's power, which is the rational [power] in essence. And it [faith] exists in the two components of the rational [part]—intellect and will. Faith exists in the intellect as follower and in the will as commander, because the will commands the act of faith and only the willing can believe. Consequently, the intellect, not the will, is in first place and subject to faith for two reasons. First, faith is followed by truth and will [is followed] by goodness; but truth is in faith and goodness is in hope and love, because we hope for goodness and love that which is good. Then, therefore, faith is in the intellect, and hope and love are in the will. Second, it is evident that faith is transformed into bright perception in the glory of the heavenly kingdom. As the Apostle says: "Now we see by the way of reflection, but then [we will see] face to face" (cf. 1 Cor 13:12). The bright and direct perception is given to the intellect and not the will. This [much about] the fourth matter.

The fifth question is: How many kinds of faith are there? It is to be known that faith is divided into three [kinds]. First, the so-called imperfect faith of demons; [they possess it] not through the grace of God but rather through their ingenious skill and by perceiving the miracles of Christ and the apostles. They [demons] were compelled to say: "I know who you are, the Holy one of God; do not torment us before time" (cf. Mk 1:24 and Mt 8:29). James says: "You believe that God is one; you do well. Even the demons believe—and shudder" (Jas 2:19). This kind of faith is imperfect and unrewardable. Second, the so-called formless and dead faith of nominal Christians. This faith is truer than the faith of demons, because it is poured in them [the nominal Christians] through the grace of God at the time of baptism, [as opposed to the] demons who lack the ability to believe in the bounties [of God], as previously demonstrated. This [kind of faith] is also formless and dead, because their [nominal Christians'] faith is dead due to evil actions. They do not possess love, which is a kind of faith, nor do they have good works, which represent the vitality of faith. Moreover, this kind of faith is unrewardable. Hence: "Faith without works is dead" (Jas 2:26). The third kind of faith is multitudinous, infinite, and perfect; that is, the faith of the saints and the chosen, who received it by loving God and doing good, as the Apostle says: "Neither circumcision nor uncircumcision counts for anything; but faith with works by love" (Gal 5:6). The reward of such faith is multitudinous and never-ending. It is with this kind of faith that all of the patriarchs, such as Noah, Abraham, Isaac, Jacob, and others, were justified. It is with this kind of faith that the prophets, such as Moses, Samuel, David, and others, spoke. It is with this kind of faith that the apostles preached throughout the universe, as the Apostle says: "So we proclaimed and so you have come to believe" (1 Cor 15:11). It is for the sake of this faith that martyrs suffered, hermits were martyred, and all the ranks of the chosen ones—whether first, middle, or last—died and were crowned. This is the perfect and rewardable faith, as the Apostle says: "I have finished the work, I have kept the faith. From now on there is reserved for me the crown of righteousness, which the Lord, the righteous judge, will give me on the day" (2 Tim 4:7–8). This [much about] the fifth matter.

The sixth question is: How many steps of faith are there? It is to be known that the steps of faith were patterned after Jacob's ladder. He saw the ladder stretching from earth unto heaven, and the Lord standing beside him, while the angels were descending and men ascending. Now, these steps indicate the height of faith by which we, believers, ascend unto heaven and angels descend unto the believers, while the Lord stands by its [faith's] side, because God rests in man through the profession of faith and [thus] we join God. Of the two sides of the tall ladder one [indicates] the incorporeal essence of God, and the other the humanization of our Lord. The steps of the ladder were [a symbol of] the fourteen steps of faith by which we fortify our minds and ascend and rise unto God. Seven of these fourteen steps are [indications of] the incorporeal essence of the three persons of God, and [the other] seven are the corporeal dispensations of Christ.

Now, in relation to divinity, there are seven steps, because God has three aspects: first, the person of God; second, the nature of God; third, the work of God. In relation to the person, there are three steps of faith: First, we ought to believe that the person of God is without beginning and unbegotten. Second, we ought to believe that the person of the Son is begotten of the Father. Third, we ought to believe that the Holy Spirit proceeds from the Father. However, the nature [of these three persons] is one, wherefore the fourth step is the belief that the Trinity is one nature and one divinity. All the works of God are of three kinds: The first is a work of nature, such as creation. The second is a work of grace, such as providing for and granting forgiveness to the faithful. The third is a work of glory and greatness, such as raising the dead and the glory of angels. Wherefore, the fifth step is to believe that God is the Creator and author of all beings, whether visible or invisible. The sixth step is the belief in the forgiveness of sins in the holy church. The seventh step is the obligation to believe that there will be general resurrection for the righteous and the sinful, and the righteous will inherit eternal life and the wicked eternal torment. This is in relation to divinity.

In relation to Christ's humanization, we ought to believe in seven things. The first step is to believe that the Son of God was conceived through the Holy Spirit by the Holy Mother of God. The second step is to believe that He was born of the Holy Virgin, with the virginity of the birth-giver remaining incorrupt. The third step is [to believe] that He suffered and died, and was buried physically. The fourth step is to believe that He descended to hell with [His] rational soul and illuminated the entrapped souls. The fifth step is to believe that He rose from the grave on the third day, destroyed hell, and liberated the entrapped souls. The sixth step is to believe that He ascended unto heaven in His body forty days later and sat on the right hand of God; that is, He settled in divine glory. The seventh step is to believe in the second coming of Christ, for He will come to judge the living and the dead. These fourteen steps of faith are the foundation and root of faith.

Summing it up, we profess in the following fashion, in simple words: We confess and believe wholeheartedly in God the Father, uncreated, unborn, and without beginning, and begetter of the Son and the cause of the proceeding of the Holy Spirit. We believe in God the Word, uncreated, begotten of and beginning from the Father before all ages; neither after nor younger [than the Father], but as much as the Father is Father, so the Son with Him is Son. We believe in the Holy Spirit, uncreated, timeless, not begotten of but proceeding from the Father, consubstantial with the Father and sharing the glory with the Son. We believe in the Holy Trinity, one nature, one divinity; not three gods but one God, one Godhead, one will, one kingship, one power; Creator of all visible and invisible things. We believe in the holy church [and] the forgiveness of sins through the communion of the saints. We believe that one of the Three Persons, God the Word, begotten by the Father before all ages, in time came down into the Mother of God, Virgin Mary, taking from her blood united it to His divinity, waited patiently in the womb of the pure Virgin for nine months, and the perfect God became perfect man in spirit, in mind, and in body; one person, one countenance, and one united nature; humanized God without mutation and without alteration; seedless conception and pure birth; without end to His humanity, as there is no beginning to His divinity, "For Jesus Christ is the same yesterday, today, and forever" (Heb 13:8). We believe that our Lord Jesus Christ wandered on earth, and that after thirty years He came to baptism; the Father testified: "This is my Son, the Beloved" (Mt 17:5), and the Holy Spirit descended upon Him in the form of a dove; He was tempted by Satan and defeated him. He proclaimed salvation for humankind, worked, labored, and experienced hunger and thirst in the body. Then He willingly came to suffer; crucified, died in the body while living as divinity. His body, unseparated from his divinity, was buried in the grave, and He descended into hell with His indivisible divinity. He preached to the souls, destroyed hell, and liberated the souls. Three days after [His burial], He rose from the dead and appeared to His disciples. We believe that our Lord Jesus Christ ascended with the same body unto heaven and sat on the right hand of the Father. And He will come to judge the living and the dead, and to recompense according to deeds—eternal life to the righteous and eternal torment to the sinners.

This is the orthodox profession of faith, which every Christian should always keep in his mind and on his tongue. For as the Apostle says: "Believing with the heart brings justification, and confessing with the mouth brings salvation" (Rom 10:10). This is the foundation, and good works should be based on it. This is the unshakeable rock; we should adhere to and establish ourselves on it. This is the lamp in the darkness of our life; we ought to always keep it in hand and be enlightened through it. This is the way, and with it we shall walk toward eternal life to our Lord Jesus Christ. Glory and praise to Him, and to His Father, and to the Holy Spirit, forever and ever, amen.

CHAPTER XIII

Homily of the same on James's verse: "Faith by itself, if it has no works, is dead" (Jas 2:17)

The doctors say that virtue is in not only knowing, but working, because to know and yet not work is useless and harmful. As James says: "Anyone who knows the right thing to do and fails to do so, commits sin" (Jas 4:17). To know by itself does not make man blessed. Our Lord said to His disciples: "If you know these things, you are blessed if you do them" (Jn 13:17). As the philosophers say, anyone who knows medicine is a doctor, but anyone who knows justice is not [necessarily] righteous. Likewise, not everyone who knows the faith is faithful; but anyone who does justice is righteous, and anyone who performs the works of faith is faithful. Faith without works is dead and empty, as James says: "Faith by itself, if it has no works, is dead" (Jas 2:17). This statement about faith indicates six things. First, the essence of faith. Second, the kinds of faith. Third, the difference between dead and living faith. Fourth, the necessity of associating faith with good works. Fifth, what we gain and benefit from faith. Sixth, what [happens] to the evil unbeliever.

Let us first discuss the essence of faith. Doctors define faith the following way: Faith is the possession of grace, poured into the rational man from the Prime Light, that he may recognize spiritual goodness. Faith is an innate habit, poured by the grace of God as a bounty of light into our rational souls. With it we recognize spiritual goodness like seeing the world, man, stone, and other things through the light of the sun when it unites with the light of our eyes. The light of faith irradiates through God in our rational soul and enlightens us, and through the light of faith we see the eternal life, the glory of the righteous, and the punishment of the sinners.

When does faith shine in us? It shines at baptism, when we face west and renounce Satan and his dark works, and then we turn eastward and profess our belief in the Holy Trinity and Christ's dispensations. Since we vowed to believe in God, we ought to keep this vow in our hearts and on our tongues from that moment [of the vow] unto death. When we are baptized, in the name of the Father, the Son, and the Holy Spirit, the covert light of faith shines in us instantly.

118

This is evident from three testimonies. First, the Prophet Joel says: "I will pour out my spirit on all flesh; your sons and your daughters shall prophesy, and your old men shall dream dreams" (Joel 2:28). The act of pouring signifies the grace of the Spirit, which [God] grants at baptism. Second, the Apostle Paul testifies: "To another prophesy, to another faith with the same spirit" (1 Cor 12:10). This means that a person receives many kinds of grace at baptism, such as prophecy, teaching, and the knowledge of languages. It also means that grace is granted by God. Third, the Gospel testifies to what [Christ] said to Peter: "Blessed are you, for flesh and blood has not revealed this to you, but my Father in heaven" (Mt 16:17). He [Christ] said that Peter's belief that Christ is the Son of God was revealed by God and not man. And He blessed him, for God's blessing goes to the believers; not to those who believe because they have seen, but to those who have not seen and yet have come to believe. As the Lord said to Thomas: "Have you believed because you have seen me? Blessed are those who have not seen and yet have come to believe" (Jn 20:29). This blessing belongs to those of us who believe in Christ, have been baptized, and have received the bounty of faith, which is the kingdom of heaven, because as we vowed to believe in Him [Christ], He promised us the kingdom. Hence: "I confer on you, just as my Father has conferred on me, a kingdom" (Lk 22:29). We were designated as children of God by grace and partakers of Christ's inheritance at our baptism. As long as we keep our vow to believe and confess, He shall keep His promise of the bounties He pledged; hence: "Everyone who acknowledges me before men, I also will acknowledge him before my Father" (Mt 10:32). But when we refuse to acknowledge and believe in Him, He will deny His promise and bounty; hence: "Whoever denies me before men, I also will deny him before my Father in heaven" (Mt 10:33). This is a terrible thing; this is a formidable command. If we deny [Him] before men, Christ our Savior will deny us before God, [saying]: "I do not know you" (Mt 25:12).

People do not recognize a person for four reasons. First, when someone's face has changed its original color and darkened. Through baptism our souls become white like snow, but later [when] it turns into black through sins, Christ does not recognize them [the souls], as Jeremiah says: "Their countenances have become as black as soot" (Lam 4:8). Second, when someone covers his face, [people] cannot recognize him; likewise, whoever commits sins after baptism, and covers them instead of confessing, Christ does not recognize him, because a sin resembles coal: when people cover it under the earth for an extended period, it remains intact, but when it is brought to the surface [and exposed] to rain and sun, it soon disintegrates. Similarly, when you hide your sins in your heart and refuse to confess them, they remain absolutely intact, but when you reveal them, they soon become erased. Third, if someone changes a sign he had originally, no one would recognize him; likewise, whoever changes the sign of faith and denies Christ, God and the angels will not recognize him, as Solomon says: "We have not seen our signs" (Ps 74:9). Fourth, when people migrate at a young age and stay away until they mature, they become unrecognizable upon their return; likewise, if someone departs from God's commandments from childhood unto old age, God does not recognize him. Then, therefore, it is true that whoever denies Christ by faith and works, Christ will deny him before God and the angels. This was [about] the first section.

The second question is: How many kinds of faith are there? The doctors say that faith has one designation, but two meanings. The first is the belief in the creed, which means acknowledging the Holy Trinity, which every individual has received from the font. That is, our belief in God the Father, our belief in God the Son, and our belief in God the Holy Spirit as plain and equal [divinities]. Neither first nor last; neither elder nor younger; neither more nor less; but consubstantial, equal in reverence and glory; one power; one dominion; one kingdom; one divinity; one nature; Creator of all beings [together]. We also believe in Christ's birth, humanization, crucifixion, burial, resurrection, ascension, and second coming. This is the first profession of faith [acknowledging] the Holy Trinity. The second [meaning is that] faith takes place when a believer does not consider the words spoken by the Holy Spirit through the mouths of the prophets and the apostles, and the holy books written by the doctors of the church myths and lies; rather, he believes that they are true and unmistakable, as if he is seeing, by his own eyes, all that happened, will happen, and is happening now. Things that occurred are things that were told; all the visible and invisible beings did not exist, and they came into being by God's command. He [the believer] believes in what is told in the Scripture— whether in the Old [Testament] or the New—about all the wonderful things and miracles of God that followed the creation of beings. And things that will occur are things that were spoken about: God will reward those who have done good, while for the wicked [there will be] eternal torment and fire, weeping of the eyes and gnashing of the teeth, a darkness where God cannot be seen, and an everlasting fire, "where their worm never dies and the fire is never quenched" (Mk 9:48). Present things are things they [prophets, apostles, and doctors] proclaimed in all of their writings: God is close to everybody, not distant from them. God knows everything that people think, be it good or evil.

He unmistakably hears whatever they speak, and He manifestly sees whatever they covertly do, "For there is no creature hidden from him" (Heb 4:13).

Now, he who wholeheartedly believes in these possesses the living faith. He would never dare to think evil, speak iniquity, or commit sins. When a man is close to God, he is prohibited from [performing] unworthy works, and when a man believes that God is seer, for God means seer, he would not dare to speak or do something evil intentionally. But whoever confesses to God in words only and not by works, his faith is dead, for his faith has become dead due to his dead works, as the Apostle says: "Faith by itself, if it has no works, is dead" (Jas 2:17). This was about the second section.

Third question: How is a dead faith differentiated from a living faith? We say that the dead and the living faiths are differentiated in ten ways. First, as we have mentioned, the dead and the living faiths are differentiated through good works, because just as the soul constitutes the vitality of the body, good works constitute [the vitality] of faith. And just as a dead body is idle, for it does not see, hear, speak, walk, work, and so on, so is a dead faith, for it does not see or hear the good, does not speak the truth, does not walk in the path of God, and does not perform good works. But he who possesses the living faith works, speaks, and hears everything that is good, and does everything else [that is good].

Second, the philosophers say that the soul is what forms man and completes him. A dead man is formless, for the form of the body would soon disintegrate and become corrupt. Similarly, the form of faith is love for God and the neighbor: to believe in good God and to love Him, and to believe in God's representatives and love the neighbor, as was said to the Galatians: "In Christ Jesus neither circumcision nor uncircumcision counts for anything; the only thing that counts is faith accomplished through love" (Gal 5:6). Whoever lacks love possesses a formless and incomplete faith; it [faith] soon disintegrates and become corrupt, for he lacks love, which adorns and completes faith. Third, as the living [man] is a true man and is referred to as man, and a dead [person] is an unreal man; likewise, whoever has the living faith is a true believer and is referred to as Christian, and whoever has a dead faith is a false believer and is referred to as a false Christian. Such a person contradicts the commands of God that say: "You shall not give the name of the Lord your God in vain for vain things" (Ex 20:7). It is as if it [the commandment] says: "If you are referred to as a Christian, perform the works of a Christian that you are commanded to; otherwise, you would be referring to yourself as a Christian in vain." For example, a person who is referred to as

121

a sultan or a king, but does not perform the works of a sultan or a king, [is falsely referred to as such]; likewise, a Christian is falsely referred to as such if he does not perform the works [of a Christian]. Fourth, it is said [that there are] dead and living faiths: when natural warmth and energy are strong in the living man he can complete the works fast, but an old man or an immature child with incomplete strength works slowly. Similarly, whoever has strong faith and warm love accomplishes good works quickly, whereas anyone whose faith is incomplete and who is aged in sins is slow in the accomplishment of good works, which is reflected in Genesis: "God appeared to Abraham at noon" (Gen 18:1). This is an indication of a bright sun as well as Abraham's warm faith. Then it [Genesis] says: "He lifted up his eyes and behold! He saw two men above him, and he ran to meet them" (Gen 18:2).[23] This means that a man of strong faith performs good works quickly.

Fifth, faith is referred to as living because it has the color of living [beings]; that is, moderate behavior. Just as the red and gay color of the living is different from the pale color of the dead, so is the behavior of the righteous different from that of sinners. Righteous people behave like angels, whereas sinners [behave] like Satan. Therefore, the doctors say that a dead faith is like the faith of demons, for the faith of the holy is [associated] with joy, whereas the faith of demons [is associated] with grief. This was reflected through Revelation: "And I saw a pale horse; its rider had Death, and hell followed with him" (cf. Rev 6:8). The pale horse signifies sins; death rides them [the sins] and [sinners] go to hell with it [death]. And the pale [yellow] color lacks whiteness and redness. Sins also are referred to as pale, because they lack the whiteness of innocence and the redness of the warm love of God. As the doctors say, the faith of a sinner not only resembles the faith of Satan, but is worse, for "demons believe and shudder" (Jas 2:19), whereas men believe and dare to kill Christ. Sixth, it is referred to as living faith, because teaching is appropriate to those who possess the living faith. Just as a burning candle is differentiated from an extinguished candle, so is the living faith [distinguished] from the dead faith, because light proceeds from a burning candle, but a bitter smoke [is what proceeds] from the extinguished one, [to the extent] that sometimes it can cause abortion to a pregnant woman. Thus, the light of truth proceeds from the living faith to guide man to the right path. Like a bright lamp that illuminates abundantly, a teacher brings more enlightenment to men, leading them to the right path, provided he possesses the living faith. However, if the preacher is

---

[23] Should be: ". . . three men . . ."

122

an extinguished candle, that is, if he has a dead faith through evil works, he cannot enlighten; instead, he produces a smoke that can cause abortion to the pregnant woman; that is, he makes imperfect [people] stumble. Eli's sons, who through their evil works turned men away from offering sacrifices to God, were reminiscent of such people.

Seventh, the living faith excludes idleness, for Aristotle says that vitality is the origin of self-initiated action, because someone moved by someone else will not be referred to as living. Likewise, whoever inclines to do good works without self-motivation—without believing through his own will and without love, but by external influence—because of fear, shame, vainglory, or avarice, lacks the living faith, because his action originates from outside and not from within. Revelation refers to those: "You have a name of being alive, but you are dead. Wake up!" (Rev 3:1–2); that is, make your vitality originate from within.

Eighth, it is known that the living faith avoids harmful things just like a living man. A fly sits on an extinguished coal, but not on a burning one; likewise, Satan's temptation flees from those who possess the living faith. As James says: "Resist the devil, and he will flee from you" (Jas 4:7). Note also that when someone stays away from food based on the suspicion alone that a deadly poison is mixed in it, he will more profoundly do so when certain [about the poison]. Similarly, worldly pleasures manifestly contain a deadly poison; whoever does not watch himself lacks the living faith, and death will follow him.

This is evident from Solomon, who in Ecclesiastes says: "Whatever my eyes desired, I withheld not from them, I withheld not my heart from all my mirth" (Eccl 2:10), and because of these he turned into a pagan, for *III Kings* says: "Women and wine turned him away from the faith" (cf. 3 Kings 11:3).

Ninth, the living faith pleases God,[24] while the dead faith displeases Him, just as whoever offers God an incorrupt lamb honors Him and whoever offers Him a fetid corpse dishonors Him. Similarly, anyone who offers God innocent behavior honors God, but [anyone who offers] evil behavior dishonors Him. God is life; therefore, anyone who provokes His anger can exist no more. A person of this caliber has the death sentence within him, just like Uriah, because every sinner has all of his sins written in his heart, and this is indicated [by the Scripture]: "Those who do such things will not inherit the kingdom of God"

---

[24] The Armenian original contains, as we believe, a typographical error. It says *haštec'uc'anē* [հաշտնցնւգանէ], which means *reconcile*, but we think it should be *heštac'uc'anē* [հեշտացունգանէ], which means *pleases*.

(Gal 5:21), as the Apostle says, [and]: "They show the works of the law written in their hearts; accusing or even excusing each other in their thoughts on the day when God will consider the secrets of men" (cf. Rom 2:15–16). On the Day of Judgment, our present thoughts will accuse us, for our current thoughts remain permanently written in our hearts. Although these thoughts are hidden presently, they will surface when it is time for opening the books—the books of conscience—where each person will read his own [thoughts].

Tenth, the dead faith intensifies the punishment for major sins. Just as ignorance of sins lightens up the sins, knowledge of sins makes them heavier. The doctors say that the faith of a sinful Christian intensifies his punishment, because just as a priest who has renounced the holy order is more despicable than one who has never received the order, and [just as] the nature of angels is most despicable in demons, so are the sins of a Christian more despicable than the sins of a disbeliever. Moreover, just as man's body is the most fetid among all dead bodies, even though the living body [of man] is the most noble [of bodies], so is a holy priest nobler than all the laity if he lives through the grace of God. A good Christian is nobler than all unbelievers. But if they [priests and lay Christians] die by sins, they are fetid before God. Those are reminiscent of the cursed fig tree: although they look green and full of leaves, they carry no fruit. But the living faith is like a tree that flourishes by pure intentions, adorned with leaves of good words, and perfect with the fruit of good works. In this way, the living and dead faiths are differentiated, as the Apostle says: "Faith by itself, if it has no works, is dead" (Jas 2:17). This [was about] the third section.

The fourth question is whether good works are necessary for faith, as was demonstrated through [the discussion on] the living faith. But first we need to examine how the kingdom can be free of charge, when remuneration is based on the works and received by us through much labor; hence: "Through much hardship we enter the rest" (cf. Heb 4:3). We say that the kingdom of heaven is free of charge for three reasons. First, because, as the Apostle says: "The sufferings of this present time are not worth comparing to the glories to come that are to be revealed to us" (Rom 8:18). What is the worth of bread that you give the poor compared with the immortal nourishment, or a cup of water compared with the immortal drink, or your clothes compared with the luminous [tunic], or your house compared with the house of the kingdom? Then, therefore, [comparatively] the kingdom is a free gift. Second, we receive the kingdom because of the hope and love of Christ, and not according to our works. Third, because we receive it from Christ through the faith by which we are justified; hence: "We are justified by our faith and not the works, so that no one may boast" (cf. Eph 2:8–9). It is evident, then, that when any two people labor in one work, one receives rewards because of his hope in Him, while the other does not, as the Gospel says: "When two grind in one millstone on that day, one will be taken and one will be left" (cf. Mt 24:41). Then, therefore, works can never justify [man].

Moreover, the grace of God's mercy truly commands: "I will give my kingdom freely" (cf. Lk 22:29). Should someone argue: Then it is not necessary to do good [works], since the kingdom is associated with faith [alone]. We say: Yes, it is necessary to associate good works with faith, and this is for ten reasons. First, because "Faith without works is barren and dead" (Jas 2:20). Works are faith's vitality, for just as works without faith are barren and vain, so is faith [barren] without works. Second, it is necessary to do the works of faith by which we are justified, and to not do the works of the old law, which cannot justify [us]. Third, by faith we were cleansed of the rust of sins, and through works we maintain our cleanliness, so that we may not be stained. Fourth, by faith we deserved the kingdom, and by works we keep ourselves always worthy. Fifth, by faith we received the promise of the kingdom, and by works we will attain the accomplishment of the promise.

Sixth, faith and hope are for [God's] mercy; love and works are for God's justice. Now, just as God's mercy is with justice and [His] justice is with mercy, so is faith an accomplished work in us and our works are illuminated by faith. Seventh, our faith adorns the soul and our works [adorn] the body. Therefore, one needs both faith and works to adorn both the soul and the body. Eighth, by faith [our] sins are forgiven, and by works the punishments for sins [are eliminated], wherefore it is necessary to receive the faith and [the determination to do] works together. Ninth, faith is a covenant and a treaty by which we obey God, while works are the execution of God's will, for the obedient person is he who keeps God's commandments and executes His will. Therefore, sacred work is required to be associated with the profession of faith. Tenth, by faith we receive grace and adoption here, and by works we inherit glory and the fruits of eternal life, because here, in this life, we have all the goodness by hope, while there [in the world to come, we will have it] in reality. Grace is here, and glory is there. [Reality] is concealed here and manifest there. Through sacred works we prepare ourselves for His grace and mercy for the life to come, as the Apostle says: "All who have this hope in Him, purify himself from sins, just as He is pure" (1 Jn 3:3).

Briefly, the following also are evident. Just as a yoke requires two oxen, the yoke of Christ's law requires faith and works. Just as an eagle flies with two wings, humanity flies to the kingdom of heaven with faith and works. Also, faith is the root and work is the fruit. Faith is the head, while works are the body and its members, linked to the head and completed only then [by association], because any one of these [members alone] is useless and incomplete without the other; likewise, faith without works and works without faith [are useless and incomplete]. Again, faith is like an immaterial luminous cord that descends from heaven, whereas works are like the successive movements of the hands by which we rise up [unto heaven]. Faith is the key to the kingdom, whereas works are the turning [of the key] to open the door and enter. Again, faith is the foundation, whereas works are the building on the foundation, as the Apostle says. Some build gold on this foundation (that is, righteousness and truth) and silver (that is, purity of the mind and holiness of the heart) and precious stones: The particles of the multitude of virtues—love, humility, almsgiving, fasting, prayer, abstinence, and so on—are the precious stones built by righteous people on the foundation of faith.

Whereas those who are fond of sins, as he [the Apostle] says, instead of these precious and durable substances, use nonprecious and easily disposable matter, such as wood, grass, and reed to build on the foundation of faith. Wood indicates the heaviest sins—murder, adultery, theft, and so on. Grass [symbolizes] evil thoughts assembled in the heart [mind]. Reed indicates abominable words, which people pronounce by mouth, and make their tongues a tool of Satan by antagonizing their neighbor with many and various blasphemous expressions, which, according to the colloquial dialect, are interpreted as swearing and according to the tradition of the Scripture [are interpreted] as curses and animosity. As David says: "Whose mouth is full of cursing and bitterness" (Ps 10:7). Lies, slanderous expressions, betrayals, and other similar things that are reminiscent of words of iniquity also indicate the reed. These two adverse buildings—the precious and the nonprecious—"will be revealed by fire," [as Paul] says (1 Cor 3:13), because the Judge will reveal them through fire. If the work established on the foundation of faith is gold, silver, or precious stones, fire cannot corrupt them; rather, it purifies them, and the worker will live and receive rewards. However, if [the work is] grass, reed, or wood, which fire can easily corrupt, the worker will be punished. For this reason, I beg you to associate righteous works with the true faith that you receive when you are born from the font, and which you maintain firmly, so that you may not enlighten yourselves with one eye; rather, be lit with two. Do not imitate the wicked slave who received the one talent but earned nothing [cf. Mt 25:24–26]; he was cast into the outer darkness, for the talent indicates the faith and the earning indicates the good work. Concerning these, he [James] says: "Faith by itself, if it has no works, is dead" (Jas 2:17). This was [about] the fourth section.

The fifth question is: What is the benefit of faith? The doctors say that faith is great and the foremost goodness; it distances man from all evil things, brings him to God's love and proximity, and befriends him with angels. We shall mention a few of the many good things in ten points.

First, faith elevates some, such as Enoch and Elijah, unto heaven. Second, faith defeats the waters of the flood, as [happened to] Noah with his household, for by faith he constructed the ark for the deluge, and he survived. Third, faith justifies man—Abraham, for example—as the Scripture says: "Abraham believed God, and it was counted to him for righteousness" (Gen 15:6). Fourth, faith rejects temporal things, as is said in Hebrews: "By faith Moses, when he was grown up, refused to be called a son of pharaoh's daughter, choosing rather to share ill treatment with the people of God than to enjoy the fleeting pleasures of sin" (Heb 11:24–25). Fifth, faith battles the world, as the Apostle says: "Saints through faith conquered kingdoms" (Heb 11:33). Sixth, faith receives whatever it seeks; hence: "Woman, your faith is great! Let it be done to you as you wish" (Mt 15:28). Seventh, faith saves man from sins and suffering, as the Lord said to the Magdalenian: "Your faith has healed you; go in peace and be freed from your suffering" (Mk 5:34). Eighth, faith brings perpetuity, as the Apostle says: "You shall live by faith" (Heb 10:38). Ninth, faith blesses man, as the Lord said to Thomas: "Have you believed because you have seen me? Blessed are those who have not seen and yet have come to believe" (Jn 20:29). And blessing is the inclusion of all good things, which faith grants us. Tenth, faith brought the dead back to life. When Lazarus's sister knelt at the feet of Jesus, He said: "'If you believe, your brother will rise again.' She said: 'Yes, I believe that you are the Christ who was supposed to come into the world'" (cf. Jn 11:23–27). Therefore, He made the man who had been dead for four days rise again. The Apostle also says: "Women received through faith their dead by resurrection" (Heb 11:35), such as the son of the widow whom the Prophet Elijah raised. Elisha did the same thing with the son of a Shunammite. And there are numerous other things that occurred because of faith and which the Apostle mentioned in his epistle to the Hebrews. "By faith the people passed through the sea" (Heb 11:29), as Moses did. By faith they [the Prophets] defeated kingdoms—that is, Joshua—and captured the camp of the strangers, and survived fire, sword, and lions, such as Daniel and the three young men. I mentioned a few of the many, so that I may not bore my audience. This was the fifth section about faith.

The sixth [question] is: What is the harm and evil of disbelief? Because just as faith brings great goodness, God's love, and the friendship of the angels to man, disbelief—the evil of all evils—distances man from God and brings him close to demons. But what is disbelief? It is to believe not and to execute none of God's commandments; rather, to be always engaged in unlawful actions and various evil things through disbelief and sacrilegious behavior, fearless of God, unashamed of man, and forgetful about God's infallible judgment.

Here I consider disbelievers not only those who do not confess the Holy Trinity but also those who are called to the faith, are nominally Christian, and yet [demonstrate] the works of a disbeliever, because to bear Christ's name in word, yet to receive Satan's works, is not profitable. [A man] is definitely a disbeliever if he does not believe in the compensation for all actions, in the unforgivable suffering, in the never-sleeping worms, in the weeping of the eyes and gnashing of the teeth, in the outer darkness, in bursting open in the middle, or in the closing of the curtain, and if he does not recall other similar threats, fear, or tremble. Disbeliever is he who does not repent for his sins and does not turn and cleanse [himself of] them by confession. Disbeliever is also he who serves mammon, has placed his hope in the wealth of this world, and does not distribute and give it [the wealth] to the poor, when [by distributing] "his righteousness endures forever" (2 Cor 9:9); nor does he believe in God who tells him: "You fool! This very night your life is being demanded of you. And the things you have prepared, whose will they be?" (Lk 12:20).

Disbeliever is he who corrupts his body by adultery, masturbation, and filthy sins, for he does not believe him who said: "You are God's temple, and God's spirit dwells in you. If anyone destroys God's temple, God will destroy him" (1 Cor 3:16). Also, disbeliever is he who deifies his belly by eating, drinking, and being drunk, for he does not believe him who said: "I tell with tears to the enemies of the cross of Christ whose God is their belly and whose glory is in their shame" (cf. Phil 3:18–19). Also, disbeliever is the arrogant, vainglorious, boastful, and haughty, for he does not believe him who said: "What is highly esteemed among men is abominable in the sight of God. And the Lord resists the arrogant, but gives grace to the humble" (cf. Lk 16:15, Prov 3:34). How would you be able to believe, since "You accept glory from man and do not seek the glory of God" (cf. Jn 5:44)? Also, disbeliever is he who steals, reviles, and complains, for he does not believe him who said: "Neither thieves, nor complainers, nor revilers will inherit the kingdom of God" (1 Cor 6:10).

Also, disbeliever is he who hates his brother, envies him, and holds a grudge against his neighbor, for he does not believe him who said: "He who hates his brother is a murderer" (1 Jn 3:15), and that "Through envy of the devil came death into the world" (Wis 2:24), and "There remember that your brother has ill will against you, leave your gift, and go and be reconciled with him" (cf. Mt 5:23–24). Also, disbeliever is he who lies and bears false witness, for he does not believe him who said: "When he lies, he speaks according to his own nature, for his father Satan also is a liar" (cf. Jn 8:44), and that "The Lord destroys all that speak falsehood" (Ps 5:5), and that "You shall not bear false witness against anyone" (Ex 20:13).

Disbeliever is anyone who speaks nonsense and makes fun, and is playful and comedian, for he does not believe him who said: "You will have to give an account for every careless word on the Day of Judgment; and woe to you who are laughing" (cf. Mt 12:36 and Lk 6:35). Also, disbeliever is anyone who does not honor his father and mother, for he does not believe him who said: "Honor your father and your mother, and whoever speaks evil of father or mother must surely die" (Mk 7:10). Also, disbeliever is anyone who loses his temper and is angry, for he does not believe him who said: "Whosoever is angry with a brother unreasonably will be liable to judgment" (Mt 5:22), and that "Their vexation is like that of a serpent" (cf. Ps 58:4). Also, disbeliever is he who does not love his brother, for he does not believe Christ who said: "I give you a new commandment, that you love one another just as I have loved you" (Jn 13:34), and "By this everyone will know that you are my disciples, if you have love for one another" (Jn 13:35). Also, disbeliever is anyone who is slothful in praying and slow in requesting, for he does not believe him who says: "Ask, and it will be given," and so on (Lk 11:9), and "Pray always so that you may not come into the time of trial" (Lk 22:40). Now, how can anyone who, [despite] the Scripture of doctrine, does not believe all of these be considered as part of the faithful? He is rather in the category of disbelievers[25] and more evil than disbelievers. Wherefore I beg you by Christ's love that you receive the good works together with the faith and be worthy of the good things to come in our Lord Jesus Christ, who is blessed forever and ever, amen.

---

[25] The original text says *individual* (*anhat* [ԱՆՀԱՏ]). We think it is a typographical mistake and should be *disbeliever* (*anhawat* [ԱՆՀԱՒԱՏ]).

CHAPTER XIV

[Homily] of the same, again, on faith, hope, and love, according to the verse:
"Faith is accomplished through love" (Gal 5:6).

Our minds and rational souls are created as light; not sensible, but intelligible and immaterial [light]. Since God is intelligible and rational light, He made our minds in the likeness of His image—intelligible and rational light. Our eyes can see colors, forms, and dimensions after combining the light of the sun with their own [light]. Similarly, the intelligible light of God, uniting with the natural light of our minds, enables us to see the difference of earthly and heavenly knowledge, believe in God, and be strengthened in our hope and love toward God. This is the light of faith, which the intelligible grace of God pours into our rational minds, and which is substantiated by faith. Faith is defined [by doctors] as [follows]: Faith is a habit poured from the prime light in the rational person, so that he may recognize spiritual goodness. It is also the light of law that enters our souls and establishes our faith and hope. The light of the Gospel follows these to establish perfect faith, hope, and love in us. Thus, through the three lights—through the rational and poured light, the written law, and the Gospel of grace—the divine virtues of faith, hope, and love are established in us.

This manifests that the patriarchs, all of them, possessed the three divine virtues partially and incompletely, because they only believed that God exists, whereas Abraham, the father of faith, who "believed in God and he reckoned it to him as righteousness" (Gen 15:6), possessed, in addition, a complete hope and love. Through the law of Moses, they [the Israelites] received the perfect faith and the corporeal hope and love. Through Christ's Gospel, however, faith, hope, and love were fulfilled, for faith was established on the three Persons of the Holy Trinity and on the humanization of Christ, hope was established in the invisible spiritual goodness, and the love of God [was established] with inseparable life, for the Apostle says: "Who will separate us from the love of Christ?" (Rom 8:35).

Let us examine the differences of the three divine virtues. First, faith, hope, and love were fulfilled during three [different] periods: before the law, during the [old] law, and during the [period of] tidings, as has been demonstrated.

Second, they were established through three [different] lights: the rational poured light, the written law, and the grace of the Gospel, as we have mentioned. Third, the three divine Persons are different according to their comparison. Faith is in the Father; hope is appropriate to the Son; and love [is appropriate] to the Holy Spirit. Fourth, [the three virtues are different] in accordance with the three faculties of the mind: [the faculty] of faith is the consent of the intellect; [the faculty] of hope is remitted from memory; and that of love is the consent of the will. Fifth, [the three virtues differ] according to the three faculties of the soul: faith is in the rational part [of the soul], hope in the passionate, and love in the covetous. Concerning the order [of these three virtues], one should know that it is conceivable through three arrangements: faith is prime, hope is born of it, and love is its procession, because hope and love proceed from faith just as the Word and the Spirit [proceeded] from the Father. Again, faith is like the root, the branches are hope, and the leaves and the fruits are love [proceeding] from [hope], or [faith] is like the soul—the mind and vitality are its processions; or like the spirit, with the word and breath [proceeding] from [the spirit]; or like the mind, which the intellect and will [proceed] from; or like number one, which two and three [proceed] from, and so on. This is the first order of these [three virtues proceeding] from one origin. Second, hope and love are naturally arranged with faith, just as the inherent (the prime) is followed by the sentient and the rational, the blossom (the prime) is followed by the leaf and fruit, the deacon (the preliminary in rank) is followed by the priest and the bishop, the servant [is inferior to and followed by] the soldier and the king; or the door [is the entrance leading to] the house and the upper room, the altar [is set before and leads to] the Holy and the Holy of Holies, the earth [is respectively inferior to] the heaven and the heaven of heavens, or the slave [is respectively inferior to] the hireling and the son [in a household]. This arrangement in accordance with nature is taught by the Apostle: "And now faith, hope, and love abide, these three; and the greatest of these is love" (1 Cor 13:13), because it [love] is lasting and eternal, for faith is in this world, hope is in the world to come, and love is everlasting after resurrection. Thus, through a natural order, these [three virtues] are arranged from the lesser to the greater. Third, [there is] the order in accordance with preference, faith and love together being first, followed by hope, because before hoping for His goodness, we believe in God and love Him. Before becoming enlightened by the light, we open our eyes to see it, or before inheriting the patrimony, a son loves his father. Similarly, love comes first, followed by hope. Or as love is first, followed respectively by work and compensation, or as the altar is first, followed by the offering, so is the love of God first, followed by our expectation from Him.

Concerning what the Apostle says: "But faith, hope, and love abide; and the greatest of these is love," we shall examine it in four ways. First, faith acquaints [man] with God, hope guides and keeps [him] firm in [his] faith, and love binds these [faith and hope] and hinders disbelief or hopelessness. It [love] also binds man with all kinds of correct behaviors, and binds the man of correct behavior with God. For this reason, love is greatest. Second, love is greatest because John in his General Epistle says: "God is love; and those who love God, abide in God, and God abides in them" (cf. 1 Jn 4:16). Love is greatest in a third way: because love, whether for God or for the neighbor, is the origin and begetter of all good things. The saints endured all kinds of troubles and were tortured and martyred by death by the sword, fire, and so on for the love of God. Hence, the Apostle says: "Who will separate us from the love of Christ?" and so on (Rom 8:35). Concerning the love of neighbor, he [the Apostle] says: "Love is not envious or boastful or irritable," and so on (cf. 1 Cor 13:4–5). Wherefore he [the Apostle] said: "Strive for the gifts that are good" (1 Cor 12:31); that is, love more than tongues, prophecy, and all other things (cf. 1 Cor 13), because if we have these, but we do not have love, we are "a noisy gong or a clanging cymbal" (1 Cor 13:1). Otherwise, if we have love, but we do not have prophecy, or the knowledge of tongues, we [still] execute all of His laws; hence: "Love is the fulfilling of the law" (Rom 13:10).

Love is greatest in a fourth way: because faith is part of man's life here, it is unnecessary after death, for there is God's vision face to face. Hope remains in the soul even after death, because [man] expects rewards and glory at the resurrection in the body; hope will be fulfilled there, because man will attain the entire bliss that he had hoped for. The love of God and the neighbor, however, will remain forever and ever; it will not decrease; rather, it will grow constantly: both the divine love for His saints and the love of the chosen ones for God and for their neighbors. For this reason, love is divine and greater than any other virtue. It is to be known that when the passionate and covetous parts [of the soul] err, the rational part can guide them through exhortation and wisdom, whereby they soon turn back from adultery and murder. But when the rational [part of the soul] errs by arrogance, envy, or other things, it cannot be straightened quickly, for it has no exhorter, unless God turns him through punishment, just like Adam whom He punished by death for his sins. Also, understand this in the same fashion: when a person is diverted from human virtues by a vice; that is, [diverted] from righteousness, fortitude, and so on, he can be easily straightened by human works through the divine virtues— faith, hope, and love. But if a person is diverted from faith, hope, and love, he cannot be straightened, lest God straightens him through exhortation and punishment, provided He wills. Therefore, if the works of the body and the senses are diverted toward sins unintentionally, the straight mind and will can easily turn them, but if the will and the mind are diverted or strayed, straightening them can be challenging, requiring God's punishment. The Word of life Himself will lift the curtain of our minds so that we may receive the rising grace. He will also straighten our reason by opening our minds and ears, so that we may receive what is worthy, and He will make the doers of good deserve a straight life here and turn from evil things, and hear the tidings of [eternal] life in the hereafter in our Lord Jesus Christ who is blessed forever and ever, amen.

CHAPTER XV

Homily of the same on hope according to the Apostle's word: "Hope never disappoints us" (Rom 5:5).

There are three divine virtues: faith, hope, and love. As the Apostle says: "These three, and the greatest of these is love" (1 Cor 13:13), for it is lasting and eternal. It is for this reason that these are called divine; that is, these three [virtues] are pertinent to God, for by faith we perceive the greater good, by hope expect the sublime good, and by love desire the ultimate good. Also, by faith we believe in God, by hope comprehend God, and by love unite with God. Whereby, these are called divine [virtues].

Concerning hope, there are three questions. First, what is hope and which part of the soul does it comprise? Second, how is hope distinguished from faith? Third, how can hope not disappoint?

In the first section, we will discuss hope. The doctors define it thus: Hope is the sure expectation of the good to come, proceeding from the grace of God and good works.

Hope is referred to as "sure expectation" because it is twofold. First, there is the hope of the living on the path of earthly life, and this hope consists of indubitable thoughts, because we act with firm belief and hope, and not with suspicion. Second, there is the hope of those who have come out of their bodies, and their hope consists of certain knowledge, because they surely know the reward they will receive. The expression "proceeding from the grace of God and good works" indicates that there are two reasons for hope: First, the grace of God and then our good works, because to hope for something—the kingdom [of heaven] or the rewards of God—without faith and good works is audacity rather than hope. But which part of the soul does hope occupy, since the soul is tripartite—reason, passion, and desire? It is to be known that faith is in the rational compartment, whereas fortitudinous hope is in the [compartment of] passion and love in the compartment of desire. This [was] the first [point].

Let us examine the difference between faith and hope. It is to be known that both are graces God poured in man, and both—faith and hope—are invisible and the same as such. Yet they are different in the following fashion. First, faith is [directed] toward the being of God, that we believe God is;

whereas hope is [directed] toward the bounty of His benevolence. Second, by faith we come to know God, whereas by hope we comprehend God. The third difference: Faith is [related] to the past and the hereafter; whereas hope is always [associated with] the hereafter. Because we believe that the Word of God created man and we believe that it will perish. Hope, however, is always [associated with] what to come—the hereafter. Fourth, they [faith and hope] are differentiated also in that hope is always related to goodness, whereas faith is directed toward good rewards and punishments. They also differ from one another because hope is the eye of faith, in the likeness of the eye of the body. Enough, however, about their differences!

Let us examine the third question: How can hope not disappoint?

We say [it does not disappoint] in two ways. First, because hope requires four things: the hoped for; a hoper; hope itself; and hoping. Now, the hoped-for is Christ; the hoper is man; hope is the object and the energy; and hoping is the action and expectation. When these four exist, hope cannot disappoint. Again, there are four requirements for the hoped-for: ability, willingness, knowing, and perpetuation. Christ is almighty, He wills goodness to everyone, He knows what is good for everyone, and He lasts forever. Wherefore, the hope we have in Christ does not disappoint us, be it here or in the hereafter. Men, however, are weak, unwilling, ignorant, and perishable; therefore, the hope placed upon them remains unfulfilled. For this reason, the Prophet instructs: "Hope not in princes, nor in the children of men, [etc.]" (Ps 146:3). Elsewhere, he [the Prophet] says: "It is better to hope in the Lord than to hope in man or in princes" (cf. Ps 117:8–9), and Isaiah[26] states: "Woe to him who trusts in man, or on the strength of his arm" (cf. Jer 17:5). It is God who fulfills everybody's hopes.

Hope brings many good things to man. First, it saves him from trouble; hence: "Our fathers hoped in you, O Lord, and you did deliver them" (Ps 22:4). Second, it delivers him from enemies, according to the psalm: "You that save them that hope in you" (Ps 17:7). Third, it provides for temporal things; hence: "The eyes of all wait upon you; and you give them food" (Ps 145:15). Fourth, hope fills the soul with joy; hence: "Let all that hope in you be glad in you; they shall exult forever, and you shall dwell among them" (Ps 5:11). It also says: "O Lord, I have hoped in you; let me never be ashamed" (Ps 31:1). The Apostle testifies: "Hope never disappoints" (Rom 5:5). All of the other infinite good things of the soul and the body are established in man through hope.

---

[26] Should be Jeremiah.

135

Whereas desperation is absolutely evil and bad. It is the heaviest of all sins and the most harmful to man. However, what is desperation?

It is that [state] when the mind finds itself without the support of law, for law assists the mind, just as the external light [assists] the eyes. When the work of law is not fulfilled, [the mind] fears the punishment of law and falls in despair; it is evident, then, that man becomes desperate because of sinful works, fear of law, and the solitude of the mind. Then, therefore, contrary to this, three things establish hope: when law assists the mind and enlightens it; when [man] fulfills the work of law; and when [man] perceives the corporeal and spiritual obligations of law. If the obligation is [derived] from faith and good works, hope is established. Consequently, the light of law—faith—and the good works are the seeds and the cause of hope, and hope is the fruit and result. Moreover, faith and [good] works are [related to] this life, in the present, whereas hope is [associated with] the hereafter. Besides, law and [good] works are visible, whereas hope is invisible, as the Apostle says: "Hope that is seen is not hope" (Rom 8:24). Then, therefore, the possessors of the light of faith and the works of law in this life possess also hope and the expectation for good things relative to the ordinances, and for life to come relative to faith. It is also evident that faith makes hope firm, and good works make hope good. The wrong faith, however, makes [man] desperate, whereas evil works [bring] the fear of suffering. For this reason, it is better to sin not or swerve not from faith; but if we are diverted [from faith] by strayed conduct or through the evil influence of accidents, we should not be severed from faith in a state of despair, nor should we swerve from [good] works by incorrigible conduct. Instead, we should place our hope in the Creator and establish ourselves in the infallible promise: "When you mourn, I shall say, Behold, here I am" (cf. Mt 28:20). We know that He does not make [judgment] according to our sins, nor does He compensate according to our conduct; rather, our Savior Christ the God grants goodness only by looking at our turning [from a misleading path] according to our faith and according to the hope for repentance. Glory, prostration, and incessant praise to Him, to His Almighty Father, and to the renewing and equally glorious Holy Spirit from all intelligible rational beings and all sensible material beings now and forever, amen.

CHAPTER XVI

A homily by another on love according to the verse: "This is my commandment, that you love one another" (Jn 15:12).

The philosophers say that enmity is a great defect in man, whereas love and unity bring a multitude of benefits and gains, and separation of the parts of the body brings great pain and death potentially. Similarly, Christians are the spiritual bodies of the church; their separation from each other causes pain to the soul, and death and destruction to the church. The first benefit [of unity] is that [people] conquer the enemy by unity, as the proverb states: "A brother helped by a brother is as a strong city" (Prov 18:19). [The Prophet] also says: "Two are better than one; for if they fall, the one will lift up his fellow; but woe to him who is alone, for when he falls, there is not a fellow to lift him up" (Eccl 4:9–10). Satan desires separation, as Goliath said: "Choose for yourselves a man to come down to me; and we will fight alone" (cf. 1 Kings 17:8–10). God, however, tries to unite His hosts, just as Moses stood at the gate of the camp and said: "Anyone who is on the Lord's side, let him come to me" (Ex 32:26),[27] and all the sons of Levi came to him. Second benefit: whatever they ask of God united, they receive, as the Lord said: "Anything you ask for by faith jointly, will be done for you by my Father, for where two or three are gathered in my name, I am there among them" (cf. Mt 18:19–20). Another benefit is that [people gathered together] can encourage one another to do good works and increase the love of God in one another. Love brings many benefits, wherefore Christ said: "This is my commandment, that you love one another" (Jn 15:12).

Now, note four things with regard to love. First, love is a unifier by nature, for every united thing is united by love: the fingers are united with the hand by love, the hand with the arm, the arm with the body, the body with the heart, and the heart with the soul [all united by love]. Also, by love water is united with the earth, air with the water, and fire with the air. The ten heavens also are united by love; that is, the heaven with the moon in the circle of fire, the

---

[27] A typographic error must have changed "on the Lord's side" (*Teaŕn ic 'ē* [Sⴕⴓⴏⴖ ⵁⴈⴓⴖⴐ hⴳⴒ]) into "sees" (*tesanic 'ē* [ⴖⴒⴑⴓⴓⴖⴑhⴳⴒ]) in the printed text.

137

seven planets up to Saturn, the firmament with Saturn, the liquid with the solid, and the fiery [elements] with the liquid. Also, holy men, apostles, prophets, martyrs, patriarchs, and others are united with the angels by love, these [angels] with powers and principalities, and dominions with seraphim, cherubim, and thrones, the latter with the Holy Mother of God, and the Holy Mother of God with the Holy Trinity. Thus, all of these are united by love. This is first.

Second, it is to be known that the members of the body are united with each other in four ways. First, all of the members have the same nature, for they are composed of bones and flesh. Second, they are united by joints and nerves. Third, the natural heat and energy of the soul extend to all of the members, uniting them. Fourth, all of the members have one rational soul. This four-faceted unity exists [also] among the spiritual members of the church. First, because all of the spiritual members have one nature; that is, all angels and men are similar either as species or kinds, because Christ is the head of not only men but also angels. This first [kind of] unity is incomplete, because it is common to all men—whether believer or disbeliever—who are of one species and one kind. This necessitates a second [kind of] unity so that [people] might unite with one another by faith, as the corporeal member [is united to another member] by joints and nerves. However, this, too, is imperfect, for there are sinful believers and heretics; and these are dried and severed members of the church. Whereby, a third [kind of] unity becomes necessary so that all believers live with good works, orthodox faith, and God's grace, like corporeal members that have rational vitality in the soul. Additionally, a fourth [kind of] unity is needed for all holy beings to unite with the one Holy Spirit that they acknowledge, like the corporeal members that have one rational soul. As the rational soul cannot give life to a dried-up and severed member, similarly the Holy Spirit does not give life to the disbeliever, the heretic, and those who separate Christ and the Christians, because they are severed members. This is the second.

Third, it is to be known that just as corporeal members love one another, so should we love one another. We phrase this in ten modes. First, so that none of the members envies another, even though it may not have the same function, for the hand does not envy the eye, nor does the foot [envy] the hand. Similarly, in the body of the church, one is a higher member, such as the primate; another is the lowermost, such as a laborer. One is middle, such as wealthy and noble men, whereas others, who serve the nobility, are poor. One should not envy another. In the second mode, members love each other, so none of the members may spare its functions from other members; rather, they may offer [the functions] freely, such as the eye, when it avails its light to the hands and the feet. Similarly, we should offer our works without expecting compensation, for priests offer the mysteries of the holy church freely. Doctors preach freely. The wealthy give alms to the poor without expecting reimbursement. The third mode of the love of members is that they do not repay for the damages one causes to another. A member wounding another is not avenged by another. Similarly, a Christian should compensate evil with goodness and not with evil, as the Apostle says: "Do not repay anyone evil for evil" (Rom 12:17). Fourth, a weak and vile member is more precious; therefore, it is necessary to care more for the poor and the sick than for the wealthy, for a wealthy person possesses means independently. Fifth, if a member is in pain, all the members are in pain, and if one [member] finds pleasure, all members are pleased. Thus, we ought to share the joys and sorrows of one another, as Paul says: "Rejoice with those who rejoice, weep with those who weep" (Rom 12:15). The physician Hippocrates says that one member's pain reduces another member's pain, because tying a mad man's foot and arm with tight rope reduces his headache. And the reason is this. Headache is due to increased heat and wetness. When other members ache, it is the head that sends the excess of heat and wetness to these other members and, therefore, it [the head] aches less. Likewise, when someone shares the sorrow of a sad man, his own pain and sorrow decreases. Sixth, whatever happens to a member, good or bad, all the members consider that it happened to them. For example, if the foot is hit, the mouth complains, [saying,] "Why do you hit me?" If the foot is washed, the mouth acknowledges that it was washed. Likewise, a Christian should consider that whatever happens to another Christian, good or bad, happens to him, as Christ commanded: "He who receives you, receives me; and he who despises you, despises me" (Lk 10:16). The seventh mode of the love of members is this: a member surrenders itself for the sake of another, for if a sword or a wood strikes the head or the eye, the hand interferes and receives [the strike]. Likewise, a Christian should surrender himself for the sake of his neighbor, just as our head, Christ, did so. He rose on the cross, carried upon Himself the anger of God, which came down upon us, and delivered us, as the psalm says: "He shall overshadow you with his shoulders, and you shall hope for the shelter of his wings" (Ps 91:4). The eighth mode is that members that receive nourishment—the stomach, the liver, and the heart—do not keep it only to themselves, but pass it on to other members. If they commit avarice and refuse to pass the nourishment on to others, they harm themselves and cause sickness. The wealthy who store possessions should give the poor a portion [of their wealth]; otherwise, it will bring them destruction in hell. Similarly, God will judge the doctors who, despite having stored spiritual knowledge, do not teach others. As Ecclesiastes says: "There is an infirmity which I have seen under the sun—wealth kept for its owner to his hurt; and his wealth shall perish" (Eccl 5:12–13). Ninth, a member is terribly frightened that it may dry up or become severed, for if severed, it will no longer be able to receive the vitality from the soul. Likewise, man should not fear other things, except potential separation from the church by sins or heresy, for if separated, he will no longer be able to receive the grace of the Holy Spirit. Tenth, there is love inside the members of the body, for when [a member] learns that the body is to be severed, he feels a great thrill of fear and both the foot and the hand begin to tremble. A Christian should feel the thrill of fear in a similar fashion when a member is separated by way of denial or by an unforgivable sin. Now, since corporeal members love each other in such a fashion [presented above], spiritual members should love one another in the same way. For this reason, Christ said: "This is my commandment, that you love one another" (Jn 15:12).

Fourth, it is to be known that Christ is a paradigm of love presented to Christians so that we may love one another just as He loves us. This [we should accomplish] in six ways. First, Christ loved us not according to our merits, but indiscriminately, [regardless of the fact] that we did not love Him. As John says in the General Epistle: "In this is his love; not that we loved him, but that he loved us" (1 Jn 4:10). Christians should love one another in this manner, and they should love not only the loved ones, but also the enemies; hence: "Love your enemies, [etc.]" (Mt 5:44). Second, He loved us with true and sacred love for our sake, not His benefit; more to give than to take something from us. It is with this sacred love that Christians should love one another, because anyone who loves someone for his benefit loves himself and not the other. Third, Christ loved us wisely, for He loved our nature but not our sins. We should love man and hate his sins in a similar fashion, because the doctors say that the definition of sacred love is that it does not ask anyone to do any inappropriate thing, and even if one asks you [to do an inappropriate thing] do not listen, as Paul says: "Love does no wrong to a neighbor" (Rom 13:10). If someone becomes drunk for the sake of the neighbor, or commits adultery, murder, or any other inappropriate thing, that is a crooked and meaningless love, not a sacred one. It is to be known that there are differences between heavenly and earthly bodies, for in the earthly bodies the light-weighted are precious and the dense are worthless. Fire is thousands-fold lighter than the earth, the air hundreds-fold, and the water tens-fold. Therefore, Aristotle says that ten handfuls of water, hundreds of air, and thousands of fire are generated by a handful of earth.[28] For this reason, earth is the most worthless of the four elements, for it is inferior to all. But in heavenly bodies, the densest are the most precious, such as the stars—the densest among the heavenly bodies. There is a great force there where the stars are gathered in great numbers. The earth indicates the wicked ones: the more love unites and brings them together, the more despicable they are, and they do many wicked things. It would be better if they were separated, for their evil works would be hampered. However, possessors of a sacred love resemble the stars, for their increased unity generates increased good works. Fourth: Christ loved us with warm and great love, as the Gospel says: "No one has greater love than this, to lay down one's life for one's friends" (Jn 15:13). For this reason, Christians ought to love one another with warm and great love, and they have to lay themselves down for one another, as John says in the General Epistle: "We know love by this, that he laid down his life for us—and we ought to lay down our lives for one another" (1 Jn 3:16). Fifth, Christ loved us with a fruitful love; that is, not only by words, but also by works. Therefore, Christians ought to love one another by works and truth, as John says in the General Epistle: "My children, let us love, not in word or speech, but in truth and action" (1 Jn 3:18). Sixth, He loved us with everlasting and never-ending love, as the Gospel says: "He loved his own who were in the world, he loved them to the end" (Jn 13:1). It is in this way that Christians ought to love one another with perpetual and eternal love, as Solomon says: "One always loves the true beloved" (cf. Eccl 9:9). Wherefore, Christ says: "This is my commandment, that you love one another" (Jn 15:12). Also, the love irrational animals nurture for each other instructs us to love one another, as Sirach says: "Every irrational animal loves his like" (Sir 13:16), be it wolf, lion, or serpent. Although they are predators to others, they have love for their friends. Then, therefore, whoever tears his friend apart and hates him is more despicable than the beasts. I wish men had loved one another as pigs do, because when a pig is caught, all the [other] pigs rush to deliver it, and if they fail to deliver, they cry over their friend with a mournful compassion. However, there are people like dogs: even when a great number of dogs attack a man and the man strikes [only] one by stone, all other dogs leave the person and go to tear their beaten friend apart. Similarly, if someone falls in poverty or trial, men wound him even deeper by demanding the debts, imprisoning him, and showing no compassion to him. It is evident from this that these people are not Christ's disciples, for

---

[28] Cf. Aristotle, *On Generation and Corruption*, Book II, Part 6.

Christ says: "By this everyone will know that you are my disciples; if you have love for one another" (Jn 13:35). Glory to Christ our God forever and ever, amen.

CHAPTER XVII

Again, a homily by another on the same verse: "This is my commandment, that you love one another" (Jn 15:12).

The doctors say that sacred love has four properties.

First, it makes man brave in spiritual war, for sacred love is heat, and heat makes man brave. Therefore, fortitudinous are those who have warm hearts, and timid are those who have cool [hearts]. Likewise, those who have spiritual love in their hearts do not fear, as John says in the General Epistle: "Perfect love casts out fear" (1 Jn 4:18). For example, when nature forms the body through conception, it forms the heart first, puts in it natural heat, and then through the intercession of that heat forms the other organs. Likewise, when the Holy Spirit renews man, it plants in his heart the spiritual heat, which is the love of God and the neighbor, and with that love [man] then accomplishes many good works.

Second property: Sacred love unites inseparably, whereas worldly love cannot unite inseparably, because its foundation is temporal and it soon turns corrupt. For example, if somebody loves somebody for his attractive body or wealth, his love shatters when the person turns ugly or poor. But everlasting is the foundation of sacred love—the divine benevolence, which is never diminished. For this reason, sacred love is an inseparable bond, as John says in the General Epistle: "Those who abide in love, abide in God, and God abides in them" (1 Jn 4:16).

Third property: Sacred love recalls the unforgettable beloved, for whoever loves God and the neighbor never forgets them, as [Solomon] says in Love: "Better it is to have no children, and to have love, for the memorial thereof is immortal" (Wis 4:1),[29] because he [the loving man] and God mutually do not forget one another. In the likeness of lovers who ask for mutual signs to remember one another, our Lord took upon Himself the five wounds as a sign for our sake, that He may never forget us, as Isaiah says: "Can a woman forget her child, or a bride her ornate girdle? Yet I will not forget you, says the Lord" (Isa 49:15).[30] The Lord, too, wants us to forget Him not, wherefore the Song

---

[29] *The Septuagint* has *virtue* instead of *love.*

of Songs says: "Set me as a seal upon your heart, and as a sign upon your arm, for your love is strong as death" (Song 8:6).

Fourth property: Perfect love brings suffering; however, [the lover] never feels it, because love changes the lover into the loved one, wherefore the lover does not feel his own suffering; rather, he feels the suffering of the loved one, for he is no longer himself but has been changed into his beloved. For this reason, martyrs felt not their agony but the agony of Christ, because the sacred love has transformed them into Christ, as Solomon says: "My heart has failed me" (Ps 40:12), and a heartless body cannot feel suffering. Sacred love is so strong that it makes man brave and fortitudinous [and] unites him inseparably [with the loved one], and man neither forgets the loved one nor feels the suffering. Wherefore Christ said: "This is my commandment, that you love one another" (Jn 15:12).

We ought to love one another for numerous reasons. First, because relatives love one another and we are relatives to one another in two ways. First, spiritually, for we all have one father in Christ and one mother church, as the Lord said: "One is your Father in heaven and you are all brothers" (cf. Mt 23:8–9). Besides, corporeally, we are of the same kind, for with respect to soul we all are created by God without intermediary. Bodily, we are similar to one another, for we all were created from the one earth. Wine, when it is from one vineyard, whether pressed earlier or later, is attributed to that one vineyard and is one wine. Likewise, we all are from the one earth, although some of us came later and others earlier. God did not create two Adams—one from gold for masters and one from clay for the poor. All, whether prominent or ordinary, came forth from the same [earth]. And here comes the question: Why did God not create all men simultaneously like the angels? Or, why did He not create two [human beings], Adam and his wife, like the irrational animals, but only Adam and [then] Eve from him?

The doctors mention two reasons. First, that Adam, the first man, may become the origin of humankind to despise Satan's arrogance. Satan wanted to be the head of all and imitate God, but he failed and [God] gave [the first] man an honor [Satan] failed to attain, because just as the one God originated everything through creation, so did Adam originate humankind through birth. Second reason: That all men love one another as [creatures] born of one father. Therefore, God did not create two [men], Adam and Eve, at the beginning, but one. Thereby, men ought to love one another more than irrational animals love

---

[30] The expression "or a bride her ornate girdle" is from Jer 2:32.

each other. Moreover, [men ought to love one another] more than the angels [do], because all angels did not originate from one angel, nor did all irrational animals originate from one irrational animal. All men, however, came forth from one man, wherefore we ought to love one another, as Christ commanded: "This is my commandment, that you love one another" (Jn 15:12).

It is to be known that this command, which Christ commanded, is luminous, useful, and brief, and is the fulfillment of all laws. It is luminous, because Christ gave His commandment manifestly as light from light and in a luminous way, so no one would say: "The commandments were hidden and I could not understand it." Since the Word of God stayed in the body for a brief period for our sake, as Isaiah says: "The Lord will make a short and brief mark in the earth" (Isa 10:22), it was appropriate [for Christ] to make the commandments of the old law concise, for the old law contains six hundred thirteen commandments and is overloaded. Christ condensed all these [old laws] in ten, and [then] the ten in two [laws], which are the love of God and the neighbor. [He further condensed] the two in one, [saying] love one another. He abridged these so no one would say: "The commandments were too long and I [therefore] could not remember them." We should also know that because Christ came into this world for our sake, His commandments needed to be useful, pleasant, and light, so no one would say: "Your commandments were heavy and hard, so I could not implement them." On the contrary, everybody, whether healthy or sick, rich or poor, can execute these [commandments]. Therefore, the Lord said: "My yoke is easy, and my burden is light" (Mt 11:30). It was also necessary for Christ "not to abolish the law or the prophets, but to fulfill" (Mt 5:17). It was also necessary for His commandments to be the fulfillment of the law and the prophets, as Paul says: "Anyone who loves his neighbor fulfills the law, and love is the fulfilling of law" (cf. Rom 13:8–10).

Now, if we are unable to read and fulfill the old law, the [books of] prophets, and the Gospel, at least we are able to fulfill this commandment of the Lord: "This is my commandment, that you love one another" (Jn 15:12). Then we would be fulfilling all the commandments of God. But corporeal and spiritual obligations differ from each other. Once the corporeal debt is paid, men are no longer indebted. However, no one is exempt from the spiritual debts—love—because the more one loves, the more he is indebted to love, wherefore Paul says: "Owe no one anything, except to love one another" (Rom 13:8). This is the first reason for love.

Second reason: We ought to love one another, because nature teaches us love and unity, and nature's teachings are very true and not at all false. But

145

how does it teach? [Nature teaches] by works, not by words, as follows. Every creature seeks unity. For example, nature forms one body from many members, and puts one nature in them. God, however, made man from two creatures that were quite different from each other. He also made man from the four elements, which are opposites. That is, warm and cold, dry and wet. Yet they united and composed one body. Things that are extremely different from each other unite through love. People, then, who are extremely similar, need to have a greater unity.

Everything loves unity, except for sins and the devil, who separates [creation] from God and lacks unity within him. It is to be known that knowledge in its entirety was founded for the sake of peace and unity, because the knowledge of divine Scripture was installed to reconcile and unite man with God. The purpose of medical knowledge is to create unity among the four opposite elements: when they are united, man is alive, but when they disunite, man dies. Justice and the knowledge of judgment were installed for the sake of peace that those who argue with one another, whether for the sake of patrimonies or other things, may unite with one another through righteous judgment. Now, since knowledge in its entirety was made for the sake of love and unity, whoever dislikes unity and love is irrational and an ass. Therefore, Christ said: "This is my commandment, that you love one another" (Jn 15:12).

The third reason for love and loving one another is that a friend is valuable and precious. This is demonstrated in three ways. First, Christ, the Son of God, gave Himself and His blood as a price for the sake of man. Had friendship been not so precious, He would not have paid such a great price, as Revelation says: "Who loved us and cleansed us from our sins by his body" (Rev 1:5). You should not consider your friend worthless, despicable, and weightless. On the contrary, you should weigh Christ on one side [of a balance] and your friend on the other, because Christ shed His blood for his [your friend's] sake; [only] then will you realize his preciousness, for he is valuable. Therefore, Paul says: "Do not cause by food the ruin of your friend for whom Christ died" (cf. Rom 14:15). In a second way, this is demonstrated thus: Angels love man and keep him throughout his journey, as the psalm says: "He has charged his angels concerning you, to keep you in all your way" (Ps 90:11). You, however, on the contrary, despise him to your fullest extent. Then Christ says: "Take care that you do not despise one of these little ones, for their angels continually see the face of the Father" (Mt 18:10). This is [also] demonstrated in a third way: man is made after the image of God, and although one loves the son of his beloved, more so he loves the one who shows extremely close resemblance to his beloved. Similarly, although we ought to love all the creatures of God, we ought to reserve greater love to man who resembles God. Therefore, He said: "This is my commandment, that you love one another" (Jn 15:12).

Fourth reason: We ought to love one another because our friend is a member of the spiritual body whose head is Christ, and whoever dislikes a member dislikes Christ the head. Again, the physician Galen describes the property of the arms as follows: whoever loves his heart places his arm on his bosom and moves it close to the heart. The heart among the members indicates Christ in the church, wherefore we ought to love anyone whom Christ our heart loves. Christ loves all of His members, but more so the saints. Therefore, He said: "You shall love your neighbor as yourself" (cf. Lk 10:27). One can interpret this verse in three ways. First, you ought to love your friend by the same means you love yourself with. [You ought] to love yourself in a fashion that would enable you to want God's grace upon you in this life, and His eternal glory in the hereafter. Similarly, you ought to want the same for your neighbor in this life and in the life to come. Second, "You shall love your neighbor as yourself" means that just as you want and try to "Love God with all your soul, and with all your strength, and with all your mind" (Lk 10:27), so you ought to want and try that your friend love God with all his soul, with all his strength, and with all his mind. Third interpretation: You shall do to your friend whatever you want him to do to you, and you shall not do to your friend whatever you do not want him to do to you. Again, you ought to want to love yourself according to the following order. First, desire the spiritual goodness, that your soul may be pure, filled with God's grace. Second, desire to have a healthy and strong body, that you may fulfill the commands of your soul. Third, desire for external things to be at your reach; that is, food, clothing, and so on, that your body may not become weak. You ought to love your friend with a similar order, because you should want for him, first, spiritual goodness; second, corporeal [well-being]; third, extrinsic [wellness]. If you love your friend contrary to this order—if you want for him wealth without health, or physical health without the salvation of soul—then you do not love him as yourself. The disorderliness of man's love becomes evident from the following. Men first love external goodness—the riches of the world and the health of the body—but no one cares for the goodness of the soul, whether for himself or for others. If you love your friend because he is a relative or a compatriot, that is good, but it is not a sacred love; but if you love him [in such a fashion] that he would become your fellow compatriot in Upper Jerusalem, this is a sacred love.

The doctors also say that love has seven steps. The first [step] is the highest of all—to love God more than anything else. Second, to love our soul more than anything else. Third, to love the soul of our friend along with our soul more than anything else. Fourth, to love our body together with our friend's soul more than anything else. Fifth, to love the body of our friend more than anything else. Sixth, to love possessions extrinsic to the body. Seventh, to love the corporeal possessions of the friend. This is the orderly love, as the Song of Songs says: "Bring me into the wine house (that is the Church); set love in me" (Song 2:4), so that we may know what to love with the greatest and the first love, and what with the last and the least [love]. It is evident, then, that we ought to love our souls more than our friends' soul, and that we should not save the souls of others at the expense of losing our soul.

It is to be known that the doctors say: "The love of God and the love of a friend are bound to each other and can never be separated from each other," because no one can truly love God, if he does not love his friend, nor can he love his friend, if he does not love God, as John says in the General Epistle: "If one says, 'I love God,' and hates his brother, he is a liar; for he who does not love his brother whom he sees, how can he love God whom he cannot see?" (1 Jn 4:20). Therefore, the philosophers say that the love of God is born from the love of the friend, and from the love of God is born the love of the friend. Also, love is like a compass that has two feet: one remains fixed, while the other circles around, and the closer it circles, the smaller the circle is, whereas the farther it moves, the greater is the circle's circumference. Likewise, love has two feet: one is the love of God; we ought to keep it firm in God and move it not, whereas the other [foot] is the love of the friend. If someone loves only those who are close to him, this [love] is a close and narrow one; it cannot reach far. If someone loves also the stranger, this is a broad love. But if someone loves his enemy for the sake of the love of God, [this love] is greater, as Christ said: "Be perfect, as your heavenly Father is perfect" (Mt 5:48).

This is to be known that love and unity find great favor before God, whereas dissension and disunity are extremely vexatious to God, as Solomon says in Proverbs: "There are six things that God hates, seven that are an abomination to him" (Prov 6:16); that is, haughty eyes, unjust tongue, a hand that sheds innocent blood, a heart that devises wicked plans, feet that run to do evil, a false witness, and one who sows discord among brothers. Quarrel and discord are evil seeds; they generate evil harvest, because these evil seeds sometimes destroy a city and sometimes a country. Quarrel and agitation are the work of the devil, as the Gospel says: "The wolf snatches them and scatters them" (Jn 10:12). It is in contrast with Christ's work, as Matthew says:

"Whoever does not gather with me, scatters" (Mt 12:30). The separation of the members of the church is more painful for Christ than the piercing of His body by the Jews, because He loves the body of the church more than His body. Wherefore, He did not allow His seamless tunic to be torn apart, but He allowed His body to be pierced, because the seamless tunic indicated the church, which He did not allow to be divided. What the Jews were unable to do, however, the heretics did: They, first, divided Christ [in His divine and human nature], then distanced Christians from one another and tore the tunic of Christ. They lifted love from [among people] and sowed hatred and adversity. Against such [heretics] Christ said: "This is my commandment, that you love one another" (Jn 15:12). May Christ make us worthy of His love, mercy, and compassion! Glory to Him with His Father and the most Holy Spirit now, always, and forever and ever, amen.

CHAPTER XVIII

Homily of the same on virtue according to the philosopher [Aristotle], the describer of the entire world [who says]: "The beautiful is praiseworthy, and the abominable is blameworthy."

According to Plato, the soul, being composed of three parts, has reason, passion, and desire.[31] By reason we speak, by passion we are provoked, and by desire we covet possessions, food, and so on. But why is it composed of three parts? The first reason is that there are three kinds of souls: inherent, sensible, and rational. [Of these] two are the two parts of our rational soul. The second reason is that desire in us is irrational, while passion is bestial. The third reason is that our souls are the image of God, [as] Moses says. Just as God is three Persons and one nature, so are our souls composed of three parts and three powers in one nature. Also, through the three parts of the soul we receive the three graces poured in us: faith, hope, and love. Faith exists in the rational part, hope in the fortitudinous, and love in the passionate. Concerning these, the philosopher Aristotle says: "The beautiful is praiseworthy." Beautiful are the virtues and the virtuous men. The praise is twofold—of tongue and of heart. The praise of tongue constitutes praising by words and demonstrating the beauty like those who relate the quality of a precious stone they possess. The praise of heart is that of loving [beauty] and wishing to have it within oneself. Concerning the statement, "Abominable things are blameworthy," all evil works and wicked men are abominable. Blaming by word means despising, whereas [blaming] by heart means hating, as the Prophet says: "I have hated those, O Lord, who hate you" (Ps 139:21). Now, we shall talk about two things: virtue and wickedness. First, there are four things to discuss about virtue. First, what is virtue? Second, how many kinds of virtue are there? Third, what is the function of virtue? Fourth, what is the merit of virtue?

Let us examine the first: What is virtue? Doctors define it as follows: Virtue is the good qualities of the mind, which God alone incites in man. This definition appropriately relates to God-given virtues. The good is called so because it is from God, who is good by nature, gives to those who are good,

---

[31] Cf. Plato, *The Republic*.

makes the recipient good, and brings things to a good conclusion. Aristotle, however, defines [virtue] as follows: Virtue is a habit of the mind, which we acquire in our midst.[32] This "in our midst" means that all virtues are moderate and [occupy the] middle [position]; whereas the excess or deficiency [of a thing] is evil, such as the upper or lower parts of a bridge, which is bad, the middle [part of the bridge] is good. It is this that Solomon says: "Travel on the King's Highway and do not swerve to the right or to the left" (cf. Prov 4:26–27). There are many other definitions to virtue, for virtue adorns, straightens, and regulates our soul, whether in whole or in part. The rational part adorns [man] and makes him prudent. The passionate [part] straightens and makes [man] fortitudinous. The covetous [part makes man] temperate. All of these [parts together] regulate the soul and make it righteous, generous, and noble. Contrary to this, evil comprises the irregularity, deviousness, and ugliness of our soul, whether in its entirety or in its parts. Wherefore he [Aristotle] says: "The beautiful is praiseworthy, and the abominable is blameworthy." This is the first.

Let us examine the second issue—how many kinds of virtue are there? First, it is divided into divine and human [kinds]. Faith, hope, and love are the divine [virtues] and are called divine. First, because they are God's grace, given to us. Also, because these three [virtues] relate to God, for by faith we believe in God who created us through His goodness alone and delivered us again. With hope we expect God's mercy, which is promised to us, for He is compassionate and true. And we love Him, because He alone is good, and we also love our neighbor for His sake, because he is the creation and image of God. This [was] about the divine virtues. There are four human virtues: prudence, which is wisdom; fortitude, which is vigor; temperance, which is purity; [and] righteousness, which is equal treatment or distribution. These are called human [virtues], first, because God gave them to men, to good men, and then, because they regulate us with regard to ourselves and our neighbors. It is evident that wickedness is the opposite of these [human virtues]. Opposite to prudence is the foolish, who is referred to as ignorant, impudent, and rascal. Opposite to fortitude is the angry person and anyone who is lazy in praying, fasting, and so on. Opposite to temperance is the lascivious and intemperate person referred to in the Holy Scripture as debauch and prodigal. Opposite to righteousness is the iniquitous and disobedient to God and man, and so on. It is evident that an unbeliever does not believe in God, in the Holy Scripture, in

---

[32] Cf. Aristotle, *Nichomachean Ethics*, Book II, Part 1.

the judgment, or in restitution. Whoever lacks hope for a different life and the kingdom [of heaven], but has bound his mind and soul only to earthly things, is desperate. Whoever has no love for God, his neighbor, or good works, but loves only himself and the sins, is hateful. Concerning these [kind of people] the Prophet says: "He who loves sins, hates his own soul" (Ps 11:5). This was the first division of virtues.

Virtues are also divided into moral, economic, and civil [categories]. A moral [virtue] is that which adorns man's own manner and regulates the parts of the soul. It keeps passion and desire obedient to reason, the body obedient to the soul, and the soul in control of its own body and will as a master. The economic [virtue] is that which is meek and sweet, sincere and agreeable, humanitarian, friendly, hospitable, and so on. The civil [virtue] is that which loves goodness and hates evil. It does not inflict pain but rather makes good. It is quiet, reconciled, and forgiving toward delinquents. Note also that man is capable of straightening his manners and putting his house into order. Anyone who regulates his manners and puts his house into order can also regulate and lead a city or a country. These virtues [are pertinent] to the righteous. There are different virtues for sinners: repentance of the heart, confession of the tongue, [and] works of penitence. The works of penitence are three kinds: fasting, prayer, and almsgiving, as Daniel says: "You shall atone for your sins by alms, and your iniquities by presents to the poor" (Dan 4:24). Solomon says: "By alms sins are purged away" (Prov 15:27). This was [about] the second with regard to the kinds virtues are divided into.

Let us examine the third issue concerning the function of virtue, because every object has a function: the eye sees, the ear hears, and so on. Likewise, every object is known by its function, whether useful or useless, such as "Each tree is known by its fruit" (Lk 6:44). Now, primarily, the function of prudence and wisdom is to choose and distinguish the good and the evil, the false and the true, and to despise evil and falsehood, to choose goodness and truth; hence: "Turn away from evil and do good" (Ps 34:14). The function of prudence is also to choose the time, place, and person, and then to speak or work, otherwise goodness may turn into its opposite. Contrary to this, the ignorant does not choose the time and place, and does not distinguish the good from evil, but rather abandons the good and commits evil acts, abandons the truth and loves falsehood. The function of fortitude is that it neither is destroyed by troubles nor softened by pleasures. It does not fear threats and remains brave and fortitudinous during trial when it encounters spiritual or corporeal temptations. It also demonstrates will, energy, diligence, and patience in spiritual labor.

Contrary to this, the slothful is lazy in spiritual learning and prayer, whereas the tardy is slow and weak in physical work. [The slothful] also takes fright and is grieved by an insignificant fear, and he is an egoist, luxurious, unengaged in profitable occupations, and idle. The function of temperance is that it makes man abstinent before lewd desires and voluptuousness—eating, drinking, and so on. Temperate is also he who remains moderate and balanced, becomes neither excessive nor deficient. If possessing excessively, he knows what it is to distribute, and if poor, he knows what it is to endure, as the Apostle says: "We know what it is to have plenty, and we know what it is to have less" (cf. Phil 4:12). Contrary to this is the lascivious or intemperate person who always seeks luxurious desires; his reason does not hinder him; he confuses and conceives the evil as good, and continuously commits sins joyfully, as Solomon says: "A fool does mischief by laughing" (Prov 10:23). Such a person tends to be more disorderly, shameless, immoderate, voluptuous, lazy, [and] contemptuous, and subjects himself to weakness of the mind and the body. For this reason, the canons stipulated that even upon his confession a fallen priest should not be allowed to offer the Liturgy, because remembering the lascivious thoughts means the renewal of sins and it corrupts the nature, as the Apostle says: "Every sin that a person commits is outside the body; but the fornicator sins against his body" (1 Cor 6:18). The Lord commands: "If salt has lost its taste, it is cast out" (cf. Mt 5:13). Referring to the prodigal son, [Christ] says: "Get the fatted calf" (Lk 15:23). There are many testimonies in the Holy Scripture that a fallen priest does not have the right to offer sacrifice. This much about the virtuous and evil works of the parts and the faculties of the soul.

The soul in its entirety has three virtues: righteousness, nobility, and magnanimity. The function of righteousness is, first, equal distribution according to merits. This is of two kinds: natural and rational. Natural [righteousness] equally distributes to all, such as the sun [distributing] its light and water its taste. The rational [righteousness] distributes by choice according to merits, proportionally, such as God's [distribution of] grace according to [one's] limits and capability; hence: "To one is given through the Spirit the utterance of wisdom, and to another the utterance of knowledge, [etc.]" (1 Cor 12:8). The function of righteousness is also to pay respect and reverence to God, obedience to lay and clerical rulers, love and peace to the equal, [and] guidance and alms to the little ones, as the Apostle says: "Pay to all what is due them—to one debt, honor, respect, [etc.]" (cf. Rom 13:7). Again, [the function of righteousness is to] think the truth, speak the truth, work the truth, fulfill the covenant, hate the wicked ones, and love the good ones. All of these constitute the function of righteousness. Iniquity is the opposite of righteousness. There are three kinds of iniquities: impiety, avarice, and meanness. First, the impious person is the unbeliever, the denier, and the heretic; he does not believe in God and does not accept the written canons of the primates and the catholicoi. Second, there is avarice in trade, which is of two kinds—evil and good; hence, the kind that gives and receives objects is good and is referred to as trading, but the kind that gives for more than the [object's] worth and receives with less [than the object's worth] in double standard "and in double weight, large and small, is hated by God," says Solomon (cf. Prov 20:10). This, too, is referred to as trading, because many lies, swearing, and crying occur [during trading]. The third kind [of iniquity] is meanness, which is cursing, blasphemy, and so on. This iniquity is useless, wherefore the philosopher Enosimos says: "Even though one knows he will gain nothing, he commits iniquity." The Holy Scripture refers to these swearwords as curses: "Whose mouth is full of cursing, and bitterness, and fraud, [etc.]" (Ps 10:7). Insult is interpreted as the remembrance of God's anger,[33] for after God has forgiven the sins of people upon provocation, the recollection of swearwords provokes Him anew. This is [about] righteousness and its opposite—iniquity.

[Concerning] the second virtue, the noble person is generous, simple, and open-minded. The function of this [nobility] is being generous in good gifts and meritorious tables, clean clothes and abode, sweetness in conduct, mercifulness, love for strangers, and so on. The ignoble, contrary to this, is of three kinds: profit-driven, greedy, and incommunicable. The profit-driven person seeks gain in everything, right or wrong, evil or good, and so on. The greedy is sordid and cruel; he spends in evil [manner]. The incommunicable is stiff; he does not spend at good occasions. Every sacred being is communicable, whereas every unholy [being] and beast is incommunicable. It is an ignoble act also to ignore a person who is in dire need; [ignoble is] a person who stores and does not spend; who has a worthless mind and despicable speech; who hates people; and so on. The third virtue is magnanimity, which endures both good and evil encounters. It does not boast with wealth, power, and glory; does not love the corporeal life; and does not love falsehood. He [the magnanimous] has simple mind, great thoughts, and truthful words. These are the works of a magnanimous person. Contrary to this is the pusillanimous person who endures

---

[33] Tat'ewac'i uses here yet another pun by treating *swearword* (*yišoc'* [ųh2ng]) and *remembrance* (*yišum* [ųh2nιũ]) as both derived from the root *yiš* [ųh2].

neither honor nor dishonor; if he encounters honor, he boasts, and if [he encounters] dishonor, he complains against his fortune and blames it in desperate and worthless words.

Now, these are the functions of a person's general and particular virtues and wickedness. Referring to these, he [Aristotle] says: "The beautiful is praiseworthy, and the abominable is blameworthy." This was about the third article.

The fourth article is about the praiseworthiness of virtues. It is to be known that the doctors of the church mention numerous praiseworthy things, a few of which we shall present in ten articles. First, God is the origin of all virtues, just as Satan is the cause of everything evil, because as it has been mentioned, God alone incites virtues in man—faith, hope, love, prudence, fortitude, temperance, and righteousness. As the Apostle says: "God enables you both to will and work" (Phil 2:13). The Lord says: "Without me you can do nothing" (Jn 15:5). Second, God gives all kinds of corporeal goodness to all people, righteous or sinful; hence: "He makes his sun rise, and sends rain on the evil and on the good" (cf. Mt 5:45). However, He gives virtues to only the righteous; hence: "To you it has been given to know the secrets of the kingdom of heaven" (Lk 8:10).

Third praise: The reward of virtue was given to an individual by the same God, according to the Apostle: "What no eye has seen, nor ear heard, [etc.]" (1 Cor 2:9). Fourth praise: virtue is good by itself, for virtue is the good habit of minds. Just as a field closer to the city is better, so is a virtue better if it is inside the soul. Fifth [praise]: It [virtue] is more precious than other good things, as the Apostle wrote in the Hebrews: "It is better for the heart to be established with grace" (Heb 13:9). Sixth [praise]: It [virtue] is precious because of the labor, for it makes man's work good and rewardable, because a work that is not generated by virtue is not rewardable, as the psalm says: "Whatsoever he shall do shall be prospered" (Ps 1:3). Seventh [praise]: It [virtue] is precious because of transformation, for it transforms a wolf into a sheep, turns darkness into light, and changes [a person] from evil sins into good grace. This was signified when Christ changed the water into wine. Eighth [praise]: It [virtue] is precious because it distinguishes the children of God from the children of Satan; hence: "By this all men will know that you are my disciples" (Jn 13:35). Ninth [praise]: It [virtue] is precious because of the model, for all the saints have exerted efforts to devote themselves to virtues: innocence is praised in Abel; obedience in Abraham; prudence in Joseph; meekness in Moses; humility in David, and so on. Tenth [praise]: Virtues were so great and precious that

Christ performed and instructed them; hence: "Learn from me, for I am gentle and humble in heart" (Mt 11:29). There are numerous other praiseworthy and beautiful things about virtues, which we shall not detail here. Thus, "The beautiful is praiseworthy." Evil and vice are the opposite of all these and are contrary to them, blamable, and abominable, as has been demonstrated at the beginning. Glory, praise, and benediction to our Lord Jesus Christ—who delivers us from evil and gives us various good gifts—with His Father and the most Holy Spirit, now and forever, amen.

CHAPTER XIX

Homily of the same on prudence according to the words of the proverb:
"He who increases knowledge will increase sorrow" (Eccl 1:18).

God created man soul and body, and adorned the soul with four things: free will, reason, passion, and desire. He did not take these away from man after man had sinned, nor did He decrease them [in man] for two reasons: first, that the reflection of God's image may remain intact in man; second, that man may again keep the commandments of God through his free will, wisdom, fortitude, and love, and stand before the judgment [accordingly]. These [four things] now exist also in the demons as they do in angels, but in a different fashion. Angels chose the good and loved it voluntarily, and they were established in goodness immutably, whereas the demons chose and loved evil voluntarily, and they were established [in evil] immutably.

Man, however, has a free will that changes into good and evil by reason's choice, as well as by the choices of passion and desire. These four things have been in man's soul since his creation and shall remain there forever. Similarly, punishment was received in the body quadruply: first, [man] was sentenced to death; second, he entered the sinful life; third, he encountered a disorderly accident; [and] fourth, he suffered through inevitable external influences and needs. Now, even God's benevolent and fine people cannot be exempted or treated differently in the present eternity, just as those who sinned voluntarily, by imposition, or unintentionally cannot be allowed in the kingdom. Likewise, the punishment for sins cannot be lifted from anyone in this eternity, and this is so for two reasons. First, as man received the free will from the beginning, so did he receive the punishment for sins from the beginning, immediately upon committing the sins. In this way, the original punishment came eternally with the original sins. The second reason, says Solomon, is that "God made punishment inevitable, that men may fear him" (cf. Eccl 3:14); that is, that man may not see the soul without body, or the body without the need for and obedience to God. Adam, the first man, envisioned himself in such a fashion and disobeyed God. Likewise, Satan disobeyed God and fell from the glory. He [God] made man's nature needy, that he may take fright of everything and trust in God and obey Him out of his fear. Wherefore the proverb says: "He who increases knowledge will increase sorrow" (Eccl 1:18).

We ought to know that there are two kinds of knowledge—divine and human or earthly. The divine and spiritual knowledge, such as that of angels and saints in heaven, is joy and happiness no matter how much it increases; hence: "I remembered God and rejoiced, and how sweet are your words to my taste! more than honey to my mouth" (Ps 77:3, 118:103). The material and earthly knowledge, however, causes pain and sorrow when increased, because, first, by understanding and reflecting upon the heavenly, the mind is enlightened and brightened, but by thinking about the earthly, it is darkened and turned ugly. Second, the natural course of the mind requires thinking about the immaterial things and the heavens, but by looking down on earth, [man] is bitterly violated, just as when man's eye is pleased by looking up and displeased by looking into deep places. Third, heavenly things strengthen hope in man through their immutability, [but] knowing that the earth is mutable makes man desperate. Fourth, because in heaven man's thoughts are directed to one thing—God—joy and happiness fill the heart of man immediately; however, on earth, [man thinks] of the many anxieties of the world and, overwhelmed, [his thoughts] become scattered and spread, wherefore he feels pain and sorrow. Fifth, there are two kinds of understanding. The first [kind] recognizes all things as singular, simple, and essential. This kind is called light and luminous [understanding]. The second [kind] recognizes through combined senses—color by the eyes, sound by the ears, and so on accordingly. This mixed and distorted understanding is called dark, for it depends on the senses and is charmed by them. Now, simple singular understanding is joy and generates happiness, whereas when [understanding is] distorted and intermingled with the senses, it is pain and bitterness to the soul, wherefore it is said: "He who increases knowledge will increase sorrow" (Eccl 1:18).

The verse "He who increases knowledge will increase sorrow" is also understood in the following fashion. First, when we increase within us our knowledge by learning, research, meditation, and remembering Him, the things we have learned and the things we have yet to learn increase our anxiety. Second, with regard to others, when we examine people's widely varying manners and conducts, and ponder about instructing and guiding them in accordance with their differences, we need many thoughts just like the physicians who think about various medicines for various pains. Third, when we find the unlearned reluctant toward various good things and inclined toward evil things, we feel sorrow and grief; hence: "Sorrow took hold upon me, because of the sinners who abandoned your law" (Ps 118:53). Fourth, when people persistently sin, their hearts harden, because the wicked are accustomed to dare to sin and persistently sin after exhortation and reproach, just as the Lord felt sorrow and wept over the Jews when He saw their blindness. Fifth, when [people] ignore the guidance of instructors and are pleased with and used to evil things, the words lose their strength and influence, and the instructors feel more pain like a man of prominence who feels pain for the refusal of his words when his command is despised. Sixth, with greater wisdom and compassion, man feels greater grief in his heart for others, in view of their evil works and the punishments for their sins. Whereby, a wise man is troubled more for the wicked than an ignorant person would be. For example, a man standing by the seashore and witnessing the sinking of a ship in the turbulent sea feels spiritual grief and depression by natural disposition, just like those who are grieved physically on the ship. But a distant person who cannot see the ship does not feel grief, just like the ignorant, be it on his own or other people's account. A wise man, however, is grieved for those who float in the midst of worldly sins and are willing to sink into hell by closing their ears [before instruction] and refusing to head for the harbor of righteousness. It was thus that the Sage [Solomon] experienced pain, the Prophet David grieved, and all of the [other] prophets mourned for the world, and they wore skins [of animals] and stuff made of goat's hair because of mourning. Again, an ignorant and foolish transgressor does not feel the weight of sins, just as a very sick person cannot comprehend his pain. However, whoever understands the burden of sins, remembers the pain and fear of punishment, and embraces the work of penance crosses into health and recovery through his knowledge. Again, those whose grace of knowledge is increased in any given field—be it in teaching, priesthood, or anything else—have to respect the grace of talent. Otherwise, when a man covers the grace he received from God with the veil of sloth, he sins knowingly, and whoever sins knowingly receives severe punishment. It was said in reference to such people: "Whoever adds sins knowingly, adds severe punishment to his grief" (cf. Eccl 1:18). Again, "Knowledge puffs up, but love builds up" (1 Cor 8:1), for wise men ought to "Destroy every summit of pride, and take every thought captive to obey Christ" (cf. 2 Cor 10:5). But we, first, ought to receive obedience ourselves, and then teach it to others; by doing so, we can build with love. Whoever boasts with his knowledge is ignorant and imitates Satan who boasted with his knowledge and was destroyed. Thus, pride is pain, vice, and destruction to the soul. "And the Lord resists and opposes the arrogant" (cf. Prov 3:34). Wherefore it was said: "He who boasts with increased knowledge will increase sorrow and his own destruction" (cf. Eccl 1:18). This was also said with regard to the heretics, for the greater knowledge they accumulate, the more they increase the pain of their own destruction. For example, a sick belly turns the healthy food into bitter gall and intensifies its pain. The same is true for the heretic who learns daily the sacred words of the Holy Scripture, twists them in his mind, and errs by following his own thoughts. He attracts to himself the first four classes—the ignorant and the insensible—for he speaks heresy with ignorance and insensibility; he is willfully diverted and driven away from orthodoxy; he boasts with his knowledge by which he speaks heresy through delusive and sweet words, thus making his words persuasive. He devours the ears like cancer with delusive and deceitful words, and by the sweetness of his words persuades the minds, which then consent to his words. Because of the sweet and passionate words, the proverb teller [Solomon] figuratively refers to their words as honey and says: "It is not good to eat much honey" (Prov 25:27). Since there are many kinds of knowledge, just like the many kinds of honey of which some are harmful and others useful, the holy and orthodox words are compared to useful honey; hence: "Your oracles are sweet to my taste, more so than honey to my mouth" (Ps 118:103), whereas the words of heretics are harmful.

This is so for many reasons. First, because just as honey tastes sweet but afflicts the body and causes madness, so do the words of heretics, as the Apostle says: "By smooth talk and flattery they deceive the souls of the innocent" (Rom 16:18). The proverb says: "Honey drops from the lips of the harlot; but afterward it will become more bitter than gall" (cf. Prov 5:3). Within the same context, David says: "Their words were smoother than oil, [etc.]" (Ps 55:21). The Lord says: "They came to you in sheep's clothing but inwardly are ravenous wolves" (Mt 7:15). Second, it has been said that a person ought to taste the honey before choosing it, and eating much of it is not good. Likewise, it is not good to subject the mind to the teachings of the heretics, lest reading enough of it to make a choice between the orthodox [teaching] and theirs. In order for the explication to oppose them [heretics] appropriately, it was accordingly said: "Answer a fool according to his folly" (Prov 26:5). Third, just as the wild bee—like the domestic bee—forms cells and gathers [nectar] from the flowers, so do the heretics gather the testimonies of the Holy Scripture, tune their words to the orthodox believers, and present them as true teaching, as the Apostle says: "They have the embodiment of knowledge" (Rom 2:20). Fourth, salt cannot be mixed to honey; similarly, the words of a heretic lack salt—the grace of the Holy Spirit; hence, the true words are formulated thus: "Let your speech always be seasoned with salt, so that it may give grace to the listeners" (cf. Col 4:6). Indeed, "a breathing man does not receive the Spirit of God, for it is foolishness to him" (1 Cor 2:14), for Solomon says: "The holy Spirit of wisdom will flee deceit" (Wis 1:5). Fifth, just as the honey, or its kneaded [version], did not find its way to the temple as offering, so should heretical teachings, whether as songs or in any other form, remain outside the church, for the Lord says: "The bad tree bears bad fruit" (Mt 7:17). Enough on comparing the words of heretics with honey. Holy words, on the contrary, are figuratively presented like domestic honey. First, because honey is manna from heaven, and words inspired by God are from the Holy Spirit, according to Peter who says: "No prophecy ever came by human will, but men moved by the Holy Spirit spoke from God" (2 Pet 1:21). Paul says: "God has revealed us through the Spirit" (1 Cor 2:10). Second, because [domestic honey] is gathered from various flowers into simple [substance]; therefore, David says: "The words of the Lord are choicer than silver, seven times purified and simplified in earth" (cf. Ps 12:6), and the doctors of the church gather from these [words]. Third, because the taste of honey is sweeter than all other sweet tastes, David compares the wisdom of holy words with honey, by saying: "Sweeter than the honey-comb" (Ps 19:10). Plato [citing Socrates's dialogue] writes about Theodorus the geometer: "O Theodorus, a greater gift than wisdom from God has never come to men, nor will ever come." Fourth, just as it heals wounds and pains, as the proverb says: "Whose labors the rich and the poor use for health" (Prov 6:8), so do wise words heal the soul and the body, as the proverb says: "Some wound as they speak, like swords; but the tongues of the wise heal" (Prov 12:18). It also says: "The wholesome tongue is a tree of life" (Prov 15:4). Fifth, just as honey comes in different kinds according to its color— although all have one and the same taste—so do all holy words have one purpose, although structured differently in different sentences: to teach and direct us through exhortation, according to the Apostle: "All scripture is inspired by God and is useful for exhorting and teaching us" (cf. 2 Tim 3:16). Enough comparing the words and honey!

Concerning the following quotation from the proverb: "Though you scourge a fool, disgracing him in the midst of the council, you will in no way remove his folly from him" (Prov 27:22), [know that] the fool refers to those who are ignorant, ungodly, cunning, and heretic. Anyone who has wickedness in the rational part [of his soul] is referred to as a fool. This fool cannot be corrected from straying because of ten reasons. First, reason comprises the upper part of the soul and has nothing above it to exhort and correct it unlike the guidance it offers to passion and desire; therefore, it cannot repent for its sins. For example, a primate or a ruler exhorts the subjects, but he cannot be corrected when he errs, because he does not have an exhorter above him. Second, even when someone exhorts the fool, he does not heed, for he thinks he is more correct than the person trying to exhort him. Third, because he [the fool] considers his wrong right and another person's right wrong and erroneous; therefore, he ignores you. As the wise man says, the insane considers himself sane; therefore, he does not learn sanity. Fourth, just as a squint eye cannot see itself, but sees others, likewise a fool does not understand his deficiencies, but understands the deficiencies of others; hence: "You see the speck in your neighbor's eye, but do not notice the log in your own eye" (Lk 6:41). Fifth, just as the wise is strengthened in holiness by thoughtfulness, so is the fool strengthened in wickedness. Sixth, just as routine work strengthens the body, so does the soul strengthen the will and the intellect. Seventh, since the light of a fool is darkened and he lacks consciousness of the mind, he cannot repent. Eighth, since persuasion—faith, hope, and love—is absent in him, he [the fool] cannot listen and repent, for he has no expectation for goodness and rewards, nor does he love God. Ninth, the prudent discerns the hidden and remote things, such as the hereafter, whereas the fool sees the superficial and the close—the pleasures of this world; therefore, he does not fear the distant fear and the punishment of God. Tenth, because the fool despises divine ordinances and God, and lacks the support of law, God, his inner thoughts, or any external source, he feels not, fears not, and is ashamed not when he is punished. This kind of fool ought to be brought to persuasion gradually, skillfully and by sweet words, just as the Apostle [Paul did with] the pagans who were fooled by paganism. May Christ the God grant us wisdom, faith, hope, and love, that we may follow His law and inherit the eternal life by following His will. Glory to Christ our God forever, amen.

CHAPTER XX

Homily of the same [on] wisdom according to the verse, "Blessed is the man who has found wisdom" (Prov 3:13).

According to the philosopher [Aristotle], wisdom is divided into [two categories]: theoretical and practical.[34] Practical wisdom is virtue performed by the body, whereas theoretical wisdom is performed by the mind. The practical [wisdom] is divided into three [categories]: moral, derivative, and divine. The moral [wisdom] is inherent, such as prudence, fortitude, temperance, and righteousness; we adorn our behavior with them. The moral [wisdom] is named so also because these [four aforementioned qualities] are found in the animals likewise—a camel is prudent, a lion is fortitudinous, a turtledove is temperate, and a stork is righteous. The derivative virtue is obtained by our choice and practiced by us—righteousness, temperance, fasting, prayers, and almsgiving. These are things by which men govern a house or a city. It is also called derivative because we perform righteousness, fasting, prayers, and almsgiving by knowing the reason, be it for prosperity, love of a brother, our soul, or something else. These are called derivative and human virtues. The divine virtues are faith, hope, and love. These are named divine, because faith, hope, and love are from the grace of God and are intended for God, because people believe in God, hope for His mercy, and love Him. These are designated as practical virtues because, although subsisting in the mind, they are fulfilled and specified through works, for faith, hope, and love are abstract and cannot be manifested without works, as the Apostle says: "Faith without works is dead" (Jas 2:26). Hope and love, alike, are incomplete without works, and these are virtues, [because], first, they regulate our behavior toward ourselves. Second, [they regulate our behavior] toward our neighbors. Third, they regulate our behavior toward God. This is the practical wisdom.

The theoretical wisdom comes in many kinds. It is found among us, the assembly of the faithful, and is useful. God is the first wisdom. He is referred to as wisdom because a person believes in Him through intellect; He is incomprehensible for the senses. He cannot be seen by eyes, cannot be touched

---

[34] Cf. Aristotle, *Nicomachean Ethics*.

by hands, and so on. Through intellect only we ought to believe "that he exists and that he rewards those who seek him" (Heb 11:6). He is called wisdom also because all intellectual and sentient creatures received from Him wisdom commensurate with their nature and abilities. Second, Christ also is referred to as wisdom, according to the Apostle: "Christ the power of God and the wisdom of God" (1 Cor 1:24). First, because the entire creation, whether visible or invisible, was created by Him. He [Christ] is referred to as wisdom also because He was wisdom, righteousness, and salvation to us; hence: "I told you what I heard from my Father" (cf. Jn 8:40). Third, the Holy Spirit also is called wisdom, according to Isaiah: "The spirit of wisdom and understanding" (Isa 11:2). [The Holy Spirit] is called wisdom because, first, it is intelligible and comprehensible God. Also, [because] it fills us with grace and enlightens us with understanding and wisdom; hence: "He will teach you everything that I have said to you" (cf. Jn 14:26). Fourth, believing in and hoping for the heavenly life also are wisdom, as instructed by the Apostle: "Set your minds on things that are above, where Christ is, seated at the right hand of God" (cf. Col 3:2). This is referred to as wisdom, first, because it is understood now through faith and hope, and then, because the wise will inherit the heavenly life. Fifth, meditating and choosing your actions also are wisdom, as David says: "His will is in the law of the Lord, and in the law of the Lord he will meditate day and night" (Ps 1:2). This is designated as wisdom because, first, before we act, we contemplate the law of God and differentiate the evil from the good. Also, we expect compensation through faith and hope, whereby we refer to it as wisdom. Sixth, the Hellenes' examination of the nature of heaven and earth, and times and beings, is likewise designated as wisdom, first, because it is performed by the intellect and the mind, and because they [the Hellenes] attained the higher wisdom of God by this intellect, such as Aristotle's observations, Plato's theology, and so on. They also attained perfection through such natural examination. First, [they attained] the understanding of God, as we have mentioned. Second, they promptly attained the faith of Christ, such as the Athenians through the Apostle's preaching. Third, they also attained the freedom of the soul when Christ went to hell [and] preached to the captives, and they came out because they believed. Should someone ask, how did they believe there [in hell], if they lacked faith when they were alive? We say that although they lacked the faith of grace, they knew God by inherent intelligence and therefore they believed in hell. Moreover, they possessed moral virtues—prudence, fortitude, temperance, and righteousness—so much, that they acknowledged wisdom as contemplation about death and thereby were saved. Should someone ask, why is this [wisdom] called earthly, carnal, and demonic? We say: It is time for you to open your mind. Wisdom is from God, be it inherent or granted. Reference to earthly, carnal, and demonic [wisdom] is made when men philosophize about earthly pleasures and find witchcraft and other evil things through that wisdom. However, when they contemplate and examine the heavenly, they arrive there and become heavenly and holy in their knowledge. For example, the minds and senses of human beings are one and the same; when a person directs them toward goodness, they become good, but if a person is accustomed to evil, they become wicked. Now, these are the theoretical and practical wisdoms as we have mentioned, wherefore the Sage [Solomon] says: "Blessed is the man who has found wisdom" (Prov 3:13). It is to be known that here he [Solomon] praises the God-related wisdom in ten ways. First, because he declares those who know wisdom blessed, for all lives and pleasures are temporal. Nevertheless, he rightfully considers anyone who hopes for and contemplates about the everlasting life blessed, for he deserves the ranks of the blessed. Second, he [Solomon] says: "The mortal knew talent" (Prov 3:13); meaning, the art and skill of immortality are wisdom for mortal man, because faith and hope lead us to immortality. Moreover, immortality is the living Christ when we find Him. Third, he [Solomon] says: "It is better to traffic of her, than for treasures of gold and silver" (Prov 3:14), meaning that treasure does not exempt man from death, but wisdom delivers him from eternal death; hence: "Treasures are powerless on the day of rage; but righteousness delivers from death" (Prov 10:2). Besides, when man approaches death, treasures become as useless as waste, but the wisdom of Christ provides us with the inheritance of incomprehensible goodness; then it is better than the treasures of gold and silver. When he says "traffic," he means the following: "The kingdom of heaven is like treasure hidden in a field, which someone found; he sold all that he had and bought it" (cf. Mt 13:44). Our Lord Jesus Christ is a treasure hidden in the field of the body, and He is referred to as treasure, first, because of His preciousness. Second, because He enriches those who receive Him. Third, because He was a ransom and price [of redemption] for us; hence: "By treasures shall be their deliverance" (Isa 33:6). In this way, we find Him by selling and giving up all that we possess, whether spiritual (faith, hope, and love) or corporeal (blood, body, pleasures, possessions, patrimonies, wealth, and other luxuries). Only then we can find wisdom. [We can do so] also by fasting, prayers, tears, and other sufferings. Such things seem difficult to us, wherefore he [Solomon] instructs us: "It is better to traffic of her" (Prov 3:14). Fourth, he

[Solomon] says: "She is more valuable than all precious things" (Prov 13:15), suggesting that if there is something precious in the world, it can only give wisdom, never incorruptibility. Besides, wisdom is goodness without adversary, for treasures and wealth have three adversaries. First, thieves and robbers steal [them]. Second, rulers violently ravish possessions. Third, the change of times [affects them]. Wisdom, however, has no adversary; thieves cannot steal it, rulers cannot ravish it, and poverty and sickness cannot remove it, because when the wise man becomes rich, he knows how to regulate; when he becomes poor, he "becomes rich toward God" (cf. Lk 12:21). If he is healthy, he thanks and glorifies God like Job; if alive, he increases his righteousness; if dead, [he] departs from this world without scrupulousness; so praiseworthy wisdom is. Fifth, he [Solomon] says: "She is well known to all that approach her" (Prov 13:15). That is, Christ's wisdom is well known to those who approach Him by faith, but it is despicable to those who do not approach [by faith], for "a carnal man does not receive God's Spirit, for it is foolishness to him" (1 Cor 2:14), since he doubts when we relate to him the resurrection of the dead, the life to come, and so on. Again, four kinds of people despise wisdom. First, the ignorant opposes it. Second, the hateful despises it. Third, [people] of strange professions become perplexed. Fourth, the voluptuous and carnal people. For this reason, wisdom does not reveal itself to them. Wisdom reveals its beauty to others—wise people and lovers—who are brought up with it and who are fond of spiritual things. Sixth, because he [Solomon] says: "Long years are in her right hand; and in her left hand are glory and wealth" (Prov 3:16). We do not find this in our unequal lives, because many wise people miss this glory, whereas the foolish become wealthy and glorified, as the proverb describes them: "Vanity beneath heaven; for there is no bread to the wise, nor wealth to men of understanding" (Eccl 9:11). Then, therefore, the "long years" are the eternal life, wherefore Christ says: "Come you blessed of my Father, inherit eternal life" (Mt 25:34). "Glory and wealth" indicate what is referred to as "The righteous will shine like the sun" (Mt 13:43). This is what the wise contemplate by faith and hope, "because we look not at what can be seen but at what cannot be seen," according to the Apostle (2 Cor 4:18). He mentions right and left; that is, the right signifies spiritual glory and the left physical glory. Moreover, the right indicates the life to come, whereas the left is this life, which can rejoice in hope. Seventh, he [Solomon] says: "Out of her mouth proceeds righteousness and law" (Prov 3:16), which is our Lord Jesus Christ himself. Besides, the wise always speaks truth and justice, because he knows that "he will be justified by his words and will be condemned by his words" (Mt 12:37), such as a person whom the profession of faith justifies and the renouncing destroys. Whereby, according to the Apostle, we ought to speak all the truth: "I am telling the truth in Christ and not lying, for the Lord destroys all who speak falsehood" (cf. 1 Tim 2:7 and Ps 5:5). Eighth, he [Solomon] says: "Her ways are good and straight" (cf. Prov 13:17). The way is our current life from birth to grave. First, because like a traveler moving always forward and never retreating, we move forward to the grave, and like the feet that take one step before the other, our will and thoughts change sometimes into evil and sometimes into good. Likewise, sadness and joy, health and sickness take turns. Just as the longer a traveler travels, the closer he gets to his destination, distancing himself from the point of initiation, so do we in this life become closer to our grave the longer we live. Some journey the path by persecuting and ravishing the poor, thus coming to an evil end, whereas the wise treat all meekly, peacefully, and lovingly, thus heading toward the good, toward life eternal. Ninth, he [Solomon] says: "She is a tree of life to all that lay hold upon her; and she is a secure help to all that rely on her, as on the Lord" (Prov 13:18). He [Solomon] likens wisdom to the tree of life planted in Paradise, which [God] deprived Adam of after he sinned. Before the sin, he [Adam] was allowed to eat [from the tree] and stay alive. Spiritual wisdom—Christ and the Word of the Holy Trinity—is reminiscent of the same: the crucifixion, the resurrection, and other [dispensations] are foolishness, weakness, and death to unbelievers, whereby they should be prohibited from these [dispensations]. For those, however, who trust in Him [Christ] by faith and wisdom, these [dispensations] are wisdom, might, and life, wherefore they should be provided for and nourish by these beneficial things. The one and same word of wisdom is nonsense to some and wisdom to others, just as Christ is considered a firm rock by some and a stumbling block by others, so that the faithful may stand and the unbelievers fall.

Similarly, the spiritual life is life to some and death to others. The concept of the cross "is foolishness to them that perish; but unto us which are saved is the power of God" (1 Cor 1:18); so is wisdom. To "lay hold upon her" means that the wise are supported by a strong wall. The "reliance" means that by relying on [God] in their hearts and becoming firm, the wise avoid stumbling, as if [they were relying] on a rode. Likewise, we are fortified in wisdom by faith and we rely on Him by hope and are strengthened, and we receive the immortal life by being established in our Lord Christ by faith and hope. Tenth, the praise says: "God by wisdom founded the earth" (Prov 3:19). Wisdom is praiseworthy in this way, because the world was founded by wisdom. Then, therefore, it is beneficial and extremely good to all. Our Lord Jesus Christ also is wisdom: God the Father put that wisdom as foundation for the new creation on earth; that is, the holy church; hence: "Behold, I lay in the foundation of Zion a choice stone, a cornerstone, and he who believes in it will not be ashamed" (Isa 28:16). "By prudence he prepared the heavens" (Prov 3:19); that is, by the Holy Spirit, for the Prophet Isaiah refers to it as "the spirit of wisdom and understanding" (Isa 11:2). He prepared the heavens as a place and station for those who love Him. "He broke up the depths by his understanding" (Prov 3:20); that is, He revealed the depths of knowledge or the depths of sins. He broke up the worldly sea by the sign of the cross, just as Moses [broke up] the Red Sea by his rod. "And the clouds dropped water" (Prov 3:20), because after His [Christ's] dispensations, men drank the rain of wisdom through the cloud of the Spirit, and He extended the pouring of grace upon the earth, as [He did] first in the Upper Room upon the Apostles, and then upon the world through them; hence: "The world was filled with the knowledge of the Lord, as much waters cover the seas" (Isa 11:9).

Now, the praise of wisdom is so great and embellished that he [Solomon] rightfully considers those who find wisdom and understanding blessed. Of all of these, may we deserve the grace of His wisdom and be appropriated to the heavenly rewards in our Lord Jesus Christ who is blessed forever and ever, amen.

CHAPTER XXI

Homily of the same on fortitude and the work [of fortitude], according to the verse: "Do not lag in zeal, be ardent in spirit" (Rom 12:11), or: "Go to the ant, O sluggard" (Prov 6:6).

We establish the merit of fortitudinous works by four things. First, by our nature, because naturally we are naked and void of all good things, be it corporeal or spiritual, for we do not have natural clothing like the animals, nor do we have armor or other things. Likewise, with regard to the soul, we lack purity, wisdom, and other things. All of these—the purity and knowledge of the soul, and the clothing and other corporeal necessities—we acquire later. We were created in this way so to find both of the following through work and labor: corporeal necessities through work, and spiritual [necessities] through virtue and education. Second, it is evident from the inception, from the commands of God, that when He created man, He put him in Paradise "to till it and keep it" (Gen 2:15), so that he may not remain idle and unoccupied. However, after the sins [Adam and Eve committed], He said: "By the sweat of your face you shall eat your bread all the days" (Gen 3:19). Now, whether prior to sinning or after, God's original command and ordinance oblige us to work and labor. Third, it is evident from the instructors of the Holy Scripture, as the Prophet says: "You shall eat the labors of your hands; blessed are you, and it shall be well" (Ps 127:2). The Apostle says: "Anyone who would not work, neither should he eat" (2 Thess 3:10), and it is said: "Eat the bread of grief" (Ps 126:3); that is, eating other people's bread without labor is a bread of grief and pain, because whoever eats whatever others have labored for, feels embarrassed and troubled mentally, and the giver feels sorrow. Wherefore, we are instructed that every person should eat of his own labor. Also, [we are instructed so] because idleness is the mother of all corporeal and spiritual sins, whereas when someone labors, his body loses the strength to commit sins, his thoughts remain pure, and he can set aside some of the results of his labor for others. Again, because an idle person possesses nothing that he could eat, he thinks of stealing, depriving, and ravishing in order to live; whereas a laborer stays away from these [inclinations]. Again, those who do not labor steadily grow heavier in the body and weaker, and become sick. For these and many other benefits, [the Scripture] instructs us to be fortitudinous in work. As [the Apostle] says: "Do not lay in zeal" (Rom 12:11). Fourth, it is evident from the examples, as the proverb teller says: "Go to the ant, O sluggard, and learn from it" (Prov 6:6). This example is given for this reason: if somebody forgets God's ordinances and the saints' instructions that are acquired by learning, he may see these diligent animals and learn, because what is seen by the eye is profounder than what is heard by the ear. Wherefore he [Solomon] says: "Go to the ant, O sluggard." He refers to the physically weak, spiritually slothful, and mentally ignorant as sluggard and wicked. Go to the ant that always works and stores, even though it is weaker than man in many ways. First, it is physically weaker and naturally small, whereas man is strong and big. Second, it is an irrational insect, whereas man is rational [being] and has intellect. Third, it cares for the body alone, whereas man's needs involve the body and the soul. Fourth, it labors without tools—no hands, [serving] oxen, iron [implements], or anything else, whereas [man] possesses these. Fifth, it has no supervisor or solicitor, whereas man has Christ as supervisor, and the law commands him to work. Sixth, there is no retribution for its idleness, whereas we have a master and a punisher if we remain idle. Seventh, it does not have a model to learn from, whereas we do have many: the prophets and the apostles who thought verbally and worked physically; for it is said: "My own hands served those who were with me" (cf. Acts 20:34). It [the ant] has these and many more weaknesses and shortcomings compared to man; however, despite being such a weak insect, it possesses wisdom and zeal, and its zeal is evident in two aspects. First, it always works. Second, it stores everything. Its wisdom is evident in three aspects. First, it knows that it cannot labor and work spiritually, and therefore it partakes from the labor of others and stores from the threshing floor, the field, the grass, and other things. Second, it knows that summer is time to work and winter is time to rest. Third, inherently it feels the rain and the drought, and takes care of the food to avoid famine, stores it in its house abundantly, locks the door [to safeguard what it has stored], practices abstinence, or cuts and dries the food in the sun. This is a paradigm for us to, first, always labor and work; to work not one day and stay idle on the next, and to pray not one day and refrain from praying on the next; rather, to work, pray, and study always, and add labor to labor, day after day. Second, to work all kinds of works and not refrain from one or another; to work all [kinds of works], including physical works, spiritual virtues, and intellectual studies. [We shall do] this for three reasons. First, because they support and comfort one another; that is, just as varying the menu is pleasant, so too varying works between physical labor, [works of] virtue, and studies is pleasant and condescending to man. Second, since we sin physically, spiritually, and intellectually, we should work physically for the sins of the body, be virtuous for the [sins of the] soul, and study for [the sins of] the intellect. Third, just as labor satisfies the needs of the body—hunger, thirst, and so on—and virtue [satisfies the needs] of the soul, while knowledge enlightens the minds here and now, so shall the body be glorified in the hereafter, and the body, the soul, and the mind shall rest respectively from labor, virtuous acts, and the knowledge of wisdom through the vision of God, directly facing Him. For this reason, we ought to learn the zeal of labor from the ant. We also ought to learn its [the ant's] wisdom [for the following reasons]. First, just as the ant stores from the labor of others—be it from the threshing floor, the field, or elsewhere—so shall we learn and gather from what others have written if we are weak, or acquaint ourselves with the labors of the prophets and the apostles and fulfill their ordinances if we cannot be lawmakers or preach like them. This is the meaning of the expression: "Others have labored, and you have entered into their labor" (Jn 4:38). If we are unable to share the suffering of Christ and the saints, we shall be their partakers through tears, prayers, presents, and gifts of alms; and if we are unable to do these, we shall at least join others in the church. Similarly, we shall complete our tasks with the help of others whether in speech or in other works. Second, the wise gathers whatever food is available during summer and rests during winter. Similarly, although the life of benevolent and wise people is spring and summer in the hereafter, in our [worldly] life summer [indicates] benevolence, gathering, harvesting, storing, and accumulating treasures in heaven; hence: "Store up for yourselves treasures in heaven" (Mt 6:20). Whereas the other life is the winter of sinners, for they cannot labor, gather, work, or find [what they seek] in any other way, reminiscent of those foolish bridesmaids who were unable to find what the wise [bridesmaids] found, because when the sun of righteousness nears, the coldness of sins and wickedness will flee, and pure people will flourish and become adorned with juvenile lush, and they will enjoy the fruits of their works. For slothful and sinful people, however, there is a winter where nothing can be found. It is this wisdom that we ought to learn from it [the ant]. Third, it [the ant] is wise, because it can predict the future and care for provision. Similarly, we ought to envision the hereafter mentally, store and nurture good works accordingly, and enrich our house of virtues, because famine and the winter of death will last long, and we shall close our doors so that Satan may not be able to steal and destroy. Also, we shall dry [things] in the sun; that is, we shall demonstrate our works to God so that He may enlighten us and take away all abominable sins that we may not perish through vainglory. Thus we shall learn from the ant's wisdom.

Concerning the wisdom of the bee, he [Solomon] says: "Go to the bee [and learn]" (Prov 6:8), because it, too, is a model of labor and diligence, although in different ways. The ant is a model of practical virtue, whereas the bee of theoretical [virtue]. First, because the ant always goes to the earth to labor, just as all corporeal virtues are always associated with the earth; that is, fasting, prayer, almsgiving, lying on the ground, humility, and so on. Second, because ants always follow one direction, just as there is one direction for virtues for everybody: "Strait and narrow, which leads unto life" (Mt 7:14). Third, just as ants do not carry each other's burden, so does everybody labor for his own virtues and carry his work to the house of eternity. Fourth, because ants gather tangible, visible, and heavy grains, just as the virtuous evidently suffer through physical work and heavy labor. For these reasons, the ant is analogous to practical [virtues]. The bee, however, [is analogous] to theoretical [virtues], because she flies up, sits upon all kinds of flowers, and gathers what is tiny and light. The theoretical [virtue], similarly, flies intellectually, lands upon the flowers of the Holy Scripture, and gathers delicate and beautiful sweet words for the health of the soul and the body, because just as the honeycomb is likened to the words of wisdom for its sweet taste, radiance, and other qualities, so too serving to the words [of wisdom] is likened to the diligent bee. This is so for ten reasons. First, she [the bee] gathers honey with relentless vigor, wherefore the proverb says: "Go to the bee and learn how diligent she is, [etc.]" (Prov 6:8). Likewise, wisdom is examined by labor, as the Lord says: "Search the scriptures, and then look" (cf. Jn 5:39, 7:52). David says: "My tongue is like the pen of a quick scribe, wherefore my heart overflowed with a good matter" (Prov 44:2). Second, just as the bee fills the cells day after day by gathering particle after particle, so shall we grow in wisdom and sacred words day after day, as Peter says: "Grow in grace and in the knowledge of the Lord" (2 Pet 3:18). Third, just as the bee stores honey in a transparent substance, so too wisdom is rested and gathered in pure thoughts, as the proverb says: "I wisdom have dwelt in counsel" (Prov 8:12). The Lord says: "Those who are pure in heart shall see God" (cf. Mt 5:8). Fourth, just as the bee works wisely in dark places, strengthening, first, the corners up the walls and then gathering the honey, so too it is appropriate for us to strengthen the practical virtues and then receive the theoretical, for the practical supports the theoretical, as the philosopher [Aristotle] says.[35] Fifth, just as [bees] love their parents and follow their leader—they follow the leader everywhere she goes and they die for her—so too we shall love our parent Christ, take the cross, travel in the footsteps of our King, die for Him every day, and depart Him not, according to Paul: "Who can separate us from the love of Christ" (Rom 8:35)? Sixth, just as [the bee] stores more [than she needs] by laboring to provide [honey] to people as well, so too we shall give to the needy from our spiritual and material earnings, "like the faithful and wise steward whom his lord made ruler over his household to give them their food in due time. Blessed is the servant whom his lord when he comes shall find so doing, [etc.]" (Lk 12:42–43). Seventh, just as [the bee] battles the enemy with her sting, so too we shall battle our enemy, Satan, as Paul the Apostle instructs: "We wrestle not against flesh and blood, but against principalities and against powers, and so on. Wherefore, take up the shield of faith, and the helmet of hope, and the sword of the Spirit, which is the Word of God, praying" (cf. Eph 6:12–18). David, similarly, says: "His truth will cover you as a shield; you shall not be afraid of terror by night, [etc.]" (Ps 91:4–5). Eight, just as the bee births through her labor and not through seed, so too the doctors shall receive spiritual children that are the disciples of the Word, that they may rejoice by them: "as a mother rejoicing over children," according to David (Ps 113:9). John writes in the General Epistle: "My joy is that when I hear that my children walk in truth" (3 Jn 4). Ninth, just as the bee flies unto heaven, so too we shall fly unto heaven "by thinking about things above, where Christ sits on the right hand of God" (Col 3:1). The Apostle also says: "Our virtue is in heaven" (cf. Phil 3:20). Tenth, the bee is bloodless by nature. We can attain this [state] through our will; that is, by fasting and hunger; therefore, the philosopher [Heraclitus] says that a dry soul is wise and virtuous. Incline not toward increasing the wetness and warmth in the mixture [of your bodies], for the Prophet says: "Jacob grew fat, became thick and broad; then he forsook the Lord God" (Deut 32:15). Also, that: "My spirit should not remain among these men, for they are flesh" (Ex 6:4). Therefore, the Lord instructs: "Take heed to yourselves, lest your hearts be overcharged with surfeiting, and darkness, and anxieties of life, and so that day come upon you; keep praying day and night that you may escape all these things and stand before the Son of Man" (cf. Lk 21:34–36). May Christ the God grant us sound judgment and virtuous behavior, that we inherit the immortal life by them; and glory to Him forever, amen.

---

[35] Cf. Aristotle, *Nicomachean Ethics*.

CHAPTER XXII

Homily of the same on work according to the verse: "And the Lord God took the man whom he had formed, and placed him in the Garden of Eden to cultivate and keep it" (Gen 2:15).

We evidently learn from this verse that to work and labor is intrinsic to man. First, however, let us find what this verse means, and then [talk] about labor. First, when it says "to cultivate and keep," it warns Adam against pleasures, for Eden means delight and joy. This indicates that [man] should work in a delightful environment and not stay idle, because delight and idleness are the mother of all wickedness and sins. Second, the Paradise was most abundant with fruits and trees; [man] did not need to work. [God] however, placed this [need to work] inherently in man for him to rather work and labor than eat his bread free of charge after exiting Paradise. Third, for [man] to not only do physical but also everlasting spiritual works after exiting Paradise— [cultivating] the trees of virtues and the spiritual fruits. Wherefore, [God] installed man as cultivator to the plant of immortality from inception. He named the worldly plants grass—waste, worthless, perishable food compared with spiritual and rational [nourishment]. The Lord in the Gospel said: "Labor not for the food that perishes, but for that which lasts forever" (Jn 6:27). Fourth, "to work and keep" means to stay pure; only then can a person keep God's Paradise as inheritance. But when [man] did not stay pure, he lost Paradise and was expelled. Fifth, regarding the second Adam [i.e. renovated humankind], people should know that the merciful God the Father sent His Word to become perfect man, and placed him and the faithful through him in the Paradise of the church. This means that He [Christ] protected his faithful through His righteous act, ascended through His suffering and death unto heaven, and sat on the right hand of the Father, not as a reward—as the unorthodox say—but in order to teach us that we enter the kingdom of heaven through suffering. As Paul says: "We must through much tribulation enter into the kingdom of heaven" (Acts 14:21). Sixth, to work and to keep are indications of works and faith, because a [spiritual] leader should live and stay in the church through work and faith, and should keep the congregation through work and faith. Seventh, it [the verse] instructs the congregation to stay in church through work and faith, and

174

to keep the kingdom of heaven through these, wherefore it was stated: "work and keep." Eighth, paradise is wisdom. It was said: "work and keep," because the theoretical is maintained by the practical, as Plato the philosopher says: "The practical shelters the theoretical, because it is sustained by it." Elsewhere, the philosopher says: "I define as philosopher not him who knows much and is verbose, but him who intrinsically behaves correctly." Ninth, it refers to the practical, because one should keep virtuous actions in himself; that is, a person should not sometimes work and sometimes refrain from working; rather, work always. Also, [it means] that a person should work the virtue and maintain it in himself, in his heart, and not learn it ostentatiously. Tenth, with regard to the theoretical, it [the verse] says that the disciples of the books and the doctrines should labor, learn, and keep: they should firmly keep whatever they have learned in their memory, for to learn is to recall. Now, in such a multifaceted fashion we ought to understand the verse: "placed the man in the Garden of Eden to cultivate and keep it" (Gen 2:15). This much was said on the spiritual cultivation.

Everybody should also practice physical work and manual labor for many reasons. First, because God's command said: "With the sweat of your face shall you eat your bread" (Gen 3:19). Behold! God taught the first work—the spiritual—in Paradise before the sins [committed by man], whereas physical [work] He commanded after the sins. For this reason, we ought to work primarily the spiritual [work] and then the physical [work]. Second, by reason of our nature [we should do so], for organs such as the hand, fingers, and others were formed in man's structure. Third, by reason of habit [we should do so], so that when we become used to the physical work, we also perform the spiritual work. Fourth, because of the danger of external factors [we should do so], for we need to have food and clothing; otherwise we would not work and [consequently] we would starve and be naked. Fifth, driven by blessing [we should do so], as the Prophet says: "You shall eat the labors of your hands; blessed are you and it shall be well with you" (Ps 127:2). Sixth, driven by blame [we should do so], as the Apostle says: "If any would not work, neither should he eat" (2 Thess 3:10), for such a person "eats the bread of grief," as the Prophet says (Ps 126:2). [A person of such character] resembles the wasp that does not produce honey but eats the labor of others. Seventh, because when the person works, his body works, his desire decreases, and his mind remains pure and clear. Eighth, because whoever eats his labor prays for himself, whereas [whoever eats the labor] of others, such as a hireling who labors for others, [prays for] others. Ninth, because others eat from a person's labor, and this is

175

a kind of almsgiving, reminiscent of the almsgiving oil of the wise bridesmaids. Tenth, because an industrious man is like a fruit-giving tree, whereas an unproductive man is like the fruitless fig tree that God cursed. A person of this [unproductive] nature contradicts the entire creation, because all [created things] are useful to others, such as the water that we drink, the soil that we till, and the plants and the shrubs that give fruits or shade. The case is the same with animals, luminous heavenly bodies, and even the stones that produce moss and are useful for building. The unproductive person is worse than these.

Tillage is best for six reasons. First, it is the first profession, and God commanded: "to cultivate and keep the Garden of Eden" (Gen 2:15). And as [Adam] was exiting, He said: "With the sweat of your face shall you eat your bread" (Gen 3:19). Other professions were invented later, because of skillful minds and needs. Second, as we have mentioned, it [tillage] is not associated with stealing, lying, ravishing, and other sins. Third, other professions benefit from time and other people, such as merchants who buy at a given time for less and sell at a different time for more, or buy in a given city and take it to another city to profit from the sale. The tiller, however, earns from the earth, the tree, the fruits, and animals that God naturally gave us as support that we may benefit from them and prosper. Fourth, a tiller or a peasant prospers more than people of other professions, because all others—whether merchant, traveler, or artisan—labor for the sake of food, drink, and clothing. The tiller possesses these: the food from the earth, the drink from the vineyard, and the clothing from the earth or from animals. Fifth, it [tillage] is honorable, because [a tiller] gathers and labors as needed, whereas others [men of other professions gather and labor] what is excessive. Our necessities are food, drink, and clothing, which the tiller, not the merchant, provides us with. Sixth, it [tillage] feeds the nobles, the kings, and everybody, because there can be no prosperity without it and no kingdom can be strengthened [without it], whereas all people can live without other professions. Behold! Tillage is the best, most righteous, and most useful of all professions because of these [reasons]. [A tiller] also produces much more benefits and results than any other man, and people, animals, and the poor enjoy [what comes out] of his soil, field, vineyard, threshing floor, well, house, and all other places, whereas one person alone—the owner of the profession—benefits from other professions. May Christ the God grant us diligence, abstinence, and the ability to work our good spiritual and physical works, and to inherit the present and the hereafter in our Lord Jesus Christ who is blessed forever, amen.

CHAPTER XXIII

Homily of the same, again, on tillers according to the verse of the proverb: "A foolish man is like a farm and like a vineyard, if you let him alone, he will remain barren and covered with weeds" (Prov 24:30).

Our heavenly Lord Jesus Christ, the true parable teller and preacher, tells in His teaching: "A sower went forth to sow; some fell by the wayside, some fell upon rocky places, some fell among thorns, but others fell into good ground" (cf. Mt 13:3–8). And he explains the parable: "He that sowed the good seed is the Son of Man; the field is the world, and the seed is the Word of God" (cf. Mt 13:37–38). There are three issues before us: first, finding the meaning of the parable; second, applying it upon us through analogy; third, relating it to the profession of tillage. Therefore, let us begin the examination of the expression "A foolish man is like a farm."

Now, the first clause stating "A sower went forth" refers to God the Word, our Lord Jesus Christ, who came forth from the paternal womb and came unto the earth, took a body from the Holy Virgin, appeared to people upon the earth, and preached the true Word, as he said: "I came forth from my Father, and have come into the world" (Jn 16:28). He [Christ] said: "The field is the world." This is a reference to the people and the lords of the world, because the human heart is a place for rational seeds, just as the earth, which we tread upon, is a place for material seeds. He divides the human heart into four [kinds]: "Some fell by the wayside and did not grow," for three reasons: first, because the seed was trodden upon; second, because fowls came and devoured them; third, because the flood covered them and they rotted. Similarly, those who always carry in them the devil's evil counsel are routes traversed by the devil; [therefore], the seed of the Word cannot grow in them, being trodden upon. Also, [the seed cannot grow], because the demons that fly in the air gather the good seed from man's heart, and also because the wet desire in man's soul makes the good seed fetid, corrupt, and fruitless. This was about the first part.

Second, He [Christ] said: "Some fell upon rocky places," and did not grow: first, because rocks lack moisture, and second, because the sun dries them up. Similarly, those extremely and firmly hardened in sins and disbelief have no room for good seeds within them. Third, when the sun of temptation, or the

177

persecution of demons befall, or a man is subjected to man's persecution because of his faith, those with rootless faith soon turn scorched and despaired, and become fruitless.

The third clause [says]: "Fell among thorns and were choked." The anxieties of life and the illusions of wealth are thorns and pains. Building, planting, sowing, caring, and everything else counter the seeds of good plants and suffocate them, for because of the anxieties of life [people] live anxiously day and night, and having forsaken the commandments of God, preoccupy themselves with wealth. Wealth also is a wounding thorn: wounds cover the body of a harvester and gatherer of thorns; similarly, as we accumulate wealth, we labor, as we maintain it, we suffer, and as it diminishes, we always grieve. Wealth is also a thorn because it always keeps us in trial and pain [inflicted] by thieves, robbers, neighbors, enemies, tyrants, and others, as the Apostle says: "Do not desire wealth that you do not fall into temptation" (cf. 1 Tim 6:9); that is, of the soul and the body. Again, a thorn is a combustible substance; likewise, wealth is a substance that burns the souls of the wealthy, like the rich man burning and thirsting in the fire. Wherefore the Lord said: "Woe unto you that are rich! for you have received your consolation" (Lk 6:24). Truly woe to the rich who were deprived of the life of eternities because of the inconsiderable physical pleasures. Behold! The seed of God's ordinances cannot grow in the hearts of such wealthy people, and if it grows, it remains fruitless, and none of its branches bears fruits.

The fourth [clause], "The good and rich ground brought forth fruit, some thirtyfold, some sixtyfold, and some hundredfold," means that if the good ground [of man] is softened by humility and freed of weeds, it opens its heart and receives God's Word upon hearing it. He also covers [the Word of God] in his soul and grows various good works in the senses. To grow means that hearing the Word is not enough by itself; it should be heard and kept in the mind. Just as the cultivator waters the seeds after sowing them, so too our Lord Jesus Christ made miracles after preaching in words and, by doing so, strengthened and covered the words in the hearts of the listeners. When he ascended unto heaven, he sent from the heavens the water and dew of knowledge of the Holy Spirit that descended upon the apostles and into the hearts of the faithful, increased their knowledge, and they were then able to give fruits thirty-, sixty-, and hundredfold. Hundredfold, such as virginity and martyrdom; sixtyfold, such as those who forsook the world, became clergymen, and repented for their sins; and thirtyfold, such as the lawfully married common believers in Christ fulfilling God's ordinances in their actions and deserving forgiveness. This was about the first issue on: "He that sowed the good seed is the Son of Man; the field is the world, and the seed is the Word of God" (cf. Mt 13:37–38).

Secondly, the essence of the parable is passed unto us through analogy. Our worldly body is [like] the ground, our mind is [like] the cultivator and tiller, and the law of God, be it natural, written, or [in the form of] Gospel, is [like] the seed. The senses of the body are [like] the yoke of the oxen, for these—the two eyes, the two ears, the two nostrils, the two tongues and the epiglottis, the two hands, and so on—set the yoke. Also, there are five senses to the soul and five to the body under the same yoke, and we till our rational ground with these [senses]. Just as the cultivator takes the seeds from the storehouse to sow, so too our minds take the seeds of the law of God from the storehouse of the Holy Scriptures and water them with the wisdom of faith as if with water, always keeping in mind that our life will depart this world: "Lift your thoughts above where Christ sits on the right hand of God" (Col 3:1); that is, like joy-bringing water and dew. The profession of faith and confession should be carried in the hearts and on the tongues in the likeness of a sun rising and nourishing the spiritual plants. [Only] then our ground will bear fruits, the roots of the plants being established in the soul and the various sweet-scented virtues being flourished in the senses of our bodies; it will bear fruits in this age through works and in the hereafter through merits and rewards commensurate with the works. The thirty-, sixty-, and hundredfold mean that, in the likeness of a plant that initially turns attractively green, then grows and takes shape, and then the grain ripens in accordance with its height, abstinence is a stunningly green plant in us, for all verdure is lavishly green and all good works, likewise, are fulfilled by abstinence—fasting, praying, asceticism, suffering, and so on. All are fulfilled by patience, as the Lord says: "It is by your patience that you will possess your souls" (Lk 21:19), because just as the salt mixes with everything and renders everything tasty, so too patience is useful to all works and brings taste and sweet-scent to everything; wherefore verdure is abstinence. Thereafter, the shaped ear is our inner sanctity, so that our souls and bodies may be cleansed and freed of all impurities like an ear lifted high up and supported by its stem. The ripened grain inside the ear is the fruit of mercy, for mercy is the fulfillment of all virtuous acts, because mercy is born of love and love is the fulfillment of the law [and the instructions of] the prophets, and the Gospel.

Behold! Mercy, born of love, is the fulfillment of all good things. Just as the fruit is the end result of the seed, so too mercy is the result of a fertile soul and body. Mercy is the oil of the lantern of virginity and of other virtues. [Conceive] in a similar fashion the thirtyfold (abstinence), the sixtyfold (sanctity and purity), and the hundredfold (the fruit of mercy). Thereafter, a man gathers these in the storehouse of his soul—the memory, because everything goes in there and goodness piles up in the memory; then it turns into spiritual bread for those who taste the Word; hence: "Man shall not live by bread alone, but by every word of God" (cf. Mt 4:4). Thus the Word of God is sown and grown within us as food for the soul, and the wisdom of God as drink. Whoever lacks this rational food is as irrational and unwise as animals. Moreover, he is hungry and thirsty for spiritual food and drink. This was the second section passed unto us through the paradigm referred to in the parable.

The third [discussion] is to be offered about the profession of tillage. It is to be known that men have four kinds of professions as means of labor. One is good, one is evil, and [the other] two are in between. Tillage, which earns from the ground, the fruits, the animals, the beasts, and other things, is good and just. This is altogether good and just. To eat bread by the sweat of one's face is a lawful earning. The other [profession], contrary to this, is altogether evil, for it is [realized] by violence and ravishing, such as the usury of gold and silver, and exorbitant interests from fines, taxes, and their likes. These are entirely evil. The two middle kinds [of professions] are a mixture of good and evil, such as [being] a trader, carpenter, blacksmith, or weaver. [In these] the more is good and the less is evil: [the latter occurs] when a person either performs a poor job, or steals from the substance, and so on. In trading, for example, evil surpasses the good, for in trading there is much lying, swearing, and ravishing, driven by ingenuity and avarice. It is evident, then, that working with the soil is the best of all [professions], for a person hopes and labors for God.

Now, let us examine the words of Solomon the Wise: "A foolish man is like a farm and like a vineyard, if you let him alone" (Prov 24:30). Man is compared with a farm and a vineyard for many reasons. We ought to wisely examine this, because it is necessary for, and useful to, everybody. First, man is referred to as a farm and a vineyard because just as the farm and the vineyard can grow everything that is sowed, so too a man's nature [can grow things], because in us we carry the evil seeds of weeds along with the good [seeds], and we grow them by our works, according to the parable of the Lord: "Did you not sow good seed? But the enemy has done the weeds" (cf. Mt 13:27–28). Second, thorns and weeds grow with the good plant and suffocate it, as the proverb says: "If they left them alone, they will become barren, and covered with weeds, and destitute" (cf. Prov 24:31). First, because they hinder the warmth of the sun and, second, because they suck the sap of the earth. Faith is a plant in us [planted] by Christ, the seed is the divine law, and the plants of evil are disbelief and despair; when various evil works grow within us, they hinder in us the rising of divine grace; hence: "Your sins separate between you and good" (Isa 59:2). They diminish in us the vivacious juice of the Holy Spirit that is [likened to] the water of the parable; hence: "The Holy Spirit of wisdom will flee deceit" (Wis 1:5). Paul says: "An unspiritual man does not accept the Spirit of God, for it is foolishness to him" (1 Cor 2:14). Third, if people gather excess day by day, then the plants will give meritorious fruit, be it thirty-, sixty-, or hundredfold. Likewise, if we depart from sins through repentance and confession, the fruits of charity will grow in us, as it has been said: "Afterward I will say that I repented and chose instruction" (cf. Prov 24:32). Even if people repent later, near death, they would be felicitous, says the commentator here. Fourth, it is said that whoever does not repent afterward is reminiscent of a man whose hedge stones are undermined; that is, the hedge of his faith is reduced to a totally useless state. Paul distinguishes such a person as foolish in the Galatians: "O foolish Galatians, having begun in the Spirit, would you now end in the flesh?" (cf. Gal 3:1–3). Fifth, he [Solomon] refers to people as a farm and a vineyard, because one provides vivifying food and the other cheering wine—the practical and theoretical virtues by which perfect beings are adorned. The foolish and senseless person, however, lacks the Word of God in the nourishment of his soul, according to the Lord (cf. Mt 7:26), as he lacks the mixture of the wisdom of the Holy Spirit in the wine, according to Solomon (cf. Prov 18:2). Sixth, [Paul] in the Hebrews refers to such people, saying: "The earth which drinks in the rain and brings forth useful fruits receives blessing; but that which produces thorns and briers is worthless and on the verge of being cursed, and burning shall be its end" (cf. Heb 6:7–8). Blessing, because the proverb says: "Honor the Lord with your just labors, that your storehouses may be completely filled with wine and corn" (cf. Prov 3:10); and curse, because Isaiah says: "My beloved had a vineyard on a high hill in a fertile place. I waited for it to bring me grapes, but it brought forth thorns. Now, what shall I do? I will dismantle its hedge, [etc.]" (cf. Isa 5:1–5). Seventh, just as various plants are cut in different ways in the farm, for the tares and the thorns are primarily gathered to be burned according to the parable of the Lord: "I will say to the reapers, Gather you together the tares to burn them, but gather the wheat into my storehouse" (cf. Mt 13:30), so too does the Lord refer to the vineyard: "My Father cultivates" (Jn 15:1), for He purges the fruit bearing [branches] and cuts and burns in fire the fruitless [branches], as [Christ] says:

"Men gather them and cast them into the fire and it is burned" (Jn 15:6). It is the same with people who live in the same place; some profess different religions and have different appearances, while others, [although being] among us, are dried by disbelief and severed from Christ, the head, such as the ranks of the heretics who are matches for the eternal fire, for "they have gone astray from the womb and spoke lies" (Ps 58:3). Others, obeying Christ in orthodox faith, bear fruits; hence: "You bear much fruit, so shall you be my disciples" (Jn 15:8), which the Lord specified beforehand, by saying: "If two are in the field together, the one shall be taken, and the other left" (cf. Lk 17:35). Eighth, within the same plants of the farm, some, such as chaff, are good for burning by fire, while others, such as wheat, are stored in the storehouse according to John [the Baptist]: "Whose fan is in his hand" (Mt 3:12); that is, the righteous judgment is in His hand: "gather his wheat, and burn up the chaff with unquenchable fire" (Mt 3:12). Similarly, in the vineyard, the same bunch of grapes is pressed and the purified wine is brought to be tasted by a rational man, whereas the husks and residues of the pressed grapes are [made] food for pigs. Likewise, in the same congregation of Christians—planted in the house of the Lord and in the vestibules of our God, and born and nourished in the same way—some turn to be wheat and royal drink, whereas others become food for Satan that is fond of humidity, and they undergo with him the torments of the fire; hence: "Depart from me into the torments prepared for Satan and his subjects" (cf. Mt 25:41). This is what he [Christ] meant earlier by saying: "There will be two grinding in one mill together, and there will be two in one bed; one will be taken, and the other left" (cf. Lk 17:34–35). Ninth, just as a vineyard is planted once and a farm is continuously plowed year after year, so too is the faith planted in man once from the birth of the font and remains steady, so that we may be buried with Christ's baptism once and once only at death. Cutting and digging signify our confession by the same mouth all the time. We shall labor and work the lawful works day after day, for each day indicates a year, as has been said: "Each day shall be a year for you" (cf. Ezek 4:6); wherefore Paul says: "I have forgotten those things which are behind, and am reaching forth unto those things which are before toward the mark of the calling of Christ" (cf. Phil 3:13–14). Tenth, the Prophet says: "The valleys shall abound in corn" (Ps 65:13), because they are low and surrounded by water. This indicates humble men, for "He that humbles himself shall be exalted" (Lk 14:11). The [following] words of the Lord refer to the mountainlike arrogant people: "You shall say unto this mountain be lifted and cast yourself into the sea" (Mt 21:21). [Solomon] says in Proverbs: "The Lord resists the arrogant, but he gives grace to the humble" (Prov 3:34). So is the matter with the vineyard: it means kingdom in certain places; hence: "A man planted a vineyard, and gave it to the husbandmen" (Mt 21:33), but when they did not give him fruits, he [Christ] said: "He will give the vineyard to other husbandmen who will render him the fruits in due season" (Mt 21:41), and added: "Thus the kingdom shall be taken from you and given to a nation bringing forth the fruits" (Mt 21:43). In certain [other] instances. it means forsaking, as he [Isaiah] says: "I will command my clouds to rain no rain upon my vineyards" (cf. Isa 5:6). This much on this.

Question: Why does a preaching celibate priest seal his speech with blessing?

Answer: Preaching is the seed and blessing is the water; [he does] just as the tillers do when they water the seeds after sowing, so that the seeds may grow fast.

It is to be known that five things appear in a sermon: a theme, a prologue, the sermon, an exhortation, and a blessing. These are comparable with [the parable of the sower] in the following fashion. The theme is like the seed in its shell. The prologue is the plowed land that softens the ears and the hearts. The sermon is the spiritual seed. The exhortation is the scarifying tool that levels and covers the seed. The blessing is the irrigating water. The congregation is the fertile ground to be sowed. For this reason, the preacher sows the Word of life standing, and the celibate priest is a sowing husbandman.

Question: Why does the celibate priest bless after the sermon?

Answer: First, in the likeness of the husbandman who, first, sows, then covers [the seeds], and then waters. Second, in the likeness of God the Word who, first, sowed the words of preaching upon earth and then the nourishing Holy Spirit descended as sunbeams and made the preached words grow and bear fruits; hence: "He shall teach you all things to your remembrance" (Jn 14:26). Likewise, the celibate priest, first, preaches the word and then grants the grace of the Spirit to the audience, so that the words may bear fruits. Third, the sermon of the celibate priest indicates preaching in this life, since God preaches the salvation of man through prophets, apostles, and doctors; whereas blessing [indicates] the life to come, since at the end of the age [God] will bless the faithful and admit them into the eternal life. May Christ the God allow us to hear the words of the sermons of our Lord Jesus Christ, and to give fruits, whether thirty-, sixty-, or hundredfold, and inherit through them the eternal life in our Lord Jesus Christ who is blessed forever, amen.

CHAPTER XXIV

Homily of the same on the slothful as said in the psalm: "Labor forever, and live to the end, so that he should not see corruption" (Ps 49:8–9).

At the beginning of our creation, God destined man to work and labor, because He put him in the Garden of Eden to work and keep it. Although there was no concern in Paradise with regard to protecting something, be it from thieves or animals, nor was there the need to dig and plant, [God] destined man to work and labor, so that he may not stay unoccupied and empty in an idle life, but rather trim or irrigate with the water flowing in Paradise. After [man] exited Paradise, [God] repeated the same commandment to man: "With the sweat of your face shall you eat bread all your life" (Gen 3:19). Thus, to work and labor was the initial and first commandment. Now, there are two kinds of bread: spiritual and material, because man is [composed of] soul and body. The Lord refers to the spiritual bread by saying: "Man shall not live by bread alone, but by every word of God" (cf. Mt 4:4); that is, the commandment of God is bread to the soul: when we fulfill God's command through works, the soul receives nourishment. God's wisdom and knowledge are drink to the soul, as the Lord says: "If any man thirst, let him come unto me, and drink" (Jn 7:37). Concerning the bread to the body, the Lord Himself says: "Give us this day our daily bread" (Mt 6:11). These two breads, the spiritual and material, cannot be obtained without labor, because man needs to behave and acquire instruction in the press of knowledge and study for the spiritual [bread]. He also needs to suffer virtuously through asceticism, fasting, praying, and so on. It is in this way that he can find spiritual nourishment. Similarly, labor is necessary for the material [bread]: [man] shall sweat and labor before [he can] find the material [bread]. For this reason, the Prophet instructed us: "You shall eat the labors of your hands; blessed are you and it shall be well with you" (Ps 127:2). Then, therefore, if eating his own labor is a blessing and is good for man, then eating the labor of others is evil and misery for man. People of this [latter] kind eat the bread of grief. The Prophet awakens them from sloth by saying: "Rise up after resting, you that eat the bread of grief" (Ps 126:2); that is, the bread of troubles, cries, and sins, because whoever eats the labor of others eats their sins. Should someone say, the Lord commands [us] not to worry about tomorrow, or about food and clothing, we say to him that some violators of law find excuses for their sins. When [Christ] commanded [us] not to worry about tomorrow, he prohibited excessive anxiety and avarice, [meaning] do not trouble yourselves about tomorrow, which is unnecessary and useless; rather, care for what is important and necessary. He [Christ] commanded: "Go work" (Mt 21:28); that is, [work] the spiritual and physical work, and eat not the bread you have not labored for. When He [Christ] says: "Why should you trouble yourselves over food and clothing?" (cf. Mt 6:28), He means do not trouble yourselves continuously over the body; rather, care for your souls more than your bodies, because just as the body needs food and clothing, so too does the soul. [Therefore,] care for the spiritual more than the physical. He [Christ] does not say stay idle and unoccupied. However, what does He [Christ] mean by saying: "Why do you stand here all the day idle? Go work in the vineyard" (cf. Mt 20:6–7). The physical signifies the spiritual [in this case], because the physical is necessary for the spiritual. Whoever does not work physically, does not work spiritually either. O you who listen to the Gospel and accept it in this fashion, why do not you listen to the Apostle who says: "If any would not work, neither should he eat" (2 Thess 3:10)?

There are four kinds of people. Some work and eat; this is good for the soul and the body: "You shall eat the labors of your hands; blessed are you and it shall be well with you" (Ps 127:2). Some do not work and do not eat; this is bad for the soul and the body, for they are slothful and lazy. Some work and do not eat; this is the best, for they share with others. Some do not work and yet eat; this is worst, for it harms both the soul and the body. You have chosen the last of these four [approaches], which is the worst. When they say: "Do not work," why do you hear and understand it perfectly, but when they say: "You shall not eat [if you have not worked]," you do not hear it and you close your ears? The Apostle says: "Them that are such we command that they work with their hands and eat their own bread, and stay not idle" (cf. 2 Thess 3:11–12), because idleness is the mother of all evil things: an idle man is fertile ground for Satan who sows all kinds of evil thoughts in him and makes him bear evil fruits. It is also the mother of all evil things because man cannot find his soul or his body with idleness, nor can he feed the poor or love and honor his neighbor. It is also the mother of all evil things because when man does not work, the body becomes short of necessities, such as food and clothing, for it cannot endure nudity and hunger. Consequently, he will either beg and plead, or steal and ravish, if his plea is not answered. If he begs, that is a wound and shame to the body, and if he steals, that is a wound and suffering to the soul.

Again, if he begs, he should pay for it with prayers, otherwise he would remain indebted. A thief's punishment is execution and [death by] the hook if he steals, lies, or ravishes. Behold! This is the punishment of an idle and unoccupied man, which I have made clear to you somewhat.

Now, let us delve into the Holy Scriptures and find what they say about the slothful and the lazy—both the slothful in physical work and the lazy in spiritual studies and virtues. Solomon the Wise—himself a tutor and instructor to people of all ages—places blame upon the sluggish who are slow and unsteady in all that they do. We shall recite his words in ten articles.

First, he [Solomon] says: "One who hides his hand in his bosom in vain, will not be able to bring it up to his mouth" (Prov 26:15). He applies the expression "in vain" to those who have no reason to be weak. There are four reasons for the hands to be useless: the person is sick or blind, or his hand is drained [of power], or he is wounded. [In these cases], idleness is blameless; otherwise, idleness is sluggishness. In spiritual [terms], the hand indicates virtuous works: fasting, praying, almsgiving, and so on. When a person hides these [virtues] under sluggish thoughts through laziness, he cannot bring his hand up to his mouth. The mouth signifies reason, whereas the hand signifies practical virtue, because the practical is food and the theoretical is drink to the rational soul. One is water that cools only the thirst, whereas the other is wine that cools and satiates. Similarly, the knowledge of the wise people and others cools the mind with wisdom, but the knowledge of the Holy Scriptures through the Holy Spirit cools a person with wisdom and satiates him with the love of God. A lazy person does not feed the soul with the practical, nor does he water it with theoretical wisdom.

Second, he [Solomon] says: "As a door turns on the hinge, so does a sluggard on his bed" (Prov 26:14). A door turns back and forth on a hinge and cannot move away from its [original] location; likewise, the slothful, procrastinating in bed, turns to one side and another, but cannot rise up and go to do physical work. The lazy in spiritual matters is fond of the pleasures of the body, is judged by the conscience of his mind, and turns to one side and another, but cannot turn his evil thoughts into good thoughts, because his body is burdened with the pleasures of laziness, like someone who has been stupefied by sleep.

Third, a sluggard finds excuses and says: "There is a lion in the way, and there are murderers in the streets" (Prov 26:13). When you send a weak and unsteady person to a journey for any matter, he will allege that there are lions and beasts in the way, and he will not go. What would a lion do in the way?

The lion is either in the woods or in the wilderness. He [the lazy one] will also say that there are murderers in the streets. The streets are full of people; where would a murderer come from? Nevertheless, he will use this as an excuse. Spiritually [speaking], when we send a person to heaven by way of virtue, he says: "The lion is Satan in the way of my life, he will catch me"; hence "He lies in wait in secret to ravish the poor" (Ps 10:9). [He alleges] there are murderers in the streets—the natural desires and needs of the body wound me from all directions and kill me, as if I were a street—and the lion like the devil entraps the thoughts of the mind, and the desires wound the senses of the body; therefore, I do not dare to go to heaven by way of virtue. All of these are excuses for those who like laziness and sloth. Look at the first [industrious men] who destroyed the desires of the body with fortitude and were delivered from Satan's traps. In your case, however, [we say to the lazy] the pleasure of the body will be the source of your destruction, because you are lazy and slothful, and thus Satan will find you faint and weak, and will hunt you.

Fourth, he [Solomon] says: "A sluggard is wiser in his own eyes than him who brings the fulfillment of the law" (cf. Prov 26:16). When the weak and unsteady in work is asked why he does not labor, he replies: "I am wiser than everyone else; everybody labors for me. People say: 'The unfortunate person works and the fortunate eats.' They cultivate and labor for me, and I sit heedless." In [terms of] the mind, the slow in learning and the unsteady in good works thinks he is wise, because he does not learn or teach, nor does he work good works or teach others to do so. He says: "I know everything; therefore, I will not learn. I am learned for myself and not for others; why should I bother myself to teach others?" We ask: "Why don't you work?" He says: "I work covertly to avoid praises." Or he says: "A man should have faith; what is the work for? Animals always eat grass, asses always fast, trees are generous in alms, but none of these goes to the kingdom [of heaven]." Behold! The Prophet Isaiah says woe to such people: "Woe unto them that are wise in their own eyes, and prudent in their own sight" (Isa 5:21). See, they do not study and do not work because they think they are most knowledgeable and perfect, compared with the one who brings the fulfillment of tidings. The fulfillment is the perfect virtue, complete theoretically and practically. The tiding is what a priest teaches to others. He teaches truth verbally, demonstrates goodness through works, and thus everybody receives instruction to do good by seeing and hearing, as the Lord says: "They may see your good works, and glorify your Father who is in heaven" (Mt 5:16).

Fifth, he [Solomon] says: "The desires kill the sluggard, for he refuses to do any work" (Prov 21:25). Desires always torment a faint and idle person, for he needs all the goodness the earth can offer: food, drink, clothing, and so on, but he cannot obtain these, because he does not work or labor, nor is he given what he desires. Desire kills whoever always desires physical pleasure but does not work toward filling the need. Spiritually, too, "the desire kills the sluggard," for when the lazy person desires wisdom and learning he will not find it, because the pleasures of the body counter it. Similarly, if he desires good works, virtues, peace, and so on, he will not attain these, because he does not work physically; rather, he wants through the desire and suffers by it; hence: "You desire and obtain not, because you ask not. You ask and receive not, because you ask amiss, that you may consume it upon your desires" (Jas 4:2–3). Again, and otherwise: "Desire corrupts the sluggard," because the ungodly and the lazy are equally guilty: the lazy and slothful desires bodily pleasures to delight; likewise, the ungodly desires adulterous and avaricious works, so that the body may be accommodated and pleased. In other words, the sins of the ungodly and of the faint and sluggard are the same. However, they are also different in that one of them (the slothful) does not do good, whereas the other (the ungodly) does evil. It makes no difference whether you do not do good, or you do evil, wherefore he [James] says: "You adulterers, know you not that the love of the world is enmity with God?" (Jas 4:4). Whosoever loves his body hates God and is the enemy of God.

Sixth, he [Solomon] says: "He that tills his own land shall be satisfied by bread; but they that pursue vanities are void of understanding" (Prov 12:11). Tillage is the best and most righteous labor among all professions. First, because it is man's first profession. God said: "You shall till and in the sweat shall you eat bread" (cf. Gen 2:15, 3:19). Second, because there is theft, lying, or ravishing in other professions, such as in trading, which is performed by lying, or [in the case of] a weaver and a blacksmith either they are ravished of their wages or they steal from the substance. Other [professions] are alike. Tillage, however, is altogether a just work: lying, stealing, or ravishing have no room in it. It is also beneficial for nature and the plants. [By tillage] one anticipates to bear fruits through God's mercy, whereby the house and the storehouse would be filled with bread and everything that is good, be it from the farm, the vineyard, the trees, the animals, or other things. Those who stay futile and idle of such works are void of understanding, because whoever does not work during summer cannot enjoy during winter. The same applies to the spiritual tiller who diligently plows the ground of his soul through fasting, prayers, fortitude, and humility, sows the commandments of God in his heart, and irrigates [the seeds] with the water of the Holy Spirit that is referred to in the Holy Scripture; then [the seeds] will grow and bear fruits thirty-, sixty-, and hundredfold. Spiritually and physically, he will need nothing in this world, and the storehouse of the heavens will be full of all kinds of good things in the hereafter; hence: "Store up for yourselves treasures in heaven" (Mt 6:20), so that "when you lack material [treasures], they may receive you in the everlasting habitations" (cf. Lk 16:9). Whoever is slothful in [pursuing] this is void of understanding and pursues vanities, because all corporeal works are vanity and void, as Ecclesiastes says: "Vanity of vanities; all is vanity" (Eccl 1:2). Vanity is [understood] in two aspects: all matters are perishable and vain, and man is temporal and vain, as David says: "Man has become like vanity and his days have declined like a shadow" (cf. Ps 102:11).

Seventh, he [Solomon] says: "Fear casts down the sluggard; and the souls of the effeminate shall hunger" (Prov 18:8). The sluggard is the slothful and faint in work. He fears work as much as a person fears falling in thorns, as is said: "The ways of sluggards are strewn with thorns" (Prov 15:19); not that there is thorn in work, but it seems to him that there is thorn by way of his grief. "And the effeminate should perish." A slothful man and a slothful woman are equally weak: since weakness is inherent in women, a man voluntarily accepting the behavior of a woman becomes like her. Again, the same is applicable in the spiritual [field] to the lazy in good works. Some are more arrogant and evil; others are fainter and weaker, which is evil as well. Those who fear vanities alienate themselves from God and people. To this the Prophet refers [by saying]: "You have hated them that idly persist in vanities" (Ps 31:6). They grow weaker from this fear and do not work virtues, just like the man whom Christ reproached in the Gospel: "I knew you that you are a hard man; I was afraid and hid your talent" (cf. Mt 25:24–25). Fear is of two kinds: good and evil. The good fear occurs when the person fears God because of the torments of hell, and fears the law and death, and through this fear keeps God's law. The evil fear occurs when people lose their power, grieve, and do not work good works. This surmounts to despair and leads to evil, whereas the other fear is good and leads to fortitude. It is an evil fear to say: "I cannot do good." It is the devil, people, our bodies, and the world that oppose in such fashion. It is an evil [fear] when one fears the present and refrains from doing good. It is a good fear when man fears the torments of the hereafter and does good. The good and evil fears are distinguished thus from each other. Behold! Those who accept the effeminate fear and become slothful will be deprived of the sensate material bread in this age and of the spiritual life there, in the hereafter, just like the servant whom Christ called wicked and sluggard, and destined to torments.

Eighth, he [Solomon] says: "Every drunkard and whoremonger shall be poor; and every sluggard shall clothe himself with ragged garments" (Prov 23:21). That is, wine instigates the desire of those who drink it and they commit adultery, and sleep follows the act of adultery for the wine to be discharged. These will become impoverished by paying the price of wine and the price and wages of prostitution from their possessions. When they drink and sleep, they no longer work and, consequently, become poor and naked, for they drink what they have earned without earning more. Laziness and sinning as well are drunkenness. When we are intoxicated with laziness and sleep the sleep of sins, we are impoverished of all good things, for the spiritual wealth is composed of fasting, praying, almsgiving, abstinence, suffering, fortitude, and so on. [The lazy] is deprived of these in this life and is clothed with ragged garments in the hereafter, according to what has been said: "Friend, how did you get in here without a wedding garment? Take that worthless servant into outer darkness" (cf. Mt 22:12–13).

Ninth, he says: "Go to the ant, O sluggard, and envy him; or go to the bee, and learn how diligent she is" (cf. Prov 6:6–8), because God created these two weak animals for two reasons. First, to embarrass us when these gnats, the mosquitoes, the wasp, and other small animals trouble us, for the pharaoh did not suffer in the hands of bears and lions; rather, he suffered in the hands of animalcules such as the gnats, the wasps, the frogs, the dog-flies, and so on. Second, to teach us diligence through them. The ant that labors and works constantly all summer long to earn, gather, and pile up from the press, the threshing-floor, and the grass, and to enjoy throughout the winter when gathering is impossible. We should labor in a similar fashion spiritually and physically: work in the summer and enjoy in the winter, because wise people say: "Whoever moves about the thoroughfares in summer goes from door to door [begging] in winter." Now, know that if you do not work in summer, you cannot enjoy the winter, as the proverb itself says: "A sluggard when reproached is not ashamed; so also he who borrows corn in harvest" (Prov 20:4), for summer is time for gathering; if you borrow [in summer], when would you pay? Similarly, this life of ours is the summer to gather spiritual provisions, and the other [life] is the winter where there is neither seeding and gathering, nor borrowing and working; the means available in this life for labor cannot be found in the other life. Therefore, we ought to go to the ant and learn the spiritual and physical work. The bee also is a small flying animal, yet she always gathers the sweet nourishment, which the kings and the homeless take for healing. Similarly, we ought to fly with the wings of our minds to the various flowers of the Holy Scriptures and gather knowledge, which is sweet nourishment for the minds and a source of enlightenment that casts away darkness from man. Wisdom, thereby, is a divine power that turns the free will from evil into good, which neither great rulers nor tyrants can do. Not a single sword or arrow can penetrate it. The Word [alone] by wisdom can penetrate it and turn it from evil. The wisdom of God can elevate a man in this life to glory and honor, and lead him in the hereafter into the everlasting life, and it is a spiritual and physical remedy and medicine not only for itself, but also for all the listeners, whether great or humble. Behold! It is for this reason that [Solomon] mentions these two animals as models—the ant for good works and the bee for good thoughts, since the good work regulates the body, and wisdom [regulates] the soul. Wisdom is a lantern, and good work is the oil that keeps the lantern alight. The good work is nourishment and wisdom is drink, as was mentioned before. Both are necessary to us; just as food satiates the hunger of the body and drink [quenches] its thirst, so too is the matter with spiritual [nourishment]. Accordingly, we ought to be fortitudinous in both works, to feed the hungry soul and to drink wisdom for our thirst.

Tenth, he [Solomon] says: "How long will you sleep, O sluggard? When will you awake out of sleep?" (Prov 6:9). Although it has been seen that the lazy remain poor in relation to material things, whereas diligent hands enrich a person, understand this in the following fashion in relation to spiritual matters. O sluggard and slow in virtues, how long will you lie motionless in the thorn of your sins? Or, when will you wake up out of sleep? [David] refers to the sins that lead to death or sleep when he prays: "Lighten my eyes O Lord, lest I sleep in death" (Ps 13:3).

"You sleep a little" (Prov 6:10); meaning: "I am young, let me find pleasure in luxury and waste briefly," but you do not know when the thief death will come.

"I will slumber a little" (Prov 24:33); meaning: "I am wealthy with respect to possession, let me stay briefly in the thorns of the world and gather until my son matures and inherits [from me]," but you do not know, O fool, "the night your soul shall be required of you" (Lk 12:20).

"Remain with your arms crossed briefly" (cf. Prov 24:33);[36] meaning: "I

---

[36] There is a typographical error in the manuscript where crossing the arms (*ǝndgrkic'es* [ընդգրկիցես]) has become *ǝnkrkesc'es* [ընկրկեցցես].

am weak physically, let me stay idle until I recover," in the likeness of the faint servant who said: "My Lord delayed his coming, [but the Lord] will suddenly come and cut him asunder, [etc.]" (cf. Mt 24:48–51).

"Thus will come your poverty as a forerunner" (Prov 24:34); meaning, your deprivation of good works shall be a forerunner and foreteller of the torments of hell.

"And your want" (Prov 24:34); meaning, in the likeness of the foolish bridesmaids who lacked the oil.

"Will come like a swift courier" (Prov 24:34); meaning, death will take you in its last grasp like a wicked traveler and never let you go; it will rather terminate you, according to Ecclesiastes: "In the place where the tree shall fall, there it shall be" (Eccl 11:3); meaning, like a dead body, whether [it fell] northward because of God's hard-heartedness or southward because of God's warm love, for Paul says: "Now is the accepted time; now is the day of salvation" (2 Cor 6:2). Thereafter he adds: "Every one may receive the things done in his body, whether it be good or bad" (cf. 2 Cor 5:10).

Now, brethren, since the day of death comes so soon and unexpectedly, and it shall come inevitably, we ought to wake up, come out of the sleep of sins, and be ready, for this is the time of salvation, so that people may save their souls from hell. This is the time to accept the kingdom, as the Apostle says: "Now is the day of salvation; now is the accepted time. Do not give any reason, so that no stain may be found with your ministry" (cf. 2 Cor 6:2–3), because to do good works or to have seasons of life in the other life is not an option. Just as our age changes irreversibly from childhood to youth and then to old age, so too does [our life] change irrecoverably and perish. Therefore, I beg you in the love of Christ: so long as there are days and light to work; so long as it is summer and time to gather; so long as you are healthy and able to labor, and so long as the heavenly king is seated on the throne of grace, face the ground before Him and ask for mercy in due time, because when He sits on the throne of righteousness and judges infallibly, mercy will not be mixed in equitable rights, as is said: "You shall not spare a poor man in judgment" (Ex 23:3). So long as you have control over your time, ability, intellect, and will, care for piling up possessions for the other life; "When you lack it, they may receive you into everlasting habitations" (cf. Lk 16:9). Otherwise, there comes a time when you would come out of your body and be brought out of your will; it will be useless then to regret and meaningless to sigh; [God] will not listen to pleas and will not see the tears. For example, when [authorities] take a thief to execution and to the hook, regardless of his excessive begging, no one pays attention to him. The same thing will occur in the hereafter. Behold! We ought to accordingly repent for our sins today, confess today, sigh today, cry with the eyes, work with the hands, labor, share with others, and give to the poor.

This is what the Prophet instructs: "Labor forever and live to the end, so that he should not see corruption" (Ps 49:8–9). Now, the all-merciful, multicompassionate, sweet, and generous Lord himself will have merciful compassion upon you, will stir you to do good works, will take your stony heart away from you, will give you a human heart, will renew the Holy Spirit in you, and will cast away from you all the traps and deceits of Satan. May He, by keeping you in peace and free of trials in this life, make you partakers of the saints and the lovers of His name in Christ Jesus, in our Lord in the life to come. Glory and power unto Him, His Father, and the most Holy Spirit now, forever and ever, amen.

CHAPTER XXV

Homily of the same on sleep according to Luke's verse: "Why are you asleep? Rise and pray" (Lk 22:46).

There are four kinds of sleep: two are good and two are evil. First, natural sleep is good. Second, the everlasting [sleep] is best. The third [kind] is evil sleep and it is associated with sins. Fourth, the sleep of torments is worst. Similarly, watchfulness in this life is of four kinds: two are good and two evil. First, watchfulness for the body is good; it occurs during work and labor; hence: "You shall eat the labors of your hands; blessed are you, and it shall be well" (Ps 127:2). Second, the best watchfulness occurs when man is alert in mind and diligent in good works—[a watchfulness] that is cognizant of the spiritual and corporeal, distinguishes the evil and the good, and forsakes the evil and works the good. Concerning this, the Lord says: "What I say unto you, I say unto all, 'Watch'" (Lk 13:37). Third, watchfulness is evil when man is slothful and lazy, does not do physical work, does not perform spiritual labor, does not study, and does not teach. A person of this caliber, although watchful in body, is evil, for the gate of the kingdom is closed before the slothful and lazy. Fourth, the worst watchfulness occurs when man is alert in wickedness, skillful in matters of the body, ignorant in matters of the soul, [engaged in] trading, eating and drinking, ravishing and piling up; all other similar things comprise the worst watchfulness, because it would have been better to sleep than be alert in such fashion.

Now, let us go back to our first statement, that there are four kinds of sleep. First, natural sleep is good and beneficial for three reasons. First, Aristotle says that every animal should sleep, so that it may work when it is awake;[37] so shall do a person. Second, because angels appear to man a person [when he is asleep], reminiscent of Jacob's ladder. Third, so that they [sleepers] may become wiser, as God revealed all the mysteries to Solomon through a dream in his sleep, as it is mentioned in 2 Kings.

Here, however, there will come a question about dreams. Is the dream conceived by the mind or the senses? We say that the dream is conceived

---

[37] Cf. Aristotle, *On Sleep and Sleeplessness.*

neither by the mind nor by the senses. That it is not related to the senses is evident: food's steam rises up in the head like smoke [risen up] to the window, covering the senses and preventing them from performing any work. This vice is designated as physical sleep. And that it is not related to the mind's performance is evident from three things. First, the senses are tools for the mind by which it sees, hears, and so on. When they [senses] do not function, the mind also ceases to work. For example, artisans cannot do any work if they lack the tools. Second, the mind's function is to think and to judge selectively. Dreams, however, form haphazardly illusions and abominable scenery, and they are not associated with order or thoughts. Third, it is evident from those who lack the rational mind and yet they dream, such as dogs that bark in their dreams, and others. It is evident, then, that dreams are not seen through an association with the rational mind or the senses; rather, they are seen as a vision of the innate soul that is the nourishing part. It follows that this [the innate] operates better when the rational and sensate [parts of the soul] cease to function during sleep. It [the innate soul—the nourishing part] digests the food, separates and refines each [particle] for each [corresponding] part, then retrieves images from the memory, and finally projects them within itself in accordance with a person's weakness. And that the vision is not altogether separated from the senses and the minds, and that it occurs in association with them, is evident, first, from the unity by nature, which makes the living creature alive, because the separation [of senses and the mind] causes death. Contrary to alertness where the mind is leader and the sensate and innate are subservient, in sleep the innate leads and the sensate and mind serve it through visions. Second, it is evident that the dream is composed of some orderly and some disorderly elements. The orderly element belongs to the mind that affects it, whereas the disorderly element belongs to the innate that receives the mind's influence indirectly. Whoever, though, speaks, sees, hears, moves, works, or tastes in his dream [does so] because of the senses that are inseparable from him. This is what St. Gregory of Nyssa has written in his book *The Creation [of Man]*. Therefore, natural sleep is good and useful, as it has been demonstrated.

Second, the everlasting sleep. This is better for three reasons. First, because Job says: "Death is rest to man" (Job 3:22), for he has been saved from the torments of the world and the sins. Second, it is better, because man died under God's hand, as Solomon says: "But the souls of the righteous are in the hand of God, and there shall no evil touch them; in the sight of the unwise they seemed to die; but they are in peace" (cf. Wis 3:1–2). In Leviticus [God] says:

"You shall lie down and none shall awaken you" (Lev 26:6). Third, it is better, because at the resurrection it will rise to life, as David says: "I will both lie down in peace and sleep" (Ps 4:8). These two sleeps—natural sleep and the sleep of death—are good.

Evil sleep is the sleep of sins, as David says: "They have slept their sleep, and have found nothing" (cf. Ps 75:6). The worst is [the sleep] of everlasting torments and death, as David begged: "O Lord, lighten my eyes, lest I sleep in death" (Ps 13:3). Now, sin is reminiscent of sleep for many reasons. First, because man in his sleep sees many unreal visions—eating, drinking, and so on. Likewise, the sinner by avarice sees many things, but when he dies, he owns nothing, as [David] says: "They have slept their sleep, and have found nothing" (cf. Ps 76:5). Isaiah says: "As men drink and eat in sleep, and when they have arisen, the dream is vain, so shall be the wealth of the pagans" (cf. Isa 29:8). Second, the working body parts of a sleeping person cease to function; the same is true with laziness, wherefore the proverb says: "How long will you sleep, O sluggard? When will you awake out of sleep?" (Prov 6:9). Third, [man] fears in his sleep what he should not fear, and fears not what he should fear, as the psalm says: "There were they afraid where there was no fear" (Ps 53:4), as with a person who takes fright by dreaming of murder, whereas a sleeper fears not a person who has practically lifted his sword to kill. In the same fashion, the sinner fears not death, but fears life. Fourth, a sleeper feels nothing—he does not see, does not hear, and so on—and for this reason, just as the steam rises up by heat in a pot placed on fire and drips down the lid after condensation, so too functions man's stomach like a pot: the heat of the heart and the liver is like fire; they digest the food internally and the steam rises up to the top and becomes condensed there, for the top is cool. Now, the condensed steam comes down from the top and makes its way toward all the parts of the body, which consequently cease to function. The same relates to the soul of man: pleased with sins, it becomes benumbed from the numerous sins. Comprehend likewise the upper and lower parts of the reason, which consents to and is pleased with sins. Fifth, while a person is asleep, the entire heat of the body moves out, wherefore the sleeper becomes colder. Likewise, whoever sleeps in the sins casts out of himself the entire heat of loving God, his neighbor, the soul, and the law; he loves nothing but the sins. Sixth, a sleeper is not ashamed of his private parts, thus: "Souls entrapped in sins lose also their mind." Seventh, whoever loves the sleep loves it more than anything else. Likewise, sin is [the most beloved] to a sinner; that is, the avaricious is fond of money, the lustful of covetousness, the arrogant of glory, and so on.

Eighth, similar to a sleeper who neither is completely dead nor is completely alive, a sinner lacks spiritual vitality, yet he is not completely dead in his body. Ninth, sleep takes hold [of man] more in an accustomed hour, and sins—whether from demons or from within—dominate more in an accustomed hour. Just as sleep comes at night, so is the sin committed mostly at night, "for it is a work of darkness" (cf. Rom 13:12). Tenth, just as sleep is followed by awakening, whether [induced] by others or on one's own, so too are sins destroyed and erased in us through the grace of Christ if we repent. Sins are destroyed by old age, weakness, or death. "We ought to awake out of sleep" (Rom 13:11); meaning, we ought to swiftly rise from the sleep of sins for many reasons. First, to honor Christ who calls upon us to rise up. He calls upon us in three ways. First, by placing good thoughts in our minds, as Revelation says: "Behold! I stand at your door, and knock: if any man hear my voice, and open the door, I will come in to him, and will sup with him" (Rev 3:20). Second, He makes us rise up by preaching through the doctors, as the proverb says: "My son, if you become surety for your friend, give not sleep to your eyes, nor to his, that you may deliver yourself as a doe out of the toils" (cf. Prov 6:1–5). Third, He makes us rise up by striking and instructing, just as the angel smote Peter on the side in the [Book of] Acts and raised him up [Acts 12:7]. Thus, physical instruction makes us rise up from our sins. Again, we ought to rise up from sleep, because it is time, as Paul says: "Now it is time to awake out of sleep. The night of our life is far spent, and the day is at hand together with the light" (cf. Rom 13:11–12). Again, we ought to rise up of the sleep of sins, because sins lead us to the sleep of hell that is the worst sleep. As Jeremiah says: "I will make them drunk so that they shall sleep the perpetual sleep, and not wake" (cf. Jer 51:57). There are people who do not keep roosters at home that they may not awaken them. Speaking against them, Solomon says: "They shall rise up at the voice of the sparrow" (Eccl 12:4). Referring to the crowing cock, Peter says: "Recalled the word and wept bitterly" (cf. Mt 26:75). Crowing [or singing, or talking] indicates the doctors who make the sinners repent and rise up from their sins through preaching. The reason why a fowl calls thrice is that if people do not rise up from the first and middle [calls], they rise up from the last [call]. This signifies the prophets, apostles, and doctors. At churches, during major feasts, it is customary to strike the bells thrice, so that if [the congregation] is idle after the first [strike], [they] rise up upon the second or third. Likewise, at the celebration of the kingdom of heaven, the trumpets will call thrice.

First the prophets, then the apostles, and finally the doctors preach day after day. Therefore, we ought to rise up from the bed of pleasures, filth, and trouble, which is the sin, as Micah says: "Arise and go; for there is no rest for you there because of uncleanness" (Mic 2:10). Our Lord said: "Rise up! Let us go" (Mk 14:42), and: "I go to prepare a place for you, I will come again, and receive you unto myself" (Jn 14:2–3). When would this happen, though? We say that although we should always be ready, we should more so be ready when we are old, because natural motion is slow at the beginning and fast at the end, like a stone falling down the mountain. [Contrary to this], a forced motion is fast at the beginning and slow at the end, like an arrow or a stone that we have thrown by force. Similarly, the love of this world and the desires of sin are imposed upon us later. Therefore, when as young people we are hot, we ought to cool down at old age. The love of spiritual things and everlasting life are inherent within us and it should be strengthened at old age, because when an old man is prudent and fortitudinous by doing so, not only will he benefit himself, but also he will be considered the crown and pride of his offspring. Old age itself indicates wisdom and the Ancient of Times. Moreover, whiteness indicates innocence and righteousness. In an old man, however, we find wisdom and weakness, whereas fortitude and foolishness distinguish the young. Now, if a man possesses fortitude at a young age and wisdom at an old, he is a good and honorable old man, but if he possesses only one of these, he is imperfect. If he possesses both foolishness and weakness, he is sluggard. The old man is referred to as languished;[38] that is, extenuated and worn. The aged [person] is also perceived to have reached the edge of his lifetime.[39] Again, the aged [is perceived to] have reached the edge of transformation, because he will thereafter be transformed in the grave. Wherefore the Gospel says: "Be awake and watchful" (1 Pet 5:8). May Christ the God make us worthy to this, and glory unto Him forever, amen.

---

[38] Tatʿewacʿi displays a pun here. The Armenian equivalent for *old* is *cer* [ծեր], whereas the word for *languished* is *ciwr* [ծիւր].

[39] Another pun engaging the words *cer* (ծեր= aged) and *cayr* (ծայր= edge).

CHAPTER XXVI

Homily of the same on lawful marriage according to the Apostle's verse: "Marriage is honorable, and the bed undefiled, but fornicators and adulterers God will judge" (Heb 13:4).

When God created the first man and put him in the Garden of Eden, He took one of his ribs and made it body, made it woman, and gave her to man to assist him. He blessed them and said: "Be fruitful, and multiply, and replenish the earth, and subdue it" (Gen 1:28). This divine blessing and command made marriage lawful and the bed sacred. The Apostle says: "But fornicators and adulterers God will judge" (Heb 13:4). Now, holy matrimony is honorable for many reasons. First, when God did not find a helper similar to man in the entire creation, He gave him the woman as helper—to guard the house, to bear children, and so on. An adulteress, however, is not man's helper; she causes the destruction of houses, properties, and other things. Second, she [the lawful wife] helps man to stay virtuous—she holds man back from adultery and helps him in many good things: fasting, praying, and almsgiving. An adulteress or a fornicator, however, drives man to various wrongdoings and deprives him of everything good. Third, she [the lawful wife] is man's helper because she collects and keeps everything; moreover, she is a necessity for man: just as the lake receives all the rivers, so too does a woman receive, contain, and accumulate every good thing, wherefore marriage is honorable. A fornicator, however, scatters and destroys everything, wherefore God judges her. Fourth, she [the lawful wife] is called woman, which means half and companion, because she shares the life of man and makes half of his body, for "she is bone of his bones, and flesh of his flesh" (cf. Gen 3:23). An alien woman, however, is not half of man's flesh, nor is she a life companion, wherefore this [union] is not lawful. Fifth, God blessed marriage and made the man and the woman one body by the blessed crown. Fornicators, however, became one body [with men] by adultery and not through God's blessing, wherefore God judges them. Sixth, since a man and his wife are one body through the bond of love between man and woman, they will remain one body so long as the man, not the wife, is in control of her body, and the woman, not the man, is in control of his body, for "They are no more two, but one body" (Mt 19:6). Fornicators, however, are not one through love, nor are they one body; rather, they are many divided among many, wherefore God judges them. Seventh, marriage was made for childbirth, that humankind may multiply and the species may grow to serve the glory of God, wherefore marriage is honorable. A fornicator, however, is motivated by her body's lustful desire and not by childbirth, wherefore God judges her. Eighth, although copulation and pleasure are the same [whether for the lawfully married or] for the adulterer, one of them fulfills God's command through lawful matrimony, as He said: "Be fruitful and multiply" (Gen 1:28) and thereby is honorable by God's command, whereas [God] said for the other [unlawful copulation]: "You shall not commit adultery, you shall not commit fornication" (cf. Ex 20:13), and yet she challenges God's command and thereby God judges her. Ninth, Lawful matrimony is judged and dishonored neither among men, nor at God's judgment. Adulterers and fornicators, however, are judged and punished by men who have been authorized by God's command in the old and the new [law], such as stoning and burning the adulterer in the old [law], and gouging out the eyes, cutting the lips, smutting, dishonoring, or whipping in the new [law], based on [the nature of] each deed. Besides, they shall be tormented in the everlasting fire in the hereafter. Tenth, lawful matrimony occurs in the daylight, in the open, at the church, through the Word of God, with the cross and the Gospel, whereas fornication is performed at night, covertly, fearing men, and through satanic word, wherefore God judges them [fornicators]. Lawful matrimony, however, is honorable and the bed undefiled.

Although lawful matrimony is lawful, as has been said, it, too, can be defiled in three ways. First, if [a husband and wife] exercise [sex] indiscriminately and often, in a manner befitting lawless people and animals, the bed becomes defiled. However, reserved and moderate [intercourse is lawful], just as a little wine is drinkable and sacred, but too much wine is drunkenness and great sin. The same is applicable to matrimony. Second, [it could become defiled] with respect to time, for [intercourse] is lawful during allowed seasons and is unlawful and impure during forbidden [seasons]. For example, lamb and cattle meats are lawful during ferial periods, but are unlawful when fasting. Likewise, in matrimony, there are forbidden seasons one should learn. The forbidden period in bed coincides with periods during which wedding is prohibited, such as Sunday, Wednesday, and Friday, when wedding is not conducted. Likewise, wedding is not conducted during the weeks of fasting, the period of Lent, and the Eastertide. It is apparent that during these seasons wedding is not conducted because intercourse is prohibited. Likewise, [intercourse is prohibited] during other periods, such as menstruation, when pregnant, and when sick. Man should choose the time [whether to have intercourse or not], just like a sower who chooses the season in spring and autumn before sowing, and who does not sow in winter and summer, because [the seeds] will be ill-grown. Third, the choice of the place shall be according to God's command and not Satan's trap. Or, if a woman abandons her husband and sets for a different direction, or if a man [abandons] his wife, they are considered adulterers, makers of impurity, and dishonorers of the bed. Should a person ask: Why is adultery prohibited? Isn't it the same as matrimony in terms of intercourse and the fulfillment of the commands of God who said: "Be fruitful and multiply"? Moreover, didn't the patriarchs marry many women and possess concubines? We say: It is to be known that God established the love of man and woman as substance to their desire for two reasons. First, so that man may lower himself before the woman due to desire, otherwise he would not enter such an abominable place and [engage] in such an action [as intercourse]. Second, so that the woman may endure the burden of labor and the trouble of feeding infants. Now, regardless of whether childbirth takes place because of desire, or if desire is fulfilled for the sake of childbirth, the result is the growth and multiplication of humankind. Fornication, however, contradicts God's law. First, because [fornicators] hamper childbirth due to the flow of various diseases. Second, because in their desire they surrender themselves to abominable impurities and pass the whole day in the same insatiably. Third, because they lure innocent youngsters into inflamed desires, into the trap of Satan, which is eternal death. Fourth, because they also distract the youngsters from their duty of making babies as they waste their sperm. Fifth, because they also attract man's possessions and earnings with him and he, intoxicated by vice, disregards the loss of his properties. Wherefore, [the Scripture] rightfully cautions: "Give no heed to a worthless woman" (cf. Prov 5:2). The Apostle says: "Be not deceived: neither adulterers nor fornicators shall inherit the kingdom of God" (cf. 1 Cor 6:9–10).

Question: Why is polygamy, be it practiced by a man or a woman, despised not only in the Holy Scriptures but also in natural moral precepts, such as [in the case of] Joseph who was separated from his wife, Potipher, and Reuben who was dishonored for having gone into his father's bed?

Answer: First, because the bond of love that makes the two one body separates the wife from her husband and binds her with someone else, or, similarly, [binds] the husband with a different woman. They lack the voluntary love to one another, [harboring] love by imposition. Therefore, the Lord prohibits the separation [of a husband and wife] based on other vices, if the married person is flippant or thief, and makes exception "for fornication" (cf. 1 Cor 7:2), because a woman [in this case] separates herself voluntarily from her husband. Second, because the offspring would not know their father. Third, because the father would not have compassion for his son, for he would be in doubt about the authenticity. Fourth, because they will violate the divine law that coupled a man with a woman and [stipulated] no polygamy, such as our ancestors Adam and Eve, especially that He says in the law: "You shall not commit adultery" (Ex 20:14), but they [adulterers] dispute this. Besides, man should not be a fornicator of a married woman, nor should he separate her from her husband through deception.

Solomon who was instructed by God has shown the harm caused in such a situation in twelve ways: "Keep yourself from a married woman" (Prov 6:24), because when a man bound by marriage goes astray he is worse than the whore woman. There is only one punishment to those [unmarried whores] who fornicate—the fire of hell; whereas these [married women that fornicate] have threefold [punishment]. One [is associated with] the husband, the other is the punishment of judges, and the last is the judgment of God and the torment of hell.

Second, he says: "Let not the lust of a strange woman's beauty overcome you" (cf. Prov 6:25). This caused the destruction of the first man, because "the woman saw that the tree was good, and that it was pleasant to the eyes" (Gen 3:6). Similarly, sight is what bound David with the love of Bath-Sheba, wherefore the Lord commanded: "Look not on a woman lustfully" (cf. Mt 5:28), because man is compelled to the fulfillment of the act [of fornication] after a lustful look.

Third, he says: "The value of a harlot is as much as of one loaf" (Prov 6:26); that is, the price of prostitution is within reach, so why are you, then, so ill-temperedly grieved of her concupiscence? Or, like a person who has eaten a loaf, desire is swiftly diminished.

Fourth, he says: "A woman hunts for the precious souls of men" (Prov 6:26), because based on the four elements of the body, there are four hunters of the soul—the body, the world, women, and demons. The body hunts the soul by means of earth's gravity. The world hunts according to the quality of the fire by projecting diverse beauties. The demons hunt by way of the air you breathe. The woman hunts through the wet desire of the water. Just as the hunter hunts the bird using food and hinders its flight in the air, so also hunts the woman by desire. She hinders the ascending thoughts now and [prevents] the soul from moving toward the heavens after death. Moreover, she binds the soul and the body to the fire of hell after resurrection.

Fifth, he says: "Shall anyone wrap fire, and not burn the garment? Or will anyone walk on coals of fire and not burn his feet?" (Prov 6:27–28). Fire is the desire; if we wrap and hide it within us, it will inflame later, and if we physically tread upon it by the feet, it will burn; therefore we ought to cut its root—desire and familiarity with women, because thoughts, sight, speech, and location can play a role in fleeing from a woman. Desire is distanced from us in four ways: through physical suffering, fasting, hunger, and thirst, because physical comfort, rich food, eating, and drinking to one's bellyful inflame the desire, just as wood [inflames] the fire. Similarly, a person who goes to a married woman cannot be saved from God's punishment, just as the great David was unable to avoid it [punishment], and because of this one action [of going to a married woman] he was told: "The sword shall not depart from your house for ever" (2 Kings 12:10), and he was overthrown and fled from Absalom on his feet.

Sixth, he says: "Through the void of understanding he committed adultery" (cf. Prov 6:32); meaning, since the law commands lawful matrimony, only the same is appropriate—to be fruitful and multiply through childbirth. Whoever forsakes this commits adultery against the law that stipulated: "You shall not commit adultery" (Ex 20:14), does not give birth to children, and shall fall into the punishment of God and the punishment of man for his exclusively abominable act.

Seventh, he says: "The adulterer procures destruction to his soul" (cf. Prov 6:32); meaning, he shall be destroyed at the judgment of God, because he has disdained His law in the present and shall suffer pain and dishonor from the husband of the woman and from all those who have seen him, for they shall speak ill of him, slander him, sentence him to fines, beat him, curse him, and sever his organ.

Eighth, he says: "The jealousy of the husband is great; he will not spare in the day of vengeance" (Prov 6:34), because man begrudges and plans to kill when his vineyard or farm is ravished, and he surely begrudges more against the ravisher of his life companion who, although united with her husband by the bond of love, was separated bodily and lured by the fornicator. For this reason, when he [the husband] complains before the judge in the tribune, the latter does not spare in avenging him.

Ninth, the Apostle says: "Do not defraud your neighbor in any matter, because the Lord is the avenger of all such" (1 Thess 4:6); meaning, God avenges for those who have been ravished and for those who have been impoverished of their belongings, and surely God's vengeance and punishment would be greater upon those who ravish a man of his woman. [God will do this] through the judges; but if they decline to judge, they will provoke God and He will punish, as [He did] to the inhabitants of Sodom by the flood and in many other instances.

Tenth, he says: "He will not exchange enmity for anything; nor will he be reconciled for any reason" (cf. Prov 6:35). This is true. Before the law [was established], Samuel and Levi did not accept compensation for their sister [Dinah]; rather, they killed, with the sword, the inhabitants of the place [where their sister was defiled]. Ransom, then, is surely worth less to a person from whose bed the fornicator has ravished his lawful wife. Ransom is nothing to him who was in the habit of spending his entire wealth for his wife.

Eleventh, he says: "With her words she prevailed on him to go astray, having the appearances of a harlot" (cf. Prov 7:10, 21); meaning, she misled the foolish young man by way of four things: a merry appearance, an altered face, seducing words, and embellished ornaments. Misled thus, he followed her like a cattle led to be slaughtered, because his soul had lost its senses, and he was tied with a cord like a dog—for the body of a fornicator is called dog[40]— or resembled an entrapped bird, for she deceived and caught the flying mind, or he was like a hart fatally shot in the liver. Moreover, the whore sets her tongue like a bow and wounds with the arrow of her words the listener's liver, which is the container of desires, because just as reason is located in the head and passion in the heart, so is desire located in the liver, which was wounded by the whore and captivated consequently.

Twelfth, he says: "Do not follow her; for innumerable are those whom she has slain" (cf. Prov 7:26), because a woman caused Adam's exodus and death, and women caused the deluge. A woman deceived Samson and handed him to the enemies, and [a woman] cast David down from his throne. A woman distanced Solomon from God. Who beheaded John the Baptist if not a woman? There are many other [instances]. Here is how she slays: Like a man who slays the body with the sword, a woman slays the soul through the pleasures of the body. The house of a whore is the road to and the chamber of hell, for [the adulterer] in this age enters through the door [of hell] and thereafter goes down to [the chamber of] death; to the everlasting death of the soul and to the death

---

[40] In the Armenian language the noun *šun* [շուն] means *dog* and the verb *šnal* [շնալ], derived from the aforementioned noun, means to behave like a dog and to commit adultery.

where neither resurrection nor salvation exists. To death that deprives of everlasting life; hence: "Adulterers and fornicators shall not inherit the kingdom of God" (cf. 1 Cor 6:9–10).

Should someone ask: Why do you relate matters of fornication so meticulously one by one? We say: For five reasons. First, because when a person does not learn the evil [of fornication] by mind, he might learn it by the body and be deceived, wherefore we caution him. Second, every alert-minded person is aware of the bitterness [of fornication] before the act, but those who are void of understanding conceive it after committing the sin. It would be useless afterward, because what has been done is done, wherefore we teach beforehand. Third, people will not flee from evil unless the abominable nature of evil is projected to them. Fourth, [we caution beforehand] like someone who in the darkness of the night shows the way and the obstacles with a lamp, so that people see and stay watchful. Fifth, like a wise sailor who escapes the sea waves, reaches the harbor, and tells and describes the troubles of the sea to those who have come close, so that they may avoid drowning, Solomon the Wise entered into the sea of the world, tried all the trials of pleasure in person, and taught us that "Everything is falsehood and vanity" (cf. Eccl 9:2).

This is how Satan captures and a woman battles; this is [what happens to] the riches and comforts of the world; and it is in this way that the desires of the body capture men; [so] exercise caution. In likening the world to a sea, the desires are likened to waves for five reasons. First, desire is as natural to our body as the waves to a sea in motion. Second, the desires of the body are as many as the sea waves that follow one another, dominating us frequently from childhood unto old age. Third, a ship sinks when a risen wave falls upon it and survives when it passes from underneath; similarly, if the waves of desire overcome man, they will drown him into deep abysses; otherwise, he will survive, wherefore the Prophet says: "Let not the water-flood drown me, [etc.]" (Ps 69:15). Fourth, just as the sea is either quiet or wavy when clouds or winds trouble it, so too is the mind either peaceful [away] from desires, or troubled by the desire due to external sight, a thought, or the gathering of demons. Fifth, just as the waves crush at the shore, so too does our desire crush and cease due to embarrassment before people, the fear of God, the Holy Scripture, or exhortations and preachers. Whereby, our ancestors cared to teach us about the potential consequences of evil sins and punishment by torments. Wherefore he [Paul] says: "Marriage is honorable, and the bed undefiled, but fornicators and adulterers God will judge" (Heb 13:4).

May our merciful and forgiving Lord Christ the God save us from the trials of sins here and the fire of torments in the hereafter. Glory, power, and honor to Him now, always, and forever and ever, amen.

After what we said about lawful matrimony, we shall now talk about righteousness.

CHAPTER XXVII

Homily of the same on righteousness according to the verse: "Sow to yourselves righteousness, and gather the fruit of life" (Hos 10:12).

God the Creator made man in His image and in His likeness, as the great Prophet Moses says inspired by God: "God created man in his own image" (Gen 1:27). He put in this image three beauties: righteousness, goodness, and truth. He placed righteousness in our nature, goodness in our free will, and truth in the intellect. He sowed these [properties] in the substance of man at the beginning of His creation, not later. First, so that man may know the truth, choose goodness, and work righteousness. In this way, the image imitates the archetype, God. Second, so that these may be good seed in man's nature, so that when one man multiplies into humankind, good plants may grow in all kinds of people with him. Third, so that all people may be equal to the first man through these [three properties], for we, too, are images of God, with goodness, truth, and righteousness being planted in our natures. Besides, God gave four establishing witnesses in the Holy Scriptures, both in the Old Testament and New, so that all the prophets, the Holy Gospel, the apostles, and the doctors may teach us the same thing—goodness, truth, and righteous acts. Then, therefore, it is clear why these four things—nature, will, intellect, and Holy Scripture—harmoniously guide us toward righteousness, as the Prophet Hosea says: "Sow to yourselves righteousness, and gather the fruit of life" (Hos 10:12). And this is so for four reasons.

First, because the Scripture says: "Every word may be established by two or three witnesses" (Mt 18:16). Now, there are various witnesses, so that they may teach us that righteousness is good and true beyond doubt. Second, these [witnesses] are many, so that should one of them err—be it the nature, the will, or the intellect—the other may straighten it, and should all err, the Holy Scripture may straighten them and lead them to truth. Third, because both external and internal factors antagonize us. Natural passion and lustful desire for sins are internal, for these lustful desires constantly go against our souls and minds, as the Apostle says: "I see another law in my members, warring against the law of my mind" (Rom 7:23). Satan and this world are the external antagonists; wherefore God planted in us natural righteousness to defeat natural

207

passions and the desires for sins, and He gave us externally the Holy Scriptures to defeat with them the devil and the worldly pleasures, because we would not have known that the devil and this world are our enemies, had the Holy Scriptures not told us so. Had it not been said in the Scripture: "You shall not commit adultery; you shall not steal" (Ex 20:14–15), we would not have known these sins. Fourth, these [witnesses] are many, so that if the Scriptures and the law stop short of teaching a person, nature, the will, or wisdom may teach us to do good, as the Apostle says: "The Gentiles, who have not the law, do by nature according to the law, for they are a law unto themselves" (cf. Rom 2:14), such as the justification of the first patriarchs—Abel, Enoch, Noah, Abraham, and all others. Nowadays, too, heathens who lack the written law of Moses or the Gospel have natural righteousness as law to them, because nature loves goodness and righteousness, and when they do not act according to the natural [law], [God] punishes and torments them in the body in this life and forever in the soul in the hereafter. It is for so many reasons that many things instruct us to act righteously: our nature, our will, our intellect, the prophets, the apostles, the Gospel, and the doctors, as the Prophet Hosea addresses us on behalf of God, saying: "Sow to yourselves righteousness, and gather the fruit of life" (Hos 10:12).

There are three questions to be asked in this regard. First, how is righteousness sowed and its fruits gathered? Second, why does [the Prophet] liken righteousness to seeds? Third, what is righteousness and how many kinds of it are there?

Concerning the first, it is to be known that a person gathers whatever he has sown, be it the seeds of wheat, or something else. In this present age, however, righteousness and life are not the same thing, because righteousness—the good action—is fulfilled by hardship and suffering, whereas life is tranquility and repose. Then, therefore, the fruit of life cannot be gathered by sowing righteousness. We argue that life and immortality are the fruit of the true seeds of righteousness. This is evident from three things. First, from the pattern of the seeds, for their properties are twofold—death and life, because they are first buried in the soil, then they die and decompose, and afterward sprout out, become alive, and grow. Similarly, righteousness has two properties—death and life, because when we sow righteousness in our souls and in our bodies, the good work comes to life and grows in us after the sins and evil works are killed and decomposed. Moreover, the righteous act kills the body and keeps the soul alive. Second, it is evident from the opposite, for when we grow the seeds of sins in us, they result in punishment and torment, both temporal and eternal. Therefore, life and immortality are the fruits and results of the seeds of righteousness. Third, it is evident from the testimonies of the Holy Scriptures, as Solomon says: "Possessions profit not in the day of wrath, but righteousness delivers from death" (Prov 11:4). The Lord says in the Gospel: "Strait and narrow is the way that leads unto life" (Mt 7:14). We should understand this in the following fashion: the seed of righteousness is hardship and anxiety to the body, but its fruit is eternal life. This was demonstrated through the people of ancient Israel, for when they sowed various sins in themselves, [God] consequently gave them captivity in Babylon: their land was destroyed, their temple was demolished, their kingdom fell, and they themselves were subjected to captivity. However, after they recognized their sins during captivity, repented, and turned to God, saying: "We have sinned, we have committed iniquity, we have transgressed, but now we follow you with all our hearts" (cf. Ps 106:6; Dan 3:41), they were delivered again from captivity, the temple was rebuilt, and they were reinstated in their former position. Whereby God told them: When you sowed sins, I wrathfully sowed in you captivity in Babylon, now sow in yourselves righteousness and gather for yourselves the fruits of life and peace, so that I may gather you again in your abodes. Similarly, in our case, when we sow sins, we shall gather the fruits of sins—famine, [death by] sword, captivity, diseases, and sudden death; but when we sow righteousness in ourselves, we gather its fruits—peace, health, tranquility, longevity, and a wealth for the soul and the body. This was in relation to the first article of the verse: "Sow to yourselves righteousness, and gather the fruit of life" (Hos 10:12).

[Concerning] the second question—why righteousness and good works are likened to seeds—we say [this has been so] for ten reasons.

First reason. Gathering comes on the heels of sowing, and to gather without sowing is impossible. Similarly, it is impossible for man to attain the repose or the kingdom without good works, because just as the cultivator first labors, then rests, and finally receives the wages, so too shall each person labor and do good works in this life, then rest with the saints after death, and finally receive the kingdom of heaven as a wage upon resurrection, as the Apostle says: "I have finished the works, I have kept the faith, henceforth there is laid up for me a crown of righteousness, which the Lord, the righteous judge, shall give me at that day" (2 Tim 4:7–8).

Second reason. Righteousness is likened to seed, because just as the sown seed is one, but it sprouts out and grows many [plants] and not one, so too shall the one righteous act generate multiplied rewards, as Christ promised: "Shall

209

receive a hundredfold, and shall inherit everlasting life" (Mt 19:29). Because for the one loaf you give the poor, you shall receive the food of immortality, for the cold water [you offer to the thirsty you shall receive] the fountain of life, for the one garment [you give] you shall receive the luminous tunic, and for the little suffering of your body [you endure you shall receive] the eternal repose. This is how the seed of righteousness produces multiplied rewards.

Third reason. Just as it is necessary to plow and loosen the soil before sowing—to plow means to dismantle and distance from you all the plants of sins and all that is excessive in you, to subject your soul and your body to God's law, and then sow the righteous acts in you so that they may bear fruits, as the Lord commanded: "The fertile ground brings forth fruits thirty-, sixty-, and hundredfold" (cf. Mt 13:23), but if you sow it [the seed] among the thorns in rough ground that has not been plowed, or by the wayside, or into stony places, it will not sprout, nor will it bear fruits—so will righteous acts not sprout, nor will they bear fruits if you sow them among many sins. Therefore, a person ought to cleanse the sins through confession before working righteousness.

Fourth reason. When sowing, a person needs to watch for two things: first, cover the seed so that birds may not pick it up; second, watch, so that the enemy may not sow weeds over the good seeds. Likewise, when sowing righteousness, see that you keep it covered by humility in you, in order to not let the devil pull out the good seeds from your heart, and then stay alert, because the devil mixes evil seeds with the good seeds in man—pride, anger, envy, avarice, and so on—because the devil's daily occupation is to either pull out the good seeds from man, or mix evil seeds in, as the parable of the Gospel says: "Did not you sow good seeds? Where, then, do the tares come from? He said, 'An enemy has done it'" (cf. Mt 13:27–28). For this reason, a pious person should always be ready, stay alert, and keep the good seeds.

Fifth reason. Just as the seed needs water and the heat of sun to sprout and grow, so too do tears make up the water that spouts righteous acts, and the love of God [makes up] the heat, because one ought to sow righteousness with warm love and tears, so that joy may be harvested. As David says: "They went on and wept as they cast their seeds; but they shall surely come with exultation, bringing their piled sheaves with them" (Ps 125:6).

Sixth reason. They that sow cast seeds before them, not behind. We, too, ought to sow righteousness during our life and not leave it to [be sowed in] the future by way of our relatives, our beloved offspring, our brothers, or anyone else, because no one loves you more than you, and your son shall do to you whatever you have done to your parents. Whereby the Apostle exhorts: "Now is the day of salvation, now is the accepted time. Give no reason in anything that your ministry be not stained" (cf. 2 Cor 6:2).

Seventh reason. They that sow, sow with the right hand and reap with the right; our right is our soul, and our left is our body; the work of the right hand is spiritual and of the left hand is physical. We ought to always sow righteousness in our souls and not sins in our bodies, because our soul is incorrupt with its seeds, whereas our body is corruptible with its seeds, as the Apostle says: "He that sows to his flesh shall of the flesh reap corruption; but he that sows to the soul shall of the soul reap incorruption" (cf. Gal 6:8).

Eighth reason. He that sows, sows by faith, because he believes that it will multiply; otherwise, he may not cast the seeds. Similarly, a person ought to work righteousness in faith, believing that Christ will reward all [good] works, whether fasting, praying, almsgiving, and so on, and therefore work more good works, as the Apostle says: "He that sows bountifully, shall also reap bountifully, and he that sows sparingly, shall also reap sparingly and scantily" (cf. 2 Cor 9:6). A seed stricken by a storm cannot give fruits; meaning, a disbeliever makes righteousness by imposition and unwillingly.

Ninth reason. Worthy seeds, such as wheat, are sown this year and reaped during the next, whereas unworthy seeds are sown and reaped in the same year, such as millet, barley, and so on. Similarly, the truly virtuous sow righteousness in this age and reap the everlasting glory in the hereafter, whereas hypocrites sow in this age and reap the glory from people in this age, as the Lord states: "That is all the reward they will get" (Mt 6:2).

Tenth reason. [People] sow in various seasons, such as during autumn and spring, and reap in one season, during summer; and they sow in various places but gather in one place at the threshing ground. Similarly, regardless of when a person makes good—childhood, adulthood, or old age—and regardless of where he does it—at home, on the road, in church, or in the outdoors—the harvest, the fruit, and the sheaves of all deeds will be during the one day of resurrection, and they will be gathered in the one threshing floor of the judgment. There the wheat will be separated from the chaff; meaning, the sins [will be set apart] from righteousness. It is then that Christ will separate the righteous and the sinners, as the Gospel says: "Whose fan of judgment is in his hand, and he will purge his threshing floor, and gather his wheat into the garner, but will burn up the chaff with unquenchable fire" (Mt 3:12). This was the second clause on why righteousness is likened to seeds.

The third question [explores] what is righteousness and how many kinds of righteousness are there. The philosophers define it thus: Righteousness is dispensational power commensurate to every person's worthiness. The doctors, however, define it thus: Righteousness is a person's undertaking of all kinds of virtues that he gathers in himself—prudence, fortitude, temperance, faith, hope, love, and other specific good things, whether moral, economic, or civil. This is righteousness.

There are three modes of righteousness. First, in the soul and in the body. Second, in this present life and in the hereafter. Third, in God and in man. Now, the first righteousness in the soul and in the body neither allows the body to ravish the soul nor does it let the soul [deprive] the body, because the body's ravishing the soul will be iniquity and a sinful act, and the soul's ravishing the body will be self-betrayal; a person of such nature is cruel to his body. What then? The body should moderately receive what is necessary to the body, such as bread, water, and clothing, whereas the soul should receive sanctity, [such as] fasting, praying, almsgiving, and so on. The soul is the image of God; [therefore] it should be honored first as its archetype [God is dignified], and then a person should honor the body, which reflects the earth and resembles the animals, because our bodies are made of earth and have senses like the animals: they [the bodies] eat, drink, and take pleasure like them [animals]. The soul is a master and grand lady, whereas the body is a servant, be it male or female. The body ought to obey the soul, and the soul [ought to] rule the body. The body is a cart and the soul is a driver, in the likeness of a horse and an equestrian. The soul should lead and the body should follow it; thus, there will be righteousness in the soul and the body, just as God created them. This is coined as the moral order of righteousness, but if you violate this order, prefer your body to your soul, and subject your soul to your body, the natural order will then be changed and there will be iniquity in them [the soul and the body]. The second mode of righteousness is in this life and in the hereafter. We need to perceive this life as temporal and mutable, but the hereafter as everlasting and immutable. Similarly, we should understand that everything in this life is temporal—glory, authority, wealth, pleasure, eating, drinking, and everything else, whereas everything in the hereafter is everlasting and eternal—life, wealth, kingdom, joy, immortality, and so on. Besides, as Solomon says: "To give a portion to seven, and also to eight is righteousness" (cf. Eccl 11:2). [A person should] know [that] this life is [the life] of animals, whereas the other is of angels and God; this [life] is time to work, whereas the other is for reward; this life [should be] detested, whereas the other cherished. This is righteousness and is referred to as natural righteousness. On the contrary, if you perceive this life as good and everlasting, cherish and take pleasure in this [life], and if you forget the other life, treat it as if it weighs light, and hold its share to yourself, you will be iniquitous, a ravisher, and sinful.

The third mode of righteousness is toward God and men. First, because we ought to believe that God has created everything and He created all creatures for man, and we [are created] as God's servants; also we should hope for His mercy, for "The eyes of all wait upon you; and you give them their food in due season" (Ps 145:15). Moreover, [we ought] to fear Him and keep all His commandments, whether in the old or the new laws. In addition to all of these, [we ought to] "Love God with all the heart, with all the soul, with all the mind, and with all the strength" (Mk 12:33), so that there would not be a partial love toward God and a partial love toward the world, the family, the possessions, or our bodies. Instead, love God absolutely above all other things and consider His command absolutely above all commands. This is referred to as divine righteousness.

The second [mode] of righteousness [in this category] is toward people and friends, as He commanded in the law: "You shall love your neighbor as yourself" (Lev 19:18), because you should love your friend as much as you love yourself. This is the first righteousness toward man. The second righteousness is to obey your superiors, be it by age, authority, knowledge, possessions, or other things. You shall honor them, obey them, and consider yourself second to them. Besides, you shall show compassion and care to your inferiors, be it by age, possessions, or knowledge, and you shall apportion to them from your wealth, be it knowledge, possession, position, or anything else. Moreover, for those who are your equal peers, having your age, name, position, and so on, you should be a non-envious friend and consider their goodness yours. This is righteousness, as the Apostle says: "Render to all their dues; fear to whom fear; custom to whom custom; tribute to whom tribute; and owe no man anything" (cf. Rom 13:7–8). The third righteousness toward man is in trading: to be fair in measuring, in weighing, in trades, in husbandry, in barter, and in taxes. Neither overprice nor underprice when trading, but estimate justly. Solomon says: "Both double measures, and double weights, and double cubits; that is, large and small are abomination to the Lord" (cf. Prov 20:10–23). Righteousness is to give what has been received in the same measure and weight. In trades, [righteousness consists of] not robbing the cultivator, being loyal to the masters, lending without interest, asking for the principal alone, [and paying] tax without retribution, for [people] will receive the retribution and interest of both from God. The fourth mode of righteousness relates to the tongue; do not lie, bear false witness, curse, insult, speak heresy, accuse, betray, or speak ill of man; rather, speak good and be truthful about everything. Also, [a person] has to fulfill his vow and not break it, if he has made one, to not lie, if he has promised to give [something] to someone; other similar things are the righteousness of the tongue. The fifth [mode] is the righteousness of judges, primates, and rulers, for judges should judge righteously and not distort the judgment based on consideration, partiality, fear, or any other reason, because judgment is of God and the Lord says: "Judge righteous judgment" (Zech 7:9). Moreover, primates should treat their followers, the doctors their apprentices, the rulers their countries, and the masters their servants with righteousness, and they should not demand of them more than what is due. Furthermore, it is righteousness to provide for the food and needs of the cattle and animals, and to not burden them beyond their capacity. Solomon says: "A righteous man has pity for the cattle" (Prov 12:10). The judged should obey the judges regardless of their verdict, the apprentices [should obey] their doctors, and the servants [should obey] their masters, as the Apostle decrees: "Servants, obey your masters, not to serve unwillingly, but in singleness of heart" (Col 3:22), as we have mentioned earlier. The sixth [mode of] righteousness is between a husband and wife, so that they may keep their bed undefiled, for the Apostle says: "Marriage is honorable, and the bed undefiled" (Heb 13:4). They should behave not by frequent lasciviousness, nor by ravishing one another; rather, by honest and temperate marriage, in accordance with the canons of the church. It is also righteousness to take care of the offspring and relatives. Moreover, [it is righteousness] to keep the kindred, the spiritual relatives through the font, and the lawful relatives, such as guardians, and to not mix with one another by impurity; rather, keep [them] in purity, in accordance with the Christian law and the canons of the holy doctors. This constitutes righteousness and purity. Besides, I will briefly mention that there is an act of righteousness in every part of us, so that the eye may see without stain, the ear may hear with fairness and without deceit, the mind may think justly and without twist, the will may choose goodness without wickedness, and [a person] may speak justly, drink justly, gather justly, share justly, work justly, walk justly, and straighten all things in his life justly. This is what constitutes sowing righteousness and reaping afterward the goodness of everlasting life in our Lord Jesus Christ who is blessed forever, amen.

CHAPTER XXVIII

Homily of the same on righteousness according to David's verse: "The Lord is righteous, and loves righteousness; and his face beholds uprightness" (Ps 11:7).

God is good and benevolent by nature. He wanted to grant man all His goodness, because "God created man in his own image" (Gen 1:27), and created him as a partaker of His likeness and image. He also acquainted man with His goodness. Now, God gave us many good things, such as light, life, immortality, reason, wisdom, and so on. He also granted us righteousness as one of the many good things, as the Prophet says: "The Lord is righteous, and loves righteousness" (Ps 10:8), because God loves and wills everything that is good, and God gives humankind everything He loves and wills. Again, as the Prophet says: "God is holy, and lives in the holies" (cf. Ps 99:9, 22:3). Likewise, "God is righteous, and loves righteousness; God is upright, and his face beholds uprightness" (cf. Ps 10:8). However, God detests iniquity and deviousness; He does not provide for and does not want people to do these [iniquitous and devious acts]; instead, God wants and provides for what is righteous and upright in us. To this the Prophet refers [by saying]: "The Lord is righteous, and loves righteousness; and his face beholds uprightness" (Ps 10:8).

Now, righteousness by definition is moderation, because righteousness is neither absolutely good nor absolutely evil by nature, for righteousness sometimes inclines toward evil and sometimes toward good. It inclines toward evil when people possess false and corporeal righteousness, which is righteousness only within a person and lacks mercy. Referring to righteousness of this nature, Solomon says: "Be not very just; neither be very wise; lest you be confounded" (Eccl 7:17). Righteousness that is good and is inclined toward goodness comes with mercy, for mercy is altogether better than righteousness. Wherefore, whenever the prophets spoke of God's righteousness, [they] referred to Him not only as righteous but also as merciful; hence: "God is pitiful, merciful, and righteous" (Ps 112:4). Also: "I will sing you, O Lord, of mercy and judgment" (Ps 100:1). Also: "Mercy and truth shall go before him" (Ps 89:14), because God's righteousness comes with mercy, and mercy comes with righteousness, and none of these without the other. Sometimes, however,

215

mercy is apparent and righteousness is hidden, and the act of righteousness appears among us in a similar fashion. Righteousness is good and useful when it is combined with mercy, and righteousness is useful but inclines toward evil when it is not combined with mercy. Righteousness by itself, when lacking mercy, is the righteousness of the old covenant and is corporeal; that is, "to give eye for eye, and tooth for tooth" (Ex 21:23–24), in accordance with Moses' commandments.

This [kind of righteousness] was short of justifying man for two reasons. First, because they [people of the old covenant] were unable to fulfill the law, and they would have been liable to the law; as the Apostle says, the old law confined everybody to sin. Second, because the covenant was corporeal and weak, and not capable of justifying man. This is the righteousness of the ordinances. Christ's righteousness of grace, however, is combined with mercy, whereby it is good and useful, because there are four kinds of worthless and useless righteousness. First, the righteousness of the ordinances that stipulate: "Love those who love you, hate your enemies, repay evil for evil and good for good, and lend and then receive the balance." All such [provisions] are the righteousness of the old covenant, of the Saracens, of the judges of the world, and those who purchase, sell, and so on. These are corporeal and meaningless, spiritually considered. The righteousness of grace, however, that is useful and was commanded by Christ, is: "To lend to someone without the anticipation of receiving, to love your enemy, to bless those who curse you, to do good to those who hate you, to pray for those who abuse you, and so on" (cf. Lk 6:27–28). A righteousness of this nature is good and spiritual, because it is mercy, compassion, and love, and, therefore, useful. Second, there is also a different kind of righteousness that is worthless and evil: when Tephthah killed his daughter to keep his vow, his act did not please God and He judged him with manslayers, for he had held his word above bloodshed. Herod, on his part, beheaded John the Baptist to keep his promise and therefore worms ate him and he died. Similarly, if someone vows to do mischief, kill himself or others, or do evil and harm people, and if he keeps his promise for the sake of righteousness, that is evil and [spiritually] worthless righteousness. Third, there is [another spiritually] worthless righteousness, such as the corporeal cleanliness. The Jews observed the Sabbaths and washed the drinking and eating vessels while they were deviated from God's law and the elders' tradition. Presently, the Saracens observe the corporeal cleanliness, the ablution of the feet, hands, and body, and the cleanliness of the clothes and abodes, and yet these are useless for the soul, because these are corporeal and [spiritually] worthless. As the Lord stated: "You make clean the outside of the cup, but your inward part is rapacity and malice" (cf. Lk 11:39). These, He says, "are like whitened sepulchers, which look beautiful from the outside, but are within full of dead men's bones and stench" (Mt 23:27); meaning, their bodies and clothes are washed and cleansed from filth, and yet their souls are full of dead works and stinky sins. This kind of cleanliness is worthless, for God loves purity, as the Lord says: "O hypocrites, first cleanse your souls from within, that the outside also may be clean, for the pure in heart shall see God" (cf. Mt 23:26 and 5:8). Fourth, there is also [spiritually] worthless righteousness within the Christian church, which the Apostle prohibited [by saying]: "Some stricken by their conscience, forbidding to marry, and commanding to abstain from food, which God has given for the enjoyment of the faithful" (cf. 1 Tim 4:3). That is, certain Novatian heretics made their way into the church and proclaimed that marriage is corrupt, spiritual nourishment is corrupt, and there is no postresurrection forgiveness for sins. Wherefore, the Apostle wrote: "Marriage is honorable, and the bed undefiled, but fornicators and adulterers God will judge" (Heb 13:4). There is no corruption in the nourishments sanctified by God and allowed in the law. "But it is evil for those who eat with guilty conscience," it is said (Rom 14:20). Note here that if those who love virginity do so for the sake of purity and for the sake of the kingdom of heaven, [their deed] is acceptable, as the Gospel states: "There are eunuchs that have made themselves eunuchs for the sake of God" (cf. Mt 19:12). However, if [virginity] is natural, or [people] are made eunuchs by people, or if they say that marriage is impure, these are wicked and dishonored in the Holy Scripture. Similarly, if they refrain from eating meat or other animal food in order to torment their body, this is acceptable, for the Apostle says: "Though our outward man that is the body is being worn down, yet the inward man that is the soul receives fresh strength" (cf. 2 Cor 4:16). If, however, a man refrains from eating meat or drinking wine because he considers these impure, he commits deadly sin and is ranked with the heretics. Now, righteousness tainted and presented in this fashion is not true; rather, it is pretentious, such as the silver-colored tin and lead that are not truly silver, pure and clean. Similarly, these are not true righteousness; rather, they are false and imitative, wherefore [Solomon] the Wise said: "Be not very just, neither be very wise: lest you be confounded" (Eccl 7:17). As has been said, these are the four [kinds of] worthless righteousness that push man and drive him closer to evil than good. But righteousness that stems from the grace of Christ and is combined with mercy, compassion, and love for the neighbors is good and noble for the very reason [of being combined], as the Prophet says: "The Lord is righteous, and loves righteousness; and his face beholds uprightness" (Ps 11:7). We ought to know this: the good and noble righteousness can become evil and worthless, as [Solomon] the Wise says: "There is righteousness perished in its own righteousness, and there is an ungodly man remaining in his wickedness" (Eccl 7:16).

Solomon, whom God made wise and who examined man's behavior, intentions, and works, and who thought which of these were worthy or unworthy, examined also the righteous and the ungodly, and said: There are righteous men who live in righteousness and yet lose their righteousness, and there are ungodly men who are surrounded with malice, yet they live spiritually and lose their own wickedness. A pattern of this we find, first, in the Gospel through what has been said about the Pharisee and the publican. Although the Pharisee was righteous according to the law, when he boastfully and arrogantly cited his righteous works, [saying]: "I fast twice in the week, and give tithes of all that I possess, and I am not like this publican" (Lk 18:13), he was condemned. Whereas the publican, facing the ground and venturing not to raise his eyes to heaven, smote upon his breast, saying: "God be merciful to me, a sinner" (Lk 18:13). Now, this ungodly man went down to his house justified because of his humility, whereas the Pharisee went to his house with his sins because of his boastful arrogance. Thus, every righteous person that is adept in fasting, praying, almsgiving, asceticism, lying down on the ground, and so on, but has the vice of pride, will lose and defile his righteous works. For example, an impure animal that falls in a container full of holy food spoils the entire content; likewise, arrogance defiles and destroys righteous works upon entering the soul, whereas the sinner rids himself of his sins and is delivered through repentance, confession, and good works. Wherefore, it was said in Proverbs: "A humble sinner is better than a proud righteous [person]" (cf. Prov 7:8), because [a person] sometimes wants to repent humbly for evil things and bow under the law of God. A proud righteous person, however, thinks he is always righteous, stays in the same evil things, and does not yield to the commands of God, the canons of the saints, and the exhortations of the fathers [of the church], thereby destroying himself and his righteous works. The statement also refers to the Jewish people who considered themselves righteous and lawful, and refuted Christ, saying that they have laws and act according to the laws, as the Apostle says: "They being ignorant of God's righteousness, and seeking to establish their own righteousness" (Rom 10:3), because not knowing which righteousness was pleasing to God, they worked their own corporeal righteousness and did not receive the grace of righteousness from Christ, wherefore they were condemned, for [their] law ceased after Christ's crucifixion.

Doctors say that with Christ's crucifixion the law fell ill, and when the Holy Spirit descended upon the apostles and renewed the new law, the old law perished and disappeared; henceforth, those who fulfill the old law are equal to pagans and disbelievers. For example, the moon and the stars cast light at night and cease to illuminate after sunrise. Similarly, the law of Moses cast light like the moon, and other prophets made the darkness of our life brighter like stars; but when the sun of righteousness—our Lord Jesus Christ—rose, the obscure laws were abolished, as God said through the Prophet: "To those who fear my name shall rise the sun of righteousness" (Mal 4:2). The [old] laws and paradigms were thus eliminated in us and became void by the coming of the grace and truth.

Concerning these, Solomon says: "There is righteousness perished in its own righteousness" (Eccl 7:16). The pagans, who had given themselves to disbelief and evil works, were ungodly. When the apostles preached, they [pagans] believed in Christ and were justified through the grace of Christ. They replaced disbelief with faith, and wickedness with the grace of righteous works, as the Apostle says: "Christ is the end of the law for righteousness to everyone that believes" (Rom 10:4). Henceforth, those who believe in Christ will be justified by the grace of Christ, and those who do not believe cannot be justified, because justice and salvation for man are from Christ, and the Gospel says: "He that obeys not the Son shall not see life, but the wrath of God rests upon him" (Jn 3:36).

It is evident, then, that although a disbeliever, a Saracen, and a Jew might do many good things, all will be useless and vain, and they will have no salvation. This [is so] for two reasons. First, because faith is the foundation of good works and the works are constructions arranged upon them; whatever lacks a strong foundation is incapable of holding a construction. Second, because Christ is the salvation, whoever does not believe in Christ cannot receive His salvation. Solomon testifies in Ecclesiastes to this effect: "Wisdom will help the wise man more than ten princes that are in the city" (Eccl 7:20). Doctors interpret this statement in many different ways. First, wisdom consists of looking to God, knowing God, and believing [in God]. This wisdom is more capable of helping man to spiritually resist the battling demons than the troops and weapons of princes trying to defend a city against its enemies and failing to help man's soul, just as God helped the three young men stay unburned in the fire, while the corporeal troops were helpless. Likewise, [God] helped David in the pit against the lions that dared not approach him. Wisdom also constitutes the faith and hope we have in Christ who helped those who believed in Him more than the Ten Commandments that were placed in the city of Israel; that is, among the Jews, because the [old] laws were unable to justify man. [This is so], first, because [the old law] was weak and corporeal. Second, because [men] were unable to fulfill the law, for it was hard: "Eye for eye, and teeth for teeth" (Ex 21:24). They were therefore indebted to the law, and the law confined everybody to the sins, as we have mentioned. Righteousness was accomplished through Christ, since we were justified through the free grace of Christ.

That Christ's grace justifies us freely is evident from two things. First, when the people of olden times and the disbelievers of various ages come to the grace of Christ, believe [in Him], and baptize, they will find forgiveness for all their sins and be justified by the grace of Christ. Second, it is evident from the following: when [people] after baptism commit again all kinds of sins, then come and confess repentantly, they will find forgiveness for their sins and be justified by the grace of Christ. It is evident, then, that the grace of Christ helped us more than the Ten Commandments of the law of Moses. Again, the Apostle says: "Christ is the power of God, and the wisdom of God" (1 Cor 1:24). He helps those acquainted with the grace of Christ more than the ten senses of the soul and the body that rule in the city of our nature, because man is a living city and his internal senses—the mind and the will—are rulers of the city, whereas the external senses—eyes, ears, hands, and so on—are their troops; they fulfill whatever the mind commands.

Now, Christ has become greater in power and wisdom in us than our ten senses for two reasons. First, because we sinned with our internal and external senses and God's glory was diminished in us, but through Christ, we were justified and received glory. Second, because we were strengthened and received wisdom in the mutable and perishable temporal life with these senses, whereas through Christ, we gained strength and wisdom in the spiritual, everlasting, and imperishable life. It is evident, then, that Christ's wisdom helped us more than our entire wisdom. The holy church and our guardian angels also are rulers, for some rule and protect the saints, others [protect] the church, and others protect the rulers of peoples and cities, as the Prophet David said: "Your friends, O God, have been greatly honored by me; their rulers that are the angels have been greatly strengthened; I will number them, and they shall be multiplied beyond the sand" (cf. Ps 138:17–18). Elsewhere, he [David] says: "The angels of the Lord will encamp round about them that fear him, and will protect them" (Ps 34:7).

Now these, the myriad angels, are thus protectors of men, but Christ's help is superior to those that are our rulers and protectors. This [is so] for two reasons. First, because those who surround us can serve us in protecting us from the accidents of the evil thoughts of sins, but it is Christ's blood that cleanses us from fatal sins and the conscience of the mind, because our angels cannot justify us from sins; they can [only] protect us from evil thoughts. Christ's help, however, protects us from the accidents of demons and cleanses us, as the Prophet says: "The Lord is our keeper, and the Lord will receive by his right hand. The Lord shall keep our coming in and going out from henceforth and unto eternity" (cf. Ps 120:5–8). Second, because the angels cannot justify and deliver us from hell, but our Lord himself came and justified us, and delivered our souls from hell and our bodies from the evil servitude to sins. As Isaiah says: "Not an ambassador, nor a messenger, but the Lord himself will come and save us" (cf. Isa 63:9).

[As to] why [God] did not save us through messengers, doctors cite the following reasons. First, had a messenger come to save us, we would have bowed before our savior, and that would have been a grave pagan blasphemy, because it is written: "You shall bow only before your Lord God, and you shall worship him alone" (cf. Ex 20:3–4). The Lord himself, whom we worshipped and bowed before, saved us, "and all that dwell upon the earth, whether heavenly or worldly, shall worship him" (cf. Rev 13:8). Again, the salvation and justification of people required unlimited power. Angels are created and [therefore] have limited power; created beings cannot justify and save [other] created beings. For this reason, God the uncreated Word Himself, possessing almighty power, took body from the holy and immaculate virgin, became perfect man in the soul, in the body, and in the mind, justified us through our body, and saved us from the authority of darkness. Therefore, may He make us worthy of his saints and of those who love His name, whereby glory and lordship befits the almighty Father and the Savior Holy Spirit forever and ever, amen.

CHAPTER XXIX

Homily of the same on righteousness according to David's verse: "I have done judgment and justice; deliver me not up to them that injure me" (Ps 118:121).

At the beginning, [God] created man good and righteous, without sins, and put him in the Garden of Eden—a place of righteousness. Evil and sins became intrinsic to man's nature later. This is evident from six testimonies. First, the Scripture says: "God made man in his own image, and in the image of God he created him" (Gen 1:27). That is, He created man good and righteous in the likeness of His goodness and righteousness, because there was nothing sinful or evil in man's body, soul, and mind, so that he may imitate the prime Creator with his innocence. Second, it is evident from the form, because man has an upright structure, and he is not bowed or abased. This means that man's soul was upright, his mind was [directed] upwardly toward God, and he did not have any deviousness or inclination for sins. Third, it is evident from the cleanliness of the body, because man's body is not covered like other animals with hair, wings, or scale; rather, it is clear and exempt from all such things. This signifies the purity of the soul and mind, which God created without the cover of sins. Fourth, it is evident from the fact that many men kept themselves pure and righteous, such as the patriarchs, Abraham, Isaac, Jacob, Job, Moses, and other prophets and holy fathers. Had our nature been subject to sin, they would not have been able to be justified from sin, for these [sins] would have been united to man's nature as part of it. Fifth, it is evident from our Lord Jesus Christ, because God the Word took human nature: perfect soul, body, and mind, and kept the natural passions [of men] without sins, suffered hunger, thirst, sweat, and physical labor, and voluntarily endured the grievance and awe of the soul without sins. [He did so] to embarrass humankind, so that people may not say our bodies and souls are subject to sin. [He did so] also to embarrass Satan the enemy that falsely claimed that we, humans, are subject to sin by nature. He showed that man's nature was created without sin from the beginning. Sixth, it is evident from Solomon's words: "God made man upright; but they have sought out many thoughts" (Eccl 7:30), meaning man's soul, body, and mind are righteous and innocent from his birth.

222

Where did then the sins and evil things in our nature come from? He [Solomon] mentions: "They have sought many thoughts" (Eccl 7:30); that is, they have sought out and committed good and evil things alike by their own free will. Take the patriarchs, for example: Abraham and his sons and their descendants sought and followed faithful piety and goodness. Many pagans and many wicked and sluggish people of the nation of Jews preferred ungodliness and evil works, and they followed iniquity, because people commit sins for six reasons. First, because of the deceit of Satan that is the cause of all evil things, wherefore he is referred to as the author of all evil things. He deceived the first man from the beginning and made him fall in sins. He [Satan] is the origin and cause of the destruction of all people, for he stirs and encourages man to envy, be proud, get angry, fornicate, steal, murder, and commit diverse sins. For this reason, the Lord says: "Satan was murderer from the beginning" (Jn 8:44), since Satan encourages man to commit all kinds of sins, be it in the thoughts, the soul, the body, or the desires. The second cause of sins is the free will of man, since we choose and commit sins by our will, although they are not imposed upon us. Man acts according to his own will, because he has authority and control over evil and good. Third, man commits sins because of the deceit of wicked friends, for man's behavior is such that if he happens to be in a good environment with good instructors and good friends, he learns goodness from them and works goodness; hence: "I was a witty child, and a good soul fell to my lot" (Wis 8:19); but if he happens to be in a wicked environment with wicked instructors and wicked friends, he will learn wickedness and evil works from their deception and will be an evildoer. For this reason, Christians should not live among the wicked and the followers of other religions, as God instructs through the Prophet: "Go out from them and depart; and do not approach the unclean things" (Isa 52:11). Fourth, there is the pleasure of sins and becoming accustomed to them, because when man takes pleasure of and becomes accustomed to sins, he indiscriminately does evil, presuming it is good: the pleasure and the practice of sins become a tie to bond the man with sins, as the Prophet says: "The senses of sins entangled me" (Ps 118:61). Fifth, there is the natural inclination of the body, "that is established in our members and is fond of sins contrary to the law of our minds" (cf. Rom 7:23), and that at an opportune moment reveals the hidden and commits evil. For this reason, God said through Noah: "The imagination of men is intently bent upon evil things from their youth" (Gen 8:21); meaning, it is natural for man to love the delightful desire of sins from his youth. Sixth, one commits sins when he is not supervised, nor is he punished, because had he been punished for the sins he committed, he would have become fearful and cease committing them; but he commits sins indiscriminately when he is not exhorted and scorned on the spot. Moreover, he thinks himself surrounded by health, success, and joy, as David says: "Behold! These are sinners and they prosper; they live and possess wealth in this world" (Ps 73:12).

Besides, if he finds someone else exhorted by God, he remains indifferent. First, because he assumes that he is not involved in evil and [therefore] does not consider [what happens] to others. Also, some find excuses for [what happens after] others' sins, [claiming] that they deserve it. Man, thus, works evil in six ways and is unwilling to repent and turn. [Concerning] what the proverb says: "He that does justice is assisted" (Prov 28:18), [know] now that the righteous man is assisted from six sides—three external and three internal. Externally, our help comes, first, from God; hence: "O God, draw nigh to my help" (Ps 70:12). Second, angels assist us to do good; hence: "The angel that kept me from my youth" (cf. Gen 48:15–16). Third, God's laws assist man like a pillar of a house and the walls of a city, as Isaiah says: "I adorned it with vine-arbor and fenced it" (Isa 5:2); meaning, by the law. Fourth, internally, our nature helps and assists the righteous, because it rather obeys the soul than antagonizes it. For example, an assembled cart is ready to move; similarly, the body yields to a holy work. Fifth, the conscience assists [man]; it rather leads him unto peace than blame him. Sixth, the good work itself fills us with joy and strengthens us in doing justice.

These six assistants help the righteous in six directions through six motions in the following fashion. From above, God is our assistant. From the right hand, the angel. From the front, the law of God, which moves forward toward goodness. From down under, the body assists and obeys the soul. From the left hand, conscience assists, and from behind, the good works help [man]. Thus, righteousness finds help, surrounded from all directions. Whereas those who turn away from righteousness and go astray become surrounded and infected by sins from all directions, because the law of the body opposes them and captures and pulls them into sins, and the judging conscience makes man face the ground because sinful works are pleasant, weak, and heavy. Similarly, externally the demon, the world, and the desires pull man into sins and witnesses dishonor him, the ravished cry out, and [the sinner] always remains among them infected and bitter, because the light of reason perhaps is still ardent in his conscience and God's prudence balances his judgment, [whereby] he examines and understands the deviousness of sins, and suffers for this. He is not like the ungodly and foolish whose light [of reason] is quenched and balance of prudence is destroyed, the eyes are blind, the ears are deaf, the nose is stripped of distinguishing [ability], the mouth is tasteless, and the hands are benumbed; he cannot feel. He commits sin with ease and pleasure. [Solomon] says: "A fool does mischief in laughter" (Prov 10:23). May Christ the God guide our behavior, so that by doing his will, we may deserve the eternal life in our Lord Jesus Christ, glory to whom forever, amen.

CHAPTER XXX

Homily of the same on righteousness in trading and measuring according to the verse of Proverbs: "False balances are abomination before the Lord; but a just weight is acceptable to him" (Prov 11:1).

The Prophet says: "The Lord is righteousness, and loves righteousness; his face beholds uprightness" (Ps 11:7). Therefore, He wants us to work righteous works, and keep our minds and faith righteous and upright. Why does God love righteousness? First, because He created the first man righteous by nature, whereas iniquity is derivative and was associated with us later through Satan. For this reason, [God] wants to bring us to the initial righteousness through our works. Second, because righteousness is innate vitality: when the elements are distributed equally within us, we are healthy and alive, whereas iniquity that came to us unevenly is sickness and death. For this reason, God wants righteousness—vitality and health, and not iniquity—death and deficiency. Third, because righteous works lead to the everlasting life of the righteous— immortality; whereas iniquity leads into the everlasting torment—hell; the place of Satan the iniquitous. [God] wants our righteousness, because He is righteous, righteousness is the origin of creation, and righteousness is what sustains life. Righteousness guides the righteous in this life and makes them reach [in the everlasting life]. As he [Solomon] says: "False balances are abomination before the Lord; but a just weight is acceptable to him" (Prov 11:1). For this reason, God commanded through Moses: "You shall not have a great and a small measure or weight; they shall be equal" (cf. Deut 25:14–15).

Similarly, in natural civil law, [people] found a paradigm of justice through wisdom—balance, measure, and cubit. The balance equates the qualitative aspect of the heaviness and lightness [of an item] for the eyesight. The cubit, likewise, measures quantities, while the measure counts the substance. Thus, witnessing by our eyes their righteous work, we keep righteousness in our mind numerically, so that iniquity may not make its way into us from outside or inside. The benefits and gains of equal balances and measures are many. First, civil law and good order remain intact and beautiful thanks to the equality of balances and measures. Second, the strangers by hearing about the equal balances of a city come in, and the residents labor with confidence, thus

226

increasing their prosperity and gains. Third, barren and fruitless substances continuously grow, produce, and give results if sold by measure and balance. Fourth, the prosperity of cities is based on the equal profit of traders, for the seller earns the price and the buyer earns the substance, and thus cities prosper. Fifth, with an equal balance neither the poor nor the ignorant or the little one can be ravished by the wealthy. Sixth, taking and giving, and exchanging and remunerating are adjusted by these [standards]. Seventh, the tributes and services rendered to the kings and rulers are regulated by these [standards]. Eighth, the rewards and wages of the wealthy to the humble are measured by measurement. Ninth, the prosperity of families and the costs of wages are adjusted in accordance with the measurement of income and expenditure. Tenth, there is no greater spiritual benefit and gain than recalling righteousness through these [standards] if we have forgotten it otherwise. For this reason [Solomon] says: "A just weight is acceptable to God." Those, however, who cheatingly upset the just balance and seek gain from iniquity—when they practice double standards and take by the greater [standard] and give by the lesser—are abominable before God, because they disdain God's ordinances: "You shall not have a great or a small measure or weight" (cf. Deut 25:14). These [cheaters] also violate the civil law, for the law instructs receiving fair profit in trading rather than unfair.

The fair profit is of four kinds. First, in relation to a precious substance, if it is expensive. Second, in relation to the price and rate that is common to the country. Third, in relation to the locality. Fourth, in relation to time. Certain things are inexpensive at this time and expensive at some other time, [or] inexpensive in one place and expensive elsewhere. Profits such as these are fair and lawful in trading. However, whoever charges a high price to a needy person, overprices something that has lesser worth, demands a rate that exceeds the common rate, or puts less in the balance and confirms [the opposite] by swearing falsely receives an iniquitous profit, which rather is a loss, the eternal fire, and the burning of the soul than a gain. Wherefore [Solomon] says: "False balances are abomination before God" (Prov 11:1).

Such a person is abominable before God through ten major sins. First, because whoever cheats man deceives God whose image he has deceived. Second, because he does not believe that God knows every action; hence: "God is not before him. His ways are profane at all times" (Ps 10:4–5). Third, because he does not believe in God's judgment, that he will be punished with thieves. Fourth, because he is more wicked than a thief: a thief steals covertly and fearfully, whereas he [steals] explicitly seated in his booth, which is conceived to be a thief's yard. Fifth, because people avoid robbers when they hear about them, whereas they approach him [the iniquitous trader] as a beloved good person. Sixth, because a thief steals somebody's belongings [only] once, whereas he [the iniquitous trader] steals from the same person and deceives him time and again. Seventh, because the robber kills the bodies of other people, whereas he [the iniquitous trader] kills his own soul, subjecting it to hell; and just as the soul is greater than the body, so too is greater his death. Eighth, because he demonstrates greed, "which is idolatry," as the Apostle says (Col 3:5). Ninth, because he uses God's name in vain and commits [forsworn] perjury for which Christ commanded: "Swear not at all" (Mt 5:34). Tenth, because he makes those who falsely witness accomplices in his sins; and since they [accomplices] testify for him, they receive punishment with the false witnesses of Christ who deceived Pilate and were punished by the eternal fire, for the proverb says: "A false witness shall not be unpunished" (Prov 19:9).

The statement [that false balances are abomination before God] can also be understood in a different way. We may understand that people whom the Prophet referred to by saying, "The sons of man are vain, and they are deceitful in balances" (Ps 62:9), are the just balance acceptable to God, because the balance is man's free will: the soul and the body equally hang from it; the beam is the righteous mind and understanding; the two pans stand for the soul and the body; the three or four strings [signify that] the soul is composed of three parts and the body of the four elements; and the weight is the law of God and our deeds that equate to the law. Now, the free will should not allow the body and the soul to overcome one another, because that is abomination before God. If the body defeats the soul by evil sins, and if the soul defeats and slays the body, both will be corrupt and sentenced to death; but if [the free will] keeps them equal within the limits of the law and measures, it is acceptable [to God]. Otherwise, if the body defeats the soul, listen to what the Apostle said: "The widow who is self-indulgent is dead while she lives" (1 Tim 5:6), because [when] "Jacob was waxed fat and grew thick, he forsook God" (cf. Deut 32:15). If the soul defeats the body, listen again to what the Apostle told the disciples: "Drink no longer water, but take a little wine because of recurring illness" (cf. 1 Tim 5:23), because just as a soldier's horse should not be overly spirited so that it may not fall down, nor should it be lacking enough spirit, so that it may not lose strength, likewise the body [should not be] tender altogether, so that the soul may not revolt against it, nor should it be weak altogether, so that it may not cease to worship God. It [should be] moderate and balanced in accordance with the limits of the law. This is good.

Should a person argue that we cannot keep the soul and the body balanced, because, first, the soul is the image of God and the body of the earth; second, the Apostle says: "When I am weak, then I am strong; for when we are strong externally, then we are weak internally, [etc.]" (cf. 2 Cor 12:10); and third, we see numerous martyrs who tormented their bodies with excessive fasting, asceticism, martyrdom, and so on, and these disturb the balance. We say that the just balance is not complying sometimes with the will of the soul and sometimes with the will of the body, nor is it being pleased by the body while suffering by the soul, or blessing once and cursing once. These do not constitute a just balance; rather, they are iniquity. Justice is this: At the beginning, God created the first man altogether good in the body and the soul; there was not a single evil part in him—neither in the soul, nor in the body. He gave him the commandments of the law as just balance, which would have lifted him to the highest point in heaven, had he kept them. When he violated them, he became burdened with sins and fell into the lowest part on earth.

The following is now the just balance in us: to keep the soul and the body altogether in the same original goodness, and to ascend through the balance of the commandments unto the heavens. This is called just balance. Besides, there is a legal balance: to equally adjust our minds, words, and works to the commandments and to do as the law commands us. In addition, there is a personal balance: when we often bear within us the just balance of behavior and expressions, and burden ourselves with good works, the mind becomes liberated, rises, and touches God. When we reduce the weight of good things and diminish them in us, our minds incline downward and bind with the earth. Furthermore, there is a brotherly balance: to love him [the neighbor] as much as you love yourself; hence: "You shall love your neighbor as yourself" (Mt 19:19). Again, it is [a just balance] when after you see someone in wealth and glory, contrary to your condition, you thank God for having given him that, and you do not envy him; this is a brotherly balance. Thus there are many designations to the balance.

Now we will answer the questions.

Concerning the first [argument] that keeping the soul and the body equal is rather iniquity than righteousness, because the soul is master and the body servant: equalizing the master with the servant is great injustice, we say: The matter should be regulated in the following fashion. The body should be given its needs as servant, the soul should be given its needs as master, and the body should always be kept inferior to the soul; this is the natural and moral righteousness and regulation. Concerning the second [argument], we say that when the Apostle talks about weakening the body and strengthening the soul, he does not refer to weakening the nature; rather, he addresses the passions and [iniquitous] works, because when the passions of the body and the works of corruption lose their strength in us, the soul gains the strength and ability to act. Concerning the third [argument about] those who torment the body excessively and are martyred, we say that there are balances of love, borrowing, and remuneration.

Now, some fulfill the balance of love and suffer for the sake of loving Christ, preferring the love of Christ the God to themselves and considering the eternal life better than the temporal and perishable [life]. The balance of remuneration is that Christ suffered and was crucified for our sake, [therefore] we die and become crucified for Christ; some suffered in this way with the retributory balance. Some [fulfilled] the balance of borrowing; that is, they devoted themselves to an ascetic life for the sake of the postmortem life, subjected themselves to suffering so that they may rest, showed mercy "so that they may obtain mercy" (Mt 5:7), and killed their bodies so that they vitalize their souls. Thus, they all attained the balance of righteousness, for there is no charity beyond this; wherefore he says: "A just weight is acceptable before God" (Prov 11:1). He compensates all according to their balance and wage of labor: "a measure running over, pressed down, according to the true promise of the truth" (cf. Lk 6:38). May our merciful and benevolent Lord Christ the God make us partakers of the legacy of his saints, and glory unto him with his Father and the Holy Spirit forever, amen.

CHAPTER XXXI

Homily of the same on privation, according to Ecclesiastes: "I saw oppression under the sun and the tears of those oppressed, and they had no one to comfort them" (Eccl 4:1).

Oppression or deprivation is one of the numerous and diverse sins committed by man. [It occurs] when a person deprives another and places him under unwarranted condemnation. The devil, however, is the first and truly iniquitous being toward and dispossessor of man. Man follows [the devil and deprives] indirectly, because it is the devil that entices man to commit murder, theft, adultery, and various other sins. For this reason, he [the devil] is the first iniquitous toward and depriver of people. For example, a wicked ruler thinks wickedly and commands the executioner to slay a man. Now, the first killer is the ruler who commanded the killing, and the second [killer] is the executioner who fulfilled his [ruler's] will and did the killing. Likewise, the devil is the source of all human wickedness, for he exhorts and lures us toward wickedness, as the Lord says: "Satan was murderer from the beginning" (Jn 8:44). This is what is meant by: "God did not create death. Through the envy of the devil death came into the world" (Wis 2:24), because Satan deceived and killed the first man physically and spiritually. Again, it says: "from the beginning" (Jn 8:44), because the devil is the origin and source of all sins, and man's soul and body die through sins, wherefore Solomon says: "I saw oppression under the sun and the tears of those oppressed" (Eccl 4:1). He says he saw oppression and iniquity under the sun, meaning among people on earth and not among angels in heaven, where righteousness and justice prevail. Again, under the sun; meaning, during our lifetime, because after this life there is no privation and iniquity; rather, there is righteousness and truth. He [Solomon] says he saw the senselessness of people whose minds are darkened, who jump on each other like beasts, and [who] deprive one another by tearing each other apart. They have forgotten that they are destined to die, their life will end like irrational being, and they will turn into dust. They have also forgotten that death will deprive them of their own and lawful properties, and they shy not from depriving their neighbor. They impose taxes, deprive, and commit iniquity as if they were immortal, forgetful of the fear of God and the judgment awaiting all people, because the inescapable postmortem judgment is common to all people, like death, before "God who will righteously recompense the deprivers with never-ending torment and the deprived with eternal rest" (cf. 2 Thess 1:6–7), as the Apostle says.

For now, however, it is to be known that there are many ways of depriving, which the doctors relate in ten ways. The first privation occurs during trade: people deprive one another when they trade. Referring to these, the proverb says: "Double measures and diverse weights are abomination before the Lord" (cf. Prov 20:10). That is, whoever practices double standards—receives by the greater [measure] and gives by the lesser—violates righteousness, because balance and measure are mediums for justice and not for iniquity and privation.

Theft is the second way of privation: when a man covertly steals someone's properties from his home or elsewhere and deprives him, he steals and deprives his own soul and gives the goodness of his soul to him whose belongings he stole.

Robbery is the third way of privation. When they [robbers] set ambush on the road and rob people and steal, in exchange for the belongings that they forcibly take away, they [the robbers] also deprive them [the victims] of their sins with their belongings, because God renders justice to the deprived and compensates them righteously. He judges the depriver and the iniquitous, and delivers and rewards the dispossessed.

The fourth way is associated with the tyrants and evil rulers who tyrannically and explicitly deprive and take away the belongings of the poor like big fishes that swallow little ones, as Habakkuk says: "Why have you shown me trouble? For I see men as the fish, the big swallowing the small" (cf. Hab 1:3, 14); that is, they torture, tax, and always iniquitously deprive the poor. Because the more they take away the rights allowed to them [the poor], the more they are considered to have deprived, and they gather the sins of the poor [in their person].

The fifth way [of privation] relates to those who take away one another's fields and properties—houses, vineyards, lands, and so on, as Isaiah says: "Woe unto them that join house to house, field to field, for they expel the neighbor" (Isa 5:8). And they do not act like this to satisfy their needs, for man needs no more than a few properties; rather, they act so in order to do injustice and ravish one another. When Ahab and Jezebel took away Naboth's vineyard, they themselves were deprived of their kingdom and lives. The same happened to all those who ravished the Israelites.

The sixth way relates to those who ravish the wages of the laborers, wherefore Isaiah[41] complains: "The deprived among you cries out, and the complaint of the harvesters have reached the ears of the Lord of the hosts" (cf. Jas 5:4). Because, first, you ravished the person who labored and suffered physically for the sake of his wage, and, next, he cried out to you, but you did not hear him. Wherefore, he complains to God, and God hears him and makes justice to the deprived, as the Prophet says: "Since you did not hear his cry, when you cry unto God, he will not hear you" (cf. Mic 3:4). And since you have deprived him of the wage of his labor, behold! God will take away your life.

The seventh way relates to depriving one another of glory and ravishing authority, for whoever opposes an authority opposes God's command, as the Apostle says: "There is no authority except from God, and those that are established, have been established by God. Hence, anyone who resists authority resists the command of God" (Rom 13:1–2). And woe to anyone who resists God's commands for the sake of false and perishable glory and departs the eternal and immortal life.

Adultery is the eighth way of privation, when a man leaves his lawful wife and ravishes his neighbor's wife, depriving him. A person of this caliber defiles his own lawful bed, defiles also his neighbor's bed, and deprives his soul of God's blessing. Moreover, [he deprives the soul] of his accomplice who committed adultery with him. For this reason, God commanded in the commandments: "You shall not desire your neighbor's wife, nor shall you covet his belongings and properties" (cf. Deut 5:21).

Murder is the ninth way of privation, when a person deprives somebody of his life, or severs his body parts: hands, feet, and so on. And manslaughter is a very heavy [sin]: whoever has killed the body of his neighbor, or terminated his life, has [actually] murdered his own soul and deprived it of eternal life, as the Apostle says: "No murderer has eternal life abiding in him" (Jn 3:15). Likewise, whoever severs any organ of a person for the slightest reason, God will sever him and leave him out of the world of the living.

The tenth way relates to those who deprive by word, insult and slander their neighbor, and with vain words wound them worse than an arrow, as David says: "A man spoke vanity with his neighbor, with insidious lips" (cf. Ps 12:2). People in the same fashion shot arrows [against Christ] with insidious tongue, saying: "He casts out devils through Beelzebub" (Lk 11:15), wherefore he [Christ] said: "Whosoever speaks against the Holy Spirit, will not be forgiven,

---

[41] The ensuing verse is from James, not Isaiah.

neither in this age, nor in the age to come" (Mt 12:32). That is, whosoever speaks against the holy and pure Spirit, claiming it is evil, his sin will not be forgiven. Because it is said that depriving and oppressing by words is heavier than doing so in any other way.

Such is the multitude of the major oppressions, but the partial [oppressions] within these are numerous and countless. [Solomon] saw these through his wise mind and said: "I saw oppression under the sun and the tears of the oppressed" (Eccl 4:1). Because when the oppressor exercises force, ravishes belongings, appropriates fields, sets ambush on the road to rob, murders a person and robs another naked, and dishonors, taxes, or insults people, they [the oppressed] cry, sigh, and moan, and protest to God and call upon man. Many of them remain without comfort. A past owner of properties is robbed and now is hungry for a loaf. Yesterday's donor goes onward as a beggar today. Yesterday's lively and healthy person is today wounded by robbers and left half dead. Yesterday's sacredly revered person is oppressed by words today, banished with the wicked, and has no comfort at hand. Whereas people do not hear and do not make judgment, and God's comfort occurs later and therefore late, and whereas the deprived is distressed and panicked, and has no comfort in this life, for this reason the wise [Solomon] said: "I praised the dead which are already dead, more than the living which are yet alive" (Eccl 4:2), when he saw this disorder. That is, in view of such an injustice among people and in nature, he praised the dead which by virtue of being dead avoided these wicked situations in which the deprivers practice iniquity daily and the deprived cry daily. They [deprivers] perpetually and recklessly commit such evil acts, forgetful of the day of death. The dead are delivered from such evil acts and have reached the harbor of death, wherefore Job says: "Death is rest to such man" (Job 3:23), and thereby praises the dead. And yet better than these two are those who have not yet been; that is, things that do not exist and have not been brought to existence are better than those that exist. And he rightfully says so. First, because whosoever has been brought to existence and begotten will die by necessity, or is dead; whereas a non-existent person neither exists, nor will he die; therefore, it is better for him, because death is alien to him. Again, whosoever was brought to existence and came to this life and committed evil, privation, ravishing, and iniquity will die by evil; whereas the non-existent who did not come to this life, neither committed evil nor did he die by evil. Again, whosoever encountered evil accidents and died by evil, the eternal torturous torment is and will remain in him. The non-existent, however, did not come to this world, did not die, and will not be tormented eternally.

Looking into this matter, Jeremiah says: "Woe is me, my mother, that you have given birth to me to see pain and suffering" (cf. Jer 15:10); that is, [to see] physical pain and the torment of hell. And Job cursed the day he was born, saying: "Let the day be cursed wherein I was born, and the night in which it was said, There is a man-child" (Job 3:3); that is, let both the night and the day wherein I was born be cursed, since I have encountered painful torments. He also says woe, let the day wherein I was born be cursed, for I consider it night, and my life is darkness compared with the light of eternal life. The Lord, likewise, says: "It would have been better for that man not to have been born" (Mt 26:24). All of the saints teach that whosoever has not been brought to existence and has not been born is better than whosoever has come to this world by birth and encountered evil works—adultery, fornication, ravishing, theft, oppression, and other evil actions. Because that person inherits the reputation of a wicked, sluggish, and oppressing person in this life, and the impartial judge sentences him to eternal fire in the hereafter. And nobody is more despicable and abject than deprivers and ravishers. Keep this in mind, brothers. Do not deprive one another, do not steal, do not oppress, do not speak ill, and do not bring forth any wicked thing through the tongue or any other organ. On the contrary, speak whatever is good, do whatever is good. Love your neighbor. Have compassion for the poor. Give to the needy. Comfort the grieved, so that you may be worthy of the ineffable good in our Lord Jesus Christ who is blessed forever. Amen.

After what has been said about virtues in general, we shall now discuss the seven mysteries of the church, baptism being the first.

CHAPTER XXXII

Homily of the same about the seven mysteries of the church, and, first, about baptism, according to the Gospel: "Except a man be born of water and of the Spirit, that which is born of flesh is flesh, or something else" (cf. Jn 3:5–6).

First, let us ask: "Why was the order of the church given by word of mouth and not in writing?"

We say that the incarnate Word taught the apostles by word of mouth, and they did so to the patriarchs, and those [patriarchs] did so by word of mouth in the church. Thereby, the bishop grants authority to the priests and the deacons by word of mouth, and the priest baptizes, performs the Liturgy, marries, and grants absolution by word of mouth, and everything else is accomplished by word of mouth.

This is so for many reasons. First, the immaterial word moves from one mind to another; [therefore], our priesthood was granted [by Christ] through intellect, as it happened with angels through intellect. Second, all the ordinances of the old [testament] were put in writing, whereas the new truth was given by word of mouth to be distinguished from the old. Third, to hide it from the unworthy, as the designation itself identifies mystery—hidden knowledge. Fourth, so that His teachings are kept with care and dignity. Fifth, because we ought to present the teacher with fruitful results, reminiscent of those who respected the talent and were rewarded.

But why did He [Christ] teach through material signs, such as water and chrism, bread and wine, and so on? For this, we bring forth a number of reasons. First, because we are corporeal, we attain the immaterial through the medium of the matter: we see the writing first, and then we understand its potency. Second, to cover the hidden mystery with a curtain from the unworthy; because those who are unworthy by faith, mind, and behavior, should not see [the mystery]. Hence: "Give not that which is holy unto the dogs, [etc.]" (Mt 7:6). Third, since we perish physically; we shall discover physically, because the medicine should correspond to the ailment. Fourth, the patient—man—is [made of] body and spirit; therefore, we give him the spiritual medicine physically. For example, bitter medicine is coated with sweet food. Fifth, [we do so] on behalf of the healer, because God turned human; similarly, the medicine has an invisible divine grace and the grace has a visible physical aspect. Sixth, for the sake of the reward: the rewards benefit immensely if [man] believes in God, where the natural mind cannot reach. Seventh, for the sake of humility: man humbles himself and asks for redemption from things that are inferior to him.

How many are the mysteries of the church?

We say seven. First, baptism, confirmation, and Eucharist. Then, penance, anointment, order, and matrimony. Some claimed there was no need for seven, saying that there was only the need for one, because the mystery derives power from the power of God through Christ's agony. God's power is one, and Christ's agony is one: "for we were redeemed by his onetime entrance into the Holy Place" (cf. Heb 9:12).

The doctors, however, say: Although Christ's agony is one, and his power is one, a person can perform many things by many tools with one power. Likewise, [Christ] influences us with diverse thoughts as if with various tools through one divine power and one agony. Others, however, state that mystery is established against the defect of sins, and it is twofold: sin and punishment; therefore, two mysteries were enough. [The doctors] respond thus: Sin and punishment differ from each other in kind, and since there are various kinds of sins, so also there are diverse and many punishments. Then, therefore, there had to be diverse and many mysteries in conformity with the diverse and many sins and punishments, as we shall learn later.

Yet others say that mystery is associated with the ecclesiastical hierarchy, as stated by St. Dionysius. Now, priesthood has three functions: to cleanse, to enlighten, and to perfect, as categorized by the same St. Dionysius; therefore, there should be only three mysteries. We say in this regard that hierarchical duties involve three things: the performer, the recipient, and the work. The performers are the officiants of the mystery and they are associated with the order; the recipients are the seekers of the mystery who come forward with the crown; and the works are cleanliness, enlightenment, and perfection. Now, cleanliness and enlightenment are primarily associated with baptism, according to St. Dionysius. Secondarily, they relate to penance and, finally, to anointment. According to virtue, perfection is of two kinds: formal [theoretical] and terminal. Formal perfection relates to [the mystery of] confirmation, while the terminal [relates] to the Eucharist. Then, therefore, the church has seven mysteries and not three, as some claim.

Why are there seven mysteries? The doctors refer to many reasons. First, based on the diversity of the congregation. The first mystery is baptism for the

newcomers to the church. The second is confirmation for those who fight the
adversary, Satan. The third is communion—spiritual nourishment—to renew
the strength to fight [the adversary]. The fourth is penance for those who stand
up anew: those who fell through their sins and rose through penitential acts.
The fifth is the last anointment for those who leave this life and are delivered
from the battle. The sixth is the order for those who serve these mysteries—
the priests and other [clergy] in the church. The seventh is matrimony—the
mystery of bringing new soldiers in through physical birth. Again, there are
seven mysteries that prepare us to receive the seven virtues: faith, hope, and
love, and prudence, fortitude, temperance, and righteousness.

Why is baptism the mystery of faith? Because it is evident that in order to
be baptized, we have to believe first. Confirmation is the mystery of hope,
because hoping for the power of the Holy Spirit enables us to face the enemy.
Communion is the mystery of love, because through love we are united and
annexed to Christ the head: "Now you are the body of Christ and individually
members of it" (1 Cor 12:27). Penance is the mystery of justice, because
through repentance, confession, and other means we are justified from sins.
Anointment is the mystery of absolute fortitude, because after exiting the battle,
we cleanse the dust and the sweat, reminiscent of those who exit the physical
battle. Order is the mystery of prudence and knowledge, in order [for the
clergy] to serve the mystery with wisdom and knowledge, and teach the people
by exhorting them. Matrimony is the mystery of temperance, because through
temperate marriage one refrains from lascivious desires and avoids committing
adultery and fornication. For these reasons, the mysteries of the church are
seven.

Again, there is another reason for the mysteries to be seven: they are
established against the three sins and the four punishments. Baptism is against
the original sin. Penance is against mortal sins. Anointment is against venial
sins. Order is against ignorance. Communion is against wickedness.
Confirmation is against inability. Matrimony is against desire, moderating it
and exempting it from condemnation.

There is yet another reason: that people compare spiritual life and vitality
with corporeal life and vitality, as the church doctors state. But this is enough
for now.

Let us go back to the sequence of my discourse and find out what the
godfather stands for. We say that the godfather's role in the spiritual [birth] is
similar to the role of midwives and wet nurses in corporeal birth due to their
four duties. First, he [the godfather] raises the child and feeds, tutors, and

clothes him. As the mother of a child is mother, the godfather is godfather by designation—a man that raises the infant. He exhorts and feeds the child with words, and clothes him; thereby, he has to provide for the child's clothing. The baptized, whether young or old, needs a godfather, because the godfather is the interpreter of the baptized person and his intercessor before the priest. And since he is designated as godfather, he needs to be male.

Question: Why did the patriarchs establish canons prohibiting the presence of women in church at the time of baptism?

Answer: For many reasons. First, certain heretics allowed women to perform baptism. To banish such sects from the church, the holy fathers banned the presence of women in church during baptism. Second, women are the reason and cause of corrupt and corporeal birth; therefore, they should not be close to and contributing in spiritual and pure birth. Third, consenting to the serpent's advice, the woman caused the destruction and fall of our nature; she should not be close to and assistant in the rehabilitation through the font. For example, a wise physician first eliminates the cause of sickness with medicine and then cures it with remedies. Fourth, since man is [made of] spirit and body, he has a corporeal father and a birth-giving mother bodywise, and the font as spiritual mother and the godfather—who is Baal—as spiritual father with respect to spirit. No other mother is needed. We say godfather and not godmother, because through baptism we become the children of a heavenly Father, not heavenly mother. Fifth, children born of corporeal mothers are faint and weak; therefore, women are in charge of their upbringing. The spiritual mother, however, bears brave, strong, and active children; therefore, men are in charge of their upbringing. Just as Jesus, our Lord, baptized and empowered, fought and defeated the tempter, so are the baptized emboldened to defeat Satan. Sixth, women's testimonies are neither acceptable nor decisive in physical courts, and they will be much more so in the spiritual court. Seventh, the Apostle commands: "Women should cover and veil their heads in church, and should not speak, for whoever speaks or uncovers her face or head, dishonors her head, Christ" (cf. 1 Cor 3:5). Eighth, the seven mysteries of the church were delivered to men and not women. Women are not involved in officiating and so forth in other mysteries; therefore, here, too, they should not officiate or assist, for if they get involved in this, they will become also involved in other matters. Ninth, the Mother of God and other women were absent when Christ was being baptized. Also, at his resurrection, Christ disallowed [Mary of] Magdalene to approach him, saying: "Touch me not" (Jn 20:17). Our baptism embodies the mystery of entombment and resurrection:

[the act of] submerging thrice signifies the three-day-long entombment, whereas the lifting from the font signifies resurrection. Therefore, a woman should not be allowed to come near or to be made godfather. Tenth, in the Old [Testament], the circumcised were delivered to men and not women, as is practiced nowadays among followers of other faiths; more so, it is inappropriate for women to receive the baptized from the font. For this reason, caution should be exercised, to not entrust women with involvement in the mystery of the church. Enough on this.

Why should the godfather be both baptized and faithful? In order to have the ability to intercede before the priest and receive the profession of faith [on behalf of the baptized]. Further, the godfather should not be a heretic, pagan, Muslim, or Jew. First, because the newly dedicated child is renewed and turned to the godfather's faith, as Solomon says: "a true son brings his father's resemblance" (cf. Sir 20:28). Similarly, the spiritual son resembles the spiritual father, be it as a practitioner of the true faith or an ill faith. Second, the godfather is a witness to the faith of the baptized with his faith and not with his body or anything else. Third, whatever the godfather may profess—God, man, or objects—the same will profess the newly dedicated. Fourth, the baptized will be the son of, referred to as the son of, and inherit the legacy of the godfather, sharing the same faith of the godfather that happens to be his father's lot, just as we are the children of Abraham, according to our faith. Enough on this.

Here is the reason why we renounce, facing west, and then turn to face east. Satan, ignorance, and sins are darkness; therefore, we deny and renounce [these] facing west. God, knowledge, and the profession of faith are light; therefore, we receive them from east. These indicate three things. First, light and darkness, ignorance and knowledge, and evil and good cannot coexist, because they are opposites like the heat and cold, and death and life. This is what [Christ] teaches in the Gospel: "You cannot serve God and mammon" (Mt 6:24). Therefore, man should stay away from one [i.e., darkness, ignorance, and evil] and approach the other. Second, another indication is that man should first stay away from evil and then approach the good; flee from darkness and then dwell in light, because the holy should be in a holy place. It is with this intent that in all mysteries we first confess our sins and then [the priest] provides communion, officiates matrimony, grants remission, and so on. Third, another indication is that a person not only should stay away from evil but should also do good; not only abandon darkness and ignorance, but also receive light and knowledge, because those who do neither evil nor good will be neither tormented nor rewarded. Therefore, once the sins are pardoned and cleansed

240

through confession, a person should bear the yoke of penance, which is the good work, that he may be rewarded. It is with this intent that while renouncing Satan, we confess Christ, and after stripping the child, we put new bright clothes on him. Burning candles are held in hand because the child is cleansed from sins and is born anew by the spirit, coming to the light of the faith. Submerging the child thrice in the water and bringing him out signifies his death with Christ, the three-day-long entombment, and resurrection.

We will compare this, first, with a casual death and then with the death of Christ. And [we will do so], first, according to the following example. Death is the separation of things that are united, because the individual unity in the spirit is separated, but the substantial [unity] is not. It is so, because the elemental and material unity is separated from the spirit, whereas the innate and sensate is not, because although they [the innate and sensate] lose their functionality, they essentially remain components to the soul. Thus, when the baptized dies, the original and virtual sin departs him, but the root of sins and fragility remain in man, so that he may sin later. Second, just as earth covers the body of the deceased and his soul disappears, so does water cover the baptized; that is, water engulfs and covers the entire body. Third, just as death coercively deprives the body of the soul, so does the grace of baptism cleanse the sins from the body coercively. Fourth, just as the dead and buried body degenerates and transforms, so does the entombed by baptism transform and become the son of light. Fifth, desires no longer motivate a dead and entombed person. Similarly, the baptized is indifferent toward all worldly desires with every organ and sense. This [was] about casual death.

To die signifies Christ's death, as Paul says: "As we were baptized into Christ were baptized into his death. We are buried with him by baptism into death" (cf. Rom 6:3–4). First, because just as Christ has resemblance to death, for he was dead and yet alive, entombed and yet incorrupt in the body, so too does the baptized die by imitation, for he dies in terms of sins and yet is alive in terms of righteousness and purity. Second, just as Christ's death killed the death and by his entombment he disbanded corruption, so too does the baptized kill in himself the spiritual death and corruption. Third, just as Christ first killed the death on the cross and then disbanded corruption in the grave, so too are the sins of the baptized, which are death, cleansed first and then the punishment—the corruption of eternal torments—is disbanded. Fourth, Christ died voluntarily and not naturally; that is, he was not indebted to death, because "He did not sin" (1 Pet 2:22); rather, he paid our debts. Likewise, the baptized does not die a natural death; rather, he pays the debts of eternal death. Fifth, just as Christ died on the cross, was placed for three days in the grave with an incorrupt body, and resurrected with glory, so too does the baptized die with Christ and by being submerged in the water thrice come out of the water immortalized by Christ's resurrection. Hence: "Whoever suffers with him, also shares the glory" (cf. Rom 8:17). And it is to be known that because the mystery of Christ's baptism and the mystery of the cross are one and the same, the Apostle said in Romans: "Those who were baptized into Christ, were baptized there into his death; we are buried with him by baptism into death" (cf. Rom 6:3–4). First, just as there was the water of Jordan, so too was here the water of his [Christ's] side. Second, there [in the water] he was stripped, and here he was [stripped] on the cross. Third, there he destroyed the dragon's head, and here he destroyed his [Satan's] power with the cross. Fourth, there he cleansed our sins through baptism and here with the cross "He made purification of our sins" (Heb 1:3). Fifth, he was buried in the water there, and in the grave here. Sixth, he was resurrected with glory here, and he was strengthened by the Holy Spirit there. Thus, in our baptism, the mystery of baptism and the mystery of the cross are one. And the anointment with holy chrism indicates that when Christ was baptized, the Holy Spirit descended upon him, for he received it as our head and poured it on the members of those who believe in him. Hence: "Like the ointment that ran down the head, [etc.]" (cf. Ps 133:2). Thus we are baptized into Christ with the water, called children of God, and united with the grace of the Holy Spirit through the oil [chrism]. It is to be known that the anointment of the forehead, the heart, and the backbone is confirmation. The anointment of the five senses surmounts to the mystery of anointment covertly. The anointment of the organs relates to the mystery of other Christians who anoint before baptism. And should somebody ask: Anointing is mystery; why don't we have it?

We say that we do have the mystery of anointing, but covertly, as in baptism, which we have mentioned. [It is present] also in the washing of the feet and in the baptism of the Lord on the day of revelation. But why not explicitly like other Christians? Because confession would have been eliminated, as it is eliminated now among the Georgians and the Syriac. In our nation, too, [had we practiced anointment explicitly] people would not have confessed because of the oil of anointment, and they would have died in sins. Moreover, the anointment of the sick does not purify fatal sins; rather, it purifies the venial sins, whereas confession cleanses both fatal and venial sins, similar to cutting the roots for the stem to dry. Confession, then, is more useful than anointment. Again, fatal sins are erased with words uttered by the priests, whereas venial sins are cleansed both by the words of the priest and through prayers, as James says: "They call the elders, and pray over him, and he will be forgiven" (cf. Jas 5:14–15). It is with this notion that we, the priests, gather and perform services from evening until morning, blessing the Liturgy and the cross, both for the living and the dead; then, therefore, the words of the priest cleanse the venial sins in the name of God.

Should somebody say: The hand of the priest must touch all of the senses; we say that the right hand of the priest always touches the head of a Christian where the root of all senses exists. The hand of the priest is anointed and purified with chrism, and it gives the grace of holiness to those it touches. And as numerous and countless the venial sins are in the senses and the minds, so manifold forgiveness the order of priesthood grants by laying of the hand and purifying with the words of grace.

Should someone say: We do not have the initial anointment that precedes baptism; we say that we have it covertly, just like mixing the chrism crosslike in the water of the font. First, for the sake of this mystery. Second, because we baptize not into the water of John, but into the death of Christ. For this reason, we do not have a variety of oils, but only the holy chrism, so that priests may not dare to reintroduce the blessing of the oil to the church. We bless the oil on Great Thursday, so that the holy chrism may not touch the feet of the common.

Also, we have this mystery of anointing for deceased priests, because we anoint them as wrestlers, for they compete with evil spirits in the air. And should someone say: The body alone is anointed; how would that affect the soul? We say that when [the soul] was united with the body, all material things affected it through the unity, but now that it is separated, all holy things reach it separately. Otherwise, it is time for you to claim that all the orders of burial for the body are useless to the deceased. So also the prayers and services of the priests. Or [you may claim that] gifts and offerings are useless for the soul, which is absolute falsehood and evil heresy. And should someone say: You do not have confirmation, because, unlike Roman Catholics, it is not given by the bishop. We say that a Greek priest not only performs the Liturgy and baptizes but also confirms, according to St. Dionysius. And he [Dionysius] designates him who performs the Liturgy, baptizes, and confirms as high priest, because he is the head and senior person in performing the mystery, while other priests accompany him and serve the mystery. We also say that our priests possess the authority to confirm, which is given to them [the Greek] by their bishop; therefore, our priests and their bishops share equal authority. This is said in relation to contrasts.

Affirmatively speaking, the priest has the right to perform the seven mysteries of the church. In addition to this, the bishop has the right to give the order, and to bless the church and the altar. After the anointment, they put on [the baptized] bright clothes, which signify a luminous conduct, bright faith, and innocence, as we have mentioned. Moreover, [they put on] the ribbon woven in red and white, [indicating Christ's] blood and the water [that gushed] from his side. The cross [is like] the yoke that he carried on his neck. Going up to the pulpit [takes place because] after all of his dispensations Christ ascended unto heaven and sat on the right hand of the Father. The communion [follows] to link the members with the head, for communion is the fulfillment of all fulfillments; that is, of the order, matrimony, confession, and so on.

Moreover, during the birth through the font we witness five amazing works that the corporeal birth lacks. First, [the font] can give birth to a whole nation at once, be it one, a thousand, or ten thousand. Hence: "Who has heard and seen that as soon as Zion travailed, she brought forth a whole nation" (cf. Isa 66:8), thanks to the mighty authority of the priest and the advantage of the water. Second, [the font] gives birth immaculately, without corruption, thanks to the Holy Spirit and the liquidity of the water's substance. Third, [the font] always gives birth to firstborns and not juniors, for we receive the image of Christ, who is the firstborn of the Father. Fourth, we are always born as sons of God and not as daughters or female, "for there is neither male nor female in Christ Jesus," the Apostle says (cf. Gal 3:28). The font's location on the right-hand side of the church indicates this. Fifth, all of us are born equal; not some with honor and some without, [and not some] as rulers and [some] as subjects, as the Apostle says: "There is no distinction between Jew and gentile, slave and freeman; for you are all equal in Christ Jesus, and equal partakers of the kingdom" (cf. Gal 3:28). And this indicates the sameness of the form of the Word, which references the Trinity and the sameness of the faith.

Here, a person might ask: Are Christians allowed to be baptized twice? We answer that a baptized person should not be baptized again. First of all, the corporeal birth indicates the spiritual birth. Just as the corporeal birth occurs once, so shall it be with the spiritual.

Second, baptism is [performed] against the original sin, and the original sin is one, not two. Third, the baptized person is baptized in Christ's death, and Christ died once. Whoever performs baptism again, "he crucifies to himself the Son of God afresh, and puts him to shame again," as the Apostle says (Heb 6:6). Fourth, baptism is an inseparable seal in the spirit, as the order and confirmation are. Therefore, people should not be baptized twice in the name

244

of the Holy Trinity. Fifth, the baptized is stripped of Satan and the sins, and he puts on Christ and purity; hence: "Those of you who were baptized into Christ, have put on Christ" (Gal 3:27). Those who are baptized twice strip themselves of Christ and purity, and put on Satan and the sins anew. Also, whoever baptizes twice separates and distances [the baptized person] from the true Christ, and baptizes him, brings him close, and unites him into the fake Christ. A person, however, who has been affiliated with Arius, Nestorius, or the Macedonians, can be baptized. As for those who do not profess the one Holy Trinity, those of them that were baptized are eligible for [a second] baptism for the glory of the most Holy Trinity of the Father, the Son, and the Holy Spirit. Enough on this! Baptism is discussed elsewhere, too, in ten articles, according to the epistle to the Hebrews.

CHAPTER XXXIII

Homily of the same on baptism according to the Prophet Zechariah, who, on behalf of God, said: "Behold, I will dig the pits, and will touch all the inequity of the land" (Zech 3:9).

Digging indicates establishing the church: before we lay the foundation, we dig. As Isaiah says: "I hewed out a wine-press therein" (Isa 5:2). The pit is the symbolic womb of the holy font where [God] touches all our iniquities. In other words, just as touching by our hands we wash and cleanse the dirt from the body, so are we cleansed through the font from all our sins in the day of our life.

Consider that the spiritual birth from the font is analogous to our corporeal birth in six ways. It is also different from it in six ways. It is analogous and conformable thus: First, there is one corporeal birth from a mother; similarly, there is one spiritual birth from the font and not two. Second, by birth we come out of the darkness of the womb into the light of this life; similarly, by baptism we come out of the darkness of ignorance into the light of knowledge. This is demonstrated through renouncing the devil by facing west, and confessing the faith by facing east. Third, a person and a countenance are manifested by birth and included in the human count; likewise, God's countenance and image manifest themselves in us through baptism and we join the chosen ones. Fourth, we receive the designation "human" by birth; likewise, baptism brings us a new designation and name. Fifth, we receive our nourishment from the breasts and breathe the air; similarly, upon baptism, we taste the holy flesh and blood, and receive nourishment through the milk of the Old and New Testaments, along with receiving the Holy Spirit. Sixth, we inherit after we are born; likewise, we become "heirs of [the kingdom of] God" (cf. Rom 8:18) after we are baptized.

As the Lord says: "Except a man be born of water and of the Spirit, he cannot enter into the kingdom" (Jn 3:5). This much on similarities.

The differences are: First, we are born of a mother physically, but our birth from the font is spiritual; hence: "That which is born of the flesh is a flesh; and that which is born of the Spirit is spirit" (Jn 3:6). Second, we are born of a mother with the original sin; whereas, by baptism, we are born cleansed from all sins. Third, the birth from a mother indicates Adam's fall unto the earth. This is evident from our birth head down. Baptism, however, indicates standing in heaven through Christ. This is evident from our coming out of the baptismal water head up. Fourth, we are born male and female from mothers; whereas, through the font we are always born as children and as firstborns, according to the Apostle: "There is no distinction between male and female, for you are all one in Christ Jesus, and those who have been baptized in Christ, have put on Christ" (cf. Gal 3:27–28). This is demonstrated through the font, which is on the right-hand side of our mother—the church. Fifth, by birth we turn into and are named son of man, whereas by baptism we are designated children of God through grace, as the Gospel says: "To them gave the power to become the sons of God" (Jn 1:12). Since the Father testified for the Son: "This is my beloved son" (Mt 3:17), this became a testimony for all of the baptized in the font. Sixth, by birth we become heirs to people and inherit the perceptible life, whereas by baptism we inherit the spiritual life and the kingdom of heaven, and become partakers of Christ's inheritance, as the Apostle says: "Heirs of God, and joint-heirs of Christ" (Rom 8:17). This much on comparing the two births—of the body and of the soul.

The distinctions and differences are reminiscent to the similarities, for the soul is greater than the body, and the spiritual birth is more venerable than the corporeal birth. Consider that the Creator brings the corporeal birth forth through six steps that are analogous to our spiritual birth and rising. First, He creates from nothingness. Second, He makes a living and not lifeless body. Third, He makes man in the image of God and not just any animate thing. Fourth, He makes some of them male. Fifth, He keeps them in the laboring womb. Sixth, we are born into a world full of light. Everybody is born corporeally through these six stages.

The spiritual birth from the font takes place similarly. First, we become a thing from nothing. The Prophet says: "All pagans are nothing, and they were reckoned to him as nothing" (cf. Isa 40:17). Second, our souls receive life. Third, [the baptized] is shaped in the image of God. Fourth, [the baptized] is named son of God through grace. Fifth, [the baptized] is instructed in the mysteries of faith in the womb of the church. Sixth, [the baptized] is born into the light of the knowledge of God, as evidenced by the white clothes.

[The baptized] is also prepared for the general resurrection in six stages. First, we shall be re-created for the true life from nothingness and vain life. Second, there shall be a new existence and an incorrupt life. Third, we shall share the image of Christ and the angels. Fourth, we shall become the children

247

of resurrection and partakers of Christ's inheritance. Fifth, our body shall be kept in the elements, but our soul in the terminal of souls, as if in a mother's womb. Sixth, we shall rise into the light of the life to come as sons of light and sons of the day; hence: "The righteous shall radiate like the sun in the kingdom of heaven," as the Prophet says (Isa 13:43).

The following three births are comparable in these six [aforementioned] ways: the first birth is corporeal; the second is spiritual; the third is corporeal and spiritual. Again, the first is natural birth, the middle one is birth by grace, and the last is birth by glory. Moreover, the first birth lacks knowledge, because nobody knows the day the birth will take place. The second birth is by knowledge, because we know and we believe in the spiritual birth. The last birth is both with and without knowledge: it is with knowledge, because we know and believe in what has been said about resurrection; and it is without knowledge, because we do not know the time, the when, and the how. This much on this.

Baptism is one, but we see three mysteries in it: the profession of faith, baptism, and anointment. These are united in the Father, the Son, and the Holy Spirit, because the three persons have one nature. Thereby, as we believe, profess, and are anointed in the Father, so are we in the Son and the Holy Spirit; hence: "Baptize them in the name of the Father, the Son, and the Holy Spirit" (Mt 28:19). However, there is also distinction among these entities. First, given the unique countenances of the three persons, it would be appropriate to believe in the Father, be baptized in the Son, and be anointed in the Holy Spirit. Second, given the three virtues, [it would be appropriate] to profess with faith, be baptized with hope, and be anointed with love. Third, given the three parts of the soul, faith should be appropriated to reason, baptism to passion, and anointment to desire. Fourth, given the three faculties of the mind, faith should be appropriated to intelligence, baptism to the will, and anointment to the memory. Fifth, given the three essential components of man, faith should be appropriated to the holiness of the mind, baptism to the soul, and anointment to the body. It is thereby evident that we prostrate ourselves to the relics of the saints of the new covenant and not the prophets of the old covenant for the sake of the grace of anointment. Sixth, given their three potentialities, faith cleanses, baptism enlightens, and anointment brings to perfection, according to St. Dionysius. Consider that baptism requires four rites: first, the water has to be warm; second, the chrism should be poured into the font; third, the lights need to be turned on; fourth, a cross should be in place. The mystery is this: Water's warmth signifies the warmth of the Holy Spirit, because it neutralizes the coldness of hatred and warms the baptized with Christ's love. The chrism that is poured imitates the Holy Spirit that descended in the shape of a dove in the River Jordan and now is descending unto the font invisibly. The lights that are turned on signify the baptized person's enlightenment through the font. Moreover, this indicates that our Lord Jesus Christ was baptized during the day, when it was bright with a radiant sun. He was born at night of the Holy Virgin, but His baptism took place during the day in order to demonstrate that the corporeal birth relates us to the dark world, but the spiritual birth leads us to the heavenly and bright life. By placing the cross in the font we indicate that we are baptized into Christ's death, because the mystery of baptism includes the mystery of Christ's death. By submerging the baptized three times we indicate the three-day-long entombment, and by bringing the person out of the water we signify the resurrection. When we bring the baptized up to the pulpit, we refer to Christ, sitting on the right hand of the Father in heaven. The red and white ribbons indicate the blood and water that gushed out of Christ's side. The cross, fastened to the baptized, symbolizes his transformation into a partaker of Christ's cross. The white dress demonstrates that the whole body of the baptized is cleansed of sins. [Finally], the two lights indicate that the baptized is enlightened spiritually and physically.

Question: Why is it that in [the mystery of] confirmation the forehead is confirmed first?

Answer: The mystery of confirmation is different from that of baptism, because confirmation is a seal. When we say we sealed the child, we mean that the soul received the seal of confirmation, like the wax takes the seal of the ring. First, the forehead is the place where common feelings are gathered, and the mystery indicates this reality. The prophets and the apostles are the forehead and the vision of the church. They received the Holy Spirit before other believers who are Christ's body parts. Thereby, we confirm the forehead before other body parts. Also, Christ was priest and king. We receive the confirmation of the grace of priesthood by baptism and the confirmation of kingship by sealing the forehead. Also, by baptism we are born into the churches as children of God, whereas through confirmation we become Christ's soldiers in the face of the adversary, Satan. We confirm the forehead first, to armor them [Christ's soldiers] without fear before arming the rest of the body parts. Moreover, the forehead indicates that the profession of faith ought to be demonstrated before all men without embarrassment, explicitly, and courageously. It should not be covered or veiled, "For believing with the heart is righteousness, while confession with the mouth is salvation for the soul" (cf. Rom 10:10). Thereafter, the anointment of the entire body indicates the possession of all virtues covertly.

Question: What does this mean: "I baptized you with water unto repentance" (Mt 3:10)?

Answer: John's baptism was the repentance of sins. As such, it was more than the font of Moses, which was simply a physical cleanliness, and it was lesser than Christ's baptism, which is associated with the Holy Spirit, because, first, [the latter] forgave the sins. Second, it gave the Holy Spirit. Third, it made [man] son of God. Fourth, it opened the gate of the kingdom.

Question: What is associated with Adam's old image in us and what is new?

Answer: Adam's old image makes up three things within us: nature, sin, and punishment. Our body is nature, the original sin is our sin, and our death is the punishment. When we are born of a mother, we possess the image of old Adam—man. Through the font, we receive the image of new Adam—Christ.

This makes up three things: grace, righteousness, and glory. Through our birth by the font we are designated children of God by grace, and we receive the diverse bounties of the Spirit in the likeness of Christ's baptism, when the Father testified Christ's true sonhood through the descending Holy Spirit in the shape of a dove. The righteousness [we receive] because we are cleansed from the original sin and are justified from sins we have committed. This is signified by the holy water of the font. We are born and justified through the virgin font by the Holy Spirit in the likeness of Christ who was born of the virgin womb and the Spirit. Glory was demonstrated at the resurrection through Christ's sitting on the right hand of the Father. Through baptism we initiate within us the mystery of resurrection, because placing the cross in the font symbolizes crucifixion, the three submergences symbolize the three-day-long entombment, and the climbing up to the pulpit signifies the paternal glory. This means that by transforming the old man into a partaker of the cross, we embrace the new man and become renewed from the old sins.

Question: Why do we first baptize and then bring the baptized up to the pulpit and offer the communion?

Answer: The following four reasons are mentioned in this regard. The first reason lay in Adam whom God created on earth in His image before placing him in the garden of delight with the tree of life. Similarly, by baptism we transform into an image of God before climbing up to the pulpit to communicate with Christ's body. Second, Adam's disobedience spoiled God's image in him and he fell unto earth to feed himself along with irrational beings. Contrarily, we obey Christ in faith, and baptism renews God's image in us before we get on the pulpit to deserve the nourishment of life. Third, God the Word renewed us in this way: First, the Word became man in the virgin's womb, renewed God's image in us by his birth, took us to the garden of delight with his cross, and gave our body the food of immortality. Similarly, we come to life in God's image through the virgin font, and after tasting the holy flesh we deserve the garden of delight. Fourth reason: In the Upper Room, Christ handed out his holy flesh to the disciples after washing their feet, which is analogous to the font. Likewise, we taste Christ's flesh after we are cleansed through the font. At this juncture, consider that Christ established our baptism in the stead of the circumcision of olden days. There is a physical circumcision, and a circumcision pertinent to the soul, as Moses stated in Deuteronomy. The spiritual circumcision, which is the severance of sins, occurs in four modes. First, by faith, as Paul says in Colossians: "In whom you are circumcised with the circumcision made without hands" (Col 2:11). Second, by baptism, as [Paul] says: "Buried with him in baptism" (Col 2:12). Third, by confessing our sins. [Paul] says: "In putting off the members of our flesh" (Col 2:11). Fourth, by penance and good works, as [Paul] says in Philippians: "We are the circumcision, who worship God by the spirit" (Phil 3:3).

Why are there four modes of spiritual circumcision?

We say, because there are four kinds of sins. First, disobedience, which is counterpoised by faith. Second, the original sin, which is counterpoised by baptism. Third, the fatal sins that we commit, which are counterpoised by confession. Fourth, the venial sins, which are counterpoised by the acts of penance.

Why are these referred to as circumcision?

For three reasons, we say. First, based on designation, for circumcision indicates severance. Similarly, baptism, confession, and other [mysteries] sever and curtail the excess of sins. Second, based on the rite, for just as man's member is exposed during circumcision, so are the body and the head exposed during baptism and confession, while everything else stands as exposition of sins. [In physical circumcision] there is also the presence of a sword and the two hands of the priest, while here [in spiritual circumcision] there is the presence of the sword of the priest's authority and God's command, both officiated with the two hands of the priest. Third, based on the connotation, for circumcision indicated Abraham's covenant. Similarly, baptism, confession, and other mysteries indicate Christ's covenant. Also, as the people of the old covenant entered the land of bounties by circumcision, so too we inherit through baptism, profession of faith, confession, and good works the kingdom of heaven in our Lord Jesus Christ who is blessed with the Father and the most Holy Spirit forever and ever. Amen.

CHAPTER XXXIV

Homily of the same on communion, according to: "The bread I give as communion is my flesh; so is the cup" (Jn 6:52), and so on.

First, let us examine why it is referred to as communion. Church doctors say that this mystery has had various designations in various periods. It is referred to as sacrifice, signifying the past, in the sense that Christ was sacrificed. It is called provision, which is nourishment for the hereafter. It is also referred to as grace because of the eternal glory. Presently, however, it is called communion.

In the true act, it is designated as *communed* for many reasons. First, it communes the many with one, transforming them into Christ's members. Second, *communed* means *gathered*, for communion groups those variegated by sins in one holiness. Third, communion transforms us into partakers of the grace and the mysteries of the church. Fourth, communion also communes us with Christ the head to become his flesh and member: "a member of his members, and flesh of his flesh" (cf. Eph 5:30). Hence: "He that eats my flesh, dwells in me and I in him" (Jn 6:56). Fifth, we take part also in the sonhood, because just as Christ is the Son of God by nature, so too shall we become children of God by grace and share the inheritance of the kingdom, in addition to partaking His holiness and righteousness. The designation *communed* is also given in accordance with the object in the sense that one loaf is put together from numerous grains, and one cup of drink from many fruits, all transformed into Christ's flesh and blood. Communion is also designated as such due to noble understanding in the sense that it is communication and equalization with divinity, and it communes us with itself; hence: "You, Father, are in me, and I in you, that they also may be one in us" (Jn 12:21). Communion is also designated as perfection, because it is the fulfillment of all fulfillments; that is, of baptism, penance, order, and other mysteries, for this is the completion of all, as St. Dionysius says. For example, the head is the perfection of body parts and reason is the perfection of sentient and innate things.

Similarly, communion is the perfection of all mysteries. Some [mysteries] cleanse and others enlighten, but this one [i.e., communion] perfects. Communion is also designated as mystery, which indicates hidden things, for the form, the color, the taste, and the other attributes of bread and wine are maintained, but their substance, which is immaterial, is transformed into Christ's flesh and blood.

Again, the forms and ceremonies of the mystery, as well as their location and many other aspects, each taken individually, are expressions of many benefits. When the priest comes down from the pulpit, incenses throughout the church, and returns to the pulpit, this indicates the sweet-scented radiance descending from God unto the first class (the thrones), then unto the middle class (the dominions), and finally unto the last class (the angels). By uniting them with him, He remains in his oneness, unintermingled. Second, to begin with, the same providence descends unto the intelligible classes of angels before descending unto the rational man and the animals and the last of the beings respectively. He provides for and maintains them in sameness, and remains in his sameness unaltered and pure. Third, it refers to the humanization of the Word that presented itself to our nature through dispensation, and that as a sweet scent spread among us the scent of the Gospel; also, "Ascended into heaven and sat on the right hand of the Father" (Mk 16:19). Entering the church with music signifies the angels' conversation, which is incomprehensible to us; whereas the hymns signify the songs of the apostles originating from the prophets. Afterward, the deacon pronounces the proschume [i.e., let us attend]; that is, look up to the holy Gospels, to what they praise. Thereafter, reference is made to the three holies that make a total of nine—the nine classes of angels divided into triads.

A psalm appropriate to the day is read afterward. Consider that the psalm is chanted uninterruptedly—in the morning, at noon, and in the evening, as well as during all mysteries—confirmation, communion, order, [the last rite of] burial, and so on. This is so for three reasons. First, the psalm is heard as a song—in the old covenant, it was continuously chanted in the temple; moreover, the prophets recited it on the Sabbaths, whereby it is always chanted in the church. Second, the psalm contains the power of the Scripture in its entirety, for the Holy Scripture either cites the primary works, such as those of Moses, or foretells the last things, or presently constitutes a prayer and exhortation, such as those of Solomon. This is all-encompassing—the past, the present, and the future. Thereby, whosoever sings the psalm in holiness is filled with the grace of the Holy Spirit. Third, since David was designated Father of God, fatherly properties are more befitting to be consumed in the houses of the assembly of his son, Christ.

Why do we read the prophets before the apostles and, finally, the Gospel?

First, we say that the prophets related the humanization of the Word and the salvation of humankind as foretellers, whereas the apostles testified to it as witnesses. [Needless to say,] the act of relating precedes that of witnessing. Again, the prophets envisioned remotely, whereas the apostles were close to the incarnate Word; thereby, we read the [works of] apostles prior to [reading] the Gospel. Again, the prophets sowed and the apostles harvested. Again, the prophets told and the apostles fulfilled. And the Alleluia is the song of the angels that brought the tidings of the coming of the Word. Then [came] the Gospel of truth, bringing the good news of people's salvation and heavenly life. Before [reading] the Gospel, the Alleluia—meaning "bless the Lord"— [is sung by] those who bless the Lord through the psalm in one voice. Behold! A verse of the psalm is always associated with the Alleluia so that the songs of the angels may be intertwined with the songs of people. [Know] also this: Numbers are combined with the Alleluia to infer: "Bless the Lord and come forward to listen to the Gospel." This [is realized] with uncovered head [to indicate] that we have received the holy command in holiness. Moreover: "All things are naked and exposed unto you" (Heb 4:13). We hide nothing from you [the Lord]. Thereafter [is time for] the kiss, in a sense that we received [the Lord] by obeying physically and we joined Him spiritually. Upon resurrection, Christ first saw Peter and then Peter relayed the events to the rest of the apostles. Likewise, a person among us kisses the Gospel and delivers the tiding to us by bowing his head.

After the reading [of the Gospel] we proclaim in one voice: "Glory unto you, God," for we have received and are offering glory to your benevolence. The ensuing Nicene Creed indicates that we have received Christ's teachings and we believe in him. The creed is a manifestation of our worship, which every Christian should hold on to and pronounce. It is also the recitation of all that has happened and will happen to the end. Again, it is a thanksgiving and gratitude for all the favors God granted us: He brought us into being and gave us vitality and reason, and made us in His image before we were deprived of Him. To redeem us, He also sent His Only Begotten Son, our Lord Jesus Christ, who took blood from the immaculate virgin and united the human nature with His divinity. He became a true man, perfect in his body, spirit, and mind. One Lord, one Christ, and one God the Son, incarnate, crucified, immortally deceased, entombed without corruption, and resurrected with divine glory. He ascended unto heaven and sat on the right hand of the Father, united with Him in nature, wherefore we recall these favors and praise. Thereafter, the deacon cites: None of the catechumens, and so on, and banishes the unworthy from the church. Consider that the first unworthy are the unbelievers and those who have not been baptized, or those who disregard the prophets, the apostles, and the Gospel. They say: "We do not want to know your ways" (cf. Heb 3:10). Therefore, the omniscient God, in view of their evil intention, deprived them of His sermons: "That they may neither see with their eyes, nor understand with their ears, [etc.]" (cf. Jn 12:40). There are three worthy and three unworthy classes among churchgoers. The unbaptized catechumens, the demoniacs that are stricken by the demon—including those who are corrupt by the sins—and the penitents do not deserve to see the holy mystery. Therefore, they exit [the church] and listen only. Behold! To listen to the sermons is allowed to both the worthy and unworthy, so that they might turn from their sins. Therefore, the unworthy exit after they listen to the lectures.

Why are they banished from the sight [of the mystery]?

For the following reason. The holy mystery abounds with goodness and rightfully apportions grace according to a person's capacity; that is, to those who touch, taste, or see. The undeserved seers are harmed like those who are harmed and punished after tasting undeservedly, in the likeness of the harm the light of sun causes to a sick eye. Therefore, the caring Christ wants to protect them from being harmed.

Now, let's discuss the three unworthy classes.

First, the catechumens—the unbaptized. Like an infant that finds nourishment in the mother's womb innately and receives the rational spirit through God's procession on the fortieth day before coming into life, the catechumen gets nourished and fed in the womb of the church during his forty days, becomes a son of God, and comes into light by birth through the holy font. The unbaptized catechumen remains incomplete until he comes into light; therefore, he exits [the church] during the Liturgy. The person possessed by demons follows him out, because he [the catechumen] is incomplete in intellect, faith, love, and holy works. For this reason, the holy sermon reckons him as ill-believer. A person possessed by demons is demoniac because of idleness: he is lazy and weak mentally, and faulty in faith and love, as opposed to those who are fortitudinous in works, perfect in faith and love, and complete in intellect, and who fight the demons, defeat them, and cure people possessed by demons. Therefore, it is evident that people possessed by demons are imperfect and they [should] exit.

Those who are corrupt by various sins—the fornicators, the avaricious, the drunkards, the slanderers, and so on—follow people possessed by demons out, because they, too, resemble people possessed by demons. Just as [Satan] defeated the demoniacs by dwelling in them, so too did he defeat the sinners through their sinful acts. Again, sinners resemble people possessed by demons qualitatively, because they, too, are referred to as frenetic. Again, they resemble each other perceptively, because their faith, love, and works are faint: they have lost their intellectual strength and exchanged the everlasting life with the perishable. Their love also is weak, because they have hated the true goodness and loved the false goodness, which is imitation and unreal. They are weak also in performing and they have entangled themselves in non-existent alien pleasures, and soon they regret their abominable pleasures. Alien things are extrinsic and not innate, as the Lord says: "You have not been faithful in that which belongs to another, [etc.]" (Lk 16:12). Their faith also is weak, because they do not believe in the compensation for actions and in the judgment of God. Then, rightfully, they are banished from the holy mystery along with people possessed by demons. Here, they are banished from the church and similarly they will be banished from Christ's presence before the mighty tribunal, because they cannot see Christ's glorious divinity, let alone that they are unworthy of it; rather, they will walk out with the foolish maidens and the gate will close. And just as the listeners hear the voice but do not see the image, so too shall they in the hereafter hear from Christ the verdict of judgment "Depart from me" (Mt 25:41) but not see the divine face.

The penitents, too, who have turned from their sins and confessed but have not yet fulfilled their punishment, which is the debt of sins, do not deserve to enter the church lest they justify themselves through penance, as we who practice penance until we are completely purified in our five senses—that is, fifty [times] currently do and enter the church after we are absolved from our debts.

Should someone ask: Wouldn't confession forgive all sins?

We say that all sins are forgiven through confession; however, there is punishment, which is fulfilled by fasting and prayers, as some claim. Again, confession cleanses sins so that a sinner will no longer suffer. Penance, however, stores goodness in the soul so that man may be rewarded. Again, confession cleanses past sins, whereas penance is a fence and fortification laid for the future to prevent sins.

Should someone ask: Why, then, do people not go through communion after their confession?

We say that there are two types of confession: First, when people confess and then repent. These are in the process of penance because of punishment, and they cannot receive communion. In this, they are reminiscent of those confessing at the threshold of the quadragesimal fasting, as Isaiah says: "Wash yourselves, make yourselves clean, and come and let us discuss it with each other, [etc.]" (cf. Isa 1:16–18). Second, there is the confession of those who exercise penance through fasting, prayers, and asceticism, and then confess. These receive communion—just like those who confess when Easter approaches—and are deemed to deserve holiness.

Again, we say that there are two types of confession, as there are two types of forgiveness. Some confess their sins, but the sin is rooted deep; in other words, they intend to confess and yet sin again. The Roman Catholics, for example, have the [kind of] confession of the laity and clergy that makes forgiveness incomplete, because the confessed sin is lifted, but not the punishment. Another type of confession detaches the roots of sins from the minds through repentance for the sins; when a man is steady in his intention and has resolved to sin no more. This is the perfect confession. The priest's authority forgives the sins of a person of this caliber, along with its punishment: since sins constitute the root of punishment, with the severance of sins, the punishment of hell also is lifted. Our Lord forgave the sins of the paralytic and his punishments were lifted, as were forgiven the Canaanite and the robber. Enough on this, in the glory of Christ our God, Amen.

CHAPTER XXXV

Again, homily of the same on the same mystery [of Eucharist].

After segregating the aforementioned three unholy classes, three holy classes remain in the church—the cleansed, the enlightened, and the perfect, be them clergy or laity. The cleansed is a person purified from sins through confession and penance. The enlightened is a person baptized and enlightened in faith, works, intellect, and knowledge. The perfect is a person deemed worthy of the holy chrism, holy communion, and holy orders. These three classes remain in the church during the holy mystery, as cleansed, enlightened, and perfected as the heavenly classes of the angels in the heaven of heavens, and they are deservedly appropriated to Christ's holy mystery and to the church as well.

The cleansed move to the right [of the church] where the sacristy is, to bring the offering out to the holy altar. This symbolizes God the Word, covered in the bosom of the Father and revealed to people through the angels. The tolling bells and the interlaced songs forming a true body indicate this and thereby we officiate with uncovered heads. The priest washes his fingertips before the holy altar in the presence of the congregation. It is to be known that the priest washes his hands twice, signifying twice purification from the sins. Whatever he washes outwardly with confession indicates the fatal sins for which he has repented outside the church. Whereas this [inwardly washing] signifies the venial sins—the minute particles of the extremities; that is, corrupted in the course of life, in the mind, or in the senses. He washes [his hands] in the presence of the congregation in a sense that the minute particles [of sin] that he had received from the congregation—during matrimonial ceremony and so on—would not bind or corrupt him. He does so before the holy offering as if it is performed before God's omniscient and impartial sight, in accordance with the guidance of our conscience that is an impartial and omniscient judge within us, as John says: "Brethren, if our hearts do not condemn us, we have confidence" (1 Jn 3:21).

The holy greeting encompasses all, signifying the unifying peace and love, because thoughts, intentions, and sins no longer divide us. Know that there are divine, angelic, and human expressions in the Liturgy. God's word is: "This is my flesh, and this is my blood" (cf. Mt 26:26–28). Angels' expression is: "Holy,

holy, holy is the Lord of hosts" (Isa 6:3), whereas the songs and prayers comprise the human expressions.

Concerning the inscriptions on the table in three languages, Hebrew, Greek, and Dalmatian, [consider this]. The Hebrew says: "Hosanna in the highest" (Mk 11:10). The Greek says: "Proschume," which is: "Look up!" [although] others say that it means "God says." The Dalmatian refers to the individual languages in which the Liturgy is performed.

Blessing of the offerings is of two kinds. The first fulfills Christ's true flesh and blood in Christ's word: "This is my flesh, and this is my blood" (cf. Mt 26:26–28) and through our four words. *This* indicates one individual. *Is* refers to the present. *Flesh* designates the object. *My* indicates that the flesh belongs to Christ. The flesh and blood are fulfilled with this last word [*my*].

The second blessing is an entreaty to the Father to give the Holy Spirit. First, the Word incarnated by the will of the Father and the collaboration of the Holy Spirit. It also happens in the present. Second, the Word was real flesh, which, through a later dispensation, received the Holy Spirit in the River Jordan. It receives the Holy Spirit presently likewise. The Holy Spirit is a gift of the cross, wherefore it is signed by the cross now, before the [Word] turns flesh and blood.

Imaging the cross on the face is for the Holy Spirit to descend upon us, as it did upon the grouped apostles. Thereby, it truly turns into flesh and blood that we can believe in.

Christ honored his divine blood through bread and wine for many reasons. First, as the Prophet says: "Wine makes cheerful" (Ps 103:15) as opposed to the sadness of the ancestors, "and bread strengthens the heart of hungry man" (Ps 103:15). Second, in the archetype, Melchizedek offered bread and wine, and so did Christ the Truth. Third, in the sanctuary and the temple, bread and wine were placed daily on the altar; the Lord did the same in the Upper Room. Fourth, Solomon says: "She has killed her beasts and mingled her wine, and sent forth her maidens and said: Come, eat of my bread, and drink of my wine which I have mingled" (cf. Prov 9:2–5). Fifth, Christ wanted to give us his grace and love through wine, and his purifying power through bread, as is proclaimed during the Liturgy: "Grace, love, and purifying divine power." Sixth, we were hungry and thirsty spiritually; He gave us the sacred bread as spiritual nourishment and the cup [of sacred wine] as spiritual drink. Seventh, Christ interceded to reconcile God and humanity; He gave the bread as a sign of reconciliation and the cup as a sign of the Spirit's love. Eighth, Christ transformed the bread into his flesh and the wine into the blood pouring out of his [wounded] side. Ninth, the bread indicates the death of the body, while the wine signifies God the immortal. Tenth, the bread sustains us, whereas the wine grants us heavenly immortality. Eleventh, the bread demonstrates our holy lives, whereas the wine demonstrates the blood of martyrdom. Twelfth, the bread is the medium of our contact with Christ's flesh, whereas the wine is the medium that unites us with divinity.

Consider eight things at this juncture about the bread, which is Christ's flesh, and the drink in the chalice, which is Christ's blood. First, Christ took one loaf and blessed it on the table, as he did with a glass of wine. Second, the words have singular connotation: "This is my flesh, and this is my blood." Christ did not say "these." Third, in 1 Corinthians, the Apostle says: "We being many are one bread, and one body; for we are all partakers of that one bread" (1 Cor 10:17). The Latin church contradicts this by blessing many wafers. And should somebody claim that the priest is entitled to bless many loaves, we say that the priest's entitlement is limited to his intention, and intention is bound with one loaf, because Christ said: "This is my body." The priest, then, should not bless many loaves. Besides, if one blessed all the loaves today, how would he bless them tomorrow? This would necessitate a second blessing of what has already been blessed—which is falsehood—or [would mean that] not all the loaves are blessed.

Second, it is to be known that the bread and wine continue to hold in them all that is accidental and qualitative, and it is their substance that transforms into Christ's flesh and blood. First, because by way of chance events we sense the substance, for chance events are inseparable distinctions in the substance. Second, chance events remain to help us approach holiness: if the flesh and blood existed with explicit appearance, nobody would have dared to approach them. Third, so that we may be rewarded by faith, and faith invisibly corresponds to the substance, wherefore one ought to see the perceptible with his eyes, and examine the intelligible by the mind and be blessed, in accordance with Christ's words to Thomas: "Because you have seen me [you have believed]; blessed are those that have not seen, and yet believe" (cf. Jn 20:29). Fourth, so that it would help us understand the incarnation of the Word, for like the bread that maintains its form while transforming into Christ's flesh in substance, its apparent shape maintains the external appearance while its nature unites with the Word of God. Just as the entire wafer is one body and yet each of its divided particles is the whole and perfect body of Christ, so too are the entire body and spirit [of Christ] one God, united with the Word, each divided particle being whole and perfect God. Then, therefore, Christ's Spirit is God, as is his flesh and his blood. Therefore, we taste the divine and not human flesh and blood, and by tasting [the divine] we attain divine ability and cease to be human. This contrasts with the Nestorian diophysite heretics that separate the Word from the flesh, whereby they segregate themselves from Christ's divine grace.

[Concerning] the invocation of the saints, apostles, prophets, and others, [we say that] they do not need our invocation [to be remembered], nor are they forgotten simply because we say: "Remember them, God!" There are other reasons [for invocation]. First, soldiers are located with their king, and they serve the mystery like angels, as has been mentioned. Therefore, they ought to be recalled. Second, the entire creation needs the holy mystery, whether angels or people, whether living or dead, so that they may be renewed into Christ's grace as we recall them. Third, we recall them because they are holy and pure. We say: "Remember, God, their holiness, and have mercy upon us!" Fourth, to make the congregations hear and be motivated to imitate them. Fifth, to declare to all that they [the recalled ones] are alive with God: "For they have passed from death unto life," as the Lord says (cf. Jn 5:24).

Consider, also, that God's remembrance is different from ours, for we lacked knowledge and learned, and we forgot and then recalled again. God's remembrance is His unforgetful divine knowledge. God altogether knows the past, the present, and things to come, and this [knowledge] is called "knowing." Similarly, God's unforgetful knowledge is referred to as God's remembrance. God also knows those who are God-like—those who have become God-like through holiness; hence: "The Lord knew those who were his" (2 Tim 2:19). Remember those who died without alteration in their same holiness.

Since knowing takes place at the beginning and recalling at the end, hence: "Precious in the sight of the Lord is the death of his saints" (Ps 115:15)—those who have reached their end in holiness. Besides, God somehow knows those who have received holiness from the beginning without a mediator, and He recalls those who attained purity and holiness later, through a mediator.

Moving to the right-hand side of the altar and standing with clasped hands symbolizes those who have been invited to the right hand of God and who stand immediately next to Christ.

The left-directional praising indicates that those whom we now praise and the living that we mention are still on the left hand of the world, in the midst of the wicked; they, too, could be deemed worthy to move to the right-hand side through the intercession of those who are already in the right-hand side. Behold! Those who deserve the grace of the Eucharist are mentioned by the deacon, who then lifts [the chalice] before the eyes of the congregation, indicating that the mystery, though covered originally, was revealed through the incarnation of the Word. Repeating the lifting refers to Christ's first and second appearances, first on the high cross with his flesh and spirit separated, and then with resurrected body and spirit, whereby it is demonstrated as flesh and blood combined, concluding with his ascension unto the Father. Again, the first lifting signifies Christ's first coming, whereas the second indicates Christ's second coming when he will appear explicitly united with divinity. The last one references Christ's gathering of his followers unto the glory of the Father. This discussion on the appearing is sufficient.

What does this mystery demonstrate?

First, a person must be pure and holy, from what is evident, in order to be remembered. Second, a person must resurrect and ascend unto Christ the head. Third, the reason for a person's exaltation and vitality is his hope for resurrection, expiation, and so on. Consider that the attributes of the wafer teach us in ten ways the kind of holiness with which we ought to receive Christ's flesh. First, the wafer is white; this signifies our purity. Second, it is circular: things shaped circularly move fast; this is analogous to our fast movement toward God's commandments and all that is good. Third, it is unleavened: we ought to be exempt from all evil things. Fourth, it is small and light: indication of our humility in the soul. Fifth, it is thin: an indication of honesty. Sixth, it has the imprint of the cross: one ought to carry within himself Christ's agony. Seventh, the round circumference of the wafer implies that one must believe that Christ was God incarnate: in circles, the beginning and end are united. Eighth, the wafer reads: "Lord God Jesus Christ," meaning wisdom. It also means tasting the wafer with awe, for Christ is a judge and Lord. Ninth, the wafer is baked by fire, which symbolizes our love for Christ. Tenth, the wafer is baked on a stone or iron board, an indication of steadfast fortitude united with love.

A wafer is divided into four portions to indicate the four sanctities of the soul, the body, the thoughts, and expressions, or the four virtues, or the faithful scattered in the four corners of the world. There are others who divide the wafer into three portions to indicate Christ's flesh, spirit, and divinity, or the faith, hope, and love we have for Christ.

Consider, for now, these two things. First, the priest offers the Eucharist after receiving it himself, as Christ himself did. This is an indication for the priest that he should be a partaker of the goodness that he offers to others. To preach goodness to others, one has to first exercise it himself. To ordain someone, one should have received the grace [of ordination] beforehand. It also indicates that the priest can pass on the grace that he possesses to others—since you have the ability to receive communion, offer communion to others; if you have confessed, make others also confess, and so on. For example, the bright and clear air receives light and illuminates other things. But if the priest is unworthy of communion, he cannot make others commune. Whosoever is not baptized, cannot baptize others, in the likeness of the dense soil and rocks that neither contain light, nor spread it.

It is evident, then, that whosoever has fallen from his order cannot offer communion, marry, confirm, or perform any other mystery. Consequently, we should receive communion and only then offer communion to others. Second, consider that those who taste Christ's flesh in purity are transformed into Christ's flesh and body: ages after ages unto the end, and everywhere, they turn into the one body of Christ and become body parts to one another. Like the head that through the nerves sends to the body three things—vitality, emotion, and action—those who taste [the wafer] in faith become partakers of Christ's immortal vitality. They can sense and distinguish the evil and the good, and they flee from evil and move toward goodness. Also, just as the body parts are appropriate to the head, likewise whosoever resolves to be an appropriate member of Christ carries within him the holiness of Christ's body in accordance with his own capacity; that is, wise mind, good will, innocent soul, and righteous body, before he turns into Christ's true body and member. Like the members that are similar to one another, those who taste [the wafer] in holiness become similar to the saints that after tasting [Christ's flesh] were cleansed and enlightened by Christ.

There are two kinds of unworthy people. Some lack love. They taste [the wafer] not in faith or holiness, but rather in corruption and deficiency. Such [tasters] are separated and severed members—separated from the most holy head, Christ, in the likeness of a severed and amputated body part. Others come close undeservedly, lacking love, faith, and holiness. They, too, are dry body parts, because they have not received the vitality of the grace from the head, Christ. These [the second category of people] are subject to greater condemnation, for they have tasted undeservedly. Just as from the one and same tasting the apostles were cleansed whereas Judas was condemned, and just as the one and same fire cleanses pure silver and turns the impure into a dark substance, similarly, communion redeems the worthy eternally and condemns and torments the unworthy eternally. Then, therefore, brothers, depart not by weakness and laziness, nor receive communion by audacity and unworthiness, for all are equally punishable. Do not distance yourselves completely so as not to get cold like those who distance themselves from fire, nor come too close so as to avoid burning in the fire of Christ's divinity.

The Prophet says: "For the Lord our God is a consuming fire" (Deut 4:24), and the Apostle says: "It is a fearful thing to fall into the hands of the living God" (Heb 10:31). Choose to walk the middle road, swerving neither left nor right, for both are waste. Instead, stay in communication and attached to the head, our Lord Jesus Christ in holy heart, cleansed from the sins through confession and penance, in resolute mind, and with warm love. And unite with the Father and the Holy Spirit through Christ who says: "You, Father, are in me, and I am in you, that they also may be in us, that they may see my glory" (cf. Jn 17:21–22). So much on the mystery of communion.

CHAPTER XXXVI

A homily by another on the communion, according to the word: "Jesus took bread, blessed it, broke it, and gave it to the disciples, and said, 'Take, eat, this is my body'" (Mt 26:26).

Doctors claim that the reason for unity is love. Therefore, any two lovers resent separation from one another, and if it were possible, they would have united their souls and bodies. The almighty God is extremely loving; wherefore He is referred to as a philanthropist. And for this reason He wanted to unite with man. God's unification with man ought to have happened through the mediation of the five senses. However, of the five senses, there are three that hinder the occurrence of perfect unity, though they signal the beginning of unity: with the eyes we see the object from a distance, with the ears we hear the sound [from a distance], and with the nostrils we sense the smell [from a distance]. The fourth sense that is realized by the extremities increases unity, because we cannot touch an object from a distance: we ought to come close to that which is to be touched. Perfect unity occurs with the fifth sense, taste, because the food not only is inoculated into us but also penetrates us and unites with us.

Now, before incarnation, the Word was distant from people; therefore, people were unable to see Him or hear His voice. After His incarnation, the Word came close to us so that we may see him in the body, hear his preaching voice, and receive his sweet scent. The Word, however, was not satisfied by being seen only; He also wanted to be next to us and touched by us, as He said: "Handle me, and see" (Lk 24:39). This, too, was not a satisfactory unity; He wanted the unity with man to be perfect. Therefore, He established the mystery of the Eucharist, which is a mystery of love, and thus God and man were united perfectly, because through this mystery Christ turns bread into his flesh and wine into his blood, delivering them to us to taste, so that He may be united with us. As He said: "Lo, I am with you with the mystery of my sacrifice unto the end of the world" (cf. Mt 28:20).

For this reason, "He took bread, blessed it, broke it, and gave it to his disciples, and said, 'Take, eat, this is my body'" (Mt 26:26). Now, concerning this mystery, one can question three things. First, why did Christ establish this mystery with bread and wine? Second, what is the essence of this mystery?

Third, how do bread and wine transform into Christ's flesh and blood?

With regard to the first [question], one should ask: Why did Christ offer his flesh and blood in a transformed substance and not in the substance particular to his essence? [He did so] for two reasons. First, so that faith may continue and the reward of faith may increase, for had we seen Christ in his own particular substance, our reward would have been questionable, because faith dwells on things invisible. Second, because eating human flesh and drinking human blood would have been extremely appalling, and had this mystery been demonstrated with the substance of flesh and blood, nobody would have had the courage to taste, as John says: "The bread that I will give is my flesh. The Jews strove among themselves, saying, 'How can this man give us his flesh to eat?'" (Jn 6:51–52). When a doctor prescribes medicine to a patient, but the patient is unable to take the bitter medicine, the doctor covers the medicine with an alien substance to ease its intake by the patient. Similarly, Christ the doctor covered his spiritual medicine—his flesh and blood—with bread and wine, so that the faithful may readily receive it.

But why did he give the redeeming mystery through bread and wine, and not through a different substance? We say for six reasons. First, because bread and wine are the most common food and drink among all nourishments and their consumption does not bore us. Therefore, Christ taught the spiritual tasting through these nutrients, which are common and free of boring characteristics. Second, because more than any other nourishment, bread strengthens the mind, and more than any other drink, wine brings joy, as David says: "Wine makes man glad, and bread strengthens the heart (mind) of man" (Ps 103:15). It follows that bread and wine are sources of life and good life, whereas Christ is the source of our existence through creation, redemption, and eternal glory.

This mystery is also stronger than any other mystery and brings joy to the hearts of those who are intoxicated with love. Third, because, if touched, bread and wine are more sacred than the flesh and blood that were offered in the old covenant, where hands were plunged in blood when they touched and distributed [the offerings]. It follows that when touching Christ's body, the hands of the priest should be purified from all sins, because "When Uzzia reached out his hand to touch God's offering, he was struck dead immediately" (cf. 1 Chr 13:9–10). Because the doctors say that Uzzia married his wife that night, more so, then, a person who touches Christ's true body should have clean hands and be exempt from the wet desire for women, so that he may not be struck dead spiritually. Fourth, bread and wine, in particular, indicate Christ's true body and the spiritual body of Him who is the holy church; for as bread is made of numerous grain and wine of numerous grapes, so too is Christ's body composed of numerous members. Bread and wine also signify the holy church, which is the combination of numerous believers. The Apostle says: "You are the body of Christ, and members of it individually" (1 Cor 12:27). Also, as bread proceeds from white flour and wine from the vine of aromatic plants, so does the flesh and blood of Christ proceed from the Holy Mother of God who was purer and holier than all kinds of flour and more sweet-scented than flowers.

Fifth, bread and wine reflect Christ's agony more than any other substance, because the grain of which bread is made is crushed by the flail, and bread is baked in the oven, while wine is pressed in the wine press. Similarly, Christ was ground by the flail into torments, baked in hardship, and pressed in the wine press of the cross. And know also this: This offering was demonstrated in the old ordinances when people sometimes presented offerings of corn ear, sometimes of flour, and sometimes of bread baked in a variety of ways— sometimes baked in the oven, or in a pan, or on a gridiron.

All of these were types of Christ's agony, because, before his incarnation as a grain ear, Christ was one of the patriarchs. In Moses' ordinances and the visions of the prophets, Christ was like the flour, which, in kind, is close to bread, and became perfect bread upon incarnation. He was cooked three times: First, in the oven; that is, in the womb of the Mother of God by the fire of the Spirit. Second, in the pan; that is, in the tribulation of this world, occurring through daily suffering, preaching, labor, and Jews' insults. Third, he was cooked on the gridiron; that is, by the suffering on the cross. This indicates that bread is life-giving, for it was cooked well; then, therefore, bread and wine adequately constituted the mystery's substance.

Sixth, this mystery should have not been included in Moses' old ordinances because priesthood at that time lacked perfection and the pattern was discontinued. Therefore, in the new ordinances it was appropriate to adopt a new substance and to turn to the mystery that existed before the old ordinances, when Melchizedek offered bread and wine, as the Scripture mentions. When Abraham returned after defeating his enemies, Melchizedek, God's priest, offered him bread and wine, and blessed him. This indicates that whosoever combats against sins and defeats them deserves the mystery. But whosoever is defeated in spiritual combat, should not receive the mystery. It is evident, then, that Christ appropriately offered this mystery with bread and wine.

Second, a word should be said about the mystery's essence and rite. Doctors say that the mystery is composed of four essential components, and the absence of any of these components renders the mystery incomplete. First, the officiant should be a true priest who has received the order of priesthood. He should not be fallen from the order, nor should he be excommunicated, because if he has not received the confirmation of the priesthood, his offering is void. The second component relates to the substance: the bread should be made of grain, and wine of vine, because other kinds of bread or wine, whether from water or syrup, cannot transform into Christ's flesh and blood. The third component relates to the form, based on what Christ said: "This is my flesh, and this is my blood of the new testament, which is shed for many for the remission of sins" (cf. Mt 26:26–28). The fourth component consists of the true intention, for the officiant should possess the determination to transform bread into Christ's flesh and wine into Christ's blood by the Word of God. Thus, the mystery of the Eucharist consists of four components, and the absence of any of these components renders the offering incomplete.

Unlike this, there are many rites and adornments. First, the Eucharist is performed in the church on the blessed holy altar and not in a house or elsewhere. Second, the chalice ought to be blessed, and it should be made of gold, silver, or tin. Copper gives a rusty taste, pottery is inappropriate, wooden containers absorb the liquid, and glass is fragile. Third, the priest should make the offering with the sacred vestment, and both the vestment and the cover of the holy altar should be anointed by the bishop. Fourth, the Liturgy should be performed during the day, beginning in the morning, and at the third and sixth hours, except the lucermarium of Christmas and Easter eves. Also, the Liturgy should not be performed if the lights are turned off or when there are no servants. There are many other similar things that constitute rites and adornments; and although these are not essential components for the liturgy, they are commanded by the holy patriarchs and should not be neglected. [Officiants] should adhere with the canons of their ordinances.

Concerning the third question with regard to bread's and wine's transformation into Christ's flesh and blood, wandering disbelievers ask it in five ways. First, when they ask: How does bread turn into Christ's flesh and wine into his blood? We answer that we can in many ways confirm that bread can transform into Jesus' flesh. First testimony: Many transformations have occurred during the long-ago days of the old covenant: Lot's wife turned into a statue of salt; Moses' staff turned into a serpent; the water of the river [Nile] turned into blood. God's hand did not lose its strength, for it is as strong now as it was back then, and we believe that Christ is true and almighty God. There is nothing strange, then, when bread and wine are turned into Christ's flesh and blood by his own words. Second testimony: It is easier to transform one thing into something else, than to create something from nothing. God the Word created the heavens and the earth from nothing; then, therefore, God the Word, our Lord Jesus Christ, can transform bread into his flesh.

Third, supreme powers can do all that lesser powers can do. Nature, a lesser power, can eventually turn bread into flesh and water into wine in the body of the eater; consequently, the divine power, the greatest [of all powers], can momentarily transform bread into Christ's flesh and wine into His blood in the hand of the priest. Fourth, a big walnut tree is seeded to grow and bring forth walnuts, because the power of nature in the seed absorbs humidity and transforms it to a tree, flower, and fruit. Consequently, God, the Creator of nature, can change bread into His flesh and water into His blood. Fifth, the sages claim that the basilisk contains plenty of harmful poison and that a certain star in the heavens influences it; thus the basilisk gathers its venom in the head, turning its head into a precious stone known as lamp of night, a stone more precious than all other precious stones. Now, if the power of a single star can change venom into a precious stone, then God, the Creator of the stars, can more so transform bread into flesh and water into wine through the priest. Sixth, Aristotle says that when mercury and sulfur are mixed in the veins of the earth, they turn into a combustible substance that can melt everything, because when mercury and sulfur are mixed with the power of the stars, sometimes they turn into gold and sometimes into silver, iron, copper, or tin. Now, if the heavenly energy can transform mercury and sulfur into gold, more so God can change bread into flesh. Seventh, the seashell transforms rain into a pearl. Eighth, in the East there is water that turns submerged wood into stone, while the nonsubmerged portion of the same piece of wood maintains its wooden substance: it is evident that the stony root drinks the water and nourishes the tree. There is a certain body of water in the West; when people place a piece of wood in it, the portion of the wood that is buried in its mud turns into iron, while the portion submerged in the water transforms into marble, and the portion remaining outside the water maintains its original nature. Now, if God has empowered the water to transform wood into stone, there is nothing astonishing about God the Word's power that transforms bread into his flesh and wine into his blood through the priest. For these reasons, it is beyond doubt that the priest can change bread into Christ's flesh by the Word of God, like Christ who changed it on Great Thursday, when he said: "This is my flesh." This is how bread can be transformed into Christ's flesh and wine into his blood.

Disbelievers and ignorant people also have a second doubt as to how Christ's body in its capacity can be contained in a wafer with smaller capacity. We say that Christ's body has essence and measurable property. However, the essence of his body does not fill the space as substance per se, whereas that which is measurable fills it as measurable, and whatever fills a space fills it through the medium of the measurable. Therefore, Christ's body in heaven fills the space through the medium of the measurable, whereas in the mystery [of communion] it fills the space through the medium of essence, not through the medium of the measurable, because the substance of the bread transforms into the essence of Christ's body, not into the measurable element of the same. For this reason, the measurable property and dimension of Christ's body in this mystery are not compatible with energy transformation; here we have the measurable property of Christ's body through the medium of his substance. Since the measurable is inseparable from the body's substance, just as the body's substance does not fill the space, similarly, in this mystery, the measurable does not fill the space. According to the sages, this is a delicate thought, and since the masses of people are dumb, we must demonstrate the idea through examples. Despite being larger than the earth by manifolds, the sun is visible through a small mirror. Break the mirror into many pieces and the sun will still be visible through every piece in its entirety. Similarly, although Christ's body is much larger than the wafer, nevertheless in the blessed wafer it is complete in its substance and quantity, and otherwise. Cut the wafer into many pieces and Christ's body will still be in each piece. Whosoever takes a piece of the blessed bread, takes Christ's whole body like a person who takes the whole wafer. Again, man's rational soul, contained in the body, does not fill the space, because it is the same whether in a small or a large body. The soul in its entirety is contained in the whole body and in every part of it. Christ's body in the wafer is analogous to this and it does not occupy the [entire] space. It is the same whether in a small or a large wafer, and Christ's whole body is contained in every particle of the blessed bread.

The third doubt of the heretics and disbelievers goes like this: How is it that Christians taste Christ's body every day, yet it is not diminished, for even if Christ's body were a big mountain, it would be diminished? We speak of the following as a reason why Christ's body is not diminished, although all the people of this world taste it daily. There is a distinction between material food and this spiritual nourishment, for after the material food enters the body, it becomes corrupt and transformed. This spiritual nourishment, however— Christ's body—does not become corrupt when man tastes it, nor does it transform into his nature. On the contrary, it transforms men within themselves through love. For this reason, Christ's body is not diminished, although everybody tastes it time and again. We will confirm this through analogy. The woman from Zarephath with her children and the Prophet Elijah were fed daily over the course of a long period by a handful of flour mixed with a little oil until they were full, and yet the flour and oil did not diminish, just as the Prophet Elijah had prophesied. Similarly, the body of Christ never diminishes, although the faithful taste it daily.

The disbelievers' fourth question is: How can Christ's one body, which is in the heavens, be in many places simultaneously? Is he present wherever the Eucharist is offered? We say that the one body cannot be in many places, just like something that is fixed in one place. However, it can be [in many places] in a different fashion, which we shall confirm through an example. There is one golden apple in the middle of the earth, and there are four loaves of bread in the four corners of the world. God is capable of transforming the four loaves into the golden apple of the middle of the earth like something that is fixed in one place. And the transformation in the four corners of the earth takes place through miracle. Likewise, Christ's body is in the center of heaven and is offered throughout the world. [Here is] another example. The sound a doctor produces comes out of one mouth and enters numerous ears, and it is as whole in the one who spoke it as it is whole in the numerous listeners. Similarly, Christ's whole body is in the heavens, as it is in the whole wafer through transformation.

Fifth, disbelievers ask: How can that bread be Christ's body, since, behold, it has the color and taste of bread? The same applies to the wine [they add]. We say that the bread is composed of two things: a hidden essence and a visible accident. These are differentiated in two ways. First, bread's essence remains so long as the bread lasts, but the accidental components are mutable. Essence, the color, taste, and scent, is immutable. Second, our five senses cannot discover bread's essence, but rather only the accidental components: the eyes see the color, the palate senses the scent, the mouth feels the taste, the ear hears the sound, and the hands feel the heat and cold. However, man's intellect can reach bread's substance and uncover it. When the priest recites Christ's words, saying: "This is my body," bread's essence transforms into Christ's body, while the accidental components—color, taste, and scent—remain. And these accidental components now cover the essence of Christ's body, as they covered bread's substance before it was blessed. Thus, although the senses establish that the color, taste, and scent have remained in the bread, their intellect helps the faithful through faith, and they understand and believe that bread's substance has been transformed into the substance of Christ's body. Otherwise, one would err if he claims, after exploring the color, taste, and scent of bread and wine, that these do not constitute Christ's body and blood. Isaac was deceived by his son Jacob, because he had covered his arm and neck with the skin of a kid, and Isaac's eyes were deceived because they were darkened. He thought that he saw Esau, but his ears and nose were not deceived, for he heard Jacob's voice and smelled Jacob's fragrance. However, his mouth and extremities were deceived, because he tasted a food that seemed to have been made by Esau and his hands gave him a sensation as if he had touched Esau. Therefore, Isaac said: Your voice is Jacob's voice, but your hand is Esau's hand. Likewise, Christ's body would be covered with the shape and color of bread; therefore, one ought to not believe his eyes that would see the color of bread, nor his nose that would smell the fragrance of bread, or his mouth that would sense the taste of bread, or his extremities touching the bread. On the contrary, one ought to believe Christ's voice, saying: "This is my body, and this is my blood."

Note also that when the priest disseminates Christ's body and chews it with his teeth, Christ's body does not become crushed; it remains intact. The quantity—that is, the accidental components of the remainder of the bread—is what becomes disseminated and crushed. Although the blessed bread falls into fire or water, Christ's body becomes neither spoiled nor burned, like the ray of the sun, which never becomes spoiled when it crosses through fire or shines upon mud. Spoiled or burned are only the accidental components of bread, at which time Christ's body is no longer there. Rather, it is in the heavens, on the Father's right-hand side, as before. Now, doubts should not be cast in our minds because of the doubts of disbelievers or ignorant people; rather, we should truly understand and believe that the blessed bread and cup are Christ's true and incorrupt body and blood, of which Christ shall make us partakers. Glory to him forever and ever, amen.

CHAPTER XXXVII

Homily of the same on ordination, according to the verse "Your priests will put on justice" (cf. Ps 132:16), and so on.

First, we must know what is the definition of priesthood and what is its purpose, because everything is recognized by a name or definition, and more so by definition than name. When we ask: "What is man?" and give his name as a response, we would not know whether the man is living or dead. But when we define him as living, rational, perishable, having capacity for intellect and skills, behold, the man becomes specific. Therefore, St. Dionysius defines thus: "In my opinion, hierarchy is a sacred order; intelligence and operation to imitate God in proportion to the ability."[42] He considers the order as genus, and the rest as differentiating components. He suggests that it is a hierarchy; that is, authority on earth. It is order; that is, rank, having first, middle, and last. And it is order, for the last are regulated by the first, just as earthly bodies are regulated by heavenly bodies. And we see order in everything. First, among the angels, for they have first, middle, and last orders, categorized in three triad classes. They are the thrones, cherubim, and seraphim as first; the dominions, powers, and authorities as middle; [and] the principalities, archangels, and angels as last. And thus, in accordance with their order, all kinds of grace, splendor, and knowledge descend from God firstly unto the upper, and then through them unto the middle, and through the latter unto the lower. Thereafter, from them, unto us, human beings. First, to the superior [human beings]—the prophets, the apostles, and the patriarchs—and then to other members of the church, to each according to his order among common Christians. Hence: "It is as ointment that ran down the head and the beard of Aaron, and from the beard ran down to the fringes of the clothing of the people" (cf. Ps 133:2).

There is order in heavens, too, for the superiors are the upper ones and they encircle the inferiors. There is order among the luminous bodies also, for the smaller ones receive their light from the larger and are obscured by them, as other stars are [enlightened and obscured] by the sun. There is also order in the elements, for the simple and light are upper, such as fire and air, whereas

---

[42] Cf. Pseudo-Dionysius, *The Celestial Hierarchy*.

the dense and heavy are lower, such as water and earth. There is order also in the cardinal points of the world: east is first, south is middle, and west and north are last. And to avoid mentioning everything, there is order among the kings and the subjects, and the masters and the servants in civil society.

Similarly, hierarchy is an order in the church. These, however, are distinct, for one is corporeal order and the other spiritual; one regulates the bodies and the other the souls; one is for this life and the other for the hereafter. Nevertheless, both originate from the same source—the theocratic authority, according to Paul: "There is no power but of God: the powers that be are ordained of God" (Rom 13:1). For this reason, he [Dionysius] says that hierarchy is order. And he refers to it as sacred, because it is a sacred order, distinguishing it from the corporeal orders, which include the prominent and the humble, the master and the servant. That [corporeal order] is order, but not sacred, for it cannot sanctify them; whereas this [ecclesiastical order] is a sacred order, for it can sanctify the ordained. Again, there is corporeal purity and there is spiritual purity. Physical purity belongs to laymen, whereas spiritual purity relates to the ecclesiastical authority established in the church; wherefore, he [Dionysius] says sacred order. [He also says] "Intelligence and operation." Intelligence: sacred counsel, wisdom, and knowledge; and opearation: this order and the authority within the church motivate the hierarchs, the priests, the deacons, and others in conformity with their order. And it is to be known that this order is established upon sacred operation and sacred intelligence, which are the faith and work. For these two can host the authority of order. Then, therefore, those who are unholy in their actions and deficient in their knowledge and faith do not deserve this rank, wherefore he says: "to imitate God"; that is, through holiness, intelligence, and operation they attain godlike resemblance. This is the definition of hierarchy, which is an authority established within the church.

But what is the purpose of this; that is, what is sought, and what does the hierarchical order strive to do? It is God-like resemblance. That is, the purpose and understanding of this [order] is to attain divine imitation. What is divine imitation? There are three things observed in God: First, He is simple and pure of any dissimilitude. Second, He is good and communicates His goodness to others. Third, He perfects others. And He possesses these [attributes] by nature, by being, and without beginning. He is simple in essence, good in knowledge, and perfect in operation. Again, He cleanses and sanctifies through simpleness, enlightens through goodness, and perfects through perfection. Again, simpleness is at the beginning, goodness is at the middle, and perfection is at the end. And all of these come down from the one benevolent will and providence of God, and He communicates Himself to the beings; that is, to angels and men. But first to angels, and then to people, because the angels are closer to God by nature, glory, and place. By nature: because they are intelligible and we are perceivable. They are immutable and we are mutable. They are immortal and we are mortal. Then, therefore, they are closer to God by nature and glory, for they are established in the unintelligible glory, while we are [established] in grace and the ordinances. And by place, they have been always with God in the holy of holies, while we live in the outer hall with perceivable beings. Thereby, the proceeding of all graces, splendors, and other things is poured on them first, and then descends upon us proportionately, as we have said before. Now, the purpose of hierarchy is this: to bring us to imitate divinity; that is, [bring us] to purity, light, and perfection. And it is evident that these are within the reach of the church, for therein some are purified and some purify, some are enlightened and some enlighten, and some are dedicated and some bring perfection.

And this is the order: first, sanctification, then enlightenment, and finally perfection. To be stripped naked of dirt and darkness is purification, and to put on light is enlightenment; that is, purification occurs when a person drops down what he possesses, and enlightenment occurs when a person receives what he lacks. Thereafter, he is brought to perfection. Like whoever comes to baptism is first cleansed and renounces all evil things, then is enlightened with the light of God's knowledge according to his faith, and finally is brought to perfection through baptism and the holy chrism. Now, purification is associated with the deacon, enlightenment with the priest, and perfection with the bishop. The same order applies to those who come to the order of deaconship, priesthood, and so on: they have to be cleansed and purified, first, from all dirty works, then be enlightened with the understanding of the light and instruction of God's knowledge, and finally attain perfection in the seal of the order that they take upon.

But why are these three demanded of the devotees? First, because they have body, soul, and intellect: they are cleansed physically, enlightened intellectually, and perfected with the seal spiritually. They also have nature, person, and accident: they are cleansed from all extrinsic sins in relation to accidents, and enlightened by nature, and brought to perfection in person with the confirmation. They also have essence, potency, and operation: they are cleansed with respect to essence, enlightened with respect to potency, and perfected with respect to operation. Again, the devotee possesses nature, grace, and glory. Nature comes first, grace is obtained in the present, and glory belongs to the upper domain. He is cleansed for the sake of his nature, enlightened for the sake of his grace, and perfected for the sake of his glory.

Again, [these are obligatory] because of the three countenances—the anointer, the anointment, and the anointed. The anointer equals to the bishop, the anointment to priesthood, and the anointed to the devotee, be it deacon or priest. Now, the [devotee] has to be cleansed on his behalf, enlightened on behalf of the anointer, and perfected on behalf of the grace. Now, because of the aforementioned reasons, every devotee has to be cleansed, enlightened, and then perfected, for the essence of the order exists in the holy conduct and holy knowledge, as has been said. With regard to the grace of those who act, such as the bishop, the priest, and so on, and who cleanse, enlighten, and bring to perfection, [note that] they have to be pure and clean themselves to be able to cleanse others, like water needing to be clear to cleanse. Otherwise, how would he cleanse others if he is unclean? Likewise, those that enlighten have to be light on their own in order to enlighten others, like a mirror with dual function, which receives the light of grace and enlightens others, just like the moon, which, according to some, receives light from the sun and gives light to us, the inferiors. The same applies to the air and the glass, which are enlightened before they enlighten. But if the moon is eclipsed, the mirror rusted, and the air thickened by clouds, they cannot give light. Likewise, those who perfect—the bishop or the priest—have to be perfect before they can make others perfect.

Somebody might ask: What is perfection? It means to have clean conduct, luminous knowledge, and perfect authority to be able to perfect others. First, because of the aforementioned reasons, for a person needs to take ownership of purity, knowledge, and authority to be able to independently give them to others. Second, since he acts like God, as we have said, he has to imitate [God] by sanctity, luminescence, and perfection. Third, because he makes God; that is, he creates God, for he makes the common person son of God through baptism. Similarly, he turns the bread and wine into divine flesh and blood through blessing. It is God's prerogative to forgive the sins, give grace, and make the two one body, which the priest performs through matrimony. And as the holy fathers say, a person needs to become deified before approaching God. Fourth, these [preconditions] are required for this occupation for three reasons, related, respectively, to performance as in God, to grace as in order, and to utilization as in the bishop. For example, in an occupation requiring skilled labor, the carpenter is the performer, the trade is the grace, and the tool is the hatchet that makes the wood smooth. With respect to performance, the hatchet needs to be adequate and sharp, like the sharp mind of the artisan; otherwise, it cannot make the wood smooth. Similarly, the bishop should possess proper purity and holy knowledge in order to perfect others; otherwise, he will fail.

Should someone say: Grace is from God; it never weakens. We say that truly grace proceeds from the Holy Spirit and is absolutely potent and powerful; nevertheless, weak recipients cannot handle that which is potent, like a cracked container that cannot contain water. And the weak eye cannot see the light, and the light penetrates a simple body, like the glass, but is hindered by dense bodies, like the rock and earth. The reason for this is not the giver; rather, it is the receiver. Understand the grace of priesthood in a similar fashion, for Solomon says: "The holy spirit of wisdom will not abide in an unworthy person" (cf. Wis 1:5). The priest is also referred to as angel; hence: "The priest's lips should keep knowledge, for he is the messenger of the Lord Almighty" (Mal 2:7). Then, the priest has to be as holy in his thoughts and actions as an angel. The priest is also intercessor for reconciliation between God and men; therefore, he has to be propitious and confident to be able to intercede; and this can happen through holy conduct and orthodox faith. Holy priests, like clean animals, are fit to offering, whereas the unholy [priests], like unclean and inedible animals, are kept away from the temple. Again, the priests have to be perfect in purity and knowledge to exhort others by knowledge and be a role model for them. The priests are guards within the church, whereas the devil, sins, and the heretics are enemies; when these come to the people, the priests need to alert them with understanding, wisdom, purity, and righteousness, in order to save themselves and the congregation. Otherwise, if the guard is burdened with laziness, sleep, and ignorance, and if the sword and the enemy have entered the congregation and yet he speaks not to warn, he shall hear the terrible word of the command: "The wicked himself shall die in his iniquity; but his blood will I require at your hand" (Ezek 33:8). Again, the priest is salt with his luminous knowledge and holy conduct, bringing taste to everything that lacks taste within the congregation. But if the salt itself becomes tasteless, it shall be thrown out and despised according to the Lord's command. Again, the priests are called elder and senior, because of, first, their prudence and knowledge; second, their order; third, their righteousness and brave actions; fourth, their perfection, for they perfect others after they have been perfected; fifth, leadership and exhorting; [and] sixth, spiritual fatherhood. But a sluggish priest shall be judged: first, for his sins; second, because he did not teach goodness to the congregation, but rather he taught them evil and made them stumble; third, because sins visited the congregation and he failed to expiate them; [and] fourth, because whoever sins knowingly, shall be punished more. Similarly, a brave priest shall be rewarded, first, for his works. Second, he will be rewarded for the sake of the congregation, for he was a good shepherd. Third, he deserved rewards for the sins that he expiated. Fourth, because he worked goodness wisely and knowingly. Behold, people like this "will be counted worthy of double reward" (1 Tim 5:17). Therefore, after hearing this, beloved brothers and sons, let us examine ourselves that we may not become embarrassed before the terrible pulpit, and may not be punished like Aaron's sons, Nadab and Abihu, who burned in fire. And the sons of Eli died by the sword because of their sins and sluggishness. Let us complete our journey by holy conduct, orthodox faith, luminous mind, diligent work, and patience instead of sluggishness, sleep, drunkenness, intemperance, and profane thoughts, hoping the blessed hope and the rewards for the love of God from the crowner, Christ our God, who is blessed forever. Amen.

CHAPTER XXXVIII

Homily of the same, again, on the priesthood, according to the verse: "You are a priest forever, after the order of Melchizedek" (Ps 109:4).

We have spoken before about what the priesthood represents. Now we shall speak about the order of hierarchy. It is to be known that hierarchy is first divided into celestial and worldly; that is, related to angels and to humans. The hierarchy of angels has first, middle, and last [orders]. The classes of thrones, cherubim, and seraphim are first; they are illuminated directly by divine light. The dominions, powers, and authorities are the middle class. And the principalities, archangels, and angels are the last class. They are the lock and seal of the upper hierarchy. Just as the first pass [the divine light] on to the middle, these do so to the last [order]. And the latter receive within themselves, but do not pass it down to other classes, except for the human beings, which we shall learn later. Again, they have triple powers: cleansing, enlightening, and perfecting. Cleansing is from the Holy Spirit; enlightening is from the Only Begotten Son, and perfecting is from God the Father, whereby they perfect each other with such potency; that is, the first [in order perfects] the middle, and the middle the last, while also purifying and enlightening each other. Again, they have seniors and juniors among them, not with respect to time, nature, or cause, for all of them are even with respect to time and nature, and by existence. But they are referred to as senior and junior based on their honor and order, for the first class—the thrones, cherubim, and seraphim—being closer [to God], receive luminescence directly from God and pass it on to the lords and others. Thereby, the six classes hierarchically are junior, whereas the first three classes are senior and first in honor and order. But here comes the question: Do the demons that fell from them have hierarchy? It appears that they have [one could think], because hierarchy is inherent to the angels by essence and nature, and since the demons have the same nature as angels, they, too, have hierarchy. Again, [one could think] the demons maintained their natural characteristics after their fall, for they are incorporeal, immortal, and lucent; therefore, it seems that they have a hierarchy.

We say that the demons do not have hierarchy, because priesthood is luminous grace, understanding, activity, and divine imitation. The demons lost these by their fall; they do not possess understanding, holy activity, and divine imitation, because they are darkened by ignorance and wickedness. Also, the light of God's grace does not work in them; therefore, it is evident that they do not have hierarchy.

Now, let us answer the arguments. With regard to the first [argument], although the hierarchy of angels is essential and natural, and it is not derivative like ours, their priesthood is habitual, for they received it voluntarily, not involuntarily. Therefore, the demons do not have hierarchy, for they do not have free good will. With regard to the second [argument] we reply: Although the demons remained immortal and incorporeal after their fall, this happened to torment them eternally rather than honor them. Priesthood, however, is honor and not punishment, wherefore they [demons] do not have priesthood. Also, the demons do not possess prophecy, which is the knowledge of things to come, nor do they have kingdom, for this grace is given in man's honor; hence: "You have put all things under his feet: sheep and oxen" (Ps 8:6–7). The demons, however, do not have honor, and thereby they do not possess prophecy and kingdom. And should somebody argue that according to Paul: "We wrestle against rulers and principalities in high places" (Eph 6:12), and the Lord says: "The prince of this world comes" (Jn 14:30), we say in this regard that the devil has no authority over people; rather, he is the ruler of those who voluntarily revolted against God and obeyed him [the devil].

Again, some say that the fallen demons belonged to the classes of rulers and principalities, and they became rulers and sovereigns of diverse sins— pride, fornication, and so on—and this is what Paul means. And if somebody says: If the demons do not know the future, how can they show it through dreams and speak about things to come through idols and [pagan] priests? We say that the future is known only to God, who is universal and perfect, and to those whom He reveals it, such as the angels or prophets. The demons, however, do not know the future prophetically, for God does not reveal it to them; rather, through the sharpness of their mind, they speculate about the future; not the distant, but the near future. Concerning the future of nature, they know it from past experience. The devil does not know the future of [God's] will, but the angel reveals it to do good to somebody, as in the case of the magus Balaam. These, however, occur through angels and not demons. Know this also from the following: Had the devil known the future, he would not have antagonized the saints who defeated the demons. But they know the torments of the hereafter through their sins. Hence, some said: "Do not torture us before the appointed time" (Mt 8:29); nevertheless, they are so blinded and established in wickedness that they just increase their punishments. Then, therefore, the demons do not have prophecy, nor do they have priesthood. And should somebody say: Aren't the priests who served the idols priests? We say no, for they imitated the priest in their work, serving deceit instead of prophecy. For example, the monkey is funny imitatively and not truly; in the same fashion, their priesthood and prophecy was imitative and not true. And it served the purpose of man's loss. This was on the celestial hierarchy.

Our worldly hierarchy is bipartite: paradigm and truth—the old and new testaments, for God wanted to give this gift to man, after He had given it to the celestial bodies. Since our nature was still immature, He gave us the priesthood of ordinances as mentor and milk. And he gave lesser light, proportionate to the weak eyes, that they may not be affected. And God gave this priesthood, first, to Aaron and his sons through Moses, as the Scripture says. He also erected the tripartite tent of meeting, first, middle, and last, in the likeness of the entire world. The first, the holy of holies, wherein the golden ark was and the cherubim spread out their wings above, was an image of the luminescent heavens—the exclusive abode of the Godhead in inaccessible light, with the angels and seraphim serving Him. The middle holy, wherein the seven-branched lampstand, the altar of incense, and the bread of presence were placed, was the image of the eighth arch, where the seven luminous bodies and the sweet-scented spirits of the saints are gathered. And the holy bread there is not Christ's flesh, as certain heretics claim, because the saints by their sweet-scented spirits see Christ face to face. Later, on the judgment day, they will rise in their body and spirit unto the luminous heaven to mingle with the classes of angels. The outer hall indicated the material world, where animals were sacrificed and their flesh was cooked and the food was enjoyed. The outer hall was the prototype of the church of the new covenant, wherein are located the pulpit, the center of the church, and the door or the outer prayer house. The golden ark is the chalice, the manna is the flesh and blood, the tablets are the Gospels, the righteous scepter is Christ, the censor is his [Christ's] sweet scent, expiation is the grace, the cherubim and the flabellum are the angels in service. Entering [the tent] once a year [symbolizes] the daily offering. Similarly, the lamb and the bread of presence [symbolize] the true lamb [Christ], and the incense is the fragrance of the Holy Spirit, and the lampstand is the seven-shaded grace.

Likewise, the garments of priesthood, the offering, and everything else are paradigms for our new covenant. And there are many differences between the old and new priesthoods. First, that was paradigm; this is real. Second, that was temporal; this is everlasting. Third, that occurred through Moses' intercession; this was done through the Only Begotten Son. Fourth, that was corporeal; this is spiritual. Again, it is to be known that the priesthood of the new covenant is common and falls between the celestial hierarchy and the ordinances of the old covenant, because it is made up of substance and mystery; that is, concept and form. Now, conceptually or with respect to substance, it matches the celestial [hierarchy], whereas with its physical mystery it is associated with the ordinances of the old covenant, thus constituting a link between the two and uniting the specter with truth.

Again, the celestial hierarchy is distinguished through three [attributes]: cleansing, enlightening, and perfecting. This applies to the old covenant as well: the head priest, the priest, and the attendants. Likewise, in the new covenant, the bishop perfects, the priest enlightens, and the deacon cleanses. Again, it [the new practice] is a link between them [the celestial and old hierarchies] otherwise as well: the bishop is the equivalent of the celestial and intelligible beings, the priest [corresponds to] the new ordinances, and the deacon is [compatible with] the old ordinances. And this is evident from their respective functions: the bishop always perfects and grants like the upper classes; the priest performs all the mysteries of the church—baptism, confirmation, Eucharist, and so on; and the deacon points out with the censer of the old covenant, for the censing was the prerogative of the head priests of the old covenant. And although these—the angels in the old and new covenants, and the bishop, the priest, and the deacon—have different functions, all of them have one purpose with regard to divinity, and are bonded into one unity through the single cleansing, enlightening, and perfecting grace.

Also, it is to be known that there are nine ranks in the ecclesiastical hierarchy, divided into three triads in the likeness of the celestial hierarchy. And the reason is this. Three unconfused graces proceed from the persons of the Holy Trinity—the Father, the Son, and the Holy Spirit: cleansing, enlightening, and perfecting. Although nature, activity, and everything else are equal within the Holy Trinity, the persons' peculiarities appear in the grace. Cleansing is becoming to the Spirit, enlightening is to Christ, and perfecting is to the most perfect Father. Now, these three graces descend from the Spirit of the Godhead upon the holy church. And those who receive these graces and influence others are three: the bishop, the priest, and the deacon. Also, those who receive these graces and carry them within are three: the cleansed, the enlightened, and those brought to perfection. For this reason, there are nine ranks in the church, divided into three triads.

The first [triad] includes the catholicos, the bishop, and the priest. The second includes the deacon, the acolyte, and the seminarian; he [Dionysius] equivocally calls them servants. The third is composed of the celibate clergy that are referred to as complaisant, the holy congregation, and the catechumen; he [Dionysius] refers to them as devotees. And if you include the penitents also, the catholicos will become the tenth, just as God is the tenth above the nine classes of angels; and this is according to St. Dionysius. According to other doctors, however, [the order is categorized] upwardly. The first and most inferior is [the rank of] doorkeeper; second, the lector; third, the exorcist; fourth, the torchbearer; fifth, the acolyte; sixth, the deacon; seventh, the priest; eighth, the bishop; [and] ninth, the catholicos who encompasses all of these ranks. Know also this: I have discussed the respective functions of each of these positions elsewhere, according to the verse: "For this cause has God, your God, anointed you" (Heb 1:9). Find them there. It is also known that those who devote themselves to an order, first, they shave the summit of their head in a round shape, cut their hair moderately, and fall before the bishop at the entrance of the church naked and without girdle. And the bishop inquires about their worthiness, and the confessor witnesses to their worthiness. And he, the devotee, undertakes the canons of the bishop, first the renouncing [canons] and then those of commitment. And [the bishop] makes the sign of the cross upon the devotee and cuts the hair crosslike, reciting in the name of the Father, the Son, and the Holy Spirit. Then he hands over the key of the church, saying to him: "Receive this authority from the Holy Spirit, to open the doors of the holy church." And the deacon, who is the nearest, takes the key from the devotee's hands. All other orders are given in a similar fashion, except that this first was given at the door of the church. Other [orders] are given inside the church, gradually advancing forward. The acolyte receives his order in the chancel, whereas the deacon [receives it] on the bema, closer to the altar, as we shall mention. Know also this: [Devotees] are allowed to marry up to [the first] four ranks. As for the order of clerk, which is the fifth, marriage is not allowed, as it is not allowed to the deacon, which is the sixth [order]. As to why there are five orders up to the deacon and he is the sixth, St. Dionysius says: The five orders do the cleansing, and the deacon has authority over them and conducts the purification. The first [function] is to banish the unbaptized and the sinful from the church; and this is conducted by the doorkeeper. Second, there are the deniers to whom the lector delivers the sermon. Third, there are the demoniacs whom the exorcist heals. Fourth, there are those whose turning from the sins has been incomplete; the torchbearer enlightens them. Fifth, those who have repented fully, abandoned the sins, and are working good works are tended by the acolyte through psalms and Alleluia. Sixth, the deacon in general preaches to all and exercises authority over the congregation and all the lower ranks, as we have said.

Six things are required for those who come to the orders: first, to be male; second, to be baptized; third, to be pure in the body and in the soul; fourth, the presence of a bishop; fifth, the Word that requests divine and heavenly grace; [and] sixth, the garment and the myrrh. Now, during the blessing ceremony, there are six common elements for three orders—the bishop, the priest, and the deacon: first, the offering before the altar; second, the kneeling; third, the ordination; fourth, the cross-shaped seal; fifth, the repeated request for divine and heavenly grace; [and] sixth, the greeting at the conclusion. [Apart from these] there are unique and particular functions, [such as] placing the Gospel upon the head of the priest by the bishop, and the kneeling of the priest on two knees in contrast with the deacon's kneeling on one knee. These indicate that one is higher in rank than the other, for just as the Gospel includes all the testaments and constitutes their completion, so does the priest encompass the cleansing, enlightenment, and perfection, constituting the completion of all ranks. The bishop, too, encompasses the cleansing, enlightenment, and perfection, constituting the completion of all ranks. And just as the Gospel includes all the works and teachings of Christ, so is the bishop obliged to incorporate within his person the works and teachings of Christ, so that he may teach the divine understanding and messages verbally and show them practically. [The vestment] he [the bishop] wears on his head refers to receiving the grace and authority directly from Christ, just as the first classes of the thrones, cherubim, and seraphim [receive theirs directly from God]. Again, it infers that the bishop is first among all the ranks, and therefore the grace goes to him before it is poured down unto others; hence: "Like an ointment that ran down the head, [etc.]" (cf. Ps 133:2). The kneeling of the priest on two knees indicates his two authorities—enlightening and cleansing. He is also authorized to offer the Eucharist and to confirm, because myrrh was applied to his hands explicitly. The kneeling of the deacon on one knee indicates one authority—the cleansing only. Therefore, he wears the stole and the maniple only on his left side, symbolizing that his yoke and labor are partial. But what do these mean? First, it is common for the three ranks to approach the altar. The altar is Jesus, as has been mentioned, whereas the three ranks by the altar are reminiscent of the thrones, cherubim, and seraphim gathered around God. The deacon—the cleanser—refers to the seraphim and the Holy Spirit, the priest to the cherubim and Christ, and the bishop to the thrones and God the Father. Kneeling indicates that our entire life and wills belong to God [and also indicates] dedicating our body, spirit, and obedience to Christ. Again, the knees, the hands, and the head in their bowed position indicate offering all of our conducts, works, and senses to Christ.

Again, we dedicate three orders to Christ by cleansing, enlightening, and perfecting. And just as the summit of the head is clean, likewise we have to purify our soul, mind, and senses through confession and penitence. And just as the altar, the bishop, and the heavenly grace are holy, so too should we render ourselves worthy by holiness. And placing the hand in the likeness of Christ, who placed his hand upon the disciples and blessed them, signifies, first, the fatherly protection upon a beloved son; second, the protection from enemies; third, the distribution of grace that is in the right hand; fourth, the power of the hands, as in: "my hand shall support him" (Ps 89:21); fifth, the sacred work, for the hand signifies work; [and] sixth, teaching and instructing him to learn and keep. He says: Behold! You shall keep whatever work I have worked, just as I am entrusting to you whatever I received. Note, here, that the deacon cannot give his right hand; that [privilege] is reserved only to the priest and bishop. And this is evident from four things. First, myrrh is not applied to the deacon's hand but is applied to the priest's. Second, the deacon serves but does not perform; it is the priest who consecrates. Third, the deacon cannot expiate the sins; only the priest has the authority to absolve. Fourth, after the authority of priesthood was entrusted to Thomas, the other apostles bowed their heads and kissed the right hand that had touched the divine body. The cross-shaped haircut that was assigned after the haircut of Melchizedek in the hands of Aaron indicates, first, the severance of unnecessary desires from four things—the senses, the memory, the intellect, and the will. Moreover, [it signifies] the casting away of the diverse accidents of sins that occur through Satan, for the hair is accidental occurrence. Second, it signifies adding the suffering of the cross to one's innocence, be it virginity or something else, and endurance like Christ who, although He did not commit sin, endured the torments and the cross at the end. Wherefore the immaculate people are referred to as dead, as if they are dead for this world, to live with Christ. Concerning the depiction [of the cross] on the head [piece], it shows, first, our voluntary undertaking to commit no sin and to be crucified, as Christ himself "became obedient to the point of death—even death on a cross" (Phil 2:8). Second, because by doing so we imitate Christ, for the iconographers are accustomed to imaging the cross of salvation on the head to indicate that: First, the cross was the fulfillment of all dispensations. Second, the cross is the glory of our Savior; hence: "There was no Spirit, because Jesus was not yet glorified" (Jn 7:39); meaning, he was not yet crucified. Third, Christ is priest and king, wherefore the cross is depicted upon the crown. Fourth, since Christ voluntarily became obedient to the cross and suffering, thereby it [the cross] is depicted on the head [piece]. Fifth, while on the cross, Christ had the thorny crown on his head; so does the priest imitate Christ, indicating this resemblance through his hair and the cross-shaped cut.

Concerning the repetition of the expression "divine and heavenly grace," singing it thrice and reciting it once, [note this]. When they sing it, the bishop faces east and the devotees turn west facing the bishop. And when he recites, the devotees turn east and the bishop turns west to put his hand upon and give them the authority and grace. This indicates that the giver of authority is the Holy Spirit from whom he [the bishop] seeks it. The bishop is the servant and intercessor like a pipe that takes the water from the source and passes it on to us. Again, it shows that it is rather God that chooses and calls upon than human beings; hence: "Whom he predestined, called, and justified before the world was," says the Apostle (cf. Rom 8:30). And this is evident through four paradigms. First, Moses brought Aaron to priesthood only after God commanded him: "Take to yourself Aaron your brother to the tabernacle of the testimony and anoint him as priest" (cf. Ex 27:21–28:4). Likewise, our Lord Christ "did not glorify himself, but was appointed by the one who said to him, 'You are a priest forever'" (cf. Heb 5:5–6).

Again, the giver of the authority of priesthood to the apostles attributed the fulfillment to the Holy Spirit. "You will be baptized with the Holy Spirit, and stay in the city until you have received the power and the tiding of the Father which is the Holy Spirit" (Acts 1:15; cf. Lk 24:49). Likewise, Peter, the head of the apostles, did not add Matthias to the eleven apostles by his own authority; rather, he timidly asked God for this to happen through a lot; that is, through divine revelation, for the lot is nothing but divine revelation, which influenced the apostles to cast their lot for Matthias when Judas fell, and Matthias was elevated to become one of the twelve [apostles].

All of these indicate that the bishop is not the one who chooses as he wishes; rather "The Lord chooses whomever he wants." Wherefore it is said that the divine and heavenly grace has called upon you. And if someone chooses the unworthy for the sake of silver, it is as if he antagonizes God's will, despises what the Holy Spirit chooses, and chooses what the Holy Spirit despises. Moreover, "Despised are those who have been chosen with silver" (cf. Ps 68:30). And whoever ordains the unworthy associates himself with their

287

sins, as the Apostle says: "Do not ordain anyone hastily, [etc.]" (1 Tim 5:22).

And the holy greeting at the conclusion of [the ordination of] the bishop and the priests indicates that, first, the given devotee was purified through God's call and that God's image was beautified in him. Therefore, we all love him and greet him. Second, because he was placed in our same order and became equal to us. Third, because he defeated the adversary through God's power and became a soldier of Christ; wherefore we elevate and honor him as a victorious wrestler and martyr. Again, the holy greeting indicates the joy of our hearts and the unity of our spirits with one another with fraternal love. And now, brothers, see and contemplate the labor you have undertaken, for you have been entrusted with God-like function. And God is consuming fire, and fire needs to be handled with tongs. And what is the tongs but holiness? God is holy and through holiness we warrant ourselves to the holy, because the holy does not take unholy places as his abode. And the Holy Spirit flees the deceit of sins. See that you become intercessors between God and men. You ought to be reconciled with God, and then reconcile God with men. You are the messengers of God to men, [so] be like the good angels and not like the evil devil. Do not quench the lamps of your spirit through sluggishness and vices, so that you may not remain outside the bridegroom's wedding banquet like the foolish bridesmaids. Rather, with alertness and fortitude, like the wise bridesmaids, be worthy of the heavenly wedding. You are salt for the corrupt body of the congregation; [so] do not lose your taste through spiritual impurity and do not be thrown out to be trampled under human feet. You are installed guards to the house of God; when you see the coming of the sword, alert the congregation, so that God may not hold you accountable for their blood. You are shepherds for the rational flock of Christ; do not be after taking only the milk and fleece and neglecting the sheep; rather, tend the flock well in the nourishing pasture, and offer them the comforting water, leading them to the church. Cleanse and heal whoever is lame in [observing] the ordinances, blind toward faith, and leprous with sins, and sustain them with the comforting Word. So that you may be gathered after this life in the heavenly fold [church] with the brave head shepherd [Christ] in Christ Jesus, in our Lord, who is blessed forever. Amen.

CHAPTER XXXIX

[Homily] of the same on monks, according to the verse: "Whoever does not bear his own cross and come after me, cannot be my disciple" (Lk 14:27).[43]

As St. Dionysius says, three unconfused graces—cleansing, illuminating, and perfecting—descend in the holy church from divine benevolence and the compassionate will of the Father, the Son, and the Holy Spirit, as has been said. Some, such as the bishop, priest, or deacon, take these graces from the church and apply them to others. The deacon cleanses, the priest illuminates, while the bishop makes perfect. Whereas others only receive the graces and do not apply them to others, such as those who need to be cleansed, the holy members of a congregation needing illumination, and the monks needing perfection.

Now, those who infernally and firstly need cleansing are divided into five categories. First, the catechumen who have not yet received the spiritual birth and are not yet formed after the image of God. These are nourished in the womb of the church for forty days before they receive the divine image.

Deniers who failed to believe Christ and turned and came back to the church compose the second category. If they were baptized in orthodox ways, they do not need to be [re]baptized. They only need to confess the creed, deny their former works, and be allowed into the church. But if they were [baptized] by certain heresies, they should be baptized or confirmed.

Demoniacs [compose] the third category. These are frightened by demons due to their laziness and imperfection and need to be cleansed through fasting and prayers and healed by the Gospel and the name of God.

Fourth, [the category of] those who have turned from and confessed the sins but intend to commit them again. One ought to forgive their confessed sins and fortify them by penance, so that they may not commit [sins] again.

Fifth, [the category of] those who have totally repented for their sins, relinquished them, and are doing good works. These need to be cleansed from their sins, granted forgiveness, and put into penance, so that instead of the evil works, which they are cleansed and voided of, they store various good things

---

[43] In the original text, the verse reads: "Anyone who does not abandon his father and mother, [etc.]," which is an excerpt from Lk 14:26. We chose to replace it with the exact text of Lk 14:27.

in them and are crowned. These are the categories of those [to be] cleansed.

Those who need illumination—the middle ones, the holy members of a congregation, who do not need the cleansing [needed by] the aforementioned people and are baptized, [and] have remained steadfast in their faith and fortitudinous in implementing the commandments, fasting, praying, almsgiving, and so on—are called seers, for they are deemed worthy of seeing the Liturgy and other sacraments.

The uppermost category of these [cleansed and illuminated ones]—the monks—are referred to as executors of the will, having been named so according to their work, for they have renounced their own will, in order to implement the will of God and the will of the primate. Concerning the monks— that is, those who are cleansed, simple, and spiritual [people], who are referred to as monks because they have given up the multifarious mundane life—they are, first, called monks, because they live alone,[44] "having left their father or mother or wife or children or other things according to the Lord's command" (cf. Mt 19:29).

Second, because they stay alone in their solitary prayer, for the public prayer is reserved to priests and the congregation. Third, because having separated their minds from their senses, they touch only God, excluding all other beings. Fourth, because they make only their spirits live and they kill their bodies. Fifth, because they receive from the two lives only the life to come, and not the earthly life; hence: "The world has been crucified to me, and I to the world" (Gal 6:14). Sixth, as we have mentioned, because all of them have only one will—the will of the primate—and not individual or partial wills.

The monks are referred to as executors of will, because just as they implement God's will, so do they carry out the will of the primate.

Now, these monks are higher than all the categories of the cleansed and illuminated in two aspects. First, because the cleansed face the deacon and the illuminated face the priest, whereas these, the perfect, face the bishop, although they receive [their] order and blessing from the priest. Second, because they are thoroughly cleansed mentally, spiritually, and physically. Not only are they enlightened by sight, but also they are elevated to and in communication with the sublime intelligence and the substance of the mystery.

Now, these are called monks[45] in general, as [the priests] are called priests.

---

[44] In Armenian *miaynakeac'* [միայնակեաց] for *monastic* is a complex word, literally meaning a person who lives a solitary life.

[45] The Armenian church refers to these monks as *Abełay* (*Abīlā* in Syriac [= hermit = mourner]), which is the term used in Tat'ewac'i's original text.

However, they are divided into two categories—some are solitaries,[46] while others are monks covered with habits. The solitaries are inferior and lesser [in order], like deacons [versus priests]. They, whether male or female, vow to only stay celibate. Monks with habits are higher [in order], like priests [versus deacons]. Not only do they undertake to stay celibate, but they also abstain from eating meat and drinking wine; they suffer through vigilance and crucify themselves for Christ's sake.

Now, those dedicated to monastic life come to the priest—the abbot of the monastery—at the door of the church naked and without belt; that is, with uncovered head and loose belt, which indicates staying away from the love of the world, being stripped of everything, and having no excuse or bodily cover for sins; rather, having everything demonstrated manifestly. They enter the church holding candles and they do not kneel on one knee as the deacons do, nor do they kneel on both knees as the priests do, or lift the Gospel above their heads as the bishop does; rather, they stand close to the priest behind him and keep their heads bent down. This indicates that they do not have the order to influence others, or to cleanse them like a deacon, or to enlighten them like the priest, or to bring them to perfection like the bishop; rather, they influence only their own person and no one else. Then, therefore, a monk does not have the right to read the Gospel, incense with incense, cleanse, or deliver a sermon. Since the authority to do these things is given to the deacons, they [monks], then, cannot act as priests, nor can they baptize, officiate the Divine Liturgy, or perform the marriage ceremony. They cannot forgive the sins, cross, or perform any of the duties of the priests. Moreover, they cannot have a staff as the bishop has, nor can they bestow the order of priesthood, or take it away. Also, they cannot give orders to the priests or deacons. [The standing of a monk] close to the priest indicates that he is distanced from mundane life in numerous ways and [since] he has become close to the priest, he ought to pray, fast, and resemble God just like the priest. Thereupon, the priest turns and asks the devoted [monk] to denounce entirely the mundane life and then commit himself to keeping the yoke of the commandments wholly; and he [the devoted monk] confesses and undertakes to keep them [the commandments] wholly.

Although the act of renouncement includes numerous components, only three of these are major. First, renouncing the beloved ones; that is, the parents, the offspring, the wife, brothers, and so on, in compliance with what Christ dictated in the canon concerning such people: "Anyone who has not left his

---

[46] Tat'ewac'i distinguishes these monks using the Greek term *monozon*.

own father and mother and other things, and does not bear his own cross and come after me" (cf. Lk 14:26–27). Second, renouncing material possessions, whether from patrimony, or from trading, usury, or other things, for He [Christ] says: "You cannot serve God and mammon" (Lk 16:13). Third, renouncing the pleasures of the senses—eating, drinking, sleeping, visitations, clothing, laziness, boredom, and so on. Those are material things to be renounced. There are also three [major] spiritual things to be retired from: one's own will, that he may not be led by his own will; evil thoughts, that he may free his mind of all kinds of illusions; [and vices, such as] pride, vainglory, envy, grudge, hatred, and so on. He [the monk] confesses his retirement from these things before the priest and vows to God. Then the priest crosses and confirms [the monk] as a devotee to Christ. Thereafter, [the monk] takes the scissors in his own hands and gives it to the priest, who cuts the [monk's] hair crosslike in five places— the forehead, the crown, where the memory is [the neck], and near the ears. The crown is cleansed [of hair] entirely. This mystery is similar to what is pronounced during the ceremonies of [ordaining] the priests—to sever all lust and physical beauty, and to reject bedizenment, anointment [with scented oils], and the braiding of the hair. Because just as a stinky odor is a symbol of a corrupt body, similarly bedizenment is a demonstration of the vice of desire in the heart. Putting on tattered and ragged clothes as appropriate is demonstrative of how the soft cloth is exchanged with a coarse one. Likewise, [the monk] exchanges the conduct appropriate to the laity with an austere and coarse one. Lay people have many excusable things for which they should not be condemned, such as lawful matrimony, birthing children, soft clothes, patrimony and possessions, and selling and profiting, which are reckoned sins for the clergy if they do so.

Now, the solitary wears five [pieces of] clothes. First, the hood, which is the cowl indicative of the grace of Christ descended upon the head—which is the noblest of all body parts—and the entire body, for the grace of God protects the soul and the body wholly. Second, the rope with narrow bottom, which indicates the stern manner and the harsh and severe life. Third, the belt, [indicative of] restraining the desires of the mind and the heart. Fourth, the slippers on the feet as a symbol of fortitude. Fifth, the square frock—a symbol of the cross.

The monk with habit, however, wears four more things; that is, a hood without nap, which is the white tubing; this means that all the senses are covered, and that the thoughts are restrained from the world and directed only toward heaven. He also wears a habit on his shoulders in the shape of the cross, which indicates the yoke of the commandment and that he is lifting the cross of Christ on his shoulder. Moreover, [he wears] stuff made of goat's hair in the likeness of John and Elijah, which is natural clothing given to people. In addition, covering the body by the cloak or mantle down to the feet indicates love and humility that covers and adorns all virtues. This is what the members of the common order [of monks] wear.

However, those who are superior and practice ascetic life to its extreme, like the Egyptian fathers, abstain with sleeveless cloak and bare feet, indicating that they have absolutely distanced themselves from worldly life and corporeal works. This is the first distinction between solitaries and monks with habits. But they are different also in other ways. The solitary receives his order in the church near the entrance, whereas the monk with habit [receives the order] near the pulpit, before the holy altar. There is also a third difference: the monk with habit stands on the inner pulpit next to the priest and receives communion by his own hand, while the solitary does not. It is also known that if a layperson wants to become a monk, he needs to be ordained, but if a priest or a deacon wants to become a monk, he does not need to be ordained but rather simply changes his garments. Thereafter, the holy greeting [is applicable on those who have become monks], indicating that they have come to share our order as Christ's soldiers and have become our beloved spiritual brothers. Lastly, they receive communion during the holy sacrament, because, first, Holy Communion is the fulfillment of all sacraments; everything else is incomplete without it. Also, just as the priest has received communion from the bishop, so did the monk receive communion from the priest. The one and same communion from one to another means that all of them have been brought to perfection in priesthood in the likeness of God in our Lord Jesus Christ who is blessed eternally, amen.

CHAPTER XL

A homily by another on the order of priesthood according to the verse:
"Priests shall be holy, and not profane the name of the Lord their God, for it
is they that offer the offering to God" (Lev 21:6).

The doctors say that the Almighty God left nothing in the world without order. He wants everything to be orderly, because He is orderly.

First, order is found in the consubstantial Holy Trinity, for the Father is unborn, the Son is begotten, and the Holy Spirit is procession, each having its own immutable countenance.

Second, order is found among the angels, for all angels are divided into three [ecclesiastical] hierarchies—thrones, dominions, and principalities, each composed of three orders. First [in these] are the thrones, seraphim and cherubim, [grouped] in one hierarchy. Dominions, powers, and authorities [are] the middle [hierarchy]. Principalities, archangels, and angels [are] the last [hierarchy]. Thus, all of the heavenly hosts are included in nine classes, whether thousands of thousands, or myriads of myriads; we do not know their number, lest they themselves know it, as well as their Creator "who numbers the multitude of stars," as the Prophet says (Ps 147:4).

Third, order is found also in heaven, for heaven is divided into three sections—foremost [among these] is the fiery heaven; it lacks stars, is motionless and luminous, and the classes of angels are stationed there. Second [in these sections] is the watery arch; it absolutely lacks stars and is called first, because it moves all of the heavens. The third is the stellar heaven, which consists of eight parts—the firmament that has infinite stars, and the seven heavens of the planets, each containing one planet. The uppermost of these [planets] is Saturn, [then] Jupiter, Mars, the Sun, Lucifer [or the Morning Star], which is Venus, Mercury, and the moon, which is the most inferior. Muslims refer to these [planets] as Zohal, Mushtari, Marekh, Shams, Zohra, Odarid, and Qamar.

Fourth, there is order also in the elements, which the philosophers divided into four [kinds], and which are the basis and root of all material beings. First [in these elements] is the circle of fire, which encircles all of the elements. Second [in these] is the air. Third is the water. Fourth is the earth—the most inferior of all [elements] and in the middle of all.

Fifth, there is order in the plants and shrubs, which have an adventitious soul by which they receive nourishment, grow, and reproduce. Nourishment sustains the substance, growth [sustains] the individual [plant], and reproduction [maintains] the species and kind. It [vegetation] also has [yet another] order, for it is divided into roots, stems, branches, leaves, flowers, and fruits.

Sixth, there is order also in the animals, for they have an innate soul by which they eat, grow, and reproduce. Moreover, they have the five senses by which they see, hear, and so on. Also, they have breath and numerous body parts according to an order by which they move and travel from one place to another.

Seventh, there is order found in humans, who possess that which is innate in the plants, that which is sentient in the animals, and, in addition to these, the rational soul—the mind and will. Besides, humans are adorned with various orders, for some are kings, some princes, some artisans, and some husbandmen.

Now, since we find order everywhere, then, therefore, the holy church also should have orders. Wherefore, the doctors say that just as there are seven planets in heaven that administer and regulate the sensible world, similarly in the holy church, which is an intelligible heaven, there are seven orders that enlighten and regulate the church of God.

Now, bottom up, first is the order of doorkeepers. Second is the lecturer of the Old Testament. Third is the exorcist. Fourth are the flambeau carriers. These are referred to as the four minor orders. Lay priests can attend to these orders. They cannot, however, go beyond these, lest they enter the order of celibate monks. Fifth is the semi-deacon, who is the acolyte. Sixth is the senior deacon. Seventh is priesthood, which is the highest and most holy of all of these orders. Therefore, God commanded Moses: "Speak to the sons of Aaron that my priests shall be holy, and they shall not profane the name of their God" (cf. Lev 21:1–6).

Now, these seven ranks of church servants are known as the sacrament of order. There are two things one must say about this sacrament. First, what does Christ expect from church servants? Second, what is the essence of the mystery of priesthood, and how is it adorned and how does it occur?

First, what does Christ expect from church servants? It is to be known that Christ expects church servants to possess three things. First, priests should have a noble origin; that is, they should be born and brought up in the bosom of the church with orthodox faith, [as] a child of chosen parents, "For every sound tree bears good fruit, [etc.]" (Mt 7:17). Anyone who receives the order [of priesthood] and becomes a servant of the true head priest, Christ, ought to be a Christian by origin and the son of chosen parents, as the epistle says: "You are a chosen race, a royal priesthood, a holy nation, God's own people, that you may declare the wonderful deeds of him who called you out of darkness into his marvelous light" (1 Pet 2:9).

Second, Christ expects a man of order to be a perfect and strong person in his stature, body, and soul, and not of immature age, or imperfect mind, for according to the old law, people received the order of priesthood at the age of twenty-five—[the limit] for soldiers was twenty years and for priesthood twenty-five. Similarly, in the new covenant, one should complete the age requirement, as the Apostle says: "He must not be young and immature, or he may fall into the condemnation of the devil" (cf. 1 Tim 3:6). Again, he must be of age twenty-five spiritually; that is, he must love God and his neighbor, which indicates the number twenty, and must relinquish the pleasures of the five senses.

Third, Christ expects the priest to be pure in his body and soul, as God commanded Moses: "No one who has a blemish shall offer an offering to me" (cf. Lev 21:21). There were twelve corporeal blemishes in the old law—anyone who was lame, blind, and short-nosed, or with mutilated ear, broken hand, broken leg, hunched back, squinted eyes, bleary eyes, boldness, cancer, or one testicle should not offer an offering to God.

A person should first learn why bodily blemishes were unacceptable in the old law. We say [this was so] for three reasons. First, that they may not be seen inferior to the pagans who rejected bodily blemishes. Second, because the offerings were pure—the [sacrificial] sheep and lambs were chosen for the offering through these twelve discriminatory steps. Therefore, those who offered the sacrifices should have been free of blemishes. Third, as a paradigm for the spiritual blemishes in the new law, for just as the twelve [bodily] blemishes excluded people from the order of priesthood or deaconship there [in the old law], similarly, in the new law, twelve spiritual blemishes exclude one from the order of priesthood.

The first blemished [person] is the blind—indicative of an ignorant person who is blind in his mind, for it is extremely inappropriate for an ignorant person to practice priesthood. Malachi says: "The lips of a priest should guard knowledge, and men should seek instruction from his mouth, for he is the messenger of the Lord of hosts" (Mal 2:7). Christ commands: "If a blind man leads a blind man, both will fall into a pit" (Mt 15:14). The priest is a leader whom people follow. When too many horses are driving a cart, there will be no harm if the middle or the last [horse] is blind, but the cart will fall into a pit if the first horse is blind. Similarly, if the common people are ignorant there will be no harm, but an ignorant priest will cause much harm and he will cause many to fall into sins.

The second blemished person is the lame. Anyone who cannot walk steadily on the road is lame. This signifies a person who does not travel on the road of virtue steadily, but changes into evil, because virtue is in the middle of two evil edges. Abundance is in the middle of stinginess and lavishness. A person lame in both legs bends on the two sides of a road; he also is driven to the two evil edges—lavish sometimes and stingy sometimes; angry at instances and timid occasionally. Referring to these, the Apostle says: "A double-minded man is unstable in all his ways" (Jas 1:8).

The third blemish is [having] an extremely short or extremely long or crooked nose. We inhale through the nostrils both sweet scents and stinky odors. The nose is a symbol of sagacity. Therefore, a person of short or long nose has either deficiency or abundance of sagacity. Besides, the short-nosed [person] is one who never punishes those who are guilty; he is reminiscent of an irrational being that cannot make a righteous judgment. The long-nosed person inflicts extreme punishment upon sinners, whereas a person with a crooked nose makes wrong judgments—he unbinds the sinners and justifies them, while punishing the innocent. Isaiah condemns them, saying: "Woe to those who put darkness for light and light for darkness, who call evil good and good evil" (Isa 5:20).

The fourth blemish relates to a person whose ears are mutilated; that is, a person who does not want to hear the words of the salvation of the soul—the divine commandments; rather, he readily opens his ears to nonsense. Again, a person with mutilated ears does not want to listen to his neighbor's good [words], but readily opens his ears to evil [counsel].

The fifth blemished person is he who has broken hands—he who does not perform good works.

The sixth [blemished person] is he who has broken legs; he cannot move from one virtue to another, as the psalm says: "He shall go from strength to strength, from glory to glory, and God shall be seen to his messengers" (cf. Ps 84:8).

The seventh blemished person is the hunchback who has a kyphosis; that is, a person with hunched soul, bent down. There are those, who have their hunches in their front, because their hearts are full of the love of the world, but if the hunch is on the back, it means the person has the loads of sins piled upon his back.

The eighth blemished person is the squint-eyed [person] whose soul is squinted—a hypocrite, who pretends before men to be with God but seeks glory and people's praise.

The ninth blemished person is he who has bleary eyes, [the blurriness] excreted from the pupil; that is, he who has stains in his mind, be it from heresy or sins. Also, a person with white pupils is considered to be bleary-eyed; it indicates an arrogant person, for just as white he seems beautiful, so does the arrogant seem joyous in his own eyes with his bright will, such as the praying Pharisee in the temple who thought of himself to be righteous and the rest sinful.

The tenth blemished person is the bold; he remains consistent; that is, he always harbors lewd desires in his heart.

The eleventh blemish is cancer; that is, a person who, wherever he may reach, makes others sin by works or by words. Moreover, cancerous is [perceived to be] a person who has the leprosy. This disease does not show the filthy wounds of the body. This indicates the greedy person whose conscience never troubles him, for he says that he piles up for the sake of bodily needs, while his soul is stained before God.

The twelfth blemished person is he who has one testicle; that is, the impotent and idle. Also, a person with a rupture is considered to be one-testicled, for his intestine dangles down, gains weight, and makes it difficult for him to walk. This indicates a person whose heart is burdened with the thoughts of lewd desires, but he cannot execute [his thoughts] out of embarrassment before men.

Those who have blemishes in their souls cannot draw near the order of priesthood.

Should someone ask: Which of the bodily blemishes is unacceptable for the priests of the new [law]? We say that in the new [law] there are two kinds of priesthood—first, those who offer Christ; second, [those who offer] themselves, whether through solitary worship, or common prayer. Now, it is the spiritual blemish, and not the corporeal, that is prohibited to those who worship individually. Whereas both spiritual and corporeal blemishes are prohibited to those who pray commonly in the church: "For brothers help one another and supply for one another's need" (cf. 2 Cor 11:9). Those who offer Christ, however, are prohibited from the blemishes of the soul and the body, for they ought to be altogether pure in all the parts of their soul and all the parts of their body. Since Christ is perfectly pure in His divinity and humanity, the priest ought to be pure in his soul and his body.

Behold! The law dictates: "One who has a blemish shall eat of the sacrifices, only he shall not draw nigh to the altar, and shall not approach the veil" (cf. Lev 21:22–23). This shows that a person who is distanced from offering receives communion through others and receives what is his rightful share, but he cannot offer Christ, nor can he perform any one of the seven sacraments.

Again, the doctors say that some of those who have corporeal blemishes and come to priesthood are rejected, whereas others are accepted. The first reason is [applicable] when the blemish is such that he [the candidate] cannot perform the sacrament of communion without harm, for if there is fear that he might fall down or [encounter] something else, he should not be called for priesthood. Second, if he [the candidate] is so filthy that people might be offended and disgusted. Although he can practice [priesthood], he should not become a priest; it would seem that he has a stinky nose, which would appear disgusting to men. Third, if [candidates] have all their body parts, but they are feeble and weak, some of them might be allowed to become priests, whereas others might not. For example, if someone is so lame that he cannot stand before the altar of God without a stick, he cannot become a priest, but if the lame person can stand [without a stick] he can become a priest. Fourth, those who have either a small or a large part of the body severed, whether by one's own will or through the will of others covertly or explicitly, if the part is large and obvious, and is severed by anger, the person cannot become a priest. For example, if the arm or the leg is severed. Or if a person severs his sexual organs, thinking that he would please God—since he would not fornicate—he cannot become a priest, for he has committed suicide; but if the body part is small, such as a part that is not used for the performance of the sacrament of communion, or if it is hidden or is severed by the surgeon, the person can become a priest.

[Note] also that there are three kinds of eunuchs. Priesthood is prohibited to those who are born of their mothers' wombs [as eunuchs] and have other sins, or to those [who have become eunuchs] because of man's violence and have other sins. But if they do not have [sins] and are worthy, they can be admitted into priesthood. However, those who for the sake of the kingdom [of God] turned themselves into eunuchs, misinterpreting the word that one should sever [his] sensible body parts, are prohibited from priesthood by the Nicene canon, [which states] that a person with castrated body part should not be admitted into priesthood, and if he is a priest, he should be dismissed. Those who turned themselves into eunuchs for the sake of the kingdom [of God]; that is, through fasting and prayers [typical to] prudent people, they deserve priesthood more. It is thus that priests are chosen to serve the pure offering of Christ our God from parents that are noble by origin, [themselves being] unblemished in their body and soul. This [was about] the first section.

Second, we need to discuss the essence of [the mystery of] priesthood and how is it adorned and how does it occur. The doctors say that the essence of the mystery of priesthood consists of six things. The absence of any one of these components nulls the mystery.

First component: A bishop must grant the rank of priesthood, because the bishop has authority over the priests and deacons, just as the king has authority over city artisans, for he appoints a supervisor to collect the tithe, and regulates each trade—smith, goldsmith, and others. Similarly, the bishop takes care of the church, which is the city of God, and assigns each a spiritual task—whether priest, deacon, semi-deacon, or other. Moreover, he blesses the church, the holy altar, and all the holy vessels; as it is said in the book of rituals, it is the bishop who should pray [over the aforementioned things]. Second, it is the bishop's prerogative, by essence and by necessity, to hand the substance of this mystery to the holy orders—the chalice and the paten to the priest, together with the wine and portion; the Gospel to the deacon; the empty chalice to the semi-deacon; and so on with others. Third, there are essential and necessary formulas, and in [the case of] each rank the confirmation is restricted to the place where the substance of the mystery is delivered to them. The formulas are as follows. The doorkeeper is first in order. The bishop seals up the key, hands it to the doorkeeper, and speaks thus: "Do it in this way to answer for this work and for the things that are locked by the keys given to you." The reader is second in order. The bishop seals up the prophetical Scriptures and hands them [to the reader], saying: "Take these scriptures and be a teller of God's word; and if you perform your task with loyalty and warm love, you shall become a partaker with those who served God's word from the beginning." The exorcist is third in order. The bishop seals up and hands the book of vows, the book of rituals, [to the exorcist,] saying: "Take this, understand it, and keep it in mind, and have the ability to place your hands upon the demoniacs who come to be baptized, or are baptized." The flambeau carrier is fourth in order. The bishop seals up the candlestick and hands it [to the flambeau carrier], saying: "Take this candelabrum with the candles and know that you have the duty of lighting the chandeliers and lanterns in the holy church." Fifth, moreover, the bishop also seals up the empty chalice and paten, and hands them to the [semi-deacon], saying: "Take and find out what kind of service is invested in you, for you were asleep and lazy in the church until now, [but] you have to be diligent and alert from now on." The bishop also says whatever else is written to this regard in the books of bishops. Deaconship is the sixth order. The bishop seals up the Gospel and hands it to the deacon, speaking the following formula: "Receive the authority of reading the Gospel in God's holy church to be heard by the living and in memory of those who died in the name of God, amen." Priesthood is the seventh order. The bishop seals up the chalice full of wine and the paten with the portion, speaking the following formula: "Receive the ability to offer the offering to God, and to offer the Eucharist for the living and the dead in the name of God, amen." These indicate that formulas constitute the third essence of the mystery.

The fourth essence of this mystery is that the recipient of the order of priesthood should be male and not female, for if the recipient is female, even if all the substances [of the mystery] are placed in her hands and all the formulas are pronounced, she will not receive the confirmation. Because the person who receives the order [of priesthood] climbs a great rank and becomes leader, but a woman does not have the right to these leadership [positions] and ranks, because she is [placed] under man's service, as God said to Eve: "Your submission shall be to your husband, and he shall rule over you" (Gen 3:16). It is for this reason that Paul says to Timothy: "Let a woman learn in silence with all submissiveness. I permit no woman to teach or to have authority over men; she is to keep silent" (1 Tim 2:12). It is for this reason that [a woman] does not befit priesthood and cannot receive the confirmation.

The fifth essence of this mystery is that the receiver of the rank of priesthood should be truly baptized; if he is not baptized, he cannot receive the confirmation of priesthood. It is to be known that nine kinds of confirmations are given at church. First, during the mystery of baptism. Second, during the mystery of confirmation. Seven [additional] confirmations are given during the mystery of ordination for priesthood, because each rank has a confirmation of its own. But there are two differences between the confirmation during baptism and the other eight confirmations. First, the baptismal confirmation is a potential power, not practical; for the baptized receives the power to accept all the mysteries of the church. But the other eight confirmations are practical power, for each seal has its own performance. For example, a seal has the ability to battle the enemy and demonstratively confess Christ's faith before unbelievers. Likewise, each of the seven [hierarchical] orders [of the church] has its own task, such as the doorkeeper and so on. The second difference is that baptism is the foundation and door to all [other] seals; therefore, no one can receive any other seal, unless he is baptized, whereas a person can take the other eight seals from another. The order of receiving [the seals] is canonized for bishops: first [they receive] baptism, then confirmation, then the minor [orders], [then] the order [of priesthood], and so on.

The sixth essence of this sacrament is that both the giver and the receiver of the order should have true intentions, for the bishop gives the order with true intention, so that it may be unambiguous, and the receiver of the order receives it as to holy church with true intention. Then, therefore, the essence of the order of priesthood is evident.

Know also this. If an essential or necessary component—whether with regard to ordination, or other mysteries—has been forgotten or neglected by them [bishops], everything should start from the initial phase and be given anew, as if nothing has been received [by the ordained]. But if [the forgotten or neglected] things are accidental or ceremonial with regard to the mystery, there will be no need to start or give everything anew; [only] that which has been left [undelivered] accidentally needs to be given in due time. And accidental are the following: Anointing the hands of the priests, the cloak, the girdle, or placing the bishop's hand over the head of the devotee during ordination, and similar things, which need to be completed in due place and due time for the glory of God and in praise for the name of Christ, our God, who is blessed with His Father and the Holy Spirit forever, amen.

CHAPTER XLI

Again, a homily by another about the order of priesthood, according to the verse: "Your priests shall clothe themselves with righteousness; and your saints shall exult" (Ps 132:9).

The doctors say that it was appropriate for the order of priesthood to exist within the church, because there are three spiritual levels—nature, grace, and glory. Nature is the lowermost, grace is the middle, and glory is the highest [level], because man's nature rises to the highest glory through the intercession of angels. Now, the holy church is at the middle level; that is, the grace of the Holy Spirit, wherefore it is in between natural life and the glory of the Heavenly [Kingdom]. There is order in nature, because heavenly bodies govern us—the inferior bodies—and enlighten us. There is order also in the natural body of man, because major members of the body govern the other members, such as the head, the heart, and the liver govern other members and affect their natural energy and motion. There is order also in the glory of the heavenly kingdom, for the orders and ranks of angels and those who live like angels are numerous there. Then, therefore, truly there should have been order in the church, which is in the middle of nature and glory, because disorder is evil all over, while order is good.

It is also a must for the church to have not one, but many orders, for three reasons. First, so that the road leading man to God's service may be broad. Because had there been only one order, the road for salvation would have been narrow and not everybody would have been able to travel on it. Second, since man is weak by nature, one order alone would not have been able to perform all the services of God—such as [how] the Prophet Moses was unable to lift the people's burden alone and he selected seventy elders from them who lifted the burden of the people. Then, therefore, truly there should have been many orders in the church. Third, so that God's wisdom may be revealed, because it is the task of the wise to regulate, for the independent philosophers perceived the wisdom of God through the order of beings. When the queen of Saba saw the orderliness of Solomon's servants, she was in ecstasy and she said: "Your wisdom exceeds what I have heard" (cf. 2 Chr 9:1–6). Solomon signifies Christ, and the queen of Seba [signifies] the congregation of pagans: when they see

303

the orderliness of Christ's servants—that is, the seven orders of the church—Christ's wisdom takes them by surprise and admiration.

Within the seven orders of the church, the highest order is priesthood, as it has been written in Kings that Solomon made an ivory throne and gilded it with gold (3 Kings 10:18). Also, he made six steps to the throne; likewise, Christ made six steps, which are the six lower orders. And He placed on top of these the highest throne, the seventh order of priesthood. And He gilded it with gold; that is, with righteousness and virtue. That is why David said: "Your priests shall clothe themselves with righteousness" (Ps 132:9). Now, concerning the order of priesthood, it needs to be pointed out that Christ honored the priests by three kinds of honors. First, He put on them diverse garments. Second, He placed His crown on their heads. Third, He seated them at His table.

The first honor is that He put six kinds of different garments on the priests. The first garment is the miter, which signifies spiritual things. First, it indicates spiritual power, because it covers the shoulders by which [the priest] lifts the burden of Christ's ordinances. Second, it points at the cover by which the Hebrews covered Christ's head and struck him, saying: "Prophesy to us! Who is it that struck you?" (Mt 26:68). And [Christ] puts on them the miter, because the five senses are there [under its cover], for the priest ought to offer the offering as if he is Christ heading for the torments. [The purpose of wearing the miter is] to prevent the eyes from looking at a stain, and [to close] the ears and the mouth before nonsense, and to cover the chest over the heart, so that he may store good thoughts in the heart.

Alb is the second garment. The white garment indicates what Herod put on Christ in order to be mocked; it also indicates the holy conduct by which a priest ought to clothe himself. The white garment is appropriate for the priest during the Liturgy, because the priest acts like the angels, and when the Gospel speaks of the garments of angels, it presents their garments in white color: "they saw the angel dressed in a white robe; and they were amazed" (Mk 16:5). And in the Acts of the Apostles it is said: "Behold, two men appeared to them in white robes" (Acts 1:10). For this reason, the life of a priest ought to be holy like angels. The third garment is the girdle, which indicates the whip used for beating Christ while he was bound to the pole. The girdle also indicates restraining lewd desires, exercising temperance, and being alert, as the Gospel says: "Let your loins be girdled and your lamps burning" (Lk 12:35), for anyone who has not girdled his loins can put nothing in his chest: he will not be able to keep his temperance and the good works will be spilled out of him. It should be known that in the old law Elijah girdled his loins with leather, but in the new law Christ had a golden girdle. There are two differences between Christ and Elijah as follows: Christ's girdle was golden, while Elijah's girdle was leather. Second, Christ's girdle was around his breast, while Elijah's girdle was around his loins. Now, Elijah's girdle indicates the temperance of the priests of the old law, because their temperance was due to their fear of the ordinances; in the new law, however, temperance is to be exercised not because of fear, but because of the love of Christ, for gold signifies the divine love. Again, in the old law committing adultery was prohibited and therefore Elijah's girdle was around his loins. In the new law, however, committing fornication and the lust of the heart are forbidden, as the Lord said: "Everyone who looks at a woman lustfully has already committed adultery with her in his heart" (Mt 5:28). Therefore, Christ's girdle was around His breasts, which are close to the heart, and indicates restraining the lust of the heart.

The fourth garment is the maniple, which indicates the ties by which the Hebrews tied Christ's hands when they seized Him. It also signifies bundles of corn—good works gathered together. That is why it [the maniple] is worn on the left forearm, which shows this life, and [wearing] the maniple on both forearms [means that] in this life one should sow goodness by the left [hand] and in the hereafter harvest by the right [hand]. The maniple also signifies the cleansing of forgivable sins, because it looks like a small towel by which people cleanse. Although [people] in this life can stay away from mortal sins, they cannot avoid forgivable sins, whereby the face of the soul ought to be cleansed from forgivable sins.

The fifth garment is the stole, which shows the ties by which Christ was tied to the pole. It also shows the yoke of God's commandments, which is light and agreeable, as Christ said: "My yoke is agreeable" (Mt 11:30). The sixth garment is the cloak. It indicates Christ's scarlet robe [which He had on] while He was taken to be tortured. It also indicates the divine love, for as the cloak is the uppermost garment that covers all [other garments], so does God's love cover all sins, as the Apostle says: "Love covers a multitude of sins" (1 Pet 4:8). Just as the cloak is atop of all garments, likewise love is higher than all [other] virtues. One should also know this: The priest can clothe himself with all the garments pertinent to the six orders that are inferior to him, and he can perform every task they perform. This shows that all virtues that cover the men of inferior orders should be gathered in the priest. It is evident from this that Christ honored the priests extremely, for He clothed them with His own robe. The garments [worn] at the Liturgy signify the garments associated with Christ's torments. There are people who ignorantly despise the holy garment of the Liturgy, which in the old law [priests] wore by God's command before offering their offerings, as Aaron and his sons did. If [a priest] was required to adorn himself with garments during the offering of irrational animals, [a priest] that offers the Lamb of God in order to lift the sins of people should be under greater obligation to adorn himself [with garments]. That is why David says: "Your priests shall clothe themselves with righteousness" (Ps 132:9). This [was] the first honor by which Christ honored the priests.

The second honor was that of placing the crown on their heads, just as the crown of thorns was placed on Christ's head as a sign of kingship. Therefore, the priest has a crown on his head; that is, his head is cleansed and a circular crown is made with his hair. To serve Christ means to be king, and [to make the crown] perfectly cross-shaped means that he [the priest] shares Christ's cross. And this circular crown befits the priest for four reasons. First, the philosophers say that a circle is the most beautiful of all shapes, and the priest ought to have a conduct that is more beautiful than laypeople's conduct. Second, a circle is wide and can include many things within, and the priest ought to have a wide heart filled with love, so that [people] love not only the beloved but also the enemies. Third, a circle is the most holy, because it does not have any corner where one might hide a stain. Similarly, the soul of the priest should be pure of sins, lacking the corners of deceit or envy, where he might hide the stains of his sins. Fourth, it [a circle] is simpler than other shapes, because other shapes consist of many lines, while a circle [consists] of one line; it does not have a beginning and an end, and it is perfect. Therefore, this shape was placed in this world like the four elements, the stars, and the heavens. Likewise, the mind of the priest ought to be most uncomplicated and simple like a dove. Also, they [priests] serve God, who is without beginning and without end, and since they intercede for the entire world before God, their hair is made like a circle crown.

Again, the Apostle says: "Hair is given for a covering instead" (1 Cor 11:15), wherefore the servants of the church ought to clean the crown of their head circularly, like a crown. This indicates that their hearts or minds are open and uncovered before God. Hair also symbolizes the wealth and possessions of the world. Just as the long hair covers the visual and auditory senses and hinders their function, likewise the mind of a person who is fond of worldly wealth and possessions is covered with worldly preoccupation and he cannot see the afterlife glory or hear the word of God, or taste the sweetness of the divine commandments. And just as one who has thick hair on his head experiences headache, for the hair does not let the steam of the head out, likewise a person whose mind is preoccupied with worldly concerns experiences a lot of pain and fears thieves and robbers at all times. But a person who does not possess possessions has neither pain nor fear. Therefore, the priest ought to cleanse the crown of his head and make his hair circular like the crown of Christ who placed the crown on his [priest's] head. It is evident from this that Christ honored the priests so much that He clothed them with His robe and placed on their heads His own crown.

Christ's third honor to the priests is that He seated them at his table, which is the table of angels, as Solomon says: "Man ate angels' bread" (Ps 78:25). Not only did He make them sit on the angels' table, but he also honored them more than angels. Because although angels sit at this table and eat the bread of life comprehensibly—for they rejoice during the mystery of the Liturgy—they are not allowed to offer this offering and to change the bread and wine into Christ's body and blood. This capacity is also given neither to kings, nor rulers, patriarchs, or prophets, but rather only to priests. Although it is a great honor for a person to eat from a king's table, even if he was seated at the farthest end, it is more honorable to be seated immediately next to the king. The priest sits on Christ's table immediately next to God, as Solomon says: "I will go in to the altar of God" (Ps 43:4). For this reason, the priest, who sits close to God at Christ's table, ought to be purer and wash[47] his own hands of the sins through confession, as the Scripture of Leviticus says: "The priests that offer offerings to their God should be unblemished" (cf. Lev 21:21). And this is [so] for four reasons. First, priests touch Christ's body on the altar, which angels tremble from; therefore, priests should be holy. For example, in the old [covenant] the ark of God that the priests carried was covered with gold on the outside and contained a golden urn full of manna. The golden urn full of manna is the body of Christ full of divinity. And the priest that lifts Him [Christ's body] in his hands is reminiscent of the ark of God, wherefore he ought to be covered with gold from inside and outside, with the divine love from inside and the love of neighbor from outside. Again, [the priest ought to be covered] with spiritual temperance from inside and corporeal temperance from outside. Second, the priest serves and waits the heavenly king. Those who serve the worldly kings feel extremely embarrassed when they serve the food and the glass of wine with dirty hands. Likewise, whoever offers the body and blood of the Lamb of God as bread and as wine offers [these] before God. Therefore, if his hand is

---

[47] The original says *enlighten* (*lusaworesc'ē* [լուսաւորեսցէ]). We think it should read *wash* (*luasc'ē* [լուասցէ]).

stained by sins, he will bear a great embarrassment before God and His angels. For this reason, when the priest comes to offer the offering, he washes his fingers with water, saying: "I will wash my hands in innocence, and compass your altar" (Ps 26:6). This indicates that one ought to cleanse himself even from the most minuscule sins.

Third reason: Of the eaters from the king's table the cleanliness of the hands is required particularly of those who eat with the king from the same plate. Now, the priest that offers the offering eats and drinks with Christ from one plate and one cup, just as He ate in the Upper Room with His disciples; therefore he [the priest] ought to have his hands pure of sinful works. It is for this reason that Moses made the basin of the mirrors of the women, for there the priests washed their hands and feet, and cleansed the filth of their minds looking in the mirror, and then [only] they went in to offer the offering. This basin signifies the mystery of confession, for a person ought to look into it and cleanse his stains, and wash his sins with the water of his tears. And [only] then offer the body and blood of Christ as offering.

Fourth, because everything the priest does has divine nature—through Eucharist he turns the bread and wine into the body and blood of God; likewise, through baptism he turns the children of man into children of God; similarly, he grants forgiveness to sins—as the Gospel says, it is God's prerogative to forgive sins. Likewise, by marrying a man and a woman [that are] strangers, he makes them one body, and this, too, is the work of God; hence: "What God has joined together, let not man put asunder" (Mt 19:6). Now, all the works of the priest are thus the works of God; therefore he [the priest] first ought to become divine, and then approach God and do the works of God—to become divine through a heart that is pure, a tongue that speaks the truth, a soul that is innocent, and works that are good. And by gathering within him all the components of benevolence and human and divine virtues, he [the priest] will be able to imitate God to his best ability. Also, he shall have compassion for people as fathers have for their children and God for His creation. And as a good shepherd he shall lead Christ's flock in the manner of a man who will answer to Him on the Day of Judgment for the sake of Christ's congregation and rational flock. By doing so, he shall become a companion of the good head shepherd, Christ, in the right-hand side, saying: "Here am I, and the children God has given me" (Heb 2:13). And he shall hear the heavenly voice, saying: "Good and faithful servant, enter into the joy of your master" (Mt 25:21), in the glory of the most Holy Trinity forever and ever, amen.

CHAPTER XLII

[Homily] of the same on priests, according to the verse of the Prophet: "The priest's lips should keep knowledge, and they should seek the law at his mouth: for he is the messenger of the Lord Almighty" (Mal 2:7).

First and foremost, a person should understand this verse as follows. When the intended word [i.e., idea] reaches the mouth through the larynx, he [the priest] should hold it back by his lips, adorn it with knowledge and wisdom, and then speak.

Second, he should know and understand [his idea] before addressing other people.

Third, since the lips of his soul—the intellect and mind—cautiously embrace knowledge and wisdom, therefore he is called senior—a person who attained greatness through wisdom and good works.

Fourth, the knowledge and wisdom of the Father is the Only Begotten Son, and the priest should be watchful in keeping Him embraced, so that He [the Son] may not flee from his unworthy works, because cursing in vain, slandering, insulting, betraying someone, lying, and so on make Christ flee and depart from us, for God's wisdom cannot abide in a malicious person. Solomon says: "The Holy Spirit flees from deceit and a body enslaved to sin" (cf. Wis 1:4–5).

Fifth, the mind of the priest should attentively learn and recognize the sins of the members of his congregation from their lips, so that he may be able to heal them from the wounds [of the sins].

Sixth, he should not read the Scripture, pray, or sing psalms with his lips only; rather, he should do so knowingly and intelligently, as the Apostle says: "Sing psalms by your mind, sing psalms by your soul, sing psalms and learn them by heart" (1 Cor 14:15), because if a person prays unknowingly, God will ignore his request and leave it unfulfilled.

Seventh, he should be watchful through the prayers of his lips and through fasting, and be aware that demons and those influenced by them are persecuted and rejected by these [prayers and fasting], as the Lord said: "This kind is driven out by prayer and fasting alone" (Mt 17:21).

Eighth, he should be watchful with the lips against all harmful things and unclean food that is not befitting for priests to be nourished with—pork, according to the canons of the fathers; [meat] torn by beasts, slaughtered by Muslims, or suffocated. He should be cognizant of his worthiness and then move close to the body and blood of the Lord, so that he may avoid crucifying Christ anew to his own damnation. He should also be watchful by his lips and mind to avoid abridging the psalm; for if he does so, the demon will claim the remainder of the psalm, and at the end of the age, the demon will enter with him before the judgment of God, saying: "You have excluded us once by your silence during benediction and you have stripped us naked from our glory; look at your image and see how extensively you are robbed of and reduced from your own blessing."

Thus we would bring shame to Christ and [therefore] we will be persecuted by the Lord by means of shame.

He [Malachi] says: "They should seek the law at his mouth," so that, first, he [the priest] may speak rather lawful than unlawful words, and not speak nonsense, jest, and do similar things, as Solomon says: "My throat shall meditate truth" (Prov 8:7). Second, because God seeks whatever is commanded in the ordinances and the Gospel through the priest's mouth, and the priest should be watchful to avoid hearing: "I will condemn you out of your own mouth, you wicked servant" (Lk 19:22). Third, the priest should always establish law and order among people through his speech, and he should not cause slander and stumbling, for the Lord says: "Woe to anyone who causes one of these little ones sin" (Mt 18:6). Fourth, the priest by his own mouth should teach the congregation the ordinances and the orthodox faith, the confession and other things, so that the enlightened congregation may become accustomed to pleasing God.

After these, he [Malachi] says: "He is the messenger of the Lord Almighty." The priest resembles an angel in many ways.

First, the angel is in a lofty place, and the priest is lofty by his reverence and rank.

Second, the first [classes of] the hierarchy—the thrones, the seraphim, and the cherubim—are equally honorable; that is, the thrones face the Father, the seraphim face the Son, and the cherubim face the Holy Spirit. Likewise, the priest, the bishop, and the catholicos are equally honorable in officiating the offering, for the officiant priest is referred to as Lord. [It is conceived that] the catholicos faces the thrones and the Father, the bishop faces the seraphim and the Son, and the priest faces the cherubim and the Holy Spirit.

Third, those three [classes of angels] receive the wisdom of God directly;

likewise, these three orders [of priesthood] receive God's grace and wisdom directly, wherefore they are three; that is, the deacon, the acolyte, and so on.

Fourth, they [the angels] are incorporeal and invisible among us; likewise, the priest ought to be incorporeal in his body, so that people may not see in him any stain or blemish. Hence: "The eye of the vulture has not seen it" (Job 28:7).

Fifth, they [the angels] are imperishable in their vitality; likewise, the priest ought to be imperishable spiritually through good works, and not perish through sins, according to the philosophers: "That is not death for you, the perishable; rather, it is immortal evil."

Sixth, the angels do not have passions or needs; likewise, the priest ought to lack the passion for sins and the need for worldly possessions.

Seventh, the angels' meditations are directed upwardly to God like fire; hence: "Who makes his angels spirits, and his ministers a flaming fire" (Ps 104:4). Likewise, priests ought to "set their minds on things that are above where Christ is, seated at the right hand of God" (Col 3:1) and not on things that are on earth, according to the Apostle.

Eighth, the angels relentlessly praise God; likewise, the priest ought to always bless God—pray, learn, and teach—as David says: "I shall praise the Lord at all times" (Ps 34:1).

Ninth, the angels are always light, as the hymn says: "You created the angels from light."[48] Likewise, the priest ought to be intellectually luminous and wise, and then he ought to enlighten the congregation, because an ignorant priest is blind and sightless, and the Lord says: "If a blind man leads a blind man, he will err and both will fall into a pit" (cf. Mt 15:14).

Tenth, [the angels] are incorrupt in nature; the priest also ought to embrace an incorrupt and pure conduct, which is holiness, righteousness, cleanliness, prudence, and so on, so that his soul may not be stained by dirty works, he may not turn into worthless salt that is thrown away and trodden upon, and he may not hear: "If the light in you is darkness, how great is the darkness!" (Mt 6:23).

Eleventh, the angels receive God's wisdom always and yet are not satisfied and desire more of it; similarly, the priest ought to always train himself in education and piety, as the Apostle stated in Timothy: "Always pay attention to the reading of scripture, and train yourself in godliness" (cf. 1 Tim 4).

Twelfth, God installed the angels as protectors and caretakers of people. Similarly, the priest should take care of the congregation and protect them from

---

[48] *Šarakan* (Jerusalem, 1936), p. 709, "Canon of the Archangels," the "Patrum" hymn.

the conceivable beast, Satan, and heretic wolves.

Thirteenth, the angels present good people's good works before God, and make them worthy of rewards and mercy, as in the case of Cornelius, and they punish the evil; hence: "He sent out against them affliction by evil angel" (cf. Ps 78:49). Thus, the priest ought to pray for goodness, offer to the congregation the flesh and the blood of the Lord, and cast the wicked and the impenitent outside the church until they repent.

Fourteenth, [the angels] burn and give warmth. Similarly, the priest ought to burn, cleanse, and expiate the sins of the congregation through holiness, and bring to them the warmth of divine love through wisdom.

Fifteenth, the angels refuse to move toward evil, particularly since they are stationed [in goodness], and they always move toward goodness. Similarly, the priest ought to completely stay away from evil and sins, and always move toward goodness.

Sixteenth, due to the simpleness and delicacy of an angel, others see what an angel has within. Similarly, the priests should not hide their sins, their thoughts, or the word from each other; rather, they should expose these through confession and teach the congregation to do the same, so that they may live in this world with proper manner and true faith, and be worthy of the glory to come in Christ Jesus our Lord, who is blessed forever, amen.

Question: Why do the orders of monks and cenobites currently wear woolen clothes made of the wool of sheep and lambs and not cotton, as they did in the past?

Answer: First of all, because before God was born and intermingled with [human] nature, He ordered the garments of priests be made of cotton, but when he united and intermingled with reproducible nature and was named Lamb [of God], He ordered the garments of priests be made of lambs and then offer the lamb, in order to lift the sins of men.

Second, so that by seeing the wool, we realize that we are wearing Christ—because John called Him Lamb, and the fleece is what covers the lamb—and, thereby, be as innocent as the lambs and sin not.

Third, the fleece is coarse and tormenting: the priest needs to live a coarse, harsh, and vexatious life, and not find comfort in laziness.

Fourth, the fleece is best cleansed from its dirt when it is washed, and it cleanses others. Likewise, the priest needs to be cleansed from sins more than others and turn holy, and also cleanse others from their sins through all kinds of instructions.

Fifth, the fleece is soft and tender. Likewise, the priest should be meek, humble, and God's comfort, according to the Apostle,[49] saying: "Where do I rest, if not in the humble and contrite in spirit, who tremble at my words?" (cf. Isa 66:1–2).

Sixth, [the fleece] is a cover and garment for animals. Likewise, the priest needs to be a cover for all the sins of the congregation, protect them from all harmful things, and not expose the sins to the congregation because of jealousy and bribes.

Seventh, the fleece is sheared annually. Likewise, a priest ought to sever the excess of sins and cleanse them with the sword of the Word of God day in and day out.

Eighth, the fleece sprouts out of an animal, although it is inanimate. Likewise, although the priest sprouts out from living parents, he ought to kill his body and the vice of sins, according to the Apostle: "Put to death the members of your earthly body" (Col 3:5).

Ninth, [the priest] ought to be as innocent as a lamb and then offer Christ the unblemished lamb.

Tenth, the fleece is dry and naturally warm. Likewise, the priest needs to be dry and exempt from the wetness of physical vice and pleasures, and warm toward the love of God, his brethren, and prayers, and then [only] he shall be able to worthily offer Christ the lamb.

Question: Why in the Old [Testament] was it commanded that the tunic of the priests be made of cotton?

Answer: This was for many reasons.

First, [cotton] is born healthy; likewise, the priest should not be born with diseases. If he is born [with diseases], he should not become priest, as Moses said: "Remove the sandals from your feet" (Ex 3:5).

Second, [cotton] is inanimate and insensible. The priest should kill all his worldly members, because they desire what goes against the spirit.

Third, [cotton] is an upwardly shooting plant. The Apostle commands the priest to "Seek and contemplate the things that are above where Christ is, seated at the right hand of God" (cf. Col 3:1); to not [seek and contemplate] the worldly.

Fourth, [cotton] holds the flower and the fruit high. [The Lord] commands the priests to store in heaven: "Store up for yourselves treasures in heaven" (Mt 6:20).

Fifth, the fruit [of the cotton] is plump. The priest gets fattened through

---

[49] It should read *according to the prophet*.

multiplied virtues and good works.

Sixth, [cotton] is substance for light. The priest illuminates himself with wisdom, and [illuminates] others with the preaching of God's ordinances: "they enlighten the eyes" (Ps 19:8), as the Prophet says.

Seventh, turning [cotton] into garment is difficult. The priest ought to become a temple to the Holy Spirit and its grace by tormenting his body and mind; hence: "Those who belong to Christ have crucified their flesh with the affections and lust" (Gal 5:24).

Eighth, the fruit [of the cotton] is edible. The priest feeds the congregation with words of instruction and good works, so that they may be filled with goodness.

Ninth, [cotton] heals pains. The priest is a healer of men's souls that are diseased with various sins.

Tenth, people hold cotton more precious when it has become flax. Likewise, [the priest] has to adorn himself with all kinds of venerable works, be loved by many, and be revered: "So that they may see your good works and give glory to your Father in heaven" (Mt 5:16).

Since we received this from the Old [Testament] with regard to the priests' officiating garment and so on, and [we received] the wool as garment for common and every day [use], for the Lord said: "I have come not to abolish but to fulfill" (Mt 5:17), this much is enough on this.

Question: What is the meaning of the uncovered garment of beneficed clergymen of the church?

Answer: Untying the girdle is a demonstration for their authority. And this is so for six reasons.

First, it signifies that they are free of shame and have no fear, like kings who do not fear anybody and are not embarrassed before anybody.

Second, it shows their free, bold, and unrestricted permission toward inferiors, as is the case of lords with their servants.

Third, they are not under the binds of corporeal authorities or their taxes, unlike the case of rulers over the ruled.

Fourth, they do not have the binds and fears of servitude. Rather, they have filial love, as the Lord said: "I do not call you servants any longer, but I have called you friends, because I have made known to you everything" (cf. Jn 15:15). These are them who want to and love Christ.

Fifth, it shows their envy-free and untied conduct, for they give and disseminate grace, authority, and wisdom to each other without any restriction.

Sixth, it shows the abundance and unending bounties and grace that they possess and give freely, without giving the impression of diminution.

Question: What does *beneficed clergymen of the church* mean?

Answer: First, they inherit a share and rights in the church that are arranged by the holy fathers. Second, they inherit spiritual authority at the church. Third, they inherit reverence and glory from the congregation. Fourth, they inherit the bounties and the grace descended upon them from God. Fifth, they inherit the upper church, which is mother to all of us; this, thanks to their meritorious conduct.

Question: Why did Christ go to the wedding?

Answer: First, to manifest that this [the wedding] is what blessed the matrimony of Adam and other patriarchs and made them multiply. Second, to embarrass those who reckoned the lawful matrimony to be impure. Third, the first curse occurred with the ancestors [regarding matrimony] because of sins. Likewise, as his first miracle, the new Adam blessed this matrimony and changed the former curse into blessing.

Question: Why did He turn the water into wine?

Answer: First, by transforming water into wine, He demonstrated that He will transform the cold love of worldly desires into the warmth of divine desires with his fire that He came to cast on earth. Second, because men had become like cold water with regard to the divine love and were not moving toward good works; hence [they were] "unstable like water" (Gen 49:4). By transforming water into wine, the Lord intoxicated them with the love of the spirit, as was said: "Who will separate us from the love of Christ? Hardship or distress? Nothing that is present, nor anything to come" (cf. Rom 8:35–38). Third, by transforming water into wine, He transformed the earthly and living wisdom into heavenly and spiritual wisdom. Fourth, water signifies the old law that was fulfilled by Christ, as He said: "I have come not to abolish but to fulfill" (Mt 5:17). He also said: "Fill up" (Mt 23:32). With Christ's coming, [the Old Testament] turned into spiritual Gospels. Fifth, the color of the water remained visible; only the nature and taste turned into wine, so that He may show that the human body that the Lord took remained with his density and color, but His essence became divine by uniting with God; not lost or confused in each other, but united inseparably. Sixth, He took away Adam's disobedience by obeying His mother, as Luke says: "He was obedient to them" (Lk 2:51). Seventh, just as in the Old [Testament] Adam listened to Eve, ate, and left the garden of delight, so too in the new [testament] the new Adam listened to the daughter of Eve, Mary, and put [humankind back] in the garden of delight by tasting the wine with the Lord's command, which signified the Lord's blood.

Eighth, by transforming water into wine, He dissolved Eve's grief through the grief of born children, "For wine makes glad a man" (Ps 103:15), as David says. Ninth, God departed our predecessors because of their sins and rejected them; "Your iniquities have been barrier between me and you" (Isa 59:2) God said. Here [in the New Testament, Christ] dissembled the barrier of the fence, approached us, and revealed Himself to us through his miracles.

When the Lord said to His mother, "What have you to do with me?" (Mk 5:7), He meant that there is no distinction between His divine nature and human nature, which is from her—there is no duality and separation; rather, [the two natures] are united and inseparable. Another approach to "What have you to do with me?" (Mk 5:7)—although united but not confused and altered, there is no longer a God and a man, as Eutychus said. Rather, perfect God and perfect man; not perfect two, but perfect one with inseparable and unconfused unity.

The six water pots filled with water signify, first, the six ages where people were filled with the lewd desires of this world and that were impeded when the Lord came and turned them into the warm desire of the kingdom of heaven; and second, it means that the old Adam was created after six days and was corrupted by six movements, and that the new Adam [the Lord] renewed and vivified [the people].

Moreover, tenth, [the Lord] transformed water into wine, so that the man and the woman may stay as unique and separate in their body, and be the same in their words, hearts, wills, and love. Also, He made [the water] taste like wine but did not change the color, because the water has three properties: coldness, wetness, and satiability, whereas the wine has, contrary to these, warmth, dryness, and insatiableness. This is so [to serve] as instruction to the wedded, so that they may not become addicts to evil desire by fervent love, for the sage refers to them as "souls entrapped in sins lose also their mind." Rather, [the wedded] should be cold toward desire, and should not be dry and hardened against the instructions of the Holy Scriptures and the primates. Moreover, they should be soft and heed to, and accept the instructions. They should not be insatiate in copulation; rather moderate and [abiding with] the permissions of the canons, as the Apostle says: "[let] those who have wives be as though they had none" (1 Cor 7:29). Furthermore, they should have warm love for God and for their neighbors, dry and steady against Satan's counsel, and insatiate and incessant with regard to good works. Also, they should consider the worldly, corporeal, and material love as cold water, while [considering] the love of everything spiritual, divine, and related to heavenly life as warm wine, making the soul happy and cool.

Again, since water enters the vine and turns into grape, is gathered in the press after collection, and turns into wine after pressing, cooking, and purifying, so too the man and the woman have to train each other in God's joy; hence: "The Lord shall rejoice in his creation" (Ps 103:31). Thus they shall please God, the angels, and people, and inherit eternal life from Christ the God who is blessed forever, amen.

CHAPTER XLIII

A homily by another on confessors: "The lips of a priest should guard knowledge, and people should seek the law from his mouth, for he is the messenger of the Lord Almighty" (Mal 2:7).

Now, [a priest] needs to be cautious for four reasons. First, because he is God's servant, wherefore the Prophet [Malachi] refers to him as messenger; and God's servants ought to be wise to be able to serve in a God-pleasing way, as Solomon says: "A wise servant is acceptable to a king" (Prov 14:35). Second, because a priest is an intercessor between God and people; therefore, he ought to be knowledgeable and wise to intercede according to God's will. Third, the Prophet says: "He who brings forth the precious from the worthless is called the mouth of God" (cf. Jer 15:19). Therefore, [a priest] ought to be skilled in wisdom to be able to cast the sins out of the hearts of sinners by his artful charm, and to be the mouth of God by doing so. Fourth, the unknown and hidden sins of people should be revealed and the confessor ought to guard knowledge to be able to recognize the multitude of sins and unmistakably heal the sinful spirit of the sinner. For this reason, we shall discuss the know-how of being confessor to a degree, so that [a priest] may guard the redeeming knowledge, as the Prophet [Malachi] stated, and wisely make his spirit and the spirits of many live.

First and foremost, the confessor, who is a spiritual healer, ought to be knowledgeable and ready to open his ears to the confession; otherwise, he would cause destruction to many if he fails to recognize the sins, fails to find their cure, or prescribes a remedy that does not heal when a prescription is needed. For example, when a person who suffers from pride or anger makes confession, [the priest] may [choose] to oblige the person to abstain from food; this, however, is not a healing remedy for pride or anger, because pride is remedied by humility and anger by patience, whereas abstinence from food is the remedy for gluttony and licentiousness.

Second, the confessor ought to examine people's conduct to determine how to make the obligations of repentance acceptable to them and to know how the conditions of men differ from those of women. In times of hardship, one should prescribe for penitents regimens that differ from those instructed for peaceful

318

times. Regimens prescribed for the distressed poor ought to be different from those mandated upon the wealthy that live in the lap of luxury. One ought to prescribe one regimen for those who have just begun to sin and another for those who are seasoned sinners; one for the young and another for the old; one for men and another for women; and one for leaders who are distinguished and another for common people who occupy insignificant positions.

Third, the healer of the body does not offer medicine to a dying patient to avoid making the patient's nature weaker and [to avoid expediting] his death. The spiritual healer ought to act in a similar fashion: when he finds the sinner exposed to malady that entails physical pain, he has to listen to the sins of the patient, and instead of prescribing a regimen for the patient, he has to deliver the patient's soul to God and show a regimen appropriate for the sins, to fulfill it in the case the patient was cured.

Fourth, the confessor should know the cures of all pains, so that he may prescribe remedies opposite to the sins. For example: humility contrary to arrogance; love contrary to envy and hatred; kindness contrary to anger; diligence contrary to laziness; gifting and almsgiving contrary to greed and avarice; modesty contrary to gluttony, because a person should not become intoxicated by wine and satiated by flesh; fasting, prayers, and physical torment contrary to lasciviousness; confession and praise [to the Lord] contrary to swearwords and blasphemy; tears and spiritual words contrary to mucking and laughing; [and] silence contrary to slander. Similarly, [the priest] should prescribe regimens to other [sins] commensurate with the intensity of the sickness; that is, lesser requirements for forgivable sins and greater obligations for fatal sins. The heaviest regimens should be imposed for the disease of sins that has been persistent for ten or twenty years, whereas those who have committed sins recently should encounter the lightest regimens.

Fifth, [the confessor] ought to know whether the disease of sins is complex or simple; that is, if a person has committed a variety of sins, the remedy should be manifold, such as fasting, prayers, almsgiving, and all kinds of repentance; whereas if the sin is simple, the repentance also should be simple. For example, if the only wrongdoing has been eating on Friday, a sinner should commit himself, according to his ability and as much as he can, to consume [only] bread and water on Friday, although a more complex remedy for simple sins would be preferable.

Sixth, receiving money as a fee for confession by the priest is against the holy church and is simony; therefore, [the confessor] should not sell the grace of the Holy Spirit: the canons forbid it, because Christ said: "You received without payment; give without payment" (Mt 10:8).

Seventh, priests should not disclose a confession, although they do so partially, because many would [otherwise] fear and discontinue to confess, and would die and go to hell without confession; [if so] God will demand their blood from priests that disclose a confession, because the heart of a priest should be like a locked chest-box, and he should keep it in a way that even if the chest-box is broken, the lock remains sealed.

Eighth, a spiritual healer has to give the medicine of confession with plenty of advice to those who have hidden their sins in their hearts, so that he may pull their spiritual pain out of their hearts through their mouth and confession.

Ninth, if the sins have hardened and petrified a person, he needs to be prepared by confession and softened by the hope of God's mercy. He needs to be told: "Do not fear! Although you have many sins, if you truly confess all and hide none because of embarrassment or fear, they will all immediately disappear like a spark of a fire cast in the ocean, for the sea is limitless, whereas the fire is limited. God's mercy also is unlimited in a similar fashion, whereas the multitude of your sins is limited; when you cast them in the sea of God's mercy through a true confession before the priest, it will immediately disappear like a spark of fire."

Tenth, if someone has tightened his spiritual belly to resist casting sins out of his body, he should be given a releasing medicine; that is, he needs to be frightened by the torments of hell, saying, according to Isaiah: "The fire of sinners is unquenchable and their worm is ever active" (cf. Isa 66:24), for there is no end to their sorrow, no limit to their torment, no remedy to their pain, no release to their chain, no liberation from their prison, no comfort to their mourning, and no lifting to their darkness. When he hears this, the belly will be set loose and he will confess his trespassing.

Eleventh, watch that if the senses [of a sinner] are diluted—that is, if he opens his eyes to stains, his ears to evil, his mouth to nonsense, and so on—he ought to be given a medicine that would tie him; that is, the fear of God's judgment, so that he may no longer be diluted in sins, since there will be a great fear at the judgment, as the proverb says: "If the righteous hardly live, where would the wicked and the sinner appear!" (cf. Prov 11:31). And Paul says: "It is a great fear to fall in the hands of God" (Heb 10:31), for a person will be accountable for every senseless thing, and those who open their eyes to stains will be liable to adultery, fornication, and other [transgressions].

Twelfth, if someone has been diseased by sins, [a priest] ought to cure him by repentance, and when he becomes healthy by spirit and strengthened, [a priest] ought to give him medicine, so that he may maintain his health. And just as those who want to maintain their bodily health frequent the baths and apply a variety of pastes to their body to stay healthy, likewise a person should maintain his spiritual health by bathing; that is, by the water of tears, and apply the paste of repentance to stay spiritually healthy.

Thirteenth, it is the duty of a confessor to visit sinners, inquire about their spiritual unwellness, console them, and strengthen them with the hope of salvation, for repentance cannot expiate the sinner if he is desperate. Judas died not because of the graveness of his sins; rather, because of hopelessness. But if hope is established in him [the unwell person] and he regrets a little, repentance can expiate him.

Fourteenth, when someone commits the heaviest sins, [the priest] should not at once separate him from the members of the church by cursing, excommunicating, or abandoning him; rather, he should treat him with care, exhort him, and turn him from the sins. But if [the sinner] refused to turn and continued to be attracted toward sins unrepentantly, then he should be banished from the church by excommunication and damnation, so that he may not corrupt others, as Moses says: "You shall purge the evil from your midst" (Deut 13:5).

Fifteenth, a confessor, if experienced, ought to try to turn the sinner with very gentle words and light regimens; but if he fails to turn him from the sins, he ought to frighten him with harsh and overwhelming words, and impose heavy repentance upon him, so that he may abandon the pleasure of sins due to the fear of toilsome repentance.

Sixteenth, the confessor should state from the beginning that [a sinner] confesses before God and not man, and that God is merciful and has come for the sake of the sinners. God showed mercy to Peter, Paul, Mary of Magdalene, and other sinners when they repented, and He will treat similarly those who confess truly. But if the wound remains closed despite this sweet medicine, then it needs to be cut open by a surgeon's knife or hot red iron; that is, by terrifying and frightening words; and he needs to be scared by the fear of torments, so that he may be prompted to turn from sins and repent.

Seventeenth, it is to be known that when a person has committed many sins, has encouraged many to commit sins, and has caused destruction to many souls through evil example or counsel, or has been reluctant in his work after assuming leadership, to repent or confess for the sake of those whom he enticed to sin or the many souls he destroyed is insufficient, for God holds him accountable for them [and their sins].

Here, a question might come up: What kind of regimen should the confessor impose upon a person who has caused destruction to many? Will fasting and almsgiving be enough? Doctors answer that it is not enough, because if a person suffering from a headache applied the medicine to his feet, he is unintelligent, for medicine should be applied where the pain is. He ought to bring to confession those whom he caused destruction. It is also known that theft is of two kinds: spiritual and physical, and that the spiritual [theft] is worse. Now, whoever has encouraged others to sin is a thief, for he has taken them away from God's treasure house. Therefore, it is not enough for him to expiate his sins by fasting, prayers, and almsgiving; rather, he ought to reinstate the lost souls by encouraging them to be good, and he has to bring them back to God's treasure house. Again, when a person robs and strips someone naked, and the confessor commands him to fast, he cannot heal him by doing so, because the unwellness has affected the backs of those whom he stripped of their clothes, whereas [the confessor] is applying the balm over the chest; that is, the fasting that weakens the heart. Instead, he has to put the medicine where the pain is, and because [the thief] has stripped people naked, he ought to cover them with clothes and give back whatever he has taken away. Glory to Christ with his Father and the Holy Spirit now and always and forever and ever, amen.

CHAPTER XLIV

Homily of the same on matrimony, according to the verse: "God created man
in his image; male and female he created them; he blessed them and said:
'Be fruitful and multiply, and fill the earth'" (Gen 1:27–28).

When God the Creator created Adam, He said: "It is not good that man should be alone; I will make him a helper" (Gen 2:18). This, first, indicates that man's helper is human, for although there were animals helping man in carrying, plowing, and [fulfilling] other needs, man's helper in [matters of] heart's virtue and holiness was a human being. The woman is man's helper in childbearing and family formation; therefore [God] said: "It is not good that man should be alone" (Gen 2:18). Again, to be alone befits only God, for His nature needs nothing and He is uncreated. Other beings, however, are created and need each other. The multitude of people on earth is as good as the nine classes of angels that glorify God by thousands of thousands and myriads of myriads in heaven. First, they [the human beings] demonstrate God's abundant philanthropy. Second, they help each other in building, planting, crafts, bodily needs, and educating the soul, and in bringing joy to one another. We also find numerous other good things from each other. For this reason, [God] said: "It is not good that man should be alone" (Gen 2:18).

Should a person argue that the woman is the reason for man's engagement in sin; how can she, then, be good? We answer, first, thus. God is foreknowing. He knew that, unlike the angels, man was unable to grow without sin. Therefore, He created man in the body and gave him the woman as helper, so that they multiply and increase humankind through animalistic recreation, as He blessed them and said: "Be fruitful and multiply, and fill the earth" (Gen 1:28). Again, we say that God is good by nature, and He is generous and benevolent; [therefore] one man's sin cannot hinder and prevent God's entire goodness; rather, it is the sinner alone that becomes deprived of [God's] goodness. For example, the sun shines over everybody, and if one man closes his eyes, he cannot prevent the sunlight; rather, he deprives only himself [of it]. Likewise, although the woman committed sin, many fine and righteous men were born of her, such as the patriarchs and the prophets, and all the chosen ones [shall be born] until the end of the age. And [God] attended to and protected the woman because of good offspring, although she became the cause of sins.

Nowadays, too, there are many evil and sinful men on earth, but God allows them to stay on earth for many reasons. First, although they are evil and sinful, there would be good people among their offspring. It is for the sake of the good descendant that God keeps the evil parents. Second, if their parents were good, God forgives the wicked descendants for the sake of the good parents, just as He forgave the Hebrews because of their good patriarchs: Abraham, Isaac, Jacob, and others. Third, if the evil person has a hidden good part of which we are unaware, that [good] part counterbalances his [worldly] life. Fourth, although they are wicked, they cause goodness to others, whether countries, provinces, properties, or peace. For example, the thorns do not bear any fruit, but they protect the fruit-bearers, wherefore we nurture them. Fifth, through them [the wicked] others find spiritual goodness: wicked tyrants oppress the Christians and the poor, and thereby they [the Christians and the poor] find multiplied reward and recompense. Sixth, God does not want a sinner's death; hence: "I do not wish any sinner to perish; rather, to turn and live" (cf. 2 Pet 3:9). Wherefore, He keeps them on earth so that they may repent and turn from sins. In addition to what we have said, there are many more reasons for which God forgives a sinner, be it for his [a given individual's] or for others' good.

Likewise, although Eve the proto-mother sinned, later she repented and many sons were to be born of her; therefore, God forgave her. Again, and most importantly, had the woman not sinned, God the Word would have not incarnated and all the goodness that happened through Christ would have been hampered. Although sinless righteous people would have entered the kingdom of heaven in the stead of the fallen angels, this would have not happened through the grace of Christ. And our nature would have not united with God or been glorified by angels, and we would have not seen a human as human's creator, as we do now. Moreover, the generous philanthropy would not have appeared, nor would the preciousness of a person have become visible, whereas it happens now, since God the Word had come to examine us and honor us in this world through His agony, crucifixion, and death. Without God's humanization, we would have not been the children of God or the brothers and partakers of Christ, and we would have not born by the Holy Spirit or tasted the flesh and blood of the Son of God. And had we transformed from paradise, none of those who have been Christ's physical predecessors would have received the crown of martyrdom, austerity, apostleship, prophecy, or patriarchate. Moreover, all works of art, constructions, planting, tilling, skills, education, compassion for each other, and all other good things that, without elaboration, followed Eve's transgression would have been hampered.

Should somebody ask ignorantly: Since Eve's transgression is the cause of all these good things, why, then, was she punished? We say that sin, by itself, is evil and is the absence of goodness and righteousness. Besides, Eve herself did not purposefully sin to generate all these good things for us; rather, our salvation was conceived by God's love toward humans and His most wise knowledge. He did not want the destruction of humankind; rather, He made us good from evil, facilitated our transformation from sins to righteousness, from death to life, and from earth to heaven. This reveals God's goodness and providence, for He brought us out of wickedness into goodness, and granted us, the unworthy and sinful, salvation and bounties. Then, therefore, the cause of our redemption is not Eve; rather, it is Christ, whose grace justified us and our evil deeds.

And should somebody wonder how our human nature would have developed had Eve and Adam maintained their innocence, we say, some claim that Paradise would have become corrupt with acts of copulation between males and females, along with desire and childbirth. These people write many fictitious things that contradict the Holy Scriptures and the [teachings of] orthodox fathers. First, because the divine command says: "Be fruitful and multiply, and fill the earth" (Gen 1:28). He commanded growth on earth and not in the garden of delight. Second, the garden of delight is an incorrupt place; there could not have been impure menstruations of human beings or plants. Now, without menstruation, there would not have been physical corruption or corrupt birth. Third, the holy church is patterned after the garden of delight. Now, it is the matrimonial blessing that takes place in the church, not the making of children. Likewise, in the garden of delight, it was the blessed matrimony that took place and not the making of children. Fourth, had there [in the garden of delight] been corrupt birth, as it occurs on earth, the man would have lacked all the needs of the child, be it nourishment, development, caretaking, and so on, for none of these exist in the garden of delight, nor do there exist garments for the body. Fifth, before they transgressed, Adam and Eve were naked and yet not ashamed, because they lacked the mutual lascivious desire. Now, had they always remained innocent, they would not have had the lascivious desire. Sixth, one more evident thing: Why would [God] have removed corrupt Adam from the garden of delight, had Adam been destined to corruption? Obviously, the garden of delight is not subject to corruption and it does not allow corrupt dwellers. Seventh, St. Gregory of Nyssa states in his book, *On the Making of Man*, that virginity, purity, and resemblance to the angels were the original [form of] life in the garden of delight, and upon resurrection, we shall be restored in the purity of the original life in the garden of delight as equals to angels. Now, if Adam's original life incorporated matrimony and childbirth, as some claim, it would be so also after the final resurrection. According to the Muslim sect, there shall be material kingdom, food, marriage, and other nonsense. The holy church anathematizes those who speak and think nonsense, and they should be anathema.

Should somebody ask: Why, then, were the reproductive organs created, if reproduction was not supposed to happen in the garden of delight? We say that God is foreknowing—He knew beforehand that they [Adam and Eve] would not be able to multiply innocently like the angels in the garden of delight, so He crafted their bodies in a way that would enable them to multiply through intercourse. And should somebody insist on [learning] the type and method of innocent birth, the holy doctors say that just as the angels were multiplied in heaven, so would human beings have done in the garden of delight. And should [the person] argue: The angels were created from nothing and not from one another, whereas humankind has to be born from one man, the saints liken this to many lights that have been lit from one light. And should people argue that our birth is imperfect, the holy doctors say that, for example, the Mother of God, Virgin Mary, gave perfect and true birth as a virgin without semen; likewise, in the garden of delight, perfect human beings could have been born of Adam's nature without intercourse. Or [they could have been born like] Eve from Adam's ribs, or in any other way, as the omniscient Creator deemed appropriate. But not only do we not know the things to come—for only God knows what has not yet happened—but also we find the things that happened or exist with much effort, for that is all what we conceive, such as the lawful matrimony of a male with a female. For matrimony is defined thus: Matrimony is the lawful union of a male and a female who live inseparably. Now, matrimony begins with engagement, is established through the consent of hearts when spelled out—for matrimony is confirmed through the consent of two wills—and is accomplished by the blessing of the priest and through physical union. It is for this reason that a sign is placed [i.e., an engagement takes place]. Like a tree that first flowers and then gives fruits, the sign is the flower of matrimony, because thence the bride would be assigned to the groom and the groom appropriated to the bride. This was established as law through [God's] word when He did not find a helper for man and said: "It is not good that man should be alone; I will make him a helper" (Gen 2:18). Because God the begetter and Creator thought of Adam's wedding and made Eve his helper by engaging her to him. Similarly, the groom's parents care for their son and engage the bride to him. After Gabriel the Archangel delivered the tiding to the Holy Virgin, saying: "Rejoice, favored one, the Lord is with you," she began to ponder what sort of greeting this might be (Lk 1:28–30), but when she heard: "The Holy Spirit will come upon you" (Lk 1:38), she consented and said: "Here I am, the servant of the Lord; let it be with me according to your word" (Lk 1:38). Afterward, she conceived and gave birth to God the Word, incarnate and humanized. Similarly, first, a sign is placed upon the bride. The consent of the two wills is the confirmation of matrimony, because matrimony cannot be confirmed by force and without the mutual agreement of the bride and groom. This was evident in the Scripture's verse: "the Lord brought the rib that He had turned into a woman to Adam" (cf. Gen 2:22). [The woman] was brought to Adam in order for them to see one another and consent. Moreover, the member should be close to the head. Furthermore, they [the bride and groom] have to receive the holy matrimony together. For this purpose, before matrimony, the bride and groom have to see each other, consent by their wills and hearts to one another, and then [only] marry each other. Matrimony takes place, first, by the priest's blessing, which is followed by a physical union, like Christ's blessing by saying: "Come you that are blessed by my father" (Mt 25:34), before He was united with the holy church so that [the congregation] may inherit the kingdom. Therefore, the priest's blessing precedes the physical union [of a couple], for [God] first blessed and said: "Be fruitful and multiply, and fill the earth" (Gen 1:28). Later, [Christ] said: "And the two shall become one flesh" (Mk 10:8), because it is the divine word that marries and blesses them, like the communion that takes place by this word of God: "This is my body and this is my blood" (cf. Mt 26:26–28). It is also the word of God that makes a man and a woman one body.

Should somebody say: It was said to Adam: "Let the two become one flesh" (cf. Gen 2:24), we say that the manifestly uttered "God blessed" is God's word, whilst the covert blessing "the two shall be one flesh" God revealed to Adam in a prophetic spirit. And should somebody argue that the verse should have been phrased in present tense, as in "This is my body" (Mt 26:26), whereas this is [phrased in] future tense, saying "The two shall become one flesh" (Mk 10:8), we say that "blessing" and "being fruitful" have present connotation, whereas "shall become" is futuristic in order to indicate that matrimony is fulfilled in two steps: presently, with words of blessing, and in the future through physical union. Therefore, He blessed and said "shall be." Also, "shall be" indicates those who will marry through physical union unto the end of the age. Again, matrimony is defined as the lawful reward of two matching people in one union. Again, matrimony is the lawful union of a man and a woman who live an inseparable life. The term *lawful union* is used to indicate that [matrimony] takes place only for the purpose of birthing children in the service of God, for the doctors say that a man who loves the woman immoderately is an adulterer.

Now, there are three components to a good matrimony: loyalty, offspring, and mystery. Loyalty, for neither the husband nor the wife should experience corruption in an unfamiliar bed, unlike those abandoning their faith by renouncing it by their words, severing their links with faith, and seeing their faith become corrupt. Similarly, whoever corrupts the bond of matrimony in an unfamiliar bed is separated from the blessing and the holy bed is defiled, as the Apostle says: "Honorable is the marriage and holy is the bed; for God will judge fornicators and adulterers" (Heb 13:4). Children, for they are born and nourished to serve God, because the matrimonial command is given for birthing children. Mystery, so that they may remain inseparable, for although the church can separate them because of prohibitions—there are many prohibitions for marriage, such as spiritual or physical relationship through kinship or marriage, or weak nature, adultery, demoniacal state, slavery, forced marriage, or other similar reasons, which separate a man and a woman—nevertheless, married couples should not be separated if they have been married lawfully; hence: "What God has joined, let no one separate" (Mt 19:6). Death, however, sets the bond of marriage loose and unties it. And there are two kinds of bonds of marriage, as there are two kinds of deaths corresponding to them. There is a spiritual bond (that of the hearts) and there is a physical bond (that of the intermingling of genders). Death [also] is of two kinds: spiritual and physical. Spiritual death sets the spiritual bond loose; that is, when the person dies for this world by accepting the monastic life. The corporeal bond is set loose by physical death, wherefore lawfully wedded people should not be separated so long as they live.

And marriage occurs for three reasons. Either due to one's turning away from adultery with disgust, or for the sake of childbirth. Now, these two [kinds] are honorable and holy. The third [kind], however, occurs because of lustful desire, and this is sin. Therefore, a person should know and choose the when, where, what, and how of marriage in order to make it honorable, holy, and worthy of God's blessing. Without these choices, goodness could transform into its opposite, and the honorable could become corrupt and worthless, reckoned to be abominable sin. This [transformation] happens through the deceit and machinations of the devil, because he opposes and hampers every good thing. Sometimes he leads to sins through love and desire, and sometimes causes separation and disunity through hatred, because in both cases he destroys and despises God's precepts. May Christ the God save all those who believe in his name from the machinations of the devil, and bless the chaste matrimony of those who are married in holiness, amen.

CHAPTER XLV

Homily of the same, again, on matrimony, according to the verse: "So the Lord caused a deep sleep to fall upon Adam, and he slept; and he made a woman from Adam, [etc.]" (cf. Gen 2:21–22).

The deep sleep that befell Adam is not a sleep caused by physical work or food, nor is it unpleasant lethargy or illusion. It is the exaltation of the mind toward God, enchanted by the spiritual prophesy, like Abraham's vision when he was asleep, or when Paul was being caught up in the third heaven. But why did Adam undergo a deep sleep?

First, so that he might not feel the pain of the rib. God could have taken the rib without causing pain to Adam while he was awake, but He had a purpose. Like the earth that did not feel pain when He took earth to make Adam, Adam felt no pain when the rib was taken from him.

Second, so that he might see many things during his sleep through the uplifted mind with regard to Christ and the church, which he prophesied upon awakening.

Third, because the church was made from Christ's rib when the blood and water gushed out to establish the church while he was asleep on the cross—the water for the baptismal font and the blood for communion. Similarly, while Adam was asleep, the woman was made of his rib: "Took one of his ribs and closed up its place with flesh" (Gen 2:21).

But why did God not create Eve from the earth as He did with Adam?

First, so that they may not be equal in honor, age, and time, the man being first and preeminent, and the woman being second to him and younger, for Adam was created during the first hour and the woman during the second. Therefore, in a lawful marriage, the bride should be younger than the groom.

Second, had she been created from earth, the man and the woman would have treated each other as strangers and without compassion; but [she was created] from Adam's body, so that the man may love the woman as his own flesh, and they share each other's pains.

Third, had they both been made of earth, they would have been unlike each other and of different kinds, like an ox and a horse that have different natures, although they are from the same earth. Consequently, their children would have been unlike their parents and of different kinds.

Fourth, had the woman been from the earth, she would have required a different [divine] blowing and breath of life, as well as a different blessing and command, as was the case with Adam. Wherefore, she was created from Adam, for through Adam's faculties she received the blessing, the blow of grace, and so on, just like the Apostle Thomas who received the blow of the Spirit from other apostles, although he was not with them in the Upper Room.

Fifth, had the woman also been created from the earth, humankind would have had two origins and not one. Man resembles the Creator in this regard— the first man alone is the origin of humankind, just as God alone is the origin of the entire world. Again, just as God the Father is the origin of the Son's birth and the Spirit's proceeding, so too is Adam the origin of Seth and Eve, one through birth and the other by proceeding, although this one [in Adam's case] is an imitation, whereas the other [God's action] is truth. The imitation has only a remote resemblance.

Sixth, conformably with the mystery, for just as Adam is Eve's origin, so too is Christ the origin of the church and the head of the body of the church, as the Apostle says: "This is a great mystery, and I am applying it to Christ and the church" (Eph 5:32). For the reasons mentioned above, [God] created the woman from Adam's rib and not from an unfamiliar earth.

But why [was Eve created] from the rib and not from a different part?

First, so that she may obey Adam and be silent.

Second, [God] took her from the rib so that she may be strong rather than weak, for we refer to wrestlers as *ribby* and *thick-ribbed*.

Third, desire stems from the ribs. The sides are like a container to the kidneys and a place deriving strength from the ribs. Likewise, the woman is the location of man's desire and she inseminates and nourishes the fetus.

Fourth, the rib is located in the middle [of the body]. It indicates that the dignity allotted to the woman is not equal to what is reserved to the head, nor is it worthless or subject to violation; rather, it deserves a medial affection.

Fifth, since the rib is a curved bone, it means that the woman is a point of attraction and gathering for man and possessions, for the man is like a river, whereas the woman is like a lake where all rivers are gathered.

Sixth, the rib has a shiny surface, but internally it is muddy. Similarly, the woman appears with a beautiful countenance, but her heart is full of knavery, for her words and her feelings do not match.

Seventh, the rib has two faces, so is the woman—one for familiar people and another for strangers.

Eighth, the rib has a sharp mouth; so does the woman have a sharp and cutting tongue, and she tears apart with her tongue like a wild beast. For this reason, Secundus the philosopher refers to the woman as a familiar beast [and source for] daily strife. And these four qualities apply rather to knavish than temperate women.

Ninth, like Adam who gave the rib and received the flesh, for it is said: "closed up its place with flesh" (Gen 2:21), chaste men give strength to the women and receive weakness and tenderness. Besides, since [God] took one rib and made one woman for the one man, a woman should have one man, and a man should have one woman; and this complies with God's precepts. To have a second [wife or husband] is possible through forgiveness and allowance, but not through law. Discover this from the process: people who have been married do not put the crown on their head, nor do they stand before the sanctuary; rather, their [second] wedding takes place in the middle of the church. The third and consequent [marriages], however, are adultery and there is no wedding, as if the person is taking a second wife while the first is still alive. And just as the rib initially was Adam's body part before it was made woman and consequently turned into one inseparable flesh with him, so too is the lawful wife inseparable from her husband, because nobody can undo the nuptial blessing; hence: "What God has joined together, let no one separate" (Mt 19:6), as we have indicated before. And since God took the rib and made it woman, all men have to have a holy conduct so long as a man has a woman by God's provision and blessing.

Despicable are those who defile themselves with mad desires. First, just as a man is unable to take his own rib out, so too is he unable to bring a woman by himself. Second, should someone sever his own rib, he would not be able to close up the spot with flesh. Similarly, nobody can perform the matrimonial rite by himself, or receive a wife by adultery, for that [woman] will not be a wife to the man; rather, she will be corruption for him, because both he and his semen will be defiled.

There are two things that defile the semen. First, the semen is defiled when it is separated from man [by way of masturbation]. Second, it is defiled through adultery when it falls in strange body. It is obvious, then, that the semen is holy when it is contained within us, and that marriage is holy and honorable when the semen falls in the lawful place—inside the woman who is man's flesh.

Tenth, concurrent with the mystery, as has been demonstrated before, for the woman was made of Adam's rib, and from Christ's rib was made the holy church with the baptismal water and communion of blood. Based on this concept, it is a tradition of the church to commune the lawfully wedded with the holy mystery after the wedding, or to offer them the blessed wine. Because the bride-church was united with the groom-Christ through the communion of blood. Christ blessed the wine at the wedding in Cana of Galilee. Again, Holy Communion is the fulfillment of all mysteries, as St. Dionysius says; wherefore, people receive communion after a wedding.

Should somebody ask: Which side did [God] take it [the rib] from: the right, or left? The doctors say that [God took the rib] from the left side, which is obvious. First, the woman takes shape in the left-hand side in the womb; also, because the woman has an additional rib on her left side. Again, after our pattern, [God] created and took the rib with His right hand; it is orderly [then] to take it from the left-hand side of an object facing Him. Based on this concept, when the groom enters the church, he keeps the bride to his right-hand side and holds her hand with his right hand. The bride sits on the right-hand side of the groom in the high place. This indicates three transformations: God created the woman from the rib with His right hand, and put her on the right-hand side in an elevated place in the garden of delight. Because the woman caused the fall unto earth on the left-hand side, [the groom] exits the church—the garden of delight on earth—holding the left hand [of the bride].

Should somebody say: Since Eve is from Adam's rib, she, then, is Adam's daughter and not his wife. We say that there are three requirements for childbirth. First, the child should be born from a man and a woman. Second, [the child should be born] from semen or blood. Third, [the child should be born] from a reproductive organ. Now, the [first] woman was from Adam's rib and neither from semen or blood nor from a reproductive organ. She came forth by divine power from the rib and not from [the first] man's action. Then, therefore, Eve is not Adam's daughter. When the shoots of branches or the tendrils of vines are planted, they potentially have everything—the flowers, leaves, fruits, and so on. Likewise, the rib on its own potentially had everything—flesh, blood, nerves, skin, and so on. These were later shaped and formed by operation, as the Scripture says: "The rib that He had taken from Adam He made into woman" (Gen 2:22).

[The scripture] refers to the woman as made by God. First, because she is made by God. Nobody can disassemble her except for the maker, just as nobody can unbind the spirit and the body except for him who bound them [the spirit and the body] and who can bind them again inseparably. Again, He says "made," because a house is nothing but ruins without the woman, and the woman is the prosperity of a house. Also, because a man's city, district, and home is his wife. She is the resting, dwelling, and gathering place, as we have mentioned earlier. This has become a custom and the wife is referred to as home, as in: Do you have a home? Have you taken a home? Wherefore it is said: "The rib that God made [into woman] He had taken from Adam" (cf. Gen 2:22).

When Adam saw [the woman], first, he was astonished, and then he declined, saying: "Is this now a bone of my bones?" (cf. Gen 2:23); meaning, is that naked and worthless rib this beautiful image? Second, he affirmatively and believably said: Indeed this is bone from my bones, which took flesh by the same power. Third, he prophetically said: Now this is a bone and flesh taken from the man; this will never happen again; rather, [the person born] should be seeded by the man and the woman. "This one shall be called Woman, for out of Man this was taken" (Gen 2:23).

He [Adam] himself offered an explanation to the name Woman; that is, man's [other] half, or the rib that constitutes a power, or [an entity] taken from a living creature, or sprouted out or born from the rib. This is the explanation of the name Woman. "Therefore, a man leaves his father and his mother, and clings to his wife" (Gen 2:24). This is a prophesy to the effect that they shall become father and mother later, and sons and daughters shall be born. They will become brides and grooms, and leave their fathers and mothers just as he [Adam] did originally, for he left God the Father and Creator according to the command, and the mother nature of which he was created, went away with his woman, then listened to her, and exited the garden of delight where he was no longer fit. Thereafter, it became a tradition for the groom to leave his parents and cling to the bride. And then the bride [also] leaves her parents and goes with the groom to be wedded.

Again, should a confusion rise at home, the man leaves his parents and clings to his wife. However, the lawful way is for the lesser good to go with the greater good. That is, the wife shall go to the house of her father-in-law, as it happened at the conclusion of the great mystery, for our Lord came with his inseparable divinity from the Father, left his mother in sadness, and went after the cross with the church. Thereafter, the wedded church abandoned everything—pagan paternal customs and customary maternal sins—and went with the groom-Christ to the paternal house, to the holy faith and works, and with them to the kingdom of heavens. "And the two shall be one flesh" (1 Cor 6:16). Reference is made [here] to the abject first—the body, and not to the spirit; hence: "Anyone united to the Lord becomes one spirit with him, and anyone united to a woman becomes one body with her" (cf. 1 Cor 6:16–17); that is, both possess the same voluptuousness and desire. Again, [they are reckoned] one body, because they come to share each other's pains and joys, according to the Apostle: "If one member suffers, all suffer together with it, if one member is honored, all rejoice together with it" (1 Cor 12:26). Again, the two are one body, and one is half a human being without the other.

Should someone say: If they are half a human being without each other, then the husband should do nothing without his wife, be it praying or anything else. We say that the husband and his wife become one body but not one person, for each can do whatever he or she wants as an independent person. Fourth, again [they are reckoned] one body, because the semen of the two are coagulated in the one body of their offspring. Fifth, they become one body, for the husband takes ownership of his wife's beauty and modesty, and the wife takes ownership of her husband's possessions and honor. Sixth, the more awesome: Christ is the head and the church is the body, and, according to Paul, the head and the members are one: "We are flesh of his flesh and bone of his bones" (cf. Eph 5:30).

May Christ the true head bless you for the glory and honor of his members, to exist and remain in your bodies for the purpose of blessed child birthing, the completion of the holy church, and the multiplication of heavenly rewards in our Lord Jesus Christ who is blessed forever, amen.

CHAPTER XLVI

[Homily] of the same, again, on matrimony, according to the verse: "This is a great mystery, and I am applying it to Christ and the church" (Eph 5:32).

Mystery is the revelation of hidden things. And the mysteries of the church are seven—baptism, confirmation, Eucharist, penance, anointment, order of priesthood, and matrimony. Each of these mysteries is [established] against a past evil, except for matrimony, which is [established] against the evil to come. Moreover, it is a control over desire, for it instructs us to exercise chastity. Furthermore, it is against death, for death corrupts our nature, but this [matrimony] multiplies and replenishes through childbirth. Therefore, during the first creation, [God] blessed the marriage and said: "Be fruitful and multiply and fill the earth" (Gen 1:28). During the second creation, our Lord Jesus Christ attended the wedding in Cana of Galilee, blessed them [the bride and groom], and transformed water into wine, wherefore the Apostle says: "This is a great mystery, and I am applying it to Christ and the church" (Eph 5:32). We are obliged to follow and explain the great mystery step by step.

First, marriage begins with a sign [i.e., engagement], which is accomplished by two things: words of acceptance and a ring or other things as a token. If the two parties are not equally willing and content, the marriage could be shaky, as if it were forced or imposed against the will. The willful consent occurs through eyesight and conversation, and by the token, be it a ring or something else. These take place through the intercession of a priest and men and women. This is so for two reasons. First, the word of engagement is confirmed through two or three witnesses. Second, the priest is who blesses the engagement and the wedding, which cannot take place without him. The men and the women—the folks related to the bride and the groom—[represent] the bride and the groom. The ring symbolizes the one, entire, and complete love of the bride and the groom. Just as the ring is for one finger, so also is the bride to one groom and the groom to one bride. Also, just as the ring is round and is [worn] on one finger where the heart's artery [passes through], so too should the love of the bride and groom be round and perfect. This was seen initially in relation to the first father, Adam, on whom God said: "It is not good that the man should be alone; I will make him a helper. So he took one of his ribs and made it into a woman, and brought her to Adam to see her" (cf. Gen 2:18–22). This "seeing" was the mutual acceptance. God was the performer of the marriage and the giver of the blessing. At the time, the angels were those related to the bride and the groom. How is this evident?

First, because God was acting like a priest, the angels had to serve; besides, at the time the first created [man and woman] were innocent and peers to the angels. Thenceforth, people began to discuss the words of acceptance—whether through mediators or directly, and then place a sign upon the bride and the groom through the intercession of the priests and men and women, as has been mentioned. When God the Word decided to take our nature and become man, He sent the Archangel Gabriel to the virgin for the tiding. [Gabriel] came to her and said: "'Rejoice, favored one! The Lord is with you.' But she was much perplexed by his greeting words" (Lk 1:28–29). But when she learned from the angel: "The Holy Spirit will come upon you, and the power of the Most High will overshadow you" (Lk 1:35), she accepted and said: "Here I am, the servant of the Lord; let it be with me according to your word" (Lk 1:38). [Only] thereafter God the Word came and became man from the Holy Virgin. With this concept, the groom places a sign upon the bride and then the bride [places a sign] upon the groom. This corporeal wedding is the mystery of the spiritual wedding and the unity of our spirits with God, as the Apostle says: "This is a great mystery, and I am applying it to Christ and the church" (Eph 5:32).

The first matrimonial mediators were the prophets who foretold the humanization of the Word and our salvation covertly and to a single nation— the Jews. Thereafter, when the Word was incarnate and appeared to men, the Apostles and the followers became paranymphs, just as John was a forerunner and inviter, for he said: "He who has the bride is the bridegroom, and I am a friend of the bridegroom" (Jn 3:29). And the Apostle says: "I have espoused you to one husband, that I may present [you as] a chaste virgin to Christ" (2 Cor 11:2). The token of the ring is the faith placed on the finger to distinguish the work. Likewise, God places faith in man's reason so that he may differentiate the good and the evil.

Second, just as the ring is placed on one of the five fingers, so too is faith placed in our intellect, which is one of the five inner senses.

Third, the ring is [placed] on the finger that the artery of the heart runs through; likewise, our faith in Christ is established by the warm love of the heart, as the Apostle says: "Circumcision is nothing, and uncircumcision is nothing; the only thing that counts is faith made effective through love" (Gal 5:6).

Fourth, just as the ring needs to be neither loose nor tight, similarly our faith in Christ needs to be neither excessive nor insufficient; that is, [we should] not attribute to Him what He lacks or deny to Him what He has.

Fifth, the ring surrounds the finger from all sides; similarly, it is the entire and complete faith that keeps our spirit and body from all kinds of vices and wickedness.

Sixth, the ring is round; so should our faith be in Christ—whole, without blemishes or hesitation.

Seventh, the ring is made of precious matter, be it gold or silver; so should our faith be in Christ—precious and pure.

Eighth, it [the ring] has yellow or white color, indicating the radiance of our faith—the white color [denoting] our spiritual innocence and the yellow the fear and fright with our virtuous body.

Ninth, the matter [of the ring] is loud [when it resonates]; so should our faith be known to everybody as a lamp placed on a lampstand and not under the bed.

Tenth, the seal of a ring is one in various stamped waxes; likewise, the faith in us—the many [believers]—is one and the same impression between us and Christ, edged and imaged in our souls by Him, as was said by the philosopher Porphyry. The one and the same seal of faith was created before the many [believers], in the many, and above the many.

Again, faith is placed upon a Christian as a sign in this life; and in death, he sees the groom-Christ in hope, for hope is the foundation of faith, and he unites with the groom [Christ] with love after resurrection. Because here [in this world] faith is complete in us, and after death hope [will be complete], as Solomon says: "Their hope is full of immortality" (Wis 3:4). At the resurrection, we will be perfect by love, as the Apostle says: "Faith, hope, and love abide, these three; and the greatest of these is love" (1 Cor 13:13). There [in the hereafter], faith abides with a dim sight, [and] hope is distant, lifted, and decreased, whereas love is increased to unite with the groom-Christ, like the wise maiden that assembled the lamps and entered the chamber of the groom.

In the parable of the wedding, we see that the wealthy man organized his son's wedding, and a crowd gathered to watch, and so on. This indicates that here [in this life] we shall believe and accept, and there [in the hereafter] we shall unite with the groom-Christ. This is the mystery [of matrimony].

The paradigm of the bride and the groom indicates the perfect love that Christ has for the church, because the love of a groom and a bride is perfect and superior among all material loves, as the church is referenced in songs: "Your love for me is like the love of the bride, [etc.]" This is the mystery of the sign.

Thereafter, there comes the wedding. First, the groom visits the bride's house and takes the bride to the church for the wedding, as the Scripture says: "A man leaves his father and his mother and clings to his wife, and they become one flesh" (Gen 2:24). This is a dual mystery. First, there is the humanization of the Word. Second, [there is] the unity with the church, which has become a bride.

First, [let us look into] the former. God the Word descended from the heavens with His indivisible unity from the Father and the Spirit into the womb of the Holy Virgin, took from the virgin's blood in the likeness of Adam's rib, united it to His divinity, and became perfect man. This was so because of the many properties of the rib. First, just as [God] took the rib and made it into a woman there [in heaven], so too did God the Word take blood from the virgin here [on earth] and became man by blending it in Him. Second, just as the rib potentially included the other body parts, so too did the virgin's blood potentially include all of the members of the body—bones, flesh, blood, veins, skin, and so on. Third, the rib had no resemblance to Adam in its unshaped, lifeless, and worthless form, yet took shape and life and became Adam's equal after it was assembled. Likewise, the blood of the virgin had no resemblance to God, yet it became God and equal to God with its vitality and form through unity; hence: "Who thought he was in the form of God, did not regard equality with God as something exploited" (Phil 2:6); that is, the human nature. Fourth, there [in heaven], God took one rib and shaped it. Likewise, the Word took one individual nature from the virgin and united it with Him. He did not take the whole [nature], which is an assumption on our part. Fifth, the one rib became a basis and foundation upon which the body and the countenance were assembled. Likewise, the one person of God the Word became a foundation and platform for humankind, and personified human nature by blending it in Him as one person, one countenance, and the one nature of the incarnate Word, according to the fathers [of the church]. Sixth, God's right hand took Adam's rib and made it woman. Likewise, God's right—the Only Begotten Word—took the left rib, which is Adam's sinful nature, and by uniting it with Him, gave birth to the innocent and pure body, revealing the first rightward and unmistakable nature that Adam possessed before he sinned. Seventh, the rib is in the middle [of the body], closer to the legs. Likewise, God the Word became man at a time that is close to the last ages of our life. Eighth, the rib is strength, for we refer to wrestlers as thick-ribbed. Likewise, the Word became strong in the body and defeated the adversary; hence: "The Lord is robed in majesty; he is girded with strength" (Ps 93:1). Ninth, the rib is the place of desire and the incarnation is the love of the Word, for God's love for us was expressed through the humanization [of the Word]; hence: "God so loved the world that he gave his Only Begotten Son" (Jn 3:16). Tenth, the rib was in Adam before it was taken, but it joined him inseparably afterward. Likewise, humanity is the creation of the Word. The Word took [human nature] and by taking it joined it to the same Word inseparably, because just as there is no beginning to His divinity, so too there is no end to His humanity. Consequently, it was said: "the two shall become one flesh" (Gen 2:24); that is, one countenance by the inseparable unity of the two natures, one person, and one united nature. However, this is paradigm, mystery, and shadow; whereas He is truth and reality. Hence: "The body is Christ" (Col 2:17). [We have said] enough on the mystery of the humanization of the Word. Many more and various theories of the unity of the Word and the body, however, remain unexplained and revered silently.

The second unity is that of the bride-church with the groom-Christ. First, Adam preceded the woman who was made from his rib. Similarly, there was the groom-Christ before the Christian church became His bride. Second, the rib was taken and made into woman when Adam was in a deep sleep. Similarly, Christ's side was opened and the church formed the two streams of blood and water when Christ was asleep on the cross, that we may cleanse ourselves by the water and taste the blood. Third, the rib occupies the middle space between the head and the feet, and Christ is united with the church with a medial love— below His real body and above the common partakers of His body, because He united with the body by His person and His nature, and with the faithful by His grace and His love, whereas He united with the unbelievers and the wicked only by His providence and righteous examination, which are the ulterior feet and appendages of His body. Fourth, the rib is a bosom and gatherer. Similarly, Christ gathers the faithful around Him, "as a hen gathers her brood and protects them under her wing" (Mt 23:37). Fifth, the rib is where desire exists. Likewise, the church is the subject of Christ's love like the bride who is [the subject] of the groom's [love]. Sixth, Adam and Eve turned into one flesh with the rib; so too became Christ one body with the faithful. Hence: "We are body of his body and members of his member" (cf. Eph 5:30). Seventh, the woman [Eve] was empowered by Adam's rib and [God] covered the spot with flesh—rest, which applies to all men and women sacredly. Likewise, our Lord Christ empowers

and helps the church, and rests in his believers. Eighth, Adam is the origin of
Eve and the rib. Likewise, Christ is the origin of the church, "the firstborn of
all creation" (Col 1:15), of grace and of righteousness, and the first to resurrect
from death. Ninth, Adam and Eve gave corporeal birth through pain and
condemnation. Likewise, in the church, a spiritual birth takes place and a
blessed child comes forth according to the Prophet: "God has blessed the
children and their offspring with them" (cf. Isa 61:9). Tenth, the rib was called
Eve—half the body which is one side, or born from the rib, or sprouted from
the rib. Likewise, the church is known as born of Christ's side, or as an offshoot
of His side, or half of Christ's body, for we were born and grown through
Christ's side, and we are His members, whereas Christ is our head. Because as
the animate motions and feelings descend from the head into the members, so
too the motions of liveliness and the spiritual feelings descend into us from
Christ through faith.

The husband takes ownership of the beauty and modesty of his wife, and
the wife takes ownership of her husband's possessions and glory. Similarly,
our virtue is attributed to our head, Christ, and Christ's glory, possessions, and
heritage are reckoned to belong to His bride, the church. The groom's visit to
the bride's house to bring her to the wedding is a reflection of the verse: "A
man leaves his father and his mother, and clings to his wife" (Gen 2:24). Just
as the groom leaves his father and mother to go with his bride, so too Christ,
coming with His inseparable divinity from the Father, left His mother in grief
and went to the cross for the love of the church. Again, Christ the groom will
come at the end of the age, enter into the house of humankind, and take people
to His patrimony. Hence, "Come, you that are blessed by the Father" (Mt
25:34). Thereafter, He will place them in the kingdom of heaven. And as the
groom holds the left hand of the bride with his right hand until they reach the
church, so too the Only Begotten Son, the right hand of God, holds in His right
hand the churches that are still on the left-hand side of humankind. He will
keep holding their right hand until [men] enter the heavenly church of the
firstborn, at which point they will change [place] to stand at the right-hand side
[of Christ]; hence: "You have holden my right hand. You have guided me with
your counsel, and you have received me with glory (Ps 73:23–24). When [the
bride and groom] exit the church, the bride is on the left-hand side of the groom,
but when they sit on the high place, which is called throne, [the groom] changes
[position] and offers the bride to sit on his right-hand side. This is so, because
Adam had the woman to his right-hand side in the garden of delight, and when
they left it, the woman was on the left-hand side of Adam causing the fall.

When God the Word wanted to become human, He changed our lefty [i.e., erring] nature into righty [i.e., straight], and for this reason, He dwelled in the right side of the virgin's womb, as it is the order for male infants to be formed in the right-hand side of their mother, whereas female [infants are formed] in the left-hand side. Also, He [God the Word] wanted to give birth to us—His children—on the cross; wherefore, He opened His right side and built the church on His right-hand side, like the [baptismal] font which is located currently on the right-hand side of the church. Again, at His second coming, "He will place the church on his right" (cf. Mt 25:33), as the Gospel says. And the Apostle says: "So shall we ever be with the Lord" (1 Thess 4:16).

As for the new dress and the ornamented garments of the bride and the groom, they are seven in count—four are for the entire body, and three are for the head. This indicates that Adam and Eve lived in the garden of delight gloriously, with pure body and luminous glory, for, evidently, they did not see each other's nudity. And [these are] seven in count, because they [Adam and Eve] were adorned with seven graces before violating the commandments; that is, four physical and three spiritual [graces], which we shall reclaim at the resurrection.

When they [Adam and Eve] transgressed with the seven sins, they were stripped of the seven graces and suffered seven punishments. Therefore, it has been said: "The eyes of both were opened, and they knew that they were naked" (Gen 3:7). Likewise, our Lord Jesus Christ, with the mystery of His humanization, took the seven luminous graces as our Lord and gave them to His members—to those who are born of the spiritual font, or when they are renewed in purity, as He says in the parable of the dishonest manager: "Take off of him his old sins and put on him the former robe" (cf. Lk 15:22). After this worldly life, when the groom-Christ comes on the day of resurrection, He will adorn the holy church with seven decorations, of which three[50] are related to the body and three to the spirit, because the bodies of the holy men are adorned with four things: first, the radiance of the body: "Then the righteous will shine like the sun in the kingdom of heavens" (Mt 13:43); second, the absence of suffering, for they shall not be subjected to it and they shall be immortal; third, lightness, for they shall be delicate and light, and not thick and heavy; fourth, speed, since they will encounter nothing that would hinder them. They will be so fast and penetrative that their body will be able to reach wherever their minds want. Besides, before His agony, Christ showed these

---

[50] It appears that this should be *four*.

four [properties] in His holy body: radiance through transfiguration; speed by walking over the waters; lightness, for being born in the body incorrupt, without alteration; and impassibility in the Upper Room during supper, when He offered His holy body to His disciples, for it is to be understood that He was impassible in His energy, but not in His [human] nature. These four [attributes] adorn the body. The spirit, however, is adorned in three ways. First, the knowledge of the intellectual faculties without ignorance, for they see God face to face. Second, enchantment with divine joy and love, for there will be joy without grief; hence: "I will see you again, and your hearts will rejoice, and no one will take your joy from you" (Jn 16:22). Third, understanding and learning without loss of memory, for here [in this life] we learn and forget many things, whereas there [in the hereafter] we will keep things without forgetfulness. These are the seven fineries given to the bride in the church. Therefore, Isaiah says: "My whole being shall exult in my God; for he has clothed me with the garment of salvation, he has covered me with the robe of joy [righteousness], gave me a garland as to a bridegroom, and adorned me with finery as to a bride" (Isa 61:60). Also, the corporeal bride is given three things—quotas, dowry, and presents. The quotas are given by the bride's father to cover the wedding's necessities; the dowry is given by the groom, whereas the presents are offered by friends. Likewise, the spiritual bride of the church receives the kingdom of heaven as her quota; her dowry is the joy she will experience by seeing Christ; and her present will be her association with the saints and the classes of angels.

The veil that covers the face of the bride and the new garments of the bride and the groom suggest that for so long as the first-created man and woman lived in the garden of delight, their garment consisted of purity and radiant glory, and they did not possess [the habit of] looking lasciviously at one another. In a similar fashion, the veil is placed upon the face [of the bride], so that the groom may not look at the bride with lust. Again, so long as we are corporeal beings in this life, we see Christ the groom obscurely, be it in the past, the present, or the future. However, later [in the life to come], we shall see Him clearly and with uncovered face, as the Apostle says: "Now we see in a mirror dimly, but then we will see face to face, as a God" (cf. 1 Cor 13:12). "Thereupon, our humble bodies will be renewed in the likeness of the body of his glory, for the righteous will shine like the sun in the kingdom of heavens" (2 Cor 3:18; Mt 13:43). This is what the new garments and the veil indicate.

Placing the crown upon the head symbolizes Adam's kingdom, for he was installed lord and ruler upon all living creatures; moreover, he was installed head and lord upon the woman. Here, then, the groom became his wife's lord and king, and the bride [became] queen, for they have become one flesh by the crowning. It is referred to as [placing the] crown, because it [the crown] is whole and perfect, for through marriage the man and the woman receive perfection wholly.

The red and the white colors of the headband carry in themselves the mystery of the blood and water that gushed out of the life-giving side of Christ and bonded and married Him with the church.

The diadem [symbolizes] the thorny crown that the heavenly groom received on His head, as the song says: "Look at King Solomon, the crown with which his mother crowned him on the day of the wedding, on the day of the gladness of his heart" (Song 3:11).

Just as friends during the wedding communicate through three senses—sight, hearing, and taste—whereas unity through touching is reserved to the bride and the groom only, so too the angels share the joys of human beings through sight, hearing, and other means, but only the church is considered to be the bride that unites [humankind] with Christ the groom. During the wedding, what takes place is the unity of nature, and angels lack this [capacity], for they are not partakers of Christ's nature.

At a second wedding, the crown will not be placed and the wedding will take place rather in the middle of the church than close to the pulpit, to signify that the marrying persons possess neither the crown of virginity nor the same position. The doctors of the church say that of the classes of angels, only virgins would be mixed with those who have been impaired [by sins], whereas those that are married chastely, would be classified separately and will comprise classes in the likeness of the nine classes of angels.

The wedding lasts three days because Adam and Eve spent three joyful hours together in the garden of delight before taking shelter under the tree. The corporeal joy occurs in three times—past, present, and future; that is, yesterday, today, and tomorrow. Therefore, the wedding [celebration] lasts three days. Again, one day is [reckoned to be dedicated] to the groom, one day to the bride, and one [day] to the unity, for they become one flesh. Upon completion of seven days, on the eighth day, the crown is removed and permission is given for corporeal copulation. This suggests that the first-created human beings spent seven days in the garden of delight before they were cast out. Adam was created during the first hour of Friday; then the woman [was created] from his rib during the second hour; thereafter, the serpent deceived Eve during the third hour; they ate the fruit at the sixth hour, and at the ninth hour, toward the evening, they were cast out of the garden of delight. Adam's joy with Eve occupied three of these hours, and the other four they spent in grief. For this reason, after the conclusion of the three days, on the eighth day they [the bride and groom] go to the church for the crown to be removed. Again, there is yet another mystery—the seven days symbolize the seven ages of our life along with the corporeal diadem and crown in this life, whereas during the life to come, in the eighth age, all diadems and crowns will be lifted.

Concerning the permission of the priest on the eighth day to the bride and the groom to copulate, it indicates that the bed should be kept undefiled for the sake of the seven graces of the spirit and the seven mysteries of the church. Again, the creation extended over seven days; therefore, a person should keep the number seven pure. We are made of four elements and our soul is composed of three components—reason, passion, and desire. Moreover, we have four acquired virtues—prudence, fortitude, chastity, and righteousness, and three divine [virtues]—faith, hope, and love that sum up to seven. For this reason, the seven days should be observed sacredly. Concerning the spiritual [aspect of wedding], the church is Christ's bride, and there is no unity [with Christ] during the seven ages of our life here, but in the eighth age, the congregation will truly unite with Christ the groom and, through Him, with the Father and the Holy Spirit. Therefore, [Christ] said: "As you, Father, are in me, I am in you, may they also be in us, so that they may see my glory" (cf. Jn 17:21–22). Let us all be worthy of seeing the immortal groom and unite with Him in love, for He is blessed forever and ever, amen.

CHAPTER XLVII

Homily of the same on sins according to the verse of John: "There are sins that are sins, and there are sins that are mortal" (1 Jn 5:16).

God created all rational beings with inherent discretion. There is inherent discretion in the mind, for it recognizes and separates the good and evil, and distinguishes them from each other like an eye that sees and distinguishes the black from the white. Then there is a second choice that is made of working what is good and maintaining it, while withdrawing from wickedness. The first discretion is related to the intellect, because a person judges according to the rational light. The second discretion relates to the will, because a person willfully works that which is good and stays away from evil, for evil by itself is to be avoided by everybody, whereas goodness is to be desired by everybody.

Now, those who have intellectual wisdom make the distinction between the good and evil in this fashion: they withdraw from the evil and choose the good. However, the foolish and senseless cannot recognize and withdraw from the evil—like a blind person who cannot see colors—and commit all kinds of sins indiscriminately.

Transgressors are distinguished in three ways. There are those that sin unintentionally and unknowingly, such as the children. They deserve forgiveness and expiation, as David says: "Do not remember the sins of my youth and my ignorance" (cf. Ps 25:7). There are those who commit the sin unwillingly, although they know what the sins are; and there are those who commit sins intentionally and knowingly.

Presently, we do not recall those [sins] that are [committed] unknowingly and unintentionally, such as the [sins of] children; rather, we preach to adults, because every sin [committed] by adults is distinguished based on two considerations. First, he who unintentionally sins in the body and makes it stumble does so by a secondary will. Whereas he who sins by the primary will and intentionally is more wicked and ungodly, such as an evildoer who finds pleasure in the sins and transgresses without regret, like the pagans and heathens who are hardened in transgression and take evil for good. Their sins are of various scales: "There are sins that are sins, and there are sins that are mortal" (1 Jn 5:16).

follow his will. Hence: "I let them go after the ways of their own hearts, so they will go on in their own ways" (Ps 81:12).

Should someone ask: "Why does not [God] pull people out of the sins by force to bring them to righteousness?" We say there are two reasons for this. First, had He pulled [people] out by force, He would have removed our free will; therefore, He lets us find the direction independently. Second, had He brought us [to direction] by force, His justice would have been twisted. Since God is righteous and not unrighteous, He does not force a person into righteousness.

Twelfth, the involuntary [sinner] repents and regrets for his sinful actions; whereas [he who sins] voluntarily does so without regret, like Satan who is void of repentance. Therefore, he finds no forgiveness, as the Apostle says: "For those who willfully sin, there remains no more sacrifice for sins, but a fearful prospect of judgment and a fury of fire that will consume the adversaries" (cf. Heb 10:26). The evangelist refers to these sins when he says: "Whosoever falls again in sin willfully after receiving the Lord's mercy, shall be indebted for his former sins as well" (cf. Heb 10:26). And the Prophet refers to these sins, saying: "When the sinner commits wickedness, his righteousness which he has done shall not be remembered" (cf. Ezek 3:20); that is, when man sins willfully, he loses his former good works and takes back upon him the punishment of forgiven sins. For example, a perfect justice erases the sins committed formerly along with their punishment; likewise, a voluntary sin [is as if] "the dog turns back to its own vomit and the sow is washed only to wallow in the mud" (2 Pet 2:22). This is the distinction between voluntary and involuntary sins; thereby, the Apostle says: "There are sins that are sins, and there are sins that are mortal" (1 Jn 5:16).

It needs to be observed that when a person reaches the depths of wickedness he points at God as the cause of sins; as if He made us lustful to [make us] fornicate, and angry to [make us] kill, and needing nourishment to [make us] avaricious. We say that this is untrue pretext. First, because everything placed in man by God is placed for the sake of goodness; we turn them into evil. Reason is placed in us to recognize and choose the good God, but we choose wickedness. Anger is given to us to show anger against evil; we alter it and are provoked against the ordinances. Desire also is given for the sake of goodness; we desire wickedness. Likewise, He made us needing food and clothing so that we obtain these by daily work and avoid committing evil by staying idle. In this way, everything God placed in us is good. Again, He gave us everything in moderation; we stretch them to immoderation and excess.

For example, our needs can be satisfied by moderate food and this is what our nature demands; but through our own choice we become gluttonous. Similarly, one garment is enough for one person; many [garments] are excessive. We ride one horse; many [horses] are excessive. Although there is plenty of water, our thirst is quenched by a little, and we suck a little air; if we receive more, we die. Examine all of the sins in this manner—desire is moderate; anger is moderate; truth is the limit of knowledge; but cunningness, killing, and fornication often occur by our own choice. Therefore, a person should not blame God, for we are the cause of our sins.

Again, when a person has reached the depths of sins, disbelief captures him and his disbelief makes him despise four things. First, God, for "The fool said in his heart, 'There is no God'" (Ps 13:1). Second, he despises God's judgment and restitution for sinners. Third, he disdains God's commandments: "You shall not commit adultery and you shall not steal, [etc.]" (cf. Ex 20:14). Fourth, he repulses within himself the good deeds because he wills goodness neither in his mind, nor by his tongue or in his body; rather, he twists his mind and thoughts in wickedness and disbelief, his tongue in lie and profanity, and his body in various evil deeds. The ungodly belittles in this fashion these four [aforementioned] things. Then, at this point, the sinner himself will be repulsed and dishonored, as the Prophet says: "Whoso despises things will be despised by them" (Prov 13:13). A person of such caliber will be despised by God and then by people through God's command, as well as by lay and religious authorities and leaders who punish the wicked and lawless by God's command; or God will torment them here [on earth] by sword, slavery, or famine, and there [in the hereafter] by eternal fire.

Second, God will seek revenge proportionate to their transgressions through His judgment, and He will punish them so that those who did not remember the good works during the judgment may remember the revenge and keep in mind that there is a righteous judgment.

Third, God punishes through laws, be they natural or written, and through the Gospel. These [laws] torment those who received the laws but did not keep them: "All who have sinned under the law will be judged by the law, and all who have sinned apart from the law, will perish apart from the law" (cf. Rom 2:12).

Fourth, good deeds punish those who dishonor people and do evil, be it mentally, verbally, or practically, for a person's suffering with the soul and the body will be proportionate to the evil he has committed with the soul and the body. Now, when a man brings harm or deficiency upon someone with regard

350

to something, he is considered enemy—he harms either the possessions, or the glory, whether verbally or by any action. Now, sin is such an enemy that causes harm and deficiency not only in one thing, but everything—possessions, life, glory, spirit, and body. It causes harm and destruction to possessions and wealth, which people spend and lose through association with the wicked. It dishonors the glory, for [the wicked] loses God's favor and is detested by man. It destroys life, because it shortens the corporeal life here [on earth] and becomes eternal deficiency and harm for the soul and the body there [in the hereafter]. Then, therefore, it is detestable and reckoned to be enemy, because sin causes a great deal of harm to the spirit and the body alike.

First, the conscience always judges a sinner and torments him internally. Second, it brings sadness and shame to the countenance, like Cain whose countenance fell after he killed Abel. Third, fear, fright, and anticipation for punishment come to mind, as it happened to Eve and Adam, when they turned naked and went into hiding. Fourth, everybody hates and blames them; hence: "They lost God's favor and are detestable to all men" (cf. 1 Thess 2:15). Fifth, the mind of a sinner goes astray and he stops short of putting his thoughts in the right direction, because they are scattered by various sins and his vision is darkened. Sixth, he [the sinner] gives away his boldness and replaces the warm love of God with coldness. Seventh, his perpetual desire languishes him, for sinful deeds are insatiable and the fire always devours him; hence: "You may consume it upon your lust" (Jas 4:3). Eighth, he is lazy and a coward, and his body is plunged into voluptuousness. Ninth, he is condemned and tortured by lay authorities for various sins—he is fined for depriving others, stoned for adultery, his blood is shed for the blood he has shed, his body parts are mutilated, and so on. Tenth, [his share is] physical disaster, drought,[51] dissension, captivity, trap, and other mischief, such as the flood and [the disasters] that befell the Sodomeans.

Now, these are physical punishments for sins. Concerning the spirit, sin is likewise harmful in many ways.

First, it makes a person guilty before God and subject to His punishment. Second, he is an offender, for he has despised God's ordinances. Third, he loses the image of God in himself and stains it with sins. Fourth, he corrupts the temple of God through sins: "You are temples of the living God" (2 Cor 6:16). Fifth, Satan rests in him and he turns into a shelter for Satan. Sixth, sin takes

---

[51] Due to a typographic error, in the printed text *drought* (*erašt* [երաշտ]) has become *music* (eražštut΄iwn [երաժշտութիւն]).

away the light of grace from man. Seventh, [a sinner] loses the path that leads to God. Eighth, [sin] conjoins the spirit with death. Ninth, he [the sinner] hides from Christ's voice with a head bent down and a soul grieved disgracefully and shamefully during the judgment, in the likeness of the foolish bridesmaids. Tenth, a frightful judgment [awaits him]: "Everlasting torment prepared for the devil and his angels" (cf. Mt 25:41).

Why do people commit sins, when they are so harmful to the spirit and the body?

It is to be known that God created man good and straight, for [man] is created good with the body, the spirit, and the mind. As God Himself is good, His creations also are good, with the difference that God is good immutably, while people are mutable—we can change from good to evil with the body and the spirit, and from straight thoughts to crooked in this mutable life. Two things cause this. First, Satan who is our adversary and always wants to deceive us to change us from good to evil. Second, Satan deceives our free will to present wickedness as goodness and make us commit [wickedness]. Had he presented them as evil, we would not have committed them, because everybody flees from evil. He beautifies and attires evil as goodness and deceives us with it. And we with our free will become deceived in our choice to commit evil, and so long as we continue to commit, the body and the soul find pleasure inadvertently. People can easily recover from sins that are in the thoughts and have not been committed yet, but if a man takes his time staying in a sinful state, his body takes pleasure in it and the senses become lethargic because of the sins and do not feel the weight. For example, a fish that swallows the hook plays in the water and does not consider [the situation] until it is pulled out of the water. Likewise, a man does not understand the evilness of sins until he comes to repent and come out of the sins, or die and come out of life. At that point, he would faint, groan, and regret but find no forgiveness, for every sinful person will regret in the life to come because of the inevitable suffering, but will not be healed.

Should someone ask, since it is the same compassionate God and the same sinner, why then is the sinner not forgiven when he regrets? We say [this is so] for three reasons. First, bodies do not exist there [in the hereafter] to repent with—be it with fasting, prayers, almsgiving, or otherwise; therefore, [the sinner] is not forgiven. Second, man repents in the life to come involuntarily, not willfully; therefore, he is not forgiven. Third, the opportunity for repentance is missed and the door is closed, like it was closed before the foolish bridesmaids who, despite asking for alms, did not receive them from the wise.

Repentance, therefore, is needed in this life, when man can work with the body and repent willfully, and when the time is acceptable, according to the Apostle: "Behold, now is the accepted time; behold, now is the day of salvation" (2 Cor 6:2).

Should someone say, although I [cannot] repent, someone else [can] repent for me; we say that the prayer of the righteous and the worship, offering, and gifts to the poor are good, but these benefit those who have repented for the sins and have confessed. We help them with prayers and pay their debts, but nothing helps those who died without repentance. For example, praying to saints during a lifetime benefits the believers but not the unbelievers; likewise, nothing benefits those who died without repentance; only penitents are benefitted. Also, for example, a person ailing in the body can heal with medicine, but a dead man cannot heal, as we mentioned earlier. Likewise, a person who is ailing with sins benefits after repenting for the sins, but he who dies without repenting for the sins, nothing is useful to him. A dried tree does not benefit from the abundance of water. Likewise, a man blinded with disbelief or dried by transgressions does not benefit from the abundance of prayers. Not only do they [prayers] not help, on the contrary, they cause more harm like a hot iron in naked hands; or, as the bright sunlight darkens the insignificant light of bleary eyes, likewise the posterior remembrance is useless for disbelievers and for those who died with sins. Therefore, we have to turn from the sins today and become worthy of the mercy of God through our Lord Jesus Christ, who is blessed forever, amen.

CHAPTER XLVIII

Homily of the same, again, on sins. The Prophet Moses says: "God makes mercy for thousands, and brings the iniquity of the fathers upon the children, to the third and fourth generation" (Ex 34:7).

To make mercy for thousands of generations has two meanings. First, it shows the abundance of God's bounties. He rather compensates manifold and by thousands than in a manner commensurate with the deeds, which indicates the immortal life of eternities. Second, it shows that He brings goodness to the good children of thousands of generations thanks to their righteous fathers, and lightens the burden of sins, as the only begotten Word of God made mercy by remembering our early righteous ancestors. Hence, "He shall remember his eternal covenant and his commandments to a thousand generations" (cf. Deut 7:9). That He brings the sins of the fathers upon the children, to the third and fourth generation, this has many explanations and I shall offer six explanations for them.

First, the third and fourth generations, which [combined] make seven [generations], indicate the seven ages of our life—from Adam's exodus from Paradise unto the last generation, which is the end of the world. There begins the eighth age, when all people will be judged and all deeds will be compensated, whether good or evil.

Second explanation: The four generations indicate the four kinds of coming to being of all sinners who are compensated according to their deeds. God wiped out all sinners of the first generation by the flood in accordance with their natural sins. During the second occurrence, He drowned in the Red Sea those who had sinned through paganism. The third occurrence took place when He killed through war those who had sinned against Moses' written ordinances. The fourth occurrence will take place with the last fire, after sentencing those who have sinned against the Gospel to eternal torment.

Third explanation: [The verse] covers four ages of evil nations and kings; that is, four hundred years, because each hundred years is referred to as an age. Henceforth, the first age passed after God gave the land of Canaan to great Abraham, and He did not kill them. The same applies to the second and third ages. In the fourth age, however, He called upon the Hebrews and they rose up and killed the thirty-two kings [of the Amorites], for they returned from Egypt during the fourth age; that is, after four hundred years.

The fourth explanation is that God forgives the sins of unrighteous ancestors up to three generations, but the fourth generation will compensate for the sins of their ancestors. He will not bring the fathers' iniquity upon their children; rather, He will forgive the fathers' sins and be patient up to the children of [their] children that they may turn from sins. But if the sons and grandchildren fail to benefit from the forgiveness, He will then punish and wipe the memory of the evil generation, as David says: "The face of the Lord is against them that do evil, to destroy their memorial from the earth" (Ps 34:16).

Fifth notion: People sin in four ways: by thoughts, by words, by works, and by persistently committing sins. Bringing the iniquity upon the third and fourth generations means that God will torment for their deeds those who have persistently committed sins.

Sixth explanation: Man goes through four phases of age: childhood, adolescence, adulthood, and senility. If God forgave the sins of three of these phases, and a person continued to go without repentance, He then will punish him.

Up to here, we discussed the first expression. Let us now discuss the second and see why God punishes the sinners. We say for many reasons:

First, to make them grieve and beg; to avoid consequently the eternal punishment of the pure wrath.

Second, here [on earth] the bodily punishment results in penitence, which leads to forgiveness of sins—torments cleanse the sinners like files that cleanse the iron and furnaces that cleanse the rust.

Third, the visible torments evidence the torments of the hereafter; whereby, God spares them and physically chastens them. Hence: "When we are judged by the Lord, we are chastened so that we may not be condemned along with the world" (1 Cor 11:32).

Fourth, since this torment relates to the body alone and not the soul, He torments here physically in order to exempt from all [torments] in the hereafter, like a physician who cauterizes or cuts a part of the body to heal the entire body.

Fifth, the worldly torments lighten and shorten the eternal torments, as was the case with the people of Sodom. Hence: "it shall be more tolerable on the Day of Judgment for the land of Sodom" (Mt 10:15).

Sixth, [God punishes] to awaken the sinners who are asleep and entangled in the love of the world, so that through the worldly hardship they may seek life for the hereafter, as he tormented the Israelites in Egypt, so that they would leave it. A mother weans the child from her breast milk by [applying] a bitter medicine. The Prophet says: "You must constrain their jaws with bit and curb" (Ps 32:9). Elsewhere, [the Prophet says]: "Fill their faces with dishonor" (Ps 83:16). This [much] on the second.

The third question relates to those who wonder: What happens to disbelievers—or believers who have committed deadly sins—who do goodness, or to those who sin after doing goodness?

The doctors say that the good works of a disbeliever or a person entangled in sins are dead, and that God does not accept their works, because the first is dead by disbelief, whereas the other is dead by sins. As for those who have done goodness at the beginning and then fell in sins, there is a distinction. [For a] believer who has worked good works initially and later fell in sin and repented, the good works he has performed during his innocent period will be remembered after his repentance. Whereas the works of a person who does goodness while he is entangled in disbelief or in mortal sins will not be remembered even after he repents. As if you have planted two plants, one with roots and one without. If you keep both without watering, and then water them, the rooted plant will turn green, whereas the rootless will dry.

Likewise, a doer of goodness who has not committed mortal sins but has fallen in sins for a given duration will come back to life after repentance, thanks to the roots he had. But those who do goodness as disbelievers or sinners will not come back to life even if they have repented, because they lack the roots, as the Prophet says: "they did not remember the multitude of your kindness" (Ps 106:7). Although this is so, good works have their benefits, whether worked by disbelievers or by those who committed mortal sins, for God is righteous. Even if the unbeliever dies impenitently and descends unto hell, there are many benefits from good works. First, the torments of hell will be lighter for doers of goodness. Second, on earth, God will give them tangible wealth, as was the case of the wealthy, on whom it was told: "in your lifetime you received your good things" (Lk 16:25). Third, because, thanks to the good works, God makes the divine knowledge shine in the person's heart, as happened with Cornelius [Acts 10]. Fourth, God saves one from physical traps, as happened to Ahab [3 Kings 21:27] thanks to his repentance, because the punishment that was set for him visited him after his worldly days were completed. Fifth, the world would not remain in a good state without people doing good works. Therefore, everybody, whether righteous or sinner, should work good works, so that the world may stay in a good state. Sixth, even when a person has committed mortal sins or is a disbeliever, when he works good works, it is beneficial to the extent that he will learn and exercise goodness. When he becomes faithful or repents, benevolence will not seem difficult, for he has become accustomed to it. Seventh, disbelievers or committers of mortal sins have ailing spirit. A physically sick man needs food, which, although short of nourishing the ailing person, prevents death stemming from lack of strength. In a similar fashion, the food of benevolence is needed not only for the righteous, but also for the sinners, because although it does not make the sinners worthy of the kingdom of heaven, it prevents the total weakening of their soul. Eighth, all disbelievers and committers of mortal sins are under Satan's control, as Christ said: "every one who commits sin is a slave to sin" (Jn 8:34). Those, however, who do goodness, Satan will have less than total control over them.

But why wouldn't disbelievers or committers of mortal sins receive full reward for their good works? For the following reason: people's dried and severed members do not receive animate strength; likewise, those who have been severed from Christ do not receive perfect recompense.

And it is to be known, so long as a person lives on earth, he cannot know whether God favors him or is at odds with him, until he comes out of his body. Doctors say, however, that a person might know whether God favors him or is at odds with him in four ways. First, when a person repents for committed or past sins, that is a sign of goodness. Second, when he does not commit the sins that come to his mind. Third, when he listens to God's word and instruction, and finds them pleasant. Fourth, when he hastens to make all kinds of good works. Contrary to these, when these four signs do not appear, know, then, that you are at odds with God. First, when you do not repent for committed sins. Second, when you do not refrain from committing sins. Third, when God's commandment and human instructions seem difficult. Fourth, when a person does not haste to do goodness. This [much] concerning the third matter.

Fourth, let us discuss the difference between sins. It is to be known that the difference between sins is evident from four divisions. First, when sins are excessive quantitatively and qualitatively, they are absolutely evil. The quality of [such] sins consists of the fact that they are committed willingly, knowingly, and skillfully. These are mortal sins committed premeditatedly. Second [kind of] sin. When the quantity and quality of the sins are lesser, it is lesser evil, and this is a forgivable sin, for it has been committed unknowingly, unwillingly, and unskillfully. Third, when the quantity surpasses the quality; like a lay person who commits sin unknowingly. Fourth, when the quantity of sins is lesser than the quality; like a priest who commits sins with knowledge. These [two categories] are subject to equal punishment.

A sin committed with knowledge is as punishable as many sins committed without knowledge, as [happened] when the head priest offered one sacrifice and the people as a whole offered another. Israel sinned once by adopting paganism, whereas pagans sinned many times, but both were enslaved equally, because the Israelites sinned knowingly, whereas the pagans did so unknowingly.

In reference to this, the Apostle said: "There will be tribulation and distress for every human being who does evil, the Jew first and also the heathen" (Rom 2:9). Conclude the contrary with regard to goodness. When good works are extremely good quantitatively and qualitatively, they are absolutely good and perfect. When the quantity and quality are lesser, [the good works] are less good and are imperfect. [There are good works] where the quantity surpasses the quality, as with laity who do goodness without knowledge. And [there are good works] where the quality surpasses the quantity, as with priests who do goodness with knowledge. These are rewarded equally and with the same measure, for a priest's one [good] work is as fruitful as the many works of a layperson, because the priest's is [worked] with knowledge, whereas the layperson's [is worked] without knowledge. In reference to this, the Apostle says: "Glory and honor and peace for everyone who does good, the Jew first and also the heathen" (Rom 2:10).

Should someone counter this with the Gospel, saying: "Every one to whom much is given, of him will much be required" (Lk 12:48), we say: The Lord does not say that the honor and reward of priests and laity are equal, for, behold, he who had the two talents made two talents more, and [this is pertinent] to laity. He who had five [talents] earned ten and ruled over ten cities. This [pertains] to priests. Rather, the Lord commands that since the priest has seven more ranks as compared to laity, he is under sevenfold more obligation to do goodness. The bishop has eight ranks more [than laity], and the catholicos nine. [Therefore,] likewise, they ought to do more goodness because of their additional ranks. A celibate priest has seven ranks like the married priest, but five more honors, for the Apostle says: "in church I would rather speak five words with my mind" (1 Cor 14:19). These ranks pertain to celibate priests and therefore they are under greater obligation than the bishop and the catholicos to do goodness. Proportionate to their good works, they receive different and more honors and glorious rewards from Christ our God, who is blessed forever, amen.

CHAPTER XLIX

Homily of the same, again, on sins, according to the verse: "A conceived desire gives birth to sin, and sin gives birth to death" (Jas 1:15).

The serpent that spoke to Eve and deceived her indicates voluptuous desires that deceive us, and there are fourteen reasons for this. First, because the serpent is a poisonous animal and physical desires are death to the soul, for "A conceived desire gives birth to sin, and sin gives birth to death" (Jas 1:15). Second, the serpent moves covertly, and desire entraps covertly. Third, [the serpent] trails on earth, and desire pulls man down to the earth. Fourth, [the serpent] crawls on its side and abdomen, and desire initially bonds the heart with pleasure and then makes one work it bodily. Fifth, [the serpent] eats soil, and desire finds pleasure on earth. Sixth, the serpent makes five curls, and there are five desires in the senses. Seventh, [the serpent] is spotted, and desire is variegated in the senses. Eighth, [the serpent's] head is feeble, and desire is weak. Ninth, [the serpent] pulls its body along everywhere it inserts its head, and action follows the voluptuous desire. Tenth, [the serpent] pulls itself out with difficulty because of the spittle, and desire departs the body with difficulty because of the pleasure. Eleventh, [the serpent] gives birth to numerous younglings, and desire has multiparous daughters. Twelfth, [the serpent] fits large objects in its mouth, and desire grows more dominant by tasting. Thirteenth, [the serpent] watches for the heels, and desire entraps the steps of the body. Fourteenth, we crush the [serpent's] head, and we ought to kill desire in us from its inception, to be able to defeat passions, according to the Lord's instruction: "it shall watch against your head, and you shall watch against its heel" (Gen 1:15).

First, let us see what differentiates desire from pleasure. It is to be known that desire and pleasure are different in four ways. First, desire is a component of the soul, whereas pleasure relates to the body. Second, desire is intrinsic, whereas pleasure is extrinsic. Third, desire precedes pleasure. Fourth, to desire is to act; to take pleasure is to carry it. Thus, they are different in these four ways. Besides, desire is futuristic, [and] voluptuousness belongs to the past, whereas pleasure relates to the present. Vice and uncleanliness too are different in a similar fashion, for vice is innate, whereas uncleanliness is extrinsic.

Similarly, the blemish is part of the soul, whereas the defect is part of bodily senses. Likewise, evil proceeds from the heart and defiles us, whereas we sin because of external factors.

Second, let us discuss the differences between sin and lawlessness. We say that they have six differences. First, to sin is to transgress before a law [is established,] whereas to break the law takes place after a law [is established]. Second, to sin is to transgress against a friend, whereas to break the law is to transgress against God. Third, to sin is to transgress unknowingly, whereas to break the law is to transgress knowingly. Fourth, sin is forgivable, whereas breaking the law is mortal. Fifth, sin is physical transgression, whereas breaking the law is spiritual transgression. Sixth, sin is committed before confession, whereas breaking the law is a transgression committed anew after confession, "as when a dog goes to his own vomit" (Prov 26:11).

Third, let us examine sin, death, and mortal [transgression]. We say that sin occurs when a person practicing a given religion commits a sin and repents. Death occurs when a person, although unaware, transgresses unintentionally— his soul dies. The mortal [transgression] constitutes a deliberately committed sin—this is the bitter eternal death.

Should someone ask: What is the intentional transgression? We say that when a person knows the truth but chooses falsehood. This has three facets. First, with regard to the act and punishment: the person knows that the act is sinful; nevertheless, he commits it knowing that the sins entail heavy punishment. Second, with regard to the doer: although he knows the truth somewhat, he neglects it and commits the sin. Third, with regard to knowing God: the person has come to the true faith, yet he neglects it and commits sins. Thus, sinning deliberately is threefold, wherefore John [Chrysostom] says: "If you transgress unknowingly, God forgives you; but if you transgress deliberately, He will demand [answer] for also the former [sins]." Although the sins committed by people occur because of the devil's deception and because of their weak and voluptuous will, there are sins that proceed from the four elements that compose the body, such as anger, onanism, laziness, and pride. As Gregory of Nyssa says, irascible people are apt to be angry, and this is caused by fire. Sanguine people are lecherous, and this is caused by air. Melancholic people are sad, and this is caused by earth. And those who have aqueous humor are lazy and sluggish. Concerning air, it is either dry and cool, or moist and warm. The blood in us is attributed to moisture, whereas the dryness stemming from the storm makes us impulsive, inconsistent, and arrogant. And a strange thing takes place, because man has the good and evil within him and is created as a communicative animate being. Whatever he possesses, he shares with others, as the sun shares its rays and a tree its fruits. Now, if he kept the good to himself and did not share it with others, he is evil, but if he shared it, he is good, be it knowledge, virtue, or anything else. Likewise, if he shared evil with others, he is evil, but if he kept it to himself, he is good, for evil will perish in him. For example, a snake's poison and the sting of a scorpion are good per se, but are evil if they were shed in others. Thus, evil things, such as lechery and anger, are not evil when concealed within us; but they are evil to others and to ourselves when they are transmitted to others.

Fourth, let us see what Job meant by saying: "You would number my steps and you would seal my transgression in a bag" (cf. Job 14:16–17). We say that God does not know our deeds in numbers, but [Job] refers to numbering for four reasons. First, he who numbers knows what comes first, what follows, and so on. Similarly, God knows all our deeds by order: those of adolescence, adulthood, and old age, and He compensates accordingly. Second, we keep everything unforgettable by numbering. This means that God has not forgotten our deeds. Although we work our works and forget them, He knows [the results] of thoughts, words, and works, whether we work them willingly or unwillingly, consciously or unconsciously. Third, through numbering, we know the quantity unmistakably, be it ten, more, or less. God knows our works precisely—neither more, nor less. Fourth, since the numbered object is variable, when we increase the numbering, the number grows, and if we decrease it, it decreases. Likewise, we can increase or decrease the number of our transgressions by works, for we have control over increasing or decreasing.

He also says: "You would seal my transgression in a bag," because, first, one who seals and saves something in a bag brings it out at the time of need. Similarly, God [seals and saves] our works, words, and thoughts to bring them out during the judgment if we did not turn from our transgressions. Second, since we know that He has all our deeds saved in His bag, we will repent our sins and He will bring them out of the bag and eliminate them. Moses, too, says: "Are not these things stored up and sealed among my treasures? In the day of vengeance I will recompense" (Deut 32:34–35). Therefore, we ought to think about and fear that although we could forget our transgressions, God keeps them in His mind and recompenses [accordingly]. And when we confess and recall our transgressions, God will forget them and forgive, for He is benevolent and merciful. And to Him glory forever, amen.

CHAPTER L

A homily and guidance by another on the original sin
according to the verse: "I was conceived in iniquities, and in sins did my
mother conceive me" (Ps 51:5).

The designation *sin* is divided into three [kinds]: original, mortal, and venial. These divisions are not similar to kinds in species, or species in individuals, or anything else. They are reminiscent of the whole in the parts.

The original [sin] is distinguished from the other two—the mortal and venial—in four ways: by unity, commonality, equality, and quality. [It is distinguished] by unity, because there is one original sin and it is not divisible like the mortal into seven and venial into three [kinds]. [It is distinguished] by commonality, because commonly anyone associated with nature is also associated with it; that is, with the original [sin]. Mortal [sins] did not exist in Jeremiah and John, who were cleansed from the womb, although they could not avoid venial [sins]. Whereas Virgin Mary the Mother of God was exempt from both mortal and venial [sins], and was cleansed from the original [sin] at the point of conception through the Holy Spirit. Only our Savior Christ was exempt from the original [sin], because He was not [conceived] by semen; rather, He took body from the clean blood of the virgin. [It is distinguished] by equality, because the original [sin] is in everybody equally, and it is not lesser or greater like mortal [sins], where the sin of adultery is greater than fornication and manslaughter is greater than theft. Concerning the qualitative difference, [note that] the original [sin] dominates by necessity and involuntarily, whereas these [mortal and venial sins dominate] willingly. Second, the original [sin] accompanies the nature [of a person], whereas these [mortal and venial sins] belong to the person; therefore, the natural sin is passed on to the descendants naturally, whereas the personal [sins] are not, because they are acquired by [individual] activities.

This was about the distinction of the original [sin] from others.

The mortal and venial sins differ quantitatively, be it more or less. Just as the sting of a serpent is greater than that of a flea, or [the sting of] an arrow [is greater than that] of a thorn, or the pain of the whole [is greater than the pain] of the parts, so too mortal [sins] are greater than venial [sins].

They differ also based on numbers, because mortal [sins] are divided into seven capital [sins], such as pride, anger, and so on, whereas venial [sins], although divided into three kinds according to their dimension, whether greater or lesser, like "wood, stubble, and hay" according to the Apostle (1 Cor 3:12), are countless in their details, such as laughing, condescending, and so on.

It is to be known that the original sin causes four wounds to our soul. When the body is stricken by a serious disease, a residual disease is left [behind], or weakness [is left] in the case of strength, or desire [is left] in the case of taste. Likewise, with regard to us, the original sin leaves residues in our souls, and these are called wounds and strikes; that is, [they are left behind] in the parts of desire, passion, intellect, and will.

The first is desire, which is an incurable wound; it is the soul's covert enemy. For instance, the animal known as idoros is enemy with the crocodile and bonds with the grass. By eating the grass, the crocodile swallows the idoros and dies of its poison. Similarly, desire bonds with voluptuous things, and the soul dies by performing [voluptuous acts], as Daniel told the elders who were burning with Shushan's desire: "Her beauty deceived you, and your desire changed your heart" (Dan 13:56). It is incurable, because when it changes the heart, it changes also all of the senses along.

The second strike is ignorance, which wounds the intellect, as the psalm says: "[As for] the light of my eyes, it also is gone from me" (Ps 38:10). Also, when the sight is lost, so too are lost all visible things. Wherefore Tobit said: "Where would I find joy, for I sit in darkness, and the light of heavens I see not." Among all senses, sight is the most desirable, and the sight of the soul is more [desirable] than the sight of the body. The strike that turns us to the darkness of mind occurs from the sins.

Anger is the third strike that wounds the soul, like a disease that strikes the body. Anger changes the order [of the soul]. Instead of feeling anger against evil, we feel anger against the good. This is comparable to a handicapped person who moves in opposite direction in order to put himself to order. Wherefore, the Apostle says: "I do not do the good that I want, but the evil I do not want is what I do" (Rom 7:19).

Wickedness is the fourth strike that wounds the wills, even when the will does not perform any transgression with its wickedness, as St. Dionysius says in his *Divine Names*. Nobody performs [evil] by looking at evil, because evil cannot exist by its own will—the usurer or ravisher does not haste to God when he stumbles; rather, he rushes to multiply the money. The lascivious wants the bodily pleasure without stumbling before God, but prefers transgression by stumbling before God over abandoning the bodily pleasure.

These are the four wounds and strikes that occur in our soul from the original [sin], which the first man did not have until he sinned in the garden of delight. This much on this.

CHAPTER LI

On Mortal Sins

We already spoke about the original sin; now, we shall talk about the mortal [sins].

First, however, we need to ask, is there mortal sin? Seemingly not, because death corrupts and disintegrates anything it comes across, as [happens] with living creatures. [One could argue,] although the mortal sin is in the soul, the soul remains immortal. Besides, death impedes the proper actions—a dead man cannot act; whereas the sinful soul, [despite] existing in the midst of mortal sins, accomplishes many things vigorously and understands delicacies; it appears, then, that the mortal sin is non-existent.

However, the existence of mortal sin is evident from the following. A deadly sin corrupts lives, eliminates the energy, abandons the journey, and binds [the sinner] with hell.

First, the sin corrupts lives as follows. Death, which is the corruption of the body, occurs when the temperature of the heart is reduced, for temperature gradually runs short in the extremities of the body and is accumulated where the origin of life is—the heart; and when it is consumed there too, the body dies. Similarly, when the love of God is consumed, the soul dies.

The love of God is twofold: toward God, when we love God, and for God, when we love the neighbor, as John says: "He who loves God must love his brother also" (1 Jn 4:21). The love of God is consumed by mortal sins— blasphemy, swearing, heresy, and so on. The love of neighbor is consumed by killing, fornication, theft, false witnessing, and so on. Just as the body is alive with the soul, so also the soul is alive with God; and just as separation of the soul is death for the body, so also separation from God is death to the soul. Sin is the cause of separation from God.

Second, the mortal sin eliminates the energy, for a man fallen into the sins by himself cannot rise by himself, except with the grace of the Savior, as Solomon says: "A wind that passes away returns not" (Ps 78:39). That is, since man heads toward the sins on his own, he cannot rise from them on his own. For example, when someone throws himself in the fire, the ability to throw [himself] is his, but he lacks the ability to come out. Again, man proceeds to death on his own, but cannot rise from death by himself, for "Souls entrapped in sins lose also their mind."

Third, the deadly sin abandons the journey, because anything that begins hastens toward the completion of the initiated journey, such as [toward] a specific destination. God is the beginning and end of all things, as He said through the Prophet: "I am alpha and omega" (Rev 1:8); meaning, the beginning and end. Then, therefore, the man who originated from Him as His image ought to end his journey at Him with intact resemblance. This fulfillment is attained through "the narrow and hard road that leads to life," as the Lord says (Mt 7:14). Sins [make man] abandon this journey, begin with the opposite of all of these, and end at the opposite; that is: "The wide and free road that leads to destruction" (Mt 7:13). And the Apostle says: "I tell the enemies of the cross of Christ with tears, whose god is their belly, [etc.]" (cf. Phil 3:18–19).

This is how the mortal and venial sins are differentiated from each other. The venial [sin] diverts briefly or insignificantly from the path but does not change the course of the journey. The mortal [sin,] however, distances and [makes a person] turn back from the journey, consequently moving farther and farther away from the destination, as Solomon says: "Salvation is far from sinners" (Ps 119:155); that is, from the Savior who is the last destiny of all people.

Fourth, [the sin] binds with hell as follows. Through sin a person is bound with Satan, the origin of evil, and through him [is bound] with his place—the fire, as the Lord says: "You that are accursed, depart from me into the eternal fire prepared for the devil and his angels" (Mt 25:41).

It seems that it is inappropriate for a person to eternally suffer from the little pleasure of sins.

The doctors of the church say that the punishment for sins is measured and defined according to how a sinner sins, as he who strikes a soldier sins more than he who strikes a common man. [He who sins against] the king [sins] more than [he who sins against] the soldier. Then, therefore, he who sins against God, commits a terrible evil and deservedly falls in limitless torments for harming and offending the divine greatness. Because of the abysmal sins, the length of punishments becomes immeasurable. These obviously demonstrate that sin is mortal.

Now, first, [in response to] those who say that the soul is immortal and cannot die, the doctors of the church say that death is twofold: natural death and death caused by the sins. In terms of natural death, the soul is immortal, but in terms of death caused by the sins, the soul is mortal, as has been said, for the soul dies through sins.

With regard to the second [argument] that states that death destroys the activity of the object, the doctors of the church say that the mortally sinful person cannot do good acts, because a good act is unacceptable when one sins at the same time. It is evident that when [a sinner] turns and repents, the good acts performed before the sins are remembered, but [good acts performed] while being in the state of sinning are not remembered. Then, therefore, it is evident that sins destroy the rewards of good actions. This much on mortal sins.

CHAPTER LII

On Venial Sins

We have already spoken about mortal sins. Now, let us examine what the venial sins are. It is to be known that the venial, which is forgivable, manifests itself through three things: occurrence, cause, and intrinsicalness. By occurrence, the mortal sin is conceived to be venial through repentance and confession. By cause, when a person commits it out of ignorance or weakness, without perceiving it as sin, it [the mortal sin] warrants pardon. Intrinsicalness relates to exaggerated laughing, disdaining, talking nonsense, and so on. This was a definition of the venial sins. Know that although venial sins do not have a defined quantity, for they are many, a definition is applicable to them based on the way they are viewed as wood, grass, or stubble, for they can easily be burned and cleansed. The wood indicates the heaviest venial sins; the stubble indicates the lightest, whereas grass relates to medial sins. There are three [categories of] sins, because every creation comes with three properties: essence, power, and operation. Besides, all actions take place in three modes: beginning, middle, and end. Likewise, the human being is made of three things: body, soul, and mind. Similarly, the mind consists of memory, intellect, and will. Likewise, the original sin came forth because of three things: from the serpent to the woman, and from the woman to the man. The cleansing of this [original sin] took place through three things: baptism in the name of the Father, the Son, and the Holy Spirit. The mortal sin also is cleansed through three things: repentance, confession, and penance. The soul's perfection also is attained through three things: faith, hope, and love. It is to be known that the human being can exist without mortal sins but cannot [exist] without venial sins. This is so because so long as human beings are alive, they fall in venial sins. Wherefore John in the epistle says: "If we say that we have no sin, we deceive ourselves, and the truth is not in us" (1 Jn 1:8). And as we commit venial sins time and again, so are we cured time and again; that is, when we confess collectively, [we] pound on our hearts, [we] say prayers, [we] make the sign of the cross, the priest crosses us, [we] sing the three holies, [we] say the Lord's prayer, or [we] do other similar things, we expiate our venial sins.

What is the harm that comes to us in general from all sins? It is to be known that sins kill beings. They make the stations contemptible, eternalize the punishments, and obfuscate the sight.

First, they kill the being, for the four elements that compose the human body were amalgamated with so much love before the sins that it was impossible to separate them. Had it not been for sins, human beings would not have died, or become ill, aged, and so on. However, because we were exposed to sins, the bonds of love disunited and a fight began among the four elements: warmth and cold, wetness and dryness. This fight caused the deterioration of the body: indisposition, illness, mutation, and death. As the Apostle says: "The body dies because of sins" (Rom 8:10). The young and old die, and death spares nobody because of this.

Second, sins make the station contemptible. We see that every noble object reaches a noble place, as is evident from the human eye: the more the object is seen as noble, the loftier is the place where it is placed. For example, in a house, the base is formed of rough and hard rocks, whereas the ceiling [is formed] with wood. Likewise, in our world, the ignoble earth is placed at the bottom, whereas the noble stars are positioned in heaven. Similarly, the human beings are the noblest of all creations, so they are supposed to be emplaced in the loftiest place; but they become worthless and fall into hell because of sins, as the Gospel says: "The rich man died and was buried in hell" (Lk 16:22). The reason is this: the corruption of those who have nobler birth becomes more despicable. This becomes evident at death: the human corpse is more abject and most malodorous of all corpses. The pattern of the corruption of the body is applicable also to the soul; wherefore [church] doctors say: "Sinners do not deserve the bread they eat." Moreover, sinners sin against the limits of nature, as St. Dionysius says: "It is sin to act against nature. While man ought to have a superior position by nature, he falls into the most inferior position."

Third: Sins eternalize the punishments. This seems to go against nature, for punishments ought to answer for sins. It seems astonishing that a person should encounter eternal punishment for a temporary sinful pleasure. It should be noted, however, that this happens through God's rightful judgment. And consider this: punishments should not be spared to those unwilling to abstain from sins.

Should someone say: If somebody kills somebody, they cannot live because of the sins, it needs to be said that because of mortal sins, a person positions himself in stations from where he cannot free himself. Take, for instance, someone who throws a stone. Before throwing it, he has the ability to throw it not, but once he throws, he cannot undo the throwing.

Fourth, sins darken the sight, for the fruitful evil seems to be good, just as the bitter seems sweet to a person burning in fever, and vice versa. Wherefore Isaiah says: "Ah, you who call evil good and good evil, [etc.]" (Isa 5:20).

So much on this [subject].

CHAPTER LIII

Homily of the same on the counsels of sins, according to the proverb:
"Inquiry will be made into the counsels of the ungodly" (Wis 1:9).

There are three kinds of sins committed by human beings, associated with thoughts, words, and deeds. Because man is made of three things—body, soul, and mind—he errs and sins with each one of these components.

The sin of thoughts, which the devil seeds in human minds, precedes all. Then the devil grows them in the body and makes a person commit the sin. Wherefore, [church] doctors say that it is not enough to safeguard the body alone from sins; rather, a person should beware the thoughts. This is so for ten reasons.

First, sins extend roots in the thoughts before they grow in the body. Therefore, thoughts ought to be kept holy to prevent evil from spreading roots there and growing toward the senses.

Second, the sins of thoughts branch out throughout the body like the venom of vipers, whereas the sin of the body remains in the part that committed it, be it the hand or the foot. Therefore, people have to beware [the sin of] thoughts more.

Third, the thoughts and the mind govern and lead a human being. For example, a driver keeps the cart on the right track when it swerves, but if the carter is asleep, both the cart and the driver perish. Likewise, when the body swerves, the mind can put it on the right track, but when the mind swerves and leads a voluptuous life, the body cannot guide it.

Fourth, we find the devil agreeable and befriend him through evil thought, for the devil seeds eight kinds of sinful thoughts in the heart of man to lure him to sin, and he shoots the thoughts like a secret arrow to wound man's soul and kill him. Therefore, people ought to beware sinful thoughts.

Fifth, God is spirit and not body, and He dwells in our intelligent minds and souls; hence: "You are God's temple and God's spirit dwells in you" (1 Cor 3:16).

Just as our body is a temple for our soul, so too our soul is temple for the Holy Spirit. Now, it is not enough to safeguard the body; rather, we ought to safeguard both the soul and the body that they be God's temple. Otherwise:

"The holy and wise spirit flees from deceit and foolish counsels" (Wis 1:5).

Sixth, our intelligent mind is the source of light and the lamp of the soul. If the mind is bright and pure, the soul is luminous and bright. Otherwise, if it is spoiled by sins, the soul is darkened and obscured by sins; hence: "The eye is the lamp of the body. If your eye is healthy, your whole body will be full of light; but if it is unhealthy, your entire body will be dark" (Mt 6:22).

Seventh, the minds are the mirror and image of God; with them we see God. Now, a rusty mirror is blind, cannot see, whereas a clean one reflects the image and shows it; similarly, our rational minds are mirrors with which we see God. Now, if they have become rusty with sins, they are blind and cannot see God on their own. Whereas "those who are pure in heart, will see God," commands the Lord (Mt 5:8). Therefore, the thoughts need to be kept pure and holy.

Eighth, our mind is judge over our soul and body; hence: "In a certain city there was a judge" (Lk 18:2). Now, when the judge is exempt of shameful acts and is impartial, he judges truthfully and correctly. However, when he errs, his judgment also becomes erroneous. Therefore, people ought to keep their minds pure and free of sins, to have the ability to make correct and rightful judgment with regard to their persons and others, in relation to the body and soul.

Ninth, the mind is the source of reason and wisdom in us. Now, if the source of a fountain is clear, the water gushes out clear, pure, and beautiful, but if the source of the fountain is murky, the water flows bitter and unclear. Similarly, if our soul is clear of sins, reason and knowledge proceed as clear and pure, and comfort others, but if it is spoiled with sins, reason proceeds as impure and spoiled. Therefore, people ought to keep the thoughts holy and pure.

Tenth, people with inclination for sin in their thought like to sin more and find it agreeable before they commit it. However, those who commit the sins with the body later feel sorry, regret, and repent. Thereby, the sins within the thoughts are bound with love, wherefore people do not regret them and do not perceive themselves as sinners. The sins of the body, however, are evident and people see themselves as sinners and repent. For this reason, if possible, people should keep the thoughts free from sins as much as possible.

Those were based on paradigms. Now, let us detect from the testimonies of the Holy Scripture why people should safeguard the thoughts from sins.

First, from the Lord's command: "Everyone who looks at a woman with lust has already committed adultery with her in the heart" (Mt 5:28). This is true and real, for whoever looks with lustful mind commits adultery in his will and thoughts, and even if the body fails to act at a given time and in a given place, and the intention remains hidden, the person commits sin in the heart.

Second, again, the Lord commands: "Out of the abundance of the heart the mouth speaks. The good person brings good things out of a good treasure, and the evil person brings evil things out of an evil treasure" (Mt 12:34–35). Adultery, fornication, and other things that defile a person proceed from the heart. Then, therefore, if evil proceeding from the heart defiles the person, this means the heart as birth-giver is a greater evil—it is a heap of wickedness and sins. Therefore, people ought to beware [evil] thoughts and pile a good treasure and speak good, "for the tree is known by its fruit" (Mt 12:33). Similarly, the thought is known from the tongue and the language proceeding from it.

Third, Moses commanded in the laws: "Take heed of yourself, to keep not anything evil in your heart, and provoke not God's anger" (cf. Deut 4:9). The evil in the heart refers to the sins of thoughts, for when we conceal them within us we provoke God's anger, because, like a covered fire, they kindle later. Similarly, sins hidden in the thoughts will kindle in the body and burn it. Therefore, people ought to cleanse their thoughts from sins.

Fourth, the blessed Job used to present daily offerings to God for the sake of his sons' thoughts. Although his sons were doing good, possessing, like their father, inherent righteousness; nevertheless, he used to expiate the sinful thoughts through daily offerings, every morning and evening. Our prayers, repentance, and confession for the holiness of the thoughts are reminiscent of Job's offerings.

Fifth, our hearts and counsels are like a tray and a container by which we present everything to God. Now, if the container is clean, the king will accept the entreaty and make peace, but if it is dirty, he will reject it. Likewise, when our thoughts are free of sins, all of our good works and prayers will please God, but if they are spoiled with sins, He will not accept and will reject us, as David says: "If He finds sins, let the Lord not listen to me" (cf. Ps 66:18).

Sixth, the sage says: "The holy spirit of wisdom will flee deceit and senseless counsels" (Wis 1:5). This means, just as we see the creation after the perceptible light is united with the light of the eyes, likewise, we see God, the kingdom of heaven, and the hereafter after the light of the grace of the Holy Spirit is united with our mind. The Holy Spirit will always shine the light of knowledge in those who possess the bright light of faith and contemplate good virtuous works. However, the Holy Spirit will flee the thoughts of and no longer enlighten those who entertain deceitful counsel, have ill faith and are foolish, or look at only visible things and like only them, just like the blind [person] who is not enlightened by the sun. He shall remain in the darkness of sins and disbelief. Therefore, people ought to keep their minds holy.

Seventh, God examines the heart and reins, because man looks at the face, whereas God looks into the heart, as the proverb says: "God is witness of his reins, and a police of his heart, and a hearer of his tongue" (Wis 1:6). In other words, our souls are composed of three things: reason, wrath, and desire. The tongue indicates our reason, for it is the reason's tool; the heart relates to emotions and the reins to desire. Now, the Holy Spirit is a police and overseer, as well as a hidden beholder of their works. When they swerve and commit sins, it forgives not; rather, it testifies that man's desire swerved, reason erred, and the heart became troubled. This testimony keeps us straight, as Paul says: "Gentiles, who do not possess the law, act instinctively according to the law that is written on their hearts, having their own minds as witness" (cf. Rom 2:14–15). The Holy Spirit writes the law of righteousness thus on every individual's heart, and it was this inherent law that justified the patriarchs who existed before the law and the Gospels. Should someone argue: "How is it that we sin, if God is our overseer?" We say, first, that as God oversees the parts of our souls, our souls oversee the parts of our bodies, and it is our souls that allow us and make us sin. Again, the Holy Spirit oversees us but does not dictate to us. When we voluntarily follow the Spirit, it protects us from evil, but when we voluntarily lean toward evil, it allows us to do evil but also internally judges us and reproves through our conscience. Therefore, people ought to keep the thoughts holy and follow the Holy Spirit.

The eighth reason why the thoughts should be kept holy is that all spiritual sins, such as pride, envy, hatred, rancor, grudge, deceit, and so on, are committed with thoughts. All of these are great sins, for pride and envy are the works of the devil, who became haughty against the Creator and envied Adam's glory. Likewise, hatred, grudge, and rancor are the characteristics of murderers; hence: "Whoever hates his brother is a murderer" (cf. 1 Jn 3:15). "You abhor the bloodthirsty and deceitful, O Lord," says the Prophet (cf. Ps 5:6). And "bloody and crafty men shall not live out half their days" (Ps 55:23). That is, God shortens their bodily life due to treachery and erases the days of eternity, as elsewhere David says: "But because of their treachery, you have cast them out of life and deprived them of eternal life" (cf. Ps 73:18). Therefore, people ought to keep their thoughts holy.

Ninth, people ought to cleanse the thoughts to avoid hypocrisy, imperfection in their belief, and deceiving others, because they cleanse the body only as a spectacle, in the likeness of the fasting and prayers of double-dealers. "They have received their reward," as the Lord commanded (Mt 6:2). God, who knows the heart and thoughts, does not trust those who lack perfection in their belief. Those who deceive others deceive God; wherefore, people ought to cleanse the inner thoughts in order to become holy outside their bodies. Otherwise, "They will be like whitewashed tombs, which on the outside look beautiful and adorned, but inside they are full of stench and the bones of the dead" (Mt 23:27). Similarly, a person whose thought is defiled with indecent sins sometimes will gush out stench with evil words, and people will nauseate. Therefore, people should cleanse the thoughts from evil sins.

The tenth reason people have to cleanse the counsels is because the proverb says: "Inquisition shall be made into the counsels of the ungodly" (Wis 1:9). The inquisition is twofold. First, it is the inquisition of the Word of God that examines thoroughly and tries: "until it divides breath from soul" (Heb 4:12); that is, He examines and separates the thoughts that belong to our will and knowledge and those that are accidental, caused by the devil's wickedness. The devil seeds all kinds of evil thoughts in our hearts, but it is we who voluntarily follow him and pleasantly grow the evil inside our hearts. Hence, the Prophet says: "Purge you me from my secrets, and protect your servant from strangers" (cf. Ps 18:12–13). The alien refers to the devil's accident, which we follow and take pleasure in. God examines and identifies it. The second inquisition expects us to repent in our hearts, hate the sins, go before the priest, and confess by blaming ourselves. When we do so, God will see in our repentance our innocence and the devil's seduction and deception, will justify us through confession, and will hold the devil responsible as to the cause of our vice. Since there will be such inquisition, we ought to keep our thoughts free of evil, and glory unto Christ forever, amen.

CHAPTER LIV

Homily of the same on the tongue, according to the proverb: "Death and life are in the power of the tongue" (Prov 18:21).

Our Lord and God Jesus Christ commands in the Gospel: "By your words you will be justified, and by your words you will be condemned" (Mt 12:37). This is conceived in two ways. First, there is justification by words; such as justification from the sins by professing the faith, praying, entreating, or confessing, and so on. There is also condemnation, such as denying before men, praying not, asking for forgiveness not, confessing the sins not, and so on. Second, when a person speaks evil, calumniates, or slanders, he will be condemned, because these fall under the category of major sins. However, when he keeps silence and remains patient, he will be justified, as the Prophet says: "Keep your tongue from evil, and your lips from speaking guile" (Ps 33:14), for sages say: "Silence is the measure of wisdom." The longer a person remains silent and contemplates, the clearer the speech becomes. The larynx being composed of seven tubes, one ought to think seven times, and ought to purify [the words] seven times like silver, and then utter. God, then, will find the beautiful words pleasing, and people will find them agreeable, as the Apostle says: "Let your speech always be seasoned with salt, so that they may be gracious to the hearers" (cf. Col 4:6). Otherwise, the person will indiscriminately utter whatever comes to the mouth, creating all kinds of harms and traps. Wherefore, [Solomon] says: "Death and life are in the power of the tongue" (Prov 18:21).

The tongue causes death due to three factors. First, it is flexible in shaping the speech, and it slips and errs easily. Second, the tongue is shameless—out of people's sight, it boasts and pulls out all that is in the heart, without the feeling of embarrassment before people. Third, it is fearless, being surrounded by the mouth as fortress, protected from up, down, and the sides, and gated by the teeth and the lips. Therefore, it fearlessly speaks all kinds of harmful words. Whether people pound the head or cut the hand, it does not feel any pain. Because the tongue is so daring and shameless, the Prophet David asked for a watch, saying: "Set, O Lord, a watch on my mouth, and a strong door about my lips, and incline not my heart to evil things" (Ps 141:3–4). If the evil tongue is not calmed otherwise, it is the beast of man, reminiscent of an evil beast that is detained behind sturdy doors and fastened with chains, as the Apostle says: "Every species of animals and beasts have been tamed by man, but no one can tame the tongue—a restless evil, full of deadly poison" (cf. Jas 3:7–8). Whereby the tongue has the lips as external doors and the teeth as internal; but if these fail to prevent, the Prophet asks for a strong lock, such as the beasts' chains; that is, the fear of God, for the fear of God is the tongue's curb, like the curb around a horse's head. A person has two bridle strings in hand to curb the horse and keep it on the straight path. Similarly, wisdom is the tongue's curb, and God's fear is its bridle. One is the fear of earthly punishments, and the other [is the fear] of the punishments of the hereafter to curb the tongue from evil. In the absence of these, a curb-free horse will fall from an elevation and perish along with the rider. Similarly, in the absence of the fear of God as a curb, your tongue will fall and cause its own destruction along with yours. Therefore, [the Prophet] says: "Death and life are in the power of the tongue" (Prov 18:21).

Numerous good things proceed from the tongue, whether spiritual, or physical.

First, peace is made among people with the tongue, and "the peacemaker is called Son of God," as the Prophet teaches: "Keep your tongue from evil, seek peace, and pursue it" (cf. Ps 34:14).

Second, with the tongue, we obey the neighbor and love him, and through the love of the neighbor, we love and obey God.

Third, with the tongue, we bless and glorify God through psalms and spiritual songs, and also we bless people and praise them. For man was given a tongue to always bless and praise God, and bless and praise people.

Fourth, with the tongue, we pray to God and ask for mercy and forgiveness for our sins, and so on, as we have mentioned earlier, [and] as the Lord says: "Ask, and it will be given you; search, and you will find; knock, and the door will be opened for you" (Mt 7:7).

Fifth, moreover, with the tongue, we ask people for gifts, alms, necessities, and donations, and we find them, because the act of seeking precedes the act of finding, like a child who first asks and cries, and then the mother pities and provides the food. But there is a difference between asking God and asking human beings, because we ought to always ask God continuously: if we do not receive the first time, we have to ask twice, thrice, and many more times, night and day, as He commanded: "[A person] needs to pray always and not to lose heart, because if he will not give him anything because of friendship, he will give at least because of the persistence" (cf. Lk 18:1, 11:8), as he gave the bread

377

to the widowed woman. But in order to ask from people, one has to choose the time, the place, the person, and then ask, rather humbly and entreatingly than with imposition or boastfully, as Sirach says: "He who asks gently, shall be pitied" (cf. Prov 12:13).[52]

The sixth gain of the tongue is that those who ask will be thankful to the giver, be it God or man, for thankfulness has two effects: it is the recompense of gifts received, and it obliges the other party to give again, as it is said in folk proverbs: "A thanksgiving mouth makes God indebted." Only through thanksgiving can we compensate the spiritual and physical bounties God has given us in heaven and on earth—light, life, soul, body, properties, assets, food, health, and so on. Besides, it is through blessing and thanksgiving that we merit every good thing in the hereafter and the kingdom of heaven, the classes of angels, God's vision, and evergreen crowns. Likewise, when gifts are received from people with thanksgiving and gratitude, the donor rejoices and others think of giving likewise.

The seventh gain of the tongue rests in preaching and teaching God's ordinances, turning the swerved, exhorting and straightening the wicked, teaching to the ignorant and leading them to the orthodox faith, strengthening goodness in their actions and bringing them closer to God through various speeches, reproaches, and rebukes, as the Apostle says: "reproach, rebuke, and encourage with the utmost patience" (2 Tim 4:2). That is, rebuke and persecute the demons, damn the heretics, and excommunicate verbally the unbelievers and those who do not turn from evil.

Eighth, we converse with others by words, and with the tongue we reveal the hidden knowledge of our heart, demonstrate our needs, and ask for necessities. Everything is accomplished with words: construction and destruction, business, and so on.

Ninth, we are distinguished from irrational beings by speech and wisdom. We rule as masters, princes, and kings, and move from one country to another, cross the seas, travel, and provide for our needs with words. The tenth gain is in interceding between people and God, and between people and people. With the words we help release the slaves, free the imprisoned, pity the poor, forgive the sinners, and so on. These and many other benefits proceed from the goodness of the tongue to the self and to others, whether spiritually or physically, whether poor or wealthy, and so on. Wherefore, [the Prophet] says: "Death and life are in the power of the tongue" (Prov 18:21). Everything we

---

[52] In *The Septuagint*: "He whose looks are gentle, shall be pitied."

mentioned above relates to life and the goodness of the tongue. Death and the wickedness of the tongue also are manifold, similarly. First, speaking lies. Second, bearing false witness. Third, heresy and denial. Fourth, taking a false oath and breaking an oath. Fifth, accusation and betrayal. Sixth, gossip and tale bearing. Seventh, buffoonery and useless discourse. Eighth, anger and rage. Ninth, sorcery and witchcraft. Tenth, evil swearwords, which in the Holy Scripture are referred to as curses. These ought to be identified separately, one by one, and then a person should recognize the harmfulness of an evil tongue.

First, [let us discuss] the first one: lying, which causes great harm. First, it is useless, like someone who benefits nothing from building castles in the air. Likewise, lies are useless sounds: they do not profit the listener, nor do they reward the speaker. Second, the hearers of lies will blame and reproach the liars. Third, lies contradict the truth—as it is said, the benefit of lying is that people stop believing the truth, thinking that everything is a lie. Fourth, lies cause controversy and animosity, and the oath also gets betrayed. Fifth, the liar turns into a son of the devil, as the Lord says: "He speaks according to his nature, for he is a liar and the devil is his father" (cf. Jn 8:44). Moreover, the liar himself becomes a father of lies for those who learn from him. Sixth, the Holy Spirit flees from the lies, and so does our servant angel, for they are close to and serve the truth, and they distance themselves from lies. Seventh, [the liar] manifestly acts against the ordinances, for He said: "You shall not lie, neither shall you bear false witness" (cf. Deut 5:20). Eighth, the Prophet says: "You will destroy all that speak falsehood" (Ps 5:6). Ninth, all sins are committed through falsehood: people create a lie in their mind before stealing, committing adultery or murder, and so on. All of these bring harm to the liar himself. Tenth, liars cause much harm to others; such as those who deceive, teach heresies, and make others go against the law. Thus, others work harmful works by way of falsehood, wherefore people ought to beware the tongue and words of lie.

The second harm of the tongue comes from bearing false witness. First, it is against the ordinances of God, who said: "You shall not bear false witness" (Deut 5:20). Second, it distorts the acts of justice. Third, it falsifies the truth. Fourth, it becomes associated with evildoers, for those who commit evil and those who bear false witness are punished together. Fifth, fire is the share of those who bear false witness, like those who inherited eternal fire when they acted as false witnesses against Christ. Sixth, a false witness causes a great deal of dissension between the judges, thus multiplying the dissensions and agitation. Therefore, witnesses ought to exercise caution in order to avoid condemnation. First, they will need to think long and examine, because the testimonial statements are deep and mysterious. Second, they have to examine themselves conscientiously, because a false testimony is as evil as a truthful testimony is good, for those who hide a truthful testimony commit a sin. Third, they have to bear witness before those whom the testimony relates, so that as people listen to him, they consent and justify the subject. However, those who run here and there and hastily provide a testimony, they sin in four ways. First, they demonstrate their imprudence. Second, they are bribe-receivers. Third, they are partial. Fourth, they show the statements as unrighteous, because people do not believe those who bear witness readily.

Heresy and denial are the third harm of the tongue. They fall under the same category: those who speak heresy about God, the cross, the church, and so on, and those who deny the faith and the profession of faith, because the heretic is a veiled denier, and a denier is a visible heretic, and both commit sins alike in their words. The denier is better than the heretic because of four reasons. First, the denier recognizes himself as guilty, as it is said: "Whoever denies me before others, I also will deny him before my father" (Mt 10:33). The heretic, on the other hand, thinks of himself as loyal and faithful. Second, the denier [might] repent and turn from the sins, whereas the heretic does not turn. First, because he conceives himself to be rather true and right than erroneous and false, as the proverb says: "The ungodly think their own way is right" (cf. Prov 12:15). There is a second reason, too. The heretic does not return because of presumption, for with his free will he has made the choice and became crooked. Third, because of ignorance, for he cannot distinguish the false from the true and conceives his falsehood as truth. Fourth, because of disbelief, for the heretic does not agree with what others know, if he does not have that knowledge, and therefore remains in the same disbelief.

The fourth harm of the tongue is taking a false oath and breaking an oath, wherefore God commanded in the ordinances: "You shall not take a false oath in the name of God, and you shall not take the name of the Lord your God in vain" (cf. Deut 5:7–20). That is, do not make allowance to every false thing, and do not recall God's frightful name. First, because these befit the heathens who refer to false objects as God, for heathens had referred to false objects, such as wood and stone, as God. Second, to refer to false objects as God is great blasphemy and unforgivable sin, because by doing so they use God's name as pretext and project the falsehood as truth. It is for this reason that the Lord forbade in the Gospel: "Do not swear at all, either by heaven, for it is the throne of God, or by earth, or by anything else" (cf. Mt 5:34–35). In the Old

Testament, it was commanded to swear in the name of God in order to keep the people apart from idols and keep the true God on their tongues and in their minds; in the New Testament, however, it was forbidden, because when a man gets used to swearing, he swears in vain, too. Second, a Christian should speak everything truthfully, so there should never be the need for swearing; hence: "Let your word be 'Yes, Yes' or 'No, No'" (Mt 5:37). Breaking an oath is a greater harm, because denying the faith and breaking an oath are equally sinful, for they both deny the name of God.

The fifth harm of the tongue is in speaking vain and betraying. Those who speak vanity, come across to vanity, either here before people, or in the hereafter. Thinking of it also is great sin, like Judas, who betrayed the Lord, [and] was in line with the crucifiers, and all betrayers shall be punished along with Judas. Because betrayers are categorized with killers: as the killers kill with the sword, the betrayers kill with the tongue, instigate the killing, or cause the destruction of possessions, which in this case is human blood, as people say, "That person spilled my blood." When people take away possessions, the family and the children will perish of hunger. Behold! The betrayer became a killer [in such an instance].

Gossip and tale bearing are the sixth sin of the tongue. The Apostle says that gossipers "will not inherit the kingdom of heaven" (Gal 5:21), be the gossip false or true. For if you gossip falsehood, you will become accountable for the sins of the person [in question], and if you gossip the truth, you will become an accomplice of a sinner, wherefore the Lord says: "Do not judge, so that you may not be judged" (Mt 7:1). [Or] "Who are you to pass judgment on servants of another? It is before their own lord that they stand or fall" (Rom 14:4). And the Lord commands: "You who have a log in your own eye, do not take the speck out of your brother's eye" (cf. Mt 7:4–5). The tale bearers or slanderers also are evil, for they cause much harm when they show affection to you with their tongue and listen to your words, but then take them and relay them to others. The Prophet addresses them, saying: "Who speak peace with their neighbors, but evils are in their hearts. Give them, Lord, according to their works, [etc.]" (cf. Ps 29:3–4).

Buffoonery and useless discourse are the seventh sin of the tongue. Buffoonery amounts to blame and insult, because the buffoon insults with smile, whereas a useless discourse amounts to: "If you say to your brother insane or fool, you will be liable for hell, for on the Day of Judgment you will have to give account for every useless word you utter" (cf. Mt 5:22 and 12:36). And there are three kinds of useless words. First, those associated rather with the utterance of uncontrolled and vain words than prudence, as they come on the tongue of a person. Second, words that do not profit a neighbor are useless. Third, the words of buffoons and comedians are useless words.

Anger and rage are the eighth sin of the tongue, for anger is one of the greatest sins, as the Apostle says: "Human anger does not produce God's righteousness" (Jas 1:20); that is, an angry person cannot work God's righteousness. Anger occurs when the blood surrounding the heart begins to boil, and a person wants to take revenge from those who caused him grief. Then, the smoke of anger rises to his head and makes him insane, hindering his ability to reason straight, and the smoke comes out of his nostrils, and the juice of the blood gathers in his heart, and his face turns blue and yellow, and his anger produces fights, blasphemies, insults, beating, killing, and so on. God has instilled this innate anger to provoke our anger against sins, the devil, and evil people, but if we feel anger against the good people, that is sin. Again, anger and wrath constitute the strength of the soul, but using it in excess turns it into sin, as the Prophet says: "Be you angry, and sin not" (Ps 3:4).

Sorcery and witchcraft, the ninth sin of the tongue, are deceit, which is committed and taught by those possessed by the devil in order to deceive people. The tongue's deceit also occurs when people seduce their neighbors and lead them to evil works: theft, homicide, and so on. Wherefore the Prophet says: "Woe to him who gives his neighbor to drink muddy allurement" (cf. Hab 2:15). A person of this nature is not limited to his own sin; rather, he makes others his associates in working evil, and the two together bring upon themselves eternal punishment, as happened to evil kings and their neighbors who worshipped idols and followed other religions.

The tenth sin of the tongue is using evil swearwords, which in the Holy Scripture is referred to as cursing. Hence: "Whose mouth is full of cursing, and bitterness, and fraud, [etc.]" (Ps 10:7). Of all sins, swearing and blasphemy are the most unprofitable, useless, and grave. Unprofitable, because a person who commits other sins can obtain a little benefit for the body, although the spirit is killed. For instance, people pile possessions through theft, pleasure through fornication, and so on; whereas swearing is absolutely unprofitable, because it does not satisfy hunger, nor does it cover nakedness, bring pleasure, put on weight, and so on.

The gravity of sins is evident from three factors. First, with every sin a person commits, he sins either against his own or against his neighbor's body; whereas swearing is a sinful act against God. For if people insult faith, God is faith! A Christian's mouth is the grave of Christ and the abode of the holy body, and Christ is the Christian's look. Hence: "The breath of our faces, Lord Christ"[53] (Lam 4:30).

Also, [since] a Christian's grave and remains are sealed with the cross and Gospel, [swearers] dishonor them. Second, it is a grave sin, because it provokes the anger of the throne of God against not only the swearer but also the audiences and places: wherever the voice of the swearer reaches, the provoked God reproves through heavenly and worldly punishments—causes drought to fields, reduces the rain, severs the fruits, and so on. Third, the sin is considered grave in the punishment that states: a swearer is not entitled to communion or blessed earth in the holy graves. Indeed, a mouth that dishonors communion does not deserve communion, and whoever dishonors the cross and the Gospel cannot be blessed with them. Whoever dishonors the grave cannot be buried in the grave. Thus, swearing is the greatest and gravest sin. The mouth of the swearer will swarm with worms and he will be speechless before Christ's judgment. Where the words are consumed and the deeds reign, there shameful, downward-looking, and black-faced people, with drained and groaning hearts and broken spirits, will be persecuted by the voice of the King, saying: "I know you not; depart from me, O you, the accursed, into the eternal fire" (cf. Mt 25:41). May the Savior of all save us from such people, from the evil tongue here, and from the eternal torment in the hereafter, and make us worthy of His mercy, indescribable joy, and the kingdom of heaven, in Christ our Lord, who is blessed forever and ever, amen.

---

[53] In *The Septuagint*: "The breath of our nostrils, our anointed Lord."

CHAPTER LV

A homily by another on the sins of the tongue, according to the word: "Keep your tongue from evil, and your lips from speaking guile" (Ps 34:13).

Solomon, God's sage, says: "Death and life are in the hand of the tongue" (cf. Prov 18:21). Everybody desires and wants to live but fears death. Likewise, everybody has to love his tongue and keep it from evil, as if it were his vitality. Wherefore Job says: "Does the fluent speaker think himself to be righteous" (Job 11:2); that is, he cannot be holy. We derive our example from Leviticus, where it is said: "Anyone whose member flows with his discharge, it is uncleanness for him" (Lev 15:3). The pain of discharge is a reference to the tongue, for if somebody has good words and good conversation, he produces thousands of good things, because those who hear his good words will be strengthened and encouraged for whatever is good in them, and he will be reminiscent of a fruitful tree. However, if he produces evil words—lies, blasphemy, anger, gossip, and so on—he is reminiscent of those whose members flow with their discharge and they waste their sperm painfully. Wherefore the Apostle James says: "If any think they are religious, and do not bridle their tongues, their religion is worthless" (cf. Jas 1:26). As Solomon says: "Death and life are in the power of the tongue" (Prov 18:21); that is, holiness and sinfulness. The Lord commands in the Gospel: "By your words you will be justified, and by your words you will be condemned" (Mt 12:37). Wherefore the Prophet David exhorts: "O you who desires life, loving to see good days. Keep your tongue from evil, and your lips from speaking guile" (cf. Ps 34:12–13). Then, therefore, it is evident that we ought to keep the tongue from all evil for many reasons. I shall relay this in ten parts.

First reason: God honored man and gave him the speaking tongue, which is not given to all creatures. This is not a small gift, for it would have been a great deficiency, had man lacked the tongue, as is evident from mute people.

Second reason: The tongue is a tool and pen of wisdom, and an interpreter of the heart, as the doctors claim. Now, the tool or the pen cannot move on its own, nor can the messenger do so; similarly, it is not befitting to the tongue to speak, if it does not consider wisdom and reason appropriate.

Third reason: The mouth and tongue are holier in man when he protects them, for through them we speak with God, pray, find forgiveness to our sins, and so on. But when we do not protect it [the tongue], it becomes the most corrupt of all body parts, because all other body parts show less ungodliness compared to the tongue and the mouth, which through evil words are more filthy and abominable than anything else on this world, as the Lord says: "To eat with unwashed hands does not defile, but it is all the evil that comes out of the mouth that defiles a person" (cf. Mt 15:20 and 15:11). Then, therefore, people ought to protect their mouth and tongue from evil words, unlike the senseless people who are accustomed to speaking blasphemy against the graves of the fathers, the mouth, the church, the faith, and so on.

Fourth reason: It is improper and disorderly for people to take their body parts to places not allowed by God. For example, the eyes that see the black as white and the red as green are false eyes. Likewise, God created the tongue as a tool to bless and praise God, to counsel and preach, to speak the truth and pray. Then, therefore, when, instead, one produces swearwords, blasphemy, and deceitful words, he does not deserve forgiveness. Besides, how can a person send a messenger to the king, if the messenger has already injured the king and the king hates him? The tongue, when praying, is like an interpreter or translator, but when the person utters swearwords and blasphemy, how can he pray?

Fifth reason: The place where people lay Christ's body should be kept venerable, so that it may be the holiest of all places on earth, such as the Holy Virgin Mary who was holy, because she was a place for Christ's body; moreover, she had the purest human nature. When Christ died, Joseph and Nicodemus purchased a clean, new linen cloth, wrapped him, and placed him in a new grave. Since all Christians take the same body of Christ into their mouths, but the priests take it every day, the priests have to keep their tongues and mouths clean more than others do. Since they wear the same dress that Christ wore on earth and it was revered, this is a reason for them to revere it more. However, it is more proper to keep the cleanness of the mouth where the body of Christ enters and where the teeth chew it. As the Lord says in the Gospel: "Do not give what is holy to dogs; and do not throw your pearls before swine" (Mt 7:6). There is no other dog and swine but the tongue, and no other pearl than Christ's body.

Sixth reason: When the tongue is kept clean, the spirit also is kept, as Solomon says: "He that keeps his own mouth, keeps his own life" (Prov 13:3). He who does not keep [the mouth clean] is reminiscent of a city that is open without walls. Similarly, he who does not withhold his speech cannot prohibit the words. As it is written in the biography of the fathers, an old man was going to Father Anthony with his disciples. On their way, the disciples were arguing with each other in good words. When Anthony learned their words through the Holy Spirit, he said: "Father, you have good disciples," and he replied: "They are good, but they do not have a gate. Anyone who desires can enter their house and harness their donkeys."

Seventh reason: In the Old Testament, in Numbers, God said: "Every open vessel which has not a covering bound upon it, shall be unclean" (Num 19:15), because where there is milk and honey without any covering bound upon them, flies, worms, and reptiles will swarm that place. Our mouth is a vessel of wisdom and the knowledge of God, which is more sweet and attractive than the honey and milk, as David says: "How sweet are your oracles to my palate! more so than honey to my mouth!" (Ps 119:103). The devil is like a fly that wants to be everywhere and fill the place with abomination and filth. He tries to stain our tongues and words with filth like a fly, wherefore we ought to close our mouths to not let the devil enter.

Eighth reason: Nobody rides a wild horse without bridle, and nobody enters a boat on the sea without sails and yet be in peace. Similarly, our tongues are like a fattened horse ready to charge, and like a ship driven by the wind. Wisdom and counsel are bridle for the tongue and a rudder for the boat; if we utter words lacking wisdom and counsel, we are lost, but if we bridle the horse, we will have it under our full control. James says: "If we put bits into the mouths of the horses, we make them obey us; and though the ships are so large, yet they are guided by a very small rudder wherever the will of the pilot directs. So also the tongue is a small member, yet it boasts of great exploits" (cf. Jas 3:3–5). That is, leading human beings to the kingdom of heaven is its great work, but he who is not counseled in wisdom will lead human beings to hell.

Ninth reason: The more harmful things people possess, the more they exercise caution and hide them, such as a sword, or a serpent, or a lion. Human tongues work greater wickedness than the tongues of the serpents and lions, as James says: "Every species of beast, birds, and reptiles has been tamed by human species, but no one can tame the tongue—a restless evil, full of deadly poison" (cf. Jas 3:7–8).

Now, all species of beasts, birds, and reptiles learn from human species to cause no harm, but nobody can teach the tongue or subdue it, for it is restless evil and full of deadly poison. It is difficult, then, to keep an evil of this caliber, and people ought to exercise plenty of caution. Blessed are those who do exercise it, as Sirach says: "Blessed are those who do not fall by their own words" (cf. Sir 28:22). The Holy Spirit descended like a fiery tongue upon the Apostles unlike any other descend to other members, for the fire of the heavens cleanses the fire of hell, which is the tongue of humans. Wherefore, James, the same Apostle, says: "How great a forest is set ablaze by a small fire! And our tongue is in effect a fire of inequity. And the tongue is established among our members to defile the body and set on fire the wheel of birth" (cf. Jas 3:5–6). He draws resemblance between the human tongue and fire, because just as fire is the most potent of the four elements, so too the tongue is the most potent among our members in doing evil; wherefore the Holy Spirit came from the heavens to cleanse the hellish fire of the tongue.

Tenth reason: We ought to protect our tongues from evil, because every individual is recognized through his language as to what country he is from, such as the Georgian, the Armenian, the Greek, and all others. Likewise, from the language people identify if a person belongs to God or to hell and the devil, as people said to Peter: "Certainly you are one of them, for your speech betrays you" (Mt 26:73). Sirach says: "Wisdom shall be known by speech" (Sir 4:29). He also says: "Do not praise someone before he speaks" (cf. Sir 27:8). Wherefore Solomon says: "Death and life are in the hand of the tongue" (Prov 18:21). It is death, when a human being speaks foolishly; it is life, when he speaks wisely. For instance, the philosopher Secundus wanted to put his mother through temptation. When he went to the bed where his mother would treat him with sins, Secundus said: "God forbid if I return to the place I came out from." The mother recognized him as she heard his words, and died of extreme shame. Secundus, then, said: "There is nothing worse than a tongue on earth, nor is there anything better than it, if you keep it from evil." Thereafter, he embraced silence and spoke never again.

Although all human beings have to beware the tongue, wariness befits more so the preacher. The preacher ought to pay attention to six things. First, who is his audience and who are his listeners, for a church doctor has to address the kings, the princes, the artisans, and the commoners each in distinct ways. It often happens that a word is beneficial to one but harmful to another: breathing calms the horse down, but agitates the dog. So [preachers] speak to sinners with big phrases and imperiously; to women, who are shy, with soft and light phrases; to the aged with reverence; to youngsters formidably, to inspire awe. They give hope to the poor and frighten the wealthy. As the Lord says: "Blessed are the poor in spirit, and woe to you who are rich, and woe to you who are laughing now" (cf. Mt 5:3 and Lk 6:24–25). In this fashion, they have to address different listeners in different words. They have to give comforting hope to the commoners and teach obedience to the servants, the children, and the women. To lords and fathers [they have to instruct] guardianship and so on, preaching each [properly]. Second, the preacher ought to watch the listener, so that the words he utters may not be obscure, which the listeners can neither understand nor keep in their mind. Third,[54] he ought to watch the time—what is it that he seeks—and preach within a set time. For Solomon says: "A word in season how sweet it is!" (cf. Prov 15:23), and Sirach says: "A proverb from a fool will be rejected, for he does not tell it at the proper time" (Sir 20:20).

Fourth, a doctor of the church should beware, to be able to diminish the warmth of his heart, for when it is time to show anger against sins, the anger he shows should be little; rather, he should speak calmly and artfully, showing great anger against great sins, and little anger for the little ones.

Fifth, a doctor of the church should beware to say the phrases with merciful heart, tearful eyes, and softly, in order to soften all hardened hearts and lead them to lamentation. He should not preach with cold and fast-paced words, for a pouring and sudden shower is useless and floods the earth, whereas the soft, sweet rain finds a place in the hearts and makes the earth fertile. Wherefore the Prophet says: "Let my speech be looked for as the rain, and my words come down as dew" (Deut 32:2).

Sixth, the doctor of the church has to beware, because he himself ought to exercise the good counsel he offers, before offering it to others. For goodness is in working the work, rather than preaching in words, because the word disappears, whereas the work remains solid. What the eye sees is firmer than what the ear hears. Wherefore the Apostle says: "The hard worker ought to enjoy the first fruit" (cf. 1 Tim 2:6). This suggests that the doctor should work before preaching to others. It is he who ought to partake of his own sermon before the listeners. Solomon says: "Drink waters out of your own vessels, and when the waters come out of the fountain, let them be only your own" (cf. Prov 5:15). That is, drink water from your own wise teaching. You ought to drink yourself before preaching to others, in order for the reward to be yours alone thereafter. This suggests that [a doctor of the church] should not spoil the sermon with pride, vainglory, flattery, or other evil intentions that are unprofitable. Rather, the preaching should be for the profit of the listeners and for the glory of Christ who is blessed forever, amen.

---

[54] A typographic error presents this as *second* in the original text.

CHAPTER LVI

Again, a homily about the wicked tongue: "Keep your tongue from evil, and your lips from speaking guile" (Ps 34:13).

Earlier, we discussed the goodness of the tongue: when we keep silence, exercise caution, and speak wisely, all kinds of good things happen to us thanks to the tongue, as we have said. Now, we shall discuss the harmfulness of the wicked tongue, which we can recognize in numerous ways.

First, the wicked tongue causes harm to the listener. The doctors of the church say that the words are light, but they deal a great blow to a human being, for they are very powerful.

Second, the wicked words harm the speaker himself, as Sirach says: "The words of a wise man's mouth are honor and glory; but the tongue of the fool will drown himself" (cf. Eccl 10:12).

Third, the wicked and swift tongue causes harm to man in heaven and on earth, as David says: "They have set their mouth against heaven, and their tongue has gone through upon the earth" (Ps 73:9), because in one instance people use their tongue to utter swearwords and blaspheme God in the heavens, and they enrage their own brothers in other instances.

Fourth, none of the animals or rapacious beasts can cause as much harm as the wicked tongue, for a wicked tongue can bring to a country a destruction that a thousand wolves or lions cannot cause. Wherefore, Solomon says: "In the mouth of ungodly man is a snare for citizens" (Prov 11:9), and Sirach says: "More people were destroyed by the tongue than by war" (cf. Sir 28:18). Jeremiah likens the evil tongue to an arrow, saying [it] "suddenly strikes and wounds the man as if he were in war" (cf. Jer 50:9). The evil tongue is also reminiscent of the serpent, as David says: "They have sharpened their tongue as the tongue of a serpent" (Ps 140:3). It is worse than the tongues of serpents, because a serpent kills the body only, whereas an evil tongue kills both the soul and the body. Who can quantify the multifarious wickedness of the tongue: swearwords, complaints, false testimony, false oath, slander, insult, bragging, tale bearing, arguing, shouting, betrayal, speaking in vain, and so on?

Nevertheless, we shall discuss the four most important sins that proceed from the tongue.

First, hatred. Second, blasphemy. Third, anger. Fourth, slander.

First, concerning hatred, there are ten thoughts, which we wrote before; find them in the first sermon on the wicked tongue.

Blasphemy is the second harm of the tongue. The gravity of this sin is evident from numerous things. First, the sin of blasphemy displeases and upsets God extremely, because God has given human beings a tongue to praise and glorify God, whereas [the blasphemer] turns it around and blasphemes God instead of glorifying Him. A person of this caliber is worse than the Jews and pagans, for although the Jews crucified Christ, they did so ignorantly, not knowingly, as Paul says: "For if they had known, they would not have crucified the Lord of glory" (cf. 1 Cor 2:8), whereas these [blasphemers] blaspheme knowingly. Likewise, the pagans worshipped idols ignorantly, whereas these knowingly blaspheme the true God. Moreover, these are the worst of God's abominable creatures, because God's ability, power, and goodness are evident to each creature and they somewhat praise God, whereas blasphemers blaspheme and ignore God's power, ability, and goodness. Second, the gravity of these sins is evident from the fact that whereas all other sins take aim at God's grace and goodness, these sins take aim at God's essence and power. For instance, it is sin when a man wounds a poor man, but it is a greater sin and harm when a man wounds a king in a duel. Greater is, then, the sin, when they sin before God—the king of heaven and earth, and the Creator of all things. Third, the gravity of the sins is evident [from this episode in which] Canaan was cursed because he revealed his father's nakedness. [Imagine] the graver curse that those who with their evil tongue curse the flawless God of heaven and earth will inherit. Wherefore Sirach says: "If you draw a sword on your friend, do not despair, for a way back to friendship is possible; and if you upset [your friend] with your words, there may be reconciliation. But if you expose his nakedness and secrets, you cannot return to the favor of friendship" (cf. Sir 22:21–22). Then, therefore, whoever blasphemes God complicates the forgiveness of his sins, as the Gospel says: "People will be forgiven for every blasphemy, but whoever blasphemes the Holy Spirit will not be forgiven, either in this age, or in the age to come" (cf. Mt 12:31–32). John says: "All wrongdoing is sin, but there are sins that are mortal" (cf. 1 Jn 5:16–17) before God, and these will not be forgiven to human beings. Fourth, the gravity of the sins is evident from the punishment, for in the biographies of the fathers it is told that a man had brought up his son to utter blasphemy against all sins, but one day he blasphemed God, and the devil strangled him and took him to hell. Again, another person, when playing chess, was taken over by rage and blasphemed God's eyes. He instantly lost his eyesight and was brought to the hell of eternal punishment. As it is written in Revelation: "People cursed God because of the many punishments in hell, and thereafter gnawed their tongues" (cf. Rev 16:10). At this point, a person should know that blasphemy is of two kinds. First, by way of heart; and second, through the mouth and tongue.

The blasphemy by way of heart is a great sin, for, first, it is conceived in the heart willfully and by choice, then born in the mouth and brought out by the Godless from his evil-stricken heart and thoughts. Sometimes, though, evil suddenly penetrates the thoughts of man because of the devil's temptation, unintentionally. This is a light sin, because this is the transgression of the minds, as the Prophet says: "Who will understand his transgressions? Purge you me from my secret [sins], O Lord" (cf. Ps 19:12). But whoever thinks, consents to, and accepts the thought voluntarily commits a mortal sin, and people ought to beware him as if he were a snake. For the Gospel says: "From the human heart that evil intentions come: fornication, adultery, blasphemy, and they defile the person" (cf. Mk 7:21–23).

Concerning the tongue's blasphemy, it is twofold. First, when people attribute to God things He does not possess, or take away the attributes He possesses. For example, when they speak of God's hand and head, although God does not have feet, hands, or anything else [similar to these]. Second, when they take away God's wisdom, might, and true judgment, claiming that God does not know this, God cannot do this, or God made these things bad and crooked. This is a greater and graver sin than heresy. Heretics speak out of ignorance, assuming that they are speaking the truth. A blasphemer, however, knows that it is sin and that he is blaspheming God. It is also a greater sin than idolatry, and worse than theft and murder, because the idolaters take the token of homage for God and give it to idols, whereas blasphemers take the token of homage for God and insult Him anew. They are also worse than the Jews, for when the Jews hear blasphemy, they cover their ears; for example, when they were stoning Stephen "they covered their ears" (Acts 7:57), for they knew he was blaspheming God. Blasphemers, however, blaspheme carelessly and fearlessly: they do not cover their ears, nor do they fear God; then, therefore, it appears that they rather are the children of the devil than God. It is written that a man had three sons. One day, he quarreled with his wife, and the wife said: "Two of the sons are not from you," and she died without specifying which two. Anxiety engulfed the man and he failed to know his true son. As he was dying, he established a will to the effect that his son shall inherit him. Upon their father's death, the sons argued and went to the judge. The judge said: "Bring your father's body, install it as a target for arrows, and whoever strikes best will receive his father's inheritance." The true son did not want to strike his father's body. Then the judge gave the inheritance to that son, saying: "This is the true son who did not want to strike his father's body." Likewise, those who are God's true children do not strike God with blasphemy. The bastard and the children of the devil, however, blaspheme God and thus blasphemy is the tongue's heaviest and greatest sin. May our hope Christ the Savior who is blessed forever, amen, deliver us from these sins.

After this, we shall speak on anger and slander respectively.

CHAPTER LVII

A homily by another on slander: "Do not speak evil against one another, brothers," writes James in the epistle (Jas 4:11).

Doctors [of the church] say that the spiritual theft is heavier than the corporeal [theft] for three reasons. First, a corporeal thief steals only corporeal things: precious stones and silver; whereas a spiritual thief steals and ravishes the good work and name. "A good name is better than great riches, and favor is better than silver and gold," says Solomon (Prov 22:1). Second, a corporeal thief may regret and return [the stolen items]; whereas a spiritual thief cannot return [what has been stolen]. Because one of the human deficiencies is that when a vulgar person claims that somebody is wicked and ten others witness that the person is speaking evil, people will [still] believe the evil speaker more.

Third, although a corporeal thief likes darkness, he does not allow darkness in himself; whereas a spiritual thief not only likes, but also allows darkness to be in him; that is, he will turn the good names and luminous works that are like midday into shameful evil by speaking evil and claiming that they are evil. He wants to turn everything into darkness, for he speaks evil of everything; then, therefore, spiritual theft is heavier than corporeal theft, wherefore James says: "Do not speak evil against one another" (Jas 4:11). He also establishes that a person should not speak evil, "for whoever speaks evil against another, speaks evil against the law and judges the law" (cf. Jas 4:11). Because the laws command to speak evil not, for in Leviticus Moses says: "You shall not revile the deaf, neither shall you put a stumbling block in the way of the blind" (Lev 19:14). An evil speaker violates these two commandments; that is, he speaks evil about the person that cannot hear; that is, against the deaf, and before the person who is blind and has not seen by his own eyes, but rather believes in what he hears. Then, therefore, people should not speak evil. Now, three things need to be said against evil speakers. First, we shall say what evil speakers and gossipers are like. Second, we shall say that it is greater sin when the leaders speak evil. Third, we shall say that not only those who speak evil sin, but also those who listen.

For the first item, we shall say that a person who speaks evil resembles eight species of abominable animals. First, evil speakers are like dogs, for

Sirach says: "Like an arrow stuck affects a dog, a word stuck affects a fool" (cf. Sir 19:12). Because when a dog is struck with an arrow, it will not rest lest it takes the arrow out. Likewise, evil words heard by an evil speaker are like an arrow in his heart; he cannot rest without letting them out by gossiping. But this should not be done like this, because Sirach himself exhorts: "Have you heard something? Let it die in you. Be brave, so that it may not split you and come out of you" (cf. Sir 19:10). Besides, evil speakers bite like dogs, and there are three kinds of dogs: puppies, mature dogs, and mad dogs. A puppy only eats meat and licks blood; mature dogs eat meat and bones; whereas a mad dog wanders and bites whatever it comes across, infuriating the bitten after its own pattern. Puppies indicate insignificant gossipers: those who speak evil about simple people. Adult dogs indicate great evil speakers: false doctors, bishops, and priests who speak evil about both simple and important people. Just as the bone makes a person sturdy, likewise high-ranking primates make up the bones in a church. Whoever speaks ill of them eats bones like a dog. Those who move from one place to another, speak evil, make everybody an accomplice to their wickedness, and encourage them to speak ill are like mad dogs.

Second, evil speakers are like swine. The swine cannot distinguish their mouth from their legs. First, because they bring all kinds of mud and dirt to their mouth. Similarly, evil speakers first attract all kinds of evil things, wherefore it is said in Wisdom: "Refrain your tongue from slander, for there is no word so secret, that shall go for nothing, and a lying mouth slays the soul" (Prov 1:11). It is very improper for a Christian who gives his mouth to communion, prayers, and blessing to stain it with slander afterward. Besides, when a swine enters a garden full of sweet-scented and good flowers, with a very stinky mud spread next to the bed of flowers, it will not embrace the fragrance; rather, it will approach the mud. Similarly, if a person possesses many virtues and goodness, the evil speaker disregards all, does not follow the person's suit, and settles on something bad he discovers in him and remembers it for long. Then, therefore, the evil speaker resembles dogs and swine. Wherefore, Christ says: "Do not give what is holy to dogs; and do not throw your pearls before swine" (Mt 7:6).

The mystery of the church is holiness and it should not be revealed to the doglike impious. The pearl comes out of the shell shiny: the shell exemplifies the old ordinances of the Scripture, and the pearl exemplifies the word and the meaning. The spiritual interpretation is splendid and it should not be thrown before people engulfed in the vanities of this world, for they will despise it. Just as dogs and the swine trample holiness and the pearl under foot but cannot defile them, likewise the impious and evil speakers insult but cannot defile us.

Third, evil speakers are like serpents, wherefore Ecclesiastes says: "He who covertly slanders is no less evil than a serpent that bites silently" (cf. Eccl 10:11). Four species resemble serpents: first, those who harbor animosity; second, those who bite covertly; third, those who choose a crooked path; fourth, those who eat dirt. Slanderers are no different. First, they are full of deceit, because initially they show themselves as intimate, then they bite. Second, they bite covertly, because if they know that you can hear, they would not speak evil; but because they know that you cannot hear, they speak out. Third, evil speakers travel on a crooked path, for they, first, praise [a person], saying: "I say this not because of envy. This is a good man." Later, however, they pour out poison, saying: "They cause so-and-so harm." For example, we, naturally, accept the choice foods and reject the spoiled. Likewise, evil speakers first speak good [words] in order to make the evil [words] trustworthy. Fourth, slanderers are like ash-eaters. They eat what is heavy and troubling; such as earth, which is the dregs of the elements. That is what they eat by speaking evil. They do not speak of the fire of love, the air of holiness, and the water of wisdom; rather, they speak of the dregs of sins, which denote the earth. Such a slanderer is worse than a serpent, because serpents can be tamed by charming them, but not these type of people, as Jeremiah says: "Behold, I send forth against you deadly serpents, which cannot be charmed, and they shall bite you" (Jer 8:17).

Doctors say that there is a kind of serpent with fervor in its venom; when it bites a man's leg, the venom's fervor climbs up the leg, the thighs, the abdomen, and the heart, and turns the man into a living dead. Physicians say that such people should be hanged head down in order for the venom to be accumulated in the legs and for the legs to be amputated thereafter. This serpent signifies the devil and the legs [signify] the neighbors. When the devil pours his venom in a person to slander and speak evil, such legs should be cut; hence: "If your foot causes you to stumble, cut it off" (Mk 9:45). Fourth, evil speakers are like bears, as the Prophet Daniel saw: "And behold, a second beast like a bear, and it supported itself on one side, and there were three tusks in its mouth, between its teeth, and thus they said to it, Arise, devour many bodies" (Dan 7:5). They resemble bears for three reasons. First, with its appearance, a bear resembles a human being but is not a human being. Likewise, a slanderer resembles a human being but is not a human being; rather, he is a bloodthirsty bear. Second, he [Daniel] says: "supported itself on one side," because he has no connection with others; he seems to be very pleased with himself and he disdains others. Third, that [the bear] has three tusks in its mouth, between its teeth, indicates the three entities affected [by the slanderer]: himself, his brother, and God. First, he hurts himself, because he should have sought enlightenment for his eyes, but he seeks thorns that hurt the eyes; that is, he should have sought luminous works and followed the exemplary ones, but he seeks evil and destroys himself. This is reminiscent of players who take the coal dust in a plate and put it in front of a man to blow it, and when he blows, his face immediately turns black and people make fun of him. It is in this manner that the devil, who is a player, places other people's deficiencies before slanderers, and when a slanderer blows the evil, he becomes embarrassed before God and human beings. Second, he harms the neighbor, for he puts a stumbling block before him, because by speaking evil, he makes the listeners believe: a slanderer is like the cold wind, which spoils the flourishing orchards. Initially, many were created to flourish virtuously, but when they heard the evil wind, goodness succumbed in them and they lost their flowers. Third, they harm God in two ways. First, they ravish God's judgment, for Christ commands: "Do not judge" (Mt 7:1). Second, they reduce God's portion in the good and increase the devil's portion in the wicked, for when they speak evil of the good, they reduce God's portion. Since they cause harm to everybody, everybody hates them, as Sirach says: "A whisperer defiles his own soul and is hated wheresoever he dwells" (Sir 21:31).

Fourth, he [Daniel] says that the devil is with this beast [the bear]: "Arise, devour many bodies"; that is, human bodies, for the slanderer sometimes consumes his father; that is, the primates of the church. Sometimes he [eats] his mother; that is, the church. Moreover, they eat meat during the Great Lent, for one of the saints says: "It would have been better [for slanderers] to eat the flesh of lamb than that of their brother." They also eat the dead like hyenas. These people are worse than any other beast, for beasts do not eat each other within their species, whereas a slanderer eats his like. They are also worse than the hell, for the hell devours only the wicked, whereas these [slanderers devour] both the wicked and the good.

Fifth, [the slanderer] is reminiscent of crippled and twisted birth, as the proverb says: "A wicked offspring's teeth are like a sword and the molars are like a knife, to consume and devour the humble and poor from off the earth" (cf. Prov 30:14). And David says: "Their teeth are like weapons, and their tongues are like sharp swords" (Ps 57:4), for the tongue of a slanderer is very sharp, killing three persons at once: himself, the subject of his slander, and the person next to the slandered, as Sirach says: "A backbiting tongue has driven many from nation to nation, and strong cities has it pulled down, and has worked many evil works" (cf. Sir 28:17 [14]).

Sixth, like a dirty scarab that gathers waste and tears it apart, a slanderer does the same with regard to everything evil in human beings; wherefore, Gregory [of Narek] has never kept a gossipmonger in communion. He has written a poem regarding the common meal; whoever gossips about a brother is not [a participant] of this meal.

Seventh, slanderers are the preachers of the devil: the devil, like a monkey, repeats whatever he sees God is doing, for the devil has established houses for gathering and houses for drinking. Just as God has the holy altar in the church, the devil has the backgammon.

Just as the church choristers sing according to the written notes, the devil makes them [his preachers] stumble with his sign: first, against God's unity; second, [against] the ordinances; third, [against] the Trinity; fourth, [against] the evangelists; fifth, against Christ's five wounds; sixth, against the six alms. Against the choristers, [the devil brings] folk singers and the filthy songs. He also works against the miracles, antagonizing Christ. [He makes] the seer blind, the healthy lame, the fast speaker mute, [and] the living dead, for they enter the houses of gathering sound and come out of there drunk, like a lame, blind, and dead person. Just as the Lamb of God is offered as a sacrifice at the church, there [in the devil's domain] the flesh of brothers [is offered], which they eat speaking evil of it, as the proverb says: "Be not a winebibber, neither continue long at feasts and purchases of flesh" (Prov 23:20). They release the stench of evil sins instead of incense. God's priests, however, battle against the evil preachers of the devil, as Peter the Apostle says against the Hebrews who spoke evil about Jesus in three ways. First, with regard to life, they said: "gluttonous and winebibber man" (Mt 11:19). Second, they criticized the teaching: "This is a hard saying; who can hear it?" (Jn 6:60). Third, they spoke of his birth: "Is not this the carpenter's son?" (Mt 13:55). Peter, however, was a good witness against these, when he said: "You are Christ, the son of God" (Mt 16:16). By referring to him as Christ, the first [reference to Christ as gluttonous and winebibber] was dismissed, because those who are anointed with the Spirit do not sin. The anointed are soft and sweet, refuting those who claimed: "This is a hard saying." He also said: "To whom shall we go? You have the word of eternal life" (Jn 6:68). When [Peter] referred to [Christ] as Son of God, he refuted those who said: "He is the carpenter's son."

Referring to such evil speakers, Paul says in the Romans: "whisperers, slanderers, haters of God, haughty" (Rom 1:29–30), and concludes: "Those who commit such things do not inherit the kingdom of God" (cf. Rom 1:32). Eighth, slanderers are reminiscent of Hanun, the evil king, who insulted David's servants, shaved half of their beards, and cut off their garments to reveal their nakedness. Likewise, slanderers cut off half of their beard; that is, their good deeds, for goodness is perfect only when is done for the love of God. God cuts half of them, saying they do it deceitfully. He also cuts off the garments of might and eliminates evil. It is evident, then, whom the slanderer resembles. [We said] this with regard to the first item.

Second, it is to be known that slandering a common person is a major sin, but to slander the leader or the head person is an even greater sin. This is evident from, first, Miriam, who, after "speaking against Moses, became leprous," as is mentioned in Numbers (cf. Num 12:1–10). Exodus says: "You shall not revile the gods of your people" (Ex 22:28). Second, "Ham who told the nakedness of his father was cursed with his entire people" (cf. Gen 9:22–25). Third, as is mentioned in *III Kings* [1 Kings]: "God smote and killed Uzza who put forth his hand to hold the ark" (cf. 1 Chr 13:9–10). The ark refers to leaders who possess within themselves the sweet manna, the counseling staff, and the tablet of knowledge. God shall kill anyone who brings a slandering hand close to these. Fourth, it is mentioned in *I Kings* [1 Samuel] that "David cut off the skirt of Saul's robe privily, and his heart smote him and he said, I stretched forth my hand to the anointed of the Lord" (cf. 1 Sam 24:4–6). What, then, should slanderers do, since not only do they cut off the garment but also the head of the anointed with slander?

This was about the second item.

With regard to the third item, one should mention that the slanderers are not the only sinners. Voluntary listeners also sin for six reasons. First reason, a person is reckoned to have sinned when he sees a dog biting his brother and yet does not help to separate them. The slanderer also devours his brother like a dog, and whoever does not scold and separate them is guilty. Besides, whoever does not oppose and eagerly listens resembles a dog, as Sirach says: "What resemblance has the wolf with the lamb, or the hyena with the dog?" (cf. Sir 13:21–22). Second, those who eagerly listen to slanderers, it is as if they stimulate their [slanderers'] appetite to eat more meat, for if the listeners were discontented, the slanderers would not have dared speak evil. Third, slanderers are like vipers. Vipers harbor enmity by nature. When someone sees the tongue of a slanderer stinging his brother like a snake and yet does not beat the slanderer with verbal stones, he bears the resemblance of a snake, as the Gospel says: "O generations of vipers, who has warned you to flee?" (Mt 3:7).

Fourth, when someone stays at an open and stinking sepulcher without covering it, he will die of the smell. Likewise, the mouth of a slanderer is a stinking sepulcher, which always releases filthy smells—it contradicts God's commands, as David says: "Their throat is like an open sepulcher" (Ps 5:9). Whoever sits next to a slanderer and remains seated is foolish and a sinner, because no other sepulcher releases a smell as stinking as the tongue of a slanderer, and many die from that smell. Fifth, if a bat that is fond of darkness speaks evil of the light, a man would be foolish to believe; likewise, a slanderer is like a bat—he hates the light of virtue and loves the darkness of wickedness; therefore, ignorant is he who believes him. Sixth, a person should believe if there are many witnesses, as the Gospel says: "Through two or three witnesses every word may be established" (Mt 18:16), provided they are unblemished, sworn, and tried. However, it is a sin when [foolish listeners] believe the slanderers who witness falsely, are blemished and not sworn, are not tried, and yet testify to that which does not exist.

It is to be known that an evil speaker slanders in six ways. First, he reveals the hidden transgressions of his friend. Second, he relays the evil words he heard from others in exaggerated manner. Third, he accuses others. Fourth, he denies the hidden goodness. Fifth, he belittles the manifest goodness. Sixth, he turns goodness into evil. All of these sins exist in one slander. Therefore, Christ's Apostle says: "Do not speak evil against one another, brothers" (Jas 4:11). May Christ the God save His believers from all evil tongues and slanders: to not be slandered, to not slander, to not listen to, and to not be associated with the wicked, amen.

CHAPTER LVIII

Homily of the same on the anger of the tongue, according to the verse:
"The fire tongue is a world of iniquity" (Jas 3:6).

God created man like a city. The inhabitants of this city are the soul and the free will, which is king therein. Reason, passion, and desire are his [the king's] soldiers. Diverse virtuous acts are the bounties and properties of this city. Satan is the thief and adversary; he always wants to ravish the properties and enslave the souls and the minds of the city's inhabitants. Our body is the fortification of our city. The senses are its gates and windows. Just as every traffic, whether to or from the city, occurs through the gates, likewise every good and evil thing enters and exits through the senses. The eye sees, the ear hears, the nostrils smell, the mouth tastes, [and] the hands and the rest of the body touch and find pleasure. Just as we close the door before the enemies and open it for the beloved, likewise we ought to open our senses before the good works and close and protect them before evil works. Just as the enemy battles against the city in two ways: first, manifestly and violently, then, if he fails, [by attacking] like a thief at night and covertly, likewise in our city the manifest sins and the evil devil battle and pull us into transgressions, but if they fail, they steal covertly and deceitfully. Behold! The gatekeeper—the mind—which oversees our senses has to be on the watch in order to see the enemy and battle, as the Lord commands: "Commanded the doorkeeper to be on the watch" (Mk 13:34). Now, since all of our senses are like windows, arrows enter through and wound us, as Jeremiah says: "Our senses are windows for death" (cf. Jer 9:21). The arrow of desire penetrates the soul and wounds it through sight and hearing. The mouth and the tongue, however, are folding doors; the enemy enters through them to plunder and spoil. Therefore, James says: "The fire tongue is a world of iniquity" (Jas 3:6).

The mouth and the tongue transgress more than anything else in four ways. First, enemies enter and wound through other senses from outside, whereas the tongue brings evil forth from within, as the Lord commands: "From within, from the heart evil intentions come: fornication, deceit, slander, [etc.]" (Mk 7:21). You know that the internal enemy is more dangerous, because the external enemy attacks sometimes only, whereas the internal [enemy] is always dangerous and is a familiar enemy. The mouth likewise [has double roles]. The philosopher says that it is entrance for mortal things and exit for the immortal things; that is, mortal things—eating, drinking, and acting avariciously kill the soul. When the spelled word is good, it gushes immortality and goodness out of man; otherwise, if that spelled word, too, is evil, then it [the mouth] is doubly evil from inside and outside.

Third, other senses are associated with only one evil [function], seeing or hearing; whereas the tongue has two evil [functions]. First, it speaks vain, slanders, insults the neighbor, and so on. Second, it blasphemes the faith, the cross, the church, and so on [by lifting the words] up toward God, and thus bringing forth twice the evil.

Fourth, other senses either only see or hear, if Satan has not mixed desire in them. The tongue, however, transgresses on two counts; that is, it blesses and curses, speaks good and speaks evil. The Apostle says this should not be so: "With it we bless the Lord and Father, and with it we curse men. This ought not to be so, my brothers, because the same spring does not pour sweet and bitter [water from the same opening]" (cf. Jas 3:9–11). And "the same plant cannot bear grapes and thorns" (cf. Mt 7:16).

One should know this. Although the tongue causes much harm, such as deceit, accusation, speaking ill, insult, and so on, anger surpasses all. Anger causes much harm, which we shall discuss in ten points.

First, the Apostle says: "Your anger does not produce God's righteousness" (Jas 1:20); that is, an angry man does not perform God's justice. Second, the Apostle also says: "the angry, the slanderers—none of these will inherit the kingdom of God" (cf. 1 Cor 6:10). Third, the vice of anger makes man frenetic and demoniac, as it is manifested through the look: the eyes will turn, the face discolor into blue, the lips tremble, the saliva pour, the speech become incoherent, and the voice turn into noise. Fourth, [anger] contradicts the ordinances, as [the Lord] commanded: "Do not be angry with your brother without a cause, for whoever says 'You fool' to his brother, will be liable to the judgment and the hell of fire" (cf. Mt 5:22). Fifth, anger is the origin and mother of murder. Just as the root [is the origin and mother] of the grass, so too anger [is the origin and mother] of murder. Therefore, the Lord commanded: "It was said to those of ancient times, 'You shall not murder.' But I say do not be angry" (cf. Mt 5:21–22). Sixth, anger entraps the wisdom, which constitutes the upper part of the soul, like a smoke that rises from the fire, fills the house, and darkens it. Similarly, the steam of anger rises from the heart to darken the light of the minds. Seventh, anger is vice: it captures not only those that are on the left side, but also those that are on the right side—choice men like Moses who struck the table written by God and destroyed it when his anger was provoked, or like Elijah who massacred the prophets of Baal when his anger was provoked. These angers were revenge in favor of God's ordinances and exhortation for people. Vicious anger, however, is evil [and occurs] when man is angry with his neighbor. Eight, it [anger] is the affliction and separation of the Holy Spirit, as has been said: "For the holy spirit of wisdom will flee deception and anger" (cf. Wis 1:5). The Apostle says: "Do not grieve the Holy Spirit of God, with which you were marked with a seal for the day of redemption" (Eph 4:30). Meaning, the Holy Spirit that sealed us with the profession of faith to which we shall obey and be redeemed grieves and departs with anger. Ninth, anger harms not only the soul but also the body. When anger and turbulence befall a house, members of the family will grow bitter toward each other and the household also will become bitter; the members will separate and inflict harm upon the household; the structure of the house will deteriorate and crumble; the house will be destroyed, and the homeowner will tumble down. Tenth, anger will produce quarrel and beating, trial, penalty, imprisonment, and humiliation before all people. Because whoever wanted to hate his neighbor, lie to him, ravish him, and beat him was judged before the judge and found liar and was penalized [consequently]. In this way, whatever we want for our neighbor will happen to us here and in the hereafter; here in the hand of the judges and rulers, and there before the heavenly judge.

It needs to be known that anger and rage are different from each other—rage is elevated anger, as the Prophet says: "Anger in his rage" (Ps 30:5). Anger and rage are different in four ways. First, anger relates to the soul, rage to the body, because anger is associated with coveting, which is a part of the soul, whereas rage appears when [anger] is manifested through the body. Second, anger occurs when the soul becomes bitter and irritated by the vice, and moves to the heart, rendering it bitter. Rage [however] takes place when the bitterness entices the heart and boils the blood, and [the person] tries to cause grief to the person who grieved him. Third, the tongue is anger's tool, whereas rage is expressed through the hands, wood, stone, sword, or other objects. Fourth, anger is limited to words that dishonor, insult, or chastise; whereas rage is associated with action—striking or killing. Both are cruel and outrageous, as the proverb says: "Rage is cruel and anger is outrageous" (Prov 27:4). When the storm of bitterness stirs the heart, it no longer pities or spares; man [then] insults everything by his tongue and applies [comparable] actions. Thus, anger is the beginning and rage is its culmination. All harms stem from anger—insult, slander, curse, swearwords, blasphemy, beating, striking, killing, and everything else that has been mentioned. Therefore, [the Apostle] says: "The fire tongue is a world of iniquity" (Jas 3:6). Enough about the tongue's anger!

Just as many harms come forth from anger, similarly many good things are born for the soul and the body of a peaceful and calm tongue, for the person himself and for everybody else. We shall discuss these in ten ways, compiled from the Holy Scriptures.

The first goodness is what Christ commanded: "Peacemakers are called children of God" (cf. Mt 5:9). This is perceived in four ways. First, the person who makes peace toward himself—between his soul and body, and toward others—among people resembles the Son of God, who made peace in heaven and on earth, among the angels and humans. Second, whosoever removes the vice of anger and envy from his person and others certainly acts like the Son of God, who cured diseases and demoniacs. Third, just as the Son of God removed wickedness, whims, demons, and death from people, likewise the peacemaker removed all kinds of murders and enmity. Fourth, those who make peace with everybody are like God, "who makes his sun rise on the evil and on the good" (Mt 5:45), at which time [peacemakers] become God's worthy children. This was the first goodness of a peacemaking tongue.

Second, as the proverb says: "Water will quench a flaming fire" (Sir 3:30), your calm speech will quench the fire of your neighbor's anger and will become reason for his goodness. The sages say that the strong male person is praiseworthy in everything, except in speech, where the soft [male person] and the female person are stronger and praiseworthy, because the soft speech comes out of thoughtful minds, whereas the manly [speech comes] from a harsh and angry heart.

Third, the Apostle says: "Be not overcome of evil, but overcome evil with good" (Rom 12:21), because evil cannot defeat the homogenous evil, but the good defeats the evil; that is, if you wish to overcome evil, perform good acts and you shall defeat it!

Fourth, the proverb says: "Do not answer a fool according to his folly, or you will be like him" (Prov 26:4). The fool is senseless, impudent, and angry. Now, he foolishly speaks incoherent words and [stirs] quarrel; if you do the same—quarrel against quarrel, an oath against an oath, or contention [against contention]—you will be like the fool. Rather, "Answer a fool according to his folly, or he be wise in his own eyes" (Prov 26:5). That is, answer him, by not [countering] evil with evil; rather, [being] good against evil. He is mindless; answer him wisely. He is impudent; be humble. He is bitter; be sweet. Counter his anger in this way. First, so that you look wiser, sweeter, and kinder than he looks, and then, so that you expose his falsehood, just as Christ did to the Jews. They foolishly claimed: "You are a Samaritan and have a demon" (Jn 8:48). [Jesus] did not say you are possessed with demons and are evil; rather, with soft words He exposed their foolishness by saying: "If Satan casts out Satan, his kingdom will be divided" (cf. Mt 12:26).

Fifth, the Lord says: "The good person brings good things out of a good treasure, and the evil person brings evil things out" (Mt 12:35). Now, "Out of the abundance of the heart the mouth speaks evil" (cf. Mt 12:34), because [a fool] has become an evil treasury for Satan and speaks out of the abundance of Satan's evil counsel. You have been a treasury of the good spirit; bring out, then, goodness from your heart, so that you may be a good man, and the good spirit will dwell in you and speak of good things.

Sixth, the proverb says: "A fool gives full vent to anger, but the wise quietly holds it back" (Prov 29:11). That is, a hard-hearted person utters whatever comes to the tongue—slander, insult, curse. The curses are in swearwords, the slander is in revealing hidden works, and the insult is in claiming things that have not been performed. [A fool] utters all of these indiscriminately, leaving no room to love, and then regrets and [after] waking up from his sleep feels regret, remorse, and grief. A wise man, however, passes anger in two ways. First, he remembers the ensuing regret and remorse beforehand and refrains from insulting, because he knows that there is remorse after every transgression. He brings it to his mind and refrains from doing. This is the wisdom of man—to bring the conclusion of something to mind and avoid wickedness, thus staying exempt of all evil things. Second, he [the wise] gently and quietly examines in his mind whether he erred willingly or unwillingly, or [perhaps did so] unknowingly or by being deceived by others, and thus patiently turns himself sweet.

Seventh, it [the proverb] also says: "An angry man digs up strife, and a gentle person stops transgressions"[55] (cf. Prov 29:22). A fool and angry man does not heed the Apostle, who says: "If it is possible, live peaceably with all" (Rom 12:18). But [the angry] looks for reasons in peace to battle and war. See how he acts contrary to what the Apostle says: "Make peace with a trouble maker," but if you cannot do so, coexist with peacemakers in peace and do not be disturbed; otherwise, to cause disturbance to a peacemaker is very wrong.

---

[55] In *The Septuagint*: "A furious man stirs up strife, and a passionate man digs up sin." In the traditional Armenian Bible: "An angry man stirs up strife, and a gentle man stops transgressions, and a passionate man digs up sins."

A gentle person, unlike him [the angry], stops disturbances and calms anger. Korah and Dathan, along with the people of their camp who assembled against Moses and Aaron, were like troublemakers. Gentle Moses fell on his face and begged them to stop sinning, but they did not want to stop. On the contrary, they increased their hostility and therefore "The earth opened and swallowed up them, and the flame burned up the sinners" (cf. Ps 106:17–18). God destroyed them with a death unheard of, and honored Moses and Aaron, for Aaron's rod sprouted and yielded almonds. Similarly, God will spiritually punish all those who stir strife, and will honor the gentle.

Eighth, it [the proverb] also says: "Scoffers set a city aflame, but the wise turn away it [wrath]" (Prov 29:8). Setting aflame signifies those lawless people who motivate their companions to rebel against the king, to disobey the ruler, to kill his overseer, and so on. Wise people, on the other hand, do not let such harm happen; [they act] to prevent the burning flame of the king's anger. Take Zedekiah, for example. He did not heed to Jeremiah and violated the treaty with the Babylonians, wherefore Nebuchadnezzar came, captured Jerusalem, and burned the city, which had violated the agreement. Also, Nabal invited anger upon his house when he dishonored David's messengers, whereas Nabal's wise wife, Abigail, turned David's anger, as it is written in [1] Kings. In addition, the heretics set the church aflame, whereas the wise fathers and monks quenched it through examination and the establishment of the orthodox faith.

Ninth, the Scripture also says: "Be not hasty in your spirit to be angry, for anger rests in the bosom of fools" (Eccl 7:10). That is, the vice of anger comes hastily and is fast, because anger stems from the fiery element and fire is dynamic and quick. It is in the passionate part within the soul. Therefore, the sage exhorts to delay anger and linger on choosing, to avoid rushing toward anger and be taken by an iniquitous action, as the Apostle says: "Put away from you all bitterness and anger and clamor" (cf. Eph 4:31). The fool, however, does not watch for anger, rather: "his throat is open like a grave" (cf. Rom 3:13). When the grave is covered, [the cover] prevents its malodor, but malodor always spreads from an open grave. Likewise, a fool always gushes out indecent and stinky words, and "brings out evil from the evil treasures of his heart" (cf. Mt 12:35), as the Lord commands.

Tenth, the Scripture also says: "The words of a wise man [are] grace, but the lips of a fool will swallow up himself" (Eccl 10:12). It means that the mouth of a wise man is full of grace and illuminates the listeners, as the Apostle Paul wrote in his letter: "Grace to you and peace" (Rom 1:7). The Apostle also instructs us: "Let your speech always be seasoned with salt by the grace of the Lord, so that you may give grace to the listeners" (cf. Col 4:6). The lips of a fool, however, make him fall in a trap, wherefore the Lord commands: "By your words you will be justified, and by your words you will be condemned" (Mt 12:37); also: "I will judge you by your own words, you wicked slave!" (Lk 19:22), because disbelief and nonsense are the beginning of a fool, and wicked perplexity in the mind of listeners is his end. Therefore, one should not listen to the words of a wicked man and be instructed by them, because they will torture him and disturb the peace of his mind. Every word has a beginning and end. The beginning of a word is in the heart of the speaker and on his tongue, and the end of a word is in the ears and minds of listeners. Whosoever listens to and learns from the wicked who speak evil and instruct evil, is as evil as the wicked, just like the heretics and their apprentices, and just like the slanderer and his listeners. The same applies to a wicked angry person and those who listen to him and agree with him. Similarly, whosoever speaks goodness and listens to and learns from the good, is glorified with him, just like the Apostles who thought faith and the faithful who learned and believed. When a man instructs goodness, the learner performs good acts, and when a man utters wise words, the listener attains wisdom. Likewise, those who preach peace and those who do peace practically, both rest spiritually and physically, and Christ crowns them and glorifies them. All of these and more than these, many good things proceed from a quiet tongue. Similarly, many harms and traps proceed from ignorant tongues and angry lips, both for the subject and others, both for the soul and the body, which we somewhat discussed. Therefore, the Apostle says: "The fire tongue is a world of iniquity" (Jas 3:6). Whosoever conquers the tongue, defeats all evil, and when we all defeat evil, we attain the good and deserve the good bounties of our God Christ who is blessed forever, amen.

CHAPTER LIX

Homily of the same on patience according to the verse of the proverb: "Do not say that you will avenge evil; wait for the Lord, and he will help you" (Prov 20:22).

Avenging takes place in exchange to evil and is divided into four kinds: returning evil words for evil words, such as dispute; returning works for works, such as an eye for an eye and so on; returning works for words, as superiors treat inferiors when they compensate offensive words with deeds; and returning words for works, such as the swearwords or curses of the inferiors toward superiors. [The proverb] means that you should not seek revenge hastily when you are motivated by your indignation, because if you lean toward revenge impatiently, be it by word or works, you will later regret and grieve. Even if you are a prominent person or a ruler, avenge by patience and examine those who are guilty of breaking the law. [The proverb] also implies that when a superior or a neighbor speaks evil to you or harms you, do not respond at all and do not commit evil, because if you avenge, you will encounter four [kinds of] harm.

First, if you compensated evil for evil, you acted against the Gospel. Second, you did not ask God to help you and protect you; rather, you compensated by your own hands. Third, you have ravished God's work: "Vengeance is mine, I will repay, says the Lord" (Rom 12:19). Fourth, you have lost your reward by avenging on your own, because goodness would have come to you through your endurance; by being impatient you have lost your goodness and rewards. Then, therefore, the instruction of the sage was true: Should somebody wound you with his words, speak evil to you, torture your body, or take away your belongings, endure and compensate not with evil, neither with words, nor with works, blasphemy, slandering, or cursing at all. Also, do not say things like this: God will return you in kind, or God is a great judge, because these are curses and verbal compensation, as has been said. Endure all instructions and deprivations. Be patient with the senior, the peer, and the junior.

With regard to endurance, it is to be known thus to be greater than other virtues. Just as righteousness is greater than prudence, fortitude, and chastity in acquired virtues, so too love is greater than faith and hope in divine [virtues], and prayer is greater than fasting and almsgiving in private virtues. Similarly, endurance is more sublime than all others for four reasons.

First, it is the fulfillment of each individual virtuous act, as James says: "Let patience have [her] perfect work" (Jas 1:4). Second, it is the seat and the place of all virtues, because where endurance is not present, virtue does not dwell. Third, it supports and provides firmament to other [virtues]; as the column supports a house, so also endurance supports all virtues. Fourth, it is a rod and a weapon in the hand; man battles against Satan with endurance, as Job did. Man resists and defeats all desires, anger, and transgressions with endurance. Therefore, the sage instructs: "Wait for the Lord, and he will help you" (Prov 20:22).

Here, one should know that there are many gains and benefits stemming from endurance. We shall mention these in ten points.

First, God will help you when you wait and give you the grace of endurance and a quick way out, as Paul says: "God is faithful, and he will not let you be tested beyond your strength, but he will also provide a quick way out so that you may be able to endure" (1 Cor 10:13).

Second, it produces love, as the Apostle says: "Endurance produces character, and character produces hope, and hope spreads love" (cf. Rom 5:4).

Third, God will render justice to those who wait, as the proverb says: "Do not say that you will avenge evil; wait for the Lord, and he will help you" (Prov 20:22), just as God judged Saul to compensate David's patience.

Fourth, [God] readily listens to the prayers of those who wait, as David says: "I waited patiently for the Lord, and he attended to me, and hearkened to my prayers" (Ps 40:1).

Fifth, patience brings a work close to completion, as James says: "Let patience have [her] perfect work" (Jas 1:4).

Sixth, endurance receives eternal life, according to the Lord: "By your endurance you will gain your souls, and he that endures to the end shall be live" (cf. Lk 21:29, Mt 10:22), like the ranks of the martyrs.

Seventh, endurance makes a person prominent and glorious, and instructs others to be so; hence: "You have heard of the endurance of Job" (Jas 5:11), which famed him.

Eighth, a person who waits witnesses the perishing of the multitude of impatient people, according to the Prophet who says: "Wait on the Lord, and keep his way, and he shall exalt you to inherit the land: when the wicked are destroyed, you shall see it" (Ps 37:33).

Ninth, endurance brings others to repent, as Paul says in Romans: "God's kindness is meant to lead you to repentance, but by your impenitent heart you are storing up wrath" (cf. Rom 2:4–5). With this same meaning, the Lord set the ordinance: "If anyone strikes you on the cheek [turn to him the other also]; and anyone who takes away your coat [give your cloak as well]; and if anyone forces you to go one mile [go also the second mile]" (cf. Mt 5:39–41).

Tenth, patience turns man God-like and homonymous to God, for David says: "God is merciful, gracious, and slow to anger" (cf. Ps 102:8).

How is endurance different from temperance? We say in four ways: First, to endure is to carry spiritual influences, whereas temperance relates to physical [matters]. Second, to endure is associated with the rational [part of the soul], whereas temperance is associated with the desiring [part] in particular and the coveting [part] in general. Third, enduring is caused by external grief, whereas temperance [is caused] by innate afflictions. Fourth, temperance occurs when we maintain our peace against evil desires, whereas endurance occurs when we keep virtues unaltered and undiminished. Amen.

CHAPTER LX

Homily of the same on laughing, "Woe to you who are laughing now"
(Lk 6:25).

Laughter is reprehensible for many reasons. First, Solomon says: "Like the crackling of thorns under the pot, so is the laughter of a fool" (Eccl 7:7). A fool does not smile like a wise man; rather, he laughs by crackling, similar to the thorn crackling in the fire under the pot. Second, laughter moves the senses of the body toward lewd desire and imposes upon it the performance of the act [of lewdness], reminiscent of the flame of the thorn keeping the pot active. Third, laughter is indication of foolishness—[the fool] fails to hide the joy of the heart, whereas a wise man does not laugh; rather, he shows a smiley face and confines the joy to his heart. Fourth, laughter is a demonstration of licentiousness and stupidity. As the doctors say, the Holy Spirit vanishes by the opening of the mouth [of a fool]. Therefore, the Apostle says: "Do not grieve the Holy Spirit" (Eph 4:30). The Apostle also says: "Put off all filthy communication out of your midst" (cf. Col 3:8). Fifth, the Lord says: "Woe to you who are laughing now, for you will mourn and weep" (Lk 6:25). As the Prophet[56] says: "Let your laughter be turned to mourning and your joy to grief" (Jas 4:9). This is how people depart to the hereafter: those who weep and mourn here [in this life], rejoice there [in the hereafter], as the Lord says: "Blessed are those who mourn, for they will be comforted" (Mt 5:4); while those who rejoice here, will weep there, in the eternal fire "where there will be weeping and gnashing of teeth" (Mt 8:12), like the wealthy who was dressed in purple and fine linen and fasted sumptuously every day, was thirsty and burning in the agony of the flames there [in the hereafter] [Lk 16:19–24]. Sixth, our Lord shared all of our passions except the sins—he experienced grief and fear, hunger and thirst, but never laughed, for it is a sin. Nowhere in the Gospel is there a word about Christ laughing, but there are many places where He wept, cried, and grieved. Laughter is so despicable.

Should someone say, it is natural for man to laugh, we say that the faculty of laughter is inherent to man, just as desire and indignation are innate, but

---

[56] The Armenian text speaks of a prophet. It should be corrected to *apostle*, obviously.

laughter is superfluous—whether man laughed or not, he possesses the faculty of laughter, for the soul is tripartite—reason, passion, and desire, but anger and lasciviousness are superfluous and transgressions. Likewise, the faculty of laughter is natural, but laughing is fatuity and superfluous.

Laughter is defined as follows. Laughter is aspiration associated with straying. Also, laughter is unbecoming nakedness of the body, the babbling of the breath, the contraction of the cheeks, the exposure of the teeth and the cavities of the throat, [and] the blow of irrational sound in the throat. Others define it differently. Laughter is the severance, the cutting of the breath and is nothing but foolishness and insanity.

Now, we need to know four things about laughter. First, where is laughter formed? Second, why do people laugh? Third, what is its harm? Fourth, the magnitude of its punishment.

Let us examine the first [point] as to where laughter is formed. Here, there are three questions. First, is laughter inherent or adventitious in man? David the Invincible answers in many ways that it is adventitious and not inherent. First, the inherent through growth becomes functional in us, just as reason brings us to perfection through growth. The development of reason occurs through four elements. First, reason grows with the age. Second, [it grows] through education and skills. Third, [it grows] through perfect prudence. Fourth, [it grows] through virtue. Laughing, however, is not essential; it is abdicable, as the sage say: "Do not mock a bold man." Second, it is evident from its opposite; that is, weeping is adventitious, then, obviously, laughter, its opposite, is adventitious likewise. Third, laughter and weeping are quality; sometimes [we do] this and sometimes [we do] that; and quality is adventitious. Fourth, they are influenced by sad and delightful appetites—sadness being the deficiency and delight being the fullness of appetite. Fifth, it is evident [through the fact] that they increase and decrease; increase and decrease are accident. Sixth, they change from being present to being absent—being present and being absent are accident. Seventh, it is not an attribute in someone, for by growth it corrupts its subject, as it occurred with many who were punished by death because of laughing. Eighth, strength eliminates laughter, for those who crossed the Stoponion were deprived of laughing, as it is said. It is evident, then, that laughter is adventitious and not inherent.

The second question [is]: Where is laughter formed? A person should know that [it originates] from the irrational soul of those with whom we ally ourselves; that is, [those] we communicate or associate with. Also, laughter happens through the muscles and nerves. The muscles are those two large arteries of the larynx—the air fills them, the nerves contract the cheeks, open the mouth, and cause laughter, as is evident from its definition.

The third question [is]: We and the irrational beings have the same breath, muscles, and nerves; why don't they laugh? The answer is twofold. First, according to Aristotle, they, too, laugh—the heron, the monkey, and so on, for instance. Second, he [David the Invincible] answers: although we and the irrational beings have the same breath, it affects us and them differently. Had it had the same effect, the barking of a dog and the neighing of a horse would have existed in other [beings as well]. But the same breath affects differently, like the one and same water that affects different plants differently and the one and same air that affects various beings [differently].

Again, that laughter does not exist in the rational [part] is evident from four things. First, the immaterial and simple spirits, the angels, do not have it. Second, neither do the spirits separated from the bodies [have it]. Third, passion and desire do not laugh. Fourth, the wise and the virtuous that possess augmented rationality do not laugh, and it is not the innate—generative, vegetative,[57] and nutritive faculties—that laughs in us. Then, therefore, it is evident, that it is the irrational soul that laughs.

This much on the first part.

Let us move on to the second part and see why people laugh. We say [they laugh] for many reasons.

First, because of boldness and impudence, as the Prophet says: "The fool has said in his heart, There is no God" (Ps 14:1), for buffoonery, which is bold mockery, is the beginning and cause of all evil.

The second reason is fearlessness, for they [laughers] do not fear God or the primates, for those who fear always stay in grief, as the Prophet says: "I went with a mourning countenance all the day, for my soul is filled with suffering" (Ps 38:6–7). And the psalm says: "The fear of the Lord is the beginning of prudence" (Ps 110:10), and that: "By the fear of the Lord everyone departs from evil" (Prov 15:27).

Third, mockery takes place because of the impenitence of the heart, because it does not turn and repent for sins, for true penitents weep and bewail day and night, as the Prophet did. [David] says: "I shall wash my bed every night; I shall water my couch with my tears" (Ps 6:6).

Fourth, [a man laughs] because of the evil desire of the will, for he is filled

---

[57] Typographic error. The word *ajołakan* [աջողական] should read *ačołakan* [աճողական].

with various sins and demonic joys, as the proverb says: "A fool does mischief in sports" (Prov 10:23). And the Lord [says]: "The good person brings good things out of a good treasure, and the evil person brings evil things out of an evil treasure" (Mt 12:35), and that: "Out of the abundance of the heart the mouth speaks" (Mt 12:34).

Fifth, because [the laugher] does not strive for or desire good works, or eternal life, because those who have these are in constant mourning and grief, as David says: "Woe is me that my sojourning is prolonged; I have tabernacle among the tents of Kedar" (Ps 120:5), and the Lord says: "Blessed are you who weep now, [etc.]" (Lk 6:21).

Sixth, they laugh because of unruliness, for they have no rules and limits to their words, food, or purity; rather, [they spend their time] always with useless discourse and buffoonery, and [with] their doorless mouth they turn, like lunatics, into shelter and abode for demons, as Solomon says: "Alas for those who forsake right paths, to walk in ways of darkness" (Prov 2:13).

Seventh, they laugh because of their rudeness and lack of instruction, for they have not been trained and educated with divine ordinances, nor have they been nourished and educated by the good fathers, as the proverb says: "They have forsaken the instruction of their youth and forgotten the covenant of God" (Prov 2:17), while James says: "Whosoever does not bridle his tongue, religion is useless for him" (Jas 1:26).

Eighth, [they laugh] because of the love of the world and the body, for they discover only what they see and these are the things that please them, not the everlasting things, as [the Apostle] says: "Hypocrites! Love of the world is enmity with God" (cf. Jas 4:4); Solomon also speaks of the sinfulness of the ungodly.

Ninth, the senseless mocking takes place to admire with oneself and to insult others, because the [laugher] reckons himself to be straight and others crooked, himself to be precious and good and others to be bad and worthless, as [the Apostle] says: "Do not dishonor or speak evil against one another" (cf. Jas 4:11).

Tenth, because they forget and do not care about their soul: what will happen now or after death? They rejoice and laugh like irrational animals, as [the Prophet] says: "Souls overtaken by sins decline also in their mind and laugh" (cf. Wis 4:12).

Mocking has been related to the irrational soul. See [how] all the saints, apostles, prophets, and others lived with mourning on earth and departed the earth with mourning, so that they attain ineffable joy and everlasting delight.

413

Therefore, [the Lord] says: "Woe to you who are laughing now" (Lk 6:25).

This [was] about the second part.

Let us go to the third part [to examine] the harm of laughing and extent of its harm. We say that [this is so] for many reasons.

Primarily, useless mockery is a sign of disbelief and hopelessness, and a disbeliever is worse than the demons, as [the Apostle] says: "You believe [. . .]; you do well. [Even] the demons believe and shudder" (Jas 2:19).

Second, it makes a person forget Christ's formidable coming, the impartial judgment, and the bitter suffering of hell, as [the Apostle] says: "If you sin willfully, there no longer remains a sacrifice for sins, but a fearful prospect of judgment, and a fury of fire that will consume the adversaries" (Heb 10:26–27), and that: "Woe to you who are laughing now" (Lk 6:25).

Third, it stands for despising and disdaining God and His ordinances, which prohibit laughing and reckon the mourners blessed. Those who disobey these [ordinances] dishonor God, as Paul says: "If you despise God's forgiveness, you store up wrath for yourself on the day of God's righteous judgment" (cf. Rom 2:4–5).

Fourth, the senseless and unruly laughter turns their mind mad and blind, and it impedes the good thoughts and the spiritual theories of the pious, as the proverb says: "They rejoice in their evil" (Prov 2:14), while Paul says: "The god of this world has blinded their minds" (2 Cor 4:4).

Fifth, they [laughers] resemble evil dancing demons who always rejoice with their deeds, with the destruction of people, and with the fall of the holy, as [Solomon] says: "The holy spirit will flee deceit" (Wis 1:5). A mocker and his mocking indicate that he has become Satan's abode.

Sixth, they resemble idolaters who always rejoice with filthy deeds and abomination, and engage in shameful actions before the idols, as the Apostle says: "There was time when you were enticed and led astray to idols that could not speak" (1 Cor 12:2).

Seventh, they resemble the crucifying Jews who were torturing the Lord who was stripped naked and were laughing for their unruly action.

Eighth, [a laugher] commits arrogance and hard-heartedness—the inception and mother of all evil, and separation from everything good. Mocking is arrogance and harshness, which remove all the good gestures from man.

Ninth, it is dissimilarity to all holy men who pleased God by weeping and lamenting, as John, Jeremiah, and others. These [mockers,] however, cause harm to themselves and to others by absurd and senseless mocking.

Tenth, it is evident that laughter is despised and removed from all Christian

414

regulations—from the church, the house of prayer, the Liturgy, theological discourse, during sermons, and while discussing other philosophical topics. Wise men do not laugh.

Laughter occurs in four places: [during] the weddings of the laity, impudent games, wine drinking by foolish youngsters, [and] gatherings by corrupt unbelievers. Then, therefore, it is evident that laughter causes a great deal of harm. This much is enough on the third part.

We move on to the fourth part to discuss the punishment for laughter.

First, everybody despises [the laugher] and finds fault with him, and he remains in the state of shame: no other punishment is greater than being ashamed and reproached by people, as the Prophet says: "He does not take a reproach against his neighbor; in his sight an evildoer is contemned" (cf. Ps 15:3).

Second, they are punished repeatedly by the kings and rulers because of their senseless and bold mocking, as it is known from the canons of Chalcedon: such a [mocking] person suffers death.

Third, they are punished and reproached by the ordinances and the teachings of the Holy Scriptures, which threaten them [the mockers] with Gehenna and torments, as the Lord says woe [to those who laugh], and if saying "You fool" makes a person liable to Gehenna, how much more [will] the impudent mocking [make a person liable]?

Fourth, the Lord speaks of weeping and mourning, but they do not listen; instead, they do the opposite; therefore, they are ten thousand times more liable to punishment and hell, as the Lord says: "Bring all my enemies who did not want me to be king over them and slaughter them in my presence" (Lk 19:27). Enemies to the Lord are all those who disobey God's ordinances, as [David] says: "The Lord's enemies lied to him" (Ps 81:16).

Fifth, they are punished by the Lord and they are dropped from His resemblance, for He never laughed during his lifetime, but cried in many places, such as at Lazarus's grave, upon the city. What is greater than the punishment of being dropped from the resemblance of the Lord? Because those who are dropped from His resemblance shall be deprived of and separated from His graces, and they will bear resemblance to demons and the wicked, as has been said. Those who are deprived of His resemblance will be dropped there [in the hereafter] from all resemblance to Christ and His glory, as [the Apostle] says: "We will be like him" (1 Jn 3:2).

Sixth, they are punished, because they are deprived of the comfort of the mourners and their blessing, and what is greater than the punishment of deprivation from the comfort of the Holy Spirit that comforts the mourners and the grieved, all of them, and that grieves by senseless mockery, as [the Apostle] says: "Do not grieve the Holy Spirit [of God] with which you were marked with a seal for the day of your redemption" (Eph 4:30).

Seventh, they are deprived of the kingdom of heaven and the repose of the righteous, as Isaiah says: "Let the ungodly be taken away, that he see not the glory of the Lord" (Isa 26:10); and the mocker is ungodly, as has been demonstrated.

Eighth, they inherit eternal suffering and the fire of hell, and they join the ranks of the wicked and Satan who is the cause of all evil things and suffering, as [the Lord] says: "You will be thrown into prison and you will never get out until you have paid the last penny" (Mt 5:25–26).

Ninth, with insignificant forgivable sins, they associate themselves with truly wicked and capital sins; what else would be greater punishment? And [the sin] is not minor; it is very heavy and unforgivable, because the senseless mocking is the beginning, fulfillment, and cause of impenitence, as it is evident to wise minds.

Tenth, [laughter is punishable] according to the Lord's command: "Woe to you who are laughing now" (Lk 6:25). The woe is the inclusion of all evil things, and evil as kind is divided into seven. First, there is the first evil, Satan. The second evil is sin. The third evil is the trap and temptation. The fourth evil is punishment. The fifth evil is death, for "The death of sinners is evil" (Ps 34:21). The sixth evil is the hell. The seventh evil is the suffering of Gehenna. Saying "woe" encompasses all of these and more than these. Therefore, may our hope, Christ, save us from all evil sins and the bitter suffering forever and ever, amen.

CHAPTER LXI

Homily of the same on arrogance and humility, according to the verse of the proverb: "The Lord resists the arrogant, but gives grace to the humble" (Prov 3:34).

Satan the first evil and the fallen Lucifer, who became the author and mother of all haughty transgressions, developed with his former free will the vice of arrogance in himself and sowed his corruption by deceiving others. The reason was this: he found himself incorporeal, immortal, and luminous, revolted against the Creator, [and] remaining silent refused to praise God, as Paul says in 2 Corinthians: "The wicked prince wanted to become God" (cf. 2 Cor 11:14).[58] St. [Gregory] the Illuminator seconds this. For this reason, [Lucifer] fell from the heavens, the luminous life, and the classes of angels unto the earth and into the depths of abysses. Because of this, God made man from earth as a weighty body and in want of needs by natural passions, so that he may look at his body, remain humble, and rise from where his pride made him fall, to become, despite his earthen weak creation, an embarrassment and insult to Satan by rising unto and entering the glory of God, wherefrom he [Satan] who was glorified had fallen. The devil, in view of Adam's great honor, envied him and deceived him with the same vice of arrogance that caused his destruction. For he said: "You shall be God when you eat the fruit" (cf. Gen 3:5). Thus, they [Adam and Eve] transgressed and fell unto the deadly and cursed earth; hence: "Through envy of the devil came death into the world" (Wis 2:24). So "The Lord resists the haughty" (Prov 3:34), because God cast down the arrogant Satan from the heavens and cast out Adam from Paradise. Again, although people see that Satan was destroyed when he boasted with this vice, man was deprived of Paradise because of it, and the massive, diseased, and needy bodies that possess all kinds of abominations because of the vice of pride, instead of contemplating this [reality], think that their hypothetical and minute knowledge is true and great, and go against their superiors—as do apprentices against doctors, sons against fathers, servants against masters, subjects against rulers, and so on—then God will not have mercy on them; rather, He will take

---

[58] See "Even Satan disguised himself as an angel of light."

revenge, be at war with them, and punish them. When Dathan and Abiron opposed Moses, "the earth opened and swallowed them" (Ps 106:17), for those who rise up boastfully in their mind are cast into the depths of the earth as punishment. Likewise, when Korah and his fifty followers opposed Aaron, "fire was kindled in their congregation and the fire burned them" (Ps 105:18).

Should someone ask, both Korah and his fellows and Dathan and his fellows committed the same sin, why, then, were some buried in the earth and some burned by the flames? We say that the doctors mention these three reasons.

First, priesthood is heavenly; wherefore, Korah was burned by heavenly flames. Authority, on the other hand, is worldly; thereby, "the earth opened and swallowed Dathan" (Ps 105:17). Second, [the doctors] say that the sins of priests shake the heavens, as [occurred] there [in the first instance]; whereas [the sins of] worldly rulers [shake] the earth, as the proverb says: "Under three things the earth trembles; under four it cannot bear up: first, when a slave becomes king; second, when a fool is glutted with food; third, when a maid drives out her mistress; fourth, when an odious woman happens to a good man" (cf. Prov 30:21–23). Third, [the doctors] say that priesthood is an angelic order, [and] it has to be kept in holiness; otherwise, outraged angels will burn with fire the body or the soul. Dathan committed a civil crime, which is a transgression associated with kings. Those who sin with their king receive the extreme punishment—they are wiped out with their properties and generations; [then] those who sinned against God and Moses, who was called God and prince of the people, would have received even greater punishment. While God punished them because of their insubordination, He honored Moses the humble, who was saying: "I have not been sufficient; I am weak in speech and slow-tongued" (cf. Ex 4:10). From that moment on, it has become God's habit to forbid and hold back all kinds of people when they presumptuously seek spiritual and physical glory, and to grant [glory] to those who did not seek it. For instance, when people try to catch up with their shadows, the shadows escape, and when they stop or turn back, their shadows run after them; the same applies to worldly glories. Therefore, [Solomon] says: "The Lord resists the haughty, but gives grace to the humble" (Prov 3:34).

It is known that God pities all other sinners, as He pitied the fornicator and the robber, [and] forgave the sins of the Canaanites and the publican. God pities and forgives the denier, the murderer, and all other sinners but "resists the haughty." And this is [so] for ten reasons.

First, pride belongs to the rational, judicious part [of the soul], and [people] sin willingly and knowingly; therefore, God does not forgive. Other sins, however, are passionate, covetous, or bodily in nature, and are committed inadvertently and unknowingly, because of weakness or deception; therefore [people] find forgiveness and pardon.

Second, the arrogant cannot see his mistake because of his pride; therefore, he thinks he is true and competes against his instructors; whereas other sinners see their sins, heed instruction, and receive the cure.

Third, conscience does not judge in arrogant people; therefore, they do not repent and do not find forgiveness; whereas those who commit physical transgressions are judged internally by their conscience, grieve because of their sins, repent in their heart, and therefore find forgiveness.

Fourth, pride is greater than any other transgression, because it is a sin against God's glory and essence—as was the case with Satan; whereas other sins are against God's commandment, against the neighbor, or against one's own body, which are lesser than pride. For instance, when someone closes his eyes because of the beams of light and finds himself in darkness, that darkness is lesser than the darkness caused by looking at the circle of the sun and losing the [sense of] light. Similarly, the sin of pride is a greater and heavier transgression.

Fifth, pride exists in all sins; for just as virtues are nothing without love, vices are nothing without pride. This is how pride manifests itself in all sins: all other sins are deviation from God's ordinances and deviation after bodily pleasures; whereas with pride we despise and dishonor the true goodness and then deviate after goodness is changed in us—thus pride appears in all sins.

Sixth, the arrogant disobeys the ordinances and rules through his own pride, because he does not receive the natural laws, the written laws, or the Gospel, nor does he follow rules or obey the fathers; thereby, he is referred to as lawless. There are two kinds of lawless people: those who did not receive the laws at all and those who received the laws but despised them, like the lawless proud; thereby, the sins of the lawless [proud] are not forgiven. Other sinners, however, are lawful sinners; thereby their sins are forgiven through the laws.

Seventh, the proud is referred to as ungodly and the ungodly is the sacrilegious who "said in his heart there is no God" (Ps 14:1); that is, [he is] the proud, because he does not believe in God, and [does not believe] that God judges because of that sin, and that [pride] is a sin; therefore, the path to forgiveness is lost for him; hence: "The way of the ungodly shall perish" (Ps 1:6). Other sinners, however, are not ungodly; simply, they are guilty toward

God, but they believe in God and fear God. Therefore, they receive forgiveness through faith: "Abram believed God and it was counted to him as righteousness" (Gen 15:6).

Eighth, other kinds of vices manifest something to us: theft [manifests] properties, fornication [manifests] pleasure, and so on; whereas there is no expectation in pride at all, and therefore [the proud] are always troubled mentally and physically.

Ninth, [pride] casts out every good thing that we have inside us. For instance, when darkness arrives, it casts out the light. Likewise, when pride appears, all good things leave us, because we lose [the opportunities] to perform them and we do not perform them with our pride. Other sins, however, whatever they may be, cast out their corresponding goodness and let others be—fornication [casts out] chastity, avarice [casts out] modesty, and so on.

Tenth, all kinds of sins are committed by those who are fond of sins, but pride is committed by the holy and the chosen, such as the angels in heaven. Also, all virtuous people can regain decency after other sins, but not after pride, because this [sin] is [committed] by swerving right, whereas other physical sins are [committed] by swerving left. Satan hunts people by various traps just like hunters who use various kinds of traps to trap fowl according to their behavior, since some are foolish and others are clever.

Although the following four words belong to the same kind, they possess subtle differences in meaning—haughty, arrogant, proud, and vainglorious. The haughty is the self-admirer who does not consent to others; rather, he consents only to his own will and views. The proud is a person swollen in himself and is the high-minded who considers himself superior to everybody else. The arrogant person wants to tread upon other people and wishes that everybody were lesser than and inferior to him. The vainglorious person, on the other hand, is the same as a person who is fond of glory; they like to be glorified, honored, and praised by everybody. These are the kinds and the actions of arrogant people. Therefore, the Lord says: "The Lord is against the arrogant, but gives grace to the humble" (Prov 3:34).

Humility has many praiseworthy qualities, just as pride has [many] blameworthy qualities. The philosopher says: "The beautiful is praiseworthy, and the abominable is blameworthy"; since the abominable pride was reproached, we were able to perceive the praiseworthiness of humility.

Now, with regard to humility, as Anthony the Great says, it is to be known that all evil thoughts are consumed by humility. Humility manifests itself in three ways—natural, theoretical, and practical. Natural humility occurs when you think of the baseness and corruption of it [our nature], as to where it began and where it will end; that is, it began from the earth and will dissolve in the earth. Because of corrupting vices and abomination, it will again become corrupt and abominable. Therefore, the Prophet [David] says: "Your humility is inside of you and your body." The theoretical [humility] occurs when you bind yourself to humility, saying: "I am not competent; nor am I worthy of that [good] counsel." The practical [humility] occurs when you torture your entire body by hard work and prayers; then evil counsel will flee from you. The saints say that the river of temptation is absorbed in arid places through labor.

Through the Holy Scriptures, we see that there are many benefits to humility. First, it says: "The Lord is against the arrogant, but gives grace to the humble" (Prov 3:34), for if it is a corporeal grace of professions, [people] learn it through humility, and if the spiritual instruction of knowledge and wisdom is at question, grace belongs to the humble, as was the case of the Apostles in the upper house.

Second, all ordinances—apostolic, prophetic, and canonical—are fulfilled with humility, because we obey, heed, and implement their writings. Just as the proud disobeys the ordinances and is referred to as lawless, so are the humble referred to as lawful.

Third, our sins are justified through humility: when the conscience reproves us from within, we grieve and regret. And when we are instructed from outside, we heed and repent of our sins. Know that humility is the cause of all good things, for we fulfill the ordinances through humility, and if we stumble because of bodily weakness or the deception of the adversaries, we repent again and are justified through humility.

Fourth, we attain honor and glory through humility, as Moses witnesses: "Meek is my servant Moses" (cf. Num 12:3). See how he was glorified, saw God, established ordinances, liberated the people, and was installed ruler over them. Likewise, [the Scripture] says about David: "Lord, remember David and all his meekness" (Ps 132:1) by which he attained the grace of prophesy, sat on the throne of kingship, became Christ's father bodily, and his fame covered the heavens and the earth.

Fifth, the Lord commands: "Blessed are the meek, for they shall inherit the earth" (Mt 5:5). Which earth? Not this [earth], which is associated with grief and death; rather, that which bears light and justice; that which is the heaven of the living and saints; that which is called Paradise and kingdom. Indeed, like those who were dropped from His inheritance through pride, the obedient and the humble will enter [the kingdom]. Elsewhere, [the Lord] says:

"Learn from me, for I am meek and humble in heart; and you shall find rest unto your souls" (Mt 11:29); that is, hopefully here [on earth] and practically there [in the hereafter].

Sixth, in the corporeal life also the humble and meek live in peace, as the Prophet says: "O you man, who desires to see his life in goodness; keep your tongue from evil, and your lips from speaking guile" (cf. Ps 34:12–13). Then a person lives in love and peace with everybody; the meek and humble stay away from quarrel, insult, calumny, murder, and their like.

Seventh, the Lord commands: "Whosoever shall humble himself shall be exalted, and he that shall exalt himself shall be abased" (cf. Mt 32:12). Those who humbled themselves and suffered for the love of Christ rose unto heaven and joined the ranks of the angels, and those who did not humble themselves and rose instead were destroyed in heaven and perished. The Pharisee who boasted perished; whereas the publican was justified through his humility, as the Gospel mentions [cf. Lk 18:10–13].

Eighth, God dwells in man when he is humble; hence: "Where would I rest, if not in the meek and the humble who tremble at my words?" (cf. Isa 66:2). What the heavens and earth cannot bear, a man can receive in himself through humility like the Holy Mother of God Mary. When she said: "I am the handmaid of the Lord" (Lk 1:38), God the Word dwelt in her womb and when He was born, she said: "He has regarded the humility of his handmaiden; from henceforth all generations shall call me blessed" (Lk 1:48).

Ninth, God's eye always regards the humble from heavens unto the earth; hence: "He looks upon the humble things in heaven and on earth, lifts up the poor to set them with princes" (cf. Ps 112:6–8). That is, if a person is orphan, widowed, troubled, deprived, stressed, or enslaved, God always looks upon them; He sees them and renders justice to them.

Tenth, God sees the prayers of the humble and opens His ears to their entreaties; hence: "He has had regard to the prayers of the humble and has not despised their petitions" (Ps 102:17). When a person humbles himself in his thoughts, puts the sins before his eyes, and lowers himself before God, [God] fulfills his petitions without delay, "for a pure heart and a humble soul God will not despise" (cf. Ps 51:17), because the humble soul and a broken person are an offering for God. Not only this. God satiates the humble with all kinds of bounties.

Look at the valleys! When they are low and humble, the rain gathers there from everywhere. Therefore, [the Scripture] says: "The valleys shall abound in corn" (Ps 65:13). Similarly, when the mind of a person is humble, it will abound and multiply in effect and goodness through God's grace. Look also at the trees. The fruit-bearing branch is low and humble, whereas the barren is loose and in no way humble. Similarly, whosoever has good fruits is humble, be it knowledge, instruction, virtue, and so on. Look also at the rosebush. A bush with sweet-scented flowers is small and near the ground; whereas a rough and vain bush is tall like a poplar. For this reason, God descended in the mulberry bush and appeared to Moses, because the bush is small and low; just like the humble people in whom God descends, as has been said. Wherefore Solomon, inspired by the Holy Spirit, says: "The Lord is against the arrogant, but gives grace to the humble" (Prov 3:34). And the Apostle says: "Humble yourselves under the mighty hand of God, so that he may exalt you in due time" (1 Pet 5:6). That is, when the time arrives, if we had humbled ourselves and obeyed His commandments, He will exalt us unto the universal arena in the life to come, and will say: "Come, you that are blessed by my Father, inherit the eternal life" (cf. Mt 25:34). May all of us become partakers and heirs of the kingdom of our God who is blessed forever, amen.

CHAPTER LXII

Homily of the same on envy, according to the verse of the Prophet David:
"Do not envy evildoers, nor envy the workers of inequity" (Ps 37:1).

Like a nurse who trains a breast-sucking child and instructs him to learn goodness and stay away from evil, God is a [nurturing] father to us through grace—"who beget us unto a lively hope" (1 Pet 1:3), and the church is a spiritual mother to us, begetting us through the [baptismal] font and the Holy Spirit. Our educators and tutors are the prophets and the apostles, who instruct us and teach us to stay away from evil, do good works, and thus become heirs and co-heirs to Christ in the kingdom of heaven. Therefore, the Prophet David, the father of God [Christ], instructs gently and teaches: "Do not envy evildoers, nor envy the workers of inequity" (Ps 37:1). That is, O my dear son, who heeds to the words of my mouth! There are all kinds of evil things in the world, and those who love the world love evil works. When the wicked do evil works, they perish soon. They are like the grass of the meadow, which soon dries and perishes. I bring to you recommendations, so that you become partaker of goodness. Do not envy the wicked and those who work inequity, so that you may not perish with them quickly and turn into a combustible substance in the eternal hell.

There are many works that are worked by the wicked and are disagreeable to believers—adultery, fornication, avarice, theft, lying, sloth, pride, and so on. Christians have to flee from all of these.

Among these, the main capital sin is envy. The doctors of the church say that there are seven mortal sins: pride, envy, anger, sloth, avarice, gluttony, and lust. Of these seven sins, two are heavier and greater than others: pride and envy, because Adam and Eve committed the other sins, but pride and envy were committed by Satan, who became arrogant and went against God's glory; consequently, he was deprived of honor and the class of angels, and fell on earth. Later, Satan envied Adam's glory. He defeated Adam, caused his exodus from the glorious and immortal Paradise, and had him inherit death and the thorny and cursed earth. Thereby, envy is greater and eviler than all other sins, because it associates man with and likens him to Satan, as the sage says: "God did not create death; nevertheless, through envy of the devil came death into the world" (Wis 2:24). Whoever follows him, shares his same faith.

It needs to be known that there are two kinds of envy—evil and good. Evil envy occurs when people in view of a man's good fortune feel jealousy and pain because of his goodness, glory, assets, and so on, or in view of a man's bad fortune laugh because of the mishaps. Evil envy also occurs when a man sees an evildoer, a fornicator, a drunk, a thief, and so on, and wants to do similar works. Referring to them, [the sage] says: "Do not envy evildoers." Good envy occurs when a man sees a good work and wants to do the same—fasting, prayers, almsgiving, faith, hope, love. Referring to them, the Apostle says: "Covet the graces that are good" (cf. 1 Cor 12:31). An envy of this caliber is good and God-pleasing, and it appears in good people. The evil envy, however, which is Satan's seed and is found in evil people, has five properties that are eviler than all other sins and have the greatest separation from goodness.

The first [property] is that the vice of envy constantly tortures the mind and wears, languishes and burns the body of the person stricken by it, as the interpretation of the term itself indicates—it harms himself before harming others.[59] The envious person is called broken by envy,[60] because envy always breaks and destroys his heart. Therefore, the face of the envious person is pale and blackened from the bitter sadness of the heart. We do not find this characteristic in other sins; neither in arrogant people, nor in the angry or any other people. The other people find some joy and pleasure in their [sinful] work, although they grieve later. The envious, however, is always bitter and sad, whether before or after the sins, because he sighs, groans, and moans without finding alleviation or comfort. The second property is that envy occurs toward equals and close people, not toward a stranger or a distant person, as Solomon says: "A man is envied of his neighbor" (Eccl 4:4). A civilian does not envy a military man and a prince does not envy a husbandman; rather, envy occurs among people of similar positions and associates—a king envies a king, a prince envies a prince, a poor man envies a poor man, and an artisan envies a man of the same profession.

Man has three countenances: superior, inferior, and equal. Now, pride occurs toward inferiors and equals, but not toward superiors. Contrary to this, envy does not occur toward inferiors; rather, it occurs toward equals and

---

[59] Tat'ewac'i has resorted to a pun. The Armenian word *naxanj* [նախանձ] can be broken into two parts in two ways—*nax* [նախ] and *anj* [անձ], meaning one's self in the first place, and *na* [նա] and *xanj* [խանձ], which associates a person with burning.

[60] Tat'ewac'i uses the word *naxanjabek* [նախանձաբեկ], which literally means broken by envy.

superiors. Its occurrence toward equals is dismal, so that the envious may not resemble the envied. It occurs mostly toward superiors, by feeling jealous about their good fortune.

The third property is that the envious exerts all his efforts and skills to labor and work because of the envy, as Solomon says: "I saw that all toil in work come from one person's envy of another" (Eccl 4:4), because envious people build, plant, gather, become wealthy, travel the seas to remote lands, earn, labor, [and] suffer because of envy, and all are vanity and despicable for two reasons.

First, whoever gathers great and many treasures and builds and plants, nothing more he would be able to consume for his body's needs than a man who has less and enjoys it peacefully. But what are the necessities of the body? They are those that the Apostle Paul testifies: "We have food and clothing; we will be content with these" (1 Tim 6:8). Food is needed so that we may not die of hunger, while clothing protects us against cold and nudity. Everything else is unnecessary, useless, and nothing but an unreal desire of the soul. Second, [all are] vanity and vain, because everything perishes and becomes vain by death, except the sins and the suffering that remain. The properties become belongings to others, as the Prophet says: "A man is troubled in vain: he lays up treasures, and knows not for whom he shall gather them" (Ps 39:6). If good people [have heaped], some people will inherit; if the wicked [have heaped], they do not know [who will inherit]—their own folks or strangers, beloved people, or enemies?

The fourth property is that envy is the foundation and root of all evil works. Because of envy people deprive each other, ravish, blaspheme, slander, insult, fight, oppose, kill, betray, and do many other evil works because of envy. Without envy, this land would have satisfied this king, but because of envy, even though he has his own, he ravishes what belongs to others, [paving way to] battle and a lot of bloodshed. Because of envy a husbandman deprives another from his own field, not because of natural needs, as Isaiah says: "They join house to house, lay field to field, that they may remove their neighbor" (cf. Isa 5:8). Because of envy the Jews went against Christ, accusing him that he was doing the signs by Beelzebub; He was not imposing upon them anything by healing the diseased, the lame, and the blind. Because of envy, Korah and Dathan rose against Moses and opposed him; not because he had deprived them. And see how the envious perished: "The earth opened and swallowed up Dathan, and a fire was kindled in their company, and the flame consumed them" (cf. Ps 105:17–18). Thus, fire is enflamed in the soul of the envious people—the fire of envy now, and the fire of hell later.

The fifth property is illustrated by Solomon: "The fool folds his hands together and eats his own flesh" (Eccl 4:5). This verse does not state that man eats his own flesh; rather, it shows through the paradigm that due to the bitterness of the vice, the envious becomes fool and eats his own flesh and arm in the likeness of a demoniac who becomes furious and consumes his own flesh. The arm is man's genuine brother and father [allegorically], while the entire body is his family. Now, the vice of envy turns man into a fool who eats the arm of his brother in the likeness of envious Cain who killed his brother because of the offering [that God accepted]. Similarly, Absolom struck his father and took away the kingdom from him because of envy. It is in this way that the envious fool eats his own flesh.

In this regard, the Prophet Isaiah writes: "The hungry man turns and eats his own kindred" (cf. Isa 9:20). Eating his own kindred indicates that envy occurs more toward familiar people than strangers, and the envious accomplishes the evil work by: killing, as Cain killed his brother; slandering, as Miriam and Aaron slandered Moses; taking away the rule, as Absolom [took away the rule] of his father, David; or insulting and sentencing to death, as the Jews did to Christ. And see the judgment of the envious; when he harbors evil thoughts about others and materializes them, he himself perishes with the same evil, as Solomon says: "Whoever digs a pit for his neighbor, will himself fill it" (cf. Prov 26:27), while David says: "He has opened a pit, and dug it up, and he shall fall into the ditch which he has made" (Ps 7:15). This is evident from what we have said: when Cain killed his brother because of envy, he received God's curse, his body trembled, and he was killed by Lamech. Miriam, who slandered Moses, turned into a leper. Absolom was killed in war. Haman, who had erected a gallows for Mordecai, was himself hanged from it instead. The Jews who sentenced Christ to death perished in the hands of Titus and Vespasian, and were scattered throughout the world. Envy is a bitter, harsh, and evil vice, for like an infuriated dog, it cannot recognize his kindred and the strangers, and bites everybody indiscriminately. Also, the envious cannot differentiate his kindred from the strangers, the good from the evil; rather, he harms everybody with his evil envy because of avarice, glory, power, or anything else, himself also suffering from [his actions] and perishing.

The doctors of the church also say that a spiteful and envious person resembles three things. First, he resembles a stealth dog, for there are two kinds of dogs—good and evil. The kind that faces you and barks at you is good because it shows its enmity and man can exercise caution. The evil dog, however, comes from behind silently and bites the muscle. Likewise, the angry reveals his anger through words, but the envious covers his face and then bites as he proceeds by slandering.

Second, the spiteful resembles a fire covered under the chaff and has four properties. First, it is a hidden fire. Second, it burns and devours the chaff from under. Third, it produces bitter smoke. Fourth, it is inflamed by the wind. Likewise, the envious covers his spite with affectionate face and words, while his heart and soul are internally burning and being devoured. He sighs from his heart for this reason and demonstrates the bitter smoke that is in his nostrils; and when others join him and blow air by slandering, the evil envy inflames and burns.

Third, the spiteful resembles those who are in agony, or those who are hanged by their neck. First, their eyes become drained of light. Similarly, the eyes of the envious lose their sight. Second, their eyes fall deep down and their eyelids become stiff. The same happens to the envious. Third, their eyebrows hang down and hinder the vision. The same happens to the spiteful. Fourth, their bones stick out, their nose turns sharp, and they turn pale. Similarly, the body of the envious dwindles away, his bones and the skin stick out, the nose becomes sharp, and he turns pale because of the bitter envy that appears on his face. There are also other signs, for the envious strikes one palm to another, joins his fingers and trembles, doubts in his mind, and sighs from his heart. Detestable is the face of the envious. The banquet seems bitter to him, and the joy seems sadness; this happens, because there is pain and suffering in his body and soul.

It is to be known that envy is greater evil than anger and indignation. First, anger is over the wicked, whereas envy is over the good. Our anger is provoked when we see a person turn aside from faith, or act disorderly, or harbor enmity toward us. But we envy when we see a person straight in his faith and holy, glorious in his deeds, and friendly toward us. And the sign of the envious is that when others praise [someone], he slanders; if the person is straight, he blames and dishonors, because the praise that people formulate [he considers to be] removed from him.

Second, a person who has done evil to us in the past, presently harbors evil thoughts, or speaks evil [against us] provokes our anger, but we envy him who has not done evil to us, nor does he harbor evil thoughts or speak evil [against us]. And this shows the vice of envy: a man whose anger is provoked suffers and compensates against [his suffering], whereas the envious compensates against goodness.

Third, again, the angry and indignant person sometimes regrets, calms down, and reconciles, but the envious does not calm down, does not regret, and rests only after harming the object of his envy, like the Jews who envied Christ. Although they enjoyed his remedies to all kinds of pains, their envy troubled them constantly and they hated him: "This man is not from God, for he does not observe the Sabbath" (Jn 9:16). Their envy grew so much that they crucified Him.

Fourth, again, an angry person harms others, despises with his anger, or strikes with his indignation, but the envious harms himself first, and then he might or might not harm others. For this reason, [the phenomenon] is designated as envy; that is, he turns evil against his own self in the first place. Like a wood that catches fire and then may or may not burn other things, the envious inflames from within through envy and then his wickedness may or may not catch others. For example, a flame hidden under the chaff begins to release fumes and smoke on its own, and then grows into full fire; similarly, the envious releases fumes, hatred, and knavery within himself, [and] the smoke of the envy comes out of his nostrils and kindles as fire when the occasion arrives.

Fifth, again, we clearly see that an angry and indignant person either is ashamed on his own or calms down after he is instructed, but the envious has [the envy] hidden in his heart; nobody sees it, and he is not ashamed. For example, people can see a wound on the surface of the skin and heal it quickly by applying medicine, but an internal wound is not visible and healing it is a challenge. Similarly, envy is hidden and healing it is difficult.

Sixth, again, the angry resembles a dog that barks from a distance; people are aware of it and stay out of its way. The envious, however, resembles a stealth dog that attacks a man unawares and suddenly bites the muscle from behind. The first is a well-behaved dog that announces loudly, do not come near; beware, I am your enemy. The angry in this way is good, because we identify his wickedness and protect ourselves. The envious, however, is totally evil like the stealth [dog]; it catches us unawares and slanders and speaks evil of the good people on its way.

Seventh, again, anger is directed toward those that are inferior or equal, whereas envy is directed toward those that are superior or prominent. A person provoked against inferiors or equals calms down after completing his [evil] work, but he who envies a superior and rises against him cannot fulfill his will, nor can he find rest from his envy; rather, he always remains in bitterness and spite. Therefore, envy is greater evil than anger.

Eighth, again, as we have mentioned, goodness tones anger down, while evil inflames it. Envy, on the contrary, tones down vis-à-vis evil and inflames vis-à-vis goodness. Since people in this world are good spiritually or physically, their sight will always trouble the envious. And there is no reason for the evil in the envious to rest. Therefore, the doctors of the church say that the envious should have had eyes and ears everywhere to see and hear all the goodness of people and thereby suffer always.

Ninth, again, the envious is so spiteful about other people's bounties that he loses his own bounty because of them. There is a fable going like this: There were two people envying each other. The king promised one of them: "Ask for a gift. I will grant the double of what you ask to your friend who is your enemy." [The envious] thought: "If I ask for a village, a horse, clothing, or gold and silver, he will grant the double to my enemy." So out of jealousy he said to the king: "I ask the following of you. Gouge out one of my eyes, so that you gouge out my enemy's two eyes."

Tenth, again, envy is worse than anger, because many people return to the straight path because of anger; they abandon wickedness and embrace goodness; whereas the envious remains as is. Neither the envious can be straightened, nor the subject of his envy; as has been demonstrated, [envy] is evil in every which way, and it is harmful to the soul, the body, and properties, as well as to the own comfort of the envious. And envy is so evil as vice, that when [the envious] sees, hears, or thinks that the subject of his envy is a person of good fame, his mind pricks him painfully, his soul languishes and melts, and his heart grieves and suffers; wherefore, he is called envious, because he harms himself and his soul first, and then harbors spite and envy against others.

What are, though, the envy, the spite, and the evil eye? We say that they signify one ill nature but have different characteristics. A man of evil eye looks on with an evil eye in his mind after seeing or hearing something good. The envious is a person whose vice moves to his soul because of the envious action; it is as if a person looks on with an evil eye at the beginning [of an envious action] and envy is the fulfillment. Spite is the residue of the envy. Just as rancor and grudge are the residues of anger, spite is the residue of envy. Like a flood that leaves behind a thin body of water, envy and anger, which are a flood of vices, leave behind spite, rancor, and grudge as a residue when they cease, while they remain as anger and envy when they are at work. It is also known that the evil eye occurred after the dancers sang that Saul had slain his thousands and David his ten thousands. Saul was pained and looked on with an evil eye. The envy occurred when [Saul] moved many times and wanted to kill David. And the spite occurred when [Saul] chased David, propelled with the spite of the envy. If a man wants to spend the time of his life quietly, he should stay away from the vice of envy and be content with little. As the sage Solomon instructs: "Better is a handful with quietness, than two handfuls with toil and waywardness of spirit" (Eccl 4:6).

The good instruction is this: [The sage] says it is better to have a handful. It is better for man to have a few possessions and a little sway without envy, without depriving, and without clamor, than [to have] great authority [associated] with envy, clamor, and many possessions by ravishing and depriving, because the needs of the body—food and clothing—are inconsiderable possessions and their excess adds nothing but pain and temptation. The laity for this reason say that [so and so] grew rich;[61] that is, his pain and suffering multiplied and grew proportionally with his wealth. Therefore, the Prophet says: "If wealth should flow in, set not your heart upon it" (Ps 62:10), while the Apostle instructs: "Do not want to be rich, so that you may not fall into temptation and traps" (cf. 1 Tim 6:9). Wealth poses many and diverse traps for people. Thereby, Solomon instructs: "Better is a handful with quietness" (Eccl 4:6). The handful suggests having moderate and necessary wants; that should make people more content than the excessive [wants associated] with envy and bitterness, which lead to evil and deprive [a person] of moderation.

See from the examples of those who preceded us how Judas favored the abundance of necessities to apprenticing to Christ. He filled two handfuls with his love for silver, betrayed Christ, and lost everything he had—he died by suffocation, lost the silver, and remained under curses and suffering, all because of avarice and glory. Likewise, Gehezi lived a moderate life with the Prophet Elisha, but when he turned avaricious and took the silver from Naaman, he and his descendants were destined to leprosy, generation after generation. Likewise, Ahab had a rich kingdom, but when he envied Naboth's vineyard and took it away from him, his kingdom was destroyed, his seventy children were put to the sword, and his memory was cut off from this world. Brethren, think about these and implement the instructions of the wise man; flee from the vice of envy and avarice; [and] be content with what we have at hand, so that we may enjoy quietly our few possessions.

Do not envy the wealth of other people!

---

[61] A pun by Tat'ewac'i, who treated the past tense of the verb *became wealthy* (*mecac'aw* [մեծացաւ]) as a complex word made up of two root words: *big* and *pain* (respectively, *mec* [մեծ] and *c'aw* [ցաւ]).

Do not look on other people's glory with evil eye!

Do not slander other people's honor!

Do not be jealous about other people's praise!

Do not hate your brothers because of evil envy; rather, love them with your heart! "For love is from God [. . .] and whoever loves his brother loves God" (cf. 1 Jn 4:7, 21); whereas envy and hatred are from Satan "and all who hate a brother are murderer, and murderers do not have life abiding in them" (cf. 1 Jn 3:15). Wherefore the Prophet instructs: "Do not envy evildoers, nor envy the workers of inequity, for they shall soon wither as the green herb" (Ps 37:1–2), and they shall become matches for the eternal fire. May our Savior God, Christ, save us and all of those who worship His name from this and from eternal fire and the bitter suffering of the sinners, and glory to Him forever, amen.

CHAPTER LXIII

Homily of the same on avarice, according to the verse: "Hell and destruction are never full; so the eyes of man are never satisfied"
(Prov 27:20).

There are five senses assembled in our body—sight, hearing, smell, taste, and touch, because all perceptible things are of five kinds: color, which the eye sees; sound, which the ear hears; smell, which the nostrils take in; taste, which the mouth tastes; and matter, which the hand touches. Since there are no perceptible things in this world outside these five things, we recognize them through five senses. There are also four elements in this world, which are the basis of all matter—fire, water, air, and earth. We have four senses that enable us to recognize their corresponding elements: we see the fire and light with the eyes, we perceive the air and the sound with the ear, we savor the taste and the water with the mouth, and we recognize the heavy and light with the hand. The mixture of a thin water and thick air makes up the smell that we receive with the nose. Of these five senses, the eye and the ear are never satiated, as Solomon says: "The eye is not satisfied with seeing, nor the ear filled with hearing" (Eccl 1:8). The reason is this. Other senses are made of dense matter and they sense things that are dense matter; therefore, they are satiated and cease to smell, taste, and touch. However, the eye and the ear see and hear things that are thin; they see and hear like a ghost and, therefore, are never satiated. The more they see and hear, the more they want [to see and hear].

These are similar to and a pattern of the avaricious. As the eye and the ear find pleasure in seeing and hearing, so also the avaricious finds his joy and pleasure in the color and sound of possessions. And as the eye and the ear are not satiated with what they see and hear, so also the avaricious are not satiated by seeing possessions and hearing [about them]; the more they see and hear the count of their wealth and possessions, the more they feel a want and thirst. For this reason, Solomon the Wise compares this inclination for want with hell: "Hell and destruction are never full; so the eyes of man are never satisfied" (Prov 27:20). The hell is a grave and corruption, and death is never satisfied, because death corrupts every body and the grave bears it; likewise, the eye and the mind of the avaricious never become full, neither with gold and silver, nor with stored possessions. Avarice is equivocal, because there are those who are avaricious by their eye and in their heart, as David says: "He that is proud in look and insatiable in heart, with him I have not eaten" (Ps 101:5), and there are those who are avaricious with their mouth and body, and are called glutton. Both are mortal and capital sins, but they have differences. First, the vice of avarice is related to the soul; gluttony is related to the body. Second, gluttony is related to only food and drinks, whereas avarice is associated with external possessions. Third, gluttony is associated with young people, whereas avarice is associated with older people. Fourth, gluttonous are those who love their body, whereas avarice and the love of possessions happen to the devout. Fifth, those who are avaricious with the body and the gullet are satiated and satisfied with little, but the avaricious in their heart are not satiated; they are always hungry and insatiate. This is how the insatiate with the mouth is different from the insatiate with the heart—the avaricious with the heart is the insatiate that never gets full.

Avarice is seen through three things. First, through selling—[the avaricious] man deprives his neighbor. Second, through delimitation and distribution of possessions—[the avaricious] seeks the greater portion. Third, through homage—[the avaricious] wants to be revered more. But when the avaricious sees that he was deprived during the sale, or his neighbor received a greater share during distribution or homage, he becomes troubled and suffers, fights and stirs up strife, as the proverb says: "The greedy person stirs up strife, but whoever trusts in the Lord will be protected by him" (cf. Prov 28:25); that is, he who trusts God does not stir strife and does not keep [his neighbor's] possessions; rather, he returns them to him and thinks about the temporality of possessions—that [possessions] have the size of a grave and that to be deprived is better than to deprive. First, a deprived person loses his body, but the depriver loses his soul. Also, the depriver has God as avenger, whereas the deprived has God as helper; [therefore] he prefers peace with love over possessions.

Avarice has three degrees. The first [degree] is the mental need and the presence of eyes full of vanity. The second [degree is] the avaricious habit itself, which strives to hoard. The third [degree] is the ravishing—gathering everything from everywhere indiscriminately. These are differentiated as follows. Need indicates lack (the hungriness of the body, for example); avarice is the intention of filling what is lacking (eating, for example); and ravishing is the implementation (depriving others and gathering). Again, need is the beginning of the vice, avarice is the medial [step] proceeding toward the vice, and ravishing is the fulfillment of the vice.

Avarice stems from two things: the want for possessions because of poverty, and the want by habit because of mental vanity and need. We shall discuss these two types of avarice hereinafter.

First, there are those who are poor and avaricious, like those who are poor accidentally—impoverished by the parents or deprivers, yet habitually avaricious. Therefore, those who work always, solicit others, and beg incessantly, or deprive, ravish, and steal, although they are physically poor, they have ignoble behavior and serve avarice with their desire. The Apostle refers to them, saying: "Poor men that are not innocent." These [people] are evil and bad for many reasons. First, they always suffer physically and work for temporal earnings. Second, their mind is always busy—whom to solicit from, whom to deprive, and whom to steal from? Third, when they do not find [what they seek], they grieve, mourn, and despair. Fourth, they are captives of poverty and their minds serve the possessions. Fifth, a slave always desires wealth. Every wealth is submissive to matter, for it is temporal, and avarice is [servile] more so, because [the poor] are poor in relation to possessions and grow wealthy by their desire only. Sixth, [the poor] are irrational and mindless in poverty; they lack the will and intellect. Seventh, they are rebellious, slanderous, and envious toward others. Eighth, they always think and want to exercise authority over others, wear fine clothes, gather possessions, find pleasure in food, and so on. Ninth, they do not believe him who said: "If wealth should flow in, set not your heart upon it" (Ps 62:10), nor do they believe the Apostle, who says: "Do not want to be rich, so that you may not fall in harmful traps" (cf. 1 Tim 6:9–10). The trap is this: people of authority set taxes, robbers rob and thieves steal [the possessions], and [the wealthy person] is either killed or tortured. He dies not for the sake of God, but for the sake of possessions. Tenth, those who love possessions more than they love Christ, [and are] "Lovers of silver more than lovers of God" (cf. 2 Tim 3:4), are the kinds of the poor that harbor wicked intentions; corporeally they lack possessions, and mentally they are avaricious and slave.

The second [kind of] avaricious people are wealthy in relation to possessions, but are mentally vain, narrow-hearted, and greedy. First, they resemble the people with dropsy who always drink and their thirst is never quenched—the greedy are never satisfied by accumulating. Second, they resemble a hollow container that is never full—the avaricious are hollow habitually and are never satiated. Third, they resemble the fire that catches all kinds of matter and is never satiated—the avaricious habitually are insatiable. Fourth, they resemble an empty land, which swallows the entire water and yet does not produce plants—although the avaricious receive many possessions, they bury and cover them in darkness. Fifth, they resemble an insatiable hungry wolf, as the proverb says: "A hungry lion and a thirsty wolf" (cf. Prov 28:15)— the avaricious always ravish like a wolf and treat their inferiors like a lion. Sixth, they are mindless, for they incessantly suffer not because of that which is necessary, but because of that which exceeds. Seventh, they are idolaters, as the Apostle says: "Greed which is idolatry" (Col 3:5). And this is true, because they abandon the worship of God and the prayers, and serve the possessions night and day. Eighth, they have forgotten the day of death and judgment and are preoccupied with gains, like the rich man whose land produced abundantly and he said, "I built large barns." [God] told him: "You fool! This very night your life is being demanded of you. And the things you have prepared, whose will they be?" (Lk 12:20). Ninth, the avaricious are mindless—they labor, gather, and keep for others, so that others may scatter [their riches], as Ecclesiastes says: "There is an evil which I have seen under the sun; God has given man possessions and wealth, yet did not give him power to eat thereof" (cf. Eccl 6:1). As the Prophet says: "They shall leave their wealth to strangers" (Ps 49:10), for "he lays up treasures, and knows not for whom he shall gather them" (Ps 39:6). People of this caliber are pitiable, because they lose their body and do not find their soul; it is evident, then, that the avaricious [person is avaricious] neither for the body nor for the soul. Tenth, the avaricious seek profit from everybody, from evil and good indiscriminately, from money, working, selling, by lying, by oppressing, and so on. Piling through profits is their only concept and love. Although they experience despise, suffering, and hunger, they feel nothing because of the vice of avarice. Therefore, the Apostle instructs: "Keep your lives free from the love of money, and be content with what you have" (Heb 13:5), because our nature is satisfied with moderation. But what is moderation? The Apostle says: "We have food and clothing; we will be content with these" (1 Tim 6:8). Anything more than this is from the demon.

There are two reasons for every person's avariciousness. First, God created the natural man, Adam, with glory and dominion, and put him in the garden of delight as lord and king over everything, for the Scripture says: "You have put all things under his feet [to obey him]; sheep and cattle and everything" (cf. Ps 8:6–7). After his transgression, [Adam] was expelled from the glorious Paradise and was deprived of wealth. The wealthy turned poor, the lord turned servant to sins, and the ruler [was] "compared to senseless creatures and beasts," according to David (cf. Ps 49:20). Now, finding ourselves in this poverty, we do not tolerate it; rather, recalling the natural richness, we become avaricious, [and] we deprive, steal, disobey our lords, and rebel against each other. Since naturally we were born [rich] like this and we were deprived of it because of transgressions, we strive to return to the same position by means of transgressions and oppression, and thus avarice occurs.

Second, avarice occurs because of natural want for necessities, as we need food, drinks, clothing, houses, and similar things, as [Solomon] the Wise says: "God has given to human beings an evil business to be busy with" (Eccl 1:13). Here, business relates to the want for needs. This is not evil. On the contrary, it is good for six reasons. First, God created us needy, so that there may be a reason for us to be humble. Otherwise, we would be like the first father [Adam], who because of not being needy for food, clothes, or other things in the garden of delight, turned arrogant and was destroyed. The Prophet says that God created us needy so that we may stay humble: "Your humility is inside you"; that is, the want that is within us. Second, God created us needy so that we may always work for the necessities: "by the sweat shall you eat bread," as God commanded (Gen 3:19); we do not stay idle without work, so that we may not always commit sins because of idleness—the rulers and despots never work and [therefore] they are occupied with sins. Third, [God] created us needy altogether, with want and weak soul and body, so that we may see the neediness of our soul and body, love God, and ask Him to fill us with bounties. Fourth, [God] created us needy, so that we may satisfy our needs by helping each other and [therefore] love each other and be filled with fraternal love. We need each other now with the soul and the body; we learn from one and teach to others; we buy and sell; we construct, plant, and so on; and yet we hate each other. How much more would we have hated each other had we not needed each other? Fifth, we need food and clothing. Since we tend to animals, we satisfy our needs through them, be it food, clothing, plowing, carrying loads, and so on. Sixth, [God] created us needy and naked of natural clothing, means of protection, food, and abodes, so that He may give us the reason and wisdom to create by using our skills and find our necessities, whether clothing, means of protection, food, abodes, or anything else. Now, these are not evil. These are good and a cause for goodness, given to us by the Creator. However, by following Satan's deceit and our free will, we turn the good into evil, and thus we make avarice a cause for wickedness, because when we occupy ourselves with necessary wants and take care of our food, clothing, and other things, the excessive and limitless [want] suddenly and covertly penetrates us and becomes evil in us: by taking care above the limit we deprive each other of earnings, lands, and water. This becomes oppression. And when we fail [to do so], we encounter envy, enmity, war, and killing; thus the want leads us to avarice, and many evil things result from avarice and destroy us.

Examine the first holy fathers and the hermits who received moderate food, clothing, and abodes, and were pleased with them. But those who mixed immoderation to it, their occupation turned into wickedness.

The sinful works are different from righteous works in three ways—first, by due limits; second, by time; third, by permission. First, every moderate thing which is necessary for a need is good and righteous, like the modest food and drink, modest marriage, and so on. Excessive food is avarice and excessive drink is intoxication, and frequent lasciviousness becomes fornication. Second, time makes something sinful and another righteous—for example, meat, wine, and other food are good during flesh days, but today, during Lent, they are evil. Likewise, marriage is good and lawful during allowed periods, but during prohibited periods, such as during Lent and on Sundays, it is fornication and adultery. Third, permission makes something sinful and another righteous, because when something takes place with permission and God's will, the evil becomes good, like Hosea's fornication—it was not sin, because it was [committed] with God's permission, and it was not sin when Elijah killed eight hundred fifty prophets with God's permission. Similarly, the Prophet Samuel killed King Agag of the Amalekites, and Phinehas killed Zambri and Cozbi, upon which God reconciled and lifted death from Israel, as David says: "He made atonement and stopped death, and that was counted to him as righteousness" (cf. Ps 106:30–31). Saul's offering, however, because it was offered without permission, was reckoned as sin and his kingdom was destroyed. The incense that King Uzziah offered in the temple was not allowed by God; therefore, he became a leper and was deposed. Similarly, every work accomplished by God's permission and the canons of the primates is good and righteous, and whatever is [accomplished] without [God's] permission is evil. In this instance, too, if something is moderate and allowed, it is good and necessary, and whatever is disallowed and excessive, is avarice and evil.

Avarice causes much evil. First, as the Apostle says: "Greed which is idolatry" (Col 3:5). This is a work befitting the idolaters who prevented the offerings to true God and presented them to idols which were images made of gold and silver. Likewise, avarice prevents worshipping God and kneeling and praying [before Him], and reserves these [pious actions] to gold and silver possessions, because driven by the vice of avarice, [the avaricious person] abandons the morning worship and goes after material earnings. Abandoning the Eucharist, [the avaricious person] goes after selling, and abandoning the evening prayer, he goes after the herd of cattle and piling of other possessions. Behold! He has become an idolater by his work.

Second, as has been said, avarice causes much evil, for because of avarice we deprive and ravish, lie, commit perjury, envy, become enemy through blasphemy, curse, battle, stir strife, strike and kill, and all of these evil things and turbulences—plunder, captivity, destruction of land—happen because of the avarice of tyrants.

Third, Adam the man fell from the Paradise of life because of avarice and glory, for he was not satisfied by all of the [other] fruits of the garden of delight. Avariciously he wanted to also eat the other one, and the woman [Eve] coveted God's glory, striving to rule over the man and beget her divine child, and ate the fruit before [Adam]. Because of avarice they were dropped from their glory, stripped naked of the light, fell unto the painful and thorn-bearing earth, and were captured by death and curse, until they entered the grave physically and hell spiritually. Thus, avarice, in all its forms, condemns people physically and spiritually.

Fourth, Cain killed Abel because he coveted glory, since God did not accept his offering, or, as is said, [Cain] killed Abel because of the wife and deprived the wife, or because of [pure] avarice, so that he might be the son and heir of his father, Adam, and rule over the entire land. See what his compensation was from God: instead of the offering and blessing, he received a curse from God; and instead of ruling over the land, he received the trembling and shaking, and he ran away from people wandering with the beasts; and instead of [having] a wife and children, his children and grandchildren were erased from the earth, destroyed by the flood. Avarice is an evil of such magnitude.

Fifth, the flood, which wiped all people and animals from the earth, came because of avarice and gluttony, in relation to which the Lord commands: "They were eating and drinking" (Mt 24:38). They were eating meat and drinking wine, and were committing fornication without permission. God set for them one hundred twenty years to turn, but when they did not turn and, instead, hastened to commit more evil, God abridged the twenty years, hastily brought upon the flood, and destroyed them all. Noah was the only one to survive in the ark, along with the seeds of the animals that he took with him, because they were clean of the vice of avarice and fornication. Thus, every avaricious and wicked person will be punished either physically here or spiritually in the hereafter.

Sixth, when Joshua, son of Nun, cursed Jericho so that no one could take from its properties and curse, yet Achan,[62] son of Carmi, coveted, despised the curse, stole from the properties, did not repent for abandoning the properties, and when the stolen items, along with him, his wife, his children, and possessions were uncovered, they were taken upon Joshua's order, stoned to death, and a heap of stones was raised over him. Indeed, he was stoned because of the curse, and the heap of stones was raised over him because of his avarice, to satisfy and fill his avarice with the heap. As the folk proverbs say, only a handful of earth satiates the avaricious, when his eyes are covered in the grave. But why did people stone [Achan's] wife and children? This [was done] rightfully, because they knew about the avarice and hid the stolen items and did not admit [having them]; therefore, they were punished along with Achan. The possessions and the animals were stoned for two reasons. First, so that people might see how much he possessed and [realize] that he stole because of avarice and not because of poverty, and second, because when he entered his house, he spoiled everything there because of the curse and the deprivation [he had caused]; therefore, his spoiled possessions were destroyed with him. Thus, the deprivations and ravishing inflicted upon others by the avaricious destroy the house and the landlord, either here physically or in the hereafter spiritually.

Seventh, God commanded King Saul to go to Amalek to avenge for the people of God who were met with war when they left Egypt, and He told him to put everybody through the sword and to kill their king, Agag, but to take nothing from his possessions, the booty, and his slaves. Saul set off, defeated them, and took everybody as captive and everything as booty because of his avarice, and he brought the king [Agag] alive in chains. The Prophet Samuel went to Saul to tell him: "Why did you dishonor God's command because of your avarice? God will take away your kingdom and give it to your better neighbor who executes God's will." Likewise, Ahab and Jezebel took away the vineyard of Naboth the righteous and killed him because of avarice, wherefore God told them through Elisha that in exchange for ravishing the vineyard of the righteous and killing him, dogs would devour their bodies, pigs would wash in their blood, and their seventy children would be put through the sword, which happened in the hand of Joshua, who ruled as a king. He killed Jezebel and all of her seventy children. This is the punishment of the avaricious and ravishers of other people's properties.

Eighth, when Naaman the leprous came from Damascus to the Prophet

---

[62] *Akar* both in the Armenian Bible and in Tat'ewac'i's manuscript.

Elisha, immersed himself in the Jordan, and was cleansed of his leprosy, he turned to the Prophet and said: "Take whatever you want from the piles of the gold and silver that I brought to you, for you have cured me." The Prophet took nothing from him, not even a mite. He said: "The name of the Lord cured you freely; I will receive nothing from you." Later, Gehazi, the servant of Elisha, avariciously went after Naaman and took a talent and changes of clothing. The servants [of Naaman] brought him to the gate of the Prophet. [Gehazi] deceitfully dismissed them. [The Prophet] asked him: "Where did you come from, Gehazi?" He answered and said: "From nowhere." [The Prophet] asked to see if [Gehazi] would repent, but when he did not repent, [Elisha said]: "Did I not go with you in spirit when you went to Naaman, deceived him, and took the money and brought it here? Therefore, his leprosy shall cling to you and your descendants forever." And Gehezi became leprous and leprosy was not cleansed from his descendants.

Ninth, in the New [Testament], when Ananaias and Sapphira kept back some of the proceeds of the sale, even though they did not steal from others, but rather they kept it from the common poor because of their avariciousness, they provoked the anger of the Apostle Peter, who punished them and they died, both of them. He punished them physically, so that they might not be punished spiritually. Thus, there is punishment through God's judgment for all avaricious people, both physically and spiritually.

Tenth, this is also evident from Judas, who betrayed the Savior because of avarice and caused His crucifixion. And see his great harm. Because he was a disciple, he betrayed his teacher and not a stranger. Second, he had seen Christ's miracles and had heard the preaching of the Gospel. Third, since he was one of the twelve chosen, he was not the last [in position] or an abject person. Fourth, he owned and kept the money chest, so he was not needy or poor. Fifth, he was warned many times, "Woe to anyone by whom occasions for stumbling come; the Son of Man goes [. . .], it would have been better for that one to have not been born" (cf. Lk 17:1, Mt 26:24), and that "One of you will betray me" (Mt 26:21), and "Is it with a kiss that you are betraying the Son of Man" (Lk 22:48). Nevertheless, the love of money blinded him. Sixth, since he betrayed the innocent who was not guilty to die—[guilty] neither toward him, nor toward others. Thus, for so many reasons, Judas's sin is the heaviest and unforgivable, and it was caused by avarice—he easily sold for thirty pieces of silver the innocent, the benefactor, the teacher, and the Creator of heaven and earth. Also, the sins of Judas and Peter were equal with regard to stumbling as they denied Him. However, Judas denied him voluntarily and avariciously, so he lost his hope in the Savior and went and hanged himself. Behold! Excessive avarice led him to despair, and despair led him to death by hanging; he perished physically and spiritually. Peter, on the other hand, denied [Christ] unwillingly and by accident, but he had a firm hope in the Lord. He wept bitterly and repented, and thus he found salvation spiritually and physically.

Judas suffocated rightfully—he who was suffocated with the rope of avarice, suffocated with the rope of death. He did not benefit from the money, living or dead. Moreover, he was strangled so that his death might not be similar to the death of everybody else on earth; rather, he suffered with the devils hanging in the air. His corrupt brain did not come out of his mouth, because his mouth, which kissed Christ, did not corrupt; rather, it went down to his corrupt heart where he contemplated avarice and planned to betray Christ. For this reason, both his brain and heart were corrupted together, his bowels gushed out to the ground and filled the air with malodor, to the extent that his crucifiers who were pleased with his betraying words [earlier were] disgusted and could not stand the odor. Thus, avarice is bitter and harsh to this extent, and it causes destruction to the soul and the body, as was somewhat seen through the Holy Scriptures.

May the benevolent and patient God with His unique love forgive your transgressions, take out of you the heart made of stone and give you a corporeal heart, renew in you the straight soul, cover the eyes of your heart against the avariciousness of worldly things, [and] open and enlighten [them] for the love of the heavenly life and the riches there. And with the holy blessed and chief Apostle Peter, may He give you repentance and penitence for the committed sins, and after this life, on the great day of resurrection, may He make you worthy of His sight, incomprehensible compassion, and the kingdom of heaven, to whom glory, honor, and power with His Father and the Holy Spirit forever, amen.

CHAPTER LXIV

Homily of the same on the love of money, according to the verse of Ecclesiastes: "The lover of money will not be satisfied with money; and he who loves abundant gain, this, too, is vanity" (Eccl 5:9).

God the Creator created man's soul tripartite, says Plato the philosopher—reason, passion, and desire. Reason is given to us in order to know God the beneficent and Creator. Passion [is given] so that we may become angry against evil and oppose it. Desire [is given] so that we may desire, love, and perform everything that is good. In these desirable things there are those that we take, desire, and are satisfied—such as the food and drink for the body, for we are satiated by the little necessities that we take; and there are things when there is no satiation—such as things that we see by the eyes and hear by the ears and remain insatiate, as the sage says elsewhere: "Neither shall the eye be satisfied with seeing, neither shall the ear be filled with hearing" (Eccl 1:8). Such is the matter with the love of money, so he [the sage] says: "The lover of money will not be satisfied with money" (Eccl 5:9). The reason is this: all kinds of food and drinks enter the body and make it saturated and heavy; therefore, we become full. The sight of money, however, feeds the eye externally, brings the color [of silver and gold] to the mind, diverts it, and it becomes insatiate, because the mind of man is created insatiable by God, so that he may always seek heavenly things and remain unsatisfied. On the other hand, God created the body as satiable, so that body's want may be satiated and stopped by a few things. Now, see the ill of the love of money in two modalities. First, it redirects the mind and the soul from the insatiable love of heavenly things to the love of worldly and earthly money. Second, it turns the body, which is satiable with moderate necessities, insatiable with regard to the love of money, as [the sage] says: "The lover of money will not be satisfied" (Eccl 5:9).

Know also this. Silver, gold, and their like are not necessities established by the Creator as beneficial to the body, unlike food, drink, clothing, sleep, and wakefulness. These [the latter] are necessary needs for man, but not the silver and gold, which are alien to the needs of our nature, because they are not food, drink, covers for nudity, or anything else. Nevertheless, people discovered them on account of their covetousness and pleasure as means for personal luxury, not as necessary needs. When the necessary needs are reduced, gold and silver become repulsive and worthless, whereas when the necessary needs are satisfied, [gold and silver] become desirable as luxurious adornments. The necessary need is such that its presence makes man live and its absence makes man die; such as fire, water, and so on. A luxurious item is such that its presence does not make man live and its absence does not make man die; such as silver, gold, jewels, pearls, and so on, because these are unnecessary for man's life, and are vain and useless. Therefore, [the sage] says: "The lover of money will not be satisfied with money; and he who loves abundant gain, this, too, is vanity" (Eccl 5:9).

The Apostle, on the other hand, says: "Greed, which is idolatry" (Col 3:5). Idolatry occurs in two modalities: first, when man worships idols; second, when man gathers silver and gold. These two are the same idolatry in ten ways.

First, according to substance—the Prophet says: "The idols of heathens are silver and gold" (Ps 113:4).

Second, according to love—as they [the idolaters] loved the idols, this [money lover loves] silver and gold: "Where your treasure is, there your heart will be also" (Mt 6:21), says [the Lord].

Third, according to worship—as that [idolater] abandons God, worships idols, and prostrates before them, likewise this [money lover] abandons and impedes God's worship and prayers for the sake of money.

Fifth, according to gathering—they gathered idols in abundance, and this [gathers] money in abundance and is not satisfied.

Sixth, according to keeping—they kept idols so that they may not perish, and these [money lovers keep] possessions.

Seventh, according to grief—they grieved by losing idols, and this [money lover] grieves when the possessions are diminished.

Eighth, both are useless. The idols [are useless] because: "They have eyes, but they do not see, nor do they speak or help" (cf. Ps 115:5). Likewise, money is not food, drink, clothing, or abode, and it does not save man from evil; hence: "Riches do not profit in the day of wrath, but righteousness delivers from death" (Prov 11:4).

Ninth, both are fruitless—money does not flower and does not bear fruits, nor does it give birth like the earth, the animals, and the trees and shrubs. Moreover, when he [the money lover] lends the money for profit, he harms his soul, and if he keeps it, his heart turns black and rusty, like a silver plate.

Tenth, according to occupation—the idolaters occupied themselves in adultery, drunkenness, and fornication. The occupation of [lovers of] money does the same and is equally bitter, because man commits all kinds of sins with money and thereafter suffers in hell along with the idolaters.

A wise man witnesses that the love of money and abundant gain are vanity, unreal, and nothingness. And he truly says that for many reasons the love of money is vain and futile.

First, the love of money does not comfort our body, for it is neither food nor drink nor clothing per se. Although we find food, drink, and other things sold with money, this is due to the skills and entrepreneurship of man, but in itself, it does not comfort man's body, as has been said.

Second, [the love of money] estranges man from the love of God, as the Lord says: "No one can serve two masters" (Mt 6:24), that is, [serve] God and money, because if a person loves one, he despises the other.

Third, a money lover deprives all of his brethren: first, while hoarding, he deprives, ravishes, steals, and concentrates; then, he keeps and deprives the brethren and neighbors and does not give to the poor and needy.

Fourth, this is the meaning of the verse that says: "The lover of money will not be satisfied with money" (Eccl 5:9): [the money lover] languishes with his ever-insatiable desire and never is satisfied, as the Apostle says: "You lust something and do not receive it, that you may consume it upon your lust" (cf. Jas 4:2–3). Because the conduct of a money lover is hollow and poor; the more he gathers, the more he needs, for the money lover is like a person stricken with dropsy—the more he drinks, the thirstier he becomes.

Fifth, the mind of the money lover is always tied to the earth and to money; he cannot depart them, nor can he rise unto heaven, as the Lord commands: "Where your treasure is, there your heart will be also" (Mt 6:21), because the mind is occupied with counting and with the increase and decrease of the money.

Sixth, the heart of a money lover is as blackened and rusted as silver, for when you bind the silver with a place, it blackens the plate and rusts. Likewise, the heart of man blackens and rusts when it is associated always with the love of money, as Solomon says: "Money lovers spend all their days in darkness and in grief, in vexation and sickness" (cf. Eccl 5:16). Darkness relates to the reality that the care for money holds the mind always in darkness; it is not illuminated by the divine word, as the Lord commands: "The lure of wealth chokes the word" (Mt 13:22). [The money lover] mourns when his desire is not fulfilled; his face reflects grief and sadness, and he spitefully pushes the servants and husbandmen to work, so that they may generate money everywhere, and when they collect less, he pours his anger and wrath on them, and he becomes sick and his face pouts due to excessive grief and anger. For this reason, the face of the money lover is pale and blackish, and through it, wise people would recognize that he has collected money.

Seventh, the money lover cannot find sweet sleep, as Solomon says: "A man satiated with wealth, there is none that suffers him to sleep, but the sleep of the servant is sweet" (cf. Eccl 5:11). That is, a poor man who does not have the pain of the love of money delightfully cares for needs that are necessary, not excessive, and whether he eats little or much, he satiates the abdomen's hunger and sleeps delightfully and carelessly. A wealthy person, on the other hand, because of various concerns and his servitude to the love of possessions, cannot sleep for the fear of thieves and robbers. Whether he is awake or asleep, he fastens the doors, keeps arms in his hand and fastens them to his waist, the servants surround him, and then [only] he falls asleep, so that the enemies may not come to kill him and take over his possessions, as Judith did to Holofernes. At night, she beheaded him and went out crossing through [the Assyrians' camp], and during the [following] day, [the Israelites] took all of the possessions [of Holofernes] as spoil. This happens to many people.

Eighth, money and wealth cause evil and death to those who receive them, and this happens to many people. When a man commits evil by wealth and loses his soul, God allows for his possessions to be ravished by rulers, robbers, or thieves, so that he may be deprived of his possessions and find his soul; nevertheless, [the money lover] does not think about God and the spiritual sphere; rather, he tries to gather more and grow richer, as Solomon says: "There is evil that I have seen under the sun: wealth kept for its owner to his hurt, and that wealth perishes by evil travail" (Eccl 5:12–13). The evil travail is this: he cares to become wealthy again by borrowing and profiting, buying and selling, thus falling into the former evil, because possessions and money, all of them, are perishable items. Either [the wealth] alone perishes and slips away from a person, or he who receives it perishes with it. The Lord instructs us about the perishability of possessions: "Do not store up for yourselves treasures on earth where moth corrupts and thieves break in and steal" (cf. Mt 6:19).

That [wealth] causes destruction to its receiver is evident from Sennacherib, whose sons revolted against him for the sake of ravishing the kingdom. They killed their father, but when they failed to govern, Adrammelech and Sharezer fled to Armenia. Likewise, for the sake of ravishing riches, Cyrus, the king of Persia, killed Belteshazzar, the king of Babylon, in accordance with Daniel's interpretation. There are many more men like these whose possessions and wealth cause them harm and destruction.

Ninth, when death occurs and a man dies, he leaves his wealth to strangers because of disgrace and curses, as David says: "When he shall see wise men dying, the fool and the senseless one shall perish together; and they shall leave their wealth to strangers" (Ps 49:10). We do not know whether these strangers are good or evil, beloved or enemy, worthy or unworthy. Therefore, David says: "He is troubled in vain: he lays up treasures, and knows not for whom he shall gather them" (Ps 38:7).

Tenth, money and other possessions do not remain to us, nor do they deliver us from the trap of death. We do not take them with us when we die, and the glory and riches of the world do not stay with us, because we cannot bequeath our possessions to our sons. The sons of many wealthy people and kings have become poor and enslaved; they were unable to inherit their patrimony. Saul's [grand]son, Mephibosheth the Lame, did not inherit the kingdom of his father; rather, he became a slave and a servant in the house of David. Also, [riches] do not deliver us from the trap of death, for if riches had the ability to deliver, the wealthy would not die. Therefore, the sage says: "Riches do not profit in the day of wrath, [etc.]" (Prov 11:4). Moreover, they [the riches] do not go with us to the grave, for the Apostle says: "We brought nothing into the world, so that we can take nothing out of it" (1 Tim 6:7). As we came out of our mother's womb naked, we shall return to the mother-grave naked, for he who chases the wind cannot catch the wind. Also, he [the wealthy person] cannot take his possessions with him: a basket pulled out of the water comes out vacuous and empty; likewise, people come out of this life empty of possessions and void, leaving behind all of the riches, the glories, the buildings, the lands, the properties, the treasures, the servants and maidservants, as David says: "He shall take nothing when he dies; neither shall his glory descend with him" (Ps 49:17). As Solomon says, the ill of wickedness is that we toil and labor constantly for that which becomes estranged from us when we die. And see, brethren, other wickedness and pitiful acts: possessions do not come with us; rather, the judgment of possessions, and the conscience and sins come with us in the other life and torment us. For example, the corpse of a dead animal or its foul-smelling excrement or whatever else it may discharge emits the bad odor to us. Similarly, the abominable possessions of the world remain here and the judgment comes with us, as happened to the rich man who was dying for a drop of water from excessive thirst, yet Abraham the merciful did not find him worthy. The same will happen to everybody for the following reason. Physical possessions remain with the body, whereas the sins committed, which are incorporeal, go there [to the hereafter] with the incorporeal soul and torment the soul and the body, as one of the saints phrases: "Woe to the wealthy, for the possessions and wealth will leave them, and the eternal fire will receive them."

This, however, does not happen to every wealthy person; only to the evil ones who receive wealth, employ it for the body, and lose their soul. In the case of pious people, on the other hand, along with wealth, God gives them grace by which they know how to find the soul and the body, as Solomon says: "God gave man wealth and enabled him to eat of it, and to receive his lot from his toil—this is the gift of God" (cf. Eccl 5:18). What we hear from the Scriptures is that the wealth and possessions of a good man are from God, as Satan said to God with regard to Job: "You have fortified him internally and externally" (cf. Job 1:10). The internal refers to the body's health, and the external [refers] to the possessions and wealth. As Anna says: "The Lord makes poor and makes rich" (1 Kings 2:7).

It is evident that the wealth of pious people is from God. Although the wealth of the wicked also is from God—whether it happens by accident, or succeeds through evil, or the person himself earns and receives it; these, too, are from God, but through His allowance as opposed to the wealth of the good people, which is through God's willing. Now, as God gives possessions to good people, likewise He enables them to take a portion [from the possessions] for the body and give a portion to the soul. The portion of the body is intended for keeping the body without a need to necessities, and the soul's portion is intended for giving to the poor, keeping the soul without needs, and storing up in the heavens, as our Lord commanded: "Store up for yourselves treasures in heaven" (Mt 6:20); also: "Make to yourselves friends of the mammon of unrighteousness" (Lk 16:9). A man of this caliber has received a big gift from God, is glad with his earnings, and does not care whether his wealth is destroyed or maintained, because he has stored his share in heaven. He does not care whether he will die early or late, because he is glad with his trust in eternal life, as David says: "Let all that trust in you be glad in you; they shall exult forever, [etc.]" (Ps 5:11). And Paul says: "To me, living is Christ and dying is gain" (Phil 1:21).

Nevertheless, there are poor and pitiable people on the face of [the] earth, as Solomon says: "There is an evil which I have seen under the sun; God gave man possessions and wealth, yet he did not give him power to eat from it, [etc.]" (cf. Eccl 6:1–2).

Solomon the Wise blames three kinds of money lovers.

First, when a man is alone—he has failed in marriage; has no children; has

448

not begotten a son or a daughter, or they are dead and there are no relatives, no siblings; has departed to another land and became estranged and has no children to store for, as the Apostle says: "Parents ought to store for their children" (2 Cor 12:14) and there are no relatives to possess [for them], and yet he constantly labors and toils relentlessly to heap, gather, and not spend, and is not satisfied, does not rest physically and does not receive an idle life spiritually, for idleness is goodness for the soul. This occupation also is evil, [Solomon] says, for if a father labors and suffers for his son, it happens because of a natural compassion that he has toward his children. [The lonely man,] however, suffers because of vain avarice, wherefore the occupation is evil.

Second, the money lovers are to be blamed because their possessions have caused death and wickedness, whether by robbers, thieves, or rulers, yet they want to regain the former wealth, which again will cause them evil and suffering.

Third, the avaricious money lovers are to be blamed as is said: "God gave him possessions and wealth, silver and gold and everything else" (cf. 2 Chr 1:12), but he bound them and hid them; he did not enjoy [them], nor did he share the divine bounties with others. [Solomon's verse also applies to] the rich man about whom the Gospel says: "His land produced abundantly; he pulled down his barns, built larger ones, and stored all the grains and bounties there" (cf. Lk 12:16–18). The wicked Nabal, like the latter, was so stingy and avaricious that he did not enjoy his possessions and failed to be generous toward David. Consequently, he died by God's strike upon David's threats, and a stranger, David, inherited deservedly his wife, Abigail, and enjoyed his possessions. Referring to such avaricious people, Solomon says: "A man begets a hundred children, and lives many years on the earth, but finds no grave" (cf. Eccl 6:3). God gives to such stingy people many children and longevity for the following reason. If he [the stingy person] did not have children, people would have said he does not give to strangers, because he keeps them for his children. Behold! He has children, yet he does not give them his possessions. And if he [the stingy person] did not live long, people would have said he was young and did not mature. Therefore, God gives him many years, yet because of his wicked will, he does not change to become generous, neither for the sake of his body nor for his family. His hand remains tight and he is only a keeper of possessions, not spender. He does not turn the possessions into his salvation, for goods are interpreted as salvation—whoever gives saves his body or his soul, but the stingy [person] does not give for the body and the soul; enemies catch him by surprise, take hold of his possessions, and put an end to his life, so he may not be worthy of his own grave. For instance, when the wicked king Ahab and [his wife] Jezebel avariciously took hold of the vineyard of Naboth, God stirred Jehu up and he came, took away the kingdom from him [Ahab], who was killed during the war—just like Elijah and Micaiah had prophesied—and left his wife, Jezebel, outside the walls where she died and the dogs devoured her body, the pigs bathed in her blood, and there was no burial for them [Ahab and Jezebel]. Similarly, Judas the money lover, who betrayed Christ, did not deserve a grave; rather, he was hanged to death, and his malodor was felt throughout the city.

Likewise, there are many lovers of money and properties whose bodies have been dropped without burial, as referenced by the Prophet Jeremiah: "Write you this man as outcast, for he has no burial"[63] (cf. Jer 22:30). Again, Solomon targets the avaricious money lover in a different proverb: "I said, an untimely birth is better than he" (Eccl 6:3). The Lord commands the same in the Gospel: "It would have been better for that one not to have been born" (Mt 26:24). It is not that not being born is better than being born; rather, when [a person] is of this caliber like Judas, whose corporeal life causes him the eternal fire, it would be better for him not to have been born. Solomon also says that a person who is unable to enjoy his possessions or let his children enjoy them, or does not give them to strangers, remains hungry at the table and thirsty in the water; it would have been better for him not to have been born or brought up; he is corrupt by birth like an untimely birth, because such a stingy person is comparable with an untimely birth in six ways.

First, it was in vain that [a mother] conceived and beget the untimely birth; likewise, it is vanity and useless for a man of that caliber to be born, to come to this world, and to depart this world, because he is good for nothing, for the world and humankind.

Second, just as the untimely birth went from darkness to darkness—moved from the darkness of the womb to the darkness of death—so too the avaricious [person] moves from the darkness of his dark life to the dark eternity; he neither comforted his body by eating and drinking, nor did he comfort his soul by good deeds; rather, he remained in darkness in his body, and darkness and obscurity prevailed in his mind.

Third, he [Solomon] says: "And his name shall be covered with darkness" (Eccl 6:4). That is, he did not deserve to have a grave; neither the untimely

---

[63] It must be noted that this is an amalgamation of two verses. The second part of the sentence is from Eccl. 6:30.

birth, nor the stingy [person have been deemed worthy of burial], because a man is remembered after his death by the grave, as David says: "They have called their lands after their own names" (Ps 49:11). These [stingy] people, however, did not enter the grave and departed the world without remembrance.

Fourth, just as the untimely birth has not seen the perceptible sun, he did not know either the conceivable sun that illuminates the minds with the Holy Spirit; hence: "The sun of righteousness shall rise unto those who fear me" (Mal 4:2).

Fifth, just as the untimely birth departed this life without hope, so too [the stingy] is hopeless in the hereafter, for he has done nothing good to find rest; and nobody can inherit life without good works.

Sixth, the untimely birth goes to darkness because of Adam's original sin, for in the sense that he has received God's natural soul, he possesses immortality and resurrection, but because he did not attain the grace of baptism and good works, he cannot enter the kingdom of heaven and cannot receive glory; and in the sense that he has done nothing, he will not be tortured by the fire, but because of the original sin of the first father, he will stay in darkness.

Similarly, the avaricious rich man does not have any hope for rest in heaven, because he has not performed good works; rather, he will be tormented in the fire because of his evil works and merciless conduct, as if the rich man "who was dressed in purple and fine linen, and who feasted sumptuously every day. He did not mercy Lazarus, [so] he died and descended to hell, was in agony in the flames and was in need for a drop of water, but nobody would give it to him" (cf. Lk 16:19–25). Likewise, every merciless and wicked man will remain without mercy from the benevolent God, "for judgment will be without mercy to anyone who has shown no mercy," the Apostle says. And the Lord commands the sinners: "You that are accursed, depart from me into the eternal fire prepared for the devil and his angels, for I was hungry and you gave me no food, [etc.]" (Mt 25:41–42).

A body is buried in the ground. Similarly, the soul of a sinner like the rich man enters the hell and the torments. And just as Lazarus's soul rested in the bosom of Abraham, so too the soul of the righteous will reach the repose of the heavens and the abode of the holy to rejoice with the classes of angels and the homogenous chosen saints, "for the souls of the righteous are in the hand of God, and there shall no evil touch them" (cf. Wis 3:1). They are in peace unto the last day, when they shall receive from Christ our God the crown and the glory of unending life in their body and soul. As the Apostle says: "I have finished the work, I have kept the faith. From now on there is and remains for me the crown of righteousness, which the Lord will compensate me with on that day, and not only me, but also all those who have longed for his revelation" (cf. 2 Tim 4:7–8). So may Christ Jesus our Lord, who is blessed forever, make us worthy of general resurrection and the glories and incorruptible crown, amen.

CHAPTER LXV

A homily by another on gluttony, according to the verse: "Their god is their belly, [etc.]" (Phil 3:19), or "Your hearts may not weigh down with dissipation and drunkenness," and so on (Lk 21:34).

Doctors of the church say that the excessive love of the belly is a mouth and gate for all sins. Therefore, God countered it with the first commandment, prohibiting eating the fruit, when He said: "You may eat of every tree, but of the tree, which is in the middle of the garden of delight, you shall not eat" (cf. Gen 3:3, 2:16). And because it is the gate to all evil things, Satan wanted to open this door first, when he tried Eve with this sin. One ought to know what gluttony is.

Gluttony is the intense love of an open mouth to fill the insatiable belly, and the definition is this: gluttony is the desire to love an insatiable mouth intensely. This goes against nature, against a brother, and against God; it is a failure for the body and the soul, and a joy for Satan.

Why is it against nature? Because it is written in the books of nature that animals with mouths that open bigger need to eat more due to their large size, whereas man—the head of all animals—has a narrow mouth, because the Creator God defined it so, so that he may care for food less than animals.

Again, it is against a brother, because David says: "Their throat is an open sepulcher" (Ps 5:9). Just as everybody detests open graves, so too everybody detests the drunkards and gluttons, because they serve as ill example. Again, one drunkard and lavish person spends more than ten people. Again, he [the drunkard and lavish person] is a blemish within family, beloved ones, friends, [and] neighbors, for there will be constant quarrel, fight, and anger among them because of him, as Solomon says. A drunkard stirs up arguments. He also says: "Wine is intemperate, drunkenness stirs up animosity" (Prov 20:1).

Again, it goes against God in many ways. First, it worships abominable possessions as god, as Paul said in Philippians: "Their God is their belly" (Phil 3:19). Moreover, doctors of the church say that people worship the item that they love most. The second defect is that it turns God's temple into a kitchen for the belly, for the heart of a Christian is God's temple, as Paul says: "You are God's temple" (1 Cor 3:16). Then, therefore, those who abandon the prayers to care for their bellies and abandon contemplations about God for the sake of eating and drinking seem to worship their bellies, and the steam of food and drink stands for the fume of the incenses [to them]. The third defect is that it destroys and corrupts the image of God, as Jeremiah says in Lamentations: "Their visage is blacker than soot; nobody recognized them" (Lam 4:8), and St. Jerome says that nothing in this world dazzles man's understanding more than eating and drinking to their bellyful. The fourth defect is that drunkards and gluttons hate God. Just as Esau sold his birthright, and whenever he thought that he sold his birthright, he reckoned it to be insult and mocking toward God in his heart. Likewise, when the drunkards and gluttons see that they are insult and mockery, they despise God and blaspheme. The fifth defect is that it is a chain and a road: it catches us by our feet, because it hides underneath our needs. As [St.] Gregory [of Nyssa] says about Solomon's verse: "Bring me out of my supplications, O Lord," if there is a strong chain underneath my words. Again, the doctor of the church says: "Eat your food as if it were a medicine that quiets the temptations and keeps the body healthy, like the food given to the sick in moderation, for if [the sick person] eats too much, the stomach will corrupt from the temperature of the excessive food." Wherefore, they give little food, as Sirach says: "Honor your healer for your supplications" (cf. Sir 38:1), because he gives you what you need and nothing more. Again, a person should be careful for the sake of his health, for the physicians say that patients resemble mistresses; the temperature of the stomach is like maidens who revere their mistresses in various ways. The same applies to a patient's stomach: when he eats food, the desires of eating visit him like maidens and say, "eat all kinds of food"; but when the maidens visit him frequently, the poison of his body and soul hide in him, his confused soul finds delight in what it thinks is a profit, and [eventually] he finds destruction through it. The sixth defect that proceeds from gluttony is a great pain like leprosy.

Here we need to know that gluttony results in six kinds of harms and defects that are similar to six kinds of diseases.

First, it kills people suddenly. Second, it causes a great deal of grief so long as it lasts. Third, a few people can recover. Fourth, it requires much labor for things that are more harmful than beneficial. Fifth, it is associated with all kinds of diseases that affect the soul and the body. Sixth, it makes a person lean and keeps him in poor health.

The first [kind] that kills a person quickly and suddenly resembles choking, which catches the throat suddenly and kills the person. As Paul says in Galatians: "What the flesh desires is opposed to the Spirit, and what the Spirit desires is opposed to the flesh" (Gal 5:17), because they are enemies—when one is lean and the other is fat, they oppose and eliminate each other. What is the medicine for [the illness] that catches the throat suddenly? Physicians say that they carefully take a vein from the nape of the neck to let the blood gush out abundantly and then the patient rinses his mouth with the liquid of mistletoe. Thus, we see spiritually that when a person is sickened with gluttony, the remedy is in contemplating the death of Christ, our head, and the blood of the flesh of Jesus that gushed from the thorns of the crown, His side, His hands, and His feet during the days of the agony, as is said in Maccabees: "When Judas went to war, and they had many elephants with towers placed on them, they offered the elephants the juice" (cf. 1 Mac 32–37); that is, they were aroused by the juice of mulberries to battle. Likewise, when those who suffer all kinds of temptations give much contemplation to the suffering and the blood of Christ, they surely are healed and redeemed from devilish temptations. Again, rinsing the mouth means contemplating the bitterness that Christ experienced from the gall and vinegar, as Jeremiah says in Lamentations: "Remember my poverty, my bitterness and gall" (cf. Lam 3:19), because when a man takes a taste of this world, he cannot live without contemplating Christ's death, as Paul says in 2 Corinthians: "as we share the sufferings, so also we share the consolation" (2 Cor 1:7). Such means can save us from these sins.

The physicians also say that if someone takes the milk of a pig, the waste of a dog, and the juice of lily, and passes them through a filter, [the mixture] helps a great deal [to alleviate] the pain that catches the throat. Spiritually, the milk of the pig signifies the worldly desires, the waste of the dog [signifies] the torments of hell, and the lily [signifies] the kingdom [of heaven]. When a person contemplates that we lose the lily of the kingdom because of the pig's milk and the dog's waste, he will think about Christ's suffering and not lose the kingdom of heaven because of worldly desires.

Concerning the second [harm] that causes a great deal of grief, it resembles the disease that is called bulimia, which is interpreted as a dog's stomach, which is never satisfied with food, as David says: "They hunger like a dog and go round about the city" (Ps 59:6). [St.] Jerome says that hunger brings hunger, not satiety, because a glutton has either many possessions or a few. If he has a few, he desires many possessions to fill his stomach; and if he has many, he wants to have a stomach that eats and drinks frequently, to vomit and eat again driven by the desire of the belly, as Hosea says: "They shall eat but shall not be satisfied in their soul, but the bellies of the ungodly cannot be satisfied" (cf. Hos 4:10).

Concerning the third [harm] that few people can recover from, [know this]: This sin becomes rooted like nature and associated with [the glutton] so tightly that he cannot be cured from it at all without harm—like a person who develops the habit of drinking and eating to his bellyful and cannot abandon the wine, because he either dies or falls back into [the habit of] drinking, as the proverb says: "Whosoever nourishes his children with dainty things, later finds them turned ungodly" (cf. Sir 37:32). What should be done to people of this caliber? Paul instructs them in [1] Corinthians, saying: "If food is a cause of your brother's stumbling, it is better to never eat meat and drink wine" (cf. 1 Cor 8:13). Spiritually, the soul and the body are the most precious thing to humankind. If the soul will stumble and lose its strength by eating or drinking, it is better to eat and drink moderately, so that the soul may not be lost.

Concerning the fourth [harm]—that [gluttony] requires much labor—Ecclesiastes says: "All human illness is in the mouth" (cf. Eccl 6:7). This is very ugly and abominable. It is ugly, because man is preoccupied with filling the belly and the ugliness appears from his belly hanging downward. Again, it is useless for a man to spend the possessions since he will be killed like a robber; to be more precise, he will be killed the next day. Everybody is destined to die like a thief in accordance with a command. Therefore, he who spends all of his possessions on his belly will die the morrow and become food for the worms, and this is useless, as Paul says: "Food is meant for the stomach and the stomach for food; God will destroy both one and the other" (1 Cor 6:13).

Again, it is worthless to [try to] fill a skin that never gets full. Similarly, [it is worthless to try to fill] the stomach of a man that is disposed to eat and eats the entire earnings of the man and yet is not full, as Hosea says: "They shall eat but shall not be satisfied" (Hos 4:10). It is nothing but a curse and punishment remaining upon us because of gluttony, and there can be found no one on earth to please gluttony and satiate it by eating, be it a king or a prince, a beggar or a rich man, a big man or a little one.

Concerning the fifth [harm], which refers [to gluttony] as a door for all sins, if it is closed, then it is closed before all sins, and if it is open, then it is a place for all sins, like a fattened horse that cannot be conquered and controlled, and throws the rider in the mud and the marsh of fornication.

Sixth, that gluttony causes much harm and want related to the body, [consider this]. First, it brings hunger, as Luke says about the prodigal son: "He took his share of the property, devoured it with prostitutes and drinkers, and then was dying of hunger" (cf. Lk 15:30). It is a great deal of foolishness to spend everything and die of hunger for the sake of the little pleasures of the mouth. Second, gluttony causes various kinds of poverty, as [Solomon] says in the proverbs. Whosoever loves foods remains a wanderer. How? Because he puts his possessions in a porous purse—many work hard for a long time and earn to only extravagantly spend everything in one day, as Haggai says: "He gathered his wages and put them in a purse with holes" (Hag 1:6), and remain empty-handed, poor, indebted to the lawless, and faithless. Third, gluttony brings many and diverse pains to the body, for people often turn leprous, lose their hearing or sight, become sick, and contract fever, as Sirach says: "Sicknesses overtake from overstuffed food" (cf. Sir 31 20–22). And many die of gluttony, as the proverbs say: "Those who eat, drink, and exchange gifts abundantly corrupt themselves spiritually and physically."

Now, gluttony applies to two things: first, eating, which is called stuffing; second, drinking, which is called drunkenness. Referring to these, Luke says: "Be on guard so that your hearts are not weighed down with dissipation and drunkenness and the worries of this life" (Lk 21:34).

Now, we already discussed dissipation [above], and we shall discuss drunkenness [next].

CHAPTER LXVI

Homily of the same on drunkenness, according to the words of Paul in
Ephesians: "Do not get drunk with wine that contains debauchery"
(Eph 5:18).

Now, we understand drunkenness in four ways through the Bible.

First, intoxication with wisdom, as the prophets, the apostles, and the holy fathers were intoxicated with divine wine—the intoxication of wisdom, as Jeremiah says: "I will satiate with food and drink the souls of the priests, the sons of Levi's Israelites, and my people shall be satisfied with my bounty, says the Lord" (Jer 31:14). Like a person intoxicated with wine who lets everything go and gives them to others, the [person] intoxicated with wisdom disregards the world and sets off, as the apostles did. When Christ, the Wisdom of the Father, called upon them, they left the world and went with Him. Thereafter, when they received the Holy Spirit, they were so perfectly intoxicated with wisdom and set their words loose that people thought they were intoxicated, as Sirach says: "Whosoever is wise, when gold and silver are compared with wisdom, says [wisdom] is esteemed above them" (cf. Sir 40:25). Those who are intoxicated with worldly matters do not accept this intoxication [with wisdom], as Sirach says: "The heart of fools is like broken vessel, will hold no wisdom" (cf. Sir 21:17). [The apostles] were not alone in despising the world for the sake of God's wisdom. The philosophers also held the world as nothing for the sake of wisdom, as we read about Plato and others, who despised the world and their own persons that they might attain wisdom.

The second way to drunkenness is the intoxication with God's mercy, as Solomon says: "You have thoroughly anointed my head with oil, and your cup intoxicated me like a pure wine" (Ps 23:5). The cup signifies God's mercy, for just as a man intoxicated with wine is brave and confident, so too are the saints, who, intoxicated with the wine of divine wisdom, braved and defeated the entire world.

The third intoxication is associated with the joy, exultation, and glory of the kingdom. Just as a man intoxicated with wine rejoices and laughs limitlessly, so too the holy in the kingdom rejoice infinitely, as David says: "They shall be fully satisfied with the fatness of your house; and you shall cause them to drink of the full stream of your delights" (Ps 36:8).

These three kinds of drunkenness are very good and agreeable to God and his saints.

The fourth [kind of drunkenness], however, is the intoxication with worldly wine. Concerning this intoxication, Sirach says: "Wine was made to make men glad; it was not made to make them drunk" (cf. Sir 31:30), because this kind of drunkenness is very wicked and is sin; it is the mother of all sins and fatally poisons everything good, as [St.] Gregory [of Nyssa] says. Drunkenness is a soft devil, pleasant poison, sweet honey. Whosoever practices drunkenness is deprived of his soul and has no control over himself, and whosoever commits this sin is sinful absolutely. The fathers of the church also say that as the extended drought is very harmful to the earth and brings deficiency to it, so too excessive rain and wetness are harmful to the earth, but they are good in moderation. Like a man who irrigates the earth, a moderate [satiation] of the needs is good for man's soul. Drunkenness, however, is like a torrential current that corrupts the earth and uproots every fruit. Again, [the fathers] say that drunkenness deprives man of reason, corrupts the senses, disperses the intellect, stirs [the desire for] fornication, renders the tongue imperfect, weakens all of the body parts, shortens [a] man's life, and destroys the salvation of the soul and the body. Therefore, Paul says: "Do not get drunk with wine that contains debauchery" (Eph 5:18); that is, do not drink wine that produces all kinds of wickedness and fornication.

Those who become intoxicated, in addition to fornicating with women with debauchery, apply debauchery upon God's entire creation. Nothing good comes out of drunkenness; on the contrary, it is disgraceful to all created beings. We have Noah as an example from Genesis: when he drank wine and was intoxicated, he uncovered his nakedness and his son mocked him. Man loses his senses, as is said in the same [Genesis], for Lot who was redeemed from [the destruction of] Sodom, drank wine, became intoxicated, and slept with his own daughters. Since wine is sulfur warmed by the sins of fornication and oil to the fire of fornication, wherever it exists, it kindles the fire of fornication, as is said in [folk] proverbs: "Wine is the root of fornication." [The folk proverbs] also say: "Do not receive homage from wine drinkers, for corrupt are those who are saturated with wine." Do not look at the wine when it is in the drinking glass; it has shiny color and goes in pleasantly, but bites like a serpent later. The eyes of wine drinkers see women that belong to others, they contemplate evil and turn into men sleeping in a ship without steersman; wherefore Paul says: "Do not get drunk with wine that contains debauchery" (Eph 5:18).

It is true that every wine drinker becomes corrupted and embarrasses God and man, but [drunkenness] harms three kinds of people more than others: first, all of the servants of the church; second, all the primates and bishops of the church; third, the kings and rulers.

Concerning the servants of the church, Leviticus says: "You shall not drink wine nor strong drink, you and your sons with you, whenever you go to the temple of God, lest you die" (cf. Lev 10:9). If God was so vengeful for [instances] of the old age and established for them such a great command, we, the priests and bishops who are the truth and light of ordinances, shall be even more watchful in the new age. Again, drunkenness is a gross shame for kings and rulers, as well as for all those who give their soul to God—clergy, preachers, deacons, and others, as is said in Numbers: "Whatsoever man or woman shall vow and give oneself to God, shall purely abstain from wine and strong drink" (Num 6:2–3). The New Testament does not say that it is not allowed to drink wine at all, as Paul says: "No longer drink only water, but take a little wine for the sake of your ailments" (1 Tim 5:23).

One should also know that wine is absolutely forbidden to clergymen, but it is allowed to the laity in moderation, as Evagrius [Ponticus] the Great says. "Do not drink wine at all" is stated for the clergy, but "should you drink, you have to bless the Creator" is stated for the laity. Not drinking wine at all is reminiscent of pure virginity, while drinking wine in moderation is reminiscent to lawful matrimony. Immoderate drinking, on the other hand, is reminiscent of adultery and fornication. Therefore, the Apostle says: "Fornicators, adulterers, drunkards—none of these will inherit the kingdom of God" (cf. 1 Cor 6:9).

The wine has two inherent influences: confusing and motivating. Meaning, when a man drinks wine, the fume rises to the brain and confuses the mind; it changes happiness to sadness and weeping, and changes sadness to happiness. Likewise, it changes wisdom into ignorance and ignorance into wisdom; strength into weakness and weakness into strength. This is the first influence of wine. The second influence is that it motivates the drinker to become angry, to desire, to play, to clap, to dance, and so on, as the Scripture says: "The people sat down to eat and drink, and rose up to play" (Ex 32:6).

These two influences are inherent to wine. The first, confusion, stems from the reality that the wine itself is in constant state of change. It is not like the wheat and fruits that always remain unchanged; rather, wine mutates, because it was grape and then turned into must, sour grape, wine, and vinegar, and thereby it confuses anyone who drinks it. The second, motivation, stems from the reality that when cooked, wine moves and boils, and consequently the elements become separated and it turns clear; therefore, it motivates everybody, because motion is inherent to it.

One should also know that the sage allows four kinds of people to drink wine: first, the poor and the homeless, so that they forget their misery; second, the grieved and mournful, so that they find comfort and become glad; third, the weak and the ailing, so that they recover from their ailments; fourth, the aged, for wine is strength and support to them. On the other hand, the sage says, people of prominence who are prone to anger should not drink wine; otherwise, their thoughts will scatter and they will err in judging the poor. Likewise [wine should not be touched by] happy people, to not become sad; the healthy, to not become weak, as was indicated earlier; [and] the young, to not get mentally confused and motivated by lust and anger.

Moreover, the spiritual wine, which is the wisdom of holy Scriptures, should be given to those who are poor and homeless relative to virtues, are ailing, sad, and weakened by sins, and those who are in constant pain and sadness due to their conscience, as [Christ] says: "I have come to call not the righteous but sinners" (Mt 9:13), and "Come to me, all you that are weary, and I will give you rest" (cf. Mt 11:28–29), and "Jesus Christ came into the world to save sinners—of whom I am the foremost" (1 Tim 1:15). For this kind of people, [wine] is hope, comfort, and a directing staff.

The wine of wisdom needs to be spared to those who are rich with virtues, happy with their deeds, and fortitudinous and healthy, so that they may not be satiated and filled with the rapture of their activities and theories, [and may not] treat mercilessly those that act poorly and judge ignorantly, and fail to judge them with mercy and correctly, as [Solomon] says: "Men of prominence are prone to anger, let them not drink wine" (cf. Prov 31:4). Elijah, for example, was prone to anger, filled with activity and satiated with wisdom, and he closed the heavens over Israel and punished the righteous and the sinners, those who deserved [punishment] and those who did not deserve it, alike.

On Debauchery

Now, herein follows the rest of the sins of debauchery, which is the opposite of avarice and contradicts the virtue known as generosity.

Debauchery is the opposite of generosity in four ways. First, a debauched person does not give his possessions; rather, the wind of the love of glory ravishes his possessions from him. For example, when the wind drops a fruit from a tree, people do not say that the tree gave it; rather, [they say] the wind [gave it]. The second difference [between debauchery and generosity] is that the generous person distributes but the debauched [person] wastes, like a man who pours wine over a full skin or a barrel, or empties in a broken container and wastes it. Similarly, he who gives his possessions to wicked and evil people is an indulger in dissipation and waster. Third, when [a] man gives generously [but] not for the sake of friendship or virtue, he is reminiscent of a hunter who sets baits to catch fowls; this is not generosity; it is deception. Fourth, a man who gives his own possessions is generous, but the miser often gives items that do not belong to him.

However, what does debauchery do? I say many things. First, it turns a man to a beggar—hungry and thirsty, as Luke says about the prodigal son. Second, he often falls into the hands of usurers who make him commit a great deal of mischief by borrowing and consuming. Third, it makes people thieves and robbers, and it resembles the web of a spider that weaves its strings, catches and consumes many flies, and weaves again. Fourth, it hates spiritual goodness, like Esau who sold God's blessing for the sake of lentil soup.

Although debauchery and wasting are bad for everybody, they are worst for priests for many reasons. First, St. Gregory [I the Great] says that everything the priests possess belongs to the poor; therefore, taking more than a garb and a [portion of] food is unduly great sin and robbery within the church. Why? Because everything related to the church belongs to Christ; thereby, they have to give, as [Christ] says: "Anything you own in abundance, give to the poor" (cf. Mk 10:21), and as Paul says: "We have food and clothing, we will be content with these" (1 Tim 6:8). And St. [John] Chrysostom says: Feeding the poor is much better than covering stones with gold and walls with images. Second, [because] priests should serve as good example to others; it is very inappropriate for healers, who ought to heal others, to contract ailment from them. Third, because this sin [of debauchery] disallows the priests to pray and do good deeds. Fourth, because of the fear of God's judgment, for Christ will tell them on the Day of Judgment the verse: "I was hungry and you gave me no food, [etc.]" (Mt 25:42). He applies this also to those who eat the fruits of their own labor. What would He tell the priests who eat and appropriate what belongs to Christ, if not the verse: "You that are accursed, depart from me into eternal fire" (Mt 25:41).

Since we spoke about avarice and gluttony, let us now talk about fornication.

CHAPTER LXVII

Homily of the same on Satan's deceptions and fornication, according to the proverb: "The horseleech had three dearly beloved daughters: and these three did not satisfy her; and the fourth was not contended as to say, Enough" (Prov 30:15).

The Prophet Moses told the story of the creation of the entire world, but he did not say anything about Satan for two reasons. First, at the time people were naïve and childish—they were unable to understand the intelligible and immaterial. Therefore, he established for them corporeal ordinances and promised them corporeal goodness. People understood the adversary to be corporeal and abhorred corporeal sins, so he did not say anything about angels or demons. Second, since the knowledge of God was new, he did not speak about Satan's opposition to God and enmity to man or his fall from heaven, so that they might not presume the existence of two opposite gods—the creator of the good and the creator of the evil, as the Manicheans heretically claimed later. In the New Testament, however, as people learned the worship of God [and] the knowledge of the Holy Trinity, and were filled with wisdom and the Holy Spirit, [Christ] gave them spiritual ordinances [and] promised spiritual gifts, kingdom to the believers, and eternal suffering to the disbelievers and the lawless. Afterward, the apostles and the holy fathers revealed Satan the enemy to be the adversary to God, the angels, and man, to have fallen from the heavens, and to be the cause of the destruction and sins of man.

The anterior prophets demonstrated Satan's adversity to us and his opposition to our good deeds through proverbs and examples. The Prophet David, for instance, called him lion: "He lies in wait in secret as a lion in his den" (Ps 10:9). Satan is called lion because of his ravishing nature, for he roars, ravishes man's soul, and destroys him. He [David] calls Satan dog, because Satan flatters sins, and bull, because he strikes by his nature: "Many dogs[64] have compassed me and fat bulls have beset me round" (Ps 22:12). He names [the demons] after their deeds. He designates them as slandering prince, because they speak ill of us and calumniate. He calls them persecutor and

---

[64] *Bullocks* in *The Septuagint* and other common versions of the Bible.

enemy: "Let the enemy persecuted my soul," he says (Ps 7:5), "They that afflict me are multiplied? many rise up against me" (Ps 3:2). [He says so] because they wage war against us. He calls them viper and basilisk because of their deceiving nature, and [designates them as] evil poisons, which they cast into our thoughts and souls to corrupt them. Just as the Prophet David call them crooked leviathan, lion, and beast, so too his wise son, Solomon, calls Satan the enemy horseleech, saying: "The horseleech had three dearly beloved daughters" (Prov 30:15).

Satan is called horseleech for many reasons. First, the horseleech sucks blood, which is the juice of vitality. Likewise, Satan sucks and draws the vital disposition of prudence and wrath in man, wherefore Christ says: "Satan was murderer from the beginning" (cf. Jn 8:44). Second, as people say, the leech sucks diseased blood; similarly, the disease of sins is what Satan eats. Therefore, [Satan] is allegorized as a pig in the parable of the prodigal [son]: "He would gladly have filled himself with the pods that the pigs were eating" (Lk 15:16). Third, the leech is insatiate, as [Solomon] says here: "these three did not satisfy her" (Prov 10:15); Satan, likewise, is not satisfied with evil works. Fourth, the leech is found in wet places; Satan is always in wet lusts, as [the Lord] said: "Behemoth lies in marshy places" (cf. Job 40:15–21). Ninth, the leech is a reptile, so also is Satan who sneaks into the thoughts of man creepily and secretly: "I cannot comprehend the way of a serpent upon a rock" (cf. Prov 30:18–19). Sixth, the leech has two mouths and Satan has two deceptions in his words: first, before the sinner sins, he declares God sweet, benevolent, and patient, and makes people fall into sins; later, after the sinner has sinned, he reminds him of righteousness and the punishment of the judgment, thus hopelessly destroying [the sinner]; wherefore David says: "The words of his mouth are transgression and deceit" (Ps 36:3). Seventh, the leech does not leave a body unless its belly is satisfied with blood. Likewise, when Satan catches someone in sins, he does not release him until he completes the sinful action and sins in every which way. Eighth, the leech catches conveniently at the beginning, but at the end gives the affliction of pain. Similarly, Satan shows the beginning of the sins to be sweet, but later [a sinner] becomes bitter because of his conscience, his respect for the commandments, and the fear of the ordinances, as Solomon says: "Honey drops from the lips of a harlot [. . .] but afterward you will find her more bitter than gall" (Prov 5:3–4). Ninth, the leech is rapacious and black; Satan, likewise, is called darkness; hence: "The darkness did not overcome it" (Jn 1:5), and "He has rescued us from the power of darkness" (Col 1:13). Therefore, the darkness of sins and ignorance obscures the minds of the sinners here [on earth], as the Lord says: "All who do evil hate the light and do not come to the light" (Jn 3:20), and after committing them, they suffer in the outer darkness. Tenth, the leech cannot go near the healthy part of the body, and Satan cannot approach those who have perfectly healthy spirits; hence: "The ruler of this world is coming. He has no power over me" (Jn 14:30). This also applies to all the chosen, as David says: "When evildoers drew nigh against me to eat up my flesh, my persecutors and my enemies, they fainted and fell" (Ps 27:2). Also: "A thousand shall fall at your side, [etc.]" (Ps 91:7). Because: "The angels of the Lord will encamp round about them that fear him, and will protect them" (Ps 34:7).

The three daughters of Satan the leech are hell, which is the loss in the grave; the love of women; and the Tartarus, which is the suffering in hell. These are the three daughters of Satan. However, why does [Solomon] refer to them as daughters and not sons? [He does so] for two reasons: first, to reveal their evilness through a feminine noun and, second, because they bear and receive, but they do not give; hence [the designation as] daughter, because the love of women entraps the thoughts, the grave [entraps] the body, and the Tartarus [entraps] the spirit of men and they do not release them.

Should someone say, behold! Christ liberated the spirits from hell and the bodies of people rise from the grave; besides, the female gives children. We say that the bodies of human beings rise from the earth and their spirits from hell through God's providence and power; otherwise, they [the earth and hell] bear but do not give; and this is evident through the torments of eternity, for nobody is redeemed from there. Know also through other things that they bear and do not give; thereby, [Solomon] refers to them as daughter.

Again, should someone say: How are these daughters of Satan? Behold! God gave the woman as man's helper; He also prepared the hell as suffering for sinners just like the grave: "Dust you are and unto dust shall you return" [the Lord] says (Gen 3:19). We say that these were the daughters of Satan not because they were created by him; rather, they were transformed into evil by him; he was the cause of their wickedness.

God created the woman good for the purpose of human reproduction, but Satan became the cause of voluptuous desire and adultery, because he made her see the fruit in the garden of delight with lust, and lust transformed her. He [Satan] also caused the death and the grave: "God did not create death. Through the envy of the devil came death into the world," says the proverb (cf. Prov 2:23–24), because [Adam] ate the fruit through deception and returned into

465

[being] dust. Likewise, God prepared the Tartarus and Gehenna as a destiny for sinners, but Satan from the beginning of the world took human spirits there and tortured them. Moreover, since God prepared the suffering for sinners, Satan forcibly tormented both the righteous and the sinners. Then, therefore, [Solomon] rightfully refers to the woman, the grave, and Gehenna as daughters of Satan. He refers to the grave as hell, because just as hell is the internal harsh and distressful suffering of the spirit, so too the grave is a hell for the body; hence, [God] told David: "Bring down Shimei to the hell with his blood" (cf. 3 Kings 2:8–9); meaning, to the grave. And Isaiah says: "They that are dead shall not praise you, neither shall they that are in Hades hope for your mercy" (Isa 38:18); this signifies the grave.

[Solomon] puts love for women in the midst to show that the woman caused two things: the grave of death and the torment of Gehenna. This is evident from two things. First, from the same first wife of Adam, as the Apostle says: "The man was not deceived, but the woman was deceived and became transgressor" (1 Tim 2:14), because the man ate the fruit not by his own will, but for the love of the woman. [This happened] as if to imply: Mercy my sinful wife for my sake. Later, his notion materialized. When God removed Adam's spirit from hell, He also removed his wife's, Eve's [spirit] for his sake. Their two intentions were accomplished. First, the first mother [Eve] put in her mind eating the fruit and begetting divine descendants; this was accomplished through the Holy Mother of God Virgin Mary who gave birth to the Only Begotten as incarnate and humanized God. Second, Adam's intention was materialized when our Lord Jesus Christ descended into hell and, thanks to the righteous and for their love, redeemed also the souls of the sinners from the torments of hell. It is evident, then, that the woman transgressed, not the man, just as Adam himself testified, when he said to God: "The woman whom you gave me [. . .] she gave me" (Gen 3:12), and I ate the fruit because of the natural love that I have for her. Therefore, God said: "Because you have harkened to the voice of your wife, and eaten of the tree [. . .], cursed is the ground in your labors [. . .], thorns and thistles shall it bring forth for you [. . .]. In the sweat of your face shall you eat your bread until you return to the earth out of which you were taken, for earth you are and to earth you shall return" (Gen 3:18–20).

Now see how the love for the woman took him to the hell of the grave, and as his body went into the confinement of the grave, so too his soul with the thorn of the sins entered the torments of Gehenna. There, Adam's spirit suffered six thousand years in hell until the Only Begotten of God came, became human, suffered, and redeemed him from hell. For this reason,

[Solomon] considers the love for the woman to be medial, for the woman caused the death of the body and the torments of hell. [Then], first, it is evident from this [that we said].

Second, it is evident nowadays that the woman is still causing death to the body and eternal suffering in Gehenna because of fornication and adultery, as the Apostle says: "Fornicators and adulterers will not inherit the kingdom of God" (cf. 1 Cor 6:9); this is the suffering of the spirit that women bring upon us. The death of the body also has occurred many times through women, as the waters of the flood happened because of women: "[Before the flood] they were eating and drinking, marrying and giving in marriage" (Mt 24:38). Therefore, they provoked God's anger and He destroyed them all with the flood. Noah and his two descendants were the only survivors, and he [Noah] kept his virginity for five hundred years. Because of the adultery of Dinah, Jacob's daughter, the entire population of the city of Shechem was put through sword.

Likewise, because [the Israelites] were defiled with other women and ate the sacrifices of the dead, four thousand men perished in the congregation until Phinehas killed Zambri and Chezib, and death ceased thereupon.

Likewise, in the days of the judges, because of the adultery of the concubine of the Levite, the Benjamites were smitten with the sword; fifty thousand men from eleven tribes died.

What else shall I list? Mighty Sampson was deceived and perished by the woman Delilah. The Prophet David was deceived by the woman and lost his throne but later repented and was justified through Nathan. Solomon the Wise himself lost God's favor because of a woman: "Wine and women turned him away from God" [the Scripture] says (cf. 3 Kings 11:3–4, Neh 13:26). A woman beheaded John the Baptist. [A woman] removed Adam from Eden. And plenty of harm to the body and the soul has happened and will happen until the end of the world in the hand of women. Many have dropped dead wounded by them, and countless are those who have been slain by women. The enemy, Satan, is insatiate to this extent, as insatiate is the loss [caused] by women. Satan is constantly at war with men through evil counsel; he brings them to the love of women, and women bring death to the body and the eternal suffering of Tartarus to the soul. "They will not say, It is enough" (Prov 30:16); that is, just as the grave is never satisfied or full with bodies and hell with suffering, so too the demons are not satisfied with deceiving and women with destroying, as the proverb says: "The woman hunts for the precious souls of men" (Prov 6:26).

Through his next verse, [Solomon] brings an example of women's love and the evil counsels of Satan, by saying: "The earth is not filled with water; water also and fire will not say, It is enough" (Prov 30:16). That is, irrigation will not satisfy the earth for two reasons: first, the earth itself carries and receives [water]; second, it makes various plants grow with that water. The earth signifies our rational mind, while water signifies the knowledge and thoughts that we carry.

Knowledge is of two kinds: good and evil. The good knowledge is from the Holy Spirit, the Holy Scriptures, and spiritual wisdom, and the good thoughts come from God to man. The evil knowledge is from the evil spirit of Satan who constantly dumps evil thoughts in man and destroys him. Our rational mind carries both the good and the evil, and receives them differently. Because [man is a] rational being, he is nourished with reason: some [are nourished] with divine reason, others with demonic reason. Therefore, a person should always listen to and learn the divine knowledge, and keep it in mind and contemplate it, so that the demonic thought may not enter us. For example, a container full of water cannot receive anything more; similarly, a mind contemplating goodness cannot receive Satan's evil counsel. Again, as water incessantly moves in the root, the plant, the flower, and the fruit, so too the knowledge within our mind, if good, waters good roots [and] grows in our body plants and flowers such as sweet-scented rose, violet, and so on; that is, it fruits within us prudence, fortitude, faith, hope, love, and all kinds of good works. Because the good work sends roots in the mind, grows plants in the body, gives sweet-scented flowers through works, and turns into the fruit of peace and tranquility for the body here [on earth] and into eternal life in the hereafter. The good knowledge of the holy water brings these kinds of fruits.

Likewise, evil knowledge enters our thoughts and grows the thorns of sins—licentiousness, disbelief, hatred, laziness, and so on. Similarly, these evil thoughts send roots in the soul, grow in the body, flower through works, and bring evil fruits: the [suffering of the] conscience in the soul and the punishment for sins in the body—disease, untimely death, famine, [death by the] sword, captivity, and so on, here [on earth], and the eternal suffering, the weeping and gnashing of teeth in the hereafter, which is referred to as Tartarus.

Behold, brothers! See through your eyes and understand through your minds: this is the fruit of the two counsels—the good and the evil. Choose whichever you want!

Thereafter, [Solomon] says: "water also and fire will not say, It is enough" (Prov 30:16). As we have said, water works incessantly; so also does the fire. It takes the visible things we throw in and never says it is enough, be it stone, wood, iron, or anything else; it receives everything and kindles stronger. Similarly, the fire of warm love in our soul is insatiate and kindles stronger. This fire of love is of two kinds—good and evil. The spiritual love for God is good; we possess it in a pure heart to love God absolutely. The evil love is corporeal and ill; it is the wicked love of pleasures, such as the love of woman, eating, drinking, money, glory, and so on. The Prophet refers to the ill love as [follows]: "My heart grew hot within me, and a fire kindled in my meditation" (Ps 39:3). The kindling occurs when a person inflames the fire and places the wood to burn it. Similarly, our internal desire is like a natural fire; Satan inflames it in the thought, and the external senses of vision serve as the substance that kindles the evil desire, which, when implemented, gives birth to death; hence: "When that desire has conceived, it gives birth to sin, and that sin, when is accomplished, gives birth to death" (Jas 1:15). This is the kindling of evil.

Concerning the good [fire of love], the Prophet says: "I opened my mouth and drew breath: for I earnestly longed after your commandments" (Ps 118:131); that is, every time we open the mouth of our thoughts and release them, we receive the sensation of the Holy Spirit, and when we long for God's commandment, our love for Him kindles. This is the good love, and this love is lasting; it never diminishes for three reasons—because of the beloved, because of the lover, and because of love. The beloved is God and is eternal. Likewise, love, which is a bond between our spirit and God, is eternal, as the Apostle says: "[Faith, hope, and love . . .] these three, and the greatest of these is love" (1 Cor 13:13); that is, faith is in this life, hope is [associated with] the expectation of reward after this life, and love after resurrection remains in us and toward God in the life of eternity.

The evil love of world, however, is not lasting like this in three aspects: from the beloved, from the lover, and from love. From the beloved as follows: the world perishes and gold, silver, women, and their desire perish with it; so also our bodies and the desire therein perish. Likewise, the love itself, the longer it lasts, the lesser it becomes, because the love of God and the love of the world are distinguished as follows: the longer the love for God and spirituality lasts, the more it grows and becomes stronger, whereas the longer the love for the world and man lasts, the weaker it becomes and diminishes. [This is so], because the beginning of the love of world is firm, but the end is weak, whereas the beginning of the divine love is weak, but the end is firm and inflamed. Consequently, [Solomon] says about love: "water also and fire will not say, It is enough" (Prov 30:16). That is, the water of the knowledge of the

Holy Spirit and the fire of God's love are everlasting and eternal, because just as the knowledge and love of the angels are now an eternal pouring from God, so also the wisdom and knowledge of the chosen holy men will always gush out in the hereafter from God with unending love and eternal life. May Christ make us, all the believers in His name, worthy of His heavenly wisdom and have us communicate with the immortal table, which is promised to His saints, and glory to Him forever, amen.

CHAPTER LXVIII

Homily of the same on the harm of harlots.

Solomon the sage provides systematic instruction about the harm of harlots. First, he says: "Do not gaze on a wicked woman" (Prov 5:2), for watching with lust outwardly is the cause of all evil. The Lord commands: "Everyone who looks at a woman with lust has already committed adultery with her in his heart" (Mt 5:28); even though the place and the time could have hindered the outward action, adultery was accomplished in his will. Besides, Satan interjects lust in the vision, as [he did] to the first mother, Eve: "She saw the tree beautiful" (cf. Gen 3:6).

Satan interjected pleasantness and she ate the fruit. Therefore, a person should not gaze on at all. Also, by gazing with the eyes, the lust moves and leads to action; therefore, a person should not gaze on at all. Had David not seen Bath-Sheba, he would not have desired her and committed adultery. Likewise, Judah [would not have desired] Tamar. This is the first harm—gazing with the eyes at harlots.

The second harm that Solomon mentions [is]: "The adulterer destroys his own soul and endures disgrace" (cf. Prov 6:32–33). The Apostle says in [1] Corinthians: "Anyone united to the Lord becomes one spirit with him, but whoever is united to a prostitute becomes one body with her" (cf. 1 Cor 6:15–16), because since the harlot is wicked, her entire wickedness becomes associated with [the adulterer]. This is reminiscent of a person who contracts malodor by intermingling with trash and [a person who] turns black by intermingling with soot.

The third [harm Solomon] relates [is]: "Honey drops from the lips of a harlot, but afterward she is more bitter than gall" (Prov 5:3), for she attracts a young man with flattering words, and after completion of the action, he feels more bitter than gall because of his conscience and the corporeal abominations, as it happened with Amnon in relation to Absalom's sister: the concluding hatred was more bitter than the initial pleasure. Likewise, a similar bitterness occurs to every young man eventually.

Fourth, [Solomon] says: "Sharper than a two-edged sword" (Prov 5:4) in reference to the evil action, for it severs the body from life and the spirit from

471

the kingdom; hence: "Do not be deceived! Neither fornicators nor adulterers inherit the kingdom" (1 Cor 6:9–10).

Fifth, [Solomon] says: "Her feet lead down to the grave with death" (Prov 5:5); that is, fornication results in eternal death; [for] those who go down to the grave with [the act of fornication], it torments their souls eternally. As the Apostle says: "When that desire is conceived, it gives birth to sin, and that sin [gives birth] to perfect death" (cf. Jas 1:15), because the fulfillment of the sins is the beginning of eternal death.

Sixth, "Her love is slippery" [Solomon] says, "and fades away" (cf. Prov 5:6), because her deceitful love was for the sake of the price of prostitution; once she receives it, she no longer loves you; she abandons you and loves someone else.

Seventh, [Solomon] says: "She takes away your life" (cf. Prov 5:9) in reference to possessions that we call goods, for she binds the young man with her love and with it takes away everything. And he, intoxicated with her love, overlooks the loss of possessions. Intoxication derives from many things—sins, authority, youth, richness, and so on. All of these are worse than wine's intoxication, as the Prophet says: "Woe to you that are drunken without wine" (Isa 28:1). Because of it, they do not sense any fear, shame, and instruction, for they are intoxicated and maddened with sins.

Eighth: "It makes you repent at last, when the flesh of your body is consumed" (Prov 5:11); that is, [the fornicator] repents and regrets when he ages and his strength is gone, or becomes sick and languishes, or turns poor and the food and drink diminish. These—youthfulness, health, and wealth—are advantageous to the wicked and help them, but when they diminish, the spirit gains strength and [the fornicator] suffers from his conscience. Thence, he recognizes the shame and the necessities that are gone, because a harlot deprives man of everything. She deprives them of possessions, takes away the feeling of shame, takes away their necessities, shortens their life, tortures their body, and torments their soul in the fire, as [Solomon] says: "They fell in many harms in the public and the congregation" (cf. Prov 5:14). Here [Solomon] speaks not only about slanders and shame, but also about the last judgment. When the seats of judgment are set along with the registers of the Word, and the heavens and earth are gathered together in one place, there the shame, disgrace, and suffering of the evildoer will be; hence: "All of us must appear before the judgment seat of Christ, so that each may receive recompense for what has been done in the body, whether good or evil" (2 Cor 5:10).

Ninth, when [Solomon] says: "The ways of a man are before the eyes of

God" (Prov 5:21), he means awe and fear that surpass everything, because whatever a man does, God sees; nothing is hidden from Him. Four things hide deeds from people: first, the distance of a remote land; second, the house; third, darkness; fourth, the body. Now, distance and the covers of earth cannot hide us from God's sight; hence: "The Lord looked down from heaven upon the sons of men to see" (Ps 13:2), nor can a house: "The darkness and light are both alike" (Ps 139:12), or the body: "for [God] tries the hearts and reins" (cf. Ps 7:9).

Now, God sees our deeds and recompenses, but we do not see God: "The fool said in his heart: 'There is no God'" (Ps 14:1). Someone seeing God near him will not transgress; for example, when we see a person [near us], we do not commit [an evil act against another]. Besides, one of the ordinances that He set for us in the Ten Commandments was: "You shall not commit adultery" (Ex 20:14). When we disdain it, we shall be judged by the same ordinances that ordered the adulterers to be stoned and burned.

Tenth, [Solomon] says: "iniquities ensnare a man, and [. . .] such a man dies with the uninstructed" (Prov 5:23–24). That is, the hunter is Satan and with little pleasure he envelops people in the trap of sins; hence: "The snares of sinners entangled me" (Ps 118:61), and pulls them with him to the eternal suffering, as [Solomon] says: "he dies with the uninstructed" (Prov 5:24). Now, death and suffering are corporeal here [on earth], [and they are ordered] by the rulers of countries and judges: "For rulers are not a terror to good conduct, but bad conduct" (Rom 13:3), as they punish the fornicator, adulterer, and evildoer. They take away their possessions, torture them with cudgels, and sever either their body parts or the entire head. Again, the uninstructed is Satan, for he did not obey God or the angels in the old or the new ordinances, so [the fornicator's] death will be with Satan the uninstructed, for he received Satan's instruction and disdained the instructions of God, the church, and the saints.

What is the end of these two [Satan and the fornicator]? It is the saying: "You that are accursed, depart from me into the eternal fire prepared for the devil and his angels" (Mt 25:41). This is the share and the destiny of a harlot. Therefore, [Solomon] says: "Do not gaze on a wicked woman" (Prov 5:2). As for adultery, it was said at the beginning of the ordinances of the Scripture: "You shall not commit adultery" (Ex 20:14); see there.

His word on fornication.

[Question:] Why did God command the Prophet Hosea to fornicate?
Answer: This provokes many thoughts.

First, it showed that the people of Israel were fornicators; they had abandoned the Lord God and worshipped idols.

Second, to show that their land would commit whoredom in service of their enemies.

Third, a disaster was about to befall the people, and they that had taken shelter in the temple did not believe, thinking that those were false prophesies. Therefore, a proof of their destruction was to be given to them not only verbally, but also practically.

Fourth, the prophets had spoken about many things, and the people had forgotten. Therefore, [God] made the Prophet Isaiah wander naked and barefoot as a paradigm for the Israelites' slavery and He commanded Hosea to fornicate as a sign to their destruction, because what is seen is more certain than what is heard; and this is similar to the third thought [above].

Fifth, the prophets used to intercede for the sake of the wicked people. God told [Hosea]: Take an adulteress, so that you may teach them that you as a man find the adulteress disgusting; how much more shall I [as God] be patient with my people who constantly adulterate with idols?

Sixth, [God] set the Prophet [Hosea] as a paradigm to the offensive nation, [saying]: The adulteress comes to her senses when she is humiliated; when you take her, she will no longer commit whoredom. But the Israelites did not come to their senses, although I brought them near me; instead, they abandoned me and profaned with idols.

Seventh, [the Prophet Hosea was set] as a paradigm to the effect that despite the fornication of the Jews in Egypt and with Canaanites, God had accepted them and their progeny as His people. In like manner, Christ accepted in the new [age] the heathens into His church.

Eighth, the Prophet cleansed the adulteress, because the holy is not stained by touching the impure; rather, the impure is cleansed from his or her impurity. Likewise, God took the impure people and cleansed them from their entire impurity, and named the Jews with the holy name, Israel, which means they have seen God, while the gentiles are named Christian, which means Christ is with them.

Ninth, [God] commanded [Hosea] to fornicate so that He might show the Prophet's obedience and his perfect love for God, because he despised embarrassment and disgrace before the people for the sake of God's commands. Likewise, we have to obey the ordinances of God and the will of the primates.

Tenth, [God] said in the ordinances: "You shall not commit adultery" (Ex 20:14), and yet He commanded the Prophet to commit whoredom and adultery, so that He might show that God's will is above and beyond the ordinances, not inferior to them, and that God can change the ordinances He had placed. Although it was said: "You shall not murder" (Ex 20:13), [God] commanded Samuel to kill Agag, and He accepted the killings of Phinehas and Elijah. The same [applies] to this [instance of commanding fornication].

Whoredom and adultery are differentiated as follows. The whore is known and bold; hence: "You have a whore's face; you did become shameless toward all" (Jer 3:3). Adultery, however, is committed covertly and secretively, like a dog. Therefore, the Lord says: "Everyone who looks at a woman [with lust] has already committed adultery with her in his heart" (Mt 5:28). Since Ephraim was committing whoredom openly with the idols and covertly in Jerusalem, the Prophet said: "He committed adultery in Jerusalem and whoredom in Samaria" (cf. Hos 7).

Question: How is it that Hosea remained pure when he went to the whore and the woman was cleansed through him, whereas someone else would become impure by committing whoredom?

Answer: The pure and impure are equally perceived in four aspects, for there is purity of spirit and purity of the body, and impurity of the spirit and impurity of the body alike. Now, when the impure body touches other [bodies], it turns the body impure but not the spirit, because according to philosophers, the impurity of matter and quality cannot pollute the essence; [it pollutes] only what is qualitative and accidental. Likewise, the impure spirit pollutes the spirit of others when it touches them, but cannot pollute the quality of the body. On the other hand, when the pure spirit touches others, it can purify both the spirit and the body. Likewise, the pure body can purify other bodies that it touches, because purity is stronger than impurity, so that it may be able to change both qualities [of an impure spirit and body]. For this reason, when the impure woman touched the holy Prophet, she was cleansed through him; hence: "With the holy you will be holy, [etc.]" (Ps 17:25), whereas when other people went to the whore, they became impure through her, [for] David says: "the transgressors shall be utterly destroyed together" (Ps 37:38), and the Apostle says: "Anyone united to the Lord becomes one spirit with him, but whoever is united to a prostitute becomes one body with her" (cf. 1 Cor 6:15–16).

Also, every profession is distinguished through its products, whereas the good and the evil are distinguished by their reason, and intention is the reason, for a work is recompensed according to the intention, whether good or evil, as the Lord said: "They have received their reward" (Mt 6:2).

Now, God's command was Hosea's reason and intention, which he fulfilled

475

and thereby he remained pure, whereas other human beings have the pleasure of the body as their reason and thereby they become impure. Phinehas and Elijah stand as evidence to this—they killed many people but were not indebted because of the reason. Saul offered a sacrifice and Uzzi offered incense, but both were condemned because of the reason and intention. This much on this.

CHAPTER LXIX

Homily of the same on the yoke of ordinances.

Question: Hosea says: "Ephraim was a trained heifer" (Hos 10:11).

Answer: When people abandoned God's ordinances, [Hosea] referred to the heifer as disobedient. But when people were obedient to God's ordinances, [Hosea] called her trained heifer. This has many attributes: First, in accordance with the designation, because *heifer* means *birth giver*, and people had the fruits of goodness. Second, she was trained and tamed to the yoke, and people were so with regard to God's ordinances. Third, she is righteous, for she is equal to her partner. Forth, she is laborious and productive. Fifth, she moves forward straight in the path, without swerving right or left. Sixth, she is as steady in work as in the yoke. Seventh, if she falls behind or leaves her partner behind, the rod becomes her reprimand. The Prophet [David] says: "I will fill their faces with scourge and strike their inequity with a rod" (Ps 89:32). Eighth, it is at odds with the unyoked, and the faithful have to be at odds with disbelievers. Ninth, she lowers her neck under the yoke, which signifies the cross, and accepts the leather thong of the yoke as an inseparable bond, as the Lord commanded taking the cross and following him. This indicates voluntary humility. Tenth, the neck bears the marks and signs of the yoke; this constitutes the beauty of the neck over which the yoke is placed. This is analogous to the virtues we have, by which we accept Christ's ordinances and cross, and by which our souls are beautified. These are the attributes of the trained heifer—Christ's faithful people. Whereas the unyoked heifer needs to be conceived as the opposite of all of these. She signifies the disbelievers who disobey God's ordinances. So much on this.

His words on conception according to Hosea.

"Give them, O Lord, a miscarrying womb and dry breasts" (Hos 9:14). First, this means disgrace, sterility, and barrenness among the Israelites. He damns the evil people thus, so that they may not have corporeal heirs and memory on earth. Second, parents were [conceived as] kings who multiplied the troops, and the breasts were [conceived as] priests who pressed the ordinances and fed the people. When the kings multiply idols and priests fail

477

to teach the ordinances, he damns them thus. Third, the womb of the mind births the words and feeds the tongue. Heretics, who conceive and teach vice, receive such damnation. Fourth, our soul is a womb that births goodness. And our body is a breast, for it feeds through works. Now, whosoever, contrary to these, conceives evil in the soul and works [evil] with the body will deserve such damnation. So much on this.

His words about the threats of prophets.

Question: Why did the prophets threaten the people beforehand with punishment?

Answer: For four reasons. First, they reproached their [the Israelites'] sins and spoke of punishment to inform them that they would encounter punishments commensurate with transgressions. Second, to inform them that the punishment is not purposeless; rather, God commands it and it is irreversible. Third, as the mind is lured by the evil thought before the body implements it, likewise, a threat frightens man and torments him mentally before his body suffers the punishment for his transgressions. Fourth, a punishment has two folds: the threat and the execution. Now, the prophets delivered the threats, and the kings of Assyria and Babylon brought the execution. When people open their ears to threats and repent, they escape punishment. When the residents of Nineveh, for example, took fright of the Prophet's one word and repented, they survived the punishment. Whereas the Israelites, because they did not repent despite the many threats of many prophets, were subjected to the punishment of captivity under the Assyrian kings, and then only they repented for their transgressions. Enough on this!

His words [on]: "Two legs and a piece of an ear" [Am 3:12]

Question: What does Amos mean by saying: "As a shepherd who rescues from the mouth of a lion two legs and a piece of an ear."

Answer: First, it related to Israel. God was its shepherd; hence: "The Lord is my shepherd" (Ps 22:2). He saved his people from the Assyrians and Babylonians when He brought them back from captivity. The two legs are the two kingdoms in Jerusalem and in Samaria. Whereas the piece of an ear is a part of the whole body; it indicates that the entire population of the country was taken captive. And He saved only the Israelites who obeyed God's ordinances. Also, there were two kingdoms formerly, but when they returned from captivity, they obeyed and submitted to one kingdom. Spiritually, our Lord Jesus Christ shepherds everything and everybody, whether in heaven or on earth, whether Jew or gentile; hence: "I am the good shepherd" (Jn 10:11). First, he went after death and saved humanity from it. Speaking of two legs, He [Christ] saved man—who is soul and body—and not other animals, quadrupeds, or birds. And the one piece of an ear is mentioned against the devil whom he did not save, because the devil absolutely lacked the ear to obey God. The man, however, although listening to the devil with one ear, listened to God's ordinances with the other ear and obeyed. Again, the two legs refer to Adam who approached the tree with his two feet and was expelled from Paradise. Later, Christ brought him back to the delightful Paradise in the hand of the robber. And the piece of an ear refers to Eve who listened to the serpent's voice and was pleased before she heard the damnations and grieved. And she heard the angel's voice through the Holy Virgin and felt troubled but later became fastened, joyful, and blessed; hence: "Greetings unto you, Mary full of grace, rejoice, favored one, the Lord is with you. Blessed are you among women" (cf. Lk 1:28–42). The wounds of Eve's ear healed from this greeting.

His word on the knowledge and glory of God.

Habakkuk says: "The earth was filled with the glory and the knowing of the Lord like abundant waters that cover the seas" (Hab 2:14). The seas indicate the words of the prophets: first, referring to bitterness; second, referring to the gathering for Israel; third, because the island and the mainland remained pagan. The abundant waters relate to the rainfalls, indicating that the new covenant poured down from the Holy Spirit: first, in relation to sweetness and grace; second, in relation to the abundance among Jews and gentiles; third, in relation to the ever flowing [of the Spirit] in the churches. When he says: "The earth was filled with the glory and the knowing of the Lord," understand this in four ways. First, justice constrained God's mercy before the Word's arrival, because mercy was restricted to the Jews, while there was justice for all heathens and there was judgment for Jews with just laws. However, upon the Word's arrival, mercy constrained justice, for it was transformed into grace and forgiveness. Second, at the time, Israelites were the only chosen and glorified people; whereas now gentiles [also] are chosen, "For there is no distinction between Jew and gentile," as Paul says, and as the Prophet Joel says: "I will pour out my spirit on all flesh and they shall prophesy" (Joel 2:28). Third, during the old covenant, sacrifices and offerings took place in the temple only, according to the laws of Moses, whereas during the new covenant, the temple of God's glory was built throughout the universe where Christ, the nourishment of life, is forever offered. Fourth, there [during the old covenant), the temple was material and the offering and the worship were merely corporeal, whereas here [during the new covenant], Paul says: "You are the temple of the living God" (1 Cor 3:16), and the offering and the worship are oral and spoken, because the specter and imitation were destroyed, and the essence and truth were established. Thus: "The earth was filled with the knowledge and glory of God." Because instead of one, numerous temples and numerous nations were chosen, and the corporeal was transformed into spiritual, as justice was transformed into grace and mercy. And this happened by Christ's coming and the descending of the Holy Spirit in the hearts of the faithful.

Habakkuk also says.

"Behold, you despisers and corrupters, for I work a work in your days that you would not believe though someone tell it to you" (Hab 1:5). The despised is someone whom others despise. The despiser is he who verbally despises others. Whereas the despising is he who despises by work, such as those who despise and remain impenitent in wickedness through God's allowance. Not that transgression is sweet to God and He reckons it to be good and, therefore, forgives the sinner. Rather, the repentance of a sinner is sweet and pleasant to God, and for this reason, during the last repentance God will be patient and will allow penitence. But when people remain impenitent in transgression to the end, they will provoke God's anger and He will pile past transgressions upon them and punish them here and in the hereafter, as the Apostle says: "Despite God's forgiveness, you are storing up eternal wrath for yourself on the day of God's judgment" (cf. Rom 2:5).

There are two components to being patient. First, God sees the transgressions and ignores them. Second, He thinks of subjecting the person to His mercy; whereas impatience goes like this. First, He sees the sins and remembers them. Second, He rightfully punishes. Having learned this, let us examine this verse. The first meaning of the verse is that you, despisers, have seen me so forgiving and sweet toward you, and yet you did not repent. Now, believe in my revenge and be astonished by the extent of your corruption. For I work a work that you would not believe though someone tell it to you. That is, since you did not believe in my ordinances with your ears, I will practically punish you physically—if you will not listen with the ears, you shall listen with your back. A work of this kind would seem unbelievable to you because you are intoxicated and maddened by sins, and you do not believe the tellers, but when you carry the punishment practically, you will then become astonished.

The verse also refers to Christ's first coming. This was an astonishing work of God on earth, and the despisers and disbelievers did not believe. And [understand] this in four ways. First, the God of heaven and earth dwelled in the womb of the virgin and God became man. Second, the immortal and living God died in the body on the cross and gave us life. When pagans hear this, they become astonished, whereas Jews ridicule it, for the Apostle says: "The message about the cross is foolishness to those who are perishing" (1 Cor 1:18). Third, He descended to hell, destroyed it, and saved men's souls, and He rose from the dead and ascended unto the heavens. Fourth, pagans and unbelievers believed and were delivered, whereas Jews disbelieved and were lost.

These four were a great work of the Lord, but despisers do not believe in these.

The verse also refers to the last coming of Christ and the end of the world. God rather than nature will be the cause of the mighty and marvelous works at the time—people's resurrection and world's renovation, and the glory of the righteous and punishment of the sinners. This, too, is a great work of God in four ways. First, general resurrection for all humans that are dead and decomposed into earth; they will resurrect physically and live the immortal life. Second, the renovation of the world and the elements, the transformation of orders and times, the termination of motion in moving things, and the movement of static things perpetually. Third, seeing God, the angels, human beings, and everybody's works, and hearing the inquiries of the judge and the answers. Fourth, the dead will rise from hell and the graves, while the living will descend unto hell and the graves, and those who afflict torments will be tormented, whereas those who suffer from tormenters will be saved. Those incorporeal will come down from above to submerge in the lower side of the earth, whereas those corporeal will be lifted unto the upper side; there, the first will become the last, whereas the last will become the first, and so on. For this, all creatures shall be amazed. Despising demons and evil human beings do not believe in the day of that great work, but when they see it in the works, they will be astonished by suffering unquenchable torments. Enough on this!

CHAPTER LXX

Homily of the same on paganism, according to the words that God said through the Prophet Hosea: "I am the Lord your God that established the heaven and the earth, and I do not command you to prostrate before their stars" (cf. Hos 13:4).

A person could ask here: Why did He [God] prohibit prostrating before created things? I answer: For many reasons, but primarily I will bring forth ten reasons.

First, because all creatures are created from nothingness and they would have turned into nothingness if it were not for God's will to sustain their existence. Now, had they prostrated before created things, they would have become worshippers of nothingness.

Second, because regulation requires that creatures prostrate before the Creator they have received their being from; creatures do not come to being from creatures, unless God commands so.

Third, it is disorderly for the lord to prostrate before the servant. Now, man is both lord and ruler, and all creatures serve man; they were created for this purpose.

Fourth, the Creator is one, whereas the creatures are many; had people prostrated before creatures, they would have erred and became polytheists, and they would not have found the one God.

Fifth, to receive worship is proper to the Creator, whereas to offer [worship] to Him is proper to creatures. Now, if people offered worship to creatures, the properties [of both the offerers and receivers] would have changed. It was for this reason that He said: "I will not give my glory to another" (Isa 48:11).

Sixth, all creatures depend on God relatively; they look up to Him and, therefore, they prostrate before Him. The created do not prostrate before [each other] because they do not look up to each other.

Seventh, the Creator alone is the archetype and norm for all creatures. All tend to be him. Moreover, only man is the image of God and not of creatures; therefore, he worships only Him and not the creatures.

Eighth, a prostrator seeks help from the one before whom he prostrates; creatures are weak and cannot help. Therefore, man does not worship creatures, but rather the Creator from who he receives the entire assistance.

Ninth, when somebody worships, he approaches and loves the worshipped. Now, God wanted that we love Him only and not the creatures.

Tenth, Satan, the first to become arrogant, did not worship the Creator and was destroyed. Then he made the creatures worship him and brought destruction upon them. Therefore, against him, He [God] commanded [people] to worship God the Creator and not the creatures.

Now these are the primary reasons. Worshipping idols has brought forth many and countless reasons for destruction—impurity, crime, blasphemy, murder, and so on. Wherefore, many ordinances were established through the prophets: "I am your Lord God. Go you not after another God and worship him not" (cf. Deut 6:14).

Second question: What was the pretext the pagan priests used to make the sacrifice of human beings to idols acceptable?

Answer: Obviously, there were four judgments. First, they [the priests] would say that when the calf and the heifer were erected [as idols], people offered them animals in their likeness; but now, human beings should be offered to the images of the idols which resembled them. Second, they would say that animals are different from us; therefore, you should offer your own sons and daughters as a sign of greater love. Third, they would say that animals only were slaughtered in God's temple; whereas you should slaughter human beings to distinguish yourselves from them and to demonstrate greater worship. Fourth, they would refer to the examples of the Patriarch Abraham who offered his son and was justified, and Jephthah who promised and sacrificed her daughter. And our forefathers who exited Egypt "sacrificed their sons and their daughters to the demons," as David said (Ps 105:37). Therefore, you are the descendants and you should resemble your forefathers.

Third question: Why is the sin of paganism greater than all other sins?

Answer: First, paganism is transgression against the essence and glory of God, whereas other transgressions are against a friend or one's self. Second, paganism was a transgression committed by everybody, whereas other sins are committed individually. Third, paganism was [practiced] demonstratively and presumptuously; other sins are committed covertly. Fourth, people practiced paganism as goodness, whereas other sins are committed out of evilness and conscientiously. Fifth, people worshipped the idols willingly and knowingly, whereas other sins are committed out of ignorance and reluctantly. Sixth, paganism attracts others also, whereas other sins are committed alone. And this is evident from the evil kings who forcibly turned people to the idols, but not to other sins. As to what the idols deprived God of, we say four things: first, the name, for they were referred to as God; second, the worship and offerings; third, the priests; fourth, the people.

Fourth question: Where did paganism come from?

Answer: Paganism has four sources. First, as it goes, a father of a prematurely dead son made his image. Next, other despots envied him and made their own images. Third, they took [their image] to remote worlds and the image was multiplied. Fourth, sculptors beautified the same and later [people] began to worship it.

Again, there are four reasons for paganism. First, the demons enticed people to worship them. Second, sorcerers and magicians, such as Zeus, Cronus, and Aphrodite, deified themselves by sorcery during their lifetime, and people worshipped their image after their death. Third, evil kings, such as Nebuchadnezzar, erected Baal's sixty-cubit tall image and made people prostrate before it. Fourth, people devoted to the worship of the devil, such as Julian the Apostate and other demoniacs.

Again, paganism was established for four reasons. First, because of the traditions of the ancients, sons learned from their fathers and practiced it for long time. Second, because of the beauty of images, they lasciviously worshipped them. Third, because of appearing and talking demons who revealed mysteries, such as when the demon appeared to Saul in Samuel's image and told him many things to come. Fourth, because of the pleasures of corporeal impurity during their [idols'] various holidays, as Aphrodite required fornication, Dionysius [required] intoxication, and so on. For these four reasons, people steadily worshipped the idols.

Fifth question: Why did the pagans commit so many diverse evil acts indiscriminately?

Answer: For four reasons. First, because of corporeal pleasure and habit. Second, because the idols sought the same—blood, killing, and evil works. Third, because they did not have ordinances, nor did they know sins. Fourth, because they feared not that the idols would judge and punish them. It was for this reason that God commanded in Moses' ordinances to recompense evil with evil, "eye for eye, and blood for blood" (cf. Ex 21:24), that they would fear and commit not evil acts.

Sixth question: Why did the demons sow idolatry?

Answer: For four reasons. First, to antagonize God, like him who said: "I will place my throne above the clouds; I will be like the Most High" (Isa 14:14). Second, because he [Satan] intended to do the same to the angels in the heavens—take away their glory and subject them to his rule. Third, to prevent people from worshipping God and to destroy people with him. Fourth, because he is steadfast in wickedness and blinded against goodness, he would intensify his torments through all his deeds.

Seventh question: What are curving and imaging, and what does the designation "idol" mean?

Answer: Carving is sculpting,[65] whereas imaging is painting with dyes and coloring a cast. The idol and the sketch are the image. And the designation "idol" indicates: first, the mind's blindness;[66] second, being engraved and made; third, being inanimate and idol; fourth, being contrary to God.

Eighth question: How many levels of paganism are there?

Answer: [There are] six with regard to the matter, and ten with regard to the worship. That is: First, the luminous bodies of the heavens. Second, the elements, such as fire and water. Third, the silver and the gold. Fourth, the durable stones. Fifth, the lumber and trees. Sixth, the ceramics of a potter. These are the matters, one more ignoble than the other in level. Seventh, human images. Eighth, images of animals and birds. Ninth, irrational animals and reptiles, in the case of the Egyptians. Tenth, the altar of the unknown god, in the case of the Athenians; wherefore the Apostle said: "What you worship is unknown, this I proclaim to you" (Acts 17:23).

Ninth question: What does it mean to say, He [God] claims the debts of the spirit?

Answer: Pagans disagree with this. First, they claim that all images are idols. Second, [they say that] God demands spirit from the image maker. For the first [argument] we say that the saints are different from the demons. We make the images of saints and not demons; therefore, all images are not idols, because their prototypes are different. If they argue that this image and that image are made of the same matter, such as gold and silver, and that the shapes of the images of an adult and a child are identical, we say that although the matter is identical, the application is different—a chair and a wheel are made of the same wood, and from the same stone are built a temple of God and a temple of idols. Likewise, some burn the same frankincense for God, others for idols. Behold, matter is identical [in these cases], but the applications are different. With regard to the second [argument], we say that God does not

---

[65] The Armenian text goes as *praising*. This must be a typographic error where *sculpting* (*druagel* [դրուագել]) has been changed into *praising* (*druatel* [դրուատել]).

[66] It appears that Tat'ewac'i, again, is using a pun here, considering the pronunciational proximity of the term *idol* (*kuřk'* [կուռք]) to *blindness* (*koyr/kur* [կոյր/կուր]).

demand spirit from the image maker. First, God says: "Spirit shall go forth from me, and I have created all breath" (Isa 57:16). Now, if God is the only Creator of spirits and breaths, how would He demand spirit from a human being who cannot do so? Second, the parents of children prepare only the matter of the body; they do not give spirit. How would [then] the image maker give spirit? Third, Moses erected two cherubs on the mercy seat and the huge image above the lampstand, and Solomon made two cherubs of cypress wood in the temple. Fourth, in the new covenant, the Savior made the holy image on a handkerchief. The same did the Mother of the Lord at her assumption, and spirit was not required. The same applies to other images as well. Again, we say to the adversaries: If you make the images of an animal, you become indebted to the spirit of the animal, and when you depict the trees, you become indebted to created vegetative spirits: this is falsehood. As to the statement of the wise [Solomon], "He demands the souls that were borrowed" (Wis 15:8), it means God claims the transgressions of paganism and torments in the fire of hell whosoever made the image of idols, worshipped them, and prostrated before them. May Christ our God save them and us from idolatrous blasphemy in general and from all transgressions and the bitter torments of hell, and glory unto him forever, amen.

Index of Biblical Verses

Mt 10:15, 53, 355
Mt 10:22, 408
Mt 10:28, 18
Mt 10:32, 119
Mt 10:33, 35, 119, 380
Mt 11:19, 397
Mt 11:28–29, 461
Mt 11:29, 98, 156, 422
Mt 11:30, 145, 305
Mt 12:26, 404
Mt 12:30, 149
Mt 12:31–32, 390
Mt 12:32, 35, 234
Mt 12:33, 373
Mt 12:34, 404, 413
Mt 12:34–35, 373
Mt 12:35, 404–405, 413
Mt 12:36, 36, 62, 129, 381
Mt 12:37, 166, 384, 406
Mt 13:3–8, 177
Mt 13:22, 445
Mt 13:23, 210
Mt 13:27–28, 180, 210
Mt 13:30, 181
Mt 13:37–38, 177, 179
Mt 13:43, 100, 166, 342–343
Mt 13:44, 165
Mt 13:55, 397
Mt 15:8, 12
Mt 15:11, 385
Mt 15:14, 296, 311
Mt 15:20, 385
Mt 15:28, 127
Mt 16:16, 397
Mt 16:17, 119
Mt 17:5, 117
Mt 17:21, 27, 309
Mt 18:6, 23, 310
Mt 18:6, 25:34, 70
Mt 18:10, 146
Mt 18:16, 207, 399
Mt 18:19–20, 137

Mt 18:20, 93
Mt 18:32–34, 107
Mt 19:6, 199, 308, 328, 332
Mt 19:12, 217
Mt 19:19, 229
Mt 19:29, 210
Mt 20:6–7, 185
Mt 21:21, 182
Mt 21:28, 185
Mt 21:33, 183
Mt 21:41, 183
Mt 21:43, 183
Mt 22:12–13, 190
Mt 22:44, 84
Mt 23:4, 68
Mt 23:8–9, 144
Mt 23:9, 93
Mt 23:26, 217
Mt 23:27, 217, 375
Mt 23:32, 315
Mt 23:37, 340
Mt 24:12, 68
Mt 24:38, 439, 467
Mt 24:41, 125
Mt 24:48–51, 192
Mt 24:51, 13
Mt 25:12, 119
Mt 25:21, 308
Mt 25:24–25, 189
Mt 25:24–26, 126
Mt 25:33, 342
Mt 25:34, 63, 166, 327, 341, 423
Mt 25:41, 24, 34, 41, 58, 63, 182, 257, 352, 366, 383, 462, 473
Mt 25:41–42, 451
Mt 25:42, 462
Mt 26:24, 235, 441, 450
Mt 26:26, 266, 327
Mt 26:26–28, 259–260, 269, 327
Mt 26:68, 304
Mt 26:73, 387
Mt 26:75, 197

Index of Referenced Authorities